BEYOND GOOD AND EVIL

BEYOND GOOD AND EVIL

FRIEDRICH
NIETZSCHE

This edition published in 2021 by Arcturus Publishing Limited
26/27 Bickels Yard, 151–153 Bermondsey Street,
London SE1 3HA

Cover design: Peter Ridley
Cover illustration: Peter Gray

AD006009UK

Printed in the UK

CONTENTS

INTRODUCTION

Friedrich Nietzsche was born on 15 October 1844 in the small Prussian town of Röcken in Saxony. His father, Karl Ludwig, had been appointed by King Friedrich Wilhelm IV as the Lutheran pastor for the town just before his birth. Karl passed away in 1849 when Friedrich was just five years old. After his father's death, Nietzsche's family moved to Naumburg, where he lived with his mother, younger sister, grandmother and aunt. In 1858, Friedrich was admitted to the Schulpforta, one of Germany's most prestigious boarding schools, where he studied humanities, theology and classics.

After graduating, Nietzsche enrolled at the University of Bonn, where he studied theology and classical philosophy. But he transferred to the University of Leipzig after just two terms when a professor he admired, Friedrich Wilhelm Ritschl, accepted a teaching position there. At Leipzig, Friedrich became the first student to publish a piece in Ritschl's journal, *Rheinisches Museum*.

In 1869, Ritschl recommended Friedrich for a professorship in philology at the University of Basel. The university was hesitant: Nietzsche was only 24 years old and he had yet to complete his doctoral thesis or dissertation, both of which were necessary for a German degree. However, after conferring with the University of Leipzig, Basel decided to offer Nietzsche a position as extraordinary professor of classical philology. He was promoted to full professor the following year.

In August 1870, he took leave to volunteer as a medical correspondent during the Franco-German War. While helping to transport the wounded, Nietzsche contracted dysentery and diphtheria which resulted in poor health for the rest of his life. Upon his return to Basel, Nietzsche found himself unable to continue the taxing work of his professorship and, in 1879, he resigned from his position at the age of 34.

He continued to receive a pension for his time at Basel, but his declining health slowly began to affect his mental faculties. Between 1883 and 1885 he published what he considered his masterpiece, *Thus Spoke Zarathustra*. A philosophical novel in four parts, it was the iconic statement of Nietzsche's philosophy. But it received little attention at the time due to his diminished reputation in the academic world. In 1886, disappointed by the poor response to his previous publication, he reworked his ideas into *Beyond Good and Evil*, in which he launched a scathing criticism of his fellow philosophers and articulated a new morality.

After spending some time in psychiatric asylums, Friedrich lived with his mother until her death in 1897. He then moved in with his anti-Semitic sister, Elizabeth, and her politically active, anti-Semitic husband, Bernhard Förster. After Förster's suicide in 1889, Elizabeth worked diligently to keep her and her husband's dreams of 'racial purity' alive. She took control of Friedrich's estate and used his writings to promote him in a similar light to that of Förster. This association led historians inaccurately to assert that Nietzsche was an anti-Semite and a firm supporter of Adolf Hitler.

But in *Beyond Good and Evil*, Nietzsche illustrates his deeply insightful and open-minded views of man's spirituality. In contradiction to the hateful message of his sister, his aim was to broaden the minds of his readers through careful introspection and inspiring perspectives.

PREFACE

Supposing that Truth is a woman – what then? Is there not ground for suspecting that all philosophers, in so far as they have been dogmatists, have failed to understand women – that the terrible seriousness and clumsy importunity with which they have usually paid their addresses to Truth, have been unskilled and unseemly methods for winning a woman? Certainly she has never allowed herself to be won; and at present every kind of dogma stands with sad and discouraged mien – *if*, indeed, it stands at all! For there are scoffers who maintain that it has fallen, that all dogma lies on the ground – nay more, that it is at its last gasp. But to speak seriously, there are good grounds for hoping that all dogmatizing in philosophy, whatever solemn, whatever conclusive and decided airs it has assumed, may have been only a noble puerilism and tyronism; and probably the time is at hand when it will be once and again understood *what* has actually sufficed for the basis of such imposing and absolute philosophical edifices as the dogmatists have hitherto reared: perhaps some popular superstition of immemorial time (such as the soul-superstition, which, in the form of subject- and ego-superstition, has not yet ceased doing mischief): perhaps some play upon words, a deception on the part of grammar, or an audacious generalization of very restricted, very personal, very human – all-too-human facts. The philosophy of the dogmatists, it is to be hoped, was only a promise for thousands of years afterwards, as was astrology in still earlier times, in the service of which probably more labour, gold, acuteness and patience have been spent than on any actual science hitherto: we owe to it, and to its 'super-terrestrial' pretensions in Asia and Egypt, the grand style of architecture. It seems that in order to inscribe themselves upon the heart of humanity with everlasting claims, all great things have first to wander about the earth as enormous and awe-inspiring caricatures: dogmatic philosophy has been a caricature of this kind – for instance, the Vedanta doctrine in Asia, and Platonism in Europe. Let us not be ungrateful to it, although it must certainly be confessed that the worst, the most tiresome and the most dangerous of errors hitherto has been a dogmatist error – namely, Plato's invention of Pure Spirit and the Good in Itself. But now when it has been surmounted, when Europe, rid of this nightmare, can again draw breath freely and at least enjoy a healthier – sleep, we, *whose duty is wakefulness itself*, are the heirs of all the strength which the struggle against this error has fostered. It amounted to the very inversion of truth, and the denial of the *perspective* – the fundamental condition – of life, to speak of Spirit and the Good as Plato spoke of them; indeed one might ask, as a physician: 'How did such a malady attack that finest product of antiquity, Plato? Had the wicked Socrates really corrupted him? Was Socrates after all a corrupter of youths, and deserved his hemlock?' But the struggle against Plato, or – to speak plainer, and for the 'people' – the struggle against the ecclesiastical oppression of millenniums of Christianity (*for Christianity is Platonism for the 'people')*, produced in Europe a magnificent tension of soul, such as had not existed anywhere previously; with such a tensely strained bow one can now aim at the furthest goals. As a matter of fact, the European feels this tension as a state of distress, and twice attempts have been made in grand style to unbend the bow: once by means of Jesuitism, and the second time by means of democratic enlightenment – which, with the aid of liberty of the press and newspaper reading, might, in fact, bring it about that the spirit would not so easily find itself in 'distress'! (The Germans invented gunpowder – all credit to them! but they again made things square – they invented printing.) But we, who are neither Jesuits, nor democrats nor even sufficiently Germans, we *good Europeans*, and free, *very* free spirits – we have it still, all the distress of spirit and all the tension of its bow! And perhaps also the arrow, the duty, and, who knows? *The goal to aim at...*

Sils Maria Upper Engadine, June, 1885.

CHAPTER I

Prejudices of Philosophers

1. The Will to Truth, which is to tempt us to many a hazardous enterprise, the famous Truthfulness of which all philosophers have hitherto spoken with respect, what questions has this Will to Truth not laid before us! What strange, perplexing, questionable questions! It is already a long story; yet it seems as if it were hardly commenced. Is it any wonder if we at last grow distrustful, lose patience and turn impatiently away? That this Sphinx teaches us at last to ask questions ourselves? *Who* is it really that puts questions to us here? *What* really is this 'Will to Truth' in us? In fact we made a long halt at the question as to the origin of this Will – until at last we came to an absolute standstill before a yet more fundamental question. We inquired about the *value* of this Will. Granted that we want the truth: *why not rather* untruth? And uncertainty? Even ignorance? The problem of the value of truth presented itself before us – or was it we who presented ourselves before the problem? Which of us is the Oedipus here? Which the Sphinx? It would seem to be a rendezvous of questions and notes of interrogation. And could it be believed that it at last seems to us as if the problem had never been propounded before, as if we were the first to discern it, get a sight of it, and *risk raising* it? For there is risk in raising it, perhaps there is no greater risk.

2. '*How could* anything originate out of its opposite? For example, truth out of error? or the Will to Truth out of the will to deception? or the generous deed out of selfishness? or the pure sun-bright vision of the wise man out of covetousness? Such genesis is impossible; whoever dreams of it is a fool, nay, worse than a fool; things of the highest value must have a different origin, an origin of *their* own – in this transitory, seductive, illusory, paltry world, in this turmoil of delusion and cupidity, they cannot have

their source. But rather in the lap of Being, in the intransitory, in the concealed God, in the 'Thing-in-itself – *there* must be their source, and nowhere else!' – This mode of reasoning discloses the typical prejudice by which metaphysicians of all times can be recognized, this mode of valuation is at the back of all their logical procedure; through this 'belief' of theirs, they exert themselves for their 'knowledge', for something that is in the end solemnly christened 'the Truth'. The fundamental belief of metaphysicians is *the belief in antitheses of values*. It never occurred even to the wariest of them to doubt here on the very threshold (where doubt, however, was most necessary); though they had made a solemn vow, '*de omnibus dubitandum*'. For it may be doubted, firstly, whether antitheses exist at all; and secondly, whether the popular valuations and antitheses of value upon which metaphysicians have set their seal, are not perhaps merely superficial estimates, merely provisional perspectives, besides being probably made from some corner, perhaps from below – 'frog perspectives', as it were, to borrow an expression current among painters. In spite of all the value which may belong to the true, the positive and the unselfish, it might be possible that a higher and more fundamental value for life generally should be assigned to pretence, to the will to delusion, to selfishness and cupidity. It might even be possible that *what* constitutes the value of those good and respected things, consists precisely in their being insidiously related, knotted and crocheted to these evil and apparently opposed things – perhaps even in being essentially identical with them. Perhaps! But who wishes to concern himself with such dangerous 'Perhapses'! For that investigation one must await the advent of a new order of philosophers, such as will have other tastes and inclinations, the reverse of those hitherto prevalent – philosophers of the dangerous 'Perhaps' in every sense of the term. And to speak in all seriousness, I see such new philosophers beginning to appear.

3. Having kept a sharp eye on philosophers, and having read between their lines long enough, I now say to myself that the greater part of conscious thinking must be counted among the instinctive

functions, and it is so even in the case of philosophical thinking; one has here to learn anew, as one learned anew about heredity and 'innateness'. As little as the act of birth comes into consideration in the whole process and procedure of heredity, just as little is 'being-conscious' *opposed* to the instinctive in any decisive sense; the greater part of the conscious thinking of a philosopher is secretly influenced by his instincts, and forced into definite channels. And behind all logic and its seeming sovereignty of movement, there are valuations, or to speak more plainly, physiological demands, for the maintenance of a definite mode of life. For example, that the certain is worth more than the uncertain, that illusion is less valuable than 'truth': such valuations, in spite of their regulative importance for *us*, might notwithstanding be only superficial valuations, special kinds of *niaiserie*, such as may be necessary for the maintenance of beings such as ourselves. Supposing, in effect, that man is not just the 'measure of things'.

4. The falseness of an opinion is not for us any objection to it: it is here, perhaps, that our new language sounds most strangely. The question is, how far an opinion is life-furthering, life-preserving, species-preserving, perhaps species-rearing; and we are fundamentally inclined to maintain that the falsest opinions (to which the synthetic judgments a priori belong), are the most indispensable to us, that without a recognition of logical fictions, without a comparison of reality with the purely *imagined* world of the absolute and immutable, without a constant counterfeiting of the world by means of numbers, man could not live – that the renunciation of false opinions would be a renunciation of life, a negation of life. *To recognize untruth as a condition of life*; that is certainly to impugn the traditional ideas of value in a dangerous manner, and a philosophy which ventures to do so, has thereby alone placed itself beyond good and evil.

5. That which causes philosophers to be regarded half-distrustfully and half-mockingly, is not the oft-repeated discovery how innocent they are – how often and easily they make mistakes and

lose their way, in short, how childish and childlike they are, – but that there is not enough honest dealing with them, whereas they all raise a loud and virtuous outcry when the problem of truthfulness is even hinted at in the remotest manner. They all pose as though their real opinions had been discovered and attained through the self-evolving of a cold, pure, divinely indifferent dialectic (in contrast to all sorts of mystics, who, fairer and foolisher, talk of 'inspiration'); whereas, in fact, a prejudiced proposition, idea, or 'suggestion', which is generally their heart's desire abstracted and refined, is defended by them with arguments sought out after the event. They are all advocates who do not wish to be regarded as such, generally astute defenders, also, of their prejudices, which they dub 'truths', – and *very* far from having the conscience which bravely admits this to itself, very far from having the good taste of the courage which goes so far as to let this be understood, perhaps to warn friend or foe, or in cheerful confidence and self-ridicule. The spectacle of the Tartuffery of old Kant, equally stiff and decent, with which he entices us into the dialectic by-ways that lead (more correctly mislead) to his 'categorical imperative' – makes us fastidious ones smile, we who find no small amusement in spying out the subtle tricks of old moralists and ethical preachers. Or, still more so, the hocus-pocus in mathematical form, by means of which Spinoza has, as it were, clad his philosophy in mail and mask – in fact, the 'love of *his* wisdom', to translate the term fairly and squarely – in order thereby to strike terror at once into the heart of the assailant who should dare to cast a glance on that invincible maiden, that Pallas Athene: – how much of personal timidity and vulnerability does this masquerade of a sickly recluse betray!

6. It has gradually become clear to me what every great philosophy up till now has consisted of – namely, the confession of its originator, and a species of involuntary and unconscious autobiography; and moreover that the moral (or immoral) purpose in every philosophy has constituted the true vital germ out of which the entire plant has always grown. Indeed, to understand how the

abstrusest metaphysical assertions of a philosopher have been arrived at, it is always well (and wise) to first ask oneself: 'What morality do they (or does he) aim at?' Accordingly, I do not believe that an 'impulse to knowledge' is the father of philosophy; but that another impulse, here as elsewhere, has only made use of knowledge (and mistaken knowledge!) as an instrument. But whoever considers the fundamental impulses of man with a view to determining how far they may have here acted as *inspiring genii* (or as demons and cobolds), will find that they have all practiced philosophy at one time or another, and that each one of them would have been only too glad to look upon itself as the ultimate end of existence and the legitimate *lord* over all the other impulses. For every impulse is imperious, and as *such*, attempts to philosophize. To be sure, in the case of scholars, in the case of really scientific men, it may be otherwise – 'better', if you will; there there may really be such a thing as an 'impulse to knowledge', some kind of small, independent clockwork, which, when well wound up, works away industriously to that end, *without* the rest of the scholarly impulses taking any material part therein. The actual 'interests' of the scholar, therefore, are generally in quite another direction – in the family, perhaps, or in money-making or in politics; it is, in fact, almost indifferent at what point of research his little machine is placed, and whether the hopeful young worker becomes a good philologist, a mushroom specialist or a chemist; he is not *characterized* by becoming this or that. In the philosopher, on the contrary, there is absolutely nothing impersonal; and above all, his morality furnishes a decided and decisive testimony as to *who he is*, – that is to say, in what order the deepest impulses of his nature stand to each other.

7. How malicious philosophers can be! I know of nothing more stinging than the joke Epicurus took the liberty of making on Plato and the Platonists; he called them *Dionysiokolakes*. In its original sense, and on the face of it, the word signifies 'Flatterers of Dionysius' – consequently, tyrants' accessories and lick-spittles; besides this, however, it is as much as to say, 'They are all *actors*,

there is nothing genuine about them' (for *Dionysiokolax* was a popular name for an actor). And the latter is really the malignant reproach that Epicurus cast upon Plato: he was annoyed by the grandiose manner, the *mise en scène* style of which Plato and his scholars were masters – of which Epicurus was not a master! He, the old schoolteacher of Samos, who sat concealed in his little garden at Athens, and wrote three hundred books, perhaps out of rage and ambitious envy of Plato, who knows! Greece took a hundred years to find out who the garden-god Epicurus really was. Did she ever find out?

8. There is a point in every philosophy at which the 'conviction' of the philosopher appears on the scene; or, to put it in the words of an ancient mystery:

Adventavit asinus,
Pulcher et fortissimus.

9. You desire to *live* 'according to Nature'? Oh, you noble Stoics, what fraud of words! Imagine to yourselves a being like Nature, boundlessly extravagant, boundlessly indifferent, without purpose or consideration, without pity or justice, at once fruitful and barren and uncertain: imagine to yourselves *indifference* as a power – how *could* you live in accordance with such indifference? To live – is not that just endeavouring to be otherwise than this Nature? Is not living valuing, preferring, being unjust, being limited, endeavouring to be different? And granted that your imperative, 'living according to Nature', means actually the same as 'living according to life' – how could you do *differently*? Why should you make a principle out of what you yourselves are, and must be? In reality, however, it is quite otherwise with you: while you pretend to read with rapture the canon of your law in Nature, you want something quite the contrary, you extraordinary stage-players and self-deluders! In your pride you wish to dictate your morals and ideals to Nature, to Nature herself, and to incorporate them therein; you insist that it shall be Nature 'according to the Stoa', and would like everything to be made after your own image, as a vast, eternal

glorification and generalism of Stoicism! With all your love for truth, you have forced yourselves so long, so persistently, and with such hypnotic rigidity to see Nature *falsely*, that is to say, Stoically, that you are no longer able to see it otherwise – and to crown all, some unfathomable superciliousness gives you the Bedlamite hope that *because* you are able to tyrannize over yourselves – Stoicism is self-tyranny – Nature will also allow herself to be tyrannized over: is not the Stoic a *part* of Nature?... But this is an old and everlasting story: what happened in old times with the Stoics still happens today, as soon as ever a philosophy begins to believe in itself. It always creates the world in its own image; it cannot do otherwise; philosophy is this tyrannical impulse itself, the most spiritual Will to Power, the will to 'creation of the world', the will to the *causa prima*.

10. The eagerness and subtlety, I should even say craftiness, with which the problem of 'the real and the apparent world' is dealt with at present throughout Europe, furnishes food for thought and attention; and he who hears only a 'Will to Truth' in the background, and nothing else, cannot certainly boast of the sharpest ears. In rare and isolated cases, it may really have happened that such a Will to Truth – a certain extravagant and adventurous pluck, a metaphysician's ambition of the forlorn hope – has participated therein: that which in the end always prefers a handful of 'certainty' to a whole cartload of beautiful possibilities; there may even be puritanical fanatics of conscience, who prefer to put their last trust in a sure nothing, rather than in an uncertain something. But that is Nihilism, and the sign of a despairing, mortally wearied soul, notwithstanding the courageous bearing such a virtue may display. It seems, however, to be otherwise with stronger and livelier thinkers who are still eager for life. In that they side *against* appearance, and speak superciliously of 'perspective', in that they rank the credibility of their own bodies about as low as the credibility of the ocular evidence that 'the earth stands still', and thus, apparently, allowing with complacency their securest possession to escape (for what does one at present believe in more firmly than in one's

body?), – who knows if they are not really trying to win back something which was formerly an even securer possession, something of the old domain of the faith of former times, perhaps the 'immortal soul', perhaps 'the old God', in short, ideas by which they could live better, that is to say, more vigorously and more joyously, than by 'modern ideas'? There is *distrust* of these modern ideas in this mode of looking at things, a disbelief in all that has been constructed yesterday and today; there is perhaps some slight admixture of satiety and scorn, which can no longer endure the *bric-a-brac* of ideas of the most varied origin, such as so-called Positivism at present throws on the market; a disgust of the more refined taste at the village-fair motleyness and patchiness of all these reality-philosophasters, in whom there is nothing either new or true, except this motleyness. Therein it seems to me that we should agree with those sceptical anti-realists and knowledge-microscopists of the present day; their instinct, which repels them from *modern* reality, is unrefuted... what do their retrograde by-paths concern us! The main thing about them is *not* that they wish to go 'back', but that they wish to get *away* therefrom. A little *more* strength, swing, courage and artistic power, and they would be *off* – and not back!

11. It seems to me that there is everywhere an attempt at present to divert attention from the actual influence which Kant exercised on German philosophy, and especially to ignore prudently the value which he set upon himself. Kant was first and foremost proud of his Table of Categories; with it in his hand he said: 'This is the most difficult thing that could ever be undertaken on behalf of metaphysics'. Let us only understand this 'could be'! He was proud of having *discovered* a new faculty in man, the faculty of synthetic judgment a priori. Granting that he deceived himself in this matter; the development and rapid flourishing of German philosophy depended nevertheless on his pride, and on the eager rivalry of the younger generation to discover if possible something – at all events 'new faculties' – of which to be still prouder! – But let us reflect for a moment – it is high time to do so. 'How are synthetic judgments

a priori *possible*?' Kant asks himself – and what is really his answer? '*By means of a means* (faculty)' – but unfortunately not in five words, but so circumstantially, imposingly and with such display of German profundity and verbal flourishes, that one altogether loses sight of the comical *niaiserie allemande* involved in such an answer. People were beside themselves with delight over this new faculty, and the jubilation reached its climax when Kant further discovered a moral faculty in man – for at that time Germans were still moral, not yet dabbling in the 'Politics of hard fact'. Then came the honeymoon of German philosophy. All the young theologians of the Tübingen institution went immediately into the groves – all seeking for 'faculties'. And what did they not find – in that innocent, rich and still youthful period of the German spirit, to which Romanticism, the malicious fairy, piped and sang, when one could not yet distinguish between 'finding' and 'inventing'! Above all a faculty for the 'transcendental'; Schelling christened it, intellectual intuition, and thereby gratified the most earnest longings of the naturally pious-inclined Germans. One can do no greater wrong to the whole of this exuberant and eccentric movement (which was really youthfulness, notwithstanding that it disguised itself so boldly, in hoary and senile conceptions), than to take it seriously, or even treat it with moral indignation. Enough, however – the world grew older, and the dream vanished. A time came when people rubbed their foreheads, and they still rub them today. People had been dreaming, and first and foremost – old Kant. 'By means of a means (faculty)' – he had said, or at least meant to say. But, is that – an answer? An explanation? Or is it not rather merely a repetition of the question? How does opium induce sleep? 'By means of a means (faculty)', namely the *virtus dormitiva*, replies the doctor in Molière,

> *Quia est in eo virtus dormitiva,*
> *Cujus est natura sensus assoupire.*

But such replies belong to the realm of comedy, and it is high time to replace the Kantian question, 'How are synthetic judgments a priori possible?' by another question, 'Why is belief in such judgments necessary?' – in effect, it is high time that we should understand that such judgments must be *believed* to be true, for the sake of the preservation of creatures like ourselves; though they still might naturally be *false* judgments! Or, more plainly spoken, and roughly and readily – synthetic judgments a priori should not 'be possible' at all; we have no right to them; in our mouths they are nothing but false judgments. Only, of course, the belief in their truth is necessary, as plausible belief and ocular evidence belonging to the perspective view of life. And finally, to call to mind the enormous influence which 'German philosophy' – I hope you understand its right to inverted commas (goosefeet)? – has exercised throughout the whole of Europe, there is no doubt that a certain *virtus dormitiva* had a share in it; thanks to German philosophy, it was a delight to the noble idlers, the virtuous, the mystics, the artists, the three-fourths Christians and the political obscurantists of all nations, to find an antidote to the still overwhelming sensualism which overflowed from the last century into this, in short – '*sensus assoupire*'...

12. As regards materialistic atomism, it is one of the best-refuted theories that have been advanced, and in Europe there is now perhaps no one in the learned world so unscholarly as to attach serious signification to it, except for convenient everyday use (as an abbreviation of the means of expression) – thanks chiefly to the Pole Boscovich: he and the Pole Copernicus have hitherto been the greatest and most successful opponents of ocular evidence. For while Copernicus has persuaded us to believe, contrary to all the senses, that the earth does *not* stand fast, Boscovich has taught us to abjure the belief in the last thing that 'stood fast' of the earth – the belief in 'substance', in 'matter', in the earth-residuum and particle-atom: it is the greatest triumph over the senses that has hitherto been gained on earth. One must, however, go still further, and also declare war, relentless war to the knife, against the 'atomistic requirements' which still lead a dangerous after-life in places where no one suspects them, like the more celebrated 'metaphysical requirements': one must also above all give the finishing stroke to that other and more

portentous atomism which Christianity has taught best and longest, the *soul-atomism*. Let it be permitted to designate by this expression the belief which regards the soul as something indestructible, eternal, indivisible, as a monad, as an *atomon*: *this* belief ought to be expelled from science! Between ourselves, it is not at all necessary to get rid of 'the soul' thereby, and thus renounce one of the oldest and most venerated hypotheses – as happens frequently to the clumsiness of naturalists, who can hardly touch on the soul without immediately losing it. But the way is open for new acceptations and refinements of the soul-hypothesis; and such conceptions as 'mortal soul', and 'soul of subjective multiplicity', and 'soul as social structure of the instincts and passions', want henceforth to have legitimate rights in science. In that the *new* psychologist is about to put an end to the superstitions which have hitherto flourished with almost tropical luxuriance around the idea of the soul, he is really, as it were, thrusting himself into a new desert and a new distrust – it is possible that the older psychologists had a merrier and more comfortable time of it; eventually, however, he finds that precisely thereby he is also condemned to *invent* – and, who knows? perhaps to *discover* the new.

13. Psychologists should bethink themselves before putting down the instinct of self-preservation as the cardinal instinct of an organic being. A living thing seeks above all to *discharge* its strength – life itself is *Will to Power*; self-preservation is only one of the indirect and most frequent *results* thereof. In short, here, as everywhere else, let us beware of *superfluous* teleological principles! – one of which is the instinct of self-preservation (we owe it to Spinoza's inconsistency). It is thus, in effect, that method ordains, which must be essentially economy of principles.

14. It is perhaps just dawning on five or six minds that natural philosophy is only a world-exposition and world-arrangement (according to us, if I may say so!) and *not* a world-explanation; but in so far as it is based on belief in the senses, it is regarded as more, and for a long time to come must be regarded as more – namely,

as an explanation. It has eyes and fingers of its own, it has ocular evidence and palpableness of its own: this operates fascinatingly, persuasively and *convincingly* upon an age with fundamentally plebeian tastes – in fact, it follows instinctively the canon of truth of eternal popular sensualism. What is clear, what is 'explained'? Only that which can be seen and felt – one must pursue every problem thus far. Obversely, however, the charm of the Platonic mode of thought, which was an *aristocratic* mode, consisted precisely in *resistance* to obvious sense-evidence – perhaps among men who enjoyed even stronger and more fastidious senses than our contemporaries, but who knew how to find a higher triumph in remaining masters of them: and this by means of pale, cold, grey conceptional networks which they threw over the motley whirl of the senses – the mob of the senses, as Plato said. In this overcoming of the world, and interpreting of the world in the manner of Plato, there was an *enjoyment* different from that which the physicists of today offer us – and likewise the Darwinists and anti-teleologists among the physiological workers, with their principle of the 'smallest possible effort', and the greatest possible blunder. 'Where there is nothing more to see or to grasp, there is also nothing more for men to do' – that is certainly an imperative different from the Platonic one, but it may notwithstanding be the right imperative for a hardy, laborious race of machinists and bridge-builders of the future, who have nothing but *rough* work to perform.

15. To study physiology with a clear conscience, one must insist on the fact that the sense-organs are not phenomena in the sense of the idealistic philosophy; as such they certainly could not be causes! Sensualism, therefore, at least as regulative hypothesis, if not as heuristic principle. What? And others say even that the external world is the work of our organs? But then our body, as a part of this external world, would be the work of our organs! But then our organs themselves would be the work of our organs! It seems to me that this is a complete *reductio ad absurdum*, if the conception *causa sui* is something fundamentally absurd. Consequently, the external world is *not* the work of our organs – ?

16. There are still harmless self-observers who believe that there are 'immediate certainties'; for instance, 'I think', or as the superstition of Schopenhauer puts it, 'I will'; as though cognition here got hold of its object purely and simply as 'the thing in itself', without any falsification taking place either on the part of the subject or the object. I would repeat it, however, a hundred times, that 'immediate certainty', as well as 'absolute knowledge' and the 'thing in itself', involve a *contradictio in adjecto*; we really ought to free ourselves from the misleading significance of words! The people on their part may think that cognition is knowing all about things, but the philosopher must say to himself: 'When I analyze the process that is expressed in the sentence, "I think", I find a whole series of daring assertions, the argumentative proof of which would be difficult, perhaps impossible: for instance, that it is *I* who think, that there must necessarily be something that thinks, that thinking is an activity and operation on the part of a being who is thought of as a cause, that there is an "ego", and finally, that it is already determined what is to be designated by thinking – that *I know* what thinking is. For if I had not already decided within myself what it is, by what standard could I determine whether that which is just happening is not perhaps "willing" or "feeling"? In short, the assertion "I think", assumes that I *compare* my state at the present moment with other states of myself which I know, in order to determine what it is; on account of this retrospective connection with further "knowledge", it has, at any rate, no immediate certainty for me.' – In place of the 'immediate certainty' in which the people may believe in the special case, the philosopher thus finds a series of metaphysical questions presented to him, veritable conscience questions of the intellect, to wit: 'From whence did I get the notion of "thinking"? Why do I believe in cause and effect? What gives me the right to speak of an "ego", and even of an "ego" as cause, and finally of an "ego" as cause of thought?' He who ventures to answer these metaphysical questions at once by an appeal to a sort of *intuitive* perception, like the person who says, 'I think, and know that this, at least, is true, actual and certain' – will encounter a smile and two notes of interrogation in

a philosopher nowadays. 'Sir,' the philosopher will perhaps give him to understand, 'it is improbable that you are not mistaken, but why should it be the truth?'

17. With regard to the superstitions of logicians, I shall never tire of emphasizing a small, terse fact, which is unwillingly recognized by these credulous minds – namely, that a thought comes when 'it' wishes, and not when 'I' wish; so that it is a *perversion* of the facts of the case to say that the subject 'I' is the condition of the predicate 'think'. *One* thinks; but that this 'one' is precisely the famous old 'ego', is, to put it mildly, only a supposition, an assertion, and assuredly not an 'immediate certainty'. After all, one has even gone too far with this 'one thinks' – even the 'one' contains an *interpretation* of the process, and does not belong to the process itself. One infers here according to the usual grammatical formula – 'To think is an activity; every activity requires an agency that is active; consequently'... It was pretty much on the same lines that the older atomism sought, besides the operating 'power', the material particle wherein it resides and out of which it operates – the atom. More rigorous minds, however, learnt at last to get along without this 'earth-residuum', and perhaps some day we shall accustom ourselves, even from the logician's point of view, to get along without the little 'one' (to which the worthy old 'ego' has refined itself).

18. It is certainly not the least charm of a theory that it is refutable; it is precisely thereby that it attracts the more subtle minds. It seems that the hundred-times-refuted theory of the 'free will' owes its persistence to this charm alone; some one is always appearing who feels himself strong enough to refute it.

19. Philosophers are accustomed to speak of the will as though it were the best-known thing in the world; indeed, Schopenhauer has given us to understand that the will alone is really known to us, absolutely and completely known, without deduction or addition. But it again and again seems to me that in this case

Schopenhauer also only did what philosophers are in the habit of doing – he seems to have adopted a *popular prejudice* and exaggerated it. Willing – seems to me to be above all something *complicated*, something that is a unity only in name – and it is precisely in a name that popular prejudice lurks, which has got the mastery over the inadequate precautions of philosophers in all ages. So let us for once be more cautious, let us be 'unphilosophical': let us say that in all willing there is firstly a plurality of sensations, namely, the sensation of the condition '*away from which* we go', the sensation of the condition '*towards which* we go', the sensation of this '*from*' and '*towards*' itself, and then besides, an accompanying muscular sensation, which, even without our putting in motion 'arms and legs', commences its action by force of habit, directly we 'will' anything. Therefore, just as sensations (and indeed many kinds of sensations) are to be recognized as ingredients of the will, so, in the second place, thinking is also to be recognized; in every act of the will there is a ruling thought; – and let us not imagine it possible to sever this thought from the 'willing', as if the will would then remain over! In the third place, the will is not only a complex of sensation and thinking, but it is above all an *emotion*, and in fact the emotion of the command. That which is termed 'freedom of the will' is essentially the emotion of supremacy in respect to him who must obey: 'I am free, 'he' must obey' – this consciousness is inherent in every will; and equally so the straining of the attention, the straight look which fixes itself exclusively on one thing, the unconditional judgment that 'this and nothing else is necessary now', the inward certainty that obedience will be rendered – and whatever else pertains to the position of the commander. A man who *wills* commands something within himself which renders obedience, or which he believes renders obedience. But now let us notice what is the strangest thing about the will, – this affair so extremely complex, for which the people have only one name. Inasmuch as in the given circumstances we are at the same time the commanding *and* the obeying parties, and as the obeying party we know the sensations of constraint, impulsion, pressure, resistance and motion, which usually commence immediately after the act of will; inasmuch as, on the other hand, we are accustomed to disregard this duality, and to deceive ourselves about it by means of the synthetic term 'I': a whole series of erroneous conclusions, and consequently of false judgments about the will itself, has become attached to the act of willing – to such a degree that he who wills believes firmly that willing *suffices* for action. Since in the majority of cases there has only been exercise of will when the effect of the command – consequently obedience, and therefore action – was to be *expected*, the *appearance* has translated itself into the sentiment, as if there were a *necessity of effect*; in a word, he who wills believes with a fair amount of certainty that will and action are somehow one; he ascribes the success, the carrying out of the willing, to the will itself, and thereby enjoys an increase of the sensation of power which accompanies all success. 'Freedom of Will' – that is the expression for the complex state of delight of the person exercising volition, who commands and at the same time identifies himself with the executor of the order – who, as such, enjoys also the triumph over obstacles, but thinks within himself that it was really his own will that overcame them. In this way the person exercising volition adds the feelings of delight of his successful executive instruments, the useful 'underwills' or under-souls – indeed, our body is but a social structure composed of many souls – to his feelings of delight as commander. *L'effet c'est moi.* what happens here is what happens in every well-constructed and happy commonwealth, namely, that the governing class identifies itself with the successes of the commonwealth. In all willing it is absolutely a question of commanding and obeying, on the basis, as already said, of a social structure composed of many 'souls', on which account a philosopher should claim the right to include willing-as-such within the sphere of morals – regarded as the doctrine of the relations of supremacy under which the phenomenon of 'life' manifests itself.

20. That the separate philosophical ideas are not anything optional or autonomously evolving, but grow up in connection and relationship with each other; that, however suddenly and

arbitrarily they seem to appear in the history of thought, they nevertheless belong just as much to a system as the collective members of the fauna of a Continent – is betrayed in the end by the circumstance: how unfailingly the most diverse philosophers always fill in again a definite fundamental scheme of *possible* philosophies. Under an invisible spell, they always revolve once more in the same orbit, however independent of each other they may feel themselves with their critical or systematic wills, something within them leads them, something impels them in definite order the one after the other – to wit, the innate methodology and relationship of their ideas. Their thinking is, in fact, far less a discovery than a re-recognizing, a remembering, a return and a home-coming to a far-off, ancient common-household of the soul, out of which those ideas formerly grew: philosophizing is so far a kind of atavism of the highest order. The wonderful family resemblance of all Indian, Greek and German philosophizing is easily enough explained. In fact, where there is affinity of language, owing to the common philosophy of grammar – I mean owing to the unconscious domination and guidance of similar grammatical functions – it cannot but be that everything is prepared at the outset for a similar development and succession of philosophical systems, just as the way seems barred against certain other possibilities of world-interpretation. It is highly probable that philosophers within the domain of the Ural-Altaic languages (where the conception of the subject is least developed) look otherwise 'into the world', and will be found on paths of thought different from those of the Indo-Germans and Mussulmans, the spell of certain grammatical functions is ultimately also the spell of *physiological* valuations and racial conditions. – So much by way of rejecting Locke's superficiality with regard to the origin of ideas.

21. The *causa sui* is the best self-contradiction that has yet been conceived, it is a sort of logical violation and unnaturalness; but the extravagant pride of man has managed to entangle itself profoundly and frightfully with this very folly. The desire for 'freedom of will' in the superlative, metaphysical sense, such as still

holds sway, unfortunately, in the minds of the half-educated, the desire to bear the entire and ultimate responsibility for one's actions oneself, and to absolve God, the world, ancestors, chance and society therefrom, involves nothing less than to be precisely this *causa sui*, and, with more than Munchausen daring, to pull oneself up into existence by the hair, out of the slough of nothingness. If any one should find out in this manner the crass stupidity of the celebrated conception of 'free will' and put it out of his head altogether, I beg of him to carry his 'enlightenment' a step further, and also put out of his head the contrary of this monstrous conception of 'free will': I mean 'non-free will', which is tantamount to a misuse of cause and effect. One should not wrongly *materialize* 'cause' and 'effect', as the natural philosophers do (and whoever like them naturalize in thinking at present), according to the prevailing mechanical doltishness which makes the cause press and push until it 'effects' its end; one should use 'cause' and 'effect' only as pure *conceptions*, that is to say, as conventional fictions for the purpose of designation and mutual understanding, – *not* for explanation. In 'being-in-itself' there is nothing of 'casual-connection', of 'necessity', or of 'psychological non-freedom'; there the effect does *not* follow the cause, there 'law' does not obtain. It is *we* alone who have devised cause, sequence, reciprocity, relativity, constraint, number, law, freedom, motive and purpose; and when we interpret and intermix this symbol-world, as 'being-in-itself', with things, we act once more as we have always acted – *mythologically*. The 'non-free will' is mythology; in real life it is only a question of *strong* and *weak* wills. – It is almost always a symptom of what is lacking in himself, when a thinker, in every 'causal-connection' and 'psychological necessity', manifests something of compulsion, indigence, obsequiousness, oppression and non-freedom; it is suspicious to have such feelings – the person betrays himself. And in general, if I have observed correctly, the 'non-freedom of the will' is regarded as a problem from two entirely opposite standpoints, but always in a profoundly *personal* manner: some will not give up their 'responsibility', their belief in *themselves*, the personal right to *their* merits, at any price (the vain races belong to this class); others on the contrary, do not wish to be answerable for anything, or blamed for anything, and owing to an inward self-contempt, seek to *get out of the business*, no matter how. The latter, when they write books, are in the habit at present of taking the side of criminals; a sort of socialistic sympathy is their favourite disguise. And as a matter of fact, the fatalism of the weak-willed embellishes itself surprisingly when it can pose as '*la religion de la souffrance humaine*'; that is *its* 'good taste'.

22. Let me be pardoned, as an old philologist who cannot desist from the mischief of putting his finger on bad modes of interpretation, but 'Nature's conformity to law', of which you physicists talk so proudly, as though – why, it exists only owing to your interpretation and bad 'philology'. It is no matter of fact, no 'text', but rather just a naively humanitarian adjustment and perversion of meaning, with which you make abundant concessions to the democratic instincts of the modern soul! 'Everywhere equality before the law – Nature is not different in that respect, nor better than we': a fine instance of secret motive, in which the vulgar antagonism to everything privileged and autocratic – likewise a second and more refined atheism – is once more disguised. '*Ni dieu, ni maître*' – that, also, is what you want; and therefore 'Cheers for natural law!' – is it not so? But, as has been said, that is interpretation, not text; and somebody might come along, who, with opposite intentions and modes of interpretation, could read out of the same 'Nature', and with regard to the same phenomena, just the tyrannically inconsiderate and relentless enforcement of the claims of power – an interpreter who should so place the unexceptionalness and unconditionalness of all 'Will to Power' before your eyes, that almost every word, and the word 'tyranny' itself, would eventually seem unsuitable, or like a weakening and softening metaphor – as being too human; and who should, nevertheless, end by asserting the same about this world as you do, namely, that it has a 'necessary' and 'calculable' course, *not*, however, because laws obtain in it, but because they are absolutely *lacking*, and every power effects its ultimate consequences every moment. Granted that this also is

only interpretation – and you will be eager enough to make this objection? – well, so much the better.

23. All psychology hitherto has run aground on moral prejudices and timidities, it has not dared to launch out into the depths. In so far as it is allowable to recognize in that which has hitherto been written, evidence of that which has hitherto been kept silent, it seems as if nobody had yet harboured the notion of psychology as the Morphology and *Development – doctrine of the Will to Power*, as I conceive of it. The power of moral prejudices has penetrated deeply into the most intellectual world, the world apparently most indifferent and unprejudiced, and has obviously operated in an injurious, obstructive, blinding and distorting manner. A proper physio-psychology has to contend with unconscious antagonism in the heart of the investigator, it has 'the heart' against it; even a doctrine of the reciprocal conditionalness of the 'good' and the 'bad' impulses, causes (as refined immorality) distress and aversion in a still strong and manly conscience – still more so, a doctrine of the derivation of all good impulses from bad ones. If, however, a person should regard even the emotions of hatred, envy, covetousness and imperiousness as life-conditioning emotions, as factors which must be present, fundamentally and essentially, in the general economy of life (which must, therefore, be further developed if life is to be further developed), he will suffer from such a view of things as from sea-sickness. And yet this hypothesis is far from being the strangest and most painful in this immense and almost new domain of dangerous knowledge; and there are in fact a hundred good reasons why every one should keep away from it who *can* do so! On the other hand, if one has once drifted hither with one's bark, well! very good! now let us set our teeth firmly! let us open our eyes and keep our hand fast on the helm! We sail away right *over* morality, we crush out, we destroy perhaps the remains of our own morality by daring to make our voyage thither – but what do *we* matter. Never yet did a *profounder* world of insight reveal itself to daring travellers and adventurers, and the psychologist who thus 'makes a sacrifice' – it is *not* the *sacrifizio*

dell' intelletto, on the contrary! – will at least be entitled to demand in return that psychology shall once more be recognized as the queen of the sciences, for whose service and equipment the other sciences exist. For psychology is once more the path to the fundamental problems.

CHAPTER II

The Free Spirit

24. *O sancta simplicitas!* In what strange simplification and falsification man lives! One can never cease wondering when once one has got eyes for beholding this marvel! How we have made everything around us clear and free and easy and simple! how we have been able to give our senses a passport to everything superficial, our thoughts a godlike desire for wanton pranks and wrong inferences! – how from the beginning, we have contrived to retain our ignorance in order to enjoy an almost inconceivable freedom, thoughtlessness, imprudence, heartiness and gaiety – in order to enjoy life! And only on this solidified, granite-like foundation of ignorance could knowledge rear itself hitherto, the will to knowledge on the foundation of a far more powerful will, the will to ignorance, to the uncertain, to the untrue! Not as its opposite, but – as its refinement! It is to be hoped, indeed, that *language*, here as elsewhere, will not get over its awkwardness, and that it will continue to talk of opposites where there are only degrees and many refinements of gradation; it is equally to be hoped that the incarnated Tartuffery of morals, which now belongs to our unconquerable 'flesh and blood', will turn the words round in the mouths of us discerning ones. Here and there we understand it, and laugh at the way in which precisely the best knowledge seeks most to retain us in this *simplified*, thoroughly artificial, suitably imagined and suitably falsified world: at the way in which, whether it will or not, it loves error, because, as living itself, it loves life!

25. After such a cheerful commencement, a serious word would fain be heard; it appeals to the most serious minds. Take care, ye philosophers and friends of knowledge, and beware of martyrdom! Of suffering 'for the truth's sake'! even in your own defence! It spoils all the innocence and fine neutrality of your conscience; it makes you

headstrong against objections and red rags; it stupefies, animalizes and brutalizes, when in the struggle with danger, slander, suspicion, expulsion and even worse consequences of enmity, ye have at last to play your last card as protectors of truth upon earth – as though 'the Truth' were such an innocent and incompetent creature as to require protectors! and you of all people, ye knights of the sorrowful countenance, Messrs Loafers and Cobweb-spinners of the spirit! Finally, ye know sufficiently well that it cannot be of any consequence if *ye* just carry your point; ye know that hitherto no philosopher has carried his point, and that there might be a more laudable truthfulness in every little interrogative mark which you place after your special words and favourite doctrines (and occasionally after yourselves) than in all the solemn pantomime and trumping games before accusers and law-courts! Rather go out of the way! Flee into concealment! And have your masks and your ruses, that ye may be mistaken for what you are, or somewhat feared! And pray, don't forget the garden, the garden with golden trellis-work! And have people around you who are as a garden – or as music on the waters at eventide, when already the day becomes a memory. Choose the *good* solitude, the free, wanton, lightsome solitude, which also gives you the right still to remain good in any sense whatsoever! How poisonous, how crafty, how bad, does every long war make one, which cannot be waged openly by means of force! How *personal* does a long fear make one, a long watching of enemies, of possible enemies! These pariahs of society, these long-pursued, badly persecuted ones – also the compulsory recluses, the Spinozas or Giordano Brunos – always become in the end, even under the most intellectual masquerade, and perhaps without being themselves aware of it, refined vengeance-seekers and poison-brewers (just lay bare the foundation of Spinoza's ethics and theology!), not to speak of the stupidity of moral indignation, which is the unfailing sign in a philosopher that the sense of philosophical humour has left him. The martyrdom of the philosopher, his 'sacrifice for the sake of truth', forces into the light whatever of the agitator and actor lurks in him; and if one has hitherto contemplated him only with artistic curiosity, with regard to many a philosopher it is easy to understand the dangerous desire to see him also in his deterioration (deteriorated into a 'martyr', into a stage-and-tribune-bawler). Only, that it is necessary with such a desire to be clear *what* spectacle one will see in any case – merely a satyric play, merely an epilogue farce, merely the continued proof that the long, real tragedy *is at an end*, supposing that every philosophy has been a long tragedy in its origin.

26. Every select man strives instinctively for a citadel and a privacy, where he is *free* from the crowd, the many, the majority – where he may forget 'men who are the rule', as their exception; – exclusive only of the case in which he is pushed straight to such men by a still stronger instinct, as a discerner in the great and exceptional sense. Whoever, in intercourse with men, does not occasionally glisten in all the green and grey colours of distress, owing to disgust, satiety, sympathy, gloominess and solitariness, is assuredly not a man of elevated tastes; supposing, however, that he does not voluntarily take all this burden and disgust upon himself, that he persistently avoids it, and remains, as I said, quietly and proudly hidden in his citadel, one thing is then certain: he was not made, he was not predestined for knowledge. For as such, he would one day have to say to himself: 'The devil take my good taste! but "the rule" is more interesting than the exception – than myself, the exception!' And he would go *down*, and above all, he would go 'inside'. The long and serious study of the *average* man – and consequently much disguise, self-overcoming, familiarity and bad intercourse (all intercourse is bad intercourse except with one's equals): – that constitutes a necessary part of the life-history of every philosopher; perhaps the most disagreeable, odious and disappointing part. If he is fortunate, however, as a favourite child of knowledge should be, he will meet with suitable auxiliaries who will shorten and lighten his task; I mean so-called cynics, those who simply recognize the animal, the commonplace and 'the rule' in themselves, and at the same time have so much spirituality and ticklishness as to make them talk of themselves and their like *before witnesses* – sometimes they wallow, even in books, as on their own dung-hill.

Cynicism is the only form in which base souls approach what is called honesty; and the higher man must open his ears to all the coarser or finer cynicism, and congratulate himself when the clown becomes shameless right before him, or the scientific satyr speaks out. There are even cases where enchantment mixes with the disgust – namely, whereby a freak of nature, genius is bound to some such indiscreet billy-goat and ape, as in the case of the Abbé Galiani, the profoundest, acutest and perhaps also filthiest man of his century – he was far profounder than Voltaire, and consequently also, a good deal more silent. It happens more frequently, as has been hinted, that a scientific head is placed on an ape's body, a fine exceptional understanding in a base soul, an occurrence by no means rare, especially among doctors and moral physiologists. And whenever anyone speaks without bitterness, or rather quite innocently, of man as a belly with two requirements, and a head with one; whenever anyone sees, seeks and *wants* to see only hunger, sexual instinct and vanity as the real and only motives of human actions; in short, when anyone speaks 'badly' – and not even 'ill' – of man, then ought the lover of knowledge to hearken attentively and diligently; he ought, in general, to have an open ear wherever there is talk without indignation. For the indignant man, and he who perpetually tears and lacerates himself with his own teeth (or, in place of himself, the world, God or society), may indeed, morally speaking, stand higher than the laughing and self-satisfied satyr, but in every other sense he is the more ordinary, more indifferent and less instructive case. And no one is such a *liar* as the indignant man.

27. It is difficult to be understood, especially when one thinks and lives *gangasrotogati** among those only who think and live otherwise – namely, *kurmagati*†, or at best 'frog-like', *mandeikagati*‡ (I do everything to be 'difficultly understood' myself!) – and one should be heartily grateful for the good will to some refinement of

* Like the River Ganges: *presto*.

† Like the tortoise: *lento*.

‡ Like the frog: *staccato*.

interpretation. As regards 'the good friends', however, who are always too easy-going, and think that as friends they have a right to ease, one does well at the very first to grant them a playground and romping-place for misunderstanding – one can thus laugh still; or get rid of them altogether, these good friends – and laugh then also!

28. What is most difficult to render from one language into another is the *tempo* of its style, which has its basis in the character of the race, or to speak more physiologically, in the average *tempo* of the assimilation of its nutriment. There are honestly meant translations, which, as involuntary vulgarizations, are almost falsifications of the original, merely because its lively and merry *tempo* (which overleaps and obviates all dangers in word and expression) could not also be rendered. A German is almost incapacitated for *presto* in his language; consequently also, as may be reasonably inferred, for many of the most delightful and daring *nuances* of free, free-spirited thought. And just as the buffoon and satyr are foreign to him in body and conscience, so Aristophanes and Petronius are untranslatable for him. Everything ponderous, viscous and pompously clumsy, all long-winded and wearying species of style, are developed in profuse variety among Germans – pardon me for stating the fact that even Goethe's prose, in its mixture of stiffness and elegance, is no exception, as a reflection of the 'good old time' to which it belongs, and as an expression of German taste at a time when there was still a 'German taste', which was a rococo-taste *in moribus et artibus*. Lessing is an exception, owing to his histrionic nature, which understood much, and was versed in many things; he who was not the translator of Bayle to no purpose, who took refuge willingly in the shadow of Diderot and Voltaire, and still more willingly among the Roman comedy-writers – Lessing loved also free-spiritism in the *tempo*, and flight out of Germany. But how could the German language, even in the prose of Lessing, imitate the *tempo* of Machiavelli, who in his '*Il Principe*' makes us breathe the dry, fine air of Florence, and cannot help presenting the most serious events in a boisterous *allegrissimo*, perhaps not without a malicious artistic sense of the contrast he ventures to present – long, heavy, difficult, dangerous

thoughts and a *tempo* of the gallop, and of the best, wantonest humour? Finally, who would venture on a German translation of Petronius, who, more than any great musician hitherto, was a master of *presto* in invention, ideas and words? What matter in the end about the swamps of the sick, evil world or of the 'ancient world', when like him, one has the feet of a wind, the rush, the breath, the emancipating scorn of a wind, which makes everything healthy, by making everything *run*! And with regard to Aristophanes – that transfiguring, complementary genius, for whose sake one *pardons* all Hellenism for having existed, provided one has understood in its full profundity *all* that there requires pardon and transfiguration; there is nothing that has caused me to meditate more on *Plato's* secrecy and sphinx-like nature, than the happily preserved *petit fait* that under the pillow of his death-bed there was found no 'Bible', nor anything Egyptian, Pythagorean or Platonic – but a book of Aristophanes. How could even Plato have endured life – a Greek life which he repudiated – without an Aristophanes!

29. It is the business of the very few to be independent; it is a privilege of the strong. And whoever attempts it, even with the best right, but without being *obliged* to do so, proves that he is probably not only strong, but also daring beyond measure. He enters into a labyrinth, he multiplies a thousandfold the dangers which life in itself already brings with it; not the least of which is that no one can see how and where he loses his way, becomes isolated, and is torn piecemeal by some minotaur of conscience. Supposing such a one comes to grief, it is so far from the comprehension of men that they neither feel it, nor sympathize with it. And he cannot any longer go back! He cannot even go back again to the sympathy of men!

30. Our deepest insights must – and should – appear as follies, and under certain circumstances as crimes, when they come unauthorizedly to the ears of those who are not disposed and predestined for them. The exoteric and the esoteric, as they were formerly distinguished by philosophers – among the Indians, as among the Greeks, Persians and Mussulmans, in short, wherever people believed

in gradations of rank and *not* in equality and equal rights – are not so much in contradistinction to one another in respect to the exoteric class, standing without, and viewing, estimating, measuring and judging from the outside, and not from the inside; the more essential distinction is that the class in question views things from below upwards – while the esoteric class views things *from above downwards*. There are heights of the soul from which tragedy itself no longer appears to operate tragically; and if all the woe in the world were taken together, who would dare to decide whether the sight of it would *necessarily* seduce and constrain to sympathy, and thus to a doubling of the woe?... That which serves the higher class of men for nourishment or refreshment, must be almost poison to an entirely different and lower order of human beings. The virtues of the common man would perhaps mean vice and weakness in a philosopher; it might be possible for a highly developed man, supposing him to degenerate and go to ruin, to acquire qualities thereby alone, for the sake of which he would have to be honoured as a saint in the lower world into which he had sunk. There are books which have an inverse value for the soul and the health according as the inferior soul and the lower vitality, or the higher and more powerful, make use of them. In the former case they are dangerous, disturbing, unsettling books, in the latter case they are herald-calls which summon the bravest to *their* bravery. Books for the general reader are always ill-smelling books, the odour of paltry people clings to them. Where the populace eat and drink, and even where they reverence, it is accustomed to stink. One should not go into churches if one wishes to breathe *pure* air.

31. In our youthful years we still venerate and despise without the art of *nuance*, which is the best gain of life, and we have rightly to do hard penance for having fallen upon men and things with Yea and Nay. Everything is so arranged that the worst of all tastes, *the taste for the unconditional*, is cruelly befooled and abused, until a man learns to introduce a little art into his sentiments, and prefers to try conclusions with the artificial, as do the real artists of life. The angry and reverent spirit peculiar to youth appears to allow

itself no peace, until it has suitably falsified men and things, to be able to vent its passion upon them: youth in itself even, is something falsifying and deceptive. Later on, when the young soul, tortured by continual disillusions, finally turns suspiciously against itself – still ardent and savage even in its suspicion and remorse of conscience: how it upbraids itself, how impatiently it tears itself, how it revenges itself for its long self-blinding, as though it had been a voluntary blindness! In this transition one punishes oneself by distrust of one's sentiments; one tortures one's enthusiasm with doubt, one feels even the good conscience to be a danger, as if it were the self-concealment and lassitude of a more refined uprightness; and above all, one espouses upon principle the cause *against* 'youth'. – A decade later, and one comprehends that all this was also still – youth!

32. Throughout the longest period of human history – one calls it the prehistoric period – the value or non-value of an action was inferred from its *consequences*; the action in itself was not taken into consideration, any more than its origin; but pretty much as in China at present, where the distinction or disgrace of a child redounds to its parents, the retro-operating power of success or failure was what induced men to think well or ill of an action. Let us call this period the *pre-moral* period of mankind; the imperative, 'know thyself!' was then still unknown. – In the last ten thousand years, on the other hand, on certain large portions of the earth, one has gradually got so far, that one no longer lets the consequences of an action, but its origin, decide with regard to its worth: a great achievement as a whole, an important refinement of vision and of criterion, the unconscious effect of the supremacy of aristocratic values and of the belief in 'origin', the mark of a period which may be designated in the narrower sense as the *moral* one: the first attempt at self-knowledge is thereby made. Instead of the consequences, the origin – what an inversion of perspective! And assuredly an inversion effected only after long struggle and wavering! To be sure, an ominous new superstition, a peculiar narrowness of interpretation, attained supremacy precisely thereby: the origin of an action was interpreted in the most definite sense possible, as origin out of an *intention*;

people were agreed in the belief that the value of an action lay in the value of its intention. The intention as the sole origin and antecedent history of an action: under the influence of this prejudice moral praise and blame have been bestowed, and men have judged and even philosophized almost up to the present day. – Is it not possible, however, that the necessity may now have arisen of again making up our minds with regard to the reversing and fundamental shifting of values, owing to a new self-consciousness and acuteness in man – is it not possible that we may be standing on the threshold of a period which to begin with, would be distinguished negatively as *ultra-moral*: nowadays when, at least among us immoralists, the suspicion arises that the decisive value of an action lies precisely in that which is *not intentional*, and that all its intentionalness, all that is seen, sensible or 'sensed' in it, belongs to its surface or skin – which, like every skin, betrays something, but *conceals* still more? In short, we believe that the intention is only a sign or symptom, which first requires an explanation – a sign, moreover, which has too many interpretations, and consequently hardly any meaning in itself alone: that morality, in the sense in which it has been understood hitherto, as intention-morality, has been a prejudice, perhaps a prematureness or preliminariness, probably something of the same rank as astrology and alchemy, but in any case something which must be surmounted. The surmounting of morality, in a certain sense even the self-mounting of morality – let that be the name for the long-secret labour which has been reserved for the most refined, the most upright and also the most wicked consciences of today, as the living touchstones of the soul.

33. It cannot be helped: the sentiment of surrender, of sacrifice for one's neighbour, and all self-renunciation-morality, must be mercilessly called to account, and brought to judgment; just as the aesthetics of 'disinterested contemplation', under which the emasculation of art nowadays seeks insidiously enough to create itself a good conscience. There is far too much witchery and sugar in the sentiments 'for others' and '*not* for myself', for one not needing to be doubly distrustful here, and for one asking promptly: 'Are they

not perhaps – *deceptions*?' – That they *please* – him who has them, and him who enjoys their fruit, and also the mere spectator – that is still no argument in their *favour*, but just calls for caution. Let us therefore be cautious!

34. At whatever standpoint of philosophy one may place oneself nowadays, seen from every position, the *erroneousness* of the world in which we think we live is the surest and most certain thing our eyes can light upon: we find proof after proof thereof, which would fain allure us into surmises concerning a deceptive principle in the 'nature of things'. He, however, who makes thinking itself, and consequently 'the spirit', responsible for the falseness of the world – an honourable exit, which every conscious or unconscious *advocatus dei* avails himself of – he who regards this world, including space, time, form and movement, as falsely *deduced*, would have at least good reason in the end to become distrustful also of all thinking; has it not hitherto been playing upon us the worst of scurvy tricks? and what guarantee would it give that it would not continue to do what it has always been doing? In all seriousness, the innocence of thinkers has something touching and respect-inspiring in it, which even nowadays permits them to wait upon consciousness with the request that it will give them *honest* answers: for example, whether it be 'real' or not, and why it keeps the outer world so resolutely at a distance, and other questions of the same description. The belief in 'immediate certainties' is a *moral naïveté* which does honour to us philosophers; but – we have now to cease being '*merely* moral' men! Apart from morality, such belief is a folly which does little honour to us! If in middle-class life an ever-ready distrust is regarded as the sign of a 'bad character', and consequently as an imprudence, here among us, beyond the middle-class world and its Yeas and Nays, what should prevent our being imprudent and saying: the philosopher has at length a *right* to 'bad character', as the being who has hitherto been most befooled on earth – he is now under *obligation* to distrustfulness, to the wickedest squinting out of every abyss of suspicion. – Forgive me the joke of this gloomy grimace and turn of expression; for I myself

have long ago learned to think and estimate differently with regard to deceiving and being deceived, and I keep at least a couple of pokes in the ribs ready for the blind rage with which philosophers struggle against being deceived. Why *not*? It is nothing more than a moral prejudice that truth is worth more than semblance; it is, in fact, the worst proved supposition in the world. So much must be conceded: there could have been no life at all except upon the basis of perspective estimates and semblances; and if, with the virtuous enthusiasm and stupidity of many philosophers, one wished to do away altogether with the 'seeming world' – well, granted that *you* could do that, – at least nothing of your 'truth' would thereby remain! Indeed, what is it that forces us in general to the supposition that there is an essential opposition of 'true' and 'false'? Is it not enough to suppose degrees of seemingness, and as it were lighter and darker shades and tones of semblance – different *valeurs*, as the painters say? Why might not the world *which concerns us* – be a fiction? And to any one who suggested: 'But to a fiction belongs an originator?' – might it not be bluntly replied: *Why*? May not this 'belong' also belong to the fiction? Is it not at length permitted to be a little ironical towards the subject, just as towards the predicate and object? Might not the philosopher elevate himself above faith in grammar? All respect to governesses, but is it not time that philosophy should renounce governess-faith?

35. O Voltaire! O humanity! O idiocy! There is something ticklish in 'the truth', and in the *search* for the truth; and if man goes about it too humanely – '*il ne cherche le vrai que pour faire le bien*' – I wager he finds nothing!

36. Supposing that nothing else is 'given' as real but our world of desires and passions, that we cannot sink or rise to any other 'reality' but just that of our impulses – for thinking is only a relation of these impulses to one another: – are we not permitted to make the attempt and to ask the question whether this which is 'given' does not *suffice*, by means of our counterparts, for the understanding even of the so-called mechanical (or 'material') world?

I do not mean as an illusion, a 'semblance', a 'representation' (in the Berkeleyan and Schopenhauerian sense), but as possessing the same degree of reality as our emotions themselves – as a more primitive form of the world of emotions, in which everything still lies locked in a mighty unity, which afterwards branches off and develops itself in organic processes (naturally also, refines and debilitates) – as a kind of instinctive life in which all organic functions, including self-regulation, assimilation, nutrition, secretion and change of matter, are still synthetically united with one another – as a *primary form* of life? – In the end, it is not only permitted to make this attempt, it is commanded by the conscience of *logical method*. Not to assume several kinds of causality, so long as the attempt to get along with a single one has not been pushed to its furthest extent (to absurdity, if I may be allowed to say so): that is a morality of method which one may not repudiate nowadays – it follows 'from its definition', as mathematicians say. The question is ultimately whether we really recognize the will as *operating*, whether we believe in the causality of the will; if we do so – and fundamentally our belief *in this* is just our belief in causality itself – we *must* make the attempt to posit hypothetically the causality of the will as the only causality. 'Will' can naturally only operate on 'will' – and not on 'matter' (not on 'nerves', for instance): in short, the hypothesis must be hazarded, whether will does not operate on will wherever 'effects' are recognized – and whether all mechanical action, inasmuch as a power operates therein, is not just the power of will, the effect of will. Granted, finally, that we succeeded in explaining our entire instinctive life as the development and ramification of one fundamental form of will – namely, the Will to Power, as *my* thesis puts it; granted that all organic functions could be traced back to this Will to Power, and that the solution of the problem of generation and nutrition – it is one problem – could also be found therein: one would thus have acquired the right to define *all* active force unequivocally as *Will to Power*. The world seen from within, the world defined and designated according to its 'intelligible character' – it would simply be 'Will to Power', and nothing else.

37. 'What? Does not that mean in popular language: God is disproved, but not the devil?' – On the contrary! On the contrary, my friends! And who the devil also compels you to speak popularly!

38. As happened finally in all the enlightenment of modern times with the French Revolution (that terrible farce, quite superfluous when judged close at hand, into which, however, the noble and visionary spectators of all Europe have interpreted from a distance their own indignation and enthusiasm so long and passionately, *until the text has disappeared under the interpretation*), so a noble posterity might once more misunderstand the whole of the past, and perhaps only thereby make *its* aspect endurable. – Or rather, has not this already happened? Have not we ourselves been – that 'noble posterity'? And, in so far as we now comprehend this, is it not – thereby already past?

39. Nobody will very readily regard a doctrine as true merely because it makes people happy or virtuous – excepting, perhaps, the amiable 'Idealists', who are enthusiastic about the good, true and beautiful, and let all kinds of motley, coarse and good-natured desirabilities swim about promiscuously in their pond. Happiness and virtue are no arguments. It is willingly forgotten, however, even on the part of thoughtful minds, that to make unhappy and to make bad are just as little counter-arguments. A thing could be *true*, although it were in the highest degree injurious and dangerous; indeed, the fundamental constitution of existence might be such that one succumbed by a full knowledge of it – so that the strength of a mind might be measured by the amount of 'truth' it could endure – or to speak more plainly, by the extent to which it *required* truth attenuated, veiled, sweetened, damped and falsified. But there is no doubt that for the discovery of certain *portions* of truth the wicked and unfortunate are more favourably situated and have a greater likelihood of success; not to speak of the wicked who are happy – a species about whom moralists are silent. Perhaps severity and craft are more favourable conditions for the development of strong, independent spirits and philosophers than the gentle, refined, yielding

good-nature and habit of taking things easily, which are prized, and rightly prized in a learned man. Presupposing always, to begin with, that the term 'philosopher' be not confined to the philosopher who writes books, or even introduces *his* philosophy into books! – Stendhal furnishes a last feature of the portrait of the free-spirited philosopher, which for the sake of German taste I will not omit to underline – for it is *opposed* to German taste. '*Pour être bon philosophe*,' says this last great psychologist, '*il faut être sec, clair, sans illusion. Un banquier, qui a fait fortune, a une partie du caractère requis pour faire des découvertes en philosophie, c'est-à-dire pour voir clair dans ce qui est*.'

40. Everything that is profound loves the mask: the profoundest things have a hatred even of figure and likeness. Should not the *contrary* only be the right disguise for the shame of a God to go about in? A question worth asking! – it would be strange if some mystic has not already ventured on the same kind of thing. There are proceedings of such a delicate nature that it is well to overwhelm them with coarseness and make them unrecognizable; there are actions of love and of an extravagant magnanimity after which nothing can be wiser than to take a stick and thrash the witness soundly: one thereby obscures his recollection. Many a one is able to obscure and abuse his own memory, in order at least to have vengeance on this sole party in the secret: shame is inventive. They are not the worst things of which one is most ashamed: there is not only deceit behind a mask – there is so much goodness in craft. I could imagine that a man with something costly and fragile to conceal, would roll through life clumsily and rotundly like an old, green, heavily hooped wine cask: the refinement of his shame requiring it to be so. A man who has depths in his shame meets his destiny and his delicate decisions upon paths which few ever reach, and with regard to the existence of which his nearest and most intimate friends may be ignorant; his mortal danger conceals itself from their eyes, and equally so his regained security. Such a hidden nature, which instinctively employs speech for silence and concealment, and is inexhaustible in evasion of communication, *desires* and

insists that a mask of himself shall occupy his place in the hearts and heads of his friends; and supposing he does not desire it, his eyes will some day be opened to the fact that there is nevertheless a mask of him there – and that it is well to be so. Every profound spirit needs a mask; nay, more, around every profound spirit there continually grows a mask, owing to the constantly false, that is to say, *superficial* interpretation of every word he utters, every step he takes, every sign of life he manifests.

41. One must subject oneself to one's own tests that one is destined for independence and command, and do so at the right time. One must not avoid one's tests, although they constitute perhaps the most dangerous game one can play, and are in the end tests made only before ourselves and before no other judge. Not to cleave to any person, be it even the dearest – every person is a prison and also a recess. Not to cleave to a fatherland, be it even the most suffering and necessitous – it is even less difficult to detach one's heart from a victorious fatherland. Not to cleave to a sympathy, be it even for higher men, into whose peculiar torture and helplessness chance has given us an insight. Not to cleave to a science, though it tempt one with the most valuable discoveries, apparently specially reserved for us. Not to cleave to one's own liberation, to the voluptuous distance and remoteness of the bird, which always flies further aloft in order always to see more under it – the danger of the flier. Not to cleave to our own virtues, nor become as a whole a victim to any of our specialties, to our 'hospitality' for instance, which is the danger of dangers for highly developed and wealthy souls, who deal prodigally, almost indifferently with themselves, and push the virtue of liberality so far that it becomes a vice. One must know how *to conserve oneself* – the best test of independence.

42. A new order of philosophers is appearing; I shall venture to baptize them by a name not without danger. As far as I understand them, as far as they allow themselves to be understood – for it is their nature to *wish* to remain something of a puzzle – these philosophers of the future might rightly, perhaps also wrongly, claim to

be designated as 'tempters'. This name itself is after all only an attempt, or, if it be preferred, a temptation.

43. Will they be new friends of 'truth', these coming philosophers? Very probably, for all philosophers hitherto have loved their truths. But assuredly they will not be dogmatists. It must be contrary to their pride, and also contrary to their taste, that their truth should still be truth for every one – that which has hitherto been the secret wish and ultimate purpose of all dogmatic efforts. 'My opinion is *my* opinion: another person has not easily a right to it' – such a philosopher of the future will say, perhaps. One must renounce the bad taste of wishing to agree with many people. 'Good' is no longer good when one's neighbour takes it into his mouth. And how could there be a 'common good'! The expression contradicts itself; that which can be common is always of small value. In the end things must be as they are and have always been – the great things remain for the great, the abysses for the profound, the delicacies and thrills for the refined, and, to sum up shortly, everything rare for the rare.

44. Need I say expressly after all this that they will be free, *very* free spirits, these philosophers of the future – as certainly also they will not be merely free spirits, but something more, higher, greater and fundamentally different, which does not wish to be misunderstood and mistaken? But while I say this, I feel under *obligation* almost as much to them as to ourselves (we free spirits who are their heralds and forerunners), to sweep away from ourselves altogether a stupid old prejudice and misunderstanding, which, like a fog, has too long made the conception of 'free spirit' obscure. In every country of Europe, and the same in America, there is at present something which makes an abuse of this name: a very narrow, prepossessed, enchained class of spirits, who desire almost the opposite of what our intentions and instincts prompt – not to mention that in respect to the *new* philosophers who are appearing, they must still more be closed windows and bolted doors. Briefly and regrettably, they belong to the *levellers*, these wrongly named 'free spirits' – as glib-tongued and scribe-fingered slaves of the democratic

taste and its 'modern ideas': all of them men without solitude, without personal solitude, blunt honest fellows to whom neither courage nor honourable conduct ought to be denied; only, they are not free, and are ludicrously superficial, especially in their innate partiality for seeing the cause of almost *all* human misery and failure in the old forms in which society has hitherto existed – a notion which happily inverts the truth entirely! What they would fain attain with all their strength, is the universal, green-meadow happiness of the herd, together with security, safety, comfort and alleviation of life for everyone, their two most frequently chanted songs and doctrines are called 'Equality of Rights' and 'Sympathy with all Sufferers' – and suffering itself is looked upon by them as something which must be *done away with*. We opposite ones, however, who have opened our eye and conscience to the question how and where the plant 'man' has hitherto grown most vigorously, believe that this has always taken place under the opposite conditions, that for this end the dangerousness of his situation had to be increased enormously, his inventive faculty and dissembling power (his 'spirit') had to develop into subtlety and daring under long oppression and compulsion, and his Will to Life had to be increased to the unconditioned Will to Power – we believe that severity, violence, slavery, danger in the street and in the heart, secrecy, stoicism, tempter's art and devilry of every kind, – that everything wicked, terrible, tyrannical, predatory and serpentine in man, serves as well for the elevation of the human species as its opposite: – we do not even say enough when we only say *this much*; and in any case we find ourselves here, both with our speech and our silence, at the *other* extreme of all modern ideology and gregarious desirability, as their antipodes perhaps? What wonder that we 'free spirits' are not exactly the most communicative spirits? that we do not wish to betray in every respect *what* a spirit can free itself from, and *where* perhaps it will then be driven? And as to the import of the dangerous formula, 'Beyond Good and Evil', with which we at least avoid confusion, we *are* something else than '*libres-penseurs*', '*liben pensatori*', 'freethinkers', and whatever these honest advocates of 'modern ideas' like to call themselves. Having been at home, or at least guests, in many realms of the spirit, having escaped again and again from the gloomy, agreeable nooks in which preferences and prejudices, youth, origin, the accident of men and books, or even the weariness of travel seemed to confine us; full of malice against the seductions of dependency which lie concealed in honours, money, positions or exaltation of the senses; grateful even for distress and the vicissitudes of illness, because they always free us from some rule, and its 'prejudice', grateful to the God, devil, sheep and worm in us; inquisitive to a fault, investigators to the point of cruelty, with unhesitating fingers for the intangible, with teeth and stomachs for the most indigestible, ready for any business that requires sagacity and acute senses, ready for every adventure, owing to an excess of 'free will'; with anterior and posterior souls, into the ultimate intentions of which it is difficult to pry, with foregrounds and backgrounds to the end of which no foot may run; hidden ones under the mantles of light, appropriators, although we resemble heirs and spendthrifts, arrangers and collectors from morning till night, misers of our wealth and our full-crammed drawers, economical in learning and forgetting, inventive in scheming; sometimes proud of tables of categories, sometimes pedants, sometimes night owls of work even in full day; yea, if necessary, even scarecrows – and it is necessary nowadays, that is to say, inasmuch as we are the born, sworn, jealous friends of *solitude*, of our own profoundest midnight and midday solitude: – such kind of men are we, we free spirits! And perhaps *ye* are also something of the same kind, ye coming ones? ye *new* philosophers?

CHAPTER III

The Religious Mood

45. The human soul and its limits, the range of man's inner experiences hitherto attained, the heights, depths and distances of these experiences, the entire history of the soul *up to the present time*, and its still unexhausted possibilities: this is the preordained hunting-domain for a born psychologist and lover of a 'big hunt'. But how often must he say despairingly to himself: 'A single individual! alas, only a single individual! and this great forest, this virgin forest!' So he would like to have some hundreds of hunting assistants and fine trained hounds, that he could send into the history of the human soul, to drive *his* game together. In vain: again and again he experiences, profoundly and bitterly, how difficult it is to find assistants and dogs for all the things that directly excite his curiosity. The evil of sending scholars into new and dangerous hunting-domains, where courage, sagacity and subtlety in every sense are required, is that they are no longer serviceable just when the '*big* hunt', and also the great danger commences, – it is precisely then that they lose their keen eye and nose. In order, for instance, to divine and determine what sort of history the problem of *knowledge and conscience* has hitherto had in the souls of *homines religiosi*, a person would perhaps himself have to possess as profound, as bruised, as immense an experience as the intellectual conscience of Pascal; and then he would still require that wide-spread heaven of clear, wicked spirituality, which, from above, would be able to oversee, arrange and effectively formulize this mass of dangerous and painful experiences. – But who could do me this service! And who would have time to wait for such servants! – they evidently appear too rarely, they are so improbable at all times! Eventually one must do everything *oneself* in order to know something; which means that one has *much* to do! – But a curiosity like mine is once for all the most agreeable of vices –

pardon me! I mean to say that the love of truth has its reward in heaven, and already upon earth.

46. Faith, such as early Christianity desired, and not infrequently achieved in the midst of a sceptical and southernly free-spirited world, which had centuries of struggle between philosophical schools behind it and in it, counting besides the education in tolerance which the *Imperium Romanum* gave – this faith is *not* that sincere, austere slave-faith by which perhaps a Luther or a Cromwell, or some other northern barbarian of the spirit remained attached to his God and Christianity; it is much rather the faith of Pascal, which resembles in a terrible manner a continuous suicide of reason – a tough, long-lived, worm-like reason, which is not to be slain at once and with a single blow. The Christian faith from the beginning, is sacrifice: the sacrifice of all freedom, all pride, all self-confidence of spirit; it is at the same time subjection, self-derision and self-mutilation. There is cruelty and religious Phoenicianism in this faith, which is adapted to a tender, many-sided and very fastidious conscience, it takes for granted that the subjection of the spirit is indescribably *painful*, that all the past and all the habits of such a spirit resist the *absurdissimum*, in the form of which 'faith' comes to it. Modern men, with their obtuseness as regards all Christian nomenclature, have no longer the sense for the terribly superlative conception which was implied to an antique taste by the paradox of the formula, 'God on the Cross'. Hitherto there had never and nowhere been such boldness in inversion, nor anything at once so dreadful, questioning and questionable as this formula: it promised a transvaluation of all ancient values. – It was the Orient, the *profound* Orient, it was the Oriental slave who thus took revenge on Rome and its noble, light-minded toleration, on the Roman 'Catholicism' of non-faith; and it was always not the faith, but the freedom from the faith, the half-stoical and smiling indifference to the seriousness of the faith, which made the slaves indignant at their masters and revolt against them. 'Enlightenment' causes revolt: for the slave desires the unconditioned, he understands nothing but the tyrannous, even in morals; he loves as he hates, without *nuance*, to the very depths, to the point of pain,

to the point of sickness – his many *hidden* sufferings make him revolt against the noble taste which seems to *deny* suffering. The scepticism with regard to suffering, fundamentally only an attitude of aristocratic morality, was not the least of the causes, also, of the last great slave-insurrection which began with the French Revolution.

47. Wherever the religious neurosis has appeared on the earth so far, we find it connected with three dangerous prescriptions as to regimen: solitude, fasting and sexual abstinence – but without its being possible to determine with certainty which is cause and which is effect, or *if* any relation at all of cause and effect exists there. This latter doubt is justified by the fact that one of the most regular symptoms among savage as well as among civilized peoples is the most sudden and excessive sensuality; which then with equal suddenness transforms into penitential paroxysms, world-renunciation and will-renunciation: both symptoms perhaps explainable as disguised epilepsy? But nowhere is it *more* obligatory to put aside explanations: around no other type has there grown such a mass of absurdity and superstition, no other type seems to have been more interesting to men and even to philosophers – perhaps it is time to become just a little indifferent here, to learn caution, or, better still, to look away, *to go away* – Yet in the background of the most recent philosophy, that of Schopenhauer, we find almost as the problem in itself, this terrible note of interrogation of the religious crisis and awakening. How is the negation of will *possible*? how is the saint possible? – that seems to have been the very question with which Schopenhauer made a start and became a philosopher. And thus it was a genuine Schopenhauerian consequence, that his most convinced adherent (perhaps also his last, as far as Germany is concerned), namely, Richard Wagner, should bring his own life-work to an end just here, and should finally put that terrible and eternal type upon the stage as Kundry, *type vécu*, and as it loved and lived, at the very time that the mad-doctors in almost all European countries had an opportunity to study the type close at hand, wherever the religious neurosis – or as I call it, 'the religious mood' – made its latest epidemical outbreak and display as the

'Salvation Army'. – If it be a question, however, as to what has been so extremely interesting to men of all sorts in all ages, and even to philosophers, in the whole phenomenon of the saint, it is undoubtedly the appearance of the miraculous therein – namely, the immediate *succession of opposites*, of states of the soul regarded as morally antithetical: it was believed here to be self-evident that a 'bad man' was all at once turned into a 'saint', a good man. The hitherto existing psychology was wrecked at this point; is it not possible it may have happened principally because psychology had placed itself under the dominion of morals, because it *believed* in oppositions of moral values, and saw, read and *interpreted* these oppositions into the text and facts of the case? What? 'Miracle' only an error of interpretation? A lack of philology?

48. It seems that the Latin races are far more deeply attached to their Catholicism than we Northerners are to Christianity generally, and that consequently unbelief in Catholic countries means something quite different from what it does among Protestants – namely, a sort of revolt against the spirit of the race, while with us it is rather a return to the spirit (or non-spirit) of the race. We Northerners undoubtedly derive our origin from barbarous races, even as regards our talents for religion – we have *poor* talents for it. One may make an exception in the case of the Celts, who have theretofore furnished also the best soil for Christian infection in the North: the Christian ideal blossomed forth in France as much as ever the pale sun of the North would allow it. How strangely pious for our taste are still these later French sceptics, whenever there is any Celtic blood in their origin! How Catholic, how un-German does Auguste Comte's Sociology seem to us, with the Roman logic of its instincts! How Jesuitical, that amiable and shrewd cicerone of Port Royal, Sainte-Beuve, in spite of all his hostility to Jesuits! And even Ernest Renan: how inaccessible to us Northerners does the language of such a Renan appear, in whom every instant the merest touch of religious thrill throws his refined voluptuous and comfortably couching soul off its balance! Let us repeat after him these fine sentences – and what wickedness and haughtiness is immediately

aroused by way of answer in our probably less beautiful but harder souls, that is to say, in our more German souls! – '*Disons donc hardiment que la religion est un produit de l'homme normal, que l'homme est le plus dans le vrai quand il est le plus religieux et le plus assuré d'une destinée infinie.... C'est quand il est bon qu'il veut que la virtu corresponde à un order éternal, c'est quand il contemple les choses d'une manière désintéressee qu'il trouve la mort révoltante et absurde. Comment ne pas supposer que c'est dans ces moments-là, que l'homme voit le mieux?*'... These sentences are so extremely *antipodal* to my ears and habits of thought, that in my first impulse of rage on finding them, I wrote on the margin, '*la niaiserie religieuse par excellence*!' – until in my later rage I even took a fancy to them, these sentences with their truth absolutely inverted! It is so nice and such a distinction to have one's own antipodes!

49. That which is so astonishing in the religious life of the ancient Greeks is the irrestrainable stream of *gratitude* which it pours forth – it is a very superior kind of man who takes *such* an attitude towards nature and life. – Later on, when the populace got the upper hand in Greece, *fear* became rampant also in religion; and Christianity was preparing itself.

50. The passion for God: there are churlish, honest-hearted and importunate kinds of it, like that of Luther – the whole of Protestantism lacks the Southern *delicatezza*. There is an Oriental exaltation of the mind in it, like that of an undeservedly favoured or elevated slave, as in the case of St Augustine, for instance, who lacks in an offensive manner, all nobility in bearing and desires. There is a feminine tenderness and sensuality in it, which modestly and unconsciously longs for a *unio mystica et physica*, as in the case of Madame de Guyon. In many cases it appears, curiously enough, as the disguise of a girl's or youth's puberty; here and there even as the hysteria of an old maid, also as her last ambition. The Church has frequently canonized the woman in such a case.

51. The mightiest men have hitherto always bowed reverently before the saint, as the enigma of self-subjugation and utter voluntary privation – why did they thus bow? They divined in him – and as it were behind the questionableness of his frail and wretched appearance – the superior force which wished to test itself by such a subjugation; the strength of will, in which they recognized their own strength and love of power, and knew how to honour it: they honoured something in themselves when they honoured the saint. In addition to this, the contemplation of the saint suggested to them a suspicion: such an enormity of self-negation and anti-naturalness will not have been coveted for nothing – they have said, inquiringly. There is perhaps a reason for it, some very great danger, about which the ascetic might wish to be more accurately informed through his secret interlocutors and visitors? In a word, the mighty ones of the world learned to have a new fear before him, they divined a new power, a strange, still unconquered enemy: – it was the 'Will to Power' which obliged them to halt before the saint. They had to question him.

52. In the Jewish 'Old Testament', the book of divine justice, there are men, things and sayings on such an immense scale, that Greek and Indian literature has nothing to compare with it. One stands with fear and reverence before those stupendous remains of what man was formerly, and one has sad thoughts about old Asia and its little out-pushed peninsula Europe, which would like, by all means, to figure before Asia as the 'Progress of Mankind'. To be sure, he who is himself only a slender, tame house-animal, and knows only the wants of a house-animal (like our cultured people of today, including the Christians of 'cultured' Christianity), need neither be amazed nor even sad amid those ruins – the taste for the Old Testament is a touchstone with respect to 'great' and 'small': perhaps he will find that the New Testament, the book of grace, still appeals more to his heart (there is much of the odour of the genuine, tender, stupid beadsman and petty soul in it). To have bound up this New Testament (a kind of *rococo* of taste in every respect) along with the Old Testament into one book, as the 'Bible', as 'The Book in

Itself', is perhaps the greatest audacity and 'sin against the Spirit' which literary Europe has upon its conscience.

53. Why Atheism nowadays? 'The father' in God is thoroughly refuted; equally so 'the judge', 'the rewarder'. Also his 'free will': he does not hear – and even if he did, he would not know how to help. The worst is that he seems incapable of communicating himself clearly; is he uncertain? – This is what I have made out (by questioning and listening at a variety of conversations) to be the cause of the decline of European theism; it appears to me that though the religious instinct is in vigorous growth, – it rejects the theistic satisfaction with profound distrust.

54. What does all modern philosophy mainly do? Since Descartes – and indeed more in defiance of him than on the basis of his procedure – an *attentat* has been made on the part of all philosophers on the old conception of the soul, under the guise of a criticism of the subject and predicate conception – that is to say, an *attentat* on the fundamental presupposition of Christian doctrine. Modern philosophy, as epistemological scepticism, is secretly or openly *anti-Christian*, although (for keener ears, be it said) by no means anti-religious. Formerly, in effect, one believed in 'the soul' as one believed in grammar and the grammatical subject: one said, 'I' is the condition, 'think' is the predicate and is conditioned – to think is an activity for which one *must* suppose a subject as cause. The attempt was then made, with marvellous tenacity and subtlety, to see if one could not get out of this net, – to see if the opposite was not perhaps true: 'think' the condition, and 'I' the conditioned; 'I', therefore, only a synthesis which has been *made* by thinking itself. *Kant* really wished to prove that, starting from the subject, the subject could not be proved – nor the object either: the possibility of an *apparent existence* of the subject, and therefore of 'the soul', may not always have been strange to him, – the thought which once had an immense power on earth as the Vedanta philosophy.

55. There is a great ladder of religious cruelty, with many rounds; but three of these are the most important. Once on a time men

sacrificed human beings to their God, and perhaps just those they loved the best – to this category belong the firstling sacrifices of all primitive religions, and also the sacrifice of the Emperor Tiberius in the Mithra-Grotto on the Island of Capri, that most terrible of all Roman anachronisms. Then, during the moral epoch of mankind, they sacrificed to their God the strongest instincts they possessed, their 'nature'; *this* festal joy shines in the cruel glances of ascetics and 'anti-natural' fanatics. Finally, what still remained to be sacrificed? Was it not necessary in the end for men to sacrifice everything comforting, holy, healing, all hope, all faith in hidden harmonies, in future blessedness and justice? Was it not necessary to sacrifice God himself, and out of cruelty to themselves to worship stone, stupidity, gravity, fate, nothingness? To sacrifice God for nothingness – this paradoxical mystery of the ultimate cruelty has been reserved for the rising generation; we all know something thereof already.

56. Whoever, like myself, prompted by some enigmatical desire, has long endeavoured to go to the bottom of the question of pessimism and free it from the half-Christian, half-German narrowness and stupidity in which it has finally presented itself to this century, namely, in the form of Schopenhauer's philosophy; whoever, with an Asiatic and super-Asiatic eye, has actually looked inside, and into the most world-renouncing of all possible modes of thought – beyond good and evil, and no longer like Buddha and Schopenhauer, under the dominion and delusion of morality, – whoever has done this, has perhaps just thereby, without really desiring it, opened his eyes to behold the opposite ideal: the ideal of the most world-approving, exuberant and vivacious man, who has not only learnt to compromise and arrange with that which was and is, but wishes to have it again *as it was and is*, for all eternity, insatiably calling out *da capo*, not only to himself, but to the whole piece and play; and not only the play, but actually to him who requires the play – and makes it necessary; because he always requires himself anew – and makes himself necessary. – What? And this would not be – *circulus vitiosus deus*?

57. The distance, and as it were the space around man, grows with the strength of his intellectual vision and insight: his world becomes profounder; new stars, new enigmas and notions are ever coming into view. Perhaps everything on which the intellectual eye has exercised its acuteness and profundity has just been an occasion for its exercise, something of a game, something for children and childish minds. Perhaps the most solemn conceptions that have caused the most fighting and suffering, the conceptions 'God' and 'sin', will one day seem to us of no more importance than a child's plaything or a child's pain seems to an old man; – and perhaps another plaything and another pain will then be necessary once more for 'the old man' – always childish enough, an eternal child!

58. Has it been observed to what extent outward idleness, or semi-idleness, is necessary to a real religious life (alike for its favourite microscopic labour of self-examination, and for its soft placidity called 'prayer', the state of perpetual readiness for the 'coming of God'), I mean the idleness with a good conscience, the idleness of olden times and of blood, to which the aristocratic sentiment that work is *dishonouring* – that it vulgarizes body and soul – is not quite unfamiliar? And that consequently the modern, noisy, time-engrossing, conceited, foolishly proud laboriousness educates and prepares for 'unbelief' more than anything else? Among these, for instance, who are at present living apart from religion in Germany, I find 'free-thinkers' of diversified species and origin, but above all a majority of those in whom laboriousness from generation to generation has dissolved the religious instincts; so that they no longer know what purpose religions serve, and only note their existence in the world with a kind of dull astonishment. They feel themselves already fully occupied, these good people, be it by their business or by their pleasures, not to mention the 'Fatherland', and the newspapers, and their 'family duties'; it seems that they have no time whatever left for religion; and above all, it is not obvious to them whether it is a question of a new business or a new pleasure – for it is impossible, they say to themselves, that people should go to church merely to spoil their tempers. They are by no means enemies

of religious customs; should certain circumstances, State affairs perhaps, require their participation in such customs, they do what is required, as so many things are done – with a patient and unassuming seriousness, and without much curiosity or discomfort; – they live too much apart and outside to feel even the necessity for a *for* or *against* in such matters. Among those indifferent persons may be reckoned nowadays the majority of German Protestants of the middle classes, especially in the great laborious centres of trade and commerce; also the majority of laborious scholars, and the entire University personnel (with the exception of the theologians, whose existence and possibility there always gives psychologists new and more subtle puzzles to solve). On the part of pious, or merely church-going people, there is seldom any idea of *how much* good-will, one might say arbitrary will, is now necessary for a German scholar to take the problem of religion seriously; his whole profession (and as I have said, his whole workmanlike laboriousness, to which he is compelled by his modern conscience) inclines him to a lofty and almost charitable serenity as regards religion, with which is occasionally mingled a slight disdain for the 'uncleanliness' of spirit which he takes for granted wherever anyone still professes to belong to the Church. It is only with the help of history (*not* through his own personal experience, therefore) that the scholar succeeds in bringing himself to a respectful seriousness, and to a certain timid deference in presence of religions; but even when his sentiments have reached the stage of gratitude towards them, he has not personally advanced one step nearer to that which still maintains itself as Church or as piety; perhaps even the contrary. The practical indifference to religious matters in the midst of which he has been born and brought up, usually sublimates itself in his case into circumspection and cleanliness, which shuns contact with religious men and things; and it may be just the depth of his tolerance and humanity which prompts him to avoid the delicate trouble which tolerance itself brings with it. – Every age has its own divine type of naïveté, for the discovery of which other ages may envy it: and how much naïveté – adorable, childlike and boundlessly foolish naïveté is involved in this belief of the scholar in his superiority, in the good conscience of his tolerance, in the unsuspecting, simple certainty with which his instinct treats the religious man as a lower and less valuable type, beyond, before and *above* which he himself has developed – he, the little arrogant dwarf and mob-man, the sedulously alert, head-and-hand drudge of 'ideas', of 'modern ideas'!

59. Whoever has seen deeply into the world has doubtless divined what wisdom there is in the fact that men are superficial. It is their preservative instinct which teaches them to be flighty, lightsome and false. Here and there one finds a passionate and exaggerated adoration of 'pure forms' in philosophers as well as in artists: it is not to be doubted that whoever has *need* of the cult of the superficial to that extent, has at one time or another made an unlucky dive *beneath* it. Perhaps there is even an order of rank with respect to those burnt children, the born artists who find the enjoyment of life only in trying to *falsify* its image (as if taking wearisome revenge on it); one might guess to what degree life has disgusted them, by the extent to which they wish to see its image falsified, attenuated, ultrified and deified; – one might reckon the *homines religiosi* among the artists, as their *highest* rank. It is the profound, suspicious fear of an incurable pessimism which compels whole centuries to fasten their teeth into a religious interpretation of existence: the fear of the instinct which divines that truth might be attained *too soon*, before man has become strong enough, hard enough, artist enough... Piety, the 'Life in God', regarded in this light, would appear as the most elaborate and ultimate product of the *fear* of truth, as artist-adoration and artist-intoxication in presence of the most logical of all falsifications, as the will to the inversion of truth, to untruth at any price. Perhaps there has hitherto been no more effective means of beautifying man than piety; by means of it man can become so artful, so superficial, so iridescent and so good, that his appearance no longer offends.

60. To love mankind *for God's sake* – this has so far been the noblest and remotest sentiment to which mankind has attained. That love to mankind, without any redeeming intention in the background,

is only an *additional* folly and brutishness, that the inclination to this love has first to get its proportion, its delicacy, its grain of salt and sprinkling of ambergris from a higher inclination: – whoever first perceived and 'experienced' this, however his tongue may have stammered as it attempted to express such a delicate matter, let him for all time be holy and respected, as the man who has so far flown highest and gone astray in the finest fashion!

61. The philosopher, as *we* free spirits understand him – as the man of the greatest responsibility, who has the conscience for the general development of mankind, – will use religion for his disciplining and educating work, just as he will use the contemporary political and economic conditions. The selecting and disciplining influence – destructive, as well as creative and fashioning – which can be exercised by means of religion is manifold and varied, according to the sort of people placed under its spell and protection. For those who are strong and independent, destined and trained to command, in whom the judgment and skill of a ruling race is incorporated, religion is an additional means for overcoming resistance in the exercise of authority – as a bond which binds rulers and subjects in common, betraying and surrendering to the former the conscience of the latter, their inmost heart, which would fain escape obedience. And in the case of the unique natures of noble origin, if by virtue of superior spirituality they should incline to a more retired and contemplative life, reserving to themselves only the more refined forms of government (over chosen disciples or members of an order), religion itself may be used as a means for obtaining peace from the noise and trouble of managing *grosser* affairs, and for securing immunity from the *unavoidable* filth of all political agitation. The Brahmins, for instance, understood this fact. With the help of a religious organization, they secured to themselves the power of nominating kings for the people, while their sentiments prompted them to keep apart and outside, as men with a higher and super-regal mission. At the same time, religion gives inducement and opportunity to some of the subjects to qualify themselves for future ruling and commanding the slowly ascending ranks and classes, in

which, through fortunate marriage customs, volitional power and delight in self-control are on the increase. To them religion offers sufficient incentives and temptations to aspire to higher intellectuality, and to experience the sentiments of authoritative self-control, of silence and of solitude. Asceticism and Puritanism are almost indispensable means of educating and ennobling a race which seeks to rise above its hereditary baseness and work itself upwards to future supremacy. And finally, to ordinary men, to the majority of the people, who exist for service and general utility, and are only so far entitled to exist, religion gives invaluable contentedness with their lot and condition, peace of heart, ennoblement of obedience, additional social happiness and sympathy, with something of transfiguration and embellishment, something of justification of all the commonplaceness, all the meanness, all the semi-animal poverty of their souls. Religion, together with the religious significance of life, sheds sunshine over such perpetually harassed men, and makes even their own aspect endurable to them, it operates upon them as the Epicurean philosophy usually operates upon sufferers of a higher order, in a refreshing and refining manner, almost *turning* suffering *to account*, and in the end even hallowing and vindicating it. There is perhaps nothing so admirable in Christianity and Buddhism as their art of teaching even the lowest to elevate themselves by piety to a seemingly higher order of things, and thereby to retain their satisfaction with the actual world in which they find it difficult enough to live – this very difficulty being necessary.

62. To be sure – to make also the bad counter-reckoning against such religions, and to bring to light their secret dangers – the cost is always excessive and terrible when religions do *not* operate as an educational and disciplinary medium in the hands of the philosopher, but rule voluntarily and *paramountly*, when they wish to be the final end, and not a means along with other means. Among men, as among all other animals, there is a surplus of defective, diseased, degenerating, infirm and necessarily suffering individuals; the successful cases, among men also, are always the exception; and in view of the fact that man is *the animal not yet properly adapted to*

his environment, the rare exception. But worse still. The higher the type a man represents, the greater is the improbability that he will *succeed*; the accidental, the law of irrationality in the general constitution of mankind, manifests itself most terribly in its destructive effect on the higher orders of men, the conditions of whose lives are delicate, diverse and difficult to determine. What, then, is the attitude of the two greatest religions above-mentioned to the *surplus* of failures in life? They endeavour to preserve and keep alive whatever can be preserved; in fact, as the religions *for sufferers*, they take the part of these upon principle; they are always in favour of those who suffer from life as from a disease, and they would fain treat every other experience of life as false and impossible. However highly we may esteem this indulgent and preservative care (inasmuch as in applying to others, it has applied, and applies also to the highest and usually the most suffering type of man), the hitherto *paramount* religions – to give a general appreciation of them – are among the principal causes which have kept the type of 'man' upon a lower level – they have preserved too much *that which should have perished*. One has to thank them for invaluable services; and who is sufficiently rich in gratitude not to feel poor at the contemplation of all that the 'spiritual men' of Christianity have done for Europe hitherto! But when they had given comfort to the sufferers, courage to the oppressed and despairing, a staff and support to the helpless, and when they had allured from society into convents and spiritual penitentiaries the broken-hearted and distracted: what else had they to do in order to work systematically in that fashion, and with a good conscience, for the preservation of all the sick and suffering, which means, in deed and in truth, to work for the *deterioration of the European race*? To *reverse* all estimates of value – *that* is what they had to do! And to shatter the strong, to spoil great hopes, to cast suspicion on the delight in beauty, to break down everything autonomous, manly, conquering and imperious – all instincts which are natural to the highest and most successful type of 'man' – into uncertainty, distress of conscience and self-destruction; forsooth, to invert all love of the earthly and of supremacy over the earth, into hatred of the earth and earthly things – *that* is the task the Church imposed on itself, and was obliged to impose, until, according to its standard of value, 'unworldliness', 'unsensuousness', and 'higher man' fused into one sentiment. If one could observe the strangely painful, equally coarse and refined comedy of European Christianity with the derisive and impartial eye of an Epicurean god, I should think one would never cease marvelling and laughing; does it not actually seem that some single will has ruled over Europe for eighteen centuries in order to make a *sublime abortion* of man? He, however, who, with opposite requirements (no longer Epicurean) and with some divine hammer in his hand, could approach this almost voluntary degeneration and stunting of mankind, as exemplified in the European Christian (Pascal, for instance), would he not have to cry aloud with rage, pity and horror: 'Oh, you bunglers, presumptuous pitiful bunglers, what have you done! Was that a work for your hands? How you have hacked and botched my finest stone! What have you presumed to do!' – I should say that Christianity has hitherto been the most portentous of presumptions. Men, not great enough, nor hard enough, to be entitled as artists to take part in fashioning *man*; men, not sufficiently strong and far-sighted to *allow*, with sublime self-constraint, the obvious law of the thousandfold failures and perishings to prevail; men, not sufficiently noble to see the radically different grades of rank and intervals of rank that separate man from man: – *such* men, with their 'equality before God', have hitherto swayed the destiny of Europe; until at last a dwarfed, almost ludicrous species has been produced, a gregarious animal, something obliging, sickly, mediocre, the European of the present day.

CHAPTER IV

Apophthegms and Interludes

63. He who is a thorough teacher takes things seriously – and even himself – only in relation to his pupils.

64. 'Knowledge for its own sake' – that is the last snare laid by morality: we are thereby completely entangled in morals once more.

65. The charm of knowledge would be small, were it not so much shame has to be overcome on the way to it.

65[A]. We are most dishonourable towards our God: he is not *permitted* to sin.

66. The tendency of a person to allow himself to be degraded, robbed, deceived and exploited might be the diffidence of a God among men.

67. Love to one only is a barbarity, for it is exercised at the expense of all others. Love to God also!

68. 'I did that,' says my memory. 'I could not have done that,' says my pride, and remains inexorable. Eventually – the memory yields.

69. One has regarded life carelessly, if one has failed to see the hand that – kills with leniency.

70. If a man has character, he has also his typical experience, which always recurs.

71. *The Sage as Astronomer*. – So long as thou feelest the stars as an 'above thee', thou lackest the eye of the discerning one.

72. It is not the strength, but the duration of great sentiments that makes great men.

73. He who attains his ideal, precisely thereby surpasses it.

73[A]. Many a peacock hides his tail from every eye – and calls it his pride.

74. A man of genius is unbearable, unless he possess at least two things besides: gratitude and purity.

75. The degree and nature of a man's sensuality extends to the highest altitudes of his spirit.

76. Under peaceful conditions the militant man attacks himself.

77. With his principles a man seeks either to dominate, or justify, or honour, or reproach, or conceal his habits: two men with the same principles probably seek fundamentally different ends therewith.

78. He who despises himself, nevertheless esteems himself thereby, as a despiser.

79. A soul which knows that it is loved, but does not itself love, betrays its sediment: its dregs come up.

80. A thing that is explained ceases to concern us. – What did the God mean who gave the advice, 'Know thyself!' Did it perhaps imply: 'Cease to be concerned about thyself! become objective!' – And Socrates? – And the 'scientific man'?

81. It is terrible to die of thirst at sea. Is it necessary that you should so salt your truth that it will no longer – quench thirst?

82. 'Sympathy for all' – would be harshness and tyranny for *thee*, my good neighbour.

83. *Instinct.* – When the house is on fire one forgets even the dinner. – Yes, but one recovers it from among the ashes.

84. Woman learns how to hate in proportion as she – forgets how to charm.

85. The same emotions are in man and woman, but in different *tempo*; on that account man and woman never cease to misunderstand each other.

86. In the background of all their personal vanity, women themselves have still their impersonal scorn – for 'woman'.

87. *Fettered Heart, Free Spirit* – When one firmly fetters one's heart and keeps it prisoner, one can allow one's spirit many liberties: I said this once before. But people do not believe it when I say so, unless they know it already.

88. One begins to distrust very clever persons when they become embarrassed.

89. Dreadful experiences raise the question whether he who experiences them is not something dreadful also.

90. Heavy, melancholy men turn lighter, and come temporarily to their surface, precisely by that which makes others heavy – by hatred and love.

91. So cold, so icy, that one burns one's finger at the touch of him! Every hand that lays hold of him shrinks back! – And for that very reason many think him red-hot.

92. Who has not, at one time or another – sacrificed himself for the sake of his good name?

93. In affability there is no hatred of men, but precisely on that account a great deal too much contempt of men.

94. The maturity of man – that means, to have reacquired the seriousness that one had as a child at play.

95. To be ashamed of one's immorality is a step on the ladder at the end of which one is ashamed also of one's morality.

96. One should part from life as Ulysses parted from Nausicaa – blessing it rather than in love with it.

97. What? A great man? I always see merely the play-actor of his own ideal.

98. When one trains one's conscience, it kisses one while it bites.

99. *The Disappointed One Speaks.* – 'I listened for the echo and I heard only praise.'

100. We all feign to ourselves that we are simpler than we are, we thus relax ourselves away from our fellows.

101. A discerning one might easily regard himself at present as the animalization of God.

102. Discovering reciprocal love should really disenchant the lover with regard to the beloved. 'What! *She* is modest enough to love even you? Or stupid enough? Or – or – '

103. *The Danger in Happiness.* – 'Everything now turns out best for me, I now love every fate: – who would like to be my fate?'

104. Not their love of humanity, but the impotence of their love, prevents the Christians of today – burning us.

105. The *pia fraus* is still more repugnant to the taste (*the 'piety'*) of the free spirit (the 'pious man of knowledge') than the *impia fraus*. Hence the profound lack of judgment, in comparison with the Church, characteristic of the type 'free spirit' – as *its* non-freedom.

106. By means of music the very passions enjoy themselves.

107. A sign of strong character, when once the resolution has been taken, to shut the ear even to the best counter-arguments. Occasionally, therefore, a will to stupidity.

108. There is no such thing as moral phenomena, but only a moral interpretation of phenomena.

109. The criminal is often enough not equal to his deed: he extenuates and maligns it.

110. The advocates of a criminal are seldom artists enough to turn the beautiful terribleness of the deed to the advantage of the doer.

111. Our vanity is most difficult to wound just when our pride has been wounded.

112. To him who feels himself preordained to contemplation and not to belief, all believers are too noisy and obtrusive; he guards against them.

113. 'You want to prepossess him in your favour? Then you must be embarrassed before him.'

114. The immense expectation with regard to sexual love, and the coyness in this expectation, spoils all the perspectives of women at the outset.

115. Where there is neither love nor hatred in the game, woman's play is mediocre.

116. The great epochs of our life are at the points when we gain courage to rebaptize our badness as the best in us.

117. The will to overcome an emotion, is ultimately only the will of another, or of several other, emotions.

118. There is an innocence of admiration: it is possessed by him to whom it has not yet occurred that he himself may be admired some day.

119. Our loathing of dirt may be so great as to prevent our cleaning ourselves – 'justifying' ourselves.

120. Sensuality often forces the growth of love too much, so that its root remains weak, and is easily torn up.

121. It is a curious thing that God learned Greek when he wished to turn author – and that he did not learn it better.

122. To rejoice on account of praise is in many cases merely politeness of heart – and the very opposite of vanity of spirit.

123. Even concubinage has been corrupted – by marriage.

124. He who exults at the stake, does not triumph over pain, but because of the fact that he does not feel pain where he expected it. A parable.

125. When we have to change an opinion about any one, we charge heavily to his account the inconvenience he thereby causes us.

126. A nation is a detour of nature to arrive at six or seven great men. – Yes, and then to get round them.

127. In the eyes of all true women science is hostile to the sense

of shame. They feel as if one wished to peep under their skin with it – or worse still! under their dress and finery.

128. The more abstract the truth you wish to teach, the more must you allure the senses to it.

129. The devil has the most extensive perspectives for God; on that account he keeps so far away from him: – the devil, in effect, as the oldest friend of knowledge.

130. What a person *is* begins to betray itself when his talent decreases, – when he ceases to show what he *can* do. Talent is also an adornment; an adornment is also a concealment.

131. The sexes deceive themselves about each other: the reason is that in reality they honour and love only themselves (or their own ideal, to express it more agreeably). Thus man wishes woman to be peaceable: but in fact woman is *essentially* unpeaceable, like the cat, however well she may have assumed the peaceable demeanour.

132. One is punished best for one's virtues.

133. He who cannot find the way to *his* ideal, lives more frivolously and shamelessly than the man without an ideal.

134. From the senses originate all trustworthiness, all good conscience, all evidence of truth.

135. Pharisaism is not a deterioration of the good man; a considerable part of it is rather an essential condition of being good.

136. The one seeks an *accoucheur* for his thoughts, the other seeks someone whom he can assist: a good conversation thus originates.

137. In intercourse with scholars and artists one readily makes mistakes of opposite kinds: in a remarkable scholar one not infre-

quently finds a mediocre man; and often, even in a mediocre artist, one finds a very remarkable man.

138. We do the same when awake as when dreaming: we only invent and imagine him with whom we have intercourse – and forget it immediately.

139. In revenge and in love woman is more barbarous than man.

140. *Advice as a riddle.* – 'If the band is not to break, bite it first – secure to make!'

141. The belly is the reason why man does not so readily take himself for a God.

142. The chastest utterance I ever heard: '*Dans le véritable amour c'est l'âmi qui enveloppe le corps.*'

143. Our vanity would like what we do best to pass precisely for what is most difficult to us. – Concerning the origin of many systems of morals.

144. When a woman has scholarly inclinations there is generally something wrong with her sexual nature. Barrenness itself conduces to a certain virility of taste; man, indeed, if I may say so, is 'the barren animal'.

145. Comparing man and woman generally, one may say that woman would not have the genius for adornment, if she had not the instinct for the *secondary* role.

146. He who fights with monsters should be careful lest he thereby become a monster. And if thou gaze long into an abyss, the abyss will also gaze into thee.

147. From old Florentine novels – moreover, from life: *Buona femmina e mala femmina vuol bastone*. – Sacchetti, Nov. 86.

148. To seduce their neighbour to a favourable opinion, and afterwards to believe implicitly in this opinion of their neighbour – who can do this conjuring trick so well as women?

149. That which an age considers evil is usually an unseasonable echo of what was formerly considered good – the atavism of an old ideal.

150. Around the hero everything becomes a tragedy; around the demigod everything becomes a satyr-play; and around God everything becomes – what? perhaps a 'world'?

151. It is not enough to possess a talent: one must also have your permission to possess it; – eh, my friends?

152. 'Where there is the tree of knowledge, there is always Paradise': so say the most ancient and the most modern serpents.

153. What is done out of love always takes place beyond good and evil.

154. Objection, evasion, joyous distrust and love of irony are signs of health; everything absolute belongs to pathology.

155. The sense of the tragic increases and declines with sensuousness.

156. Insanity in individuals is something rare – but in groups, parties, nations and epochs it is the rule.

157. The thought of suicide is a great consolation: by means of it one gets successfully through many a bad night.

158. Not only our reason, but also our conscience, truckles to our strongest impulse – the tyrant in us.

159. One *must* repay good and ill; but why just to the person who did us good or ill?

160. One no longer loves one's knowledge sufficiently after one has communicated it.

161. Poets act shamelessly towards their experiences: they exploit them.

162. 'Our fellow-creature is not our neighbour, but our neighbour's neighbour': – so thinks every nation.

163. Love brings to light the noble and hidden qualities of a lover – his rare and exceptional traits: it is thus liable to be deceptive as to his normal character.

164. Jesus said to his Jews: 'The law was for servants; – love God as I love him, as his Son! What have we Sons of God to do with morals!'

165. *In Sight of Every Party*. – A shepherd has always need of a bell-wether – or he has himself to be a wether occasionally.

166. One may indeed lie with the mouth; but with the accompanying grimace one nevertheless tells the truth.

167. To vigorous men intimacy is a matter of shame – and something precious.

168. Christianity gave Eros poison to drink; he did not die of it, certainly, but degenerated to Vice.

169. To talk much about oneself may also be a means of concealing oneself.

170. In praise there is more obtrusiveness than in blame.

171. Pity has an almost ludicrous effect on a man of knowledge, like tender hands on a Cyclops.

172. One occasionally embraces someone or other, out of love to mankind (because one cannot embrace all); but this is what one must never confess to the individual.

173. One does not hate as long as one disesteems, but only when one esteems equal or superior.

174. Ye Utilitarians – ye, too, love the *utile* only as a *vehicle* for your inclinations, – ye, too, really find the noise of its wheels insupportable!

175. One loves ultimately one's desires, not the thing desired.

176. The vanity of others is only counter to our taste when it is counter to our vanity.

177. With regard to what 'truthfulness' is, perhaps nobody has ever been sufficiently truthful.

178. One does not believe in the follies of clever men: what a forfeiture of the rights of man!

179. The consequences of our actions seize us by the forelock, very indifferent to the fact that we have meanwhile 'reformed'.

180. There is an innocence in lying, which is the sign of good faith in a cause.

181. It is inhuman to bless when one is being cursed.

182. The familiarity of superiors embitters one, because it may not be returned.

183. 'I am affected, not because you have deceived me, but because I can no longer believe in you.'

184. There is a haughtiness of kindness, which has the appearance of wickedness.

185. 'I dislike him.' – Why? – 'I am not a match for him.' – Did anyone ever answer so?

CHAPTER V

The Natural History of Morals

186. The moral sentiment in Europe at present is perhaps as subtle, belated, diverse, sensitive and refined, as the 'Science of Morals' belonging thereto is recent, initial, awkward and coarse-fingered: – an interesting contrast, which sometimes becomes incarnate and obvious in the very person of a moralist. Indeed, the expression, 'Science of Morals' is, in respect to what is designated thereby, far too presumptuous and counter to *good* taste, – which is always a foretaste of more modest expressions. One ought to avow with the utmost fairness *what* is still necessary here for a long time, *what* is alone proper for the present: namely, the collection of material, the comprehensive survey and classification of an immense domain of delicate sentiments of worth and distinctions of worth, which live, grow, propagate and perish – and perhaps attempts to give a clear idea of the recurring and more common forms of these living crystallizations – as preparation for a *theory of types* of morality. To be sure, people have not hitherto been so modest. All the philosophers, with a pedantic and ridiculous seriousness, demanded of themselves something very much higher, more pretentious and ceremonious, when they concerned themselves with morality as a science: they wanted to *give a basis* to morality – and every philosopher hitherto has believed that he has given it a basis; morality itself, however, has been regarded as something 'given'. How far from their awkward pride was the seemingly insignificant problem – left in dust and decay – of a description of forms of morality, notwithstanding that the finest hands and senses could hardly be fine enough for it! It was precisely owing to moral philosophers' knowing the moral facts imperfectly, in an arbitrary epitome, or an accidental abridgement – perhaps as the morality of their environment, their position, their church, their *Zeitgeist*, their climate and zone – it was precisely because they were badly instructed with regard to nations, eras and

past ages, and were by no means eager to know about these matters, that they did not even come in sight of the real problems of morals – problems which only disclose themselves by a comparison of *many* kinds of morality. In every 'Science of Morals' hitherto, strange as it may sound, the problem of morality itself has been *omitted*: there has been no suspicion that there was anything problematic there! That which philosophers called 'giving a basis to morality', and endeavoured to realize, has, when seen in a right light, proved merely a learned form of good *faith* in prevailing morality, a new means of its *expression*, consequently just a matter-of-fact within the sphere of a definite morality, yea, in its ultimate motive, a sort of denial that it is *lawful* for this morality to be called in question – and in any case the reverse of the testing, analyzing, doubting and vivisecting of this very faith. Hear, for instance, with what innocence – almost worthy of honour – Schopenhauer represents his own task, and draw your conclusions concerning the scientificness of a 'Science' whose latest master still talks in the strain of children and old wives: 'The principle,' he says (page 136 of the *Grundprobleme der Ethik**), 'the axiom about the purport of which all moralists are *practically* agreed: *neminem laede, immo omnes quantum potes juva* – is *really* the proposition which all moral teachers strive to establish,... the *real* basis of ethics which has been sought, like the philosopher's stone, for centuries.' – The difficulty of establishing the proposition referred to may indeed be great – it is well known that Schopenhauer also was unsuccessful in his efforts; and whoever has thoroughly realized how absurdly false and sentimental this proposition is, in a world whose essence is Will to Power, may be reminded that Schopenhauer, although a pessimist, *actually* – played the flute... daily after dinner: one may read about the matter in his biography. A question by the way: a pessimist, a repudiator of God and of the world, who *makes a halt* at morality – who assents to morality, and plays the flute to *laede-neminem* morals, what? Is that really – a pessimist?

---

* Pages 54–55 of Schopenhauer's *Basis of Morality*, translated by Arthur B. Bullock, M.A. (1903).

187. Apart from the value of such assertions as 'there is a categorical imperative in us', one can always ask: What does such an assertion indicate about him who makes it? There are systems of morals which are meant to justify their author in the eyes of other people; other systems of morals are meant to tranquilize him, and make him self-satisfied; with other systems he wants to crucify and humble himself, with others he wishes to take revenge, with others to conceal himself, with others to glorify himself and gave superiority and distinction, – this system of morals helps its author to forget, that system makes him, or something of him, forgotten, many a moralist would like to exercise power and creative arbitrariness over mankind, many another, perhaps, Kant especially, gives us to understand by his morals that 'what is estimable in me, is that I know how to obey – and with you it *shall* not be otherwise than with me!' In short, systems of morals are only a *sign-language of the emotions*.

188. In contrast to *laisser-aller*, every system of morals is a sort of tyranny against 'nature' and also against 'reason'; that is, however, no objection, unless one should again decree by some system of morals, that all kinds of tyranny and unreasonableness are unlawful What is essential and invaluable in every system of morals, is that it is a long constraint. In order to understand Stoicism, or Port-Royal or Puritanism, one should remember the constraint under which every language has attained to strength and freedom – the metrical constraint, the tyranny of rhyme and rhythm. How much trouble have the poets and orators of every nation given themselves! – not excepting some of the prose writers of today, in whose ear dwells an inexorable conscientiousness – 'for the sake of a folly', as utilitarian bunglers say, and thereby deem themselves wise – 'from submission to arbitrary laws', as the anarchists say, and thereby fancy themselves 'free', even free-spirited. The singular fact remains, however, that everything of the nature of freedom, elegance, boldness, dance and masterly certainty, which exists or has existed, whether it be in thought itself, or in administration, or in speaking and persuading, in art just as in

conduct, has only developed by means of the tyranny of such arbitrary law; and in all seriousness, it is not at all improbable that precisely this is 'nature' and 'natural' – and not *laisser-aller*! Every artist knows how different from the state of letting himself go, is his 'most natural' condition, the free arranging, locating, disposing and constructing in the moments of 'inspiration' – and how strictly and delicately he then obeys a thousand laws, which, by their very rigidness and precision, defy all formulation by means of ideas (even the most stable idea has, in comparison therewith, something floating, manifold and ambiguous in it). The essential thing 'in heaven and in earth' is, apparently (to repeat it once more), that there should be long *obedience* in the same direction, there thereby results, and has always resulted in the long run, something which has made life worth living; for instance, virtue, art, music, dancing, reason, spirituality – anything whatever that is transfiguring, refined, foolish or divine. The long bondage of the spirit, the distrustful constraint in the communicability of ideas, the discipline which the thinker imposed on himself to think in accordance with the rules of a church or a court, or conformable to Aristotelian premises, the persistent spiritual will to interpret everything that happened according to a Christian scheme, and in every occurrence to rediscover and justify the Christian God: – all this violence, arbitrariness, severity, dreadfulness and unreasonableness, has proved itself the disciplinary means whereby the European spirit has attained its strength, its remorseless curiosity and subtle mobility; granted also that much irrecoverable strength and spirit had to be stifled, suffocated and spoilt in the process (for here, as everywhere, 'nature' shows herself as she is, in all her extravagant and *indifferent* magnificence, which is shocking, but nevertheless noble). That for centuries European thinkers only thought in order to prove something – nowadays, on the contrary, we are suspicious of every thinker who 'wishes to prove something' – that it was always settled beforehand what *was to be* the result of their strictest thinking, as it was perhaps in the Asiatic astrology of former times, or as it is still at the present day in the innocent, Christian-moral explanation of immediate personal events 'for the glory of God', or 'for the good of the soul': – this tyranny, this arbitrariness, this severe and magnificent stupidity, has *educated* the spirit; slavery, both in the coarser and the finer sense, is apparently an indispensable means even of spiritual education and discipline. One may look at every system of morals in this light: it is 'nature' therein which teaches to hate the *laisser-aller*, the too great freedom, and implants the need for limited horizons, for immediate duties – it teaches the *narrowing of perspectives*, and thus, in a certain sense, that stupidity is a condition of life and development. 'Thou must obey some one, and for a long time; *otherwise* thou wilt come to grief, and lose all respect for thyself' – this seems to me to be the moral imperative of nature, which is certainly neither 'categorical', as old Kant wished (consequently the 'otherwise'), nor does it address itself to the individual (what does nature care for the individual!), but to nations, races, ages and ranks; above all, however, to the animal 'man' generally, to *mankind*.

189. Industrious races find it a great hardship to be idle: it was a master stroke of *English* instinct to hallow and begloom Sunday to such an extent that the Englishman unconsciously hankers for his week- and work-day again: – as a kind of cleverly devised, cleverly intercalated *fast*, such as is also frequently found in the ancient world (although, as is appropriate in southern nations, not precisely with respect to work). Many kinds of fasts are necessary; and wherever powerful influences and habits prevail, legislators have to see that intercalary days are appointed, on which such impulses are fettered, and learn to hunger anew. Viewed from a higher standpoint, whole generations and epochs, when they show themselves infected with any moral fanaticism, seem like those intercalated periods of restraint and fasting, during which an impulse learns to humble and submit itself – at the same time also to *purify* and *sharpen* itself; certain philosophical sects likewise admit of a similar interpretation (for instance, the Stoa, in the midst of Hellenic culture, with the atmosphere rank and over-charged with Aphrodisiacal odours). – Here also is a hint for the

explanation of the paradox, why it was precisely in the most Christian period of European history, and in general only under the pressure of Christian sentiments, that the sexual impulse sublimated into love (*amour-passion*).

190. There is something in the morality of Plato which does not really belong to Plato, but which only appears in his philosophy, one might say, in spite of him: namely, Socratism, for which he himself was too noble. 'No one desires to injure himself, hence all evil is done unwittingly. The evil man inflicts injury on himself; he would not do so, however, if he knew that evil is evil. The evil man, therefore, is only evil through error; if one free him from error one will necessarily make him – good.' – This mode of reasoning savours of the *populace*, who perceive only the unpleasant consequences of evil-doing, and practically judge that 'it is *stupid* to do wrong'; while they accept 'good' as identical with 'useful and pleasant', without further thought. As regards every system of utilitarianism, one may at once assume that it has the same origin, and follow the scent: one will seldom err. – Plato did all he could to interpret something refined and noble into the tenets of his teacher, and above all to interpret himself into them – he, the most daring of all interpreters, who lifted the entire Socrates out of the street, as a popular theme and song, to exhibit him in endless and impossible modifications – namely, in all his own disguises and multiplicities. In jest, and in Homeric language as well, what is the Platonic Socrates, if not – πρόοὒε Πλάτων ἄπσέυ τε Πλάτων μέσση Χίμαιρα

191. The old theological problem of 'Faith' and 'Knowledge', or more plainly, of instinct and reason – the question whether, in respect to the valuation of things, instinct deserves more authority than rationality, which wants to appreciate and act according to motives, according to a 'Why', that is to say, in conformity to purpose and utility – it is always the old moral problem that first appeared in the person of Socrates, and had divided men's minds long before Christianity. Socrates himself, following, of course, the taste of his talent – that of a surpassing dialectician – took first the side of

reason; and, in fact, what did he do all his life but laugh at the awkward incapacity of the noble Athenians, who were men of instinct, like all noble men, and could never give satisfactory answers concerning the motives of their actions? In the end, however, though silently and secretly, he laughed also at himself: with his finer conscience and introspection, he found in himself the same difficulty and incapacity. 'But why' – he said to himself – 'should one on that account separate oneself from the instincts! One must set them right, and the reason *also* – one must follow the instincts, but at the same time persuade the reason to support them with good arguments.' This was the real *falseness* of that great and mysterious ironist; he brought his conscience up to the point that he was satisfied with a kind of self-outwitting: in fact, he perceived the irrationality in the moral judgment. – Plato, more innocent in such matters, and without the craftiness of the plebeian, wished to prove to himself, at the expenditure of all his strength – the greatest strength a philosopher had ever expended – that reason and instinct lead spontaneously to one goal, to the good, to 'God'; and since Plato, all theologians and philosophers have followed the same path – which means that in matters of morality, instinct (or as Christians call it, 'Faith', or as I call it, 'the herd') has hitherto triumphed. Unless one should make an exception in the case of Descartes, the father of rationalism (and consequently the grandfather of the Revolution), who recognized only the authority of reason: but reason is only a tool, and Descartes was superficial.

192. Whoever has followed the history of a single science, finds in its development a clue to the understanding of the oldest and commonest processes of all 'knowledge and cognizance': there, as here, the premature hypotheses, the fictions, the good stupid will to 'belief' and the lack of distrust and patience are first developed – our senses learn late, and never learn completely, to be subtle, reliable and cautious organs of knowledge. Our eyes find it easier on a given occasion to produce a picture already often produced, than to seize upon the divergence and novelty of an impression: the latter requires more force, more 'morality'. It is difficult and

painful for the ear to listen to anything new; we hear strange music badly. When we hear another language spoken, we involuntarily attempt to form the sounds into words with which we are more familiar and conversant – it was thus, for example, that the Germans modified the spoken word *arcubalista* into *armbrust* (cross-bow). Our senses are also hostile and averse to the new; and generally, even in the 'simplest' processes of sensation, the emotions *dominate* – such as fear, love, hatred and the passive emotion of indolence. – As little as a reader nowadays reads all the single words (not to speak of syllables) of a page – he rather takes about five out of every twenty words at random, and 'guesses' the probably appropriate sense to them – just as little do we see a tree correctly and completely in respect to its leaves, branches, colour and shape; we find it so much easier to fancy the chance of a tree. Even in the midst of the most remarkable experiences, we still do just the same; we fabricate the greater part of the experience, and can hardly be made to contemplate any event, *except* as 'inventors' thereof. All this goes to prove that from our fundamental nature and from remote ages we have been – *accustomed to lying*. Or, to express it more politely and hypocritically, in short, more pleasantly – one is much more of an artist than one is aware of. – In an animated conversation, I often see the face of the person with whom I am speaking so clearly and sharply defined before me, according to the thought he expresses, or which I believe to be evoked in his mind, that the degree of distinctness far exceeds the *strength* of my visual faculty – the delicacy of the play of the muscles and of the expression of the eyes *must* therefore be imagined by me. Probably the person put on quite a different expression, or none at all.

193. *Quidquid luce fuit, tenebris agit*: but also contrariwise. What we experience in dreams, provided we experience it often, pertains at last just as much to the general belongings of our soul as anything 'actually' experienced; by virtue thereof we are richer or poorer, we have a requirement more or less, and finally, in broad daylight, and even in the brightest moments of our waking life, we are ruled

to some extent by the nature of our dreams. Supposing that someone has often flown in his dreams, and that at last, as soon as he dreams, he is conscious of the power and art of flying as his privilege and his peculiarly enviable happiness; such a person, who believes that on the slightest impulse, he can actualize all sorts of curves and angles, who knows the sensation of a certain divine levity, an 'upwards' without effort or constraint, a 'downwards' without descending or lowering – without *trouble*! – how could the man with such dream-experiences and dream-habits fail to find 'happiness' differently coloured and defined, even in his waking hours! How could he fail – to long *differently* for happiness? 'Flight', such as is described by poets, must, when compared with his own 'flying', be far too earthly, muscular, violent, far too 'troublesome' for him.

194. The difference among men does not manifest itself only in the difference of their lists of desirable things – in their regarding different good things as worth striving for, and being disagreed as to the greater or less value, the order of rank, of the commonly recognized desirable things: – it manifests itself much more in what they regard as actually *having* and *possessing* a desirable thing. As regards a woman, for instance, the control over her body and her sexual gratification serves as an amply sufficient sign of ownership and possession to the more modest man; another with a more suspicious and ambitious thirst for possession, sees the 'questionableness', the mere apparentness of such ownership, and wishes to have finer tests in order to know especially whether the woman not only gives herself to him, but also gives up for his sake what she has or would like to have – only *then* does he look upon her as 'possessed.' A third, however, has not even here got to the limit of his distrust and his desire for possession: he asks himself whether the woman, when she gives up everything for him, does not perhaps do so for a phantom of him; he wishes first to be thoroughly, indeed, profoundly well known; in order to be loved at all he ventures to let himself be found out. Only then does he feel the beloved one fully in his possession, when

she no longer deceives herself about him, when she loves him just as much for the sake of his devilry and concealed insatiability, as for his goodness, patience and spirituality. One man would like to possess a nation, and he finds all the higher arts of Cagliostro and Catalina suitable for his purpose. Another, with a more refined thirst for possession, says to himself: 'One may not deceive where one desires to possess' – he is irritated and impatient at the idea that a mask of him should rule in the hearts of the people: 'I must, therefore, *make* myself known, and first of all learn to know myself!' Among helpful and charitable people, one almost always finds the awkward craftiness which first gets up suitably him who has to be helped, as though, for instance, he should 'merit' help, seek just *their* help and would show himself deeply grateful, attached and subservient to them for all help. With these conceits, they take control of the needy as a property, just as in general they are charitable and helpful out of a desire for property. One finds them jealous when they are crossed or forestalled in their charity. Parents involuntarily make something like themselves out of their children – they call that 'education'; no mother doubts at the bottom of her heart that the child she has borne is thereby her property, no father hesitates about his right to *his own* ideas and notions of worth. Indeed, in former times fathers deemed it right to use their discretion concerning the life or death of the newly born (as among the ancient Germans). And like the father, so also do the teacher, the class, the priest and the prince still see in every new individual an unobjectionable opportunity for a new possession. The consequence is...

195. The Jews – a people 'born for slavery', as Tacitus and the whole ancient world say of them; 'the chosen people among the nations', as they themselves say and believe – the Jews performed the miracle of the inversion of valuations, by means of which life on earth obtained a new and dangerous charm for a couple of millenniums. Their prophets fused into one the expressions 'rich', 'godless', 'wicked', 'violent', 'sensual', and for the first time coined the word 'world' as a term of reproach. In this inversion of valua-

tions (in which is also included the use of the word 'poor' as synonymous with 'saint' and 'friend') the significance of the Jewish people is to be found; it is with *them* that the *slave-insurrection in morals* commences.

196. It is to be *inferred* that there are countless dark bodies near the sun – such as we shall never see. Among ourselves, this is an allegory; and the psychologist of morals reads the whole star-writing merely as an allegorical and symbolic language in which much may be unexpressed.

197. The beast of prey and the man of prey (for instance, Caesar Borgia) are fundamentally misunderstood, 'nature' is misunderstood, so long as one seeks a 'morbidness' in the constitution of these healthiest of all tropical monsters and growths, or even an innate 'hell' in them – as almost all moralists have done hitherto. Does it not seem that there is a hatred of the virgin forest and of the tropics among moralists? And that the 'tropical man' must be discredited at all costs, whether as disease and deterioration of mankind, or as his own hell and self-torture? And why? In favour of the 'temperate zones'? In favour of the temperate men? The 'moral'? The mediocre? – This for the chapter: 'Morals as Timidity'.

198. All the systems of morals which address themselves with a view to their 'happiness', as it is called – what else are they but suggestions for behaviour adapted to the degree of *danger* from themselves in which the individuals live; recipes for their passions, their good and bad propensities, in so far as such have the Will to Power and would like to play the master; small and great expediencies and elaborations, permeated with the musty odour of old family medicines and old-wife wisdom; all of them grotesque and absurd in their form – because they address themselves to 'all', because they generalize where generalization is not authorized; all of them speaking unconditionally, and taking themselves unconditionally; all of them flavoured not merely with one grain of salt, but rather endurable only, and sometimes even seductive, when

they are over-spiced and begin to smell dangerously, especially of 'the other world'. That is all of little value when estimated intellectually, and is far from being 'science', much less 'wisdom'; but, repeated once more, and three times repeated, it is expediency, expediency, expediency, mixed with stupidity, stupidity, stupidity – whether it be the indifference and statuesque coldness towards the heated folly of the emotions, which the Stoics advised and fostered; or the no-more-laughing and no-more-weeping of Spinoza, the destruction of the emotions by their analysis and vivisection, which he recommended so naively; or the lowering of the emotions to an innocent mean at which they may be satisfied, the Aristotelianism of morals; or even morality as the enjoyment of the emotions in a voluntary attenuation and spiritualization by the symbolism of art, perhaps as music or as love of God, and of mankind for God's sake – for in religion the passions are once more enfranchised, provided that...; or, finally, even the complaisant and wanton surrender to the emotions, as has been taught by Hafis and Goethe, the bold letting-go of the reins, the spiritual and corporeal *licentia morum* in the exceptional cases of wise old codgers and drunkards, with whom it 'no longer has much danger'. – This also for the chapter: 'Morals as Timidity'.

199. Inasmuch as in all ages, as long as mankind has existed, there have also been human herds (family alliances, communities, tribes, peoples, states, churches), and always a great number who obey in proportion to the small number who command – in view, therefore, of the fact that obedience has been most practiced and fostered among mankind hitherto, one may reasonably suppose that, generally speaking, the need thereof is now innate in every one, as a kind of *formal conscience* which gives the command: 'Thou shalt unconditionally do something, unconditionally refrain from something'; in short, 'Thou shalt'. This need tries to satisfy itself and to fill its form with a content, according to its strength, impatience and eagerness, it at once seizes as an omnivorous appetite with little selection, and accepts whatever is shouted into its ear by all sorts of commanders – parents, teachers, laws, class prejudices or public opinion. The extraordinary limitation of human development, the hesitation, protractedness, frequent retrogression and turning thereof, is attributable to the fact that the herd-instinct of obedience is transmitted best, and at the cost of the art of command. If one imagine this instinct increasing to its greatest extent, commanders and independent individuals will finally be lacking altogether, or they will suffer inwardly from a bad conscience, and will have to impose a deception on themselves in the first place in order to be able to command just as if they also were only obeying. This condition of things actually exists in Europe at present – I call it the moral hypocrisy of the commanding class. They know no other way of protecting themselves from their bad conscience than by playing the role of executors of older and higher orders (of predecessors, of the constitution, of justice, of the law or of God himself), or they even justify themselves by maxims from the current opinions of the herd, as 'first servants of their people', or 'instruments of the public weal'. On the other hand, the gregarious European man nowadays assumes an air as if he were the only kind of man that is allowable; he glorifies his qualities, such as public spirit, kindness, deference, industry, temperance, modesty, indulgence, sympathy, by virtue of which he is gentle, endurable and useful to the herd, as the peculiarly human virtues. In cases, however, where it is believed that the leader and bell-wether cannot be dispensed with, attempt after attempt is made nowadays to replace commanders by the summing together of clever gregarious men all representative constitutions, for example, are of this origin. In spite of all, what a blessing, what a deliverance from a weight becoming unendurable, is the appearance of an absolute ruler for these gregarious Europeans – of this fact the effect of the appearance of Napoleon was the last great proof: the history of the influence of Napoleon is almost the history of the higher happiness to which the entire century has attained in its worthiest individuals and periods.

200. The man of an age of dissolution which mixes the races with one another, who has the inheritance of a diversified descent in his body – that is to say, contrary, and often not only contrary,

instincts and standards of value, which struggle with one another and are seldom at peace – such a man of late culture and broken lights, will, on an average, be a weak man. His fundamental desire is that the war which is *in him* should come to an end; happiness appears to him in the character of a soothing medicine and mode of thought (for instance, Epicurean or Christian); it is above all things the happiness of repose, of undisturbedness, of repletion, of final unity – it is the 'Sabbath of Sabbaths', to use the expression of the holy rhetorician, St Augustine, who was himself such a man. – Should, however, the contrariety and conflict in such natures operate as an *additional* incentive and stimulus to life – and if, on the other hand, in addition to their powerful and irreconcilable instincts, they have also inherited and indoctrinated into them a proper mastery and subtlety for carrying on the conflict with themselves (that is to say, the faculty of self-control and self-deception), there then arise those marvellously incomprehensible and inexplicable beings, those enigmatical men, predestined for conquering and circumventing others, the finest examples of which are Alcibiades and Caesar (with whom I should like to associate the *first* of Europeans according to my taste, the Hohenstaufen, Frederick the Second), and among artists, perhaps Leonardo da Vinci. They appear precisely in the same periods when that weaker type, with its longing for repose, comes to the front; the two types are complementary to each other, and spring from the same causes.

201. As long as the utility which determines moral estimates is only gregarious utility, as long as the preservation of the community is only kept in view, and the immoral is sought precisely and exclusively in what seems dangerous to the maintenance of the community, there can be no 'morality of love to one's neighbour'. Granted even that there is already a little constant exercise of consideration, sympathy, fairness, gentleness and mutual assistance, granted that even in this condition of society all those instincts are already active which are latterly distinguished by honourable names as 'virtues', and eventually almost coincide with the conception

'morality': in that period they do not as yet belong to the domain of moral valuations – they are still *ultra-moral*. A sympathetic action, for instance, is neither called good nor bad, moral nor immoral, in the best period of the Romans; and should it be praised, a sort of resentful disdain is compatible with this praise, even at the best, directly the sympathetic action is compared with one which contributes to the welfare of the whole, to the *res publica*. After all, 'love to our neighbour' is always a secondary matter, partly conventional and arbitrarily manifested in relation to our *fear of our neighbour*. After the fabric of society seems on the whole established and secured against external dangers, it is this fear of our neighbour which again creates new perspectives of moral valuation. Certain strong and dangerous instincts, such as the love of enterprise, foolhardiness, revengefulness, astuteness, rapacity and love of power, which up till then had not only to be honoured from the point of view of general utility – under other names, of course, than those here given – but had to be fostered and cultivated (because they were perpetually required in the common danger against the common enemies), are now felt in their dangerousness to be doubly strong – when the outlets for them are lacking – and are gradually branded as immoral and given over to calumny. The contrary instincts and inclinations now attain to moral honour, the gregarious instinct gradually draws its conclusions. How much or how little dangerousness to the community or to equality is contained in an opinion, a condition, an emotion, a disposition or an endowment – that is now the moral perspective, here again fear is the mother of morals. It is by the loftiest and strongest instincts, when they break out passionately and carry the individual far above and beyond the average, and the low level of the gregarious conscience, that the self-reliance of the community is destroyed; its belief in itself, its backbone, as it were, breaks; consequently these very instincts will be most branded and defamed. The lofty independent spirituality, the will to stand alone, and even the cogent reason, are felt to be dangers, everything that elevates the individual above the herd, and is a source of fear to the neighbour, is henceforth called *evil*; the tolerant, unassuming, self-adapting, self-equalizing disposition, the *mediocrity* of desires, attains to moral distinction and honour. Finally, under very peaceful circumstances, there is always less opportunity and necessity for training the feelings to severity and rigour; and now every form of severity, even in justice, begins to disturb the conscience; a lofty and rigorous nobleness and self-responsibility almost offends, and awakens distrust, 'the lamb', and still more 'the sheep', wins respect. There is a point of diseased mellowness and effeminacy in the history of society, at which society itself takes the part of him who injures it, the part of the *criminal*, and does so, in fact, seriously and honestly. To punish, appears to it to be somehow unfair – it is certain that the idea of 'punishment' and 'the obligation to punish' are then painful and alarming to people. 'Is it not sufficient if the criminal be rendered *harmless*? Why should we still punish? Punishment itself is terrible!' – with these questions gregarious morality, the morality of fear, draws its ultimate conclusion. If one could at all do away with danger, the cause of fear, one would have done away with this morality at the same time, it would no longer be necessary, it *would not consider itself* any longer necessary! – Whoever examines the conscience of the present-day European, will always elicit the same imperative from its thousand moral folds and hidden recesses, the imperative of the timidity of the herd 'we wish that some time or other there may be *nothing more to fear*!' Some time or other – the will and the way *thereto* is nowadays called 'progress' all over Europe.

202. Let us at once say again what we have already said a hundred times, for people's ears nowadays are unwilling to hear such truths – *our* truths. We know well enough how offensive it sounds when any one plainly, and without metaphor, counts man among the animals, but it will be accounted to us almost a *crime*, that it is precisely in respect to men of 'modern ideas' that we have constantly applied the terms 'herd', 'herd-instincts', and such like expressions. What avail is it? We cannot do otherwise, for it is precisely here that our new insight is. We have found that in all the principal moral judgments, Europe has become unanimous, including likewise

the countries where European influence prevails in Europe people evidently *know* what Socrates thought he did not know, and what the famous serpent of old once promised to teach – they 'know' today what is good and evil. It must then sound hard and be distasteful to the ear, when we always insist that that which here thinks it knows, that which here glorifies itself with praise and blame, and calls itself good, is the instinct of the herding human animal: the instinct which has come and is ever coming more and more to the front, to preponderance and supremacy over other instincts, according to the increasing physiological approximation and resemblance of which it is the symptom. *Morality in Europe at present is herding-animal morality;* and therefore, as we understand the matter, only one kind of human morality, beside which, before which and after which many other moralities, and above all *higher* moralities, are or should be possible. Against such a 'possibility', against such a 'should be', however, this morality defends itself with all its strength, it says obstinately and inexorably: 'I am morality itself and nothing else is morality!' Indeed, with the help of a religion which has humoured and flattered the sublimest desires of the herding-animal, things have reached such a point that we always find a more visible expression of this morality even in political and social arrangements: the *democratic* movement is the inheritance of the Christian movement. That its *tempo*, however, is much too slow and sleepy for the more impatient ones, for those who are sick and distracted by the herding-instinct, is indicated by the increasingly furious howling, and always less disguised teeth-gnashing of the anarchist dogs, who are now roving through the highways of European culture. Apparently in opposition to the peacefully industrious democrats and Revolution-ideologues, and still more so to the awkward philosophasters and fraternity-visionaries who call themselves Socialists and want a 'free society', those are really at one with them all in their thorough and instinctive hostility to every form of society other than that of the *autonomous* herd (to the extent even of repudiating the notions 'master' and 'servant' – *ni dieu ni maître*, says a socialist formula); at one in their tenacious opposition to every special claim, every special right and privilege (this means ultimately opposition to *every* right, for when all are equal, no one needs 'rights' any longer); at one in their distrust of punitive justice (as though it were a violation of the weak, unfair to the *necessary* consequences of all former society); but equally at one in their religion of sympathy, in their compassion for all that feels, lives and suffers (down to the very animals, up even to 'God' – the extravagance of 'sympathy for God' belongs to a democratic age); altogether at one in the cry and impatience of their sympathy, in their deadly hatred of suffering generally, in their almost feminine incapacity for witnessing it or *allowing* it; at one in their involuntary beglooming and heart-softening, under the spell of which Europe seems to be threatened with a new Buddhism; at one in their belief in the morality of *mutual* sympathy, as though it were morality in itself, the climax, the *attained* climax of mankind, the sole hope of the future, the consolation of the present, the great discharge from all the obligations of the past; altogether at one in their belief in the community as the *deliverer*, in the herd, and therefore in 'themselves'.

203. We, who hold a different belief – we, who regard the democratic movement, not only as a degenerating form of political organization, but as equivalent to a degenerating, a waning type of man, as involving his mediocrising and depreciation: where have *we* to fix our hopes? In *new philosophers* – there is no other alternative: in minds strong and original enough to initiate opposite estimates of value, to transvalue and invert 'eternal valuations'; in forerunners, in men of the future, who in the present shall fix the constraints and fasten the knots which will compel millenniums to take *new* paths. To teach man the future of humanity as his *will*, as depending on human will, and to make preparation for vast hazardous enterprises and collective attempts in rearing and educating, in order thereby to put an end to the frightful rule of folly and chance which has hitherto gone by the name of 'history' (the folly of the 'greatest number' is only its last form) – for that purpose a new type of philosopher and commander will sometime or other be needed, at the very idea of which everything that has

existed in the way of occult, terrible and benevolent beings might look pale and dwarfed. The image of such leaders hovers before *our* eyes: – is it lawful for me to say it aloud, ye free spirits? The conditions which one would partly have to create and partly utilize for their genesis; the presumptive methods and tests by virtue of which a soul should grow up to such an elevation and power as to feel a *constraint* to these tasks; a transvaluation of values, under the new pressure and hammer of which a conscience should be steeled and a heart transformed into brass, so as to bear the weight of such responsibility; and on the other hand the necessity for such leaders, the dreadful danger that they might be lacking, or miscarry and degenerate: – these are *our* real anxieties and glooms, ye know it well, ye free spirits! these are the heavy distant thoughts and storms which sweep across the heaven of *our* life. There are few pains so grievous as to have seen, divined or experienced how an exceptional man has missed his way and deteriorated; but he who has the rare eye for the universal danger of 'man' himself *deteriorating*, he who like us has recognized the extraordinary fortuitousness which has hitherto played its game in respect to the future of mankind – a game in which neither the hand, nor even a 'finger of God' has participated! – he who divines the fate that is hidden under the idiotic unwariness and blind confidence of 'modern ideas', and still more under the whole of Christo-European morality – suffers from an anguish with which no other is to be compared. He sees at a glance all that could still *be made out of man* through a favourable accumulation and augmentation of human powers and arrangements; he knows with all the knowledge of his conviction how unexhausted man still is for the greatest possibilities, and how often in the past the type man has stood in presence of mysterious decisions and new paths: – he knows still better from his painfulest recollections on what wretched obstacles promising developments of the highest rank have hitherto usually gone to pieces, broken down, sunk and become contemptible. The *universal degeneracy of mankind* to the level of the 'man of the future' – as idealized by the socialistic fools and shallow-pates – this degeneracy and dwarfing of man to an absolutely gregarious animal (or as they call it, to a man of 'free society'), this brutalizing of man into a pigmy with equal rights and claims, is undoubtedly *possible*! He who has thought out this possibility to its ultimate conclusion knows *another* loathing unknown to the rest of mankind – and perhaps also a new *mission*!

CHAPTER VI

We Scholars

204. At the risk that moralizing may also reveal itself here as that which it has always been – namely, resolutely *montrer ses plaies*, according to Balzac – I would venture to protest against an improper and injurious alteration of rank, which quite unnoticed, and as if with the best conscience, threatens nowadays to establish itself in the relations of science and philosophy. I mean to say that one must have the right out of one's own *experience* – experience, as it seems to me, always implies unfortunate experience? – to treat of such an important question of rank, so as not to speak of colour like the blind, or *against* science like women and artists ('Ah! this dreadful science!' sigh their instinct and their shame, 'it always *finds things out*!'). The declaration of independence of the scientific man, his emancipation from philosophy, is one of the subtler after-effects of democratic organization and disorganization: the self-glorification and self-conceitedness of the learned man is now everywhere in full bloom, and in its best springtime – which does not mean to imply that in this case self-praise smells sweetly. Here also the instinct of the populace cries, 'Freedom from all masters!' and after science has, with the happiest results, resisted theology, whose 'handmaid' it had been too long, it now proposes in its wantonness and indiscretion to lay down laws for philosophy, and in its turn to play the 'master' – what am I saying! to play the *philosopher* on its own account. My memory – the memory of a scientific man, if you please! – teems with the naïvetés of insolence which I have heard about philosophy and philosophers from young naturalists and old physicians (not to mention the most cultured and most conceited of all learned men, the philologists and schoolmasters, who are both the one and the other by profession). On one occasion it was the specialist and the Jack Horner who instinctively stood on the defensive against all synthetic tasks and capabilities; at another time

it was the industrious worker who had got a scent of *otium* and refined luxuriousness in the internal economy of the philosopher, and felt himself aggrieved and belittled thereby. On another occasion it was the colour-blindness of the utilitarian, who sees nothing in philosophy but a series of *refuted* systems, and an extravagant expenditure which 'does nobody any good'. At another time the fear of disguised mysticism and of the boundary-adjustment of knowledge became conspicuous, at another time the disregard of individual philosophers, which had involuntarily extended to disregard of philosophy generally. In fine, I found most frequently, behind the proud disdain of philosophy in young scholars, the evil after-effect of some particular philosopher, to whom on the whole obedience had been foresworn, without, however, the spell of his scornful estimates of other philosophers having been got rid of – the result being a general ill-will to all philosophy. (Such seems to me, for instance, the after-effect of Schopenhauer on the most modern Germany: by his unintelligent rage against Hegel, he has succeeded in severing the whole of the last generation of Germans from its connection with German culture, which culture, all things considered, has been an elevation and a divining refinement of the *historical sense*; but precisely at this point Schopenhauer himself was poor, irreceptive and un-German to the extent of ingeniousness.) On the whole, speaking generally, it may just have been the humanness, all-too-humanness of the modern philosophers themselves, in short, their contemptibleness, which has injured most radically the reverence for philosophy and opened the doors to the instinct of the populace. Let it but be acknowledged to what an extent our modern world diverges from the whole style of the world of Heraclitus, Plato, Empedocles, and whatever else all the royal and magnificent anchorites of the spirit were called, and with what justice an honest man of science *may* feel himself of a better family and origin, in view of such representatives of philosophy, who, owing to the fashion of the present day, are just as much aloft as they are down below – in Germany, for instance, the two lions of Berlin, the anarchist Eugen Dühring and the amalgamist Eduard von Hartmann. It is especially the sight of those hotchpotch philosophers, who call themselves 'realists', or 'positivists', which is calculated to implant a dangerous distrust in the soul of a young and ambitious scholar those philosophers, at the best, are themselves but scholars and specialists, that is very evident! All of them are persons who have been vanquished and *brought back again* under the dominion of science, who at one time or another claimed more from themselves, without having a right to the 'more' and its responsibility – and who now, creditably, rancorously, and vindictively, represent in word and deed, *disbelief* in the master-task and supremacy of philosophy After all, how could it be otherwise? Science flourishes nowadays and has the good conscience clearly visible on its countenance, while that to which the entire modern philosophy has gradually sunk, the remnant of philosophy of the present day, excites distrust and displeasure, if not scorn and pity. Philosophy reduced to a 'theory of knowledge', no more in fact than a diffident science of epochs and doctrine of forbearance: a philosophy that never even gets beyond the threshold, and rigorously *denies* itself the right to enter – that is philosophy in its last throes, an end, an agony, something that awakens pity. How could such a philosophy – *rule*!

205. The dangers that beset the evolution of the philosopher are, in fact, so manifold nowadays, that one might doubt whether this fruit could still come to maturity. The extent and towering structure of the sciences have increased enormously, and therewith also the probability that the philosopher will grow tired even as a learner, or will attach himself somewhere and 'specialize' so that he will no longer attain to his elevation, that is to say, to his superspection, his circumspection and his *despection*. Or he gets aloft too late, when the best of his maturity and strength is past, or when he is impaired, coarsened and deteriorated, so that his view, his general estimate of things, is no longer of much importance. It is perhaps just the refinement of his intellectual conscience that makes him hesitate and linger on the way, he dreads the temptation to become a dilettante, a millepede, a milleantenna; he knows too well that as a discerner, one who has lost his self-respect no longer commands,

no longer *leads*; unless he should aspire to become a great play-actor, a philosophical Cagliostro and spiritual rat-catcher – in short, a misleader. This is in the last instance a question of taste, if it has not really been a question of conscience. To double once more the philosopher's difficulties, there is also the fact that he demands from himself a verdict, a Yea or Nay, not concerning science, but concerning life and the worth of life – he learns unwillingly to believe that it is his right and even his duty to obtain this verdict, and he has to seek his way to the right and the belief only through the most extensive (perhaps disturbing and destroying) experiences, often hesitating, doubting and dumbfounded. In fact, the philosopher has long been mistaken and confused by the multitude, either with the scientific man and ideal scholar, or with the religiously elevated, desensualized, desecularized visionary and God-intoxicated man; and even yet when one hears anybody praised, because he lives 'wisely', or 'as a philosopher', it hardly means anything more than 'prudently and apart'. Wisdom: that seems to the populace to be a kind of flight, a means and artifice for withdrawing successfully from a bad game; but the *genuine* philosopher – does it not seem so to *us*, my friends? – lives 'unphilosophically' and 'unwisely', above all, *imprudently*, and feels the obligation and burden of a hundred attempts and temptations of life – he risks *himself* constantly, he plays *this* bad game.

206. In relation to the genius, that is to say, a being who either *engenders* or *produces* – both words understood in their fullest sense – the man of learning, the scientific average man, has always something of the old maid about him; for, like her, he is not conversant with the two principal functions of man. To both, of course, to the scholar and to the old maid, one concedes respectability, as if by way of indemnification – in these cases one emphasizes the respectability – and yet, in the compulsion of this concession, one has the same admixture of vexation. Let us examine more closely: what is the scientific man? First, a commonplace type of man, with commonplace virtues: that is to say, a non-ruling, non-authoritative and non-self-sufficient type of man; he possesses industry, patient adapt-

ableness to rank and file, equability and moderation in capacity and requirement; he has the instinct for people like himself, and for that which they require – for instance: the portion of independence and green meadow without which there is no rest from labour, the claim to honour and consideration (which first and foremost presupposes recognition and recognizability), the sunshine of a good name, the perpetual ratification of his value and usefulness, with which the inward *distrust* which lies at the bottom of the heart of all dependent men and gregarious animals, has again and again to be overcome. The learned man, as is appropriate, has also maladies and faults of an ignoble kind: he is full of petty envy, and has a lynx-eye for the weak points in those natures to whose elevations he cannot attain. He is confiding, yet only as one who lets himself go, but does not *flow*; and precisely before the man of the great current he stands all the colder and more reserved – his eye is then like a smooth and irresponsive lake, which is no longer moved by rapture or sympathy. The worst and most dangerous thing of which a scholar is capable results from the instinct of mediocrity of his type, from the Jesuitism of mediocrity, which labours instinctively for the destruction of the exceptional man, and endeavours to break – or still better, to relax – every bent bow. To relax, of course, with consideration, and naturally with an indulgent hand – to *relax* with confiding sympathy: that is the real art of Jesuitism, which has always understood how to introduce itself as the religion of sympathy.

207. However gratefully one may welcome the *objective* spirit – and who has not been sick to death of all subjectivity and its confounded *ipissimosity*! – in the end, however, one must learn caution even with regard to one's gratitude, and put a stop to the exaggeration with which the unselfing and depersonalizing of the spirit has recently been celebrated, as if it were the goal in itself, as if it were salvation and glorification – as is especially accustomed to happen in the pessimist school, which has also in its turn good reasons for paying the highest honours to 'disinterested knowledge'. The objective man, who no longer curses and scolds like the pessimist, the *ideal* man of learning in whom the scientific instinct

blossoms forth fully after a thousand complete and partial failures, is assuredly one of the most costly instruments that exist, but his place is in the hand of one who is more powerful. He is only an instrument, we may say, he is a *mirror* – he is no 'purpose in himself'. The objective man is in truth a mirror: accustomed to prostration before everything that wants to be known, with such desires only as knowing or 'reflecting' imly – he waits until something comes, and then expands himself sensitively, so that even the light footsteps and gliding past of spiritual beings may not be lost on his surface and film. Whatever 'personality' he still possesses seems to him accidental, arbitrary or still oftener, disturbing, so much has he come to regard himself as the passage and reflection of outside forms and events. He calls up the recollection of 'himself' with an effort, and not infrequently wrongly, he readily confounds himself with other persons, he makes mistakes with regard to his own needs, and here only is he unrefined and negligent. Perhaps he is troubled about the health, or the pettiness and confined atmosphere of wife and friend, or the lack of companions and society – indeed, he sets himself to reflect on his suffering, but in vain! His thoughts already rove away to the *more general* case, and tomorrow he knows as little as he knew yesterday how to help himself. He does not now take himself seriously and devote time to himself: he is serene, *not* from lack of trouble, but from lack of capacity for grasping and dealing with *his* trouble. The habitual complaisance with respect to all objects and experiences, the radiant and impartial hospitality with which he receives everything that comes his way, his habit of inconsiderate good-nature, of dangerous indifference as to Yea and Nay: alas! there are enough of cases in which he has to atone for these virtues of his! – and as man generally, he becomes far too easily the *caput mortuum* of such virtues. Should one wish love or hatred from him – I mean love and hatred as God, woman and animal understand them – he will do what he can, and furnish what he can. But one must not be surprised if it should not be much – if he should show himself just at this point to be false, fragile, questionable and deteriorated. His love is constrained, his hatred is artificial, and rather *un tour de force*, a slight ostentation and exaggeration. He is only genuine so far as he can be objective; only in his serene totality is he still 'nature' and 'natural'. His mirroring and eternally self-polishing soul no longer knows how to affirm, no longer how to deny; he does not command; neither does he destroy. '*Je ne méprise presque rien*' – he says, with Leibniz: let us not overlook nor undervalue the *presque*! Neither is he a model man; he does not go in advance of anyone, nor after, either; he places himself generally too far off to have any reason for espousing the cause of either good or evil. If he has been so long confounded with the *philosopher*, with the Caesarian trainer and dictator of civilization, he has had far too much honour, and what is more essential in him has been overlooked – he is an instrument, something of a slave, though certainly the sublimest sort of slave, but nothing in himself – *presque rien*! The objective man is an instrument, a costly, easily injured, easily tarnished measuring instrument and mirroring apparatus, which is to be taken care of and respected; but he is no goal, not outgoing nor upgoing, no complementary man in whom the *rest* of existence justifies itself, no termination – and still less a commencement, an engendering or primary cause, nothing hardy, powerful, self-centred, that wants to be master; but rather only a soft, inflated, delicate, movable potter's-form, that must wait for some kind of content and frame to 'shape' itself thereto – for the most part a man without frame and content, a 'selfless' man. Consequently, also, nothing for women, *in parenthesi*.

208. When a philosopher nowadays makes known that he is not a sceptic – I hope that has been gathered from the foregoing description of the objective spirit? – people all hear it impatiently; they regard him on that account with some apprehension, they would like to ask so many, many questions… indeed among timid hearers, of whom there are now so many, he is henceforth said to be dangerous. With his repudiation of scepticism, it seems to them as if they heard some evil-threatening sound in the distance, as if a new kind of explosive were being tried somewhere, a dynamite of the spirit, perhaps a newly discovered Russian *nihiline*, a pessimism *bonae voluntatis*, that not only denies, means denial, but – dreadful

thought! *practises* denial. Against this kind of 'good-will' – a will to the veritable, actual negation of life – there is, as is generally acknowledged nowadays, no better soporific and sedative than scepticism, the mild, pleasing, lulling poppy of scepticism; and Hamlet himself is now prescribed by the doctors of the day as an antidote to the 'spirit', and its underground noises. 'Are not our ears already full of bad sounds?' say the sceptics, as lovers of repose, and almost as a kind of safety police, 'this subterranean Nay is terrible! Be still, ye pessimistic moles!' The sceptic, in effect, that delicate creature, is far too easily frightened; his conscience is schooled so as to start at every Nay, and even at that sharp, decided Yea, and feels something like a bite thereby. Yea! and Nay! – they seem to him opposed to morality; he loves, on the contrary, to make a festival to his virtue by a noble aloofness, while perhaps he says with Montaigne: 'What do I know?' Or with Socrates: 'I know that I know nothing.' Or: 'Here I do not trust myself, no door is open to me.' Or: 'Even if the door were open, why should I enter immediately?' Or: 'What is the use of any hasty hypotheses? It might quite well be in good taste to make no hypotheses at all. Are you absolutely obliged to straighten at once what is crooked? to stuff every hole with some kind of oakum? Is there not time enough for that? Has not the time leisure? Oh, ye demons, can ye not at all *wait*? The uncertain also has its charms, the Sphinx, too, is a Circe, and Circe, too, was a philosopher.' – Thus does a sceptic console himself; and in truth he needs some consolation. For scepticism is the most spiritual expression of a certain many-sided physiological temperament, which in ordinary language is called nervous debility and sickliness; it arises whenever races or classes which have been long separated, decisively and suddenly blend with one another. In the new generation, which has inherited as it were different standards and valuations in its blood, everything is disquiet, derangement, doubt and tentativeness; the best powers operate restrictively, the very virtues prevent each other growing and becoming strong, equilibrium, ballast, and perpendicular stability are lacking in body and soul. That, however, which is most diseased and degenerated in such nondescripts is the *will*; they are no longer familiar with independence of decision, or the courageous feeling of pleasure in willing – they are doubtful of the 'freedom of the will' even in their dreams Our present-day Europe, the scene of a senseless, precipitate attempt at a radical blending of classes, and *consequently* of races, is therefore sceptical in all its heights and depths, sometimes exhibiting the mobile scepticism which springs impatiently and wantonly from branch to branch, sometimes with gloomy aspect, like a cloud overcharged with interrogative signs – and often sick unto death of its will! Paralysis of will, where do we not find this cripple sitting nowadays! And yet how bedecked oftentimes! How seductively ornamented! There are the finest gala dresses and disguises for this disease, and that, for instance, most of what places itself nowadays in the show-cases as 'objectiveness', 'the scientific spirit', '*l'art pour l'art*', and 'pure voluntary knowledge', is only decked-out scepticism and paralysis of will – I am ready to answer for this diagnosis of the European disease. – The disease of the will is diffused unequally over Europe; it is worst and most varied where civilization has longest prevailed; it decreases according as 'the barbarian' still – or again – asserts his claims under the loose drapery of Western culture. It is therefore in the France of today, as can be readily disclosed and comprehended, that the will is most infirm, and France, which has always had a masterly aptitude for converting even the portentous crises of its spirit into something charming and seductive, now manifests emphatically its intellectual ascendancy over Europe, by being the school and exhibition of all the charms of scepticism. The power to will and to persist, moreover, in a resolution, is already somewhat stronger in Germany, and again in the North of Germany it is stronger than in Central Germany; it is considerably stronger in England, Spain and Corsica, associated with phlegm in the former and with hard skulls in the latter – not to mention Italy, which is too young yet to know what it wants, and must first show whether it can exercise will but it is strongest and most surprising of all in that immense middle empire where Europe as it were flows back to Asia – namely, in Russia. There the power to will has been long stored up and accumulated, there the will – uncertain whether to be negative or affirmative – waits threateningly to be discharged (to borrow their pet phrase from our physicists). Perhaps not only Indian wars and complications in Asia would be necessary to free Europe from its greatest danger, but also internal subversion, the shattering of the empire into small states, and above all the introduction of parliamentary imbecility, together with the obligation of everyone to read his newspaper at breakfast. I do not say this as one who desires it; in my heart I should rather prefer the contrary – I mean such an increase in the threatening attitude of Russia, that Europe would have to make up its mind to become equally threatening – namely, *to acquire one will*, by means of a new caste to rule over the Continent, a persistent, dreadful will of its own, that can set its aims thousands of years ahead; so that the long spun-out comedy of its petty-statism, and its dynastic as well as its democratic many-willed-ness, might finally be brought to a close. The time for petty politics is past; the next century will bring the struggle for the dominion of the world – the *compulsion* to great politics.

209. As to how far the new warlike age on which we Europeans have evidently entered may perhaps favour the growth of another and stronger kind of scepticism, I should like to express myself preliminarily merely by a parable, which the lovers of German history will already understand. That unscrupulous enthusiast for big, handsome grenadiers (who, as King of Prussia, brought into being a military and sceptical genius – and therewith, in reality, the new and now triumphantly emerged type of German), the problematic, crazy father of Frederick the Great, had on one point the very knack and lucky grasp of the genius: he knew what was then lacking in Germany, the want of which was a hundred times more alarming and serious than any lack of culture and social form – his ill-will to the young Frederick resulted from the anxiety of a profound instinct. *Men were lacking*; and he suspected, to his bitterest regret, that his own son was not man enough. There, however, he deceived himself; but who would not have deceived himself in his place? He saw his son lapsed to atheism, to the *esprit*, to the pleasant frivolity of clever Frenchmen – he saw in the background the great bloodsucker, the spider scepticism; he suspected the incurable wretchedness of a heart no longer

hard enough either for evil or good, and of a broken will that no longer commands, is no longer *able* to command. Meanwhile, however, there grew up in his son that new kind of harder and more dangerous scepticism – who knows *to what extent* it was encouraged just by his father's hatred and the icy melancholy of a will condemned to solitude? – the scepticism of daring manliness, which is closely related to the genius for war and conquest, and made its first entrance into Germany in the person of the great Frederick. This scepticism despises and nevertheless grasps; it undermines and takes possession; it does not believe, but it does not thereby lose itself; it gives the spirit a dangerous liberty, but it keeps strict guard over the heart. It is the *German* form of scepticism, which, as a continued Fredericianism, risen to the highest spirituality, has kept Europe for a considerable time under the dominion of the German spirit and its critical and historical distrust. Owing to the insuperably strong and tough masculine character of the great German philologists and historical critics (who, rightly estimated, were also all of them artists of destruction and dissolution), a *new* conception of the German spirit gradually established itself – in spite of all Romanticism in music and philosophy – in which the leaning towards masculine scepticism was decidedly prominent: whether, for instance, as fearlessness of gaze, as courage and sternness of the dissecting hand or as resolute will to dangerous voyages of discovery, to spiritualized North Pole expeditions under barren and dangerous skies. There may be good grounds for it when warm-blooded and superficial humanitarians cross themselves before this spirit, *cet esprit fataliste, ironique, méphistophélique*, as Michelet calls it, not without a shudder. But if one would realize how characteristic is this fear of the 'man' in the German spirit which awakened Europe out of its 'dogmatic slumber', let us call to mind the former conception which had to be overcome by this new one – and that it is not so very long ago that a masculinized woman could dare, with unbridled presumption, to recommend the Germans to the interest of Europe as gentle, good-hearted, weak-willed and poetical fools. Finally, let us only understand profoundly enough Napoleon's astonishment when he saw Goethe: it reveals what had been regarded for centuries as the 'German spirit'. '*Voilà un homme*!' – that was as much as to say: 'But this is a *man*! And I only expected to see a German!'

210. Supposing, then, that in the picture of the philosophers of the future, some trait suggests the question whether they must not perhaps be sceptics in the last-mentioned sense, something in them would only be designated thereby – and *not* they themselves. With equal right they might call themselves critics, and assuredly they will be men of experiments. By the name with which I ventured to baptize them, I have already expressly emphasized their attempting and their love of attempting: is this because, as critics in body and soul, they will love to make use of experiments in a new, and perhaps wider and more dangerous sense? In their passion for knowledge, will they have to go further in daring and painful attempts than the sensitive and pampered taste of a democratic century can approve of? – There is no doubt these coming ones will be least able to dispense with the serious and not unscrupulous qualities which distinguish the critic from the sceptic: I mean the certainty as to standards of worth, the conscious employment of a unity of method, the wary courage, the standing-alone and the capacity for self-responsibility; indeed, they will avow among themselves a *delight* in denial and dissection, and a certain considerate cruelty, which knows how to handle the knife surely and deftly, even when the heart bleeds. They will be *sterner* (and perhaps not always towards themselves only) than humane people may desire, they will not deal with the 'truth' in order that it may 'please' them, or 'elevate' and 'inspire' them – they will rather have little faith in '*truth*' bringing with it such revels for the feelings. They will smile, those rigorous spirits, when anyone says in their presence: 'that thought elevates me, why should it not be true?' or 'that work enchants me, why should it not be beautiful?' or 'that artist enlarges me, why should he not be great?' Perhaps they will not only have a smile, but a genuine disgust for all that is thus rapturous, idealistic, feminine and hermaphroditic, and if any one could look into their inmost hearts, he would not easily find therein the intention to reconcile 'Christian sentiments' with 'antique taste', or even with 'modern parliamentarism' (the kind of reconcil-

iation necessarily found even among philosophers in our very uncertain and consequently very conciliatory century). Critical discipline, and every habit that conduces to purity and rigour in intellectual matters, will not only be demanded from themselves by these philosophers of the future, they may even make a display thereof as their special adornment – nevertheless they will not want to be called critics on that account. It will seem to them no small indignity to philosophy to have it decreed, as is so welcome nowadays, that 'philosophy itself is criticism and critical science – and nothing else whatever!' Though this estimate of philosophy may enjoy the approval of all the Positivists of France and Germany (and possibly it even flattered the heart and taste of *Kant*: let us call to mind the titles of his principal works), our new philosophers will say, notwithstanding, that critics are instruments of the philosopher, and just on that account, as instruments, they are far from being philosophers themselves! Even the great Chinaman of Königsberg was only a great critic.

211. I insist upon it that people finally cease confounding philosophical workers, and in general scientific men, with philosophers – that precisely here one should strictly give 'each his own', and not give those far too much, these far too little. It may be necessary for the education of the real philosopher that he himself should have once stood upon all those steps upon which his servants, the scientific workers of philosophy, remain standing, and *must* remain standing: he himself must perhaps have been critic, and dogmatist, and historian, and besides, poet, and collector, and traveller, and riddle-reader, and moralist, and seer, and 'free spirit', and almost everything, in order to traverse the whole range of human values and estimations, and that he may *be able* with a variety of eyes and consciences to look from a height to any distance, from a depth up to any height, from a nook into any expanse. But all these are only preliminary conditions for his task; this task itself demands something else – it requires him *to create values*. The philosophical workers, after the excellent pattern of Kant and Hegel, have to fix and formalize some great existing body of valuations – that is to say,

former *determinations of value*, creations of value, which have become prevalent, and are for a time called 'truths' – whether in the domain of the *logical*, the *political* (moral) or the *artistic*. It is for these investigators to make whatever has happened and been esteemed hitherto, conspicuous, conceivable, intelligible and manageable, to shorten everything long, even 'time' itself, and to *subjugate* the entire past: an immense and wonderful task, in the carrying out of which all refined pride, all tenacious will, can surely find satisfaction. *The real philosophers, however, are commanders and law-givers*; they say: 'Thus *shall* it be!' They determine first the Whither and the Why of mankind, and thereby set aside the previous labour of all philosophical workers, and all subjugators of the past – they grasp at the future with a creative hand, and whatever is and was, becomes for them thereby a means, an instrument and a hammer. Their 'knowing' is *creating*, their creating is a law-giving, their will to truth is – *Will to Power*. – Are there at present such philosophers? Have there ever been such philosophers? *Must* there not be such philosophers some day?...

212. It is always more obvious to me that the philosopher, as a man *indispensable* for the morrow and the day after the morrow, has ever found himself, and *has been obliged* to find himself, in contradiction to the day in which he lives; his enemy has always been the ideal of his day. Hitherto all those extraordinary furtherers of humanity whom one calls philosophers – who rarely regarded themselves as lovers of wisdom, but rather as disagreeable fools and dangerous interrogators – have found their mission, their hard, involuntary, imperative mission (in the end, however, the greatness of their mission), in being the bad conscience of their age. In putting the vivisector's knife to the breast of the very *virtues of their age*, they have betrayed their own secret; it has been for the sake of a *new* greatness of man, a new untrodden path to his aggrandizement. They have always disclosed how much hypocrisy, indolence, self-indulgence, and self-neglect, how much falsehood was concealed under the most venerated types of contemporary morality, how much virtue was *outlived*; they have always said: 'We must remove hence

to where *you* are least at home'. In the face of a world of 'modern ideas', which would like to confine everyone in a corner, in a 'specialty', a philosopher, if there could be philosophers nowadays, would be compelled to place the greatness of man, the conception of 'greatness', precisely in his comprehensiveness and multifariousness, in his all-roundness; he would even determine worth and rank according to the amount and variety of that which a man could bear and take upon himself, according to the *extent* to which a man could stretch his responsibility Nowadays the taste and virtue of the age weaken and attenuate the will, nothing is so adapted to the spirit of the age as weakness of will: consequently, in the ideal of the philosopher, strength of will, sternness and capacity for prolonged resolution, must specially be included in the conception of 'greatness'; with as good a right as the opposite doctrine, with its ideal of a silly, renouncing, humble, selfless humanity, was suited to an opposite age – such as the sixteenth century, which suffered from its accumulated energy of will, and from the wildest torrents and floods of selfishness. In the time of Socrates, among men only of worn-out instincts, old conservative Athenians who let themselves go – 'for the sake of happiness', as they said, for the sake of pleasure, as their conduct indicated – and who had continually on their lips the old pompous words to which they had long forfeited the right by the life they led, *irony* was perhaps necessary for greatness of soul, the wicked Socratic assurance of the old physician and plebeian, who cut ruthlessly into his own flesh, as into the flesh and heart of the 'noble', with a look that said plainly enough. 'Do not dissemble before me! here – we are equal!' At present, on the contrary, when throughout Europe the herding-animal alone attains to honours, and dispenses honours, when 'equality of right' can too readily be transformed into equality in wrong: – I mean to say into general war against everything rare, strange and privileged, against the higher man, the higher soul, the higher duty, the higher responsibility, the creative plenipotence and lordliness – at present it belongs to the conception of 'greatness' to be noble, to wish to be apart, to be capable of being different, to stand alone, to have to live by personal initiative and the philosopher will betray something of his own ideal when he asserts: 'He shall be the greatest who can be the most solitary, the most concealed, the most divergent, the man beyond good and evil, the master of his virtues and of superabundance of will; precisely this shall be called *greatness*: as diversified as can be entire, as ample as can be full.' And to ask once more the question: Is greatness *possible* – nowadays?

213. It is difficult to learn what a philosopher is, because it cannot be taught: one must 'know' it by experience – or one should have the pride *not* to know it. The fact that at present people all talk of things of which they *cannot* have any experience, is true more especially and unfortunately as concerns the philosopher and philosophical matters: – the very few know them, are permitted to know them and all popular ideas about them are false. Thus, for instance, the truly philosophical combination of a bold, exuberant spirituality which runs at *presto* pace, and a dialectic rigour and necessity which makes no false step, is unknown to most thinkers and scholars from their own experience, and therefore, should anyone speak of it in their presence, it is incredible to them. They conceive of every necessity as troublesome, as a painful compulsory obedience and state of constraint; thinking itself is regarded by them as something slow and hesitating, almost as a trouble, and often enough as 'worthy of the *sweat* of the noble' – but not at all as something easy and divine, closely related to dancing and exuberance! 'To think' and to take a matter 'seriously', 'arduously' – that is one and the same thing to them; such only has been their 'experience'. – Artists have here perhaps a finer intuition; they who know only too well that precisely when they no longer do anything 'arbitrarily', and everything of necessity, their feeling of freedom, of subtlety, of power, of creatively fixing, disposing and shaping, reaches its climax – in short, that necessity and 'freedom of will' are then the same thing with them. There is, in fine, a gradation of rank in psychical states, to which the gradation of rank in the problems corresponds; and the highest problems repel ruthlessly everyone who ventures too near them, without being predestined for their solution by the loftiness and power of his spirituality. Of what use is it for nimble, everyday

intellects, or clumsy, honest mechanics and empiricists to press, in their plebeian ambition, close to such problems, and as it were into this 'holy of holies' – as so often happens nowadays! But coarse feet must never tread upon such carpets: this is provided for in the primary law of things; the doors remain closed to those intruders, though they may dash and break their heads thereon. People have always to be born to a high station, or, more definitely, they have to be *bred* for it: a person has only a right to philosophy – taking the word in its higher significance – in virtue of his descent; the ancestors, the 'blood', decide here also. Many generations must have prepared the way for the coming of the philosopher; each of his virtues must have been separately acquired, nurtured, transmitted and embodied; not only the bold, easy, delicate course and current of his thoughts, but above all the readiness for great responsibilities, the majesty of ruling glance and contemning look, the feeling of separation from the multitude with their duties and virtues, the kindly patronage and defence of whatever is misunderstood and calumniated, be it God or devil, the delight and practice of supreme justice, the art of commanding, the amplitude of will, the lingering eye which rarely admires, rarely looks up, rarely loves....

CHAPTER VII

Our Virtues

214. Our Virtues? – It is probable that we, too, have still our virtues, although naturally they are not those sincere and massive virtues on account of which we hold our grandfathers in esteem and also at a little distance from us. We Europeans of the day after tomorrow, we firstlings of the twentieth century – with all our dangerous curiosity, our multifariousness and art of disguising, our mellow and seemingly sweetened cruelty in sense and spirit – we shall presumably, *if* we must have virtues, have those only which have come to agreement with our most secret and heartfelt inclinations, with our most ardent requirements: well, then, let us look for them in our labyrinths! – where, as we know, so many things lose themselves, so many things get quite lost! And is there anything finer than to *search* for one's own virtues? Is it not almost to *believe* in one's own virtues? But this 'believing in one's own virtues' – is it not practically the same as what was formerly called one's 'good conscience', that long, respectable pigtail of an idea, which our grandfathers used to hang behind their heads, and often enough also behind their understandings? It seems, therefore, that however little we may imagine ourselves to be old-fashioned and grandfatherly respectable in other respects, in one thing we are nevertheless the worthy grandchildren of our grandfathers, we last Europeans with good consciences: we also still wear their pigtail. – Ah! if you only knew how soon, so very soon – it will be different!

215. As in the stellar firmament there are sometimes two suns which determine the path of one planet, and in certain cases suns of different colours shine around a single planet, now with red light, now with green, and then simultaneously illumine and flood it with motley colours: so we modern men, owing to the complicated mechanism of our 'firmament', are determined by *different* moralities;

our actions shine alternately in different colours, and are seldom unequivocal – and there are often cases, also, in which our actions are *motley-coloured.*

216. To love one's enemies? I think that has been well learnt: it takes place thousands of times at present on a large and small scale; indeed, at times the higher and sublimer thing takes place: – we learn to *despise* when we love, and precisely when we love best; all of it, however, unconsciously, without noise, without ostentation, with the shame and secrecy of goodness, which forbids the utterance of the pompous word and the formula of virtue. Morality as attitude – is opposed to our taste nowadays. This is *also* an advance, as it was an advance in our fathers that religion as an attitude finally became opposed to their taste, including the enmity and Voltairean bitterness against religion (and all that formerly belonged to free-thinker-pantomime). It is the music in our conscience, the dance in our spirit, to which Puritan litanies, moral sermons and goody-goodness won't chime.

217. Let us be careful in dealing with those who attach great importance to being credited with moral tact and subtlety in moral discernment! They never forgive us if they have once made a mistake *before* us (or even with *regard* to us) – they inevitably become our instinctive calumniators and detractors, even when they still remain our 'friends.' – Blessed are the forgetful: for they 'get the better' even of their blunders.

218. The psychologists of France – and where else are there still psychologists nowadays? – have never yet exhausted their bitter and manifold enjoyment of the *betise bourgeoise*, just as though... in short, they betray something thereby. Flaubert, for instance, the honest citizen of Rouen, neither saw, heard, nor tasted anything else in the end; it was his mode of self-torment and refined cruelty. As this is growing wearisome, I would now recommend for a change something else for a pleasure – namely, the unconscious astuteness with which good, fat, honest mediocrity always behaves towards

loftier spirits and the tasks they have to perform, the subtle, barbed, Jesuitical astuteness, which is a thousand times subtler than the taste and understanding of the middle-class in its best moments – subtler even than the understanding of its victims: – a repeated proof that 'instinct' is the most intelligent of all kinds of intelligence which have hitherto been discovered. In short, you psychologists, study the philosophy of the 'rule' in its struggle with the 'exception': there you have a spectacle fit for Gods and godlike malignity! Or, in plainer words, practise vivisection on 'good people', on the '*homo bonae voluntatis*', *on yourselves*!

219. The practice of judging and condemning morally, is the favourite revenge of the intellectually shallow on those who are less so, it is also a kind of indemnity for their being badly endowed by nature, and finally, it is an opportunity for acquiring spirit and *becoming* subtle – malice spiritualizes. They are glad in their inmost heart that there is a standard according to which those who are over-endowed with intellectual goods and privileges, are equal to them, they contend for the 'equality of all before God', and almost *need* the belief in God for this purpose. It is among them that the most powerful antagonists of atheism are found. If any one were to say to them 'A lofty spirituality is beyond all comparison with the honesty and respectability of a merely moral man' – it would make them furious, I shall take care not to say so. I would rather flatter them with my theory that lofty spirituality itself exists only as the ultimate product of moral qualities, that it is a synthesis of all qualities attributed to the 'merely moral' man, after they have been acquired singly through long training and practice, perhaps during a whole series of generations, that lofty spirituality is precisely the spiritualizing of justice, and the beneficent severity which knows that it is authorized to maintain *gradations of rank* in the world, even among things – and not only among men.

220. Now that the praise of the 'disinterested person' is so popular one must – probably not without some danger – get an idea of *what* people actually take an interest in, and what are the things generally

which fundamentally and profoundly concern ordinary men – including the cultured, even the learned, and perhaps philosophers also, if appearances do not deceive. The fact thereby becomes obvious that the greater part of what interests and charms higher natures, and more refined and fastidious tastes, seems absolutely 'uninteresting' to the average man: – if, notwithstanding, he perceive devotion to these interests, he calls it désintéressé, and wonders how it is possible to act 'disinterestedly.' There have been philosophers who could give this popular astonishment a seductive and mystical, other-worldly expression (perhaps because they did not know the higher nature by experience?), instead of stating the naked and candidly reasonable truth that 'disinterested' action is very interesting and 'interested' action, provided that... 'And love?' – What! Even an action for love's sake shall be 'unegoistic'? But you fools – ! 'And the praise of the self-sacrificer?' – But whoever has really offered sacrifice knows that he wanted and obtained something for it – perhaps something from himself for something from himself; that he relinquished here in order to have more there, perhaps in general to be more, or even feel himself 'more'. But this is a realm of questions and answers in which a more fastidious spirit does not like to stay: for here truth has to stifle her yawns so much when she is obliged to answer. And after all, truth is a woman; one must not use force with her.

221. 'It sometimes happens,' said a moralistic pedant and trifle-retailer, 'that I honour and respect an unselfish man: not, however, because he is unselfish, but because I think he has a right to be useful to another man at his own expense.' In short, the question is always who *he* is, and who *the other* is. For instance, in a person created and destined for command, self-denial and modest retirement, instead of being virtues, would be the waste of virtues: so it seems to me. Every system of unegoistic morality which takes itself unconditionally and appeals to every one, not only sins against good taste, but is also an incentive to sins of omission, an *additional* seduction under the mask of philanthropy – and precisely a seduction and injury to the higher, rarer and more privileged types of men. Moral

systems must be compelled first of all to bow before the *gradations of rank*; their presumption must be driven home to their conscience – until they thoroughly understand at last that it is *immoral* to say that 'what is right for one is proper for another'. – So said my moralistic pedant and bonhomme. Did he perhaps deserve to be laughed at when he thus exhorted systems of morals to practise morality? But one should not be too much in the right if one wishes to have the laughers on *one's own* side; a grain of wrong pertains even to good taste.

222. Wherever sympathy (fellow-suffering) is preached nowadays – and, if I gather rightly, no other religion is any longer preached – let the psychologist have his ears open through all the vanity, through all the noise which is natural to these preachers (as to all preachers), he will hear a hoarse, groaning, genuine note of *self-contempt*. It belongs to the overshadowing and uglifying of Europe, which has been on the increase for a century (the first symptoms of which are already specified documentarily in a thoughtful letter of Galiani to Madame d'Epinay) – *if it is not really the cause thereof*! The man of 'modern ideas', the conceited ape, is excessively dissatisfied with himself – this is perfectly certain. He suffers, and his vanity wants him only 'to suffer with his fellows'.

223. The hybrid European – a tolerably ugly plebeian, taken all in all – absolutely requires a costume: he needs history as a storeroom of costumes. To be sure, he notices that none of the costumes fit him properly – he changes and changes. Let us look at the nineteenth century with respect to these hasty preferences and changes in its masquerades of style, and also with respect to its moments of desperation on account of 'nothing suiting' us. It is in vain to get ourselves up as romantic, or classical, or Christian, or Florentine, or *barocco* or 'national', *in moribus et artibus*: it does not 'clothe us'! But the 'spirit', especially the 'historical spirit', profits even by this desperation: once and again a new sample of the past or of the foreign is tested, put on, taken off, packed up and above all *studied* – we are the first studious age *in puncto* of 'costumes', I mean as

concerns morals, articles of belief, artistic tastes and religions; we are prepared as no other age has ever been for a carnival in the grand style, for the most spiritual festival-laughter and arrogance, for the transcendental height of supreme folly and Aristophanic ridicule of the world. Perhaps we are still discovering the domain of our *invention* just here, the domain where even we can still be original, probably as parodists of the world's history and as God's Merry-Andrews, – perhaps, though nothing else of the present have a future, our *laughter* itself may have a future!

224. The *historical sense* (or the capacity for divining quickly the order of rank of the valuations according to which a people, a community or an individual has lived, the 'divining instinct' for the relationships of these valuations, for the relation of the authority of the valuations to the authority of the operating forces), – this historical sense, which we Europeans claim as our specialty, has come to us in the train of the enchanting and mad *semi-barbarity* into which Europe has been plunged by the democratic mingling of classes and races – it is only the nineteenth century that has recognized this faculty as its sixth sense. Owing to this mingling, the past of every form and mode of life, and of cultures which were formerly closely contiguous and superimposed on one another, flows forth into us 'modern souls'; our instincts now run back in all directions, we ourselves are a kind of chaos: in the end, as we have said, the spirit perceives its advantage therein. By means of our semi-barbarity in body and in desire, we have secret access everywhere, such as a noble age never had; we have access above all to the labyrinth of imperfect civilizations, and to every form of semi-barbarity that has at any time existed on earth; and in so far as the most considerable part of human civilization hitherto has just been semi-barbarity, the 'historical sense' implies almost the sense and instinct for everything, the taste and tongue for everything: whereby it immediately proves itself to be an *ignoble* sense. For instance, we enjoy Homer once more: it is perhaps our happiest acquisition that we know how to appreciate Homer, whom men of distinguished culture (as the French of the seventeenth century, like

Saint-Evremond, who reproached him for his *esprit vaste*, and even Voltaire, the last echo of the century) cannot and could not so easily appropriate – whom they scarcely permitted themselves to enjoy. The very decided Yea and Nay of their palate, their promptly ready disgust, their hesitating reluctance with regard to everything strange, their horror of the bad taste even of lively curiosity, and in general the averseness of every distinguished and self-sufficing culture to avow a new desire, a dissatisfaction with its own condition, or an admiration of what is strange: all this determines and disposes them unfavourably even towards the best things of the world which are not their property or *could not* become their prey – and no faculty is more unintelligible to such men than just this historical sense, with its truckling, plebeian curiosity. The case is not different with Shakespeare, that marvellous Spanish-Moorish-Saxon synthesis of taste, over whom an ancient Athenian of the circle of Aeschylus would have half-killed himself with laughter or irritation: but we – accept precisely this wild motleyness, this medley of the most delicate, the most coarse and the most artificial, with a secret confidence and cordiality; we enjoy it as a refinement of art reserved expressly for us, and allow ourselves to be as little disturbed by the repulsive fumes and the proximity of the English populace in which Shakespeare's art and taste lives, as perhaps on the Chiaja of Naples, where, with all our senses awake, we go our way, enchanted and voluntarily, in spite of the drain-odour of the lower quarters of the town. That as men of the 'historical sense' we have our virtues, is not to be disputed: – we are unpretentious, unselfish, modest, brave, habituated to self-control and self-renunciation, very grateful, very patient, very complaisant – but with all this we are perhaps not very 'tasteful'. Let us finally confess it, that what is most difficult for us men of the 'historical sense' to grasp, feel, taste and love, what finds us fundamentally prejudiced and almost hostile, is precisely the perfection and ultimate maturity in every culture and art, the essentially noble in works and men, their moment of smooth sea and halcyon self-sufficiency, the goldenness and coldness which all things show that have perfected themselves. Perhaps our great virtue of the historical sense is in necessary contrast to *good* taste, at least to the very bad taste; and we can only evoke in ourselves imperfectly, hesitatingly and with compulsion the small, short and happy godsends and glorifications of human life as they shine here and there: those moments and marvellous experiences when a great power has voluntarily come to a halt before the boundless and infinite, – when a superabundance of refined delight has been enjoyed by a sudden checking and petrifying, by standing firmly and planting oneself fixedly on still trembling ground. *Proportionateness* is strange to us, let us confess it to ourselves; our itching is really the itching for the infinite, the immeasurable. Like the rider on his forward panting horse, we let the reins fall before the infinite, we modern men, we semi-barbarians – and are only in *our* highest bliss when we – *are in most danger*.

225. Whether it be hedonism, pessimism, utilitarianism or eudaemonism, all those modes of thinking which measure the worth of things according to *pleasure* and *pain*, that is, according to accompanying circumstances and secondary considerations, are plausible modes of thought and naïvetés, which everyone conscious of *creative* powers and an artist's conscience will look down upon with scorn, though not without sympathy. Sympathy for *you*! – to be sure, that is not sympathy as you understand it: it is not sympathy for social 'distress', for 'society' with its sick and misfortuned, for the hereditarily vicious and defective who lie on the ground around us; still less is it sympathy for the grumbling, vexed, revolutionary slave-classes who strive after power – they call it 'freedom'. *Our* sympathy is a loftier and further-sighted sympathy: – we see how *man* dwarfs himself, how *you* dwarf him! and there are moments when we view *your* sympathy with an indescribable anguish, when we resist it, – when we regard your seriousness as more dangerous than any kind of levity. You want, if possible – and there is not a more foolish 'if possible' – *to do away with suffering*; and we? – it really seems that *we* would rather have it increased and made worse than it has ever been! Well-being, as you understand it – is certainly not a goal; it seems to us an *end*; a condition which at once renders man ludicrous and contemptible – and makes his

destruction *desirable*! The discipline of suffering, of *great* suffering – know ye not that it is only *this* discipline that has produced all the elevations of humanity hitherto? The tension of soul in misfortune which communicates to it its energy, its shuddering in view of rack and ruin, its inventiveness and bravery in undergoing, enduring, interpreting and exploiting misfortune, and whatever depth, mystery, disguise, spirit, artifice or greatness has been bestowed upon the soul – has it not been bestowed through suffering, through the discipline of great suffering? In man *creature* and *creator* are united: in man there is not only matter, shred, excess, clay, mire, folly, chaos; but there is also the creator, the sculptor, the hardness of the hammer, the divinity of the spectator and the seventh day – do ye understand this contrast? And that *your* sympathy for the 'creature in man' applies to that which has to be fashioned, bruised, forged, stretched, roasted, annealed, refined – to that which must necessarily *suffer*, and *is meant* to suffer? And *our* sympathy – do ye not understand what our *reverse* sympathy applies to, when it resists your sympathy as the worst of all pampering and enervation? – So it is sympathy *against* sympathy! – But to repeat it once more, there are higher problems than the problems of pleasure and pain and sympathy; and all systems of philosophy which deal only with these are naïvetés.

226. *We Immoralists*. – This world with which *we* are concerned, in which we have to fear and love, this almost invisible, inaudible world of delicate command and delicate obedience, a world of 'almost' in every respect, captious, insidious, sharp and tender – yes, it is well protected from clumsy spectators and familiar curiosity! We are woven into a strong net and garment of duties, and *cannot* disengage ourselves – precisely here, we are 'men of duty', even we! Occasionally, it is true, we dance in our 'chains' and betwixt our 'swords'; it is none the less true that more often we gnash our teeth under the circumstances, and are impatient at the secret hardship of our lot. But do what we will, fools and appearances say of us: 'These are men *without* duty', – we have always fools and appearances against us!

227. Honesty, granting that it is the virtue of which we cannot rid ourselves, we free spirits – well, we will labour at it with all our perversity and love, and not tire of 'perfecting' ourselves in *our* virtue, which alone remains: may its glance some day overspread like a gilded, blue, mocking twilight this aging civilization with its dull gloomy seriousness! And if, nevertheless, our honesty should one day grow weary, and sigh, and stretch its limbs, and find us too hard, and would fain have it pleasanter, easier and gentler, like an agreeable vice, let us remain *hard*, we latest Stoics, and let us send to its help whatever devilry we have in us: – our disgust at the clumsy and undefined, our '*nitimur in vetitum*', our love of adventure, our sharpened and fastidious curiosity, our most subtle, disguised, intellectual Will to Power and universal conquest, which rambles and roves avidiously around all the realms of the future – let us go with all our 'devils' to the help of our 'God'! It is probable that people will misunderstand and mistake us on that account: what does it matter! They will say: 'Their "honesty" – that is their devilry, and nothing else!' What does it matter! And even if they were right – have not all Gods hitherto been such sanctified, re-baptized devils? And after all, what do we know of ourselves? And what the spirit that leads us wants *to be called*? (It is a question of names.) And how many spirits we harbour? Our honesty, we free spirits – let us be careful lest it become our vanity, our ornament and ostentation, our limitation, our stupidity! Every virtue inclines to stupidity, every stupidity to virtue; 'stupid to the point of sanctity', they say in Russia, – let us be careful lest out of pure honesty we eventually become saints and bores! Is not life a hundred times too short for us – to bore ourselves? One would have to believe in eternal life in order to...

228. I hope to be forgiven for discovering that all moral philosophy hitherto has been tedious and has belonged to the soporific appliances – and that 'virtue', in my opinion, has been *more* injured by the *tediousness* of its advocates than by anything else; at the same time, however, I would not wish to overlook their general usefulness. It is desirable that as few people as possible should reflect upon morals,

and consequently it is very desirable that morals should not some day become interesting! But let us not be afraid! Things still remain today as they have always been: I see no one in Europe who has (or *discloses*) an idea of the fact that philosophizing concerning morals might be conducted in a dangerous, captious and ensnaring manner – that *calamity* might be involved therein. Observe, for example, the indefatigable, inevitable English utilitarians: how ponderously and respectably they stalk on, stalk along (a Homeric metaphor expresses it better) in the footsteps of Bentham, just as he had already stalked in the footsteps of the respectable Helvétius! (no, he was not a dangerous man, Helvétius, *ce sénateur Pococurante*, to use an expression of Galiani). No new thought, nothing of the nature of a finer turning or better expression of an old thought, not even a proper history of what has been previously thought on the subject: an *impossible* literature, taking it all in all, unless one knows how to leaven it with some mischief. In effect, the old English vice called *cant*, which is *moral Tartuffism*, has insinuated itself also into these moralists (whom one must certainly read with an eye to their motives if one *must* read them), concealed this time under the new form of the scientific spirit; moreover, there is not absent from them a secret struggle with the pangs of conscience, from which a race of former Puritans must naturally suffer, in all their scientific tinkering with morals. (Is not a moralist the opposite of a Puritan? That is to say, as a thinker who regards morality as questionable, as worthy of interrogation, in short, as a problem? Is moralizing not-immoral?) In the end, they all want *English* morality to be recognized as authoritative, inasmuch as mankind, or the 'general utility', or 'the happiness of the greatest number', – no! the happiness of *England*, will be best served thereby. They would like, by all means, to convince themselves that the striving after *English* happiness, I mean after *comfort* and *fashion* (and in the highest instance, a seat in Parliament), is at the same time the true path of virtue; in fact, that in so far as there has been virtue in the world hitherto, it has just consisted in such striving. Not one of those ponderous, conscience-stricken herding-animals (who undertake to advocate the cause of egoism as conducive to the general welfare) wants to have any knowledge or inkling of the facts that the 'general welfare' is no ideal, no goal, no notion that can be at all grasped, but is only a nostrum, – that what is fair to one *may not* at all be fair to another, that the requirement of one morality for all is really a detriment to higher men, in short, that there is a *distinction of rank* between man and man, and consequently between morality and morality. They are an unassuming and fundamentally mediocre species of men, these utilitarian Englishmen, and, as already remarked, in so far as they are tedious, one cannot think highly enough of their utility. One ought even to *encourage* them, as has been partially attempted in the following rhymes: –

Hail, ye worthies, barrow-wheeling,
'Longer – better', aye revealing,
Stiffer aye in head and knee;
Unenraptured, never jesting,
Mediocre everlasting,
Sans genie et sans esprit!

229. In these later ages, which may be proud of their humanity, there still remains so much fear, so much *superstition* of the fear, of the 'cruel wild beast', the mastering of which constitutes the very pride of these humaner ages – that even obvious truths, as if by the agreement of centuries, have long remained unuttered, because they have the appearance of helping the finally slain wild beast back to life again. I perhaps risk something when I allow such a truth to escape; let others capture it again and give it so much 'milk of pious sentiment'* to drink, that it will lie down quiet and forgotten, in its old corner. – One ought to learn anew about cruelty, and open one's eyes; one ought at last to learn impatience, in order that such immodest gross errors – as, for instance, have been fostered by ancient and modern philosophers with regard to tragedy – may no longer wander about virtuously and boldly. Almost everything that we call 'higher culture' is based

* An expression from Schiller's *William Tell*, Act IV, Scene 3.

upon the spiritualizing and intensifying of *cruelty* – this is my thesis; the 'wild beast' has not been slain at all, it lives, it flourishes, it has only been – transfigured. That which constitutes the painful delight of tragedy is cruelty; that which operates agreeably in so-called tragic sympathy, and at the basis even of everything sublime, up to the highest and most delicate thrills of metaphysics, obtains its sweetness solely from the intermingled ingredient of cruelty. What the Roman enjoys in the arena, the Christian in the ecstasies of the cross, the Spaniard at the sight of the faggot and stake, or of the bull-fight, the present-day Japanese who presses his way to the tragedy, the workman of the Parisian suburbs who has a homesickness for bloody revolutions, the Wagnerienne who, with unhinged will, 'undergoes' the performance of *Tristan and Isolde* – what all these enjoy, and strive with mysterious ardour to drink in, is the philtre of the great Circe 'cruelty.' Here, to be sure, we must put aside entirely the blundering psychology of former times, which could only teach with regard to cruelty that it originated at the sight of the suffering of *others*: there is an abundant, superabundant enjoyment even in one's own suffering, in causing one's own suffering – and wherever man has allowed himself to be persuaded to self-denial in the *religious* sense, or to self-mutilation, as among the Phoenicians and ascetics, or in general, to desensualization, decarnalization and contrition, to Puritanical repentance-spasms, to vivisection of conscience and to Pascal-like *sacrifizia dell' intelleto*, he is secretly allured and impelled forwards by his cruelty, by the dangerous thrill of cruelty *towards himself*. – Finally, let us consider that even the seeker of knowledge operates as an artist and glorifier of cruelty, in that he compels his spirit to perceive *against* its own inclination, and often enough against the wishes of his heart: – he forces it to say Nay, where he would like to affirm, love and adore; indeed, every instance of taking a thing profoundly and fundamentally, is a violation, an intentional injuring of the fundamental will of the spirit, which instinctively aims at appearance and superficiality, – even in every desire for knowledge there is a drop of cruelty.

230. Perhaps what I have said here about a 'fundamental will of the spirit' may not be understood without further details; I may be allowed a word of explanation. – That imperious something which is popularly called 'the spirit', wishes to be master internally and externally, and to feel itself master; it has the will of a multiplicity for a simplicity, a binding, taming, imperious and essentially ruling will. Its requirements and capacities here, are the same as those assigned by physiologists to everything that lives, grows and multiplies. The power of the spirit to appropriate foreign elements reveals itself in a strong tendency to assimilate the new to the old, to simplify the manifold, to overlook or repudiate the absolutely contradictory; just as it arbitrarily re-underlines, makes prominent and falsifies for itself certain traits and lines in the foreign elements, in every portion of the 'outside world'. Its object thereby is the incorporation of new 'experiences', the assortment of new things in the old arrangements – in short, growth; or more properly, the *feeling* of growth, the feeling of increased power – is its object. This same will has at its service an apparently opposed impulse of the spirit, a suddenly adopted preference of ignorance, of arbitrary shutting out, a closing of windows, an inner denial of this or that, a prohibition to approach, a sort of defensive attitude against much that is knowable, a contentment with obscurity, with the shutting-in horizon, an acceptance and approval of ignorance: as that which is all necessary according to the degree of its appropriating power, its 'digestive power', to speak figuratively (and in fact 'the spirit' resembles a stomach more than anything else). Here also belong an occasional propensity of the spirit to let itself be deceived (perhaps with a waggish suspicion that it is *not* so and so, but is only allowed to pass as such), a delight in uncertainty and ambiguity, an exulting enjoyment of arbitrary, out-of-the-way narrowness and mystery, of the too-near, of the foreground, of the magnified, the diminished, the misshapen, the beautified – an enjoyment of the arbitrariness of all these manifestations of power. Finally, in this connection, there is the not unscrupulous readiness of the spirit to deceive other spirits and dissemble before them – the constant pressing and straining of a creating, shaping, changeable power: the spirit enjoys therein its

craftiness and its variety of disguises, it enjoys also its feeling of security therein – it is precisely by its Protean arts that it is best protected and concealed! – *Counter to* this propensity for appearance, for simplification, for a disguise, for a cloak, in short, for an outside – for every outside is a cloak – there operates the sublime tendency of the man of knowledge, which takes, and *insists* on taking things profoundly, variously and thoroughly; as a kind of cruelty of the intellectual conscience and taste, which every courageous thinker will acknowledge in himself, provided, as it ought to be, that he has sharpened and hardened his eye sufficiently long for introspection, and is accustomed to severe discipline and even severe words. He will say: 'There is something cruel in the tendency of my spirit': let the virtuous and amiable try to convince him that it is not so! In fact, it would sound nicer, if, instead of our cruelty, perhaps our 'extravagant honesty' were talked about, whispered about and glorified – we free, *very* free spirits – and some day perhaps *such* will actually be our – posthumous glory! Meanwhile – for there is plenty of time until then – we should be least inclined to deck ourselves out in such florid and fringed moral verbiage; our whole former work has just made us sick of this taste and its sprightly exuberance. They are beautiful, glistening, jingling, festive words: honesty, love of truth, love of wisdom, sacrifice for knowledge, heroism of the truthful – there is something in them that makes one's heart swell with pride. But we anchorites and marmots have long ago persuaded ourselves in all the secrecy of an anchorite's conscience, that this worthy parade of verbiage also belongs to the old false adornment, frippery and gold-dust of unconscious human vanity, and that even under such flattering colour and repainting, the terrible original text *homo natura* must again be recognized. In effect, to translate man back again into nature; to master the many vain and visionary interpretations and subordinate meanings which have hitherto been scratched and daubed over the eternal original text, *homo natura*; to bring it about that man shall henceforth stand before man as he now, hardened by the discipline of science, stands before the *other* forms of nature, with fearless Oedipus-eyes, and stopped Ulysses-ears, deaf to the enticements of old metaphysical bird-catchers, who have piped to him far too long: 'Thou art more! thou art higher! thou hast a different origin!' – this may be a strange and foolish task, but that it is a *task*, who can deny! Why did we choose it, this foolish task? Or, to put the question differently: 'Why knowledge at all?' Everyone will ask us about this. And thus pressed, we, who have asked ourselves the question a hundred times, have not found and cannot find any better answer...

231. Learning alters us, it does what all nourishment does that does not merely 'conserve' – as the physiologist knows. But at the bottom of our souls, quite 'down below', there is certainly something unteachable, a granite of spiritual fate, of predetermined decision and answer to predetermined, chosen questions. In each cardinal problem there speaks an unchangeable 'I am this'; a thinker cannot learn anew about man and woman, for instance, but can only learn fully – he can only follow to the end what is 'fixed' about them in himself. Occasionally we find certain solutions of problems which make strong beliefs for *us*; perhaps they are henceforth called 'convictions.' Later on – one sees in them only footsteps to self-knowledge, guide-posts to the problem which we ourselves *are* – or more correctly to the great stupidity which we embody, our spiritual fate, the *unteachable* in us, quite 'down below'. – In view of this liberal compliment which I have just paid myself, permission will perhaps be more readily allowed me to utter some truths about 'woman as she is', provided that it is known at the outset how literally they are merely – *my* truths.

232. Woman wishes to be independent, and therefore she begins to enlighten men about 'woman as she is' – *this* is one of the worst developments of the general *uglifying* of Europe. For what must these clumsy attempts of feminine scientificality and self-exposure bring to light! Woman has so much cause for shame; in woman there is so much pedantry, superficiality, schoolmasterliness, petty presumption, unbridledness and indiscretion concealed – study only woman's behaviour towards children! – which has really been best restrained and dominated hitherto by the *fear* of man. Alas, if ever

the 'eternally tedious in woman' – she has plenty of it! – is allowed to venture forth! if she begins radically and on principle to unlearn her wisdom and art – of charming, of playing, of frightening away sorrow, of alleviating and taking easily; if she forgets her delicate aptitude for agreeable desires! Female voices are already raised, which, by Saint Aristophanes! make one afraid: – with medical explicitness it is stated in a threatening manner what woman first and last *requires* from man. Is it not in the very worst taste that woman thus sets herself up to be scientific? Enlightenment hitherto has fortunately been men's affair, men's gift – we remained therewith 'among ourselves'; and in the end, in view of all that women write about 'woman', we may well have considerable doubt as to whether woman really *desires* enlightenment about herself – and *can* desire it. If woman does not thereby seek a new *ornament* for herself – I believe ornamentation belongs to the eternally feminine? – why, then, she wishes to make herself feared: perhaps she thereby wishes to get the mastery. But she does not want truth – what does woman care for truth? From the very first, nothing is more foreign, more repugnant or more hostile to woman than truth – her great art is falsehood, her chief concern is appearance and beauty. Let us confess it, we men: we honour and love this very art and this very instinct in woman: we who have the hard task, and for our recreation gladly seek the company of beings under whose hands, glances and delicate follies, our seriousness, our gravity and profundity appear almost like follies to us. Finally, I ask the question: Did a woman herself ever acknowledge profundity in a woman's mind, or justice in a woman's heart? And is it not true that on the whole 'woman' has hitherto been most despised by woman herself, and not at all by us? – We men desire that woman should not continue to compromise herself by enlightening us; just as it was man's care and the consideration for woman, when the church decreed: *mulier taceat in ecclesia*. It was to the benefit of woman when Napoleon gave the too eloquent Madame de Staël to understand: *mulier taceat in politicis*! – and in my opinion, he is a true friend of woman who calls out to women today: *mulier taceat de muliere*!

233. It betrays corruption of the instincts – apart from the fact that it betrays bad taste – when a woman refers to Madame Roland, or Madame de Staël or Monsieur George Sand, as though something were proved thereby in favour of 'woman as she is'. Among men, these are the three comical women as they are – nothing more! – and just the best involuntary counter-arguments against feminine emancipation and autonomy.

234. Stupidity in the kitchen; woman as cook; the terrible thoughtlessness with which the feeding of the family and the master of the house is managed! Woman does not understand what food *means*, and she insists on being cook! If woman had been a thinking creature, she should certainly, as cook for thousands of years, have discovered the most important physiological facts, and should likewise have got possession of the healing art! Through bad female cooks – through the entire lack of reason in the kitchen – the development of mankind has been longest retarded and most interfered with: even today matters are very little better. A word to High School girls.

235. There are turns and casts of fancy, there are sentences, little handfuls of words, in which a whole culture, a whole society suddenly crystallizes itself. Among these is the incidental remark of Madame de Lambert to her son: '*Mon ami, ne vous permettez jamais que des folies, qui vous feront grand plaisir*' – the motherliest and wisest remark, by the way, that was ever addressed to a son.

236. I have no doubt that every noble woman will oppose what Dante and Goethe believed about woman – the former when he sang, '*ella guardava suso, ed io in lei*', and the latter when he interpreted it, 'the eternally feminine draws us *aloft*'; for *this* is just what she believes of the eternally masculine.

237. *Seven Apophthegms for Women*

How the longest ennui flees,
When a man comes to our knees!

Age, alas! and science staid,
Furnish even weak virtue aid.

Sombre garb and silence meet:
Dress for every dame – discreet.

Whom I thank when in my bliss?
God! – and my good tailoress!

Young, a flower-decked cavern home;
Old, a dragon thence doth roam.

Noble title, leg that's fine,
Man as well: Oh, were *he* mine!

Speech in brief and sense in mass –
Slippery for the jenny-ass!

237[A]. Woman has hitherto been treated by men like birds, which, losing their way, have come down among them from an elevation: as something delicate, fragile, wild, strange, sweet and animating – but as something also which must be cooped up to prevent it flying away.

238. To be mistaken in the fundamental problem of 'man and woman', to deny here the profoundest antagonism and the necessity for an eternally hostile tension, to dream here perhaps of equal rights, equal training, equal claims and obligations: that is a *typical* sign of shallow-mindedness; and a thinker who has proved himself shallow at this dangerous spot – shallow in instinct! – may generally be regarded as suspicious, nay more, as betrayed, as discovered; he will probably prove too 'short' for all fundamental questions of life, future as well as present, and will be unable to descend into *any* of the depths. On the other hand, a man who has depth of spirit as well as of desires, and has also the depth of benevolence which is capable of severity and harshness, and easily confounded with them, can only think of woman as *Orientals* do: he must conceive of her

as a possession, as confinable property, as a being predestined for service and accomplishing her mission therein – he must take his stand in this matter upon the immense rationality of Asia, upon the superiority of the instinct of Asia, as the Greeks did formerly; those best heirs and scholars of Asia – who, as is well known, with their *increasing* culture and amplitude of power, from Homer to the time of Pericles, became gradually *stricter* towards woman, in short, more Oriental. *How* necessary, *how* logical, even *how* humanely desirable this was, let us consider for ourselves!

239. The weaker sex has in no previous age been treated with so much respect by men as at present – this belongs to the tendency and fundamental taste of democracy, in the same way as disrespectfulness to old age – what wonder is it that abuse should be immediately made of this respect? They want more, they learn to make claims, the tribute of respect is at last felt to be well-nigh galling; rivalry for rights, indeed actual strife itself, would be preferred: in a word, woman is losing modesty. And let us immediately add that she is also losing taste. She is unlearning to *fear* man: but the woman who 'unlearns to fear' sacrifices her most womanly instincts. That woman should venture forward when the fear-inspiring quality in man – or more definitely, the *man* in man – is no longer either desired or fully developed, is reasonable enough and also intelligible enough; what is more difficult to understand is that precisely thereby – woman deteriorates. This is what is happening nowadays: let us not deceive ourselves about it! Wherever the industrial spirit has triumphed over the military and aristocratic spirit, woman strives for the economic and legal independence of a clerk: 'woman as clerkess' is inscribed on the portal of the modern society which is in course of formation. While she thus appropriates new rights, aspires to be 'master' and inscribes 'progress' of woman on her flags and banners, the very opposite realizes itself with terrible obviousness: *woman retrogrades*. Since the French Revolution the influence of woman in Europe has *declined* in proportion as she has increased her rights and claims; and the 'emancipation of woman', in so far as it is desired and demanded by women themselves (and

not only by masculine shallow-pates), thus proves to be a remarkable symptom of the increased weakening and deadening of the most womanly instincts. There is *stupidity* in this movement, an almost masculine stupidity, of which a well-reared woman – who is always a sensible woman – might be heartily ashamed. To lose the intuition as to the ground upon which she can most surely achieve victory; to neglect exercise in the use of her proper weapons; to let-herself-go before man, perhaps even 'to the book', where formerly she kept herself in control and in refined, artful humility; to neutralize with her virtuous audacity man's faith in a *veiled*, fundamentally different ideal in woman, something eternally, necessarily feminine; to emphatically and loquaciously dissuade man from the idea that woman must be preserved, cared for, protected and indulged, like some delicate, strangely wild and often pleasant domestic animal; the clumsy and indignant collection of everything of the nature of servitude and bondage which the position of woman in the hitherto existing order of society has entailed and still entails (as though slavery were a counter-argument, and not rather a condition of every higher culture, of every elevation of culture): – what does all this betoken, if not a disintegration of womanly instincts, a defeminizing? Certainly, there are enough of idiotic friends and corrupters of woman among the learned asses of the masculine sex, who advise woman to defeminize herself in this manner, and to imitate all the stupidities from which 'man' in Europe, European 'manliness', suffers, – who would like to lower woman to 'general culture', indeed even to newspaper reading and meddling with politics. Here and there they wish even to make women into free spirits and literary workers: as though a woman without piety would not be something perfectly obnoxious or ludicrous to a profound and godless man; – almost everywhere her nerves are being ruined by the most morbid and dangerous kind of music (our latest German music), and she is daily being made more hysterical and more incapable of fulfilling her first and last function, that of bearing robust children. They wish to 'cultivate' her in general still more, and intend, as they say, to make the 'weaker sex' *strong* by culture: as if history did not teach in the most emphatic manner that the 'cultivating' of mankind and his weakening – that is to say, the weakening, dissipating and languishing of his *force of will* – have always kept pace with one another, and that the most powerful and influential women in the world (and lastly, the mother of Napoleon) had just to thank their force of will – and not their schoolmasters – for their power and ascendancy over men. That which inspires respect in woman, and often enough fear also, is her *nature*, which is more 'natural' than that of man, her genuine, carnivora-like, cunning flexibility, her tiger-claws beneath the glove, her *naïveté* in egoism, her untrainableness and innate wildness, the incomprehensibleness, extent and deviation of her desires and virtues.... That which, in spite of fear, excites one's sympathy for the dangerous and beautiful cat, 'woman', is that she seems more afflicted, more vulnerable, more necessitous of love and more condemned to disillusionment than any other creature. Fear and sympathy it is with these feelings that man has hitherto stood in the presence of woman, always with one foot already in tragedy, which rends while it delights – What? And all that is now to be at an end? And the *disenchantment* of woman is in progress? The tediousness of woman is slowly evolving? Oh Europe! Europe! We know the horned animal which was always most attractive to thee, from which danger is ever again threatening thee! Thy old fable might once more become 'history' – an immense stupidity might once again overmaster thee and carry thee away! And no God concealed beneath it – no! only an 'idea', a 'modern idea'!

CHAPTER VIII

Peoples and Countries

240. I heard, once again for the first time, Richard Wagner's overture to the *Mastersinger*: it is a piece of magnificent, gorgeous, heavy, latter-day art, which has the pride to presuppose two centuries of music as still living, in order that it may be understood: – it is an honour to Germans that such a pride did not miscalculate! What flavours and forces, what seasons and climes do we not find mingled in it! It impresses us at one time as ancient, at another time as foreign, bitter and too modern, it is as arbitrary as it is pompously traditional, it is not infrequently roguish, still oftener rough and coarse – it has fire and courage, and at the same time the loose, dun-coloured skin of fruits which ripen too late. It flows broad and full: and suddenly there is a moment of inexplicable hesitation, like a gap that opens between cause and effect, an oppression that makes us dream, almost a nightmare; but already it broadens and widens anew, the old stream of delight – the most manifold delight, – of old and new happiness; including *especially* the joy of the artist in himself, which he refuses to conceal, his astonished, happy cognizance of his mastery of the expedients here employed, the new, newly acquired, imperfectly tested expedients of art which he apparently betrays to us. All in all, however, no beauty, no South, nothing of the delicate southern clearness of the sky, nothing of grace, no dance, hardly a will to logic; a certain clumsiness even, which is also emphasized, as though the artist wished to say to us: 'It is part of my intention'; a cumbersome drapery, something arbitrarily barbaric and ceremonious, a flirring of learned and venerable conceits and witticisms; something German in the best and worst sense of the word, something in the German style, manifold, formless and inexhaustible; a certain German potency and super-plenitude of soul, which is not afraid to hide itself under the *raffinements* of decadence – which, perhaps, feels itself most at ease there; a real, genuine token

of the German soul, which is at the same time young and aged, too ripe and yet still too rich in futurity. This kind of music expresses best what I think of the Germans: they belong to the day before yesterday and the day after tomorrow – *they have as yet no today*.

241. We 'good Europeans', we also have hours when we allow ourselves a warm-hearted patriotism, a plunge and relapse into old loves and narrow views – I have just given an example of it – hours of national excitement, of patriotic anguish, and all other sorts of old-fashioned floods of sentiment. Duller spirits may perhaps only get done with what confines its operations in us to hours and plays itself out in hours – in a considerable time: some in half a year, others in half a lifetime, according to the speed and strength with which they digest and 'change their material'. Indeed, I could think of sluggish, hesitating races, which even in our rapidly moving Europe, would require half a century ere they could surmount such atavistic attacks of patriotism and soil-attachment, and return once more to reason, that is to say, to 'good Europeanism'. And while digressing on this possibility, I happen to become an ear-witness of a conversation between two old patriots – they were evidently both hard of hearing and consequently spoke all the louder. '*He* has as much, and knows as much, philosophy as a peasant or a corps-student,' said the one – 'he is still innocent. But what does that matter nowadays! It is the age of the masses: they lie on their belly before everything that is massive. And so also in *politicis*. A statesman who rears up for them a new Tower of Babel, some monstrosity of empire and power, they call "great" – what does it matter that we more prudent and conservative ones do not meanwhile give up the old belief that it is only the great thought that gives greatness to an action or affair. Supposing a statesman were to bring his people into the position of being obliged henceforth to practise "high politics", for which they were by nature badly endowed and prepared, so that they would have to sacrifice their old and reliable virtues, out of love to a new and doubtful mediocrity; – supposing a statesman were to condemn his people generally to "practise politics", when they have hitherto had something better to do and think about, and

when in the depths of their souls they have been unable to free themselves from a prudent loathing of the restlessness, emptiness and noisy wranglings of the essentially politics-practising nations; – supposing such a statesman were to stimulate the slumbering passions and avidities of his people, were to make a stigma out of their former diffidence and delight in aloofness, an offence out of their exoticism and hidden permanency, were to depreciate their most radical proclivities, subvert their consciences, make their minds narrow and their tastes "national" – what! a statesman who should do all this, which his people would have to do penance for throughout their whole future, if they had a future, such a statesman would be *great*, would he?' – 'Undoubtedly!' replied the other old patriot vehemently, 'otherwise he *could not* have done it! It was mad perhaps to wish such a thing! But perhaps everything great has been just as mad at its commencement!' – 'Misuse of words!' cried his interlocutor, contradictorily – 'strong! strong! Strong and mad! *not* great!' – The old men had obviously become heated as they thus shouted their 'truths' in each other's faces, but I, in my happiness and apartness, considered how soon a stronger one may become master of the strong, and also that there is a compensation for the intellectual superficializing of a nation – namely, in the deepening of another.

242. Whether we call it 'civilization', or 'humanising', or 'progress' which now distinguishes the European, whether we call it simply, without praise or blame, by the political formula: the *democratic* movement in Europe – behind all the moral and political foregrounds pointed to by such formulas, an immense *physiological process* goes on, which is ever extending: the process of the assimilation of Europeans; their increasing detachment from the conditions under which, climatically and hereditarily, united races originate, their increasing independence of every definite *milieu*, that for centuries would fain inscribe itself with equal demands on soul and body; – that is to say, the slow emergence of an essentially *super-national* and nomadic species of man, who possesses, physiologically speaking, a maximum of the art and power of adaptation as his typical distinction. This process of the *evolving European*, which can be

retarded in its *tempo* by great relapses, but will perhaps just gain and grow thereby in vehemence and depth – the still-raging storm and stress of 'national sentiment' pertains to it, and also the anarchism which is appearing at present – this process will probably arrive at results on which its naïve propagators and panegyrists, the apostles of 'modern ideas', would least care to reckon. The same new conditions under which on an average a levelling and mediocrising of man will take place – a useful, industrious, variously serviceable and clever gregarious man – are in the highest degree suitable to give rise to exceptional men of the most dangerous and attractive qualities. For, while the capacity for adaptation, which is every day trying changing conditions, and begins a new work with every generation, almost with every decade, makes the *powerfulness* of the type impossible; while the collective impression of such future Europeans will probably be that of numerous, talkative, weak-willed and very handy workmen who *require* a master, a commander, as they require their daily bread; while, therefore, the democratizing of Europe will tend to the production of a type prepared for *slavery* in the most subtle sense of the term: the *strong* man will necessarily in individual and exceptional cases, become stronger and richer than he has perhaps ever been before – owing to the unprejudicedness of his schooling, owing to the immense variety of practice, art and disguise. I meant to say that the democratizing of Europe is at the same time an involuntary arrangement for the rearing of *tyrants* – taking the word in all its meanings, even in its most spiritual sense.

243. I hear with pleasure that our sun is moving rapidly towards the constellation *Hercules*: and I hope that the men on this earth will do like the sun. And we foremost, we good Europeans!

244. There was a time when it was customary to call Germans 'deep' by way of distinction; but now that the most successful type of new Germanism is covetous of quite other honours, and perhaps misses 'smartness' in all that has depth, it is almost opportune and patriotic to doubt whether we did not formerly deceive ourselves with that commendation: in short, whether German depth is not at

bottom something different and worse – and something from which, thank God, we are on the point of successfully ridding ourselves. Let us try, then, to relearn with regard to German depth; the only thing necessary for the purpose is a little vivisection of the German soul. – The German soul is above all manifold, varied in its source, aggregated and super-imposed, rather than actually built: this is owing to its origin. A German who would embolden himself to assert: 'Two souls, alas, dwell in my breast', would make a bad guess at the truth, or, more correctly, he would come far short of the truth about the number of souls. As a people made up of the most extraordinary mixing and mingling of races, perhaps even with a preponderance of the pre-Aryan element as the 'people of the centre' in every sense of the term, the Germans are more intangible, more ample, more contradictory, more unknown, more incalculable, more surprising and even more terrifying than other peoples are to themselves: – they escape *definition*, and are thereby alone the despair of the French. It is characteristic of the Germans that the question: 'What is German?' never dies out among them. Kotzebue certainly knew his Germans well enough: 'We are known,' they cried jubilantly to him – but Sand also thought he knew them. Jean Paul knew what he was doing when he declared himself incensed at Fichte's lying but patriotic flatteries and exaggerations, – but it is probable that Goethe thought differently about Germans from Jean Paul, even though he acknowledged him to be right with regard to Fichte. It is a question what Goethe really thought about the Germans? – But about many things around him he never spoke explicitly, and all his life he knew how to keep an astute silence – probably he had good reason for it. It is certain that it was not the 'Wars of Independence' that made him look up more joyfully, any more than it was the French Revolution, – the event on account of which he *reconstructed* his *Faust*, and indeed the whole problem of 'man', was the appearance of Napoleon. There are words of Goethe in which he condemns with impatient severity, as from a foreign land, that which Germans take a pride in, he once defined the famous German turn of mind as 'Indulgence towards its own and others' weaknesses'. Was he wrong? it is characteristic of Germans that one is seldom entirely wrong about them. The German soul has passages and galleries in it, there are caves, hiding-places and dungeons therein, its disorder has much of the charm of the mysterious, the German is well acquainted with the bypaths to chaos. And as everything loves its symbol, so the German loves the clouds and all that is obscure, evolving, crepuscular, damp and shrouded: it seems to him that everything uncertain, undeveloped, self-displacing and growing is 'deep'. The German himself does not *exist*: he is *becoming*, he is 'developing himself'. 'Development' is therefore the essentially German discovery and hit in the great domain of philosophical formulas, – a ruling idea, which, together with German beer and German music, is labouring to Germanize all Europe. Foreigners are astonished and attracted by the riddles which the conflicting nature at the basis of the German soul propounds to them (riddles which Hegel systematized and Richard Wagner has in the end set to music). 'Good-natured and spiteful' – such a juxtaposition, preposterous in the case of every other people, is unfortunately only too often justified in Germany: one has only to live for a while among Swabians to know this! The clumsiness of the German scholar and his social distastefulness agree alarmingly well with his physical rope-dancing and nimble boldness, of which all the Gods have learnt to be afraid. If anyone wishes to see the 'German soul' demonstrated *ad oculos*, let him only look at German taste, at German arts and manners: what boorish indifference to 'taste'! How the noblest and the commonest stand there in juxtaposition! How disorderly and how rich is the whole constitution of this soul! The German *drags* at his soul, he drags at everything he experiences. He digests his events badly; he never gets 'done' with them; and German depth is often only a difficult, hesitating 'digestion'. And just as all chronic invalids, all dyspeptics, like what is convenient, so the German loves 'frankness' and 'honesty'; it is so *convenient* to be frank and honest! – This confidingness, this complaisance, this showing-the-cards of German *honesty*, is probably the most dangerous and most successful disguise which the German is up to nowadays: it is his proper Mephistophelean art; with this he can 'still achieve much'! The German lets himself go, and thereby gazes with faithful, blue, empty German eyes – and other countries immediately confound him with his dressing-gown! – I meant to say that, let 'German depth' be what it will – among ourselves alone we perhaps take the liberty to laugh at it – we shall do well to continue henceforth to honour its appearance and good name, and not barter away too cheaply our old reputation as a people of depth for Prussian 'smartness', and Berlin wit and sand. It is wise for a people to pose, and *let* itself be regarded, as profound, clumsy, good-natured, honest and foolish: it might even be – profound to do so! Finally, we should do honour to our name – we are not called the '*tiusche Volk*' (deceptive people) for nothing...

245. The 'good old' time is past, it sang itself out in Mozart – how happy are *we* that his *rococo* still speaks to us, that his 'good company', his tender enthusiasm, his childish delight in the Chinese and its flourishes, his courtesy of heart, his longing for the elegant, the amorous, the tripping, the tearful and his belief in the South, can still appeal to *something left* in us! Ah, sometime or other it will be over with it! – but who can doubt that it will be over still sooner with the intelligence and taste for Beethoven! For he was only the last echo of a break and transition in style, and *not*, like Mozart, the last echo of a great European taste which had existed for centuries. Beethoven is the intermediate event between an old mellow soul that is constantly breaking down, and a future over-young soul that is always *coming*; there is spread over his music the twilight of eternal loss and eternal extravagant hope, – the same light in which Europe was bathed when it dreamed with Rousseau, when it danced round the Tree of Liberty of the Revolution, and finally almost fell down in adoration before Napoleon. But how rapidly does *this* very sentiment now pale, how difficult nowadays is even the *apprehension* of this sentiment, how strangely does the language of Rousseau, Schiller, Shelley and Byron sound to our ear, in whom *collectively* the same fate of Europe was able to *speak*, which knew how to *sing* in Beethoven! – Whatever German music came afterwards, belongs to Romanticism, that is to say, to a movement which, historically considered, was still shorter, more fleeting and more superficial than that great interlude, the transition of Europe from Rousseau to Napoleon, and to the rise of democracy. Weber – but what do *we* care

nowadays for *Der Freischutz* and *Oberon*! Or Marschner's *Hans Heiling* and *Vampyre*! Or even Wagner's *Tannhauser*! That is extinct, although not yet forgotten music. This whole music of Romanticism, besides, was not noble enough, was not musical enough, to maintain its position anywhere but in the theatre and before the masses; from the beginning it was second-rate music, which was little thought of by genuine musicians. It was different with Felix Mendelssohn, that halcyon master, who, on account of his lighter, purer, happier soul, quickly acquired admiration, and was equally quickly forgotten: as the beautiful *episode* of German music. But with regard to Robert Schumann, who took things seriously, and has been taken seriously from the first – he was the last that founded a school, – do we not now regard it as a satisfaction, a relief, a deliverance, that this very Romanticism of Schumann's has been surmounted? Schumann, fleeing into the 'Saxon Switzerland' of his soul, with a half Werther-like, half Jean-Paul-like nature (assuredly not like Beethoven! assuredly not like Byron!) – his *Manfred* music is a mistake and a misunderstanding to the extent of injustice; Schumann, with his taste, which was fundamentally a *petty* taste (that is to say, a dangerous propensity – doubly dangerous among Germans – for quiet lyricism and intoxication of the feelings), going constantly apart, timidly withdrawing and retiring, a noble weakling who revelled in nothing but anonymous joy and sorrow, from the beginning a sort of girl and *noli me tangere* – this Schumann was already merely a *German* event in music, and no longer a European event, as Beethoven had been, as in a still greater degree Mozart had been; with Schumann German music was threatened with its greatest danger, that of *losing the voice for the soul of Europe* and sinking into a merely national affair.

246. What a torture are books written in German to a reader who has a *third* ear! How indignantly he stands beside the slowly turning swamp of sounds without tune and rhythms without dance, which Germans call a 'book'! And even the German who *reads* books! How lazily, how reluctantly, how badly he reads! How many Germans know, and consider it obligatory to know, that there is *art* in every good sentence – art which must be divined, if the sentence is to be understood! If there is a misunderstanding about its *tempo*,

for instance, the sentence itself is misunderstood! That one must not be doubtful about the rhythm-determining syllables, that one should feel the breaking of the too-rigid symmetry as intentional and as a charm, that one should lend a fine and patient ear to every *staccato* and every *rubato*, that one should divine the sense in the sequence of the vowels and diphthongs, and how delicately and richly they can be tinted and retinted in the order of their arrangement – who among book-reading Germans is complaisant enough to recognize such duties and requirements, and to listen to so much art and intention in language? After all, one just 'has no ear for it'; and so the most marked contrasts of style are not heard, and the most delicate artistry is as it were *squandered* on the deaf. – These were my thoughts when I noticed how clumsily and unintuitively two masters in the art of prose-writing have been confounded: one, whose words drop down hesitatingly and coldly, as from the roof of a damp cave – he counts on their dull sound and echo; and another who manipulates his language like a flexible sword, and from his arm down into his toes feels the dangerous bliss of the quivering, over-sharp blade, which wishes to bite, hiss and cut.

247. How little the German style has to do with harmony and with the ear, is shown by the fact that precisely our good musicians themselves write badly. The German does not read aloud, he does not read for the ear, but only with his eyes; he has put his ears away in the drawer for the time. In antiquity when a man read – which was seldom enough – he read something to himself, and in a loud voice; they were surprised when anyone read silently, and sought secretly the reason of it. In a loud voice: that is to say, with all the swellings, inflections and variations of key and changes of *tempo*, in which the ancient *public* world took delight. The laws of the written style were then the same as those of the spoken style; and these laws depended partly on the surprising development and refined requirements of the ear and larynx; partly on the strength, endurance and power of the ancient lungs. In the ancient sense, a period is above all a physiological whole, inasmuch as it is comprised in one breath. Such periods as occur in Demosthenes and Cicero, swelling

twice and sinking twice, and all in one breath, were pleasures to the men of *antiquity*, who knew by their own schooling how to appreciate the virtue therein, the rareness and the difficulty in the deliverance of such a period; – *we* have really no right to the *big* period, we modern men, who are short of breath in every sense! Those ancients, indeed, were all of them dilettanti in speaking, consequently connoisseurs, consequently critics – they thus brought their orators to the highest pitch; in the same manner as in the last century, when all Italian ladies and gentlemen knew how to sing, the virtuosoship of song (and with it also the art of melody) reached its elevation. In Germany, however (until quite recently when a kind of platform eloquence began shyly and awkwardly enough to flutter its young wings), there was properly speaking only one kind of public and *approximately* artistical discourse – that delivered from the pulpit. The preacher was the only one in Germany who knew the weight of a syllable or a word, in what manner a sentence strikes, springs, rushes, flows and comes to a close; he alone had a conscience in his ears, often enough a bad conscience: for reasons are not lacking why proficiency in oratory should be especially seldom attained by a German, or almost always too late. The masterpiece of German prose is therefore with good reason the masterpiece of its greatest preacher: the *Bible* has hitherto been the best German book. Compared with Luther's *Bible*, almost everything else is merely 'literature' – something which has not grown in Germany, and therefore has not taken and does not take root in German hearts, as the *Bible* has done.

248. There are two kinds of geniuses: one which above all engenders and seeks to engender, and another which willingly lets itself be fructified and brings forth. And similarly, among the gifted nations, there are those on whom the woman's problem of pregnancy has devolved, and the secret task of forming, maturing and perfecting – the Greeks, for instance, were a nation of this kind, and so are the French; and others which have to fructify and become the cause of new modes of life – like the Jews, the Romans and, in all modesty be it asked: like the Germans? – nations tortured and enraptured by

unknown fevers and irresistibly forced out of themselves, amorous and longing for foreign races (for such as 'let themselves be fructified'), and withal imperious, like everything conscious of being full of generative force, and consequently empowered 'by the grace of God'. These two kinds of geniuses seek each other like man and woman; but they also misunderstand each other – like man and woman.

249. Every nation has its own 'Tartuffery', and calls that its virtue. – One does not know – cannot know, the best that is in one.

250. What Europe owes to the Jews? – Many things, good and bad, and above all one thing of the nature both of the best and the worst: the grand style in morality, the fearfulness and majesty of infinite demands, of infinite significations, the whole Romanticism and sublimity of moral questionableness – and consequently just the most attractive, ensnaring and exquisite element in those iridescences and allurements to life, in the aftersheen of which the sky of our European culture, its evening sky, now glows – perhaps glows out. For this, we artists among the spectators and philosophers, are – grateful to the Jews.

251. It must be taken into the bargain, if various clouds and disturbances – in short, slight attacks of stupidity – pass over the spirit of a people that suffers and *wants* to suffer from national nervous fever and political ambition: for instance, among present-day Germans there is alternately the anti-French folly, the anti-Semitic folly, the anti-Polish folly, the Christian-romantic folly, the Wagnerian folly, the Teutonic folly, the Prussian folly (just look at those poor historians, the Sybels and Treitschkes, and their closely bandaged heads), and whatever else these little obscurations of the German spirit and conscience may be called. May it be forgiven me that I, too, when on a short daring sojourn on very infected ground, did not remain wholly exempt from the disease, but like everyone else, began to entertain thoughts about matters which did not concern me – the first symptom of political infection. About the Jews, for instance, listen to the following: – I have never yet met a German

who was favourably inclined to the Jews; and however decided the repudiation of actual anti-Semitism may be on the part of all prudent and political men, this prudence and policy is not perhaps directed against the nature of the sentiment itself, but only against its dangerous excess, and especially against the distasteful and infamous expression of this excess of sentiment; – on this point we must not deceive ourselves. That Germany has amply *sufficient* Jews, that the German stomach, the German blood, has difficulty (and will long have difficulty) in disposing only of this quantity of 'Jew' – as the Italian, the Frenchman and the Englishman have done by means of a stronger digestion: – that is the unmistakable declaration and language of a general instinct, to which one must listen and according to which one must act. 'Let no more Jews come in! And shut the doors, especially towards the East (also towards Austria)!' – thus commands the instinct of a people whose nature is still feeble and uncertain, so that it could be easily wiped out, easily extinguished, by a stronger race. The Jews, however, are beyond all doubt the strongest, toughest and purest race at present living in Europe, they know how to succeed even under the worst conditions (in fact better than under favourable ones), by means of virtues of some sort, which one would like nowadays to label as vices – owing above all to a resolute faith which does not need to be ashamed before 'modern ideas'; they alter only, *when* they do alter, in the same way that the Russian Empire makes its conquest – as an empire that has plenty of time and is not of yesterday – namely, according to the principle, 'as slowly as possible'! A thinker who has the future of Europe at heart, will, in all his perspectives concerning the future, calculate upon the Jews, as he will calculate upon the Russians, as above all the surest and likeliest factors in the great play and battle of forces. That which is at present called a 'nation' in Europe, and is really rather a *res facta* than *nata* (indeed, sometimes confusingly similar to a *res ficta et picta*), is in every case something evolving, young, easily displaced and not yet a race, much less such a race *aere perennius*, as the Jews are: such 'nations' should most carefully avoid all hot-headed rivalry and hostility! It is certain that the Jews, if they desired – or if they were driven to it, as the anti-Semites seem to wish – *could* now have the ascendancy, nay, literally the supremacy, over Europe, that they are *not* working and planning for that end is equally certain. Meanwhile, they rather wish and desire, even somewhat importunely, to be insorbed and absorbed by Europe, they long to be finally settled, authorized and respected somewhere, and wish to put an end to the nomadic life, to the 'wandering Jew'; – and one should certainly take account of this impulse and tendency, and *make advances* to it (it possibly betokens a mitigation of the Jewish instincts): for which purpose it would perhaps be useful and fair to banish the anti-Semitic bawlers out of the country. One should make advances with all prudence, and with selection; pretty much as the English nobility do. It stands to reason that the more powerful and strongly marked types of new Germanism could enter into relation with the Jews with the least hesitation, for instance, the nobleman officer from the Prussian border: it would be interesting in many ways to see whether the genius for money and patience (and especially some intellect and intellectuality – sadly lacking in the place referred to) could not in addition be annexed and trained to the hereditary art of commanding and obeying – for both of which the country in question has now a classic reputation. But here it is expedient to break off my festal discourse and my sprightly Teutonomania: for I have already reached my *serious topic*, the 'European problem', as I understand it, the rearing of a new ruling caste for Europe.

252. They are not a philosophical race – the English: Bacon represents an *attack* on the philosophical spirit generally, Hobbes, Hume and Locke, an abasement, and a depreciation of the idea of a 'philosopher' for more than a century. It was *against* Hume that Kant uprose and raised himself; it was Locke of whom Schelling *rightly* said, '*je méprise Locke*'; in the struggle against the English mechanical stultification of the world, Hegel and Schopenhauer (along with Goethe) were of one accord; the two hostile brother-geniuses in philosophy, who pushed in different directions towards the opposite poles of German thought, and thereby wronged each other as only brothers will do. – What is lacking in England, and has always been lacking,

that half-actor and rhetorician knew well enough, the absurd muddle-head, Carlyle, who sought to conceal under passionate grimaces what he knew about himself: namely, what was *lacking* in Carlyle – real *power* of intellect, real *depth* of intellectual perception, in short, philosophy. It is characteristic of such an unphilosophical race to hold on firmly to Christianity – they *need* its discipline for 'moralizing' and humanizing. The Englishman, more gloomy, sensual, headstrong and brutal than the German – is for that very reason, as the baser of the two, also the most pious: he has all the *more need* of Christianity. To finer nostrils, this English Christianity itself has still a characteristic English taint of spleen and alcoholic excess, for which, owing to good reasons, it is used as an antidote – the finer poison to neutralize the coarser: a finer form of poisoning is in fact a step in advance with coarse-mannered people, a step towards spiritualization. The English coarseness and rustic demureness is still most satisfactorily disguised by Christian pantomime, and by praying and psalm-singing (or, more correctly, it is thereby explained and differently expressed); and for the herd of drunkards and rakes who formerly learned moral grunting under the influence of Methodism (and more recently as the 'Salvation Army'), a penitential fit may really be the relatively highest manifestation of 'humanity' to which they can be elevated: so much may reasonably be admitted. That, however, which offends even in the humanest Englishman is his lack of music, to speak figuratively (and also literally): he has neither rhythm nor dance in the movements of his soul and body; indeed, not even the desire for rhythm and dance, for 'music.' Listen to him speaking; look at the most beautiful Englishwoman *walking* – in no country on earth are there more beautiful doves and swans; finally, listen to them singing! But I ask too much...

253. There are truths which are best recognized by mediocre minds, because they are best adapted for them, there are truths which only possess charms and seductive power for mediocre spirits: – one is pushed to this probably unpleasant conclusion, now that the influence of respectable but mediocre Englishmen – I may mention Darwin, John Stuart Mill and Herbert Spencer – begins

to gain the ascendancy in the middle-class region of European taste. Indeed, who could doubt that it is a useful thing for *such* minds to have the ascendancy for a time? It would be an error to consider the highly developed and independently soaring minds as specially qualified for determining and collecting many little common facts, and deducing conclusions from them; as exceptions, they are rather from the first in no very favourable position towards those who are 'the rules.' After all, they have more to do than merely to perceive: – in effect, they have to *be* something new, they have to *signify* something new, they have to *represent* new values! The gulf between knowledge and capacity is perhaps greater, and also more mysterious, than one thinks: the capable man in the grand style, the creator, will possibly have to be an ignorant person; – while on the other hand, for scientific discoveries like those of Darwin, a certain narrowness, aridity and industrious carefulness (in short, something English) may not be unfavourable for arriving at them. – Finally, let it not be forgotten that the English, with their profound mediocrity, brought about once before a general depression of European intelligence. What is called 'modern ideas', or 'the ideas of the eighteenth century' or 'French ideas' – that, consequently, against which the *German* mind rose up with profound disgust – is of English origin, there is no doubt about it. The French were only the apes and actors of these ideas, their best soldiers, and likewise, alas! their first and profoundest *victims*; for owing to the diabolical Anglomania of 'modern ideas', the *âme Français* has in the end become so thin and emaciated, that at present one recalls its sixteenth and seventeenth centuries, its profound, passionate strength, its inventive excellency, almost with disbelief. One must, however, maintain this verdict of historical justice in a determined manner, and defend it against present prejudices and appearances: the European *noblesse* – of sentiment, taste and manners, taking the word in every high sense – is the work and invention of *France*; the European ignobleness, the plebeianism of modern ideas – is *England's* work and invention.

254. Even at present France is still the seat of the most intellectual and refined culture of Europe, it is still the high school of taste; but

one must know how to find this 'France of taste'. He who belongs to it keeps himself well concealed: – they may be a small number in whom it lives and is embodied, besides perhaps being men who do not stand upon the strongest legs, in part fatalists, hypochondriacs, invalids, in part persons over-indulged, over-refined, such as have the *ambition* to conceal themselves. They have all something in common: they keep their ears closed in presence of the delirious folly and noisy spouting of the democratic *bourgeois*. In fact, a besotted and brutalized France at present sprawls in the foreground – it recently celebrated a veritable orgy of bad taste, and at the same time of self-admiration, at the funeral of Victor Hugo. There is also something else common to them: a predilection to resist intellectual Germanizing – and a still greater inability to do so! In this France of intellect, which is also a France of pessimism, Schopenhauer has perhaps become more at home, and more indigenous than he has ever been in Germany; not to speak of Heinrich Heine, who has long ago been reincarnated in the more refined and fastidious lyrists of Paris; or of Hegel, who at present, in the form of Taine – the *first* of living historians – exercises an almost tyrannical influence. As regards Richard Wagner, however, the more French music learns to adapt itself to the actual needs of the *âme moderne*, the more will it 'Wagnerize'; one can safely predict that beforehand, – it is already taking place sufficiently! There are, however, three things which the French can still boast of with pride as their heritage and possession, and as indelible tokens of their ancient intellectual superiority in Europe, in spite of all voluntary or involuntary Germanizing and vulgarizing of taste. *Firstly*, the capacity for artistic emotion, for devotion to 'form', for which the expression, *l'art pour l'art*, along with numerous others, has been invented: – such capacity has not been lacking in France for three centuries; and owing to its reverence for the 'small number', it has again and again made a sort of chamber music of literature possible, which is sought for in vain elsewhere in Europe. – The *second* thing whereby the French can lay claim to a superiority over Europe is their ancient, many-sided, *moralistic* culture, owing to which one finds on an average, even in the petty *romanciers* of the newspapers and chance *boulevardiers de Paris*, a psychological sensitiveness and curiosity, of which, for example, one has no conception (to say nothing of the thing itself!) in Germany. The Germans lack a couple of centuries of the moralistic work requisite thereto, which, as we have said, France has not grudged: those who call the Germans 'naïve' on that account give them commendation for a defect. (As the opposite of the German inexperience and innocence *in voluptate psychologica*, which is not too remotely associated with the tediousness of German intercourse, – and as the most successful expression of genuine French curiosity and inventive talent in this domain of delicate thrills, Henri Beyle may be noted; that remarkable anticipatory and forerunning man, who, with a Napoleonic *tempo*, traversed *his* Europe, in fact, several centuries of the European soul, as a surveyor and discoverer thereof: – it has required two generations to *overtake* him one way or other, to divine long afterwards some of the riddles that perplexed and enraptured him – this strange Epicurean and man of interrogation, the last great psychologist of France). – There is yet a *third* claim to superiority: in the French character there is a successful half-way synthesis of the North and South, which makes them comprehend many things, and enjoins upon them other things, which an Englishman can never comprehend. Their temperament, turned alternately to and from the South, in which from time to time the Provençal and Ligurian blood froths over, preserves them from the dreadful, northern grey-in-grey, from sunless conceptual-spectrism and from poverty of blood – our *German* infirmity of taste, for the excessive prevalence of which at the present moment, blood and iron, that is to say 'high politics', has with great resolution been prescribed (according to a dangerous healing art, which bids me wait and wait, but not yet hope). – There is also still in France a pre-understanding and ready welcome for those rarer and rarely gratified men, who are too comprehensive to find satisfaction in any kind of fatherlandism, and know how to love the South when in the North and the North when in the South – the born Midlanders, the 'good Europeans'. For them *Bizet* has made music, this latest genius, who has seen a new beauty and seduction, – who has discovered a piece of the *South in music*.

255. I hold that many precautions should be taken against German music. Suppose a person loves the South as I love it – as a great school of recovery for the most spiritual and the most sensuous ills, as a boundless solar profusion and effulgence which o'erspreads a sovereign existence believing in itself – well, such a person will learn to be somewhat on his guard against German music, because, in injuring his taste anew, it will also injure his health anew. Such a Southerner, a Southerner not by origin but by *belief*, if he should dream of the future of music, must also dream of it being freed from the influence of the North; and must have in his ears the prelude to a deeper, mightier and perhaps more perverse and mysterious music, a super-German music, which does not fade, pale and die away, as all German music does, at the sight of the blue, wanton sea and the Mediterranean clearness of sky – a super-European music, which holds its own even in presence of the brown sunsets of the desert, whose soul is akin to the palm tree, and can be at home and can roam with big, beautiful, lonely beasts of prey... I could imagine a music of which the rarest charm would be that it knew nothing more of good and evil; only that here and there perhaps some sailor's homesickness, some golden shadows and tender weaknesses might sweep lightly over it; an art which, from the far distance, would see the colours of a sinking and almost incomprehensible *moral* world fleeing towards it, and would be hospitable enough and profound enough to receive such belated fugitives.

256. Owing to the morbid estrangement which the nationality-craze has induced and still induces among the nations of Europe, owing also to the short-sighted and hasty-handed politicians, who with the help of this craze, are at present in power, and do not suspect to what extent the disintegrating policy they pursue must necessarily be only an interlude policy – owing to all this and much else that is altogether unmentionable at present, the most unmistakable signs that *Europe wishes to be one*, are now overlooked, or arbitrarily and falsely misinterpreted. With all the more profound and large-minded men of this century, the real general tendency of the mysterious labour of their souls was to prepare the way for that

new *synthesis*, and tentatively to anticipate the European of the future; only in their simulations, or in their weaker moments, in old age perhaps, did they belong to the 'fatherlands' – they only rested from themselves when they became 'patriots'. I think of such men as Napoleon, Goethe, Beethoven, Stendhal, Heinrich Heine, Schopenhauer: it must not be taken amiss if I also count Richard Wagner among them, about whom one must not let oneself be deceived by his own misunderstandings (geniuses like him have seldom the right to understand themselves), still less, of course, by the unseemly noise with which he is now resisted and opposed in France: the fact remains, nevertheless, that Richard Wagner and the *later French Romanticism* of the forties, are most closely and intimately related to one another. They are akin, fundamentally akin, in all the heights and depths of their requirements; it is Europe, the *one* Europe, whose soul presses urgently and longingly, outwards and upwards, in their multifarious and boisterous art – whither? into a new light? towards a new sun? But who would attempt to express accurately what all these masters of new modes of speech could not express distinctly? It is certain that the same storm and stress tormented them, that they *sought* in the same manner, these last great seekers! All of them steeped in literature to their eyes and ears – the first artists of universal literary culture – for the most part even themselves writers, poets, intermediaries and blenders of the arts and the senses (Wagner, as musician is reckoned among painters, as poet among musicians, as artist generally among actors); all of them fanatics for *expression* 'at any cost' – I specially mention Delacroix, the nearest related to Wagner; all of them great discoverers in the realm of the sublime, also of the loathsome and dreadful, still greater discoverers in effect, in display, in the art of the show-shop; all of them talented far beyond their genius, out and out *virtuosi*, with mysterious accesses to all that seduces, allures, constrains and upsets; born enemies of logic and of the straight line, hankering after the strange, the exotic, the monstrous, the crooked and the self-contradictory; as men, Tantaluses of the will, plebeian parvenus, who knew themselves to be incapable of a noble *tempo* or of a *lento* in life and action – think of Balzac, for instance, – unrestrained workers, almost destroying themselves by work; antinomians and rebels in manners, ambitious and insatiable, without equilibrium and enjoyment; all of them finally shattering and sinking down at the Christian cross (and with right and reason, for who of them would have been sufficiently profound and sufficiently original for an *anti-Christian* philosophy?); – on the whole, a boldly daring, splendidly overbearing, high-flying and aloft-up-dragging class of higher men, who had first to teach their century – and it is the century of the *masses* – the conception 'higher man'.... Let the German friends of Richard Wagner advise together as to whether there is anything purely German in the Wagnerian art, or whether its distinction does not consist precisely in coming from *super-German* sources and impulses: in which connection it may not be underrated how indispensable Paris was to the development of his type, which the strength of his instincts made him long to visit at the most decisive time – and how the whole style of his proceedings, of his self-apostolate, could only perfect itself in sight of the French socialistic original. On a more subtle comparison it will perhaps be found, to the honour of Richard Wagner's German nature, that he has acted in everything with more strength, daring, severity and elevation than a nineteenth-century Frenchman could have done – owing to the circumstance that we Germans are as yet nearer to barbarism than the French; – perhaps even the most remarkable creation of Richard Wagner is not only at present, but for ever inaccessible, incomprehensible and inimitable to the whole latter-day Latin race: the figure of Siegfried, that *very free* man, who is probably far too free, too hard, too cheerful, too healthy, too *anti-Catholic* for the taste of old and mellow civilized nations. He may even have been a sin against Romanticism, this anti-Latin Siegfried: well, Wagner atoned amply for this sin in his old sad days, when – anticipating a taste which has meanwhile passed into politics – he began, with the religious vehemence peculiar to him, to preach, at least, *the way to Rome*, if not to walk therein. – That these last words may not be misunderstood, I will call to my aid a few powerful rhymes, which will even betray to less delicate ears what I mean – what I mean *counter to* the 'last Wagner' and his *Parsifal* music: –

– Is this our mode? –
From German heart came this vexed ululating?
From German body, this self-lacerating?
Is ours this priestly hand-dilation,
This incense-fuming exaltation?
Is ours this faltering, falling, shambling,
This quite uncertain ding-dong-dangling?
This sly nun-ogling, Ave-hour-bell ringing, This wholly false enraptured heaven-o'erspringing?
– Is this our mode? –
Think well! – ye still wait for admission –
For what ye hear is *Rome – Rome's faith by intuition*!

CHAPTER IX

What is Noble?

257. Every elevation of the type 'man', has hitherto been the work of an aristocratic society and so it will always be – a society believing in a long scale of gradations of rank and differences of worth among human beings, and requiring slavery in some form or other. Without the *pathos of distance*, such as grows out of the incarnated difference of classes, out of the constant out-looking and down-looking of the ruling caste on subordinates and instruments, and out of their equally constant practice of obeying and commanding, of keeping down and keeping at a distance – that other more mysterious pathos could never have arisen, the longing for an ever new widening of distance within the soul itself, the formation of ever higher, rarer, further, more extended, more comprehensive states, in short, just the elevation of the type 'man', the continued 'self-surmounting of man', to use a moral formula in a supermoral sense. To be sure, one must not resign oneself to any humanitarian illusions about the history of the origin of an aristocratic society (that is to say, of the preliminary condition for the elevation of the type 'man'): the truth is hard. Let us acknowledge unprejudicedly how every higher civilization hitherto has *originated*! Men with a still natural nature, barbarians in every terrible sense of the word, men of prey, still in possession of unbroken strength of will and desire for power, threw themselves upon weaker, more moral, more peaceful races (perhaps trading or cattle-rearing communities), or upon old mellow civilizations in which the final vital force was flickering out in brilliant fireworks of wit and depravity. At the commencement, the noble caste was always the barbarian caste: their superiority did not consist first of all in their physical, but in their psychical power – they were more *complete* men (which at every point also implies the same as 'more complete beasts').

258. Corruption – as the indication that anarchy threatens to break out among the instincts, and that the foundation of the emotions, called 'life', is convulsed – is something radically different according to the organization in which it manifests itself. When, for instance, an aristocracy like that of France at the beginning of the Revolution, flung away its privileges with sublime disgust and sacrificed itself to an excess of its moral sentiments, it was corruption: – it was really only the closing act of the corruption which had existed for centuries, by virtue of which that aristocracy had abdicated step by step its lordly prerogatives and lowered itself to a *function* of royalty (in the end even to its decoration and parade-dress). The essential thing, however, in a good and healthy aristocracy is that it should not regard itself as a function either of the kingship or the commonwealth, but as the *significance* and highest justification thereof – that it should therefore accept with a good conscience the sacrifice of a legion of individuals, who, *for its sake*, must be suppressed and reduced to imperfect men, to slaves and instruments. Its fundamental belief must be precisely that society is *not* allowed to exist for its own sake, but only as a foundation and scaffolding, by means of which a select class of beings may be able to elevate themselves to their higher duties, and in general to a higher *existence*: like those sun-seeking climbing plants in Java – they are called *Sipo Matador*, – which encircle an oak so long and so often with their arms, until at last, high above it, but supported by it, they can unfold their tops in the open light, and exhibit their happiness.

259. To refrain mutually from injury, from violence, from exploitation, and put one's will on a par with that of others: this may result in a certain rough sense in good conduct among individuals when the necessary conditions are given (namely, the actual similarity of the individuals in amount of force and degree of worth, and their co-relation within one organization). As soon, however, as one wished to take this principle more generally, and if possible even as the *fundamental principle of society*, it would immediately disclose what it really is – namely, a Will to the *denial* of life, a principle of dissolution and decay. Here one must think profoundly to the very basis

and resist all sentimental weakness: life itself is *essentially* appropriation, injury, conquest of the strange and weak, suppression, severity, obtrusion of peculiar forms, incorporation and at the least, putting it mildest, exploitation; – but why should one for ever use precisely these words on which for ages a disparaging purpose has been stamped? Even the organization within which, as was previously supposed, the individuals treat each other as equal – it takes place in every healthy aristocracy – must itself, if it be a living and not a dying organization, do all that towards other bodies, which the individuals within it refrain from doing to each other it will have to be the incarnated Will to Power, it will endeavour to grow, to gain ground, attract to itself and acquire ascendancy – not owing to any morality or immorality, but because it *lives*, and because life *is* precisely Will to Power. On no point, however, is the ordinary consciousness of Europeans more unwilling to be corrected than on this matter; people now rave everywhere, even under the guise of science, about coming conditions of society in which 'the exploiting character' is to be absent: – that sounds to my ears as if they promised to invent a mode of life which should refrain from all organic functions. 'Exploitation' does not belong to a depraved, or imperfect and primitive society: it belongs to the *nature* of the living being as a primary organic function; it is a consequence of the intrinsic Will to Power, which is precisely the Will to Life. – Granting that as a theory this is a novelty – as a reality it is the *fundamental fact* of all history: let us be so far honest towards ourselves!

260. In a tour through the many finer and coarser moralities which have hitherto prevailed or still prevail on the earth, I found certain traits recurring regularly together, and connected with one another, until finally two primary types revealed themselves to me, and a radical distinction was brought to light. There is *master-morality* and *slave-morality*, – I would at once add, however, that in all higher and mixed civilizations, there are also attempts at the reconciliation of the two moralities, but one finds still oftener the confusion and mutual misunderstanding of them, indeed sometimes their close juxtaposition – even in the same man, within one soul. The distinctions

of moral values have either originated in a ruling caste, pleasantly conscious of being different from the ruled – or among the ruled class, the slaves and dependents of all sorts. In the first case, when it is the rulers who determine the conception 'good', it is the exalted, proud disposition which is regarded as the distinguishing feature, and that which determines the order of rank. The noble type of man separates from himself the beings in whom the opposite of this exalted, proud disposition displays itself: he despises them. Let it at once be noted that in this first kind of morality the antithesis 'good' and 'bad' means practically the same as 'noble' and 'despicable'; – the antithesis 'good' and 'evil' is of a different origin. The cowardly, the timid, the insignificant and those thinking merely of narrow utility are despised; moreover, also, the distrustful, with their constrained glances, the self-abasing, the dog-like kind of men who let themselves be abused, the mendicant flatterers and above all the liars: – it is a fundamental belief of all aristocrats that the common people are untruthful. 'We truthful ones' – the nobility in ancient Greece called themselves. It is obvious that everywhere the designations of moral value were at first applied to *men*, and were only derivatively and at a later period applied to *actions*; it is a gross mistake, therefore, when historians of morals start with questions like, 'Why have sympathetic actions been praised?' The noble type of man regards *himself* as a determiner of values; he does not require to be approved of; he passes the judgment: 'What is injurious to me is injurious in itself'; he knows that it is he himself only who confers honour on things; he is a *creator of values*. He honours whatever he recognizes in himself: such morality equals self-glorification. In the foreground there is the feeling of plenitude, of power, which seeks to overflow, the happiness of high tension, the consciousness of a wealth which would fain give and bestow: – the noble man also helps the unfortunate, but not – or scarcely – out of pity, but rather from an impulse generated by the super-abundance of power. The noble man honours in himself the powerful one, him also who has power over himself, who knows how to speak and how to keep silence, who takes pleasure in subjecting himself to severity and hardness, and has reverence for all that is severe and hard. 'Wotan placed a hard heart in my breast,' says an old Scandinavian Saga: it is thus rightly expressed from the soul of a proud Viking. Such a type of man is even proud of not being made for sympathy; the hero of the Saga therefore adds warningly: 'He who has not a hard heart when young, will never have one.' The noble and brave who think thus are the furthest removed from the morality which sees precisely in sympathy, or in acting for the good of others, or in *désintéressement*, the characteristic of the moral; faith in oneself, pride in oneself, a radical enmity and irony towards 'selflessness', belong as definitely to noble morality, as do a careless scorn and precaution in presence of sympathy and the 'warm heart'. – It is the powerful who *know* how to honour, it is their art, their domain for invention. The profound reverence for age and for tradition – all law rests on this double reverence, – the belief and prejudice in favour of ancestors and unfavourable to newcomers, is typical in the morality of the powerful; and if, reversely, men of 'modern ideas' believe almost instinctively in 'progress' and the 'future', and are more and more lacking in respect for old age, the ignoble origin of these 'ideas' has complacently betrayed itself thereby. A morality of the ruling class, however, is more especially foreign and irritating to present-day taste in the sternness of its principle that one has duties only to one's equals; that one may act towards beings of a lower rank, towards all that is foreign, just as seems good to one, or 'as the heart desires', and in any case 'beyond good and evil': it is here that sympathy and similar sentiments can have a place. The ability and obligation to exercise prolonged gratitude and prolonged revenge – both only within the circle of equals, – artfulness in retaliation, *raffinement* of the idea in friendship, a certain necessity to have enemies (as outlets for the emotions of envy, quarrelsomeness, arrogance – in fact, in order to be a good *friend*): all these are typical characteristics of the noble morality, which, as has been pointed out, is not the morality of 'modern ideas', and is therefore at present difficult to realize, and also to unearth and disclose. – It is otherwise with the second type of morality, *slave-morality*. Supposing that the abused, the oppressed, the suffering, the unemancipated, the weary and those uncertain of themselves should moralize, what will be the common element in their moral estimates? Probably a pessimistic suspicion with regard to the entire situation of man will find expression, perhaps a condemnation of man, together with his situation. The slave has an unfavourable eye for the virtues of the powerful; he has a scepticism and distrust, a *refinement* of distrust of everything 'good' that is there honoured – he would fain persuade himself that the very happiness there is not genuine. On the other hand, *those* qualities which serve to alleviate the existence of sufferers are brought into prominence and flooded with light; it is here that sympathy, the kind, helping hand, the warm heart, patience, diligence, humility and friendliness attain to honour; for here these are the most useful qualities, and almost the only means of supporting the burden of existence. Slave-morality is essentially the morality of utility. Here is the seat of the origin of the famous antithesis 'good' and 'evil': – power and dangerousness are assumed to reside in the evil, a certain dreadfulness, subtlety and strength, which do not admit of being despised. According to slave-morality, therefore, the 'evil' man arouses fear; according to master-morality, it is precisely the 'good' man who arouses fear and seeks to arouse it, while the bad man is regarded as the despicable being. The contrast attains its maximum when, in accordance with the logical consequences of slave-morality, a shade of depreciation – it may be slight and well-intentioned – at last attaches itself to the 'good' man of this morality; because, according to the servile mode of thought, the good man must in any case be the *safe* man: he is good-natured, easily deceived, perhaps a little stupid, *un bonhomme*. Everywhere that slave-morality gains the ascendancy, language shows a tendency to approximate the significations of the words 'good' and 'stupid'. – A last fundamental difference: the desire for *freedom*, the instinct for happiness and the refinements of the feeling of liberty belong as necessarily to slave-morals and morality, as artifice and enthusiasm in reverence and devotion are the regular symptoms of an aristocratic mode of thinking and estimating. – Hence we can understand without further detail why love *as a passion* – it is our European specialty – must absolutely be of noble origin; as is well known, its invention is due to the Provençal poet-cavaliers, those brilliant, ingenious men of the '*gai saber*', to whom Europe owes so much, and almost owes itself.

261. Vanity is one of the things which are perhaps most difficult for a noble man to understand: he will be tempted to deny it, where another kind of man thinks he sees it self-evidently. The problem for him is to represent to his mind beings who seek to arouse a good opinion of themselves which they themselves do not possess – and consequently also do not 'deserve', – and who yet *believe* in this good opinion afterwards. This seems to him on the one hand such bad taste and so self-disrespectful, and on the other hand so grotesquely unreasonable, that he would like to consider vanity an exception, and is doubtful about it in most cases when it is spoken of. He will say, for instance: 'I may be mistaken about my value, and on the other hand may nevertheless demand that my value should be acknowledged by others precisely as I rate it: – that, however, is not vanity (but self-conceit, or, in most cases, that which is called "humility", and also "modesty").' Or he will even say: 'For many reasons I can delight in the good opinion of others, perhaps because I love and honour them, and rejoice in all their joys, perhaps also because their good opinion endorses and strengthens my belief in my own good opinion, perhaps because the good opinion of others, even in cases where I do not share it, is useful to me, or gives promise of usefulness: – all this, however, is not vanity.' The man of noble character must first bring it home forcibly to his mind, especially with the aid of history, that, from time immemorial, in all social strata in any way dependent, the ordinary man *was* only that which he *passed for*: – not being at all accustomed to fix values, he did not assign even to himself any other value than that which his master assigned to him (it is the peculiar *right of masters* to create values). It may be looked upon as the result of an extraordinary atavism, that the ordinary man, even at present, is still always *waiting* for an opinion about himself, and then instinctively submitting himself to it; yet by no means only to a 'good' opinion, but also to a bad and unjust one (think, for instance, of the greater part of the self-appreciations and self-depreciations which believing women learn from their confessors, and which in general the believing Christian learns from his Church). In fact, conformably to the slow rise of the democratic social order (and its cause, the blending of the blood of masters and slaves), the originally noble and rare impulse of the masters to assign a value to themselves and to 'think well' of themselves, will now be more and more encouraged and extended; but it has at all times an older, ampler and more radically ingrained propensity opposed to it – and in the phenomenon of 'vanity' this older propensity overmasters the younger. The vain person rejoices over *every* good opinion which he hears about himself (quite apart from the point of view of its usefulness, and equally regardless of its truth or falsehood), just as he suffers from every bad opinion: for he subjects himself to both, he *feels* himself subjected to both, by that oldest instinct of subjection which breaks forth in him. – It is 'the slave' in the vain man's blood, the remains of the slave's craftiness – and how much of the 'slave' is still left in woman, for instance! – which seeks to *seduce* to good opinions of itself; it is the slave, too, who immediately afterwards falls prostrate himself before these opinions, as though he had not called them forth. – And to repeat it again: vanity is an atavism.

262. A *species* originates, and a type becomes established and strong in the long struggle with essentially constant *unfavourable* conditions. On the other hand, it is known by the experience of breeders that species which receive superabundant nourishment, and in general a surplus of protection and care, immediately tend in the most marked way to develop variations, and are fertile in prodigies and monstrosities (also in monstrous vices). Now look at an aristocratic commonwealth, say an ancient Greek *polis*, or Venice, as a voluntary or involuntary contrivance for the purpose of *rearing* human beings; there are there men beside one another, thrown upon their own resources, who want to make their species prevail, chiefly because they *must* prevail, or else run the terrible danger of being exterminated. The favour, the superabundance, the protection are there lacking under which variations are fostered; the species needs itself as species, as something which, precisely by virtue of its hardness, its uniformity and simplicity of structure, can in general prevail and make itself permanent in constant struggle with its neighbours, or with rebellious or rebellion-threatening vassals. The

most varied experience teaches it what are the qualities to which it principally owes the fact that it still exists, in spite of all Gods and men, and has hitherto been victorious: these qualities it calls virtues, and these virtues alone it develops to maturity. It does so with severity, indeed it desires severity; every aristocratic morality is intolerant in the education of youth, in the control of women, in the marriage customs, in the relations of old and young, in the penal laws (which have an eye only for the degenerating): it counts intolerance itself among the virtues, under the name of 'justice'. A type with few, but very marked features, a species of severe, warlike, wisely silent, reserved and reticent men (and as such, with the most delicate sensibility for the charm and *nuances* of society) is thus established, unaffected by the vicissitudes of generations; the constant struggle with uniform *unfavourable* conditions is, as already remarked, the cause of a type becoming stable and hard. Finally, however, a happy state of things results, the enormous tension is relaxed; there are perhaps no more enemies among the neighbouring peoples, and the means of life, even of the enjoyment of life, are present in superabundance. With one stroke the bond and constraint of the old discipline severs: it is no longer regarded as necessary, as a condition of existence – if it would continue, it can only do so as a form of *luxury*, as an archaizing *taste*. Variations, whether they be deviations (into the higher, finer and rarer), or deteriorations and monstrosities, appear suddenly on the scene in the greatest exuberance and splendour; the individual dares to be individual and detach himself. At this turning-point of history there manifest themselves, side by side, and often mixed and entangled together, a magnificent, manifold, virgin-forest-like up-growth and up-striving, a kind of *tropical tempo* in the rivalry of growth, and an extraordinary decay and self-destruction, owing to the savagely opposing and seemingly exploding egoisms, which strive with one another 'for sun and light', and can no longer assign any limit, restraint or forbearance for themselves by means of the hitherto existing morality. It was this morality itself which piled up the strength so enormously, which bent the bow in so threatening a manner: – it is now 'out of date', it is getting 'out of date'. The dangerous and disquieting point has been reached when the greater, more manifold, more comprehensive life *is lived beyond* the old morality; the 'individual' stands out, and is obliged to have recourse to his own law-giving, his own arts and artifices for self-preservation, self-elevation and self-deliverance. Nothing but new 'Whys', nothing but new 'Hows', no common formulas any longer, misunderstanding and disregard in league with each other, decay, deterioration and the loftiest desires frightfully entangled, the genius of the race overflowing from all the cornucopias of good and bad, a portentous simultaneousness of Spring and Autumn, full of new charms and mysteries peculiar to the fresh, still inexhausted, still unwearied corruption. Danger is again present, the mother of morality, great danger; this time shifted into the individual, into the neighbour and friend, into the street, into their own child, into their own heart, into all the most personal and secret recesses of their desires and volitions. What will the moral philosophers who appear at this time have to preach? They discover, these sharp onlookers and loafers, that the end is quickly approaching, that everything around them decays and produces decay, that nothing will endure until the day after tomorrow, except one species of man, the incurably *mediocre*. The mediocre alone have a prospect of continuing and propagating themselves – they will be the men of the future, the sole survivors; 'be like them! become mediocre!' is now the only morality which has still a significance, which still obtains a hearing. – But it is difficult to preach this morality of mediocrity! it can never avow what it is and what it desires! it has to talk of moderation and dignity and duty and brotherly love – it will have difficulty *in concealing its irony*!

263. There is an *instinct for rank*, which more than anything else is already the sign of a *high* rank; there is a *delight* in the *nuances* of reverence which leads one to infer noble origin and habits. The refinement, goodness and loftiness of a soul are put to a perilous test when something passes by that is of the highest rank, but is not yet protected by the awe of authority from obtrusive touches and incivilities: something that goes its way like a living touchstone, undistinguished, undiscovered and tentative, perhaps voluntarily

veiled and disguised. He whose task and practice it is to investigate souls, will avail himself of many varieties of this very art to determine the ultimate value of a soul, the unalterable, innate order of rank to which it belongs: he will test it by its *instinct for reverence. Différence engendre haine*: the vulgarity of many a nature spurts up suddenly like dirty water, when any holy vessel, any jewel from closed shrines, any book bearing the marks of great destiny, is brought before it; while on the other hand, there is an involuntary silence, a hesitation of the eye, a cessation of all gestures, by which it is indicated that a soul *feels* the nearness of what is worthiest of respect. The way in which, on the whole, the reverence for the *Bible* has hitherto been maintained in Europe, is perhaps the best example of discipline and refinement of manners which Europe owes to Christianity: books of such profoundness and supreme significance require for their protection an external tyranny of authority, in order to acquire the *period* of thousands of years which is necessary to exhaust and unriddle them. Much has been achieved when the sentiment has been at last instilled into the masses (the shallow-pates and the boobies of every kind) that they are not allowed to touch everything, that there are holy experiences before which they must take off their shoes and keep away the unclean hand – it is almost their highest advance towards humanity. On the contrary, in the so-called cultured classes, the believers in 'modern ideas', nothing is perhaps so repulsive as their lack of shame, the easy insolence of eye and hand with which they touch, taste and finger everything; and it is possible that even yet there is more *relative* nobility of taste, and more tact for reverence among the people, among the lower classes of the people, especially among peasants, than among the newspaper-reading *demimonde* of intellect, the cultured class.

264. It cannot be effaced from a man's soul what his ancestors have preferably and most constantly done: whether they were perhaps diligent economizers attached to a desk and a cash-box, modest and citizen-like in their desires, modest also in their virtues; or whether they were accustomed to commanding from morning till night, fond of rude pleasures and probably of still ruder duties

and responsibilities; or whether, finally, at one time or another, they have sacrificed old privileges of birth and possession, in order to live wholly for their faith – for their 'God', – as men of an inexorable and sensitive conscience, which blushes at every compromise. It is quite impossible for a man *not* to have the qualities and predilections of his parents and ancestors in his constitution, whatever appearances may suggest to the contrary. This is the problem of race. Granted that one knows something of the parents, it is admissible to draw a conclusion about the child: any kind of offensive incontinence, any kind of sordid envy, or of clumsy self-vaunting – the three things which together have constituted the genuine plebeian type in all times – such must pass over to the child, as surely as bad blood; and with the help of the best education and culture one will only succeed in *deceiving* with regard to such heredity. – And what else does education and culture try to do nowadays! In our very democratic, or rather, very plebeian age, 'education' and 'culture' *must* be essentially the art of deceiving – deceiving with regard to origin, with regard to the inherited plebeianism in body and soul. An educator who nowadays preached truthfulness above everything else, and called out constantly to his pupils: 'Be true! Be natural! Show yourselves as you are!' – even such a virtuous and sincere ass would learn in a short time to have recourse to the *furca* of Horace, *naturam expellere*: with what results? 'Plebeianism' *usque recurret.**

265. At the risk of displeasing innocent ears, I submit that egoism belongs to the essence of a noble soul, I mean the unalterable belief that to a being such as 'we', other beings must naturally be in subjection, and have to sacrifice themselves. The noble soul accepts the fact of his egoism without question, and also without consciousness of harshness, constraint or arbitrariness therein, but rather as something that may have its basis in the primary law of things: – if he sought a designation for it he would say: 'It is justice itself'. He acknowledges under certain circumstances, which made him hesitate

* Horace's *Epistles*, I. x. 24.

at first, that there are other equally privileged ones; as soon as he has settled this question of rank, he moves among those equals and equally privileged ones with the same assurance, as regards modesty and delicate respect, which he enjoys in intercourse with himself – in accordance with an innate heavenly mechanism which all the stars understand. It is an *additional* instance of his egoism, this artfulness and self-limitation in intercourse with his equals – every star is a similar egoist; he honours *himself* in them, and in the rights which he concedes to them, he has no doubt that the exchange of honours and rights, as the *essence* of all intercourse, belongs also to the natural condition of things. The noble soul gives as he takes, prompted by the passionate and sensitive instinct of requital, which is at the root of his nature. The notion of 'favour' has, *inter pares*, neither significance nor good repute; there may be a sublime way of letting gifts as it were light upon one from above, and of drinking them thirstily like dew-drops; but for those arts and displays the noble soul has no aptitude. His egoism hinders him here: in general, he looks 'aloft' unwillingly – he looks either *forward*, horizontally and deliberately, or downwards – *he knows that he is on a height.*

266. 'One can only truly esteem him who does not *look out for* himself.' – Goethe to Rath Schlosser.

267. The Chinese have a proverb which mothers even teach their children: '*Siao-sin*' ('*make thy heart small*'). This is the essentially fundamental tendency in latter-day civilizations. I have no doubt that an ancient Greek, also, would first of all remark the self-dwarfing in us Europeans of today – in this respect alone we should immediately be 'distasteful' to him.

268. What, after all, is ignobleness? – Words are vocal symbols for ideas; ideas, however, are more or less definite mental symbols for frequently returning and concurring sensations, for groups of sensations. It is not sufficient to use the same words in order to understand one another: we must also employ the same words for the same kind of internal experiences, we must in the end have

experiences *in common*. On this account the people of one nation understand one another better than those belonging to different nations, even when they use the same language; or rather, when people have lived long together under similar conditions (of climate, soil, danger, requirement, toil) there *originates* therefrom an entity that 'understands itself' – namely, a nation. In all souls a like number of frequently recurring experiences have gained the upper hand over those occurring more rarely: about these matters people understand one another rapidly and always more rapidly – the history of language is the history of a process of abbreviation; on the basis of this quick comprehension people always unite closer and closer. The greater the danger, the greater is the need of agreeing quickly and readily about what is necessary; not to misunderstand one another in danger – that is what cannot at all be dispensed with in intercourse. Also in all loves and friendships one has the experience that nothing of the kind continues when the discovery has been made that in using the same words, one of the two parties has feelings, thoughts, intuitions, wishes or fears different from those of the other. (The fear of the 'eternal misunderstanding': that is the good genius which so often keeps persons of different sexes from too hasty attachments, to which sense and heart prompt them – and *not* some Schopenhauerian 'genius of the species'!) Whichever groups of sensations within a soul awaken most readily, begin to speak, and give the word of command – these decide as to the general order of rank of its values, and determine ultimately its list of desirable things. A man's estimates of value betray something of the *structure* of his soul, and wherein it sees its conditions of life, its intrinsic needs. Supposing now that necessity has from all time drawn together only such men as could express similar requirements and similar experiences by similar symbols, it results on the whole that the easy *communicability* of need, which implies ultimately the undergoing only of average and *common* experiences, must have been the most potent of all the forces which have hitherto operated upon mankind. The more similar, the more ordinary people, have always had and are still having the advantage; the more select, more refined, more unique and difficultly comprehensible, are liable to stand alone; they succumb to accidents in their isolation, and seldom propagate themselves. One must appeal to immense opposing forces, in order to thwart this natural, all-too-natural *progressus in simile*, the evolution of man to the similar, the ordinary, the average, the gregarious – to the *ignoble* – !

269. The more a psychologist – a born, an unavoidable psychologist and soul-diviner – turns his attention to the more select cases and individuals, the greater is his danger of being suffocated by sympathy: he *needs* sternness and cheerfulness more than any other man. For the corruption, the ruination of higher men, of the more unusually constituted souls, is in fact, the rule: it is dreadful to have such a rule always before one's eyes. The manifold torment of the psychologist who has discovered this ruination, who discovers once, and then discovers *almost* repeatedly throughout all history, this universal inner 'desperateness' of higher men, this eternal 'too late!' in every sense – may perhaps one day be the cause of his turning with bitterness against his own lot, and of his making an attempt at self-destruction – of his 'going to ruin' himself. One may perceive in almost every psychologist a tell-tale inclination for delightful intercourse with commonplace and well-ordered men: the fact is thereby disclosed that he always requires healing, that he needs a sort of flight and forgetfulness, away from what his insight and incisiveness – from what his 'business' – has laid upon his conscience. The fear of his memory is peculiar to him. He is easily silenced by the judgment of others; he hears with unmoved countenance how people honour, admire, love and glorify, where he has *perceived* – or he even conceals his silence by expressly assenting to some plausible opinion. Perhaps the paradox of his situation becomes so dreadful that, precisely where he has learnt *great sympathy*, together with *great contempt*, the multitude, the educated and the visionaries, have on their part learnt great reverence – reverence for 'great men' and marvellous animals, for the sake of whom one blesses and honours the fatherland, the earth, the dignity of mankind and one's own self, to whom one points the young, and in view of whom one educates them. And who knows but in all great instances hitherto just the

same happened: that the multitude worshipped a God, and that the 'God' was only a poor sacrificial animal! *Success* has always been the greatest liar – and the 'work' itself is a success; the great statesman, the conqueror, the discoverer, are disguised in their creations until they are unrecognizable; the 'work' of the artist, of the philosopher, only invents him who has created it, is *reputed* to have created it; the 'great men', as they are reverenced, are poor little fictions composed afterwards; in the world of historical values spurious coinage *prevails*. Those great poets, for example, such as Byron, Musset, Poe, Leopardi, Kleist, Gogol (I do not venture to mention much greater names, but I have them in my mind), as they now appear, and were perhaps obliged to be: men of the moment, enthusiastic, sensuous and childish, light-minded and impulsive in their trust and distrust; with souls in which usually some flaw has to be concealed; often taking revenge with their works for an internal defilement, often seeking forgetfulness in their soaring from a too true memory, often lost in the mud and almost in love with it, until they become like the will-o'-the-wisps around the swamps, and *pretend to be* stars – the people then call them idealists, – often struggling with protracted disgust, with an ever-reappearing phantom of disbelief, which makes them cold, and obliges them to languish for *gloria* and devour 'faith as it is' out of the hands of intoxicated adulators: – what a *torment* these great artists are and the so-called higher men in general, to him who has once found them out! It is thus conceivable that it is just from woman – who is clairvoyant in the world of suffering, and also unfortunately eager to help and save to an extent far beyond her powers – that *they* have learnt so readily those outbreaks of boundless devoted *sympathy*, which the multitude, above all the reverent multitude, do not understand, and overwhelm with prying and self-gratifying interpretations. This sympathizing invariably deceives itself as to its power; woman would like to believe that love can do *everything* – it is the *superstition* peculiar to her. Alas, he who knows the heart finds out how poor, helpless, pretentious and blundering even the best and deepest love is – he finds that it rather *destroys* than saves! – It is possible that under the holy fable and travesty of the life of Jesus there is hidden one of the most painful cases of the martyrdom of *knowledge about love*: the martyrdom of the most innocent and most craving heart, that never had enough of any human love, that *demanded* love, that demanded inexorably and frantically to be loved and nothing else, with terrible outbursts against those who refused him their love; the story of a poor soul insatiated and insatiable in love, that had to invent hell to send thither those who *would not* love him – and that at last, enlightened about human love, had to invent a God who is entire love, entire *capacity* for love – who takes pity on human love, because it is so paltry, so ignorant! He who has such sentiments, he who has such *knowledge* about love – *seeks* for death! – But why should one deal with such painful matters? Provided, of course, that one is not obliged to do so.

270. The intellectual haughtiness and loathing of every man who has suffered deeply – it almost determines the order of rank *how* deeply men can suffer – the chilling certainty, with which he is thoroughly imbued and coloured, that by virtue of his suffering he *knows more* than the shrewdest and wisest can ever know, that he has been familiar with, and 'at home' in, many distant, dreadful worlds of which '*you* know nothing'! – this silent intellectual haughtiness of the sufferer, this pride of the elect of knowledge, of the 'initiated', of the almost sacrificed, finds all forms of disguise necessary to protect itself from contact with officious and sympathizing hands, and in general from all that is not its equal in suffering. Profound suffering makes noble: it separates. – One of the most refined forms of disguise is Epicurism, along with a certain ostentatious boldness of taste, which takes suffering lightly, and puts itself on the defensive against all that is sorrowful and profound. They are 'gay men' who make use of gaiety, because they are misunderstood on account of it – they *wish* to be misunderstood. There are 'scientific minds' who make use of science, because it gives a gay appearance, and because scientificness leads to the conclusion that a person is superficial – they *wish* to mislead to a false conclusion. There are free insolent minds which would fain conceal and deny that they are broken, proud, incurable hearts (the cynicism of Hamlet

– the case of Galiani); and occasionally folly itself is the mask of an unfortunate *over-assured* knowledge. – From which it follows that it is the part of a more refined humanity to have reverence 'for the mask', and not to make use of psychology and curiosity in the wrong place.

271. That which separates two men most profoundly is a different sense and grade of purity. What does it matter about all their honesty and reciprocal usefulness, what does it matter about all their mutual good-will: the fact still remains – they 'cannot smell each other!' The highest instinct for purity places him who is affected with it in the most extraordinary and dangerous isolation, as a saint: for it is just holiness – the highest spiritualization of the instinct in question. Any kind of cognizance of an indescribable excess in the joy of the bath, any kind of ardour or thirst which perpetually impels the soul out of night into the morning, and out of gloom, out of 'affliction' into clearness, brightness, depth and refinement: – just as much as such a tendency *distinguishes* – it is a noble tendency – it also *separates*. – The pity of the saint is pity for the *filth* of the human, all-too-human. And there are grades and heights where pity itself is regarded by him as impurity, as filth.

272. Signs of nobility: never to think of lowering our duties to the rank of duties for everybody; to be unwilling to renounce or to share our responsibilities; to count our prerogatives, and the exercise of them, among our *duties*.

273. A man who strives after great things, looks upon everyone whom he encounters on his way either as a means of advance, or a delay and hindrance – or as a temporary resting-place. His peculiar lofty *bounty* to his fellow-men is only possible when he attains his elevation and dominates. Impatience, and the consciousness of being always condemned to comedy up to that time – for even strife is a comedy, and conceals the end, as every means does – spoil all intercourse for him; this kind of man is acquainted with solitude, and what is most poisonous in it.

The Problem of those who Wait. – Happy chances are necessary, and many incalculable elements, in order that a higher man in whom the solution of a problem is dormant, may yet take action, or 'break forth', as one might say – at the right moment. On an average it *does not* happen; and in all corners of the earth there are waiting ones sitting who hardly know to what extent they are waiting, and still less that they wait in vain. Occasionally, too, the waking call comes too late – the chance which gives 'permission' to take action – when their best youth, and strength for action have been used up in sitting still; and how many a one, just as he 'sprang up', has found with horror that his limbs are benumbed and his spirits are now too heavy! 'It is too late', he has said to himself – and has become self-distrustful and henceforth forever useless. – In the domain of genius, may not the 'Raphael without hands' (taking the expression in its widest sense) perhaps not be the exception, but the rule? – Perhaps genius is by no means so rare: but rather the five hundred *hands* which it requires in order to tyrannize over the καιρὸς 'the right time' – in order to take chance by the forelock!

274. He who does not *wish* to see the height of a man, looks all the more sharply at what is low in him, and in the foreground – and thereby betrays himself.

275. In all kinds of injury and loss the lower and coarser soul is better off than the nobler soul: the dangers of the latter must be greater, the probability that it will come to grief and perish is in fact immense, considering the multiplicity of the conditions of its existence. – In a lizard a finger grows again which has been lost; not so in man. –

276. It is too bad! Always the old story! When a man has finished building his house, he finds that he has learnt unawares something which he *ought* absolutely to have known before he – began to build. The eternal, fatal 'Too late!' The melancholia of everything *completed* – !

277. – Wanderer, who art thou? I see thee follow thy path without scorn, without love, with unfathomable eyes, wet and sad as a plummet which has returned to the light insatiated out of every depth – what did it seek down there? – with a bosom that never sighs, with lips that conceal their loathing, with a hand which only slowly grasps: who art thou? what hast thou done? Rest thee here: this place has hospitality for everyone – refresh thyself! And whoever thou art, what is it that now pleases thee? What will serve to refresh thee? Only name it, whatever I have I offer thee! 'To refresh me? To refresh me? Oh, thou prying one, what sayest thou! But give me, I pray thee –' What? what? Speak out! 'Another mask! A second mask!'

278. Men of profound sadness betray themselves when they are happy: they have a mode of seizing upon happiness as though they would choke and strangle it, out of jealousy – ah, they know only too well that it will flee from them!

279. 'Bad! Bad! What? Does he not – go back?' Yes! But you misunderstand him when you complain about it. He goes back like everyone who is about to make a great spring.

280. – 'Will people believe it of me? But I insist that they believe it of me: I have always thought very unsatisfactorily of myself and about myself, only in very rare cases, only compulsorily, always without delight in "the subject", ready to digress from "myself", and always without faith in the result, owing to an unconquerable distrust of the *possibility* of self-knowledge, which has led me so far as to feel a *contradictio in adjecto* even in the idea of "direct knowledge" which theorists allow themselves: – this matter of fact is almost the most certain thing I know about myself. There must be a sort of repugnance in me to *believe* anything definite about myself. – Is there perhaps some enigma therein? Probably; but fortunately nothing for my own teeth. – Perhaps it betrays the species to which I belong? – but not to myself, as is sufficiently agreeable to me.'

281. – 'But what has happened to you?' – 'I do not know,' he said, hesitatingly; 'perhaps the Harpies have flown over my table.' – It sometimes happens nowadays that a gentle, sober, retiring man becomes suddenly mad, breaks the plates, upsets the table, shrieks, raves and shocks everybody – and finally withdraws, ashamed, and raging at himself – whither? for what purpose? To famish apart? To suffocate with his memories? – To him who has the desires of a lofty and dainty soul, and only seldom finds his table laid and his food prepared, the danger will always be great – nowadays, however, it is extraordinarily so. Thrown into the midst of a noisy and plebeian age, with which he does not like to eat out of the same dish, he may readily perish of hunger and thirst – or, should he nevertheless finally 'fall to', of sudden nausea. – We have probably all sat at tables to which we did not belong; and precisely the most spiritual of us, who are most difficult to nourish, know the dangerous *dyspepsia* which originates from a sudden insight and disillusionment about our food and our messmates – the *after-dinner nausea*.

282. If one wishes to praise at all, it is a delicate and at the same time a noble self-control, to praise only where one *does not* agree – otherwise in fact one would praise oneself, which is contrary to good taste: – a self-control, to be sure, which offers excellent opportunity and provocation to constant *misunderstanding*. To be able to allow oneself this veritable luxury of taste and morality, one must not live among intellectual imbeciles, but rather among men whose misunderstandings and mistakes amuse by their refinement – or one will have to pay dearly for it! – 'He praises me, *therefore* he acknowledges me to be right' – this asinine method of inference spoils half of the life of us recluses, for it brings the asses into our neighbourhood and friendship.

283. To live in a vast and proud tranquility; always beyond... To have, or not to have, one's emotions, one's For and Against, according to choice; to lower oneself to them for hours; to *seat* oneself on them as upon horses, and often as upon asses: – for one must know how to make use of their stupidity as well as of their fire. To conserve

one's three hundred foregrounds; also one's black spectacles: for there are circumstances when nobody must look into our eyes, still less into our 'motives'. And to choose for company that roguish and cheerful vice, politeness. And to remain master of one's four virtues, courage, insight, sympathy and solitude. For solitude is a virtue with us, as a sublime bent and bias to purity, which divines that in the contact of man and man – 'in society' – it must be unavoidably impure. All society makes one somehow, somewhere, or sometime – 'commonplace'.

284. The greatest events and thoughts – the greatest thoughts, however, are the greatest events – are longest in being comprehended: the generations which are contemporary with them do not *experience* such events – they live past them. Something happens there as in the realm of stars. The light of the furthest stars is longest in reaching man; and before it has arrived man *denies* – that there are stars there. 'How many centuries does a mind require to be understood?'– that is also a standard, one also makes a gradation of rank and an etiquette therewith, such as is necessary for mind and for star.

285. 'Here is the prospect free, the mind exalted.'* – But there is a reverse kind of man, who is also upon a height, and has also a free prospect – but looks *downwards*.

286. – What is noble? What does the word 'noble' still mean for us nowadays? How does the noble man betray himself, how is he recognized under this heavy overcast sky of the commencing plebeianism, by which everything is rendered opaque and leaden? – It is not his actions which establish his claim – actions are always ambiguous, always inscrutable; neither is it his 'works.' One finds nowadays among artists and scholars plenty of those who betray by their works that a profound longing for nobleness impels them; but this very *need of* nobleness is radically different from the needs of the noble soul itself, and is in fact the eloquent and dangerous

* Goethe's *Faust*, Part II, Act V. The words of Dr Marianus.

sign of the lack thereof. It is not the works, but the *belief* which is here decisive and determines the order of rank – to employ once more an old religious formula with a new and deeper meaning – it is some fundamental certainty which a noble soul has about itself, something which is not to be sought, is not to be found and perhaps, also, is not to be lost. – *The noble soul has reverence for itself.* –

287. There are men who are unavoidably intellectual, let them turn and twist themselves as they will, and hold their hands before their treacherous eyes – as though the hand were not a betrayer; it always comes out at last that they have something which they hide – namely, intellect. One of the subtlest means of deceiving, at least as long as possible, and of successfully representing oneself to be stupider than one really is – which in everyday life is often as desirable as an umbrella, – is called *enthusiasm*, including what belongs to it, for instance, virtue. For as Galiani said, who was obliged to know it: *vertu est enthousiasme.*

288. In the writings of a recluse one always hears something of the echo of the wilderness, something of the murmuring tones and timid vigilance of solitude; in his strongest words, even in his cry itself, there sounds a new and more dangerous kind of silence, of concealment. He who has sat day and night, from year's end to year's end, alone with his soul in familiar discord and discourse, he who has become a cave-bear, or a treasure seeker, or a treasure guardian and dragon in his cave – it may be a labyrinth, but can also be a gold-mine – his ideas themselves eventually acquire a twilight colour of their own, and an odour, as much of the depth as of the mould, something uncommunicative and repulsive, which blows chilly upon every passer-by. The recluse does not believe that a philosopher – supposing that a philosopher has always in the first place been a recluse – ever expressed his actual and ultimate opinions in books: are not books written precisely to hide what is in us? – indeed, he will doubt whether a philosopher *can* have 'ultimate and actual' opinions at all; whether behind every cave in him there is not, and must necessarily be, a still deeper cave: an ampler, stranger,

richer world beyond the surface, an abyss behind every bottom, beneath every 'foundation'. Every philosophy is a foreground philosophy – this is a recluse's verdict: 'There is something arbitrary in the fact that the *philosopher* came to a stand here, took a retrospect and looked around; that he *here* laid his spade aside and did not dig any deeper – there is also something suspicious in it.' Every philosophy also *conceals* a philosophy; every opinion is also a *lurking-place*, every word is also a *mask*.

289. Every deep thinker is more afraid of being understood than of being misunderstood. The latter perhaps wounds his vanity; but the former wounds his heart, his sympathy, which always says: 'Ah, why would you also have as hard a time of it as I have?'

290. Man, a *complex*, mendacious, artful and inscrutable animal, uncanny to the other animals by his artifice and sagacity, rather than by his strength, has invented the good conscience in order finally to enjoy his soul as something *simple*; and the whole of morality is a long, audacious falsification, by virtue of which generally enjoyment at the sight of the soul becomes possible. From this point of view there is perhaps much more in the conception of 'art' than is generally believed.

291. A philosopher: that is a man who constantly experiences, sees, hears, suspects, hopes and dreams extraordinary things; who is struck by his own thoughts as if they came from the outside, from above and below, as a species of events and lightning flashes *peculiar to him*; who is perhaps himself a storm pregnant with new lightnings; a portentous man, around whom there is always rumbling and mumbling and gaping and something uncanny going on. A philosopher: alas, a being who often runs away from himself, is often afraid of himself – but whose curiosity always makes him 'come to himself' again.

292. A man who says: 'I like that, I take it for my own, and mean to guard and protect it from everyone'; a man who can conduct a

case, carry out a resolution, remain true to an opinion, keep hold of a woman, punish and overthrow insolence; a man who has his indignation and his sword, and to whom the weak, the suffering, the oppressed and even the animals willingly submit and naturally belong; in short, a man who is a *master* by nature – when such a man has sympathy, well! *That* sympathy has value! But of what account is the sympathy of those who suffer! Or of those even who preach sympathy! There is nowadays, throughout almost the whole of Europe, a sickly irritability and sensitiveness towards pain, and also a repulsive irrestrainableness in complaining, an effeminizing, which, with the aid of religion and philosophical nonsense, seeks to deck itself out as something superior – there is a regular cult of suffering. The *unmanliness* of that which is called 'sympathy' by such groups of visionaries, is always, I believe, the first thing that strikes the eye. – One must resolutely and radically taboo this latest form of bad taste; and finally I wish people to put the good amulet, '*gai saber*' ('gay science', in ordinary language), on heart and neck, as a protection against it.

293. *The Olympian Vice*. – Despite the philosopher who, as a genuine Englishman, tried to bring laughter into bad repute in all thinking minds – 'Laughing is a bad infirmity of human nature, which every thinking mind will strive to overcome' (Hobbes), – I would even allow myself to rank philosophers according to the quality of their laughing – up to those who are capable of *golden* laughter. And supposing that Gods also philosophize, which I am strongly inclined to believe, owing to many reasons – I have no doubt that they also know how to laugh thereby in an overman-like and new fashion – and at the expense of all serious things! Gods are fond of ridicule: it seems that they cannot refrain from laughter even in holy matters.

294. The genius of the heart, as that great mysterious one possesses it, the tempter-god and born rat-catcher of consciences, whose voice can descend into the netherworld of every soul, who neither speaks a word nor casts a glance in which there may not be some motive

or touch of allurement, to whose perfection it pertains that he knows how to appear, – not as he is, but in a guise which acts as an *additional* constraint on his followers to press ever closer to him, to follow him more cordially and thoroughly; – the genius of the heart, which imposes silence and attention on everything loud and self-conceited, which smoothes rough souls and makes them taste a new longing – to lie placid as a mirror, that the deep heavens may be reflected in them; – the genius of the heart, which teaches the clumsy and too hasty hand to hesitate, and to grasp more delicately; which scents the hidden and forgotten treasure, the drop of goodness and sweet spirituality under thick dark ice, and is a divining-rod for every grain of gold, long buried and imprisoned in mud and sand; the genius of the heart, from contact with which everyone goes away richer; not favoured or surprised, not as though gratified and oppressed by the good things of others; but richer in himself, newer than before, broken up, blown upon and sounded by a thawing wind; more uncertain, perhaps, more delicate, more fragile, more bruised, but full of hopes which as yet lack names, full of a new will and current, full of a new ill-will and counter-current... but what am I doing, my friends? Of whom am I talking to you? Have I forgotten myself so far that I have not even told you his name? Unless it be that you have already divined of your own accord who this questionable God and spirit is, that wishes to be *praised* in such a manner? For, as it happens to everyone who from childhood onward has always been on his legs, and in foreign lands, I have also encountered on my path many strange and dangerous spirits; above all, however, and again and again, the one of whom I have just spoken: in fact, no less a personage than the god *Dionysus*, the great equivocator and tempter, to whom, as you know, I once offered in all secrecy and reverence my first-fruits – the last, as it seems to me, who has offered a *sacrifice* to him, for I have found no one who could understand what I was then doing. In the meantime, however, I have learned much, far too much, about the philosophy of this god, and, as I said, from mouth to mouth – I, the last disciple and initiate of the god Dionysus: and perhaps I might at last begin to give you, my friends, as far as I am allowed, a little taste of this philosophy? In a hushed voice, as is but seemly: for it has to do with much that is secret, new, strange, wonderful and uncanny. The very fact that Dionysus is a philosopher, and that therefore gods also philosophize, seems to me a novelty which is not unensnaring, and might perhaps arouse suspicion precisely among philosophers; – among you, my friends, there is less to be said against it, except that it comes too late and not at the right time; for, as it has been disclosed to me, you are loth nowadays to believe in God and gods. It may happen, too, that in the frankness of my story I must go further than is agreeable to the strict usages of your ears? Certainly the god in question went further, very much further, in such dialogues, and was always many paces ahead of me... Indeed, if it were allowed, I should have to give him, according to human usage, fine ceremonious titles of lustre and merit, I should have to extol his courage as investigator and discoverer, his fearless honesty, truthfulness and love of wisdom. But such a god does not know what to do with all that respectable trumpery and pomp. 'Keep that', he would say, 'for thyself and those like thee, and whoever else require it! I – have no reason to cover my nakedness!' One suspects that this kind of divinity and philosopher perhaps lacks shame? – He once said: 'Under certain circumstances I love mankind' – and referred thereby to Ariadne, who was present; 'in my opinion man is an agreeable, brave, inventive animal, that has not his equal upon earth, he makes his way even through all labyrinths. I like man, and often think how I can still further advance him, and make him stronger, more evil and more profound.' – 'Stronger, more evil and more profound?' I asked in horror. 'Yes', he said again, 'stronger, more evil and more profound; also more beautiful' – and thereby the tempter-god smiled with his halcyon smile, as though he had just paid some charming compliment. One here sees at once that it is not only shame that this divinity lacks; – and in general there are good grounds for supposing that in some things the gods could all of them come to us men for instruction. We men are – more human. –

295. Alas! what are you, after all, my written and painted thoughts! Not long ago you were so variegated, young and malicious, so full

of thorns and secret spices, that you made me sneeze and laugh – and now? You have already doffed your novelty, and some of you, I fear, are ready to become truths, so immortal do they look, so pathetically honest, so tedious! And was it ever otherwise? What then do we write and paint, we mandarins with Chinese brush, we immortalizers of things which *lend* themselves to writing, what are we alone capable of painting? Alas, only that which is just about to fade and begins to lose its odour! Alas, only exhausted and departing storms and belated yellow sentiments! Alas, only birds strayed and fatigued by flight, which now let themselves be captured with the hand – with *our* hand! We immortalize what cannot live and fly much longer, things only which are exhausted and mellow! And it is only for your *afternoon*, you, my written and painted thoughts, for which alone I have colours, many colours, perhaps, many variegated softenings, and fifty yellows and browns and greens and reds; – but nobody will divine thereby how ye looked in your morning, you sudden sparks and marvels of my solitude, you, my old, beloved – *evil* thoughts!

FROM THE HEIGHTS

By F. W. Nietzsche

Translated by L. A. Magnus

1.

MIDDAY of Life! Oh, season of delight!
 My summer's park!
Uneaseful joy to look, to lurk, to hark: –
I peer for friends, am ready day and night, –
Where linger ye, my friends? The time is right!

2.

Is not the glacier's grey today for you
 Rose-garlanded?
The brooklet seeks you; wind, cloud, with longing thread
And thrust themselves yet higher to the blue,
To spy for you from farthest eagle's view.

3.

My table was spread out for you on high: –
 Who dwelleth so
Star-near, so near the grisly pit below? –
My realm – what realm hath wider boundary?
My honey – who hath sipped its fragrancy?

4.

Friends, ye are there! Woe me, – yet I am not
He whom ye seek?
Ye stare and stop – better your wrath could speak!
I am not I? Hand, gait, face, changed? And what
I am, to you my friends, now am I not?

5.

Am I an other? Strange am I to Me?
Yet from Me sprung?
A wrestler, by himself too oft self-wrung?
Hindering too oft my own self's potency,
Wounded and hampered by self-victory?

6.

I sought where-so the wind blow keenest. There
I learned to dwell
Where no man dwells, on lonesome ice-lorn fell,
And unlearned Man and God and curse and prayer?
Became a ghost haunting the glaciers bare?

7.

Ye, my old friends! Look! Ye turn pale, filled o'er
With love and fear!
Go! Yet not in wrath. Ye could ne'er live here.
Here in the farthest realm of ice and scaur,
A huntsman must one be, like chamois soar.

8.

An evil huntsman was I? See how taut
My bow was bent!
Strongest was he by whom such bolt were sent –
Woe now! That arrow is with peril fraught,
Perilous as none. – Have yon safe home ye sought!

9.

Ye go! Thou didst endure enough, oh, heart; –
Strong was thy hope;
Unto new friends thy portals widely ope,
Let old ones be. Bid memory depart!
Wast thou young then, now – better young thou art!

10.

What linked us once together, one hope's tie –
(Who now doth con
Those lines, now fading, Love once wrote thereon?) –
Is like a parchment, which the hand is shy
To touch – like crackling leaves, all seared, all dry.

11.

Oh! Friends no more! They are – what name for those? –
Friends' phantom-flight
Knocking at my heart's window-pane at night,
Gazing on me, that speaks 'We were' and goes, –
Oh, withered words, once fragrant as the rose!

12.

Pinings of youth that might not understand!
For which I pined,
Which I deemed changed with me, kin of my kind:
But they grew old, and thus were doomed and banned:
None but new kith are native of my land!

13.

Midday of life! My second youth's delight!
My summer's park!
Unrestful joy to long, to lurk, to hark!
I peer for friends! – am ready day and night,
For my new friends. Come! Come! The time is right!

14.

This song is done, – the sweet sad cry of rue
Sang out its end;
A wizard wrought it, he the timely friend,
The midday friend, – no, do not ask me who;
At midday 'twas, when one became as two.

15.

We keep our Feast of Feasts, sure of our bourne,
Our aims self-same:
The Guest of Guests, friend Zarathustra, came!
The world now laughs, the grisly veil was torn,
And Light and Dark were one that wedding-morn.

ON THE GENEALOGY OF MORALS

ON THE GENEALOGY OF MORALS

FRIEDRICH NIETZSCHE

This edition published in 2021 by Arcturus Publishing Limited
26/27 Bickels Yard, 151–153 Bermondsey Street,
London SE1 3HA

Cover design: Peter Ridley
Cover illustration: Peter Gray

AD007621UK

Printed in the UK

CONTENTS

INTRODUCTION

Friedrich Nietzsche was born on 15 October 1844 in the small Prussian town of Röcken bei Lützen in Saxony. His father, Karl Ludwig, was appointed Röcken's Lutheran minister by King Friedrich Wilhelm IV. In 1849, Karl died and the family moved to Naumburg, where Nietzsche lived with his mother, sister, grandmother and two aunts. In 1858, he was accepted into the Schulpforta, one of Germany's most prestigious boarding schools.

Upon graduating in 1864, Nietzsche enrolled as a theology and classical philology student at the University of Bonn. Two terms later, he transferred to the University of Leipzig to follow Professor Friedrich Wilhelm Ritschl. Under Ritschl's tutelage Nietzsche thrived in Leipzig, learning the philosophy of Arthur Schopenhauer and Immanuel Kant.

In 1869, Ritschl recommended the 24-year-old Nietzsche for a professorship in philology at the University of Basel. Basel was hesitant; Nietzsche had left the university for a year of military service and hadn't completed his doctoral thesis. But Ritschl heaped praise on Nietzsche, stating that he hadn't found another student like him in 40 years of teaching. So the University of Basel appointed him as an extraordinary professor of classical philology, and promoted him to full professor the following year.

Nietzsche took leave in August 1870 to work as a medical orderly during the Franco-German War. While helping transport the wounded, he contracted dysentery and diphtheria, which resulted in poor health, migraines, insomnia and near blindness for the rest of his life. In October, he returned to university, but found himself struggling between his deteriorating health and the demands of teaching. In 1879, he resigned from his position at the age of 34.

While he battled with illness between 1883 and 1885, he wrote *Thus Spake Zarathustra*, intended to be the culmination of his philosophical career. The work received a poor reception initially, leading Nietzsche to rework his ideas into *Beyond Good and Evil* in 1886. A year later, he published *On the Genealogy of Morals*, a collection of essays on the history of ethics and morality, hoping to draw attention to his earlier works. In these essays, he explored the binary divisions of 'good' and 'evil' and questioned the Christian and humanist foundations of the ideas that governed late-19th-century Europe. Through these writings, he aimed to show that the ethical assumptions people took for granted were not absolute, timeless dictates but had evolved from a conflict of different value systems. The radical, sometimes disturbing, arguments he presented in this book made it one of the most important works of modern European philosophy.

Two years after its publication, Nietzsche suffered a nervous breakdown and spent a number of years in psychiatric asylums, before returning to live with his mother until her death in 1897. He then moved into the household of his sister Elisabeth and her husband Bernhard Förster, a politically active anti-Semite. After Förster's suicide in 1889, Elisabeth worked diligently to keep her husband's racist philosophy alive. While living with his sister, Nietzsche's health continued to worsen. He suffered a number of strokes before eventually succumbing to pneumonia in 1900. Control of his estate passed to Elisabeth, and she attempted to use Nietzsche's writings to paint him as a supporter of Förster's work.

But in truth, Nietzsche offered an insightful and open-minded view of man's spirituality. Contrary to the hateful message of his sister, he aimed to broaden the minds of his readers and urged them to take control of their own lives.

PREFACE

1

We are unknown, we knowers, ourselves to ourselves: this has its own good reason. We have never searched for ourselves – how should it then come to pass, that we should ever *find* ourselves? Rightly has it been said: 'Where your treasure is, there will your heart be also.' *Our* treasure is there, where stand the hives of our knowledge. It is to those hives that we are always striving; as born creatures of flight, and as the honey-gatherers of the spirit, we care really in our hearts only for one thing – to bring something 'home to the hive!'

As far as the rest of life with its so-called 'experiences' is concerned, which of us has even sufficient serious interest? or sufficient time? In our dealings with such points of life, we are, I fear, never properly to the point; to be precise, our heart is not there, and certainly not our ear. Rather like one who, delighting in a divine distraction, or sunken in the seas of his own soul, in whose ear the clock has just thundered with all its force its twelve strokes of noon, suddenly wakes up, and asks himself, 'What has in point of fact just struck?' so do we at times rub afterwards, as it were, our puzzled ears, and ask in complete astonishment and complete embarrassment, 'Through what have we in point of fact just lived?' further, 'Who are we in point of fact?' and count, *after they have struck*, as I have explained, all the twelve throbbing beats of the clock of our experience, of our life, of our being – ah! – and count wrong in the endeavour. Of necessity we remain strangers to ourselves, we understand ourselves not, in ourselves we are bound to be mistaken, for of us holds good to all eternity the motto, 'Each one is the farthest away from himself' – as far as ourselves are concerned we are not 'knowers.'

2

My thoughts concerning the *genealogy* of our moral prejudices – for they constitute the issue in this polemic – have their first, bald, and provisional expression in that collection of aphorisms entitled *Human, all-too-Human, a Book for Free Minds*, the writing of which was begun in Sorrento, during a winter which allowed me to gaze over the broad and dangerous territory through which my mind had up to that time wandered. This took place in the winter of 1876-77; the thoughts themselves are older. They were in their substance already the same thoughts which I take up again in the following treatises: we hope that they have derived benefit from the long interval, that they have grown riper, clearer, stronger, more complete. The fact, however, that I still cling to them even now, that in the meanwhile they have always held faster by each other, have, in fact, grown out of their original shape and into each other, all this strengthens in my mind the joyous confidence that they must have been originally neither separate disconnected capricious nor sporadic phenomena, but have sprung from a common root, from a fundamental '*fiat*' of knowledge, whose empire reached to the soul's depth, and that ever grew more definite in its voice, and more definite in its demands. That is the only state of affairs that is proper in the case of a philosopher.

We have no right to be '*disconnected*'; we must neither err 'disconnectedly' nor strike the truth 'disconnectedly.' Rather with the necessity with which a tree bears its fruit, so do our thoughts, our values, our Yes's and No's and If's and Whether's, grow connected and interrelated, mutual witnesses of *one* will, *one* health, *one* kin gdom, *one* sun – as to whether they are to *your* taste, these fruits of ours? But what matters that to the trees? What matters that to us, us the philosophers?

3

Owing to a scrupulosity peculiar to myself, which I confess reluctantly – it concerns indeed *morality* – a scrupulosity, which manifests itself in my life at such an early period, with so much spontaneity, with so chronic a persistence and so keen an opposition to environment, epoch, precedent, and ancestry that I should have been almost entitled to style it my '*â priori*' – my curiosity and my suspicion felt themselves betimes bound to halt at the question, of what in point of actual fact was the *origin* of our 'Good' and of our 'Evil.' Indeed, at the boyish age of thirteen the problem of the origin of Evil already haunted me: at an age 'when games and God divide one's heart,' I devoted to that problem my first childish attempt at the literary game, my first philosophic essay – and as regards my infantile solution of the problem, well, I gave quite properly the honour to God, and made him the *father* of evil. Did my own '*â priori*' demand that precise solution from me? that new, immoral, or at least 'amoral' '*â priori*' and that 'categorical imperative' which was its voice (but oh! how hostile to the Kantian article, and how pregnant with problems!), to which since then I have given more and more attention, and indeed what is more than attention. Fortunately I soon learned to separate theological from moral prejudices, and I gave up looking for a *supernatural* origin of evil. A certain amount of historical and philological education, to say nothing of an innate faculty of psychological discrimination *par excellence* succeeded in transforming almost immediately my original problem into the following one: Under what conditions did Man invent for himself those judgements of values, 'Good' and 'Evil'? *And what intrinsic value do they possess in themselves?* Have they up to the present hindered or advanced human well-being? Are they a symptom of the distress, impoverishment, and degeneration of Human Life? Or, conversely, is it in them that is manifested the fullness, the strength, and the will of Life, its courage, its self-confidence, its future? On this point I found and hazarded in my mind the most diverse answers, I established distinctions in periods, peoples, and castes, I became a specialist in my problem, and from my answers grew new questions, new investigations, new conjectures, new probabilities; until at last I had a land of my own and a soil of my own, a whole secret world growing and flowering, like hidden gardens of whose existence no one could have an inkling – oh, how happy are we, we finders of knowledge, provided that we know how to keep silent sufficiently long.

4

My first impulse to publish some of my hypotheses concerning the origin of morality I owe to a clear, well-written, and even precocious little book, in which a perverse and vicious kind of moral philosophy (your real *English* kind) was definitely presented to me for the first time; and this attracted me – with that magnetic attraction, inherent in that which is diametrically opposed and antithetical to one's own ideas. The title of the book was *The Origin of the Moral Emotions*; its author, Dr Paul Rée; the year of its appearance, 1877. I may almost say that I have never read anything in which every single dogma and conclusion has called forth from me so emphatic a negation as did that book; albeit a negation tainted by either pique or intolerance. I referred accordingly both in season and out of season in the previous works, at which I was then working, to the arguments of that book, not to refute them – for what have I got to do with mere refutations but substituting, as is natural to a positive mind, for an improbable theory one which is more probable, and occasionally no doubt, for one philosophic error, another. In that early period I gave, as I have said, the first public expression to those theories of origin to which these essays are devoted, but with a clumsiness which I was the last to conceal from myself, for I was as yet cramped, being still without a special language for these special subjects, still frequently liable to relapse and to vacillation. To go into details, compare what I say in *Human, all-too-Human*, part i., about the parallel early history of Good and Evil, Aph. 45 (namely, their origin from the castes of the aristocrats and the slaves); similarly, Aph. 136 et. seq., concerning the birth and value of ascetic morality; similarly,

Aphs. 96, 99, vol. ii., Aph. 89, concerning the Morality of Custom, that far older and more original kind of morality which is *toto cœlo* different from the altruistic ethics (in which Dr Rée, like all the English moral philosophers, sees the ethical 'Thing-in-itself'); finally, Aph. 92. Similarly, Aph. 26 in *Human, all-too-Human*, part ii., and Aph. 112, the *Dawn of Day*, concerning the origin of Justice as a balance between persons of approximately equal power (equilibrium as the hypothesis of all contract, consequently of all law); similarly, concerning the origin of Punishment, *Human, all-too-Human*, part ii., Aphs. 22, 23, in regard to which the deterrent object is neither essential nor original (as Dr Rée thinks: rather is it that this object is only imported, under certain definite conditions, and always as something extra and additional).

5

In reality I had set my heart at that time on something much more important than the nature of the theories of myself or others concerning the origin of morality (or, more precisely, the real function from my view of these theories was to point an end to which they were one among many means). The issue for me was the value of morality, and on that subject I had to place myself in a state of abstraction, in which I was almost alone with my great teacher Schopenhauer, to whom that book, with all its passion and inherent contradiction (for that book also was a polemic), turned for present help as though he were still alive. The issue was, strangely enough, the value of the 'un-egoistic' instincts, the instincts of pity, self-denial, and self-sacrifice which Schopenhauer had so persistently painted in golden colours, deified and etherealized, that eventually they appeared to him, as it were, high and dry, as 'intrinsic values in themselves,' on the strength of which he uttered both to Life and to himself his own negation. But against *these very* instincts there voiced itself in my soul a more and more fundamental mistrust, a scepticism that dug ever deeper and deeper: and in this very instinct I saw the *great* danger of mankind, its most sublime temptation and seduction – seduction to what? to nothingness? – in these very instincts I saw the beginning of the end, stability, the exhaustion that gazes backwards, the will turning *against* Life, the last illness announcing itself with its own mincing melancholy: I realized that the morality of pity which spread wider and wider, and whose grip infected even philosophers with its disease, was the most sinister symptom of our modern European civilization; I realized that it was the route along which that civilization slid on its way to – a new Buddhism? – a European Buddhism? – *Nihilism*? This exaggerated estimation in which modern philosophers have held pity, is quite a new phenomenon: up to that time philosophers were absolutely unanimous as to the *worthlessness* of pity. I need only mention Plato, Spinoza, La Rochefoucauld, and Kant – four minds as mutually different as is possible, but united on one point; their contempt of pity.

6

This problem of the value of pity and of the pity-morality (I am an opponent of the modern infamous emasculation of our emotions) seems at the first blush a mere isolated problem, a note of interrogation for itself; he, however, who once halts at this problem, and learns how to put questions, will experience what I experienced: a new and immense vista unfolds itself before him, a sense of potentiality seizes him like a vertigo, every species of doubt, mistrust, and fear springs up, the belief in morality, nay, in all morality, totters, – finally a new demand voices itself. Let us speak out this *new demand*: we need a *critique* of moral values, *the value of these values* is for the first time to be called into question – and for this purpose a knowledge is necessary of the conditions and circumstances out of which these values grew, and under which they experienced their evolution and their distortion (morality as a result, as a symptom, as a mask, as Tartuffism, as disease, as a misunderstanding; but also morality as a cause, as a remedy, as a stimulant, as a fetter, as a drug), especially as such a knowledge has neither existed up to the present time nor is even now generally desired. The value of these 'values' was taken for granted as an indisputable fact, which was beyond all question. No one has, up to the present, exhibited the faintest doubt or hesitation in judging the 'good man' to be of a higher value than the 'evil man,' of a higher value with regard specifically to human progress, utility, and prosperity generally, not forgetting the future. What? Suppose the converse were the truth! What? Suppose there lurked in the 'good man' a symptom of retrogression, such as a danger, a temptation, a poison, a *narcotic*, by means of which the present *battened on the future*! More comfortable and less risky perhaps than its opposite, but also pettier, meaner! So that morality would really be saddled with the guilt, if the *maximum potentiality of the power and splendour* of the human species were never to be attained? So that really morality would be the danger of dangers?

7

Enough, that after this vista had disclosed itself to me, I myself had reason to search for learned, bold, and industrious colleagues (I am doing it even to this very day). It means traversing with new clamorous questions, and at the same time with new eyes, the immense, distant, and completely unexplored land of morality – of a morality which has actually existed and been actually lived! and is this not practically equivalent to first *discovering* that land? If, in this context, I thought, amongst others, of the aforesaid Dr Rée, I did so because I had no doubt that from the very nature of his questions he would be compelled to have recourse to a truer method, in order to obtain his answers. Have I deceived myself on that score? I wished at all events to give a better direction of vision to an eye of such keenness, and such impartiality. I wished to direct him to the real *history of morality*, and to warn him, while there was yet time, against a world of English theories that culminated in *the blue vacuum of heaven*. Other colours, of course, rise immediately to one's mind as being a hundred times more potent than blue for a genealogy of morals: for instance, *grey*, by which I mean authentic facts capable of definite proof and having actually existed, or, to put it shortly, the whole of that long hieroglyphic script (which is so hard to decipher) about the past history of human morals. This script was unknown to Dr Rée; but he had read Darwin: – and so in his philosophy the Darwinian beast and that pink of modernity, the demure weakling and dilettante, who 'bites no longer,' shake hands politely in a fashion that is at least instructive, the latter exhibiting a certain facial expression of refined and good-humoured indolence, tinged with a touch of pessimism and exhaustion; as if it really did not pay to take all these things – I mean moral problems – so seriously. I, on the other hand, think that there are no subjects which *pay* better for being taken seriously; part of this payment is that perhaps eventually they admit of being taken *gaily*. This gaiety indeed, or, to use my own language, this *joyful wisdom*, is a payment; a payment for a protracted, brave, laborious, and burrowing seriousness, which, it goes without saying, is the attribute of but a few. But on that day on which we say from the fullness of our hearts, 'Forward! Our old morality too is fit material *for Comedy*,' we shall have discovered a new plot, and a new possibility for the Dionysian drama entitled *The Soul's Fate* – and he will speedily utilize it, one can wager safely, he, the great ancient eternal dramatist of the comedy of our existence.

8

If this writing be obscure to any individual, and jar on his ears, I do not think that it is necessarily I who am to blame. It is clear enough, on the hypothesis which I presuppose, namely, that the reader has first read my previous writings and has not grudged them a certain amount of trouble: it is not, indeed, a simple matter to get really at their essence. Take, for instance, my *Zarathustra*; I allow no one to pass muster as knowing that book, unless every single word therein has at some time wrought in him a profound wound, and at some time exercized on him a profound enchantment: then and not till then can he enjoy the privilege of participating reverently in the halcyon element, from which that work is born, in its sunny brilliance, its distance, its spaciousness, its certainty. In other cases the aphoristic form produces difficulty, but this is only because this form is treated *too casually*. An aphorism properly coined and cast into its final mould is far from being 'deciphered' as soon as it has been read; on the contrary, it is then that it first requires *to be expounded* – of course for that purpose an art of exposition is necessary. The third essay in this book provides an example of what is offered, of what in such cases I call exposition: an aphorism is prefixed to that essay, the essay itself is its commentary. Certainly one *quality* which nowadays has been best forgotten – and that is why it will take some time yet for my writings to become readable – is essential in order to practise reading as an art – a quality for the exercise of which it is necessary to be a cow, and under *no circumstances* a modern man! – *rumination*.

Sils-Maria, Upper Engadine,
July 1887.

FIRST ESSAY.

'GOOD AND EVIL,'
'GOOD AND BAD.'

‘GOOD AND EVIL,’ ‘GOOD AND BAD.’

1

Those English psychologists, who up to the present are the only philosophers who are to be thanked for any endeavour to get as far as a history of the origin of morality – these men, I say, offer us in their own personalities no paltry problem – they even have, if I am to be quite frank about it, in their capacity of living riddles, an advantage over their books – *they themselves are interesting!* These English psychologists – what do they really mean? We always find them voluntarily or involuntarily at the same task of pushing to the front the *partie honteuse* of our inner world, and looking for the efficient, governing, and decisive principle in that precise quarter where the intellectual self-respect of the race would be the most reluctant to find it (for example, in the *vis inertiæ* of habit, or in forgetfulness, or in a blind and fortuitous mechanism and association of ideas, or in some factor that is purely passive, reflex, molecular, or fundamentally stupid) – what is the real motive power which always impels these psychologists in precisely *this* direction? Is it an instinct for human disparagement somewhat sinister, vulgar, and malignant, or perhaps incomprehensible even to itself? or perhaps a touch of pessimistic jealousy, the mistrust of disillusioned idealists who have become gloomy, poisoned, and bitter? or a petty subconscious enmity and rancour against Christianity (and Plato), that has conceivably never crossed the threshold of consciousness? or just a vicious taste for those elements of life which are bizarre, painfully paradoxical, mystical, and illogical? or, as a final alternative, a dash of each of these motives – a little vulgarity, a little gloominess, a little anti-Christianity, a little craving for the necessary piquancy?

But I am told that it is simply a case of old frigid and tedious frogs crawling and hopping around men and inside men, as if they were as thoroughly at home there, as they would be in a *swamp*.

I am opposed to this statement, nay, I do not believe it; and if, in the impossibility of knowledge, one is permitted to wish, so do I wish from my heart that just the converse metaphor should apply, and that these analysts with their psychological microscopes should be, at bottom, brave, proud, and magnanimous animals who know how to bridle both their hearts and their smarts, and have specifically trained themselves to sacrifice what is desirable to what is true, *any* truth in fact, even the simple, bitter, ugly, repulsive, unchristian, and immoral truths – for there are truths of that description.

2

All honour, then, to the noble spirits who would fain dominate these historians of morality. But it is certainly a pity that they lack the *historical sense* itself, that they themselves are quite deserted by all the beneficent spirits of history. The whole train of their thought runs, as was always the way of old-fashioned philosophers, on *thoroughly* unhistorical lines: there is no doubt on this point. The crass ineptitude of their genealogy of morals is immediately apparent when the question arises of ascertaining the origin of the idea and judgement of 'good.' 'Man had originally,' so speaks their decree, 'praised and called 'good' altruistic acts from the standpoint of those on whom they were conferred, that is, those to whom they were *useful*; subsequently the origin of this praise was *forgotten*, and altruistic acts, simply because, as a sheer matter of habit, they were praised as good, came also to be felt as good – as though they contained in themselves some intrinsic goodness.' The thing is obvious: this initial derivation contains already all the typical and idiosyncratic traits of the English psychologists – we have 'utility,' 'forgetting,' 'habit,' and finally 'error,' the whole assemblage forming the basis of a system of values, on which the higher man has up to the present prided himself as though it were a kind of privilege of man in general.

This pride *must* be brought low, this system of values *must* lose its values: is that attained?

Now the first argument that comes ready to my hand is that the real homestead of the concept 'good' is sought and located in the wrong place: the judgement 'good' did *not* originate among those to whom goodness was shown. Much rather has it been the good themselves, that is, the aristocratic, the powerful, the high-stationed, the high-minded, who have felt that they themselves were good, and that their actions were good, that is to say of the first order, in contradistinction to all the low, the low-minded, the vulgar, and the plebeian. It was out of this pathos of distance that they first arrogated the right to create values for their own profit, and to coin the names of such values: what had they to do with utility? The standpoint of utility is as alien and as inapplicable as it could possibly be, when we have to deal with so volcanic an effervescence of supreme values, creating and demarcating as they do a hierarchy within themselves: it is at this juncture that one arrives at an appreciation of the contrast to that tepid temperature, which is the presupposition on which every combination of worldly wisdom and every calculation of practical expediency is always based – and not for one occasional, not for one exceptional instance, but chronically. The pathos of nobility and distance, as I have said, the chronic and despotic *esprit de corps* and fundamental instinct of a higher dominant race coming into association with a meaner race, an 'under race,' this is the origin of the antithesis of good and bad.

(The masters' right of giving names goes so far that it is permissible to look upon language itself as the expression of the power of the masters: they say 'this *is* that, and that,' they seal finally every object and every event with a sound, and thereby at the same time take possession of it.) It is because of this origin that the word 'good' is far from having any necessary connection with altruistic acts, in accordance with the superstitious belief of these moral philosophers. On the contrary, it is on the occasion of the *decay* of aristocratic values, that the antitheses between 'egoistic' and 'altruistic' presses more and more heavily on the human conscience – it is, to use my own language, the *herd instinct* which finds in this antithesis an expression in many ways. And even then it takes a considerable time for this instinct to become sufficiently dominant, for the valuation to be inextricably dependent on this antithesis (as is the case in contemporary Europe); for today that prejudice is predominant, which, acting even now with all the intensity of an obsession and brain disease, holds that 'moral,' 'altruistic,' and '*désintéressé*' are concepts of equal value.

3

In the second place, quite apart from the fact that this hypothesis as to the genesis of the value 'good' cannot be historically upheld, it suffers from an inherent psychological contradiction. The utility of altruistic conduct has presumably been the origin of its being praised, and this origin has become *forgotten*: But in what conceivable way is this forgetting *possible*! Has perchance the utility of such conduct ceased at some given moment? The contrary is the case. This utility has rather been experienced every day at all times, and is consequently a feature that obtains a new and regular emphasis with every fresh day; it follows that, so far from vanishing from the consciousness, so far indeed from being forgotten, it must necessarily become impressed on the consciousness with ever-increasing distinctness. How much more logical is that contrary theory (it is not the truer for that) which is represented, for instance, by Herbert Spencer, who places the concept 'good' as essentially similar to the concept 'useful,' 'purposive,' so that in the judgements 'good' and 'bad' mankind is simply summarizing and investing with a sanction its *unforgotten* and *unforgettable* experiences concerning the 'useful-purposive' and the 'mischievous-non-purposive.' According to this theory, 'good' is the attribute of that which has previously shown itself useful; and so is able to claim to be considered 'valuable in the highest degree,' 'valuable in itself.' This method of explanation is also, as I have said, wrong, but at any rate the explanation itself is coherent, and psychologically tenable.

4

The guide-post which first put me on the *right* track was this question – what is the true etymological significance of the various symbols for the idea 'good' which have been coined in the various languages? I then found that they all led back to *the same evolution of the same idea* – that everywhere 'aristocrat,' 'noble' (in the social sense), is the root idea, out of which have necessarily developed 'good' in the sense of 'with aristocratic soul,' 'noble,' in the sense of 'with a soul of high calibre,' 'with a privileged soul' – a development which invariably runs parallel with that other evolution by which 'vulgar,' 'plebeian,' 'low,' are made to change finally into 'bad.' The most eloquent proof of this last contention is the German word '*schlecht*' itself: this word is identical with '*schlicht*' – (compare '*schlechtweg*' and '*schlechterdings*') – which, originally and as yet without any sinister innuendo, simply denoted the plebeian man in contrast to the aristocratic man. It is at the sufficiently late period of the Thirty Years' War that this sense becomes changed to the sense now current. From the standpoint of the Genealogy of Morals this discovery seems to be substantial: the lateness of it is to be attributed to the retarding influence exercised in the modern world by democratic prejudice in the sphere of all questions of origin. This extends, as will shortly be shown, even to the province of natural science and physiology, which, *prima facie* is the most objective. The extent of the mischief which is caused by this prejudice (once it is free of all trammels except those of its own malice), particularly to Ethics and History, is shown by the notorious case of Buckle: it was in Buckle that that *plebeianism* of the modern spirit, which is of English origin, broke out once again from its malignant soil with all the violence of a slimy volcano, and with that salted, rampant, and vulgar eloquence with which up to the present time all volcanoes have spoken.

5

With regard to *our* problem, which can justly be called an *intimate* problem, and which elects to appeal to only a limited number of ears: it is of no small interest to ascertain that in those words and roots which denote 'good' we catch glimpses of that arch-trait, on the strength of which the aristocrats feel themselves to be beings of a higher order than their fellows. Indeed, they call themselves in perhaps the most frequent instances simply after their superiority in power (*e.g.* 'the powerful,' 'the lords,' 'the commanders'), or after the most obvious sign of their superiority, as for example 'the rich,' 'the possessors' (that is the meaning of *arya*; and the Iranian and Slav languages correspond). But they also call themselves after some *characteristic idiosyncrasy*; and this is the case which now concerns us. They name themselves, for instance, 'the truthful': this is first done by the Greek nobility whose mouthpiece is found in Theognis, the Megarian poet. The word ἐσθλος, which is coined for the purpose, signifies etymologically 'one who *is*,' who has reality, who is real, who is true; and then with a subjective twist, the 'true,' as the 'truthful': at this stage in the evolution of the idea, it becomes the motto and party cry of the nobility, and quite completes the transition to the meaning 'noble,' so as to place outside the pale the lying, vulgar man, as Theognis conceives and portrays him – till finally the word after the decay of the nobility is left to delineate psychological *noblesse*, and becomes as it were ripe and mellow. In the word as in δειλός (the plebeian in contrast to the ἀγαθός) the cowardice is emphasized. This affords perhaps an inkling on what lines the etymological origin of the very ambiguous ἀγαθός is to be investigated. In the Latin *malus* (which I place side by side with μέλας) the vulgar man can be distinguished as the dark-coloured, and above all as the black-haired ('*hic niger est*'), as the pre-Aryan inhabitants of the Italian soil, whose complexion formed the clearest feature of distinction from the dominant blondes, namely, the Aryan conquering race: at any rate Gaelic has afforded me the exact analogue – *Fin* (for instance, in the name *Fin-Gal*), the distinctive word of the nobility, finally – good, noble, clean, but originally the blonde-haired man in contrast to the dark black-haired aboriginals. The Celts, if I may make a parenthetic statement, were throughout a blonde race; and it is wrong to connect, as Virchow still connects, those traces of an essentially dark-haired population which are to be seen on the more elaborate ethnographical maps of Germany with any Celtic ancestry or with any admixture of Celtic blood: in this context it is rather the *pre-Aryan* population of Germany which surges up to these districts. (The same is true substantially of the whole of Europe: in point of fact, the subject race has finally again obtained the upper hand, in complexion and the shortness of the skull, and perhaps in the intellectual and social qualities. Who can guarantee that modern democracy, still more modern anarchy, and indeed that tendency to the 'Commune,' the most primitive form of society, which is now common to all the Socialists in Europe, does not in its real essence signify a monstrous reversion – and that the conquering and *master* race – the Aryan race, is not also becoming inferior physiologically?) I believe that I can explain the Latin *bonus* as the 'warrior': my hypothesis is that I am right in deriving *bonus* from an older *duonus* (compare *bellum* = *duellum* = *duen-lum*, in which the word *duonus* appears to me to be contained). *Bonus* accordingly as the man of discord, of variance, '*entzweiung*' (*duo*), as the warrior: one sees what in ancient Rome 'the good' meant for a man. Must not our actual German word *gut* mean '*the godlike*, the man of godlike race'? and be identical with the national name (originally the nobles' name) of the *Goths*?

The grounds for this supposition do not appertain to this work.

6

Above all, there is no exception (though there are opportunities for exceptions) to this rule, that the idea of political superiority always resolves itself into the idea of psychological superiority, in those cases where the highest caste is at the same time the *priestly* caste, and in accordance with its general characteristics confers on itself the privilege of a title which alludes specifically to its priestly function. It is in these cases, for instance, that 'clean' and 'unclean' confront each other for the first time as badges of class distinction; here again there develops a 'good' and a 'bad,' in a sense which has ceased to be merely social. Moreover, care should be taken not to take these ideas of 'clean' and 'unclean' too seriously, too broadly, or too symbolically: all the ideas of ancient man have, on the contrary, got to be understood in their initial stages, in a sense which is, to an almost inconceivable extent, crude, coarse, physical, and narrow, and above all essentially *unsymbolical*. The 'clean man' is originally only a man who washes himself, who abstains from certain foods which are conducive to skin diseases, who does not sleep with the unclean women of the lower classes, who has a horror of blood – not more, not much more! On the other hand, the very nature of a priestly aristocracy shows the reasons why just at such an early juncture there should ensue a really dangerous sharpening and intensification of opposed values: it is, in fact, through these opposed values that gulfs are cleft in the social plane, which a veritable Achilles of free thought would shudder to cross. There is from the outset a certain *diseased taint* in such sacerdotal aristocracies, and in the habits which prevail in such societies – habits which, *averse* as they are to action, constitute a compound of introspection and explosive emotionalism, as a result of which there appears that introspective morbidity and neurasthenia, which adheres almost inevitably to all priests at all times: with regard, however, to the remedy which they themselves have invented for this disease – the philosopher has no option but to state, that it has proved itself in its effects a hundred times more dangerous than the disease, from which it should have been the deliverer. Humanity itself is still diseased from the effects of the naïvetés of this priestly cure. Take, for instance, certain kinds of diet (abstention from flesh), fasts, sexual continence, flight into the wilderness (a kind of Weir-Mitchell isolation, though of course without that system of excessive feeding and fattening which is the most efficient antidote to all the hysteria of the ascetic ideal); consider too the whole metaphysic of the priests, with its war on the senses, its enervation, its hair-splitting; consider its self-hypnotism on the fakir and Brahman principles (it uses Brahman as a glass disc and obsession), and that climax which we can understand only too well of an unusual satiety with its panacea of *nothingness* (or God – the demand for a *unio mystica* with God is the demand of the Buddhist for nothingness, Nirvana – and nothing else!). In sacerdotal societies *every* element is on a more dangerous scale, not merely cures and remedies, but also pride, revenge, cunning, exaltation, love, ambition, virtue, morbidity: further, it can fairly be stated that it is on the soil of this *essentially dangerous* form of human society, the sacerdotal form, that man really becomes for the first time an *interesting animal*, that it is in this form that the soul of man has in a higher sense attained *depths* and become *evil* – and those are the two fundamental forms of the superiority which up to the present man has exhibited over every other animal.

7

The reader will have already surmised with what ease the priestly mode of valuation can branch off from the knightly aristocratic mode, and then develop into the very antithesis of the latter: special impetus is given to this opposition, by every occasion when the castes of the priests and warriors confront each other with mutual jealousy and cannot agree over the prize. The knightly-aristocratic 'values' are based on a careful cult of the physical, on a flowering, rich, and even effervescing healthiness, that goes considerably beyond what is necessary for maintaining life, on war, adventure, the chase, the dance, the tourney – on everything, in fact, which is contained in strong, free, and joyous action. The priestly-aristocratic mode of valuation is – we have seen – based on other hypotheses: it is bad enough for this class when it is a question of war! Yet the priests are, as is notorious, *the worst enemies* – why? Because they are the weakest. Their weakness causes their hate to expand into a monstrous and sinister shape, a shape which is most crafty and most poisonous. The really great haters in the history of the world have always been priests, who are also the cleverest haters – in comparison with the cleverness of priestly revenge, every other piece of cleverness is practically negligible. Human history would be too fatuous for anything were it not for the cleverness imported into it by the weak – take at once the most important instance. All the world's efforts against the 'aristocrats,' the 'mighty,' the 'masters,' the 'holders of power,' are negligible by comparison with what has been accomplished against those classes by *the Jews* – the Jews, that priestly nation which eventually realized that the one method of effecting satisfaction on its enemies and tyrants was by means of a radical transvaluation of values, which was at the same time an act of the *cleverest revenge*. Yet the method was only appropriate to a nation of priests, to a nation of the most jealously nursed priestly revengefulness. It was the Jews who, in opposition to the aristocratic equation (good = aristocratic = beautiful = happy = loved by the gods), dared with a terrifying logic to suggest the contrary equation, and indeed to maintain with the teeth of the most profound hatred (the hatred of weakness) this contrary equation, namely, 'the wretched are alone the good; the poor, the weak, the lowly, are alone the good; the suffering, the needy, the sick, the loathsome, are the only ones who are pious, the only ones who are blessed, for them alone is salvation – but you, on the other hand, you aristocrats, you men of power, you are to all eternity the evil, the horrible, the covetous, the insatiate, the godless; eternally also shall you be the unblessed, the cursed, the damned!' We know who it was who reaped the heritage of this Jewish transvaluation. In the context of the monstrous and inordinately fateful initiative which the Jews have exhibited in connection with this most fundamental of all declarations of war, I remember the passage which came to my pen on another occasion (*Beyond Good and Evil*, Aph. 195) – that it was, in fact, with the Jews that the *revolt of the slaves* begins in the sphere *of morals*; that revolt which has behind it a history of two millennia, and which at the present day has only moved out of our sight, because it has achieved victory.

8

But you understand this not? You have no eyes for a force which has taken two thousand years to achieve victory? There is nothing wonderful in this: all *lengthy* processes are hard to see and to realize. But *this* is what took place: from the trunk of that tree of revenge and hate, Jewish hate – that most profound and sublime hate, which creates ideals and changes old values to new creations, the like of which has never been on earth – there grew a phenomenon which was equally incomparable, *a new love*, the most profound and sublime of all kinds of love; and from what other trunk could it have grown? But beware of supposing that this love has soared on its upward growth, as in any way a real negation of that thirst for revenge, as an antithesis to the Jewish hate! No, the contrary is the truth! This love grew out of that hate, as its crown, as its triumphant crown, circling wider and wider amid the clarity and fullness of the sun, and pursuing in the very kingdom of light and height its goal of hatred, its victory, its spoil, its strategy, with the same intensity with which the roots of that tree of hate sank into everything which was deep and evil with increasing stability and increasing desire. This Jesus of Nazareth, the incarnate gospel of love, this 'Redeemer' bringing salvation and victory to the poor, the sick, the sinful – was he not really temptation in its most sinister and irresistible form, temptation to take the tortuous path to those very *Jewish* values and those very Jewish ideals? Has not Israel really obtained the final goal of its sublime revenge, by the tortuous paths of this 'Redeemer,' for all that he might pose as Israel's adversary and Israel's destroyer? Is it not due to the black magic of a really *great* policy of revenge, of a far-seeing, burrowing revenge, both acting and calculating with slowness, that Israel himself must repudiate before all the world the actual instrument of his own revenge and nail it to the cross, so that all the world – that is, all the enemies of Israel – could nibble without suspicion at this very bait? Could, moreover, any human mind with all its elaborate ingenuity invent a bait that was more truly *dangerous*? Anything that was even equivalent in the power of its seductive, intoxicating, defiling, and corrupting influence to that symbol of the holy cross, to that awful paradox of a 'god on the cross,' to that mystery of the unthinkable, supreme, and utter horror of the self-crucifixion of a god for the *salvation of man*? It is at least certain that *sub hoc signo* Israel, with its revenge and transvaluation of all values, has up to the present always triumphed again over all other ideals, over all more aristocratic ideals.

9

'But why do you talk of nobler ideals? Let us submit to the facts; that the people have triumphed – or the slaves, or the populace, or the herd, or whatever name you care to give them – if this has happened through the Jews, so be it! In that case no nation ever had a greater mission in the world's history. The 'masters' have been done away with; the morality of the vulgar man has triumphed. This triumph may also be called a blood-poisoning (it has mutually fused the races) – I do not dispute it; but there is no doubt but that this intoxication has succeeded. The 'redemption' of the human race (that is, from the masters) is progressing swimmingly; everything is obviously becoming Judaized, or Christianized, or vulgarized (what is there in the words?). It seems impossible to stop the course of this poisoning through the whole body politic of mankind – but its *tempo* and pace may from the present time be slower, more delicate, quieter, more discreet – there is time enough. In view of this context has the Church nowadays any necessary purpose? Has it, in fact, a right to live? Or could man get on without it? *Quæritur*. It seems that it fetters and retards this tendency, instead of accelerating it. Well, even that might be its utility. The Church certainly is a crude and boorish institution, that is repugnant to an intelligence with any pretence at delicacy, to a really modern taste. Should it not at any rate learn to be somewhat more subtle? It alienates nowadays, more than it allures. Which of us would, forsooth, be a freethinker if there were no Church? It is the Church which repels us, not its poison – apart from the Church we like the poison.' This is the epilogue of a freethinker to my discourse, of an honourable animal (as he has given abundant proof), and a democrat to boot; he had up to that time listened to me, and could not endure my silence, but for me, indeed, with regard to this topic there is much on which to be silent.

10

The revolt of the slaves in morals begins in the very principle of *resentment* becoming creative and giving birth to values – a resentment experienced by creatures who, deprived as they are of the proper outlet of action, are forced to find their compensation in an imaginary revenge. While every aristocratic morality springs from a triumphant affirmation of its own demands, the slave morality says 'no' from the very outset to what is 'outside itself,' 'different from itself,' and 'not itself': and this 'no' is its creative deed. This volte-face of the valuing standpoint – this *inevitable* gravitation to the objective instead of back to the subjective – is typical of 'resentment': the slave-morality requires as the condition of its existence an external and objective world, to employ physiological terminology, it requires objective stimuli to be capable of action at all – its action is fundamentally a reaction. The contrary is the case when we come to the aristocrat's system of values: it acts and grows spontaneously, it merely seeks its antithesis in order to pronounce a more grateful and exultant 'yes' to its own self; its negative conception, 'low,' 'vulgar,' 'bad,' is merely a pale late-born foil in comparison with its positive and fundamental conception (saturated as it is with life and passion), of 'we aristocrats, we good ones, we beautiful ones, we happy ones.'

When the aristocratic morality goes astray and commits sacrilege on reality, this is limited to that particular sphere with which it is *not* sufficiently acquainted – a sphere, in fact, from the real knowledge of which it disdainfully defends itself. It misjudges, in some cases, the sphere which it despises, the sphere of the common vulgar man and the low people: on the other hand, due weight should be given to the consideration that in any case the mood of contempt, of disdain, of superciliousness, even on the supposition that it *falsely* portrays the object of its contempt, will always be far removed from that degree of falsity which will always characterize the attacks – in effigy, of course – of the vindictive hatred and revengefulness of the weak in onslaughts on their enemies. In point of fact, there is in contempt too strong an admixture of nonchalance, of casualness, of boredom, of impatience, even of personal exultation, for it to be capable of distorting its victim into a real caricature or a real monstrosity. Attention again should be paid to the almost benevolent *nuances* which, for instance, the Greek nobility imports into all the words by which it distinguishes the common people from itself; note how continuously a kind of pity, care, and consideration imparts its honeyed *flavour*, until at last almost all the words which are applied to the vulgar man survive finally as expressions for 'unhappy,' 'worthy of pity' (compare δειλο, δείλαιος, πονηρός, μοχθηρός; the latter two names really denoting the vulgar man as labour-slave and beast of burden) – and how, conversely, 'bad,' 'low,' 'unhappy' have never ceased to ring in the Greek ear with a tone in which 'unhappy' is the predominant note: this is a heritage of the old noble aristocratic morality, which remains true to itself even in contempt (let philologists remember the sense in which ὀιζυρός, ἄνολβος, τλήμων, δυστυχεῖν, ξυμφορά used to be employed). The 'well-born' simply *felt* themselves the 'happy'; they did not have to manufacture their happiness artificially through looking at their enemies, or in cases to talk and *lie themselves* into happiness (as is the custom with all resentful men); and similarly, complete men as they were, exuberant with strength, and consequently *necessarily* energetic, they were too wise to dissociate happiness from action – activity becomes in their minds necessarily counted as happiness (that is the etymology of εὖ πρᾶττειν) – all in sharp contrast to the 'happiness' of the weak and the oppressed, with their festering venom and malignity, among whom happiness appears essentially as a narcotic, a deadening, a quietude, a peace, a 'Sabbath,' an enervation of the mind and relaxation of the limbs – in short, a purely *passive* phenomenon. While the aristocratic man lived in confidence and openness with himself (γενναῖος, 'noble-born,' emphasizes the nuance 'sincere,' and perhaps also 'naïf'), the resentful man, on the other hand, is neither sincere nor naïf, nor honest and candid with himself. His soul *squints*; his mind loves hidden crannies, tortuous paths and back-doors, everything secret appeals to him as *his* world, *his* safety, *his* balm; he is past master in silence, in not forgetting, in waiting, in provisional self-depreciation and self-abasement. A race of such *resentful* men will of necessity eventually prove more *prudent* than any aristocratic race, it will honour prudence on quite a distinct scale, as, in fact, a paramount condition of existence, while prudence among aristocratic men is apt to be tinged with a delicate flavour of luxury and refinement; so among them it plays nothing like so integral a part as that complete certainty of function of the governing *unconscious* instincts, or as indeed a certain lack of prudence, such as a vehement and valiant charge, whether against danger or the enemy, or as those ecstatic bursts of rage, love, reverence, gratitude, by which at all times noble souls have recognized each other. When the resentment of the aristocratic man manifests itself, it fulfils and exhausts itself in an immediate reaction, and consequently instills no *venom*: on the other hand, it never manifests itself at all in countless instances, when in the case of the feeble and weak it would be inevitable. An inability to take seriously for any length of time their enemies, their disasters, their *misdeeds* – that is the sign of the full strong natures who possess a superfluity of moulding plastic force, that heals completely and produces forgetfulness: a good example of this in the modern world is Mirabeau, who had no memory for any insults and meannesses which were practised on him, and who was only incapable of forgiving because he forgot. Such a man indeed shakes off with a shrug many a worm which would have buried itself in another; it is only in characters like these that we see the possibility (supposing, of course, that there is such a possibility in the world) of the real '*love* of one's enemies.' What respect for his enemies is found, forsooth, in an aristocratic man – and such a reverence is already a bridge to love! He insists on having his enemy to himself as his distinction. He tolerates no other enemy but a man in whose character there is nothing to despise and much to honour! On the other hand, imagine the 'enemy' as the resentful man conceives him – and it is here exactly that we see his work, his creativeness; he has conceived 'the evil enemy,' the 'evil one,' and indeed that is the root idea from which he now evolves as a contrasting and corresponding figure a 'good one,' himself – his very self!

11

The method of this man is quite contrary to that of the aristocratic man, who conceives the root idea 'good' spontaneously and straight away, that is to say, out of himself, and from that material then creates for himself a concept of 'bad'! This 'bad' of aristocratic origin and that 'evil' out of the cauldron of unsatisfied hatred – the former an imitation, an 'extra,' an additional nuance; the latter, on the other hand, the original, the beginning, the essential act in the conception of a slave-morality – these two words 'bad' and 'evil,' how great a difference do they mark, in spite of the fact that they have an identical contrary in the idea 'good.' But the idea 'good' is not the same: much rather let the question be asked, 'Who is really evil according to the meaning of the morality of resentment?' In all sternness let it be answered thus: *just* the good man of the other morality, just the aristocrat, the powerful one, the one who rules, but who is distorted by the venomous eye of resentfulness, into a new colour, a new signification, a new appearance. This particular point we would be the last to deny: the man who learnt to know those 'good' ones only as enemies, learnt at the same time not to know them only as '*evil enemies*' and the same men who *inter pares* were kept so rigorously in bounds through convention, respect, custom, and gratitude, though much more through mutual vigilance and jealousy *inter pares*, these men who in their relations with each other find so many new ways of manifesting consideration, self-control, delicacy, loyalty, pride, and friendship, these men are in reference to what is outside their circle (where the foreign element, a *foreign* country, begins), not much better than beasts of prey, which have been let loose. They enjoy there freedom from all social control, they feel that in the wilderness they can give vent with impunity to that tension which is produced by enclosure and imprisonment in the peace of society, they *revert* to the innocence of the beast-of-prey conscience, like jubilant monsters, who perhaps come from a ghastly bout of murder, arson, rape, and torture, with bravado and a moral equanimity, as though merely some wild student's prank had been played, perfectly convinced that the poets have now an ample theme to sing and celebrate. It is impossible not to recognize at the core of all these aristocratic races the beast of prey; the magnificent *blonde brute*, avidly rampant for spoil and victory; this hidden core needed an outlet from time to time, the beast must get loose again, must return into the wilderness – the Roman, Arabic, German, and Japanese nobility, the Homeric heroes, the Scandinavian Vikings, are all alike in this need. It is the aristocratic races who have left the idea 'Barbarian' on all the tracks in which they have marched; nay, a consciousness of this very barbarianism, and even a pride in it, manifests itself even in their highest civilization (for example, when Pericles says to his Athenians in that celebrated funeral oration, 'Our audacity has forced a way over every land and sea, rearing everywhere imperishable memorials of itself for *good* and for *evil*'). This audacity of aristocratic races, mad, absurd, and spasmodic as may be its expression; the incalculable and fantastic nature of their enterprises, Pericles sets in special relief and glory the ραθυμία of the Athenians, their nonchalance and contempt for safety, body, life, and comfort, their awful joy and intense delight in all destruction, in all the ecstasies of victory and cruelty – all these features become crystallized, for those who suffered thereby in the picture of the 'barbarian,' of the 'evil enemy,' perhaps of the 'Goth' and of the 'Vandal.' The profound, icy mistrust which the German provokes, as soon as he arrives at power – even at the present time – is always still an aftermath of that inextinguishable horror with which for whole centuries Europe has regarded the wrath of the blonde Teuton beast (although between the old Germans and ourselves there exists scarcely a psychological, let alone a physical, relationship). I have once called attention to the embarrassment of Hesiod, when he conceived the series of social ages, and endeavoured to express them in gold, silver, and bronze. He could only dispose of the contradiction, with which he was confronted, by the Homeric world, an age magnificent indeed, but at the same time so awful and so violent, by making two ages out of one, which he henceforth placed one behind each other – first, the age of the heroes and demigods, as that world had remained in the memories of the aristocratic families, who found therein their own ancestors; secondly, the bronze age, as that corresponding age appeared to the descendants of the oppressed, spoiled, ill-treated, exiled, enslaved; namely, as an age of bronze, as I have said, hard, cold, terrible, without feelings and without conscience, crushing everything, and bespattering everything with blood. Granted the truth of the theory now believed to be true, that the very *essence of all civilization* is to *train* out of man, the beast of prey, a tame and civilized animal, a domesticated animal, it follows indubitably that we must regard as the real *tools of civilization* all those instincts of reaction and resentment, by the help of which the aristocratic races, together with their ideals, were finally degraded and overpowered; though that has not yet come to be synonymous with saying that the bearers of those tools also *represented* the civilisation. It is rather the contrary that is not only probable – nay, it is *palpable* to-day; these bearers of vindictive instincts that have to be bottled up, these descendants of all European and non-European slavery, especially of the pre-Aryan population – these people, I say, represent the *decline* of humanity! These 'tools of civilization' are a disgrace to humanity, and constitute in reality more of an argument against civilization, more of a reason why civilization should be suspected. One may be perfectly justified in being always afraid of the blonde beast that lies at the core of all aristocratic races, and in being on one's guard: but who would not a hundred times prefer to be afraid, when one at the same time admires, than to be immune from fear, at the cost of being perpetually obsessed with the loathsome spectacle of the distorted, the dwarfed, the stunted, the envenomed? And is that not our fate? What produces today our repulsion towards 'man'? – for we *suffer* from 'man,' there is no doubt about it. It is not fear; it is rather that we have nothing more to fear from men; it is that the worm 'man' is in the foreground and pullulates; it is that the 'tame man,' the wretched mediocre and unedifying creature, has learnt to consider himself a goal and a pinnacle, an inner meaning, an historic principle, a 'higher man'; yes, it is that he has a certain right so to consider himself, in so far as he feels that in contrast to that excess of deformity, disease, exhaustion, and effeteness whose odour is beginning to pollute present-day Europe, he at any rate has achieved a relative success, he at any rate still says 'yes' to life.

12

I cannot refrain at this juncture from uttering a sigh and one last hope. What is it precisely which I find intolerable? That which I alone cannot get rid of, which makes me choke and faint? Bad air! Bad air! That something misbegotten comes near me; that I must inhale the odour of the entrails of a misbegotten soul! That excepted, what can one not endure in the way of need, privation, bad weather, sickness, toil, solitude? In point of fact, one manages to get over everything, born as one is to a burrowing and battling existence; one always returns once again to the light, one always lives again one's golden hour of victory – and then one stands as one was born, unbreakable, tense, ready for something more difficult, for something more distant, like a bow stretched but the tauter by every strain. But from time to time do ye grant me – assuming that 'beyond good and evil' there are goddesses who can grant – one glimpse, grant me but one glimpse only, of something perfect, fully realized, happy, mighty, triumphant, of something that still gives cause for fear! A glimpse of a man that justifies the existence of man, a glimpse of an incarnate human happiness that realizes and redeems, for the sake of which one may hold fast to *the belief in man*! For the position is this: in the dwarfing and levelling of the European man lurks *our* greatest peril, for it is this outlook which fatigues – we see today nothing which wishes to be greater, we surmise that the process is always still backwards, still backwards towards something more attenuated, more inoffensive, more cunning, more comfortable, more mediocre, more indifferent, more Chinese, more Christian – man, there is no doubt about it, grows always 'better' – the destiny of Europe lies even in this – that in losing the fear of man, we have also lost the hope in man, yea, the will to be man. The sight of man now fatigues. What is present-day Nihilism if it is not *that*? We are tired of *man*.

13

But let us come back to it; the problem of *another* origin of the *good* – of the good, as the resentful man has thought it out – demands its solution. It is not surprising that the lambs should bear a grudge against the great birds of prey, but that is no reason for blaming the great birds of prey for taking the little lambs. And when the lambs say among themselves, 'These birds of prey are evil, and he who is as far removed from being a bird of prey, who is rather its opposite, a lamb, is he not good?' then there is nothing to cavil at in the setting up of this ideal, though it may also be that the birds of prey will regard it a little sneeringly, and perchance say to themselves, '*We* bear no grudge against them, these good lambs, we even like them: nothing is tastier than a tender lamb.' To require of strength that it should *not* express itself as strength, that it should not be a wish to overpower, a wish to overthrow, a wish to become master, a thirst for enemies and antagonisms and triumphs, is just as absurd as to require of weakness that it should express itself as strength. A quantum of force is just such a quantum of movement, will, action – rather it is nothing else than just those very phenomena of moving, willing, acting, and can only appear otherwise in the misleading errors of language (and the fundamental fallacies of reason which have become petrified therein), which understands, and understands wrongly, all working as conditioned by a worker, by a 'subject.' And just exactly as the people separate the lightning from its flash, and interpret the latter as a thing done, as the working of a subject which is called lightning, so also does the popular morality separate strength from the expression of strength, as though behind the strong man there existed some indifferent neutral *substratum*, which enjoyed a *caprice and option* as to whether or not it should express strength. But there is no such *substratum*, there is no 'being' behind doing, working, becoming; 'the doer' is a mere appanage to the action. The action is everything. In point of fact, the people duplicate the doing, when they make the lightning lighten, that is a 'doing-doing': they make the same phenomenon first a cause, and then, secondly, the effect of that cause. The scientists fail to improve matters when they say, 'Force moves, force causes,' and so on. Our whole science is still, in spite of all its coldness, of all its freedom from passion, a dupe of the tricks of language, and has never succeeded in getting rid of that superstitious changeling 'the subject' (the atom, to give another instance, is such a changeling, just as the Kantian 'Thing-in-itself'). What wonder, if the suppressed and stealthily simmering passions of revenge and hatred exploit for their own advantage this belief, and indeed hold no belief with a more steadfast enthusiasm than this – 'that the strong has the *option* of being weak, and the bird of prey of being a lamb.' Thereby do they win for themselves the right of attributing to the birds of prey the *responsibility* for being birds of prey: when the oppressed, down-trodden, and overpowered say to themselves with the vindictive guile of weakness, 'Let us be otherwise than the evil, namely, good! And good is every one who does not oppress, who hurts no one, who does not attack, who does not pay back, who hands over revenge to God, who holds himself, as we do, in hiding; who goes out of the way of evil, and demands, in short, little from life; like ourselves the patient, the meek, the just,' yet all this, in its cold and unprejudiced interpretation, means nothing more than 'once for all, the weak are weak; it is good to do *nothing for which we are not strong enough*'; but this dismal state of affairs, this prudence of the lowest order, which even insects possess (which in a great danger are fain to sham death so as to avoid doing 'too much'), has, thanks to the counterfeiting and self-deception of weakness, come to masquerade in the pomp of an ascetic, mute, and expectant virtue, just as though the *very* weakness of the weak – that is, forsooth, its *being*, its working, its whole unique inevitable inseparable reality – were a voluntary result, something wished, chosen, a deed, an act of *merit.* This kind of man finds the belief in a neutral, free-choosing 'subject' *necessary* from an instinct of self-preservation, of self-assertion, in which every lie is fain to sanctify itself. The subject (or, to use popular language, the *soul*) has perhaps proved itself the best dogma in the world simply because it rendered possible to the horde of mortal, weak, and oppressed individuals of every kind, that most sublime specimen of self-deception, the interpretation of weakness as freedom, of being this, or being that, as *merit.*

14

Will any one look a little into – right into – the mystery of how *ideals* are *manufactured* in this world? Who has the courage to do it? Come!

Here we have a vista opened into these grimy workshops. Wait just a moment, dear Mr Inquisitive and Foolhardy; your eye must first grow accustomed to this false changing light – Yes! Enough! Now speak! What is happening below down yonder? Speak out that what you see, man of the most dangerous curiosity – for now *I* am the listener.

'I see nothing, I hear the more. It is a cautious, spiteful, gentle whispering and muttering together in all the corners and crannies. It seems to me that they are lying; a sugary softness adheres to every sound. Weakness is turned to *merit*, there is no doubt about it – it is just as you say.'

Further!

'And the impotence which requites not, is turned to 'goodness,' craven baseness to meekness, submission to those whom one hates, to obedience (namely, obedience to one of whom they say that he ordered this submission – they call him God). The inoffensive character of the weak, the very cowardice in which he is rich, his standing at the door, his forced necessity of waiting, gain here fine names, such as 'patience,' which is also called 'virtue'; not being able to avenge one's self, is called not wishing to avenge one's self, perhaps even forgiveness (for *they* know not what they do – we alone know what *they* do). They also talk of the 'love of their enemies' and sweat thereby.'

Further!

'They are miserable, there is no doubt about it, all these whisperers and counterfeiters in the corners, although they try to get warm by crouching close to each other, but they tell me that their misery is a favour and distinction given to them by God, just as one beats the dogs one likes best; that perhaps this misery is also a preparation, a probation, a training; that perhaps it is still more something which will one day be compensated and paid back with a tremendous interest in gold, nay in happiness. This they call 'Blessedness."

Further!

'They are now giving me to understand, that not only are they better men than the mighty, the lords of the earth, whose spittle they have got to lick (*not* out of fear, not at all out of fear! But because God ordains that one should honour all authority) – not only are they better men, but that they also have a 'better time,' at any rate, will one day have a 'better time.' But enough! Enough! I can endure it no longer. Bad air! Bad air! These workshops *where ideals are manufactured* – verily they reek with the crassest lies.'

Nay. Just one minute! You are saying nothing about the masterpieces of these virtuosos of black magic, who can produce whiteness, milk, and innocence out of any black you like: have you not noticed what a pitch of refinement is attained by their *chef d'œuvre*, their most audacious, subtle, ingenious, and lying artist-trick? Take care! These cellar-beasts, full of revenge and hate – what do they make, forsooth, out of their revenge and hate? Do you hear these words? Would you suspect, if you trusted only their words, that you are among men of resentment and nothing else?

'I understand, I prick my ears up again (Ah! Ah! Ah! and I hold my nose). Now do I hear for the first time that which they have said so often: 'We good, *we are the righteous*' – what they demand they call not revenge but 'the triumph of *righteousness*'; what they hate is not their enemy, no, they hate 'unrighteousness,' 'godlessness'; what they believe in and hope is not the hope of revenge, the intoxication of sweet revenge ('sweeter than honey,' did Homer call it?), but the victory of God, of the *righteous God* over the 'godless'; what is left for them to love in this world is not their brothers in hate, but their 'brothers in love,' as they say, all the good and righteous on the earth.'

And how do they name that which serves them as a solace against all the troubles of life – their phantasmagoria of their anticipated future blessedness?

'How? Do I hear right? They call it "the last judgment," the advent of *their* kingdom, "the kingdom of God" – but *in the meanwhile* they live "in faith," "in love," "in hope."'

Enough! Enough!

15

In the faith in what? In the love for what? In the hope of what? These weaklings! – they also, forsooth, wish to be the strong some time; there is no doubt about it, some time *their* kingdom also must come – 'the kingdom of God' is their name for it, as has been mentioned: they are so meek in everything! Yet in order to experience *that* kingdom it is necessary to live long, to live beyond death, – yes, *eternal* life is necessary so that one can make up for ever for that earthly life 'in faith,' 'in love,' 'in hope.' Make up for what? Make up by what? Dante, as it seems to me, made a crass mistake when with awe-inspiring ingenuity he placed that inscription over the gate of his hell, 'Me too made eternal love': at any rate the following inscription would have a much better right to stand over the gate of the Christian Paradise and its 'eternal blessedness' – 'Me too made eternal hate' – granted of course that a truth may rightly stand over the gate to a lie! For what is the blessedness of that Paradise? Possibly we could quickly surmise it; but it is better that it should be explicitly attested by an authority who in such matters is not to be disparaged, Thomas of Aquinas, the great teacher and saint. '*Beati in regno celesti*' says he, as gently as a lamb, '*videbunt pœnas damnatorum, ut beatitudo illis magis complaceat*.' Or if we wish to hear a stronger tone, a word from the mouth of a triumphant father of the Church, who warned his disciples against the cruel ecstasies of the public spectacles – But why? Faith offers us much more – says he, *de Spectac*., c. 29 ss. something much stronger; thanks to the redemption, joys of quite another kind stand at our disposal; instead of athletes we have our martyrs; we wish for blood, well, we have the blood of Christ – but what then awaits us on the day of his return, of his triumph. And then does he proceed, does this enraptured visionary: '*at enim supersunt alia spectacula, ille ultimas et perpetuus judicii dies, ille nationibus insperatus, ille derisus, cum tanta sæculi vetustas et tot ejus nativitates uno igne haurientur. Quæ tunc spectaculi latitudo! Quid admirer! quid rideam! Ubigaudeam! Ubi exultem, spectans tot et tantos reges, qui in cœlum recepti nuntiabantur, cum ipso Jove et ipsis suis testibus in imis tenebris congemescentes! Item præsides*' (the provincial governors) '*persecutores dominici nominis sævioribus quam ipsi flammis sævierunt insultantibus contra Christianos liquescentes! Quos præterea sapientes illos philosophos coram discipulis suis una conflagrantibus erubescentes, quibus nihil ad deum pertinere suadebant, quibus animas aut nullas aut non in pristina corpora redituras affirmabant! Etiam poetas non ad Rhadamanti nec ad Minois, sed ad inopinati Christi tribunal palpitantes! Tunc magis tragœdi audiendi, magis scilicet vocales*' (with louder tones and more violent shrieks) '*in sua propria calamitate; tunc histriones cognoscendi, solutiores multo per ignem; tunc spectandus auriga in flammea rota totus rubens, tunc xystici contemplandi non in gymnasiis, sed in igne jaculati, nisi quod ne tunc quidem illos velim vivos, ut qui malim ad eos potius conspectum insatiabilem conferre, qui in dominum scevierunt. Hic est ille, dicam fabri aut quæstuariæ filius*' (as is shown by the whole of the following, and in particular by this well-known description of the mother of Jesus from the Talmud, Tertullian is henceforth referring to the Jews), '*sabbati destructor, Samarites et dæmonium habens. Hic est quem a Juda redemistis, hic est ille arundine et colaphis diverberatus, sputamentis de* *decoratus, felle et acete potatus. Hic est, quem clam discentes subripuerunt, ut resurrexisse dicatur vel hortulanus detraxit, ne lactucæ suæ frequentia commeantium laderentur. Ut talia species, ut talibus exultes, quis tibi prætor aut consul aut sacerdos de sua liberalitate prastabit? Et tamen hæc jam habemus quodammodo per fidem spiritu imaginante repræsentata. Ceterum qualia illa sunt, quæ nec oculus vidit nec auris audivit nec in cor hominis ascenderunt?'**

---

* Tertullian, *De Spectactulis*, ch XXX. English translation by Reverend S. Thelwall: 'Yes, and there are other sights: that last day of judgement, with its everlasting issues; that day unlooked for by the nations, the theme of their derision, when the world hoary with age, and all its many products, shall be consumed in one great flame! How vast a spectacle then bursts upon the eye! What there excites my admiration? What my derision? Which sight gives me joy? Which rouses me to exultation? As I see so many illustrious monarchs, whose reception into the heavens was publicly announced, groaning now in the lowest darkness with great Jove himself, and those, too, who bore witness of their exultation; governors of provinces, too, who persecuted the Christian name, in fires more fierce than those with which in the days of their pride they raged against the followers of Christ. What world's wise men besides, the very philosophers, in fact, who taught their followers that God had no concern in ought that is sublunary, and were wont to assure them that either they had no souls, or that they would never return to the bodies which at death they had left, now covered with shame before the poor deluded ones, as one fire consumes them! Poets also, trembling not before the judgement-seat of Rhadamanthus or Minos, but of the unexpected Christ! I shall have a better opportunity then of hearing the tragedians, louder-voiced in their own calamity; of viewing the play-actors, much more "dissolute" in the dissolving flame; of looking upon the charioteer, all glowing in his chariot of fire; of beholding the wrestlers, not in their gymnasia, but tossing in the fiery billows; unless even then I shall not care to attend to such ministers of sin, in my eager wish rather to fix a gaze insatiable on those whose fury vented itself against the Lord. "This," I shall say, "this is that carpenter's or hireling's son, that Sabbath-breaker, that Samaritan and devil-possessed! This is He whom you purchased from Judas! This is He whom you struck with reed and fist, whom you contemptuously spat upon, to whom you gave gall and vinegar to drink! This is He whom His disciples secretly stole away, that it might be said He had risen again, or the gardener abstracted, that his lettuces might come to no harm from the crowds of visitants!" What quaestor or priest in his munificence will

(1 Cor. ii. 9.) '*Credo circo et utraque cavea*' (first and fourth row, or, according to others, the comic and the tragic stage) '*et omni studio gratiora.*' *Per fidem*: so stands it written.

16

Let us come to a conclusion. The two *opposing values*, 'good and bad,' 'good and evil,' have fought a dreadful, thousand-year fight in the world, and though indubitably the second value has been for a long time in the preponderance, there are not wanting places where the fortune of the fight is still undecisive. It can almost be said that in the meanwhile the fight reaches a higher and higher level, and that in the meanwhile it has become more and more intense, and always more and more psychological; so that nowadays there is perhaps no more decisive mark of the *higher nature*, of the more psychological nature, than to be in that sense self-contradictory, and to be actually still a battleground for those two opposites. The symbol of this fight, written in a writing which has remained worthy of perusal throughout the course of history up to the present time, is called 'Rome against Judaea, Judaea against Rome.' Hitherto there has been no greater event than *that* fight, the putting of *that* question, *that* deadly antagonism. Rome found in the Jew the incarnation of the unnatural, as though it were its diametrically opposed monstrosity, and in Rome the Jew was held to be *convicted of hatred* of the whole human race: and rightly so, in so far as it is right to link the well-being and the future of the human race to the unconditional mastery of the aristocratic values, of the Roman values. What, conversely, did the Jews feel against Rome? One can surmise

---

bestow on you the favour of seeing and exulting in such things as these? And yet even now we in a measure have them by faith in the picturings of imagination. But what are the things which eye has not seen, ear has not heard, and which have not so much as dimly dawned upon the human heart? Whatever they are, they are nobler, I believe, than circus, and both theatres, and every race-course.'

it from a thousand symptoms, but it is sufficient to carry one's mind back to the Johannian Apocalypse, that most obscene of all the written outbursts, which has revenge on its conscience. (One should also appraise at its full value the profound logic of the Christian instinct, when over this very book of hate it wrote the name of the Disciple of Love, that self-same disciple to whom it attributed that impassioned and ecstatic Gospel – therein lurks a portion of truth, however much literary forging may have been necessary for this purpose.) The Romans were the strong and aristocratic; a nation stronger and more aristocratic has never existed in the world, has never even been dreamed of; every relic of them, every inscription enraptures, granted that one can divine *what* it is that writes the inscription. The Jews, conversely, were that priestly nation of resentment *par excellence*, possessed by a unique genius for popular morals: just compare with the Jews the nations with analogous gifts, such as the Chinese or the Germans, so as to realize afterwards what is first rate, and what is fifth rate.

Which of them has been provisionally victorious, Rome or Judaea? But there is not a shadow of doubt; just consider to whom in Rome itself nowadays you bow down, as though before the quintessence of all the highest values – and not only in Rome, but almost over half the world, everywhere where man has been tamed or is about to be tamed – to *three Jews*, as we know, and *one Jewess* (to Jesus of Nazareth, to Peter the fisher, to Paul the tent-maker, and to the mother of the aforesaid Jesus, named Mary). This is very remarkable: Rome is undoubtedly defeated. At any rate there took place in the Renaissance a brilliantly sinister revival of the classical ideal, of the aristocratic valuation of all things: Rome herself, like a man waking up from a trance, stirred beneath the burden of the new Judaized Rome that had been built over her, which presented the appearance of an ecumenical synagogue and was called the 'Church': but immediately Judaea triumphed again, thanks to that fundamentally popular (German and English) movement of revenge, which is called the Reformation, and taking also into account its inevitable corollary, the restoration of the Church – the restoration also of the ancient graveyard peace of classical Rome. Judaea proved yet once more victorious over the classical ideal in the French Revolution, and in a sense which was even more crucial and even more profound: the last political aristocracy that existed in Europe, that of the *French* seventeenth and eighteenth centuries, broke into pieces beneath the instincts of a resentful populace – never had the world heard a greater jubilation, a more uproarious enthusiasm: indeed, there took place in the midst of it the most monstrous and unexpected phenomenon; the ancient ideal *itself* swept before the eyes and conscience of humanity with all its life and with unheard-of splendour, and in opposition to resentment's lying war-cry of *the prerogative of the most*, in opposition to the will to lowliness, abasement, and equalization, the will to a retrogression and twilight of humanity, there rang out once again, stronger, simpler, more penetrating than ever, the terrible and enchanting counter-warcry of *the prerogative of the few*! Like a final signpost to other ways, there appeared Napoleon, the most unique and violent anachronism that ever existed, and in him the incarnate problem *of the aristocratic ideal in itself* – consider well what a problem it is: Napoleon, that synthesis of Monster and Superman.

17

Was it therewith over? Was that greatest of all antitheses of ideals thereby relegated *ad acta* for all time? Or only postponed, postponed for a long time? May there not take place at some time or other a much more awful, much more carefully prepared flaring up of the old conflagration? Further! Should not one wish *that* consummation with all one's strength? Will it one's self? Demand it one's self? He who at this juncture begins, like my readers, to reflect, to think further, will have difficulty in coming quickly to a conclusion – ground enough for me to come myself to a conclusion, taking it for granted that for some time past what I mean has been sufficiently clear, what I exactly *mean* by that dangerous motto which is inscribed on the body of my last book: *Beyond Good and Evil* – at any rate that is not the same as 'Beyond Good and Bad.'

Note. I avail myself of the opportunity offered by this treatise to express, openly and formally, a wish which up to the present has only been expressed in occasional conversations with scholars, namely, that some Faculty of philosophy should, by means of a series of prize essays, gain the glory of having promoted the further study of the *history of morals* – perhaps this book may serve to give forcible impetus in such a direction. With regard to a possibility of this character, the following question deserves consideration. It merits quite as much the attention of philologists and historians as of actual professional philosophers.

'*What indication of the history of the evolution of the moral ideas is afforded by philology, and especially by etymological investigation?*'

On the other hand, it is of course equally necessary to induce physiologists and doctors to be interested in these problems (*of the value* of the *valuations* which have prevailed up to the present): in this connection the professional philosophers may be trusted to act as the spokesmen and intermediaries in these particular instances, after, of course, they have quite succeeded in transforming the relationship between philosophy and physiology and medicine, which is originally one of coldness and suspicion, into the most friendly and fruitful reciprocity. In point of fact, all tables of values, all the 'thou shalts' known to history and ethnology, need primarily a *physiological*, at any rate in preference to a psychological, elucidation and interpretation; all equally require a critique from medical science. The question, 'What is the *value* of this or that table of 'values' and morality?' will be asked from the most varied standpoints. For instance, the question of 'valuable *for what*' can never be analysed with sufficient nicety. That, for instance, which would evidently have value with regard to promoting in a race the greatest possible powers of endurance (or with regard to increasing its adaptability to a specific climate, or with regard to the preservation of the greatest number) would have nothing like the same value, if it were a question of evolving a stronger species. In gauging values, the good of the majority and the good of the minority are opposed standpoints: we leave it to the naïveté of English biologists to regard the former standpoint as *intrinsically* superior. *All* the sciences have now to pave the way for the future task of the philosopher; this task being understood to mean, that he must solve the problem of *value*, that he has to fix the *hierarchy of values*.

SECOND ESSAY.

'GUILT,' 'BAD CONSCIENCE,' AND THE LIKE.

'GUILT,' 'BAD CONSCIENCE,' AND THE LIKE.

1

The breeding of an animal that *can promise* – is not this just that very paradox of a task which nature has set itself in regard to man? Is not this the very problem of man? The fact that this problem has been to a great extent solved, must appear all the more phenomenal to one who can estimate at its full value that force of *forgetfulness* which works in opposition to it. Forgetfulness is no mere *vis inertiæ*, as the superficial believe, rather is it a power of obstruction, active and, in the strictest sense of the word, positive – a power responsible for the fact that what we have lived, experienced, taken into ourselves, no more enters into consciousness during the process of digestion (it might be called psychic absorption) than all the whole manifold process by which our physical nutrition, the so-called 'incorporation,' is carried on. The temporary shutting of the doors and windows of consciousness, the relief from the clamant alarums and excursions, with which our subconscious world of servant organs works in mutual co-operation and antagonism; a little quietude, a little *tabula rasa* of the consciousness, so as to make room again for the new, and above all for the more noble functions and functionaries, room for government, foresight, predetermination (for our organism is on an oligarchic model) – this is the utility, as I have said, of the active forgetfulness, which is a very sentinel and nurse of psychic order, repose, etiquette; and this shows at once why it is that there can exist no happiness, no gladness, no hope, no pride, no real *present*, without forgetfulness. The man in whom this preventative apparatus is damaged and discarded, is to be compared to a dyspeptic, and it is something more than a comparison – he can 'get rid of' nothing. But this very animal who finds it necessary to be forgetful, in whom, in fact, forgetfulness represents a force and a form of *robust* health, has reared for himself an opposition-power, a memory, with whose help forgetfulness is, in certain instances, kept in check – in the cases, namely, where promises have to be made – so that it is by no means a mere passive inability to get rid of a once indented impression, not merely the indigestion occasioned by a once pledged word, which one cannot dispose of, but an *active* refusal to get rid of it, a continuing and a wish to continue what has once been willed, an actual *memory of the will*; so that between the original 'I will,' 'I shall do,' and the actual discharge of the will, its *act*, we can easily interpose a world of new strange phenomena, circumstances, veritable volitions, without the snapping of this long chain of the will. But what is the underlying hypothesis of all this? How thoroughly, in order to be able to regulate the future in this way, must man have first learnt to distinguish between necessitated and accidental phenomena, to think causally, to see the distant as present and to anticipate it, to fix with certainty what is the end, and what is the means to that end; above all, to reckon, to have power to calculate – how thoroughly must man have first become *calculable, disciplined, necessitated* even for himself and his own conception of himself, that, like a man entering into a promise, he could guarantee himself *as a future.*

2

This is simply the long history of the origin of *responsibility*. That task of breeding an animal which can make promises, includes, as we have already grasped, as its condition and preliminary, the more immediate task of first *making* man to a certain extent, necessitated, uniform, like among his like, regular, and consequently calculable. The immense work of what I have called, 'morality of custom'* (cp. *Dawn of Day*, Aphs. 9, 14, and 16), the actual work of man

* The German is: "*Sittlichkeit der Sitte.*" H. B. S.

on himself during the longest period of the human race, his whole prehistoric work, finds its meaning, its great justification (in spite of all its innate hardness, despotism, stupidity, and idiocy) in this fact: man, with the help of the morality of customs and of social strait-waistcoats, was *made* genuinely calculable. If, however, we place ourselves at the end of this colossal process, at the point where the tree finally matures its fruits, when society and its morality of custom finally bring to light that to which it was only the means, then do we find as the ripest fruit on its tree the *sovereign individual*, that resembles only himself, that has got loose from the morality of custom, the autonomous 'super-moral' individual (for 'autonomous' and 'moral' are mutually-exclusive terms), in short, the man of the personal, long, and independent will, *competent to promise*, and we find in him a proud consciousness (vibrating in every fibre), of *what* has been at last achieved and become vivified in him, a genuine consciousness of power and freedom, a feeling of human perfection in general. And this man who has grown to freedom, who is really *competent* to promise, this lord of the *free* will, this sovereign – how is it possible for him not to know how great is his superiority over everything incapable of binding itself by promises, or of being its own security, how great is the trust, the awe, the reverence that he awakes – he 'deserves' all three – not to know that with this mastery over himself he is necessarily also given the mastery over circumstances, over nature, over all creatures with shorter wills, less reliable characters? The 'free' man, the owner of a long unbreakable will, finds in this possession his *standard of value*: looking out from himself upon the others, he honours or he despises, and just as necessarily as he honours his peers, the strong and the reliable (those who can bind themselves by promises) – that is, every one who promises like a sovereign, with difficulty, rarely and slowly, who is sparing with his trusts but confers *honour* by the very fact of trusting, who gives his word as something that can be relied on, because he knows himself strong enough to keep it even in the teeth of disasters, even in the 'teeth of fate' – so with equal necessity will he have the heel of his foot ready for the lean and empty jackasses, who promise when they have no business to do so, and his rod of chastisement ready for the liar, who already breaks his word at the very minute when it is on his lips. The proud knowledge of the extraordinary privilege of *responsibility*, the consciousness of this rare freedom, of this power over himself and over fate, has sunk right down to his innermost depths, and has become an instinct, a dominating instinct – what name will he give to it, to this dominating instinct, if he needs to have a word for it? But there is no doubt about it – the sovereign man calls it his *conscience*.

3

His conscience? One apprehends at once that the idea 'conscience,' which is here seen in its supreme manifestation, supreme in fact to almost the point of strangeness, should already have behind it a long history and evolution. The ability to guarantee one's self with all due pride, and also at the same time to *say yes* to one's self – that is, as has been said, a ripe fruit, but also a *late* fruit: How long must needs this fruit hang sour and bitter on the tree! And for an even longer period there was not a glimpse of such a fruit to be had – no one had taken it on himself to promise it, although everything on the tree was quite ready for it, and everything was maturing for that very consummation. 'How is a memory to be made for the man-animal? How is an impression to be so deeply fixed upon this ephemeral understanding, half dense, and half silly, upon this incarnate forgetfulness, that it will be permanently present?' As one may imagine, this primeval problem was not solved by exactly gentle answers and gentle means; perhaps there is nothing more awful and more sinister in the early history of man than his *system of mnemonics*. 'Something is burnt in so as to remain in his memory: only that which never stops *hurting* remains in his memory.' This is an axiom of the oldest (unfortunately also the longest) psychology in the world. It might even be said that wherever solemnity, seriousness, mystery, and gloomy colours are now found in the life of the men and of nations of the world, there is some *survival* of that horror which was once the universal concomitant of all promises, pledges, and obligations. The past, the past with all its length, depth, and hardness, wafts to us its breath, and bubbles up in us again, when we become 'serious.' When man thinks it necessary to make for himself a memory, he never accomplishes it without blood, tortures, and sacrifice; the most dreadful sacrifices and forfeitures (among them the sacrifice of the first-born), the most loathsome mutilation (for instance, castration), the most cruel rituals of all the religious cults (for all religions are really at bottom systems of cruelty) – all these things originate from that instinct which found in pain its most potent mnemonic. In a certain sense the whole of asceticism is to be ascribed to this: certain ideas have got to be made inextinguishable, omnipresent, 'fixed,' with the object of hypnotizing the whole nervous and intellectual system through these 'fixed ideas' – and the ascetic methods and modes of life are the means of freeing those ideas from the competition of all other ideas so as to make them 'unforgettable.' The worse memory man had, the ghastlier the signs presented by his customs; the severity of the penal laws affords in particular a gauge of the extent of man's difficulty in conquering forgetfulness, and in keeping a few primal postulates of social intercourse ever present to the minds of those who were the slaves of every momentary emotion and every momentary desire. We Germans do certainly not regard ourselves as an especially cruel and hard-hearted nation, still less as an especially casual and happy-go-lucky one; but one has only to look at our old penal ordinances in order to realize what a lot of trouble it takes in the world to evolve a 'nation of thinkers' (I mean: *the* European nation which exhibits at this very day the maximum of reliability, seriousness, bad taste, and positiveness, which has on the strength of these qualities a right to train every kind of European mandarin). These Germans employed terrible means to make for themselves a memory, to enable them to master their rooted plebeian instincts and the brutal crudity of those instincts: think of the old German punishments, for instance, stoning (as far back as the legend, the millstone falls on the head of the guilty man), breaking on the wheel (the most original invention and speciality of the German genius in the sphere of punishment), dart-throwing, tearing, or trampling by horses ('quartering'), boiling the criminal in oil or wine (still prevalent in the fourteenth and fifteenth centuries), the highly popular flaying ('slicing into strips'), cutting the flesh out of the breast; think also of the evil-doer being besmeared with honey, and then exposed to the flies in a blazing sun. It was by the help of such images and precedents that man eventually kept in his memory five or six 'I will nots' with regard to which he had already given his *promise*, so as to be able to enjoy the advantages of society – and verily with the help of this kind of memory man eventually attained 'reason'! Alas! Reason, seriousness, mastery over the emotions, all these gloomy, dismal things which are called reflection, all these privileges and pageantries of humanity: how dear is the price that they have exacted! How much blood and cruelty is the foundation of all 'good things'!

4

But how is it that that other melancholy object, the consciousness of sin, the whole 'bad conscience,' came into the world? And it is here that we turn back to our genealogists of morals. For the second time I say – or have I not said it yet? – that they are worth nothing. Just their own five-spans-long limited modern experience; no knowledge of the past, and no wish to know it; still less a historic instinct, a power of 'second sight' (which is what is really required in this case) – and despite this to go in for the history of morals. It stands to reason that this must needs produce results which are removed from the truth by something more than a respectful distance.

Have these current genealogists of morals ever allowed themselves to have even the vaguest notion, for instance, that the cardinal moral idea of 'ought'* originates from the very material idea of 'owe'? Or that punishment developed as a *retaliation* absolutely independently of any preliminary hypothesis of the freedom or

* The German world '*schuld*' means both debt and guilt. Cp. the English 'owe' and 'ought,' by which I occasionally render the double meaning. – H. B. S.

determination of the will? And this to such an extent, that a *high* degree of civilization was always first necessary for the animal man to begin to make those much more primitive distinctions of 'intentional,' 'negligent,' 'accidental,' 'responsible,' and their contraries, and apply them in the assessing of punishment. That idea – 'the wrong-doer deserves punishment *because* he might have acted otherwise,' in spite of the fact that it is nowadays so cheap, obvious, natural, and inevitable, and that it has had to serve as an illustration of the way in which the sentiment of justice appeared on earth, is in point of fact an exceedingly late, and even refined form of human judgement and inference; the placing of this idea back at the beginning of the world is simply a clumsy violation of the principles of primitive psychology. Throughout the longest period of human history punishment was *never* based on the responsibility of the evil-doer for his action, and was consequently *not* based on the hypothesis that only the guilty should be punished; on the contrary, punishment was inflicted in those days for the same reason that parents punish their children even nowadays, out of anger at an injury that they have suffered, an anger which vents itself mechanically on the author of the injury – but this anger is kept in bounds and modified through the idea that every injury has somewhere or other its *equivalent* price, and can really be paid off, even though it be by means of pain to the author. Whence is it that this ancient deep-rooted and now perhaps ineradicable idea has drawn its strength, this idea of an equivalency between injury and pain? I have already revealed its origin, in the contractual relationship between *creditor* and *ower*, that is as old as the existence of legal rights at all, and in its turn points back to the primary forms of purchase, sale, barter, and trade.

5

The realization of these contractual relations excites, of course (as would be already expected from our previous observations), a great deal of suspicion and opposition towards the primitive society which made or sanctioned them. In this society promises will be made; in this society the object is to provide the promiser with a memory; in this society, so may we suspect, there will be full scope for hardness, cruelty, and pain: the 'ower,' in order to induce credit in his promise of repayment, in order to give a guarantee of the earnestness and sanctity of his promise, in order to drill into his own conscience the duty, the solemn duty, of repayment, will, by virtue of a contract with his creditor to meet the contingency of his not paying, pledge something that he still possesses, something that he still has in his power, for instance, his life or his wife, or his freedom or his body (or under certain religious conditions even his salvation, his soul's welfare, even his peace in the grave; so in Egypt, where the corpse of the ower found even in the grave no rest from the creditor – of course, from the Egyptian standpoint, this peace was a matter of particular importance). But especially has the creditor the power of inflicting on the body of the ower all kinds of pain and torture – the power, for instance, of cutting off from it an amount that appeared proportionate to the greatness of the debt; – this point of view resulted in the universal prevalence at an early date of precise schemes of valuation, frequently horrible in the minuteness and meticulosity of their application, *legally* sanctioned schemes of valuation for individual limbs and parts of the body. I consider it as already a progress, as a proof of a freer, less petty, and more *Roman* conception of law, when the Roman Code of the Twelve Tables decreed that it was immaterial how much or how little the creditors in such a contingency cut off, '*si plus minusve secuerunt, ne fraude esto*.' Let us make the logic of the whole of this equalization process clear; it is strange enough. The equivalence consists in this: instead of an advantage directly compensatory of his injury (that is, instead of an equalization in money, lands, or some kind of chattel), the creditor is granted by way of repayment and compensation a certain *sensation of satisfaction* – the satisfaction of being able to vent, without any trouble, his power on one who is powerless, the delight '*de faire le mal pour le plaisir de le faire*,' the joy in sheer violence: and this joy will be relished in proportion to the lowness and humbleness of the creditor in the social scale, and is quite apt to have the effect of the most delicious dainty, and even seem the foretaste of a higher social position. Thanks to the punishment of the 'ower,' the creditor participates in the rights of the masters. At last he too, for once in a way, attains the edifying consciousness of being able to despise and ill-treat a creature – as an 'inferior' – or at any rate of *seeing* him being despised and ill-treated, in case the actual power of punishment, the administration of punishment, has already become transferred to the 'authorities.' The compensation consequently consists in a claim on cruelty and a right to draw thereon.

6

It is then in *this* sphere of the law of contract that we find the cradle of the whole moral world of the ideas of 'guilt,' 'conscience,' 'duty,' the 'sacredness of duty,' – their commencement, like the commencement of all great things in the world, is thoroughly and continuously saturated with blood. And should we not add that this world has never really lost a certain savour of blood and torture (not even in old Kant; the categorical imperative reeks of cruelty). It was in this sphere likewise that there first became formed that sinister and perhaps now indissoluble association of the ideas of 'guilt' and 'suffering.' To put the question yet again, why can suffering be a compensation for 'owing'? Because the *infliction* of suffering produces the highest degree of happiness, because the injured party will get in exchange for his loss (including his vexation at his loss) an extraordinary counter-pleasure: the *infliction* of suffering – a real *feast*, something that, as I have said, was all the more appreciated the greater the paradox created by the rank and social status of the creditor. These observations are purely conjectural; for, apart from the painful nature of the task, it is hard to plumb such profound depths: the clumsy introduction of the idea of 'revenge' as a connecting-link simply hides and obscures the view instead of rendering it clearer (revenge itself simply leads back again to the identical problem – 'How can the infliction of suffering be a satisfaction?'). In my opinion it is repugnant to the delicacy, and still more to the hypocrisy of tame domestic animals (that is, modern men; that is, ourselves), to realize with all their energy the extent to which *cruelty* constituted the great joy and delight of ancient man, was an ingredient which seasoned nearly all his pleasures, and conversely the extent of the naïveté and innocence with which he manifested his need for cruelty, when he actually made as a matter of principle 'disinterested malice' (or, to use Spinoza's expression, the *sympathia malevolens*) into a *normal* characteristic of man – as consequently something to which the conscience says a hearty yes. The more profound observer has perhaps already had sufficient opportunity for noticing this most ancient and radical joy and delight of mankind; in *Beyond Good and Evil*, Aph. 188 (and even earlier, in *The Dawn of Day*, Aphs. 18, 77, 113), I have cautiously indicated the continually growing spiritualization and 'deification' of cruelty, which pervades the whole history of the higher civilization (and in the larger sense even constitutes it). At any rate the time is not so long past when it was impossible to conceive of royal weddings and national festivals on a grand scale, without executions, tortures, or perhaps an *auto-da-fé*, or similarly to conceive of an aristocratic household, without a creature to serve as a butt for the cruel and malicious baiting of the inmates. (The reader will perhaps remember Don Quixote at the court of the Duchess: we read nowadays the whole of *Don Quixote* with a bitter taste in the mouth, almost with a sensation of torture, a fact which would appear very strange and very incomprehensible to the author and his contemporaries – they read it with the best conscience in the world as the gayest of books; they almost died with laughing at it.) The sight of suffering does one good, the infliction of suffering does one more good – this is a hard maxim, but none the less a fundamental maxim, old, powerful, and 'human, all-too-human'; one, moreover, to which perhaps even the apes as well would subscribe: for it is said that in inventing bizarre cruelties they are giving abundant proof of their future humanity, to which, as it were, they are playing the prelude. Without cruelty, no feast: so teaches the oldest and longest history of man – and in punishment too is there so much of the *festive*.

7

Entertaining, as I do, these thoughts, I am, let me say in parenthesis, fundamentally opposed to helping our pessimists to new water for the discordant and groaning mills of their disgust with life; on the contrary, it should be shown specifically that, at the time when mankind was not yet ashamed of its cruelty, life in the world was brighter than it is nowadays when there are pessimists. The darkening of the heavens over man has always increased in proportion to the growth of man's shame *before man*. The tired pessimistic outlook, the mistrust of the riddle of life, the icy negation of disgusted ennui, all those are not the signs of the *most evil* age of the human race: much rather do they come first to the light of day, as the swamp-flowers, which they are, when the swamp to which they belong, comes into existence – I mean the diseased refinement and moralization, thanks to which the 'animal man' has at last learnt to be ashamed of all his instincts. On the road to angelhood (not to use in this context a harder word) man has developed that dyspeptic stomach and coated tongue, which have made not only the joy and innocence of the animal repulsive to him, but also life itself: so that sometimes he stands with stopped nostrils before his own self, and, like Pope Innocent the Third, makes a black list of his own horrors ('unclean generation, loathsome nutrition when in the maternal body, badness of the matter out of which man develops, awful stench, secretion of saliva, urine, and excrement'). Nowadays, when suffering is always trotted out as the first argument *against* existence, as its most sinister query, it is well to remember the times when men judged on converse principles because they could not dispense with the *infliction* of suffering, and saw therein a magic of the first order, a veritable bait of seduction to life.

Perhaps in those days (this is to solace the weaklings) pain did not hurt so much as it does nowadays: any physician who has treated negroes (granted that these are taken as representative of the prehistoric man) suffering from severe internal inflammations which would bring a European, even though he had the soundest constitution, almost to despair, would be in a position to come to this conclusion. Pain has *not* the same effect with negroes. (The curve of human sensibilities to pain seems indeed to sink in an extraordinary and almost sudden fashion, as soon as one has passed the upper ten thousand or ten millions of over-civilized humanity, and I personally have no doubt that, by comparison with one painful night passed by one single hysterical chit of a cultured woman, the suffering of all the animals taken together who have been put to the question of the knife, so as to give scientific answers, are simply negligible.) We may perhaps be allowed to admit the possibility of the craving for cruelty not necessarily having become really extinct: it only requires, in view of the fact that pain hurts more nowadays, a certain sublimation and subtilization, it must especially be translated to the imaginative and psychic plane, and be adorned with such smug euphemisms, that even the most fastidious and hypocritical conscience could never grow suspicious of their real nature ('Tragic pity' is one of these euphemisms: another is '*les nostalgies de la croix*'). What really raises one's indignation against suffering is not suffering intrinsically, but the senselessness of suffering; such a *senselessness*, however, existed neither in Christianity, which interpreted suffering into a whole mysterious salvation-apparatus, nor in the beliefs of the naive ancient man, who only knew how to find a meaning in suffering from the standpoint of the spectator, or the inflictor of the suffering. In order to get the secret, undiscovered, and unwitnessed suffering out of the world it was almost compulsory to invent gods and a hierarchy of intermediate beings, in short, something which wanders even among secret places, sees even in the dark, and makes a point of never missing an interesting and painful spectacle. It was with the help of such inventions that life got to learn the *tour de force*, which has become part of its stock-in-trade, the *tour de force* of self-justification, of the justification of evil; nowadays this would perhaps require other auxiliary devices (for instance, life as a riddle, life as a problem of knowledge). 'Every evil is justified in the sight of which a god finds edification,' so rang the logic of primitive sentiment – and, indeed, was it only of primitive? The gods conceived as friends of spectacles of cruelty – oh how far does this primeval conception extend even nowadays into our European civilization! One would perhaps like in this context to consult Luther and Calvin. It is at any rate certain that even the Greeks knew no more piquant seasoning for the happiness of their gods than the joys of cruelty. What, do you think, was the mood with which Homer makes his gods look down upon the fates of men? What final meaning have at bottom the Trojan War and similar tragic horrors? It is impossible to entertain any doubt on the point: they were intended as festival games for the gods, and, in so far as the poet is of a more godlike breed than other men, as festival games also for the poets. It was in just this spirit and no other, that at a later date the moral philosophers of Greece conceived the eyes of God as still looking down on the moral struggle, the heroism, and the self-torture of the virtuous; the Heracles of duty was on a stage, and was conscious of the fact; virtue without witnesses was something quite unthinkable for this nation of actors. Must not that philosophic invention, so audacious and so fatal, which was then absolutely new to Europe, the invention of 'free will,' of the absolute spontaneity of man in good and evil, simply have been made for the specific purpose of justifying the idea, that the interest of the gods in humanity and human virtue was *inexhaustible*?

There would never on the stage of this free-will world be a dearth of really new, really novel and exciting situations, plots, catastrophes. A world thought out on completely deterministic lines would be easily guessed by the gods, and would consequently soon bore them – sufficient reason for these *friends of the gods*, the philosophers, not to ascribe to their gods such a deterministic world. The whole of ancient humanity is full of delicate consideration for the spectator, being as it is a world of thorough publicity and theatricality, which could not conceive of happiness without spectacles and festivals. And, as has already been said, even in great *punishment* there is so much which is festive.

8

The feeling of 'ought,' of personal obligation (to take up again the train of our inquiry), has had, as we saw, its origin in the oldest and most original personal relationship that there is, the relationship between buyer and seller, creditor and ower: here it was that individual confronted individual, and that individual *matched himself against* individual. There has not yet been found a grade of civilization so low, as not to manifest some trace of this relationship. Making prices, assessing values, thinking out equivalents, exchanging – all this preoccupied the primal thoughts of man to such an extent that in a certain sense it constituted *thinking* itself: it was here that was trained the oldest form of sagacity, it was here in this sphere that we can perhaps trace the first commencement of man's pride, of his feeling of superiority over other animals. Perhaps our word 'Mensch' (*manas*) still expresses just something of *this* self-pride: man denoted himself as the being who measures values, who values and measures, as the 'assessing' animal *par excellence*. Sale and purchase, together with their psychological concomitants, are older than the origins of any form of social organization and union: it is rather from the most rudimentary form of individual right that the budding consciousness of exchange, commerce, debt, right, obligation, compensation was first transferred to the rudest and most elementary of the social complexes (in their relation to similar complexes), the habit of comparing force with force, together with that of measuring, of calculating. His eye was now focussed to this perspective; and with that ponderous consistency characteristic of ancient thought, which, though set in motion with difficulty, yet proceeds inflexibly along the line on which it has started, man soon arrived at the great generalization, 'everything has its price, *all* can be paid for,' the oldest and most naive moral canon of *justice*, the beginning of all 'kindness,' of all 'equity,' of all 'goodwill,' of all 'objectivity' in the world. Justice in this initial phase is the goodwill among people of about equal power to come to terms with each other, to come to an understanding again by means of a settlement, and with regard to the less powerful, to *compel* them to agree among themselves to a settlement.

9

Measured always by the standard of antiquity (this antiquity, moreover, is present or again possible at all periods), the community stands to its members in that important and radical relationship of creditor to his 'owers.' Man lives in a community, man enjoys the advantages of a community (and what advantages! We occasionally underestimate them nowadays), man lives protected, spared, in peace and trust, secure from certain injuries and enmities, to which the man outside the community, the 'peaceless' man, is exposed – a German understands the original meaning of 'Elend' (*êlend*) – secure because he has entered into pledges and obligations to the community in respect of these very injuries and enmities. What happens *when this is not the case*? The community, the defrauded creditor, will get itself paid, as well as it can, one can reckon on that. In this case the question of the direct damage done by the offender is quite subsidiary: quite apart from this the criminal* is above all a breaker, a breaker of word and covenant *to the whole*, as regards all the advantages and amenities of the communal life in which up to that time he had participated. The criminal is an 'ower' who not only fails to repay the advances and advantages that have been given to him, but even sets out to attack his creditor: consequently he is in the future not only, as is fair, deprived of all these advantages and amenities – he is in addition reminded of the *importance* of those advantages. The wrath of the injured creditor, of the community, puts him back in the wild and outlawed status from which he was previously protected: the community repudiates him – and now every kind of enmity can vent itself on him. Punishment is in this stage of civilization simply the copy, the mimic, of the normal treatment of the hated, disdained, and conquered enemy, who is not only

* German: '*Verbrecher*.' – H.B.S.

deprived of every right and protection but of every mercy; so we have the martial law and triumphant festival of the *væ victis* in all its mercilessness and cruelty. This shows why war itself (counting the sacrificial cult of war) has produced all the forms under which punishment has manifested itself in history.

10

As it grows more powerful, the community tends to take the offences of the individual less seriously, because they are now regarded as being much less revolutionary and dangerous to the corporate existence: the evil-doer is no more outlawed and put outside the pale, the common wrath can no longer vent itself upon him with its old licence – on the contrary, from this very time it is against this wrath, and particularly against the wrath of those directly injured, that the evil-doer is carefully shielded and protected by the community. As, in fact, the penal law develops, the following characteristics become more and more clearly marked: compromise with the wrath of those directly affected by the misdeed; a consequent endeavour to localize the matter and to prevent a further, or indeed a general spread of the disturbance; attempts to find equivalents and to settle the whole matter (*compositio*); above all, the will, which manifests itself with increasing definiteness, to treat every offence as in a certain degree capable of *being paid off*, and consequently, at any rate up to a certain point, to *isolate* the offender from his act. As the power and the self-consciousness of a community increases, so proportionately does the penal law become mitigated; conversely every weakening and jeopardizing of the community revives the harshest forms of that law. The creditor has always grown more humane proportionately as he has grown more rich; finally the amount of injury he can endure without really suffering becomes the criterion of his wealth. It is possible to conceive of a society blessed with so great a *consciousness of its own power* as to indulge in the most aristocratic luxury of letting its wrong-doers go *scot-free*. 'What do my parasites matter to me?' might society say. 'Let them live and flourish!

I am strong enough for it.' The justice which began with the maxim, 'Everything can be paid off, everything must be paid off,' ends with connivance at the escape of those who cannot pay to escape – it ends, like every good thing on earth, by *destroying itself*. The self-destruction of Justice! We know the pretty name it calls itself *Grace!* It remains, as is obvious, the privilege of the strongest, better still, their super-law.

11

A deprecatory word here against the attempts, that have lately been made, to find the origin of justice on quite another basis – namely, on that of *resentment*. Let me whisper a word in the ear of the psychologists, if they would fain study revenge itself at close quarters: this plant blooms its prettiest at present among Anarchists and anti-Semites, a hidden flower, as it has ever been, like the violet, though, forsooth, with another perfume. And as like must necessarily emanate from like, it will not be a matter for surprise that it is just in such circles that we see the birth of endeavours (it is their old birthplace – compare above, First Essay, paragraph 14), to sanctify *revenge* under the name of *justice* (as though Justice were at bottom merely a development of the consciousness of injury), and thus with the rehabilitation of revenge to reinstate generally and collectively all the *reactive* emotions. I object to this last point least of all. It even seems *meritorious* when regarded from the standpoint of the whole problem of biology (from which standpoint the value of these emotions has up to the present been underestimated). And that to which I alone call attention, is the circumstance that it is the spirit of revenge itself, from which develops this new nuance of scientific equity (for the benefit of hate, envy, mistrust, jealousy, suspicion, rancour, revenge). This scientific 'equity' stops immediately and makes way for the accents of deadly enmity and prejudice, so soon as another group of emotions comes on the scene, which in my opinion are of a much higher biological value than these reactions, and consequently have a paramount claim to the valuation and appreciation of science: I mean the really *active* emotions, such as personal and material ambition, and so forth. (E. Dühring, *Value of Life; Course of Philosophy*, and *passim.*) So much against this tendency in general: but as for the particular maxim of Dühring's, that the home of Justice is to be found in the sphere of the reactive feelings, our love of truth compels us drastically to invert his own proposition and to oppose to him this other maxim: the *last* sphere conquered by the spirit of justice is the sphere of the feeling of reaction! When it really comes about that the just man remains just even as regards his injurer (and not merely cold, moderate, reserved, indifferent: being just is always a *positive* state); when, in spite of the strong provocation of personal insult, contempt, and calumny, the lofty and clear objectivity of the just and judging eye (whose glance is as profound as it is gentle) is untroubled, why then we have a piece of perfection, a past master of the world – something, in fact, which it would not be wise to expect, and which should not at any rate be too easily *believed.* Speaking generally, there is no doubt but that even the justest individual only requires a little dose of hostility, malice, or innuendo to drive the blood into his brain and the fairness *from* it. The active man, the attacking, aggressive man is always a hundred degrees nearer to justice than the man who merely reacts; he certainly has no need to adopt the tactics, necessary in the case of the reacting man, of making false and biassed valuations of his object. It is, in point of fact, for this reason that the aggressive man has at all times enjoyed the stronger, bolder, more aristocratic, and also *freer* outlook, the *better* conscience. On the other hand, we already surmise who it really is that has on his conscience the invention of the 'bad conscience' – the resentful man! Finally, let man look at himself in history. In what sphere up to the present has the whole administration of law, the actual need of law, found its earthly home? Perchance in the sphere of the reacting man? Not for a minute: rather in that of the active, strong, spontaneous, aggressive man? I deliberately defy the above-mentioned agitator (who himself makes this self-confession, 'the creed of revenge has run through all my works and endeavours like the red thread of Justice'), and say, that judged historically law in the world represents the very war *against* the reactive feelings, the very war waged on those feelings by the powers of activity and aggression, which devote some of their strength to damming and keeping within bounds this effervescence of hysterical reactivity, and to forcing it to some compromise. Everywhere where justice is practised and justice is maintained, it is to be observed that the stronger power, when confronted with the weaker powers which are inferior to it (whether they be groups, or individuals), searches for weapons to put an end to the senseless fury of resentment, while it carries on its object, partly by taking the victim of resentment out of the clutches of revenge, partly by substituting for revenge a campaign of its own against the enemies of peace and order, partly by finding, suggesting, and occasionally enforcing settlements, partly by standardizing certain equivalents for injuries, to which equivalents the element of resentment is henceforth finally referred. The most drastic measure, however, taken and effectuated by the supreme power, to combat the preponderance of the feelings of spite and vindictiveness – it takes this measure as soon as it is at all strong enough to do so – is the foundation of *law*, the imperative declaration of what in its eyes is to be regarded as just and lawful, and what unjust and unlawful: and while, after the foundation of law, the supreme power treats the aggressive and arbitrary acts of individuals, or of whole groups, as a violation of law, and a revolt against itself, it distracts the feelings of its subjects from the immediate injury inflicted by such a violation, and thus eventually attains the very opposite result to that always desired by revenge, which sees and recognizes nothing but the standpoint of the injured party. From henceforth the eye becomes trained to a more and more *impersonal* valuation of the deed, even the eye of the injured party himself (though this is in the final stage of all, as has been previously remarked) – on this principle 'right' and 'wrong' first manifest themselves after the foundation of law (and *not*, as Dühring maintains, only after the act of violation). To talk of intrinsic right and intrinsic wrong is absolutely nonsensical; intrinsically, an injury, an oppression, an exploitation, an annihilation can be nothing wrong, inasmuch as life is *essentially* (that is, in its cardinal functions) something which functions by injuring, oppressing, exploiting, and annihilating, and is absolutely inconceivable without such a character. It is necessary to make an even more serious confession: viewed from the most advanced biological standpoint, conditions of legality can be only *exceptional conditions*, in that they are partial restrictions of the real life-will, which makes for power, and in that they are subordinated to the life-will's general end as particular means, that is, as means to create *larger* units of strength. A legal organization, conceived of as sovereign and universal, not as a weapon in a fight of complexes of power, but as a weapon *against* fighting, generally something after the style of Dühring's communistic model of treating every will as equal with every other will, would be a principle *hostile to life*, a destroyer and dissolver of man, an outrage on the future of man, a symptom of fatigue, a secret cut to Nothingness.

12

A word more on the origin and end of punishment – two problems which are or ought to be kept distinct, but which unfortunately are usually lumped into one. And what tactics have our moral genealogists employed up to the present in these cases? Their inveterate naïveté. They find out some 'end' in the punishment, for instance, revenge and deterrence, and then in all their innocence set this end at the beginning, as the *causa fiendi* of the punishment, and – they have done the trick. But the patching up of a history of the origin of law is the last use to which the 'End in Law'* ought to be put. Perhaps there is no more pregnant principle for any kind of history than the following, which, difficult though it is to master, *should* none the less be *mastered* in every detail. The origin of the existence of a thing and its final utility, its practical application and incorporation in a system of ends, are *toto cœlo* opposed to each other – everything, anything, which exists and which prevails anywhere,

* An allusion to *Der Zweck im Recht*, by the great German jurist, Professor Ihering.

will always be put to new purposes by a force superior to itself, will be commandeered afresh, will be turned and transformed to new uses; all 'happening' in the organic world consists of *overpowering* and dominating, and again all overpowering and domination is a new interpretation and adjustment, which must necessarily obscure or absolutely extinguish the subsisting 'meaning' and 'end.' The most perfect comprehension of the utility of any physiological organ (or also of a legal institution, social custom, political habit, form in art or in religious worship) does not for a minute imply any simultaneous comprehension of its origin: this may seem uncomfortable and unpalatable to the older men – for it has been the immemorial belief that understanding the final cause or the utility of a thing, a form, an institution, means also understanding the reason for its origin: to give an example of this logic, the eye was made to see, the hand was made to grasp. So even punishment was conceived as invented with a view to punishing. But all ends and all utilities are only *signs* that a Will to Power has mastered a less powerful force, has impressed thereon out of its own self the meaning of a function; and the whole history of a 'Thing,' an organ, a custom, can on the same principle be regarded as a continuous 'sign-chain' of perpetually new interpretations and adjustments, whose causes, so far from needing to have even a mutual connection, sometimes follow and alternate with each other absolutely haphazard. Similarly, the evolution of a 'thing,' of a custom, is anything but its *progressus* to an end, still less a logical and direct *progressus* attained with the minimum expenditure of energy and cost: it is rather the succession of processes of subjugation, more or less profound, more or less mutually independent, which operate on the thing itself; it is, further, the resistance which in each case invariably displayed this subjugation, the Protean wriggles by way of defence and reaction, and, further, the results of successful counter-efforts. The form is fluid, but the meaning is even more so – even inside every individual organism the case is the same: with every genuine growth of the whole, the 'function' of the individual organs becomes shifted – in certain cases a partial perishing of these organs, a diminution of their numbers (for instance, through annihilation of the connecting members), can be a symptom of growing strength and perfection. What I mean is this: even partial *loss of utility*, decay, and degeneration, loss of function and purpose, in a word, death, appertain to the conditions of the genuine *progressus*; which always appears in the shape of a will and way to *greater* power, and is always realised at the expense of innumerable smaller powers. The magnitude of a 'progress' is gauged by the greatness of the sacrifice that it requires: humanity as a mass sacrificed to the prosperity of the one *stronger* species of Man – that *would be* a progress. I emphasize all the more this cardinal characteristic of the historic method, for the reason that in its essence it runs counter to predominant instincts and prevailing taste, which much prefer to put up with absolute casualness, even with the mechanical senselessness of all phenomena, than with the theory of a power-will, in exhaustive play throughout all phenomena. The democratic idiosyncrasy against everything which rules and wishes to rule, the modern *misarchism* (to coin a bad word for a bad thing), has gradually but so thoroughly transformed itself into the guise of intellectualism, the most abstract intellectualism, that even nowadays it penetrates and *has the right* to penetrate step by step into the most exact and apparently the most objective sciences: this tendency has, in fact, in my view already dominated the whole of physiology and biology, and to their detriment, as is obvious, in so far as it has spirited away a radical idea, the idea of true *activity*. The tyranny of this idiosyncrasy, however, results in the theory of 'adaptation' being pushed forward into the van of the argument, exploited; adaptation – that means to say, a second-class activity, a mere capacity for 'reacting'; in fact, life itself has been defined (by Herbert Spencer) as an increasingly effective internal adaptation to external circumstances. This definition, however, fails to realize the real essence of life, its will to power. It fails to appreciate the paramount superiority enjoyed by those plastic forces of spontaneity, aggression, and encroachment with their new interpretations and tendencies, to the operation of which adaptation is only a natural corollary: consequently the sovereign office of the highest functionaries in the organism itself (among which the life-will appears as an active and formative principle) is repudiated. One remembers Huxley's reproach to Spencer of his 'administrative Nihilism': but it is a case of something much *more* than 'administration.'

13

To return to our subject, namely *punishment*, we must make consequently a double distinction: first, the relatively permanent *element*, the custom, the act, the 'drama,' a certain rigid sequence of methods of procedure; on the other hand, the fluid element, the meaning, the end, the expectation which is attached to the operation of such procedure. At this point we immediately assume, *per analogiam* (in accordance with the theory of the historic method, which we have elaborated above), that the procedure itself is something older and earlier than its utilization in punishment, that this utilization was *introduced* and interpreted into the procedure (which had existed for a long time, but whose employment had another meaning), in short, that the case is *different* from that hitherto supposed by our *naïf* genealogists of morals and of law, who thought that the procedure was *invented* for the purpose of punishment, in the same way that the hand had been previously thought to have been invented for the purpose of grasping. With regard to the other element in *punishment*, its fluid element, its meaning, the idea of punishment in a very late stage of civilization (for instance, contemporary Europe) is not content with manifesting merely one meaning, but manifests a whole synthesis 'of meanings.' The past general history of punishment, the history of its employment for the most diverse ends, crystallizes eventually into a kind of unity, which is difficult to analyse into its parts, and which, it is necessary to emphasize, absolutely defies definition. (It is nowadays impossible to say definitely *the precise reason* for punishment: all ideas, in which a whole process is promiscuously comprehended, elude definition; it is only that which has no history, which can be defined.) At an earlier stage, on the contrary, that synthesis of meanings appears much less rigid and much more elastic; we can realize how in each individual case the elements of the synthesis change their value and their position, so that now one element and now another stands out and predominates over the others, nay, in certain cases one element (perhaps the end of deterrence) seems to eliminate all the rest. At any rate, so as to give some idea of the uncertain, supplementary, and accidental nature of the meaning of punishment and of the manner in which one identical procedure can be employed and adapted for the most diametrically opposed objects, I will at this point give a scheme that has suggested itself to mc, a scheme itself based on comparatively small and accidental material. Punishment, as rendering the criminal harmless and incapable of further injury. Punishment, as compensation for the injury sustained by the injured party, in any form whatsoever (including the form of sentimental compensation). Punishment, as an isolation of that which disturbs the equilibrium, so as to prevent the further spreading of the disturbance. Punishment as a means of inspiring fear of those who determine and execute the punishment. Punishment as a kind of compensation for advantages which the wrong-doer has up to that time enjoyed (for example, when he is utilized as a slave in the mines). Punishment, as the elimination of an element of decay (sometimes of a whole branch, as according to the Chinese laws, consequently as a means to the purification of the race, or the preservation of a social type). Punishment as a festival, as the violent oppression and humiliation of an enemy that has at last been subdued. Punishment as a mnemonic, whether for him who suffers the punishment – the so-called 'correction,' or for the witnesses of its administration. Punishment, as the payment of a fee stipulated for by the power which protects the evil-doer from the excesses of revenge. Punishment, as a compromise with the natural phenomenon of revenge, in so far as revenge is still maintained and claimed as a privilege by the stronger races. Punishment as a declaration and measure of war against an enemy of peace, of law, of order, of authority, who is fought by society with the weapons which war provides, as a spirit dangerous to the community, as a breaker of the contract on which the community is based, as a rebel, a traitor, and a breaker of the peace.

14

This list is certainly not complete; it is obvious that punishment is overloaded with utilities of all kinds. This makes it all the more permissible to eliminate one *supposed* utility, which passes, at any rate in the popular mind, for its most essential utility, and which is just what even now provides the strongest support for that faith in punishment which is nowadays for many reasons tottering. Punishment is supposed to have the value of exciting in the guilty the consciousness of guilt; in punishment is sought the proper *instrumentum* of that psychic reaction which becomes known as a 'bad conscience,' 'remorse.' But this theory is even, from the point of view of the present, a violation of reality and psychology: and how much more so is the case when we have to deal with the longest period of man's history, his primitive history! Genuine remorse is certainly extremely rare among wrong-doers and the victims of punishment; prisons and houses of correction are not *the* soil on which this worm of remorse pullulates for choice – this is the unanimous opinion of all conscientious observers, who in many cases arrive at such a judgement with enough reluctance and against their own personal wishes. Speaking generally, punishment hardens and numbs, it produces concentration, it sharpens the consciousness of alienation, it strengthens the power of resistance. When it happens that it breaks the man's energy and brings about a piteous prostration and abjectness, such a result is certainly even less salutary than the average effect of punishment, which is characterized by a harsh and sinister doggedness. The thought of those *prehistoric* millennia brings us to the unhesitating conclusion, that it was simply through punishment that the evolution of the consciousness of guilt was most forcibly retarded – at any rate in the victims of the punishing power. In particular, let us not underestimate the extent to which, by the very sight of the judicial and executive procedure, the wrong-doer is himself prevented from feeling that his deed, the character of his act, is *intrinsically* reprehensible: for he sees clearly the same kind of acts practised in the service of justice, and then called good, and practised with a good conscience; acts such as espionage, trickery, bribery, trapping, the whole intriguing and insidious art of the policeman and the informer – the whole system, in fact, manifested in the different kinds of punishment (a system not excused by passion, but based on principle), of robbing, oppressing, insulting, imprisoning, racking, murdering. All this he sees treated by his judges, not as acts meriting censure and condemnation *in themselves*, but only in a particular context and application. It was not on this soil that grew the 'bad conscience,' that most sinister and interesting plant of our earthly vegetation – in point of fact, throughout a most lengthy period, no suggestion of having to do with a 'guilty man' manifested itself in the consciousness of the man who judged and punished. One had merely to deal with an author of an injury, an irresponsible piece of fate. And the man himself, on whom the punishment subsequently fell like a piece of fate, was occasioned no more of an 'inner pain' than would be occasioned by the sudden approach of some uncalculated event, some terrible natural catastrophe, a rushing, crushing avalanche against which there is no resistance.

15

This truth came insidiously enough to the consciousness of Spinoza (to the disgust of his commentators, who (like Kuno Fischer, for instance) give themselves no end of *trouble* to misunderstand him on this point), when one afternoon (as he sat raking up who knows what memory) he indulged in the question of what was really left for him personally of the celebrated *morsus conscientiæ* – Spinoza, who had relegated 'good and evil' to the sphere of human imagination, and indignantly defended the honour of his 'free' God against those blasphemers who affirmed that God did everything *sub ratione boni* ('but this was tantamount to subordinating God to fate, and would really be the greatest of all absurdities'). For Spinoza the world had returned again to that innocence in which it lay before the discovery of the bad conscience: what, then, had happened to the *morsus conscientiæ*? 'The antithesis of *gaudium*,' said he at last to himself – 'A sadness accompanied by the recollection of a past event which has turned out contrary to all expectation' (*Eth.* III., Propos. XVIII. Schol. i. ii.). Evil-doers have throughout thousands of years felt when overtaken by punishment *exactly like Spinoza*, on the subject of their 'offence': 'here is something which went wrong contrary to my anticipation,' *not* 'I ought not to have done this.' They submitted themselves to punishment, just as one submits one's self to a disease, to a misfortune, or to death, with that stubborn and resigned fatalism which gives the Russians, for instance, even nowadays, the advantage over us Westerners, in the handling of life. If at that period there was a critique of action, the criterion was prudence: the real *effect* of punishment is unquestionably chiefly to be found in a sharpening of the sense of prudence, in a lengthening of the memory, in a will to adopt more of a policy of caution, suspicion, and secrecy; in the recognition that there are many things which are unquestionably beyond one's capacity; in a kind of improvement in self-criticism. The broad effects which can be obtained by punishment in man and beast, are the increase of fear, the sharpening of the sense of cunning, the mastery of the desires: so it is that punishment *tames* man, but does not make him 'better' – it would be more correct even to go so far as to assert the contrary ('Injury makes a man cunning,' says a popular proverb: so far as it makes him cunning, it makes him also bad. Fortunately, it often enough makes him stupid).

16

At this juncture I cannot avoid trying to give a tentative and provisional expression to my own hypothesis concerning the origin of the bad conscience: it is difficult to make it fully appreciated, and it requires continuous meditation, attention, and digestion. I regard the bad conscience as the serious illness which man was bound to contract under the stress of the most radical change which he has ever experienced – that change, when he found himself finally imprisoned within the pale of society and of peace.

Just like the plight of the water-animals, when they were compelled either to become land-animals or to perish, so was the plight of these half-animals, perfectly adapted as they were to the savage life of war, prowling, and adventure – suddenly all their instincts were rendered worthless and 'switched off.' Henceforward they had to walk on their feet – 'carry themselves,' whereas heretofore they had been carried by the water: a terrible heaviness oppressed them. They found themselves clumsy in obeying the simplest directions, confronted with this new and unknown world they had no longer their old guides – the regulative instincts that had led them unconsciously to safety – they were reduced, were those unhappy creatures, to thinking, inferring, calculating, putting together causes and results, reduced to that poorest and most erratic organ of theirs, their 'consciousness.' I do not believe there was ever in the world such a feeling of misery, such a leaden discomfort – further, those old instincts had not immediately ceased their demands! Only it was difficult and rarely possible to gratify them: speaking broadly, they were compelled to satisfy themselves by new and, as it were, hole-and-corner methods. All instincts which do not find a vent without, *turn inwards* – this is what I mean by the growing 'internalization' of man: consequently we have the first growth in man, of what subsequently was called his soul. The whole inner world, originally as thin as if it had been stretched between two layers of skin, burst apart and expanded proportionately, and obtained depth, breadth, and height, when man's external outlet became *obstructed*. These terrible bulwarks, with which the social organization protected itself against the old instincts of freedom (punishments belong pre-eminently to these bulwarks), brought it about that all those instincts of wild, free, prowling man became turned backwards *against man himself*. Enmity, cruelty, the delight in persecution, in surprises, change, destruction – the turning all these instincts against their own possessors: this is the origin of the 'bad conscience.' It was man, who, lacking external enemies and obstacles, and imprisoned as he was in the oppressive narrowness and monotony of custom, in his own impatience lacerated, persecuted, gnawed, frightened, and ill-treated himself; it was this animal in the hands of the tamer, which beat itself against the bars of its cage; it was this being who, pining and yearning for that desert home of which it had been deprived, was compelled to create out of its own self, an adventure, a torture-chamber, a hazardous and perilous desert – it was this fool, this homesick and desperate prisoner – who invented the 'bad conscience.' But thereby he introduced that most grave and sinister illness, from which mankind has not yet recovered, the suffering of man from the disease called man, as the result of a violent breaking from his animal past, the result, as it were, of a spasmodic plunge into a new environment and new conditions of existence, the result of a declaration of war against the old instincts, which up to that time had been the staple of his power, his joy, his formidableness. Let us immediately add that this fact of an animal ego turning against itself, taking part against itself, produced in the world so novel, profound, unheard-of, problematic, inconsistent, and *pregnant* a phenomenon, that the aspect of the world was radically altered thereby. In sooth, only divine spectators could have appreciated the drama that then began, and whose end baffles conjecture as yet – a drama too subtle, too wonderful, too paradoxical to warrant its undergoing a non-sensical and unheeded performance on some random grotesque planet! Henceforth man is to be counted as one of the most unexpected and sensational lucky shots in the game of the 'big baby' of Heracleitus, whether he be called Zeus or Chance – he awakens on his behalf the interest, excitement, hope, almost the confidence, of his being the harbinger and forerunner of something, of man being no end, but only a stage, an interlude, a bridge, a great promise.

17

It is primarily involved in this hypothesis of the origin of the bad conscience, that that alteration was no gradual and no voluntary alteration, and that it did not manifest itself as an organic adaptation to new conditions, but as a break, a jump, a necessity, an inevitable fate, against which there was no resistance and never a spark of resentment. And secondarily, that the fitting of a hitherto unchecked and amorphous population into a fixed form, starting as it had done in an act of violence, could only be accomplished by acts of violence and nothing else – that the oldest 'State' appeared consequently as a ghastly tyranny, a grinding ruthless piece of machinery, which went on working, till this raw material of a semi-animal populace was not only thoroughly kneaded and elastic, but also *moulded*. I used the word 'State': my meaning is self-evident, namely, a herd of blonde beasts of prey, a race of conquerors and masters, which with all its warlike organization and all its organizing power pounces with its terrible claws on a population, in numbers possibly tremendously superior, but as yet formless, as yet nomad. Such is the origin of the 'State.' That fantastic theory that makes it begin with a contract is, I think, disposed of. He who can command, he who is a master by 'nature,' he who comes on the scene forceful in deed and gesture – what has he to do with contracts? Such beings defy calculation, they come like fate, without cause, reason, notice, excuse, they are there like the lightning is there, too terrible, too sudden, too convincing, too 'different,' to be personally even hated. Their work is an instinctive creating and impressing of forms, they are the most involuntary, unconscious artists that there are: their appearance produces instantaneously a scheme of sovereignty which is *live*, in which the functions are partitioned and apportioned, in which above all no part is received or finds a place, until pregnant with a 'meaning' in regard to the whole. They are ignorant of the meaning of guilt, responsibility, consideration, are these born organizers; in them predominates that terrible artist-egoism, that gleams like brass, and that knows itself justified to all eternity, in its work, even as a mother in her child. It is not in *them* that there grew the bad conscience, that is elementary – but it would not have grown *without them*, repulsive growth as it was, it would be missing, had not a tremendous quantity of freedom been expelled from the world by the stress of their hammer-strokes, their artist violence, or been at any rate made invisible and, as it were, *latent*. This *instinct of freedom* forced into being latent – it is already clear – this instinct of freedom forced back, trodden back, imprisoned within itself, and finally only able to find vent and relief in itself; this, only this, is the beginning of the 'bad conscience.'

18

Beware of thinking lightly of this phenomenon, by reason of its initial painful ugliness. At bottom it is the same active force which is at work on a more grandiose scale in those potent artists and organizers, and builds states, which here, internally, on a smaller and pettier scale and with a retrogressive tendency, makes itself a bad science in the 'labyrinth of the breast,' to use Goethe's phrase, and which builds negative ideals; it is, I repeat, that identical *instinct of freedom* (to use my own language, the will to power): only the material, on which this force with all its constructive and tyrannous nature is let loose, is here man himself, his whole old animal self – and *not* as in the case of that more grandiose and sensational phenomenon, the *other* man, *other* men. This secret self-tyranny, this cruelty of the artist, this delight in giving a form to one's self as a piece of difficult, refractory, and suffering material, in burning in a will, a critique, a contradiction, a contempt, a negation; this sinister and ghastly labour of love on the part of a soul, whose will is cloven in two within itself, which makes itself suffer from delight in the infliction of suffering; this wholly *active* bad conscience has finally (as one already anticipates) – true fountainhead as it is of idealism and imagination – produced an abundance of novel and amazing beauty and affirmation, and perhaps has really been the first to give birth to beauty at all. What would beauty be, forsooth, if its contradiction had not first been presented to consciousness, if the ugly had not first said to itself, 'I am ugly'? At any rate, after this hint the problem of how far idealism and beauty can be traced in such opposite ideas as '*selflessness*,' *self-denial*, *self-sacrifice*, becomes less problematical; and indubitably in future we shall certainly know the real and original character of the *delight* experienced by the self-less, the self-denying, the self-sacrificing: this delight is a phase of cruelty. So much provisionally for the origin of 'altruism' as a *moral* value, and the marking out the ground from which this value has grown: it is only the bad conscience, only the will for self-abuse, that provides the necessary conditions for the existence of altruism as a *value*.

19

Undoubtedly the bad conscience is an illness, but an illness like pregnancy is an illness. If we search out the conditions under which this illness reaches its most terrible and sublime zenith, we shall see what really first brought about its entry into the world. But to do this we must take a long breath, and we must first of all go back once again to an earlier point of view. The relation at civil law of the ower to his creditor (which has already been discussed in detail), has been interpreted once again (and indeed in a manner which historically is exceedingly remarkable and suspicious) into a relationship, which is perhaps more incomprehensible to us moderns than to any other era; that is, into the relationship of the *existing* generation to its *ancestors*. Within the original tribal association – we are talking of primitive times – each living generation recognizes a legal obligation towards the earlier generation, and particularly towards the earliest, which founded the family (and this is something much more than a mere sentimental obligation, the existence of which, during the longest period of man's history, is by no means indisputable). There prevails in them the conviction that it is only thanks to sacrifices and efforts of their ancestors, that the race *persists* at all – and that this has to be *paid back* to them by sacrifices and services. Thus is recognized the *owing* of a debt, which accumulates continually by reason of these ancestors never ceasing in their subsequent life as potent spirits to secure by their power new privileges and advantages to the race. Gratis, perchance? But there is no gratis for that raw and 'mean-souled' age. What return can be made? Sacrifice (at first, nourishment, in its crudest sense), festivals, temples, tributes of veneration, above all, obedience – since all customs are, *quâ* works of the ancestors, equally their precepts and commands – are the ancestors ever given enough? This suspicion remains and grows: from time to time it extorts a great wholesale ransom, something monstrous in the way of repayment of the creditor (the notorious sacrifice of the first-born, for example, blood, human blood in any case). The *fear* of ancestors and their power, the consciousness of owing debts to them, necessarily increases, according to this kind of logic, in the exact proportion that the race itself increases, that the race itself becomes more victorious, more independent, more honoured, more feared. This, and not the contrary, is the fact. Each step towards race decay, all disastrous events, all symptoms of degeneration, of approaching disintegration, always *diminish* the fear of the founders' spirit, and whittle away the idea of his sagacity, providence, and potent presence. Conceive this crude kind of logic carried to its climax: it follows that the ancestors of the *most powerful* races must, through the growing fear that they exercise on the imaginations, grow themselves into monstrous dimensions, and become relegated to the gloom of a divine mystery that transcends imagination – the ancestor becomes at last necessarily transfigured into a *god*. Perhaps this is the very origin of the gods, that is, an origin from *fear*! And those who feel bound to add, 'but from piety also,' will have difficulty in maintaining this theory, with regard to the primeval and longest period of the human race. And of course this is even more the case as regards the *middle* period, the formative period of the aristocratic races – the aristocratic races which have given back with interest to their founders, the ancestors (heroes, gods), all those qualities which in the meanwhile have appeared in themselves, that is, the aristocratic qualities. We will later on glance again at the ennobling and promotion of the gods (which of course is totally distinct from their 'sanctification'): let us now provisionally follow to its end the course of the whole of this development of the consciousness of 'owing.'

20

According to the teaching of history, the consciousness of owing debts to the deity by no means came to an end with the decay of the clan organization of society; just as mankind has inherited the ideas of 'good' and 'bad' from the race-nobility (together with its fundamental tendency towards establishing social distinctions), so with the heritage of the racial and tribal gods it has also inherited the incubus of debts as yet unpaid and the desire to discharge them. The transition is effected by those large populations of slaves and bondsmen, who, whether through compulsion or through submission and '*mimicry*,' have accommodated themselves to the religion of their masters; through this channel these inherited tendencies inundate the world. The feeling of owing a debt to the deity has grown continuously for several centuries, always in the same proportion in which the idea of God and the consciousness of God have grown and become exalted among mankind. (The whole history of ethnic fights, victories, reconciliations, amalgamations, everything, in fact, which precedes the eventual classing of all the social elements in each great race-synthesis, are mirrored in the hotch-potch genealogy of their gods, in the legends of their fights, victories, and reconciliations. Progress towards universal empires invariably means progress towards universal deities; despotism, with its subjugation of the independent nobility, always paves the way for some system or other of monotheism.) The appearance of the Christian god, as the record god up to this time, has for that very reason brought equally into the world the record amount of guilt consciousness. Granted that we have gradually started on the *reverse* movement, there is no little probability in the deduction, based on the continuous decay in the belief in the Christian god, to the effect that there also already exists a considerable decay in the human consciousness of owing (ought); in fact, we cannot shut our eyes to the prospect of the complete and eventual triumph of atheism freeing mankind from all this feeling of obligation to their origin, their *causa prima*. Atheism and a kind of second innocence complement and supplement each other.

21

So much for my rough and preliminary sketch of the interrelation of the ideas 'ought' (owe) and 'duty' with the postulates of religion. I have intentionally shelved up to the present the actual moralization of these ideas (their being pushed back into the conscience, or more precisely the interweaving of the *bad* conscience with the idea of God), and at the end of the last paragraph used language to the effect that this moralization did not exist, and that consequently these ideas had necessarily come to an end, by reason of what had happened to their hypothesis, the credence in our 'creditor,' in God. The actual facts differ terribly from this theory. It is with the moralization of the ideas 'ought' and 'duty,' and with their being pushed back into the *bad* conscience, that comes the first actual attempt to *reverse* the direction of the development we have just described, or at any rate to arrest its evolution; it is just at this juncture that the very hope of an eventual redemption *has to* put itself once for all into the prison of pessimism, it is at this juncture that the eye *has to* recoil and rebound in despair from off an adamantine impossibility, it is at this juncture that the ideas 'guilt' and 'duty' have to turn backwards – turn backwards against *whom*? There is no doubt about it; primarily against the 'ower,' in whom the bad conscience now establishes itself, eats, extends, and grows like a polypus throughout its length and breadth, all with such virulence, that at last, with the impossibility of paying the debt, there becomes conceived the idea of the impossibility of paying the penalty, the thought of its inexpiability (the idea of 'eternal punishment') – finally, too, it turns against the 'creditor,' whether found in the *causa prima* of man, the origin of the human race, its sire, who henceforth becomes burdened with a curse ('Adam,' 'original sin,' 'determination of the will'), or in Nature from whose womb man springs, and on whom the responsibility for the principle of evil is now cast ('Diabolization of Nature'), or in existence generally, on this logic an absolute *white elephant*, with which mankind is landed (the Nihilistic flight from life, the demand for Nothingness, or for the opposite of existence, for some other existence, Buddhism and the like) – till suddenly we stand before that paradoxical and awful expedient, through which a tortured humanity has found a temporary alleviation, that stroke of genius called Christianity: God personally immolating himself for the debt of man, God paying himself personally out of a pound of his own flesh, God as the one being who can deliver man from what man had become unable to deliver himself – the creditor playing scapegoat for his debtor, from *love* (can you believe it?), from love of his debtor!

22

The reader will already have conjectured what took place on the stage and *behind the scenes* of this drama. That will for self-torture, that inverted cruelty of the animal man, who, turned subjective and scared into introspection (encaged as he was in 'the State,' as part of his taming process), invented the bad conscience so as to hurt himself, after the *natural* outlet for this will to hurt, became blocked – in other words, this man of the bad conscience exploited the religious hypothesis so as to carry his martyrdom to the ghastliest pitch of agonized intensity. Owing something to *God*: this thought becomes his instrument of torture. He apprehends in God the most extreme antitheses that he can find to his own characteristic and ineradicable animal instincts, he himself gives a new interpretation to these animal instincts as being against what he 'owes' to God (as enmity, rebellion, and revolt against the 'Lord,' the 'Father,' the 'Sire,' the 'Beginning of the world'), he places himself between the horns of the dilemma, 'God' and 'Devil.' Every negation which he is inclined to utter to himself, to the nature, naturalness, and reality of his being, he whips into an ejaculation of 'yes,' uttering it as something existing, living, efficient, as being God, as the holiness of God, the judgement of God, as the hangmanship of God, as transcendence, as eternity, as unending torment, as hell, as infinity of punishment and guilt. This is a kind of madness of the will in the sphere of psychological cruelty which is absolutely unparalleled: man's *will* to find himself guilty and blameworthy to the point of inexpiability, his *will* to think of himself as punished, without the punishment ever being able to balance the guilt, his *will* to infect and to poison the fundamental basis of the universe with the problem of punishment and guilt, in order to cut off once and for all any escape out of this labyrinth of 'fixed ideas,' his will for rearing an ideal – that of the 'holy God' – face to face with which he can have tangible proof of his own un-worthiness. Alas for this mad melancholy beast man! What phantasies invade it, what paroxysms of perversity, hysterical senselessness, and *mental bestiality* break out immediately, at the very slightest check on its being the beast of action. All this is excessively interesting, but at the same time tainted with a black, gloomy, enervating melancholy, so that a forcible veto must be invoked against looking too long into these abysses. Here is *disease*, undubitably, the most ghastly disease that has as yet played havoc among men: and he who can still hear (but man turns now deaf ears to such sounds), how in this night of torment and nonsense there has rung out the cry of *love*, the cry of the most passionate ecstasy, of redemption in *love*, he turns away gripped by an invincible horror – in man there is so much that is ghastly – too long has the world been a mad-house.

23

Let this suffice once for all concerning the origin of the 'holy God.' The fact that *in itself* the conception of gods is not bound to lead necessarily to this degradation of the imagination (a temporary representation of whose vagaries we felt bound to give), the fact that there exist *nobler* methods of utilizing the invention of gods than in this self-crucifixion and self-degradation of man, in which the last two thousand years of Europe have been past masters – these facts can fortunately be still perceived from every glance that we cast at the Grecian gods, these mirrors of noble and grandiose men, in which the *animal* in man felt itself deified, and did *not* devour itself in subjective frenzy. These Greeks long utilized their gods as simple buffers against the 'bad conscience' – so that they could continue to enjoy their freedom of soul: this, of course, is diametrically opposed to Christianity's theory of its god. They went *very far* on this principle, did these splendid and lion-hearted children; and there is no lesser authority than that of the Homeric Zeus for making them realize occasionally that they are taking life too casually. 'Wonderful,' says he on one occasion – it has to do with the case of Ægistheus, a *very* bad case indeed –

> 'Wonderful how they grumble, the mortals against the immortals,
> *Only from us*, they presume, *comes evil*, but in their folly,
> Fashion they, spite of fate, the doom of their own disaster.'

Yet the reader will note and observe that this Olympian spectator and judge is far from being angry with them and thinking evil of them on this score. 'How *foolish* they are,' so thinks he of the misdeeds of mortals – and 'folly,' 'imprudence,' 'a little brain disturbance,' and nothing more, are what the Greeks, even of the strongest, bravest period, have admitted to be the ground of much that is evil and fatal. Folly, *not* sin, do you understand?... But even this brain disturbance was a problem – 'Come, how is it even possible? How could it have really got in brains like ours, the brains of men of aristocratic ancestry, of men of fortune, of men of good natural endowments, of men of the best society, of men of nobility and virtue?' This was the question that for century on century the aristocratic Greek put to himself when confronted with every (to him incomprehensible) outrage and sacrilege with which one of his peers had polluted himself. 'It must be that a god had infatuated him,' he would say at last, nodding his head. This solution is *typical* of the Greeks... accordingly the gods in those times subserved the functions of justifying man to a certain extent even in evil – in those days they took upon themselves not the punishment, but, what is more noble, the guilt.

24

I conclude with three queries, as you will see. 'Is an ideal actually set up here, or is one pulled down?' I am perhaps asked.... But have ye sufficiently asked yourselves how dear a payment has the setting up of *every* ideal in the world exacted? To achieve that consummation how much truth must always be traduced and misunderstood, how many lies must be sanctified, how much conscience has got to be disturbed, how many pounds of 'God' have got to be sacrificed every time? To enable a sanctuary to be set up *a sanctuary has got to be destroyed*: that is a law – show me an instance where it has not been fulfilled!... We modern men, we inherit the immemorial tradition of vivisecting the conscience, and practising cruelty to our animal selves. That is the sphere of our most protracted training, perhaps of our artistic prowess, at any rate of our dilettantism and our perverted taste. Man has for too long regarded his natural proclivities with an 'evil eye,' so that eventually they have become in his system affiliated to a bad conscience. A converse endeavour would be intrinsically feasible – but who is strong enough to attempt it? – namely, to affiliate to the 'bad conscience' all those *unnatural* proclivities, all those transcendental aspirations, contrary to sense, instinct, nature, and animalism – in short, all past and present ideals, which are all ideals opposed to life, and traducing the world. To whom is one to turn nowadays with *such* hopes and pretensions? It is just the *good* men that we should thus bring about our ears; and in addition, as stands to reason, the indolent, the hedgers, the vain, the hysterical, the tired.... What is more offensive or more thoroughly calculated to alienate, than giving any hint of the exalted severity with which we treat ourselves? And again how conciliatory, how full of love does all the world show itself towards us so soon as we do as all the world does, and 'let ourselves go' like all the world. For such a consummation we need spirits of *different* calibre than seems really feasible in this age; spirits rendered potent through wars and victories, to whom conquest, adventure, danger, even pain, have become a need; for such a consummation we need habituation to sharp, rare air, to winter wanderings, to literal and metaphorical ice and mountains; we even need a kind of sublime malice, a supreme and most self-conscious insolence of knowledge, which is the appanage of great health; we need (to summarise the awful truth) just this *great health*!

Is this even feasible today?... But some day, in a stronger age than this rotting and introspective present, must he in sooth come to us, even the *redeemer* of great love and scorn, the creative spirit, rebounding by the impetus of his own force back again away from every transcendental plane and dimension, he whose solitude is misunderstanded of the people, as though it were a flight *from* reality; while actually it is only his diving, burrowing, and penetrating *into* reality, so that when he comes again to the light he can at once bring about by these means the *redemption* of this reality; its redemption from the curse which the old ideal has laid upon it. This man of the future, who in this wise will redeem us from the old ideal, as he will from that ideal's necessary corollary of great nausea, will to nothingness, and Nihilism; this tocsin of noon and of the great verdict, which renders the will again free, who gives back to the world its goal and to man his hope, this Antichrist and Antinihilist, this conqueror of God and of Nothingness – *he must one day come.*

25

But what am I talking of? Enough! Enough? At this juncture I have only one proper course, silence: otherwise trespass on a domain open alone to one who is younger than I, one stronger, more '*future*' than I – open alone to *Zarathustra, Zarathustra the godless.*

THIRD ESSAY.

WHAT IS THE MEANING OF ASCETIC IDEALS?

'Careless, mocking, forceful – so does wisdom wish us: she is a woman, and never loves any one but a warrior.'

Thus Spake Zarathustra.

WHAT IS THE MEANING OF ASCETIC IDEALS?

1

What is the meaning of ascetic ideals? In artists, nothing, or too much; in philosophers and scholars, a kind of 'flair' and instinct for the conditions most favourable to advanced intellectualism; in women, at best an *additional* seductive fascination, a little *morbidezza* on a fine piece of flesh, the angelhood of a fat, pretty animal; in physiological failures and whiners (in the *majority* of mortals), an attempt to pose as 'too good' for this world, a holy form of debauchery, their chief weapon in the battle with lingering pain and ennui; in priests, the actual priestly faith, their best engine of power, and also the supreme authority for power; in saints, finally a pretext for hibernation, their *novissima gloriæ cupido*, their peace in nothingness ('God'), their form of madness.

But in the very fact that the ascetic ideal has meant so much to man, lies expressed the fundamental feature of man's will, his *horror vacui: he needs a goal* – and he will sooner will nothingness than not will at all. Am I not understood? Have I not been understood? 'Certainly not, sir?' Well, let us begin at the beginning.

2

What is the meaning of ascetic ideals? Or, to take an individual case in regard to which I have often been consulted, what is the meaning, for example, of an artist like Richard Wagner paying homage to chastity in his old age? He had always done so, of course, in a certain sense, but it was not till quite the end, that he did so in an ascetic sense. What is the meaning of this 'change of attitude,' this radical revolution in his attitude – for that was what it was? Wagner veered thereby straight round into his own opposite. What is the meaning of an artist veering round into his own opposite? At this point (granted that we do not mind stopping a little over this question), we immediately call to mind the best, strongest, gayest, and boldest period, that there perhaps ever was in Wagner's life: that was the period, when he was genuinely and deeply occupied with the idea of 'Luther's Wedding.' Who knows what chance is responsible for our now having the *Meistersingers* instead of this wedding music? And how much in the latter is perhaps just an echo of the former? But there is no doubt but that the theme would have dealt with the praise of chastity. And certainly it would also have dealt with the praise of sensuality, and even so, it would seem quite in order, and even so, it would have been equally Wagnerian. For there is no necessary antithesis between chastity and sensuality: every good marriage, every authentic heart-felt love transcends this antithesis. Wagner would, it seems to me, have done well to have brought this *pleasing* reality home once again to his Germans, by means of a bold and graceful 'Luther Comedy,' for there were and are among the Germans many revilers of sensuality; and perhaps Luther's greatest merit lies just in the fact of his having had the courage of his *sensuality* (it used to be called, prettily enough, 'evangelistic freedom'). But even in those cases where that antithesis between chastity and sensuality does exist, there has fortunately been for some time no necessity for it to be in any way a tragic antithesis. This should, at any rate, be the case with all beings who are sound in mind and body, who are far from reckoning their delicate balance between 'animal' and 'angel,' as being on the face of it one of the principles opposed to existence – the most subtle and brilliant spirits, such as Goethe, such as Hafiz, have even seen in this a *further* charm of life. Such 'conflicts' actually allure one to life. On the other hand, it is only too clear that when once these ruined swine are reduced to worshipping chastity – and there are such swine – they only see and worship in it the antithesis to themselves, the antithesis to ruined swine. Oh what a tragic grunting and eagerness! You can just think of it – they worship that painful and superfluous contrast, which Richard Wagner in his latter days undoubtedly wished to set to music, and to place on the stage! '*For what purpose, forsooth?*' as we may reasonably ask. What did the swine matter to him; what do they matter to us?

3

At this point it is impossible to beg the further question of what he really had to do with that manly (ah, so unmanly) country bumpkin, that poor devil and natural, Parsifal, whom he eventually made a Catholic by such fraudulent devices. What? Was this Parsifal really meant *seriously*? One might be tempted to suppose the contrary, even to wish it – that the Wagnerian Parsifal was meant joyously, like a concluding play of a trilogy or satyric drama, in which Wagner the tragedian wished to take farewell of us, of himself, above all of *tragedy*, and to do so in a manner that should be quite fitting and worthy, that is, with an excess of the most extreme and flippant parody of the tragic itself, of the ghastly earthly seriousness and earthly woe of old – a parody of that *most crude phase* in the unnaturalness of the ascetic ideal, that had at length been overcome. That, as I have said, would have been quite worthy of a great tragedian; who like every artist first attains the supreme pinnacle of his greatness when he can look *down* into himself and his art, when he can *laugh* at himself. Is Wagner's Parsifal his secret laugh of superiority over himself, the triumph of that supreme artistic freedom and artistic transcendency which he has at length attained. We might, I repeat, wish it were so, for what can Parsifal, *taken seriously*, amount to? Is it really necessary to see in it (according to an expression once used against me) the product of an insane hate of knowledge, mind, and flesh? A curse on flesh and spirit in one breath of hate? An apostasy and reversion to the morbid Christian and obscurantist ideals? And finally a self-negation and self-elimination on the part of an artist, who till then had devoted all the strength of his will to the contrary, namely, the *highest* artistic expression of soul and body. And not only of his art; of his life as well. Just remember with what enthusiasm Wagner followed in the footsteps of Feuerbach. Feuerbach's motto of 'healthy sensuality' rang in the ears of Wagner during the thirties and forties of the century, as it did in the ears of many Germans (they dubbed themselves '*Young* Germans'), like the word of redemption. Did he eventually *change his mind* on the subject? For it seems at any rate that he eventually wished to *change his teaching* on that subject ... and not only is that the case with the Parsifal trumpets on the stage: in the melancholy, cramped, and embarrassed lucubrations of his later years, there are a hundred places in which there are manifestations of a secret wish and will, a despondent, uncertain, unavowed will to preach actual retrogression, conversion, Christianity, medievalism, and to say to his disciples, 'All is vanity! Seek salvation elsewhere!' Even the 'blood of the Redeemer' is once invoked.

4

Let me speak out my mind in a case like this, which has many painful elements – and it is a typical case: it is certainly best to separate an artist from his work so completely that he cannot be taken as seriously as his work. He is after all merely the presupposition of his work, the womb, the soil, in certain cases the dung and manure, on which and out of which it grows – and consequently, in most cases, something that must be forgotten if the work itself is to be enjoyed. The insight into the *origin* of a work is a matter for psychologists and vivisectors, but never either in the present or the future for the aesthetes, the artists. The author and creator of Parsifal was as little spared the necessity of sinking and living himself into the terrible depths and foundations of medieval soul-contrasts, the necessity of a malignant abstraction from all intellectual elevation, severity, and discipline, the necessity of a kind of mental *perversity* (if the reader will pardon me such a word), as little as a pregnant woman is spared the horrors and marvels of pregnancy, which, as I have said, must be forgotten if the child is to be enjoyed. We must guard ourselves against the confusion, into which an artist himself would fall only too easily (to employ the English terminology) out of psychological 'contiguity'; as though the artist himself actually *were* the object which he is able to represent, imagine, and express. In point of fact, the position is that even if he conceived he were such an object, he would certainly not represent, conceive, express it. Homer would not have created an Achilles, nor Goethe a Faust, if Homer had been an Achilles or if Goethe had been a Faust. A complete and perfect artist is to all eternity separated from the 'real,' from the actual; on the other hand, it will be appreciated that he can at times get tired to the point of despair of this eternal 'unreality' and falseness of his innermost being – and that he then sometimes attempts to trespass on to the most forbidden ground, on reality, and attempts to have real *existence*. With what success? The success will be guessed – it is the *typical velleity* of the artist; the same velleity to which Wagner fell a victim in his old age, and for which he had to pay so dearly and so fatally (he lost thereby his most valuable friends). But after all, quite apart from this velleity, who would not wish emphatically for Wagner's own sake that he had taken farewell of us and of his art in a *different* manner, not with a *Parsifal*, but in more victorious, more self-confident, more Wagnerian style – a style less misleading, a style less ambiguous with regard to his whole meaning, less Schopenhauerian, less Nihilistic?...

5

What, then, is the meaning of ascetic ideals? In the case of an artist we are getting to understand their meaning: *Nothing at all*... or so much that it is as good as nothing at all. Indeed, what is the use of them? Our artists have for a long time past not taken up a sufficiently independent attitude, either in the world or against it, to warrant their valuations and the changes in these valuations exciting interest. At all times they have played the valet of some morality, philosophy, or religion, quite apart from the fact that unfortunately they have often enough been the inordinately supple courtiers of their clients and patrons, and the inquisitive toadies of the powers that are existing, or even of the new powers to come. To put it at the lowest, they always need a rampart, a support, an already constituted authority: artists never stand by themselves, standing alone is opposed to their deepest instincts. So, for example, did *Richard Wagner* take, 'when the time had come,' the philosopher Schopenhauer for his covering man in front, for his rampart. Who would consider it even thinkable, that he would have had the *courage* for an ascetic ideal, without the support afforded him by the philosophy of Schopenhauer, without the authority of Schopenhauer, which *dominated* Europe in the seventies? (This is without consideration of the question whether an artist without the milk* of an orthodoxy would have been possible at all.) This brings us to the more serious question: What is the meaning of a real *philosopher* paying homage to the ascetic ideal, a really self-dependent intellect like Schopenhauer, a man and knight with a glance of bronze, who has the courage to be himself, who knows how to stand alone without first waiting for men who cover him in front, and the nods of his superiors? Let us now consider at once the remarkable attitude of Schopenhauer towards *art*, an attitude which has even a fascination for certain types. For that is obviously the reason why Richard Wagner *all at once* went over to Schopenhauer (persuaded thereto, as one knows, by a poet, Herwegh), went over so completely that there ensued the cleavage of a complete theoretic contradiction between his earlier and his later aesthetic faiths – the earlier, for example, being expressed in *Opera and Drama*, the later in the writings which he published from 1870 onwards. In particular, Wagner from that time onwards (and this is the volte-face which alienates us the most) had no scruples about changing his judgement concerning the value and position of music itself. What did he care if up to that time he had made of music a means, a medium, a 'woman,' that in order to thrive needed an end, a man – that is, the drama? He suddenly realized that *more* could be effected by the novelty of the Schopenhauerian theory in *majorem musicæ gloriam* – that is to say, by means of the *sovereignty* of music, as Schopenhauer

* An allusion to the celebrated monologue in William Tell.

understood it; music abstracted from and opposed to all the other arts, music as the independent art-in-itself, *not* like the other arts, affording reflections of the phenomenal world, but rather the language of the will itself, speaking straight out of the 'abyss' as its most personal, original, and direct manifestation. This extraordinary rise in the value of music (a rise which seemed to grow out of the Schopenhauerian philosophy) was at once accompanied by an unprecedented rise in the estimation in which the *musician* himself was held: he became now an oracle, a priest, nay, more than a priest, a kind of mouthpiece for the 'intrinsic essence of things,' a telephone from the other world – from henceforward he talked not only music, did this ventriloquist of God, he talked metaphysic; what wonder that one day he eventually talked *ascetic ideals*.

6

Schopenhauer has made use of the Kantian treatment of the aesthetic problem – though he certainly did not regard it with the Kantian eyes. Kant thought that he showed honour to art when he favoured and placed in the foreground those of the predicates of the beautiful, which constitute the honour of knowledge: impersonality and universality. This is not the place to discuss whether this was not a complete mistake; all that I wish to emphasize is that Kant, just like other philosophers, instead of envisaging the aesthetic problem from the standpoint of the experiences of the artist (the creator), has only considered art and beauty from the standpoint of the spectator, and has thereby imperceptibly imported the spectator himself into the idea of the 'beautiful'! But if only the philosophers of the beautiful had sufficient knowledge of this 'spectator'! Knowledge of him as a great fact of personality, as a great experience, as a wealth of strong and most individual events, desires, surprises, and raptures in the sphere of beauty! But, as I feared, the contrary was always the case. And so we get from our philosophers, from the very beginning, definitions on which the lack of a subtler personal experience squats like a fat worm of crass error, as it does on Kant's famous definition of the beautiful. 'That is beautiful,' says Kant, 'which pleases without interesting.' Without interesting! Compare this definition with this other one, made by a real 'spectator' and 'artist' – by Stendhal, who once called the beautiful *une promesse de bonheur*. Here, at any rate, the one point which Kant makes prominent in the aesthetic position is repudiated and eliminated – *le désintéressement*. Who is right, Kant or Stendhal? When, forsooth, our aesthetes never get tired of throwing into the scales in Kant's favour the fact that under the magic of beauty men can look at even naked female statues 'without interest,' we can certainly laugh a little at their expense: in regard to this ticklish point the experiences of *artists* are more 'interesting,' and at any rate Pygmalion was not necessarily an 'unaesthetic man.' Let us think all the better of the innocence of our aesthetes, reflected as it is in such arguments; let us, for instance, count to Kant's honour the country-parson naïveté of his doctrine concerning the peculiar character of the sense of touch! And here we come back to Schopenhauer, who stood in much closer neighbourhood to the arts than did Kant, and yet never escaped outside the pale of the Kantian definition; how was that? The circumstance is marvellous enough: he interprets the expression, 'without interest,' in the most personal fashion, out of an experience which must in his case have been part and parcel of his regular routine. On few subjects does Schopenhauer speak with such certainty as on the working of aesthetic contemplation: he says of it that it simply counteracts sexual interest, like lupulin and camphor; he never gets tired of glorifying this escape from the 'Life-will' as the great advantage and utility of the aesthetic state. In fact, one is tempted to ask if his fundamental conception of Will and Idea, the thought that there can only exist freedom from the 'will' by means of 'idea,' did not originate in a generalization from this sexual experience. (In all questions concerning the Schopenhauerian philosophy, one should, by the bye, never lose sight of the consideration that it is the conception of a youth of twenty-six, so that it participates not only in what is peculiar to Schopenhauer's life, but in what is peculiar to that special period of his life.) Let us listen, for instance, to one of the most expressive among the countless passages which he has written in honour of the aesthetic state (*World as Will and*

Idea, i. 231); let us listen to the tone, the suffering, the happiness, the gratitude, with which such words are uttered: 'This is the painless state which Epicurus praised as the highest good and as the state of the gods; we are during that moment freed from the vile pressure of the will, we celebrate the Sabbath of the will's hard labour, the wheel of Ixion stands still.' What vehemence of language! What images of anguish and protracted revulsion! How almost pathological is that temporal antithesis between 'that moment' and everything else, the 'wheel of Ixion,' 'the hard labour of the will,' 'the vile pressure of the will.' But granted that Schopenhauer was a hundred times right for himself personally, how does that help our insight into the nature of the beautiful? Schopenhauer has described one effect of the beautiful – the calming of the will – but is this effect really normal? As has been mentioned, Stendhal, an equally sensual but more happily constituted nature than Schopenhauer, gives prominence to another effect of the 'beautiful.' 'The beautiful *promises* happiness.' To him it is just the *excitement* of the 'will' (the 'interest') by the beauty that seems the essential fact. And does not Schopenhauer ultimately lay himself open to the objection, that he is quite wrong in regarding himself as a Kantian on this point, that he has absolutely failed to understand in a Kantian sense the Kantian definition of the beautiful – that the beautiful pleased him as well by means of an interest, by means, in fact, of the strongest and most personal interest of all, that of the victim of torture who escapes from his torture? And to come back again to our first question, 'What is the *meaning* of a philosopher paying homage to ascetic ideals?' We get now, at any rate, a first hint; he wishes to *escape from a torture*.

7

Let us beware of making dismal faces at the word 'torture' – there is certainly in this case enough to deduct, enough to discount – there is even something to laugh at. For we must certainly not underestimate the fact that Schopenhauer, who in practice treated sexuality as a personal enemy (including its tool, woman, that '*instrumentum diaboli*'), needed enemies to keep him in a good humour; that he loved grim, bitter, blackish-green words; that he raged for the sake of raging, out of passion; that he would have grown ill, would have become a *pessimist* (for he was not a pessimist, however much he wished to be), without his enemies, without Hegel, woman, sensuality, and the whole 'will for existence' 'keeping on.' Without them Schopenhauer would not have 'kept on,' that is a safe wager; he would have run away: but his enemies held him fast, his enemies always enticed him back again to existence, his wrath was just as theirs' was to the ancient Cynics, his balm, his recreation, his recompense, his *remedium* against disgust, his *happiness*. So much with regard to what is most personal in the case of Schopenhauer; on the other hand, there is still much which is typical in him – and only now we come back to our problem. It is an accepted and indisputable fact, so long as there are philosophers in the world and wherever philosophers have existed (from India to England, to take the opposite poles of philosophic ability), that there exists a real irritation and rancour on the part of philosophers towards sensuality. Schopenhauer is merely the most eloquent, and if one has the ear for it, also the most fascinating and enchanting outburst. There similarly exists a real philosophic bias and affection for the whole ascetic ideal; there should be no illusions on this score. Both these feelings, as has been said, belong to the type; if a philosopher lacks both of them, then he is – you may be certain of it – never anything but a 'pseudo.' What does this mean? For this state of affairs must first be interpreted: in itself it stands there stupid, to all eternity, like any 'Thing-in-itself.' Every animal, including *la bête philosophe*, strives instinctively after an *optimum* of favourable conditions, under which he can let his whole strength have play, and achieves his maximum consciousness of power; with equal instinctiveness, and with a fine perceptive flair which is superior to any reason, every animal shudders mortally at every kind of disturbance and hindrance which obstructs or could obstruct his way to that optimum (it is not his way to happiness of which I am talking, but his way to power, to action, the most powerful action, and in point of fact in many cases his way to unhappiness). Similarly, the philosopher shudders mortally at *marriage*, together with all that could persuade him to it – marriage as a fatal hindrance on the way to the *optimum*. Up to the present what great philosophers have been married? Heracleitus, Plato, Descartes, Spinoza, Leibnitz, Kant, Schopenhauer – they were not married, and, further, one cannot *imagine* them as married. A married philosopher belongs to *comedy*, that is my rule; as for that exception of a Socrates – the malicious Socrates married himself, it seems, *ironice*, just to prove this *very* rule. Every philosopher would say, as Buddha said, when the birth of a son was announced to him: 'Râhoula has been born to me, a fetter has been forged for me' (Râhoula means here 'a little demon'); there must come an hour of reflection to every 'free spirit' (granted that he has had previously an hour of thoughtlessness), just as one came once to the same Buddha: 'Narrowly cramped,' he reflected, 'is life in the house; it is a place of uncleanness; freedom is found in leaving the house.' Because he thought like this, he left the house. So many bridges to *independence* are shown in the ascetic ideal, that the philosopher cannot refrain from exultation and clapping of hands when he hears the history of all those resolute ones, who on one day uttered a nay to all servitude and went into some *desert*; even granting that they were only strong asses, and the absolute opposite of strong minds. What, then, does the ascetic ideal mean in a philosopher? This is my answer – it will have been guessed long ago: when he sees this ideal the philosopher smiles because he sees therein an *optimum* of the conditions of the highest and boldest intellectuality; he does not thereby deny 'existence,' he rather affirms thereby *his* existence and *only* his existence, and this perhaps to the point of not being far off the blasphemous wish, *pereat mundus, fiat philosophia, fiat philosophus, fiam!*...

8

These philosophers, you see, are by no means uncorrupted witnesses and judges of the *value* of the ascetic ideal. They think *of themselves* – what is the 'saint' to them? They think of that which to them personally is most indispensable; of freedom from compulsion, disturbance, noise: freedom from business, duties, cares; of clear head; of the dance, spring, and flight of thoughts; of good air – rare, clear, free, dry, as is the air on the heights, in which every animal creature becomes more intellectual and gains wings; they think of peace in every cellar; all the hounds neatly chained; no baying of enmity and uncouth rancour; no remorse of wounded ambition; quiet and submissive internal organs, busy as mills, but unnoticed; the heart alien, transcendent, future, posthumous – to summarize, they mean by the ascetic ideal the joyous asceticism of a deified and newly fledged animal, sweeping over life rather than resting. We know what are the three great catch-words of the ascetic ideal: poverty, humility, chastity; and now just look closely at the life of all the great fruitful inventive spirits – you will always find again and again these three qualities up to a certain extent. *Not* for a minute, as is self-evident, as though, perchance, they were part of their virtues – what has this type of man to do with virtues? – but as the most essential and natural conditions of their *best* existence, their *finest* fruitfulness. In this connection it is quite possible that their predominant intellectualism had first to curb an unruly and irritable pride, or an insolent sensualism, or that it had all its work cut out to maintain its wish for the 'desert' against perhaps an inclination to luxury and dilettantism, or similarly against an extravagant liberality of heart and hand. But their intellect did effect all this, simply because it was the *dominant* instinct, which carried through its orders in the case of all the other instincts. It effects it still; if it ceased to do so, it would simply not be dominant. But there is not one iota of 'virtue' in all this. Further, the *desert*, of which I just spoke, in which the strong, independent, and well-equipped spirits retreat into their hermitage – oh, how different is it from the cultured classes' dream of a desert! In certain cases, in fact, the cultured classes themselves are the desert. And it is certain that all the actors of the intellect would not endure this desert for a minute. It is nothing like romantic and Syrian enough for them, nothing like enough of a stage desert! Here as well there are plenty of asses, but at this point the resemblance ceases. But a desert nowadays is something like this – perhaps a deliberate obscurity; a getting-out-of the way of one's self; a fear of noise, admiration, papers, influence; a little office, a daily task, something that hides rather than brings to light; sometimes associating with harmless, cheerful beasts and fowls, the sight of which refreshes; a mountain for company, but not a dead one, one with *eyes* (that is, with lakes); in certain cases even a room in a crowded hotel where one can reckon on not being recognized, and on being able to talk with impunity to every one: here is the desert – oh, it is lonely enough, believe me! I grant that when Heracleitus retreated to the courts and cloisters of the colossal temple of Artemis, that 'wilderness' was worthier; why do we *lack* such temples? (perchance we do not lack them: I just think of my splendid study in the *Piazza di San Marco*, in spring, of course, and in the morning, between ten and twelve). But that which Heracleitus shunned is still just what we too avoid nowadays: the noise and democratic babble of the Ephesians, their politics, their news from the 'empire' (I mean, of course, Persia), their market-trade in 'the things of today' – for there is one thing from which we philosophers especially need a rest – from the things of 'today.' We honour the silent, the cold, the noble, the far, the past, everything, in fact, at the sight of which the soul is not bound to brace itself up and defend itself – something with which one can speak without *speaking aloud*. Just listen now to the tone a spirit has when it speaks; every spirit has its own tone and loves its own tone. That thing yonder, for instance, is bound to be an agitator, that is, a hollow head, a hollow mug: whatever may go into him, everything comes back from him dull and thick, heavy with the echo of the great void. That spirit yonder nearly always speaks hoarse: has he, perchance, *thought* himself hoarse? It may be so – ask the physiologists – but he who thinks in *words*, thinks as a speaker and not as a thinker (it shows that he does not think of objects or think objectively, but only of his relations with objects – that, in point of fact, he only thinks of himself and his audience). This third one speaks aggressively, he comes too near our body, his breath blows on us – we shut our mouth involuntarily, although he speaks to us through a book: the tone of his style supplies the reason – he has no time, he has small faith in himself, he finds expression now or never. But a spirit who is sure of himself speaks softly; he seeks secrecy, he lets himself be awaited, A philosopher is recognized by the fact that he shuns three brilliant and noisy things – fame, princes, and women: which is not to say that they do not come to him. He shuns every glaring light: therefore he shuns his time and its 'daylight.' Therein he is as a shadow; the deeper sinks the sun, the greater grows the shadow. As for his humility, he endures, as he endures darkness, a certain dependence and obscurity: further, he is afraid of the shock of lightning, he shudders at the insecurity of a tree which is too isolated and too exposed, on which every storm vents its temper, every temper its storm. His 'maternal' instinct, his secret love for that which grows in him, guides him into states where he is relieved from the necessity of taking care of *himself*, in the same way in which the '*mother*' instinct in woman has thoroughly maintained up to the present woman's dependent position. After all, they demand little enough, do these philosophers, their favourite motto is, 'He who possesses is possessed.' All this is *not*, as I must say again and again, to be attributed to a virtue, to a meritorious wish for moderation and simplicity; but because their supreme lord so demands of them, demands wisely and inexorably; their lord who is eager only for one thing, for which alone he musters, and for which alone he hoards everything – time, strength, love, interest. This kind of man likes not to be disturbed by enmity, he likes not to be disturbed by friendship, it is a type which forgets or despises easily. It strikes him as bad form to play the martyr, 'to *suffer* for truth' – he leaves all that to the ambitious and to the stage-heroes of the intellect, and to all those, in fact, who have time enough for such luxuries (they themselves, the philosophers, have something *to do* for truth). They make a sparing use of big words; they are said to be adverse to the word 'truth' itself: it has a 'high falutin" ring. Finally, as far as the chastity of philosophers is concerned, the fruitfulness of this type of mind is manifestly in another sphere than that of children; perchance in some other sphere, too, they have the survival of their name, their little immortality (philosophers in ancient India would express themselves with still greater boldness: 'Of what use is posterity to him whose soul is the world?'). In this attitude there is not a trace of chastity, by reason of any ascetic scruple or hatred of the flesh, any more than it is chastity for an athlete or a jockey to abstain from women; it is rather the will of the dominant instinct, at any rate, during the period of their advanced philosophic pregnancy. Every artist knows the harm done by sexual intercourse on occasions of great mental strain and preparation; as far as the strongest artists and those with the surest instincts are concerned, this is not necessarily a case of experience – hard experience – but it is simply their 'maternal' instinct which, in order to benefit the growing work, disposes recklessly (beyond all its normal stocks and supplies) of the *vigour* of its *animal* life; the greater power then *absorbs* the lesser. Let us now apply this interpretation to gauge correctly the case of Schopenhauer, which we have already mentioned: in his case, the sight of the beautiful acted manifestly like a resolving irritant on the chief power of his nature (the power of contemplation and of intense penetration); so that this strength exploded and became suddenly master of his consciousness. But this by no means excludes the possibility of that particular sweetness and fulness, which is peculiar to the aesthetic state, springing directly from the ingredient of sensuality (just as that 'idealism' which is peculiar to girls at puberty originates in the same source) – it may be, consequently, that sensuality is not removed by the approach of the aesthetic state, as Schopenhauer believed, but merely becomes transfigured, and ceases to enter into the consciousness as sexual excitement. (I shall return once again to this point in connection with the more delicate problems of the *physiology of the aesthetic*, a subject which up to the present has been singularly untouched and unelucidated.)

9

A certain asceticism, a grimly gay whole-hearted renunciation, is, as we have seen, one of the most favourable conditions for the highest intellectualism, and, consequently, for the most natural corollaries of such intellectualism: we shall therefore be proof against any surprise at the philosophers in particular always treating the ascetic ideal with a certain amount of predilection. A serious historical investigation shows the bond between the ascetic ideal and philosophy to be still much tighter and still much stronger. It may be said that it was only in the *leading strings* of this ideal that philosophy really learnt to make its first steps and baby paces – alas how clumsily, alas how crossly, alas how ready to tumble down and lie on its stomach was this shy little darling of a brat with its bandy legs! The early history of philosophy is like that of all good things; for a long time they had not the courage to be themselves, they kept always looking round to see if no one would come to their help; further, they were afraid of all who looked at them. Just enumerate in order the particular tendencies and virtues of the philosopher – his tendency to doubt, his tendency to deny, his tendency to wait (to be 'ephectic'), his tendency to analyse, search, explore, dare, his tendency to compare and to equalize, his will to be neutral and objective, his will for everything which is '*sine ira et studio*': has it yet been realized that for quite a lengthy period these tendencies went counter to the first claims of morality and conscience? (To say nothing at all of *Reason*, which even Luther chose to call *Frau Klüglin*,* the sly whore.) Has it been yet appreciated that a philosopher, in the event of his *arriving* at self-consciousness, must needs feel himself an incarnate '*nitimur in vetitum*' – and consequently guard himself against 'his own sensations,' against self-consciousness? It is, I repeat, just the same with all good things, on which we now pride ourselves; even judged by the standard of the ancient Greeks, our whole modern life, in so far as it is not weakness, but power and the consciousness of power, appears pure 'Hybris' and godlessness: for the things which are the very reverse of those which we honour today, have had for a long time conscience on their side, and God as their guardian. 'Hybris' is our whole attitude to nature nowadays, our violation of nature with the help of machinery, and all the unscrupulous ingenuity of our scientists and engineers. 'Hybris' is our attitude to God, that is, to some alleged teleological and ethical spider behind the meshes

* Mistress Sly. – Tr.

of the great trap of the causal web. Like Charles the Bold in his war with Louis the Eleventh, we may say, '*je combats l'universelle araignée*'; 'Hybris' is our attitude to ourselves – for we experiment with ourselves in a way that we would not allow with any animal, and with pleasure and curiosity open our soul in our living body: what matters now to us the 'salvation' of the soul? We heal ourselves afterwards: being ill is instructive, we doubt it not, even more instructive than being well – inoculators of disease seem to us today even more necessary than any medicine men and 'saviours.' There is no doubt we do violence to ourselves nowadays, we crackers of the soul's kernel, we incarnate riddles, who are ever asking riddles, as though life were naught else than the cracking of a nut; and even thereby must we necessarily become day by day more and more worthy to be asked questions and *worthy* to ask them, even thereby do we perchance also become worthier to – live?

... All good things were once bad things; from every original sin has grown an original virtue. Marriage, for example, seemed for a long time a sin against the rights of the community; a man formerly paid a fine for the insolence of claiming one woman to himself (to this phase belongs, for instance, the *jus primæ noctis*, today still in Cambodia the privilege of the priest, that guardian of the 'good old customs').

The soft, benevolent, yielding, sympathetic feelings – eventually valued so highly that they almost became 'intrinsic values,' were for a very long time actually despised by their possessors: gentleness was then a subject for shame, just as hardness is now (compare *Beyond Good and Evil*, Aph. 260). The submission to law: oh, with what qualms of conscience was it that the noble races throughout the world renounced the *vendetta* and gave the law power over themselves! Law was long a *vetitum*, a blasphemy, an innovation; it was introduced with force, *like* a force, to which men only submitted with a sense of personal shame. Every tiny step forward in the world was formerly made at the cost of mental and physical torture. Nowadays the whole of this point of view – 'that not only stepping forward, nay, stepping at all, movement, change, all needed their countless martyrs,' rings in our ears quite strangely. I have put it forward in the *Dawn of Day*, Aph. 18. 'Nothing is purchased more dearly,' says the same book a little later, 'than the modicum of human reason and freedom which is now our pride. But that pride is the reason why it is now almost impossible for us to feel in sympathy with those immense periods of the "Morality of Custom," which lie at the beginning of the "world's history," constituting as they do the real decisive historical principle which has fixed the character of humanity; those periods, I repeat, when throughout the world suffering passed for virtue, cruelty for virtue, deceit for virtue, revenge for virtue, repudiation of the reason for virtue; and when, conversely, well-being passed current for danger, the desire for knowledge for danger, pity for danger, peace for danger, being pitied for shame, work for shame, madness for divinity, and *change* for immorality and incarnate corruption!'

10

There is in the same book, Aph. 12, an explanation of the *burden* of unpopularity under which the earliest race of contemplative men had to live – despised almost as widely as they were first feared! Contemplation first appeared on earth in a disguised shape, in an ambiguous form, with an evil heart and often with an uneasy head: there is no doubt about it. The inactive, brooding, unwarlike element in the instincts of contemplative men long invested them with a cloud of suspicion: the only way to combat this was to excite a definite *fear*. And the old Brahmans, for example, knew to a nicety how to do this! The oldest philosophers were well versed in giving to their very existence and appearance, meaning, firmness, background, by reason whereof men learnt to *fear* them; considered more precisely, they did this from an even more fundamental need, the need of inspiring in themselves fear and self-reverence. For they found even in their own souls all the valuations turned *against* themselves; they had to fight down every kind of suspicion and antagonism against 'the philosophic element in themselves.' Being men of a terrible age, they did this with terrible means: cruelty to themselves, ingenious self-mortification – this was the chief method of these ambitious hermits and intellectual revolutionaries, who were obliged to force down the gods and the traditions of their own soul, so as to enable themselves to *believe* in their own revolution. I remember the famous story of the King Vicvamitra, who, as the result of a thousand years of self-martyrdom, reached such a consciousness of power and such a confidence in himself that he undertook to build a *new heaven*: the sinister symbol of the oldest and newest history of philosophy in the whole world. Every one who has ever built anywhere a '*new heaven*' first found the power thereto in his *own hell*.... Let us compress the facts into a short formula. The philosophic spirit had, in order to be *possible* to any extent at all, to masquerade and disguise itself as one of the *previously fixed* types of the contemplative man, to disguise itself as priest, wizard, soothsayer, as a religious man generally: the *ascetic ideal* has for a long time served the philosopher as a superficial form, as a condition which enabled him to exist.... To be able to be a philosopher he had to exemplify the ideal; to exemplify it, he was bound to *believe* in it. The peculiarly etherealized abstraction of philosophers, with their negation of the world, their enmity to life, their disbelief in the senses, which has been maintained up to the most recent time, and has almost thereby come to be accepted as the ideal *philosophic attitude* – this abstraction is the result of those enforced conditions under which philosophy came into existence, and continued to exist; inasmuch as for quite a very long time philosophy would have been *absolutely impossible* in the world without an ascetic cloak and dress, without an ascetic self-misunderstanding. Expressed plainly and palpably, the *ascetic priest* has taken the repulsive and sinister form of the caterpillar, beneath which and behind which alone philosophy could live and slink about....

Has all that really changed? Has that flamboyant and dangerous winged creature, that 'spirit' which that caterpillar concealed within itself, has it, I say, thanks to a sunnier, warmer, lighter world, really and finally flung off its hood and escaped into the light? Can we today point to enough pride, enough daring, enough courage, enough self-confidence, enough mental will, enough will for responsibility, enough freedom of the will, to enable the philosopher to be now in the world really – *possible*?

11

And now, after we have caught sight of the *ascetic priest*, let us tackle our problem. What is the meaning of the ascetic ideal? It now first becomes serious – vitally serious. We are now confronted with the *real representatives of the serious*. 'What is the meaning of all seriousness?' This even more radical question is perchance already on the tip of our tongue: a question, fairly, for physiologists, but which we for the time being skip. In that ideal the ascetic priest finds not only his faith, but also his will, his power, his interest. His *right* to existence stands and falls with that ideal. What wonder that we here run up against a terrible opponent (on the supposition, of course, that we are the opponents of that ideal), an opponent fighting for his life against those who repudiate that ideal!... On the other hand, it is from the outset improbable that such a biased attitude towards our problem will do him any particular good; the ascetic priest himself will scarcely prove the happiest champion of his own ideal (on the same principle on which a woman usually fails when she wishes to champion 'woman') – let alone proving the most objective critic and judge of the controversy now raised. We shall therefore – so much is already obvious – rather have actually to help him to defend himself properly against ourselves, than we shall have to fear being too well beaten by him. The idea, which is the subject of this dispute, is the *value* of our life from the standpoint of the ascetic priests: this life, then (together with the whole of which it is a part, 'Nature,' 'the world,' the whole sphere of becoming and passing away), is placed by them in relation to an existence of quite another character, which it excludes and to which it is opposed, unless it *deny* its own self: in this case, the case of an ascetic life, life is taken as a bridge to another existence. The ascetic treats life as a maze, in which one must walk backwards till one comes to the place where it starts; or he treats it as an error which one may, nay *must*, refute by action: for he *demands* that he should be followed; he enforces, where he can, *his* valuation of existence. What does this mean? Such a monstrous valuation is not an exceptional case, or a curiosity recorded in human history: it is one of the most general and persistent facts that there are. The reading from the vantage of a distant star of the capital letters of our earthly life, would perchance lead to the conclusion that the earth was the especially *ascetic planet*, a den of discontented, arrogant, and repulsive creatures, who never got rid of a deep disgust of themselves, of the world, of all life, and did themselves as much hurt as possible out of pleasure in hurting – presumably their one and only pleasure. Let us consider how regularly, how universally, how practically at every single period the ascetic priest puts in his appearance: he belongs to no particular race; he thrives everywhere; he grows out of all classes. Not that he perhaps bred this valuation by heredity and propagated it – the contrary is the case. It must be a necessity of the first order which makes this species, *hostile*, as it is, to *life*, always grow again and always thrive again. *Life* itself must certainly *have an interest* in the continuance of such a type of self-contradiction. For an ascetic life is a self-contradiction: here rules resentment without parallel, the resentment of an insatiate instinct and ambition, that would be master, not over some element in life, but over life itself, over life's deepest, strongest, innermost conditions; here is an attempt made to utilize power to dam the sources of power; here does the green eye of jealousy turn even against physiological well-being, especially against the expression of such well-being, beauty, joy; while a sense of pleasure is experienced and *sought* in abortion, in decay, in pain, in misfortune, in ugliness, in voluntary punishment, in the exercizing, flagellation, and sacrifice of the self. All this is in the highest degree paradoxical: we are here confronted with a rift that *wills* itself to be a rift, which *enjoys* itself in this very *suffering*, and even becomes more and more certain of itself, more and more triumphant, in proportion as its own presupposition, physiological vitality, *decreases*. 'The triumph just in the supreme agony' under this extravagant emblem did the ascetic ideal fight from of old; in this mystery of seduction, in this picture of rapture and torture, it recognized its brightest light, its salvation, its final victory. *Crux, nux, lux* – it has all these three in one.

12

Granted that such an incarnate will for contradiction and unnaturalness is induced to *philosophize*; on what will it vent its pet caprice? On that which has been felt with the greatest certainty to be true, to be real; it will look for *error* in those very places where the life instinct fixes truth with the greatest positiveness. It will, for instance, after the example of the ascetics of the Vedanta Philosophy, reduce matter to an illusion, and similarly treat pain, multiplicity, the whole logical contrast of '*Subject*' and '*Object*' – errors, nothing but errors! To renounce the belief in one's own ego, to deny to one's self one's own 'reality' – what a triumph! And here already we have a much higher kind of triumph, which is not merely a triumph over the senses, over the palpable, but an infliction of violence and cruelty on *reason*; and this ecstasy culminates in the ascetic self-contempt, the ascetic scorn of one's own reason making this decree: *there is* a domain of truth and of life, but reason is specially *excluded* therefrom... By the bye, even in the Kantian idea of 'the intellegible character of things' there remains a trace of that schism, so dear to the heart of the ascetic, that schism which likes to turn reason against reason; in fact, 'intelligible character' means in Kant a kind of quality in things of which the intellect comprehends this much, that for it, the intellect, it is *absolutely incomprehensible*. After all, let us, in our character of knowers, not be ungrateful towards such determined reversals of the ordinary perspectives and values, with which the mind had for too long raged against itself with an apparently futile sacrilege! In the same way the very seeing of another vista, the very *wishing* to see another vista, is no little training and preparation of the intellect for its eternal '*Objectivity*' – objectivity being understood not as 'contemplation without interest' (for that is inconceivable and non-sensical), but as the ability to have the pros and cons *in one's power* and to switch them on and off, so as to get to know how to utilize, for the advancement of knowledge, the *difference* in the perspective and in the emotional interpretations. But let us, forsooth, my philosophic colleagues, henceforward guard ourselves more carefully against this mythology of dangerous ancient ideas, which has set up a 'pure, will-less, painless, timeless subject of knowledge'; let us guard ourselves from the tentacles of such contradictory ideas as 'pure reason,' 'absolute spirituality,' 'knowledge-in-itself': in these theories an eye that cannot be thought of is required to think, an eye which *ex hypothesi* has no direction at all, an eye in which the active and interpreting functions are cramped, are absent; those functions, I say, by means of which 'abstract' seeing first became seeing something; in these theories consequently the absurd and the non-sensical is always demanded of the eye. There is only a seeing from a perspective, only a 'knowing' from a perspective, and the *more* emotions we express over a thing, the *more* eyes, different eyes, we train on the same thing, the more complete will be our 'idea' of that thing, our 'objectivity.' But the elimination of the will altogether, the switching off of the emotions all and sundry, granted that we could do so, what! would not that be called intellectual *castration*?

13

But let us turn back. Such a self-contradiction, as apparently manifests itself among the ascetics, 'Life turned against Life,' is – this much is absolutely obvious – from the physiological and not now from the psychological standpoint, simply nonsense. It can only be an *apparent* contradiction; it must be a kind of provisional expression, an explanation, a formula, an adjustment, a psychological misunderstanding of something, whose real nature could not be understood for a long time, and whose *real essence* could not be described; a mere word jammed into an old *gap* of human knowledge. To put briefly the facts against its being real: *the ascetic ideal springs from the prophylactic and self-preservative instincts which mark a decadent life*, which seeks by every means in its power to maintain its position and fight for its existence; it points to a partial physiological depression and exhaustion, against which the most profound and intact life-instincts fight ceaselessly with new weapons and discoveries. The ascetic ideal is such a weapon: its position is consequently exactly the reverse of that which the worshippers of the ideal imagine – life struggles in it and through it with death and against death; the ascetic ideal is a dodge for the *preservation* of life. An important fact is brought out in the extent to which, as history teaches, this ideal could rule and exercise power over man, especially in all those places where the civilization and taming of man was completed: that fact is, the diseased state of man up to the present, at any rate, of the man who has been tamed, the physiological struggle of man with death (more precisely, with the disgust with life, with exhaustion, with the wish for the 'end'). The ascetic priest is the incarnate wish for an existence of another kind, an existence on another plane – he is, in fact, the highest point of this wish, its official ecstasy and passion: but it is the very *power* of this wish which is the fetter that binds him here; it is just that which makes him into a tool that must labour to create more favourable conditions for earthly existence, for existence on the human plane – it is with this very *power* that he keeps the whole herd of failures, distortions, abortions, unfortunates, *sufferers from themselves* of every kind, fast to existence, while he as the herdsman goes instinctively on in front. You understand me already: this ascetic priest, this apparent enemy of life, this denier – he actually belongs to the really great *conservative* and *affirmative* forces of life.... What does it come from, this diseased state? For man is more diseased, more uncertain, more changeable, more unstable than any other animal, there is no doubt of it – he is *the* diseased animal: what does it spring from? Certainly he has also dared, innovated, braved more, challenged fate more than all the other animals put together; he, the great experimenter with himself, the unsatisfied, the insatiate, who struggles for the supreme mastery with beast, Nature, and gods, he, the as yet ever uncompelled, the ever future, who finds no more any rest from his own aggressive strength, goaded inexorably on by the spur of the future dug into the flesh of the present: how should not so brave and rich an animal also be the most endangered, the animal with the longest and deepest sickness among all sick animals?... Man is sick of it, oft enough there are whole epidemics of this satiety (as about 1348, the time of the Dance of Death): but even this very nausea, this tiredness, this disgust with himself, all this is discharged from him with such force that it is immediately made into a new fetter. His 'nay,' which he utters to life, brings to light as though by magic an abundance of graceful 'yeas'; even when he *wounds* himself, this master of destruction, of self-destruction, it is subsequently the wound itself that forces him to live.

14

The more normal is this sickliness in man – and we cannot dispute this normality – the higher honour should be paid to the rare cases of psychical and physical powerfulness, the *windfalls* of humanity, and the more strictly should the sound be guarded from that worst of air, the air of the sick-room. Is that done? The sick are the greatest danger for the healthy; it is not from the strongest that harm comes to the strong, but from the weakest. Is that known? Broadly considered, it is not for a minute the fear of man, whose diminution should be wished for; for this fear forces the strong to be strong, to be at times terrible – it preserves in its integrity the sound type of man. What is to be feared, what does work with a fatality found in no other fate, is not the great fear of, but the great *nausea* with, man; and equally so the great pity for man. Supposing that both these things were one day to espouse each other, then inevitably the maximum of monstrousness would immediately come into the world – the 'last will' of man, his will for nothingness, Nihilism. And, in sooth, the way is well paved thereto. He who not only has his nose to smell with, but also has eyes and ears, he sniffs almost wherever he goes today an air something like that of a mad-house, the air of a hospital – I am speaking, as stands to reason, of the cultured areas of mankind, of every kind of 'Europe' that there is in fact in the world. The *sick* are the great danger of man, *not* the evil, *not* the 'beasts of prey.' They who are from the outset botched, oppressed, broken, those are they, the weakest are they, who most undermine the life beneath the feet of man, who instil the most dangerous venom and scepticism into our trust in life, in man, in ourselves. Where shall we escape from it, from that covert look (from which we carry away a deep sadness), from that averted look of him who is misborn from the beginning, that look which betrays what such a man says to himself – that look which is a groan? 'Would that I were something else,' so groans this look, 'but there is no hope. I am what I am: how could I get away from myself? And, verily – *I am sick of myself!*' On such a soil of self-contempt, a veritable swamp soil, grows that weed, that poisonous growth, and all so tiny, so hidden, so ignoble, so sugary. Here teem the worms of revenge and vindictiveness; here the air reeks of things secret and unmentionable; here is ever spun the net of the most malignant conspiracy – the conspiracy of the sufferers against the sound and the victorious; here is the sight of the victorious *hated*. And what lying so as not to acknowledge this hate as hate! What a show of big words and attitudes, what an art of 'righteous' calumniation! These abortions! What a noble eloquence gushes from their lips! What an amount of sugary, slimy, humble submission oozes in their eyes! What do they really want? At any rate to *represent* righteousness, love, wisdom, superiority, that is the ambition of these 'lowest ones,' these sick ones! And how clever does such an ambition make them! You cannot, in fact, but admire the counterfeiter dexterity with which the stamp of virtue, even the ring, the golden ring of virtue, is here imitated. They have taken a lease of virtue absolutely for themselves, have these weaklings and wretched invalids, there is no doubt of it; 'We alone are the good, the righteous,' so do they speak, 'we alone are the *homines bonæ voluntatis*.' They stalk about in our midst as living reproaches, as warnings to us – as though health, fitness, strength, pride, the sensation of power, were really vicious things in themselves, for which one would have some day to do penance, bitter penance. Oh, how they themselves are ready in their hearts to *exact* penance, how they thirst after being *hangmen*!

Among them is an abundance of revengeful ones disguised as judges, who ever mouth the word righteousness like a venomous spittle – with mouth, I say, always pursed, always ready to spit at everything, which does not wear a discontented look, but is of good cheer as it goes on its way. Among them, again, is that most loathsome species of the vain, the lying abortions, who make a point of representing 'beautiful souls,' and perchance of bringing to the market as 'purity of heart' their distorted sensualism swathed in verses and other bandages; the species of 'self-comforters' and masturbators of their own souls. The sick man's will to represent *some* form or other of superiority, his instinct for crooked paths, which lead to a tyranny over the healthy – where can it not be found, this will to power of the very weakest? The sick woman especially: no one surpasses her in refinements for ruling, oppressing, tyrannizing. The sick woman, moreover, spares nothing living, nothing dead; she grubs up again the most buried things (the Bogos say, 'Woman is a hyena'). Look into the background of every family, of every body, of every community: everywhere the fight of the sick against the healthy – a silent fight for the most part with minute poisoned powders, with pin-pricks, with spiteful grimaces of patience, but also at times with that diseased pharisaism of *pure* pantomime, which plays for choice the rôle of 'righteous indignation.' Right into the hallowed chambers of knowledge can it make itself heard, can this hoarse yelping of sick hounds, this rabid lying and frenzy of such 'noble' Pharisees (I remind readers, who have ears, once more of that Berlin apostle of revenge, Eugen Dühring, who makes the most disreputable and revolting use in all present-day Germany of moral refuse; Dühring, the paramount moral blusterer that there is today, even among his own kidney, the Anti-Semites). They are all men of resentment, are these physiological distortions and worm-riddled objects, a whole quivering kingdom of burrowing revenge, indefatigable and insatiable in its outbursts against the happy, and equally so in disguises for revenge, in pretexts for revenge: when will they really reach their final, fondest, most sublime triumph of revenge? At that time, doubtless, when they succeed in pushing their own misery, in fact, all misery, *into the consciousness* of the happy; so that the latter begin one day to be ashamed of their happiness, and perchance say to themselves when they meet, 'It is a shame to be happy! *there is too much misery!*' ... But there could not possibly be a greater and more fatal misunderstanding than that of the happy, the fit, the strong in body and soul, beginning in this way to doubt their right to happiness. Away with this 'perverse world'! Away with this shameful soddenness of sentiment! Preventing the sick making the healthy sick – for that is what such a soddenness comes to – this ought to be our supreme object in the world – but for this it is above all essential that the healthy should remain *separated* from the sick, that they should even guard themselves from the look of the sick, that they should not even associate with the sick. Or may it, perchance, be their mission to be nurses or doctors? But they could not mistake and disown *their* mission more grossly – the higher *must* not degrade itself to be the tool of the lower, the pathos of distance must to all eternity keep their missions also separate. The right of the happy to existence, the right of bells with a full tone over the discordant cracked bells, is verily a thousand times greater: they alone are the *sureties* of the future, they alone are *bound* to man's future. What they can, what they must do, that can the sick never do, should never do! But if *they are to* be enabled to do what *only* they must do, how can they possibly be free to play the doctor, the comforter, the 'Saviour' of the sick?... And therefore good air! Good air! And away, at any rate, from the neighbourhood of all the madhouses and hospitals of civilization! And therefore good company, *our own* company, or solitude, if it must be so! But away, at any rate, from the evil fumes of internal corruption and the secret worm-eaten state of the sick! That, forsooth, my friends, we may defend ourselves, at any rate for still a time, against the two worst plagues that could have been reserved for us – against the *great nausea with man*! Against the *great pity for man*!

15

If you have understood in all their depths – and I demand that you should *grasp them profoundly* and understand them profoundly – the reasons for the impossibility of its being the business of the healthy to nurse the sick, to make the sick healthy, it follows that you have grasped this further necessity – the necessity of doctors and nurses *who themselves are sick*. And now we have and hold with both our hands the essence of the ascetic priest. The ascetic priest must be accepted by us as the predestined saviour, herdsman, and champion of the sick herd: thereby do we first understand his awful historic mission. The *lordship over sufferers* is his kingdom, to that points his instinct, in that he finds his own special art, his master-skill, his kind of happiness. He must himself be sick, he must be kith and kin to the sick and the abortions so as to understand them, so as to arrive at an understanding with them; but he must also be strong, even more master of himself than of others, impregnable, forsooth, in his will for power, so as to acquire the trust and the awe of the weak, so that he can be their hold, bulwark, prop, compulsion, overseer, tyrant, god. He has to protect them, protect his herds – *against* whom? Against the healthy, doubtless also against the envy towards the healthy. He must be the natural adversary and *scorner* of every rough, stormy, reinless, hard, violently-predatory health and power. The priest is the first form of the more delicate animal that scorns more easily than it hates. He will not be spared the waging of war with the beasts of prey, a war of guile (of 'spirit') rather than of force, as is self-evident – he will in certain cases find it necessary to conjure up out of himself, or at any rate to represent practically a new type of the beast of prey – a new animal monstrosity in which the polar bear, the supple, cold, crouching panther, and, not least important, the fox, are joined together in a trinity as fascinating as it is fearsome. If necessity exacts it, then will he come on the scene with bearish seriousness, venerable, wise, cold, full of treacherous superiority, as the herald and mouthpiece of mysterious powers, sometimes going among even the other kind of beasts of prey, determined as he is to sow on their soil, wherever he can, suffering, discord, self-contradiction, and only too sure of his art, always to be lord of *sufferers* at all times. He brings with him, doubtless, salve and balsam; but before he can play the physician he must first wound; so, while he soothes the pain which the wound makes, *he at the same time poisons the wound*. Well versed is he in this above all things, is this wizard and wild beast tamer, in whose vicinity everything healthy must needs become ill, and everything ill must needs become tame. He protects, in sooth, his sick herd well enough, does this strange herdsman; he protects them also against themselves, against the sparks (even in the centre of the herd) of wickedness, knavery, malice, and all the other ills that the plaguey and the sick are heir to; he fights with cunning, hardness, and stealth against anarchy and against the ever imminent break-up inside the herd, where *resentment*, that most dangerous blasting-stuff and explosive, ever accumulates and accumulates. Getting rid of this blasting-stuff in such a way that it does not blow up the herd and the herdsman, that is his real feat, his supreme utility; if you wish to comprise in the shortest formula the value of the priestly life, it would be correct to say the priest is the *diverter of the course of resentment*. Every sufferer, in fact, searches instinctively for a cause of his suffering; to put it more exactly, a doer – to put it still more precisely, a sentient *responsible* doer – in brief, something living, on which, either actually or in *effigie*, he can on any pretext vent his emotions. For the venting of emotions is the sufferer's greatest attempt at alleviation, that is to say, *stupefaction*, his mechanically desired narcotic against pain of any kind. It is in this phenomenon alone that is found, according to my judgement, the real physiological cause of resentment, revenge, and their family is to be found – that is, in a demand for the *deadening of pain through emotion*: this cause is generally, but in my view very erroneously, looked for in the defensive parry of a bare protective principle of reaction, of a 'reflex movement' in the case of any sudden hurt and danger, after the manner that a decapitated frog still moves in order to get away from a corrosive acid. But the difference is fundamental. In one case the object is to prevent being hurt any more; in the other case the object is to *deaden* a racking, insidious, nearly unbearable pain by a more violent emotion of any kind whatsoever, and at any rate for the time being to drive it out of the consciousness – for this purpose an emotion is needed, as wild an emotion as possible, and to excite that emotion some excuse or other is needed. 'It must be somebody's fault that I feel bad' – this kind of reasoning is peculiar to all invalids, and is but the more pronounced, the more ignorant they remain of the real cause of their feeling bad, the physiological cause (the cause may lie in a disease of the *nervus sympathicus*, or in an excessive secretion of bile, or in a want of sulphate and phosphate of potash in the blood, or in pressure in the bowels which stops the circulation of the blood, or in degeneration of the ovaries, and so forth). All sufferers have an awful resourcefulness and ingenuity in finding excuses for painful emotions; they even enjoy their jealousy, their broodings over base actions and apparent injuries, they burrow through the intestines of their past and present in their search for obscure mysteries, wherein they will be at liberty to wallow in a torturing suspicion and get drunk on the venom of their own malice – they tear open the oldest wounds, they make themselves bleed from the scars which have long been healed, they make evil-doers out of friends, wife, child, and everything which is nearest to them. 'I suffer: it must be somebody's fault' – so thinks every sick sheep. But his herdsman, the ascetic priest, says to him, 'Quite so, my sheep, it must be the fault of someone; but thou thyself art that someone, it is all the fault of thyself alone – *it is the fault of thyself alone against thyself*': that is bold enough, false enough, but one thing is at least attained; thereby, as I have said, the course of resentment is – *diverted*.

16

You can see now what the remedial instinct of life has at least *tried* to effect, according to my conception, through the ascetic priest, and the purpose for which he had to employ a temporary tyranny of such paradoxical and anomalous ideas as 'guilt,' 'sin,' 'sinfulness,' 'corruption,' 'damnation.' What was done was to make the sick *harmless* up to a certain point, to destroy the incurable by means of themselves, to turn the milder cases severely on to themselves, to give their resentment a backward direction ('man needs but one thing'), and to *exploit* similarly the bad instincts of all sufferers with a view to self-discipline, self-surveillance, self-mastery. It is obvious that there can be no question at all in the case of a 'medication' of this kind, a mere emotional medication, of any real *healing* of the sick in the physiological sense; it cannot even for a moment be asserted that in this connection the instinct of life has taken healing as its goal and purpose. On the one hand, a kind of congestion and organization of the sick (the word 'Church' is the most popular name for it): on the other, a kind of provisional safeguarding of the comparatively healthy, the more perfect specimens, the cleavage of a *rift* between healthy and sick – for a long time that was all! And it was much! It was *very* much!

I am proceeding, as you see, in this essay, from an hypothesis which, as far as such readers as I want are concerned, does not require to be proved; the hypothesis that 'sinfulness' in man is not an actual fact, but rather merely the interpretation of a fact, of a physiological discomfort – a discomfort seen through a moral religious perspective which is no longer binding upon us. The fact, therefore, that any one feels 'guilty,' 'sinful,' is certainly not yet any proof that he is right in feeling so, any more than any one is healthy simply because he feels healthy. Remember the celebrated witch-ordeals: in those days the most acute and humane judges had no doubt but that in these cases they were confronted with guilt – the 'witches' *themselves had no doubt on the point* – and yet the guilt was lacking. Let me elaborate this hypothesis: I do not for a minute accept the very 'pain in the soul' as a real fact, but only as an explanation (a casual explanation) of facts that could not hitherto be precisely formulated; I regard it therefore as something as yet absolutely in the air and devoid of scientific cogency – just a nice fat word in the place of a lean note of interrogation. When any one fails to get rid of his 'pain in the soul,' the cause is, speaking crudely, to be found *not* in his 'soul' but more probably in his stomach (speaking crudely, I repeat, but by no means wishing thereby that you should listen to me or understand me in a crude spirit). A strong and well-constituted man digests his experiences (deeds and misdeeds all included) just as he digests his meats, even when he has some tough morsels to swallow. If he fails to 'relieve himself' of an experience, this kind of indigestion is quite as much physiological as the other indigestion – and indeed, in more ways than one, simply one of the results of the other. You can adopt such a theory, and yet *entre nous* be nevertheless the strongest opponent of all materialism.

17

But is he really a *physician*, this ascetic priest? We already understand why we are scarcely allowed to call him a physician, however much he likes to feel a 'saviour' and let himself be worshipped as a saviour.* It is only the actual suffering, the discomfort of the sufferer, which he combats, *not* its cause, not the actual state of sickness – this needs must constitute our most radical objection to priestly medication. But just once put yourself into that point of view, of which the priests have a monopoly, you will find it hard to exhaust your amazement, at what from that standpoint he has completely seen, sought, and found. The *mitigation* of suffering, every kind of 'consoling' – all this manifests itself as his very genius: with what ingenuity has he interpreted his mission of consoler, with what aplomb and audacity has he chosen weapons necessary for the part. Christianity in particular should be dubbed a great treasure-chamber of ingenious consolations – such a store of refreshing, soothing, deadening drugs has it accumulated within itself; so many of the most dangerous and daring expedients has it hazarded; with such subtlety, refinement, Oriental refinement, has it divined what emotional stimulants can conquer, at any rate for a time, the deep depression, the leaden fatigue, the black melancholy of physiological cripples – for, speaking generally, all religions are mainly concerned

* In the German text 'Heiland.' This has the double meaning of 'healer' and 'saviour.' – H. B. S.

with fighting a certain fatigue and heaviness that has infected everything. You can regard it as *prima facie* probable that in certain places in the world there was almost bound to prevail from time to time among large masses of the population a *sense of physiological depression*, which, however, owing to their lack of physiological knowledge, did not appear to their consciousness as such, so that consequently its 'cause' and its *cure* can only be sought and essayed in the science of moral psychology (this, in fact, is my most general formula for what is generally called a '*religion*'). Such a feeling of depression can have the most diverse origins; it may be the result of the crossing of too heterogeneous races (or of classes – genealogical and racial differences are also brought out in the classes: the European 'Weltschmerz,' the 'Pessimism' of the nineteenth century, is really the result of an absurd and sudden class-mixture); it may be brought about by a mistaken emigration – a race falling into a climate for which its power of adaptation is insufficient (the case of the Indians in India); it may be the effect of old age and fatigue (the Parisian pessimism from 1850 onwards); it may be a wrong diet (the alcoholism of the Middle Ages, the nonsense of vegetarianism – which, however, have in their favour the authority of Sir Christopher in Shakespeare); it may be blood-deterioration, malaria, syphilis, and the like (German depression after the Thirty Years' War, which infected half Germany with evil diseases, and thereby paved the way for German servility, for German pusillanimity). In such a case there is invariably recourse to a *war* on a grand scale with the feeling of depression; let us inform ourselves briefly on its most important practices and phases (I leave on one side, as stands to reason, the actual *philosophic* war against the feeling of depression which is usually simultaneous – it is interesting enough, but too absurd, too practically negligible, too full of cobwebs, too much of a hole-and-corner affair, especially when pain is proved to be a mistake, on the *naïf* hypothesis that pain must needs *vanish* when the mistake underlying it is recognized – but behold! It does anything but vanish...). That dominant depression is *primarily fought* by weapons which reduce the consciousness of life itself to the lowest degree. Wherever possible, no more wishes, no more wants; shun everything which produces emotion, which produces 'blood' (eating no salt, the fakir hygiene); no love; no hate; equanimity; no revenge; no getting rich; no work; begging; as far as possible, no woman, or as little woman as possible; as far as the intellect is concerned, Pascal's principle, '*il faut s'abêtir.*' To put the result in ethical and psychological language, 'self-annihilation,' 'sanctification'; to put it in physiological language, 'hypnotism' – the attempt to find some approximate human equivalent for what *hibernation* is for certain animals, for what *æstivation* is for many tropical plants, a minimum of assimilation and metabolism in which life just manages to subsist without really coming into the consciousness. An amazing amount of human energy has been devoted to this object – perhaps uselessly? There cannot be the slightest doubt but that such *sportsmen* of 'saintliness,' in whom at times nearly every nation has abounded, have really found a genuine relief from that which they have combated with such a rigorous *training* – in countless cases they really escaped by the help of their system of hypnotism *away* from deep physiological depression; their method is consequently counted among the most universal ethnological facts. Similarly it is improper to consider such a plan for starving the physical element and the desires, as in itself a symptom of insanity (as a clumsy species of roast-beef-eating 'freethinkers' and Sir Christophers are fain to do); all the more certain is it that their method can and does pave the way to all kinds of mental disturbances, for instance, 'inner lights' (as far as the case of the Hesychasts of Mount Athos), auditory and visual hallucinations, voluptuous ecstasies and effervescences of sensualism (the history of St Theresa). The explanation of such events given by the victims is always the acme of fanatical falsehood; this is self-evident. Note well, however, the tone of implicit gratitude that rings in the very *will* for an explanation of such a character. The supreme state, salvation itself, that final goal of universal hypnosis and peace, is always regarded by them as the mystery of mysteries, which even the most supreme symbols are inadequate to express; it is regarded as an entry and homecoming to the essence of things, as a liberation from all illusions, as 'knowledge,' as 'truth,' as 'being' as an escape from every end, every wish, every action, as something even beyond Good and Evil.

'Good and Evil,' quoth the Buddhists, 'both are fetters. The perfect man is master of them both.'

'The done and the undone,' quoth the disciple of the Vedânta, 'do him no hurt; the good and the evil he shakes from off him, sage that he is; his kingdom suffers no more from any act; good and evil, he goes beyond them both.' An absolutely Indian conception, as much Brahmanist as Buddhist. Neither in the Indian nor in the Christian doctrine is this 'Redemption' regarded as attainable by means of virtue and moral improvement, however high they may place the value of the hypnotic efficiency of virtue: keep clear on this point – indeed it simply corresponds with the facts. The fact that they remained *true* on this point is perhaps to be regarded as the best specimen of realism in the three great religions, absolutely soaked as they are with morality, with this one exception. 'For those who know, there is no duty.' 'Redemption is not attained by the acquisition of virtues; for redemption consists in being one with Brahman, who is incapable of acquiring any perfection; and equally little does it consist in the *giving up of faults*, for the Brahman, unity with whom is what constitutes redemption, is eternally pure' (these passages are from the Commentaries of the Cankara, quoted from the first real European *expert* of the Indian philosophy, my friend Paul Deussen). We wish, therefore, to pay honour to the idea of 'redemption' in the great religions, but it is somewhat hard to remain serious in view of the appreciation meted out to the *deep sleep* by these exhausted pessimists who are too tired even to dream – to the deep sleep considered, that is, as already a fusing into Brahman, as the attainment of the *unio mystica* with God. 'When he has completely gone to sleep,' says on this point the oldest and most venerable 'script,' 'and come to perfect rest, so that he sees no more any vision, then, oh dear one, is he united with Being, he has entered into his own self – encircled by the Self with its absolute knowledge, he has no more any consciousness of that which is without or of that which is within. Day and night cross not these bridges, nor age, nor death, nor suffering, nor good deeds, nor evil deeds.' 'In deep sleep,' say similarly the believers in this deepest of the three great religions, 'does the soul lift itself from out this body of ours, enters the supreme light and stands out therein in its true shape: therein is it the supreme spirit itself, which travels about, while it jests and plays and enjoys itself, whether with women, or chariots, or friends; there do its thoughts turn no more back to this appanage of a body, to which the '*prâna*' (the vital breath) is harnessed like a beast of burden to the cart.' None the less we will take care to realize (as we did when discussing 'redemption') that in spite of all its pomps of Oriental extravagance this simply expresses the same criticism on life as did the clear, cold, Greekly cold, but yet suffering Epicurus. The hypnotic sensation of nothingness, the peace of deepest sleep, anaesthesia in short – that is what passes with the sufferers and the absolutely depressed for, forsooth, their supreme good, their value of values; that is what *must* be treasured by them as something positive, be felt by them as the essence of *the* Positive (according to the same logic of the feelings, nothingness is in all pessimistic religions called God).

18

Such a hypnotic deadening of sensibility and susceptibility to pain, which presupposes somewhat rare powers, especially courage, contempt of opinion, intellectual stoicism, is less frequent than another and certainly easier *training* which is tried against states of depression. I mean *mechanical activity*. It is indisputable that a suffering existence can be thereby considerably alleviated. This fact is called today by the somewhat ignoble title of the 'Blessing of work.' The alleviation consists in the attention of the sufferer being absolutely diverted from suffering, in the incessant monopoly of the consciousness by action, so that consequently there is little room left for suffering – for *narrow* is it, this chamber of human consciousness! Mechanical activity and its corollaries, such as absolute regularity, punctilious unreasoning obedience, the chronic routine of life, the complete occupation of time, a certain liberty to be impersonal, nay, a training in 'impersonality,' self-forgetfulness, '*incuria sui*' – with what thoroughness and expert subtlety have all these methods been exploited by the ascetic priest in his war with pain!

When he has to tackle sufferers of the lower orders, slaves, or prisoners (or women, who for the most part are a compound of labour-slave and prisoner), all he has to do is to juggle a little with the names, and to rechristen, so as to make them see henceforth a benefit, a comparative happiness, in objects which they hated – the slave's discontent with his lot was at any rate *not* invented by the priests. An even more popular means of fighting depression is the ordaining of a *little joy*, which is easily accessible and can be made into a rule; this medication is frequently used in conjunction with the former ones. The most frequent form in which joy is prescribed as a cure is the joy in *producing* joy (such as doing good, giving presents, alleviating, helping, exhorting, comforting, praising, treating with distinction); together with the prescription of 'love your neighbour.' The ascetic priest prescribes, though in the most cautious doses, what is practically a stimulation of the strongest and most life-assertive impulse – the Will for Power. The happiness involved in the 'smallest superiority' which is the concomitant of all benefiting, helping, extolling, making one's self useful, is the most ample consolation, of which, if they are well-advised, physiological distortions avail themselves: in other cases they hurt each other, and naturally in obedience to the same radical instinct. An investigation of the origin of Christianity in the Roman world shows that co-operative unions for poverty, sickness, and burial sprang up in the lowest stratum of contemporary society, amid which the chief anti-dote against depression, the little joy experienced in mutual benefits, was deliberately fostered. Perchance this was then a novelty, a real discovery? This conjuring up of the will for co-operation, for family organization, for communal life, for '*Cœnacula*' necessarily brought the Will for Power, which had been already infinitesimally stimulated, to a new and much fuller manifestation. The herd organization is a genuine advance and triumph in the fight with depression. With the growth of the community there matures even to individuals a new interest, which often enough takes him out of the more personal element in his discontent, his aversion to himself, the '*despectus sui*' of Geulincx. All sick and diseased people strive instinctively after a herd-organization, out of a desire to shake off their sense of oppressive discomfort and weakness; the ascetic priest divines this instinct and promotes it; wherever a herd exists it is the instinct of weakness which has wished for the herd, and the cleverness of the priests which has organized it, for, mark this: by an equally natural necessity the strong strive as much for *isolation* as the weak for *union*: when the former bind themselves it is only with a view to an aggressive joint action and joint satisfaction of their Will for Power, much against the wishes of their individual consciences; the latter, on the contrary, range themselves together with positive *delight* in such a muster – their instincts are as much gratified thereby as the instincts of the 'born master' (that is, the solitary beast-of-prey species of man) are disturbed and wounded to the quick by organization. There is always lurking beneath every oligarchy – such is the universal lesson of history – the desire for tyranny. Every oligarchy is continually quivering with the tension of the effort required by each individual to keep mastering this desire. (Such, *e.g.*, was the Greek; Plato shows it in a hundred places, Plato, who knew his contemporaries – and *himself*.)

19

The methods employed by the ascetic priest, which we have already learnt to know – stifling of all vitality, mechanical energy, the little joy, and especially the method of 'love your neighbour' herd-organization, the awaking of the communal consciousness of power, to such a pitch that the individual's disgust with himself becomes eclipsed by his delight in the thriving of the community – these are, according to modern standards, the 'innocent' methods employed in the fight with depression; let us turn now to the more interesting topic of the 'guilty' methods. The guilty methods spell one thing: to produce *emotional excess* – which is used as the most efficacious anaesthetic against their depressing state of protracted pain; this is why priestly ingenuity has proved quite inexhaustible in thinking out this one question: '*By what means* can you produce an emotional excess?' This sounds harsh: it is manifest that it would sound nicer and would grate on one's ears less, if I were to say, forsooth: 'The ascetic priest made use at all times of the enthusiasm contained in all strong emotions.' But what is the good of still soothing the delicate ears of our modern effeminates? What is the good *on our side* of budging one single inch before their verbal Pecksniffianism. For us psychologists to do that would be at once *practical Pecksniffianism*, apart from the fact of its nauseating us. The *good taste* (others might say, the righteousness) of a psychologist nowadays consists, if at all, in combating the shamefully moralized language with which all modern judgements on men and things are smeared. For, do not deceive yourself: what constitutes the chief characteristic of modern souls and of modern books is not the lying, but the *innocence* which is part and parcel of their intellectual dishonesty. The inevitable running up against this 'innocence' everywhere constitutes the most distasteful feature of the somewhat dangerous business which a modern psychologist has to undertake: it is a part of *our* great danger – it is a road which perhaps leads us straight to the great nausea – I know quite well the purpose which all modern books will and can serve (granted that they last, which I am not afraid of, and granted equally that there is to be at some future day a generation with a more rigid, more severe, and *healthier* taste) – the *function* which all modernity generally will serve with posterity: that of an emetic – and this by reason of its moral sugariness and falsity, its ingrained feminism, which it is pleased to call 'Idealism,' and at any rate believes to be idealism. Our cultured men of today, our 'good' men, do not lie – that is true; but it does *not* redound to their honour! The real lie, the genuine, determined, 'honest' lie (on whose value you can listen to Plato) would prove too tough and strong an article for them by a long way; it would be asking them to do what people have been forbidden to ask them to do, to open their eyes to their own selves, and to learn to distinguish between 'true' and 'false' in their own selves. The dishonest lie alone suits them: everything which feels a good man is perfectly incapable of any other attitude to anything than that of a dishonourable liar, an absolute liar, but none the less an innocent liar, a blue-eyed liar, a virtuous liar. These 'good men,' they are all now tainted with morality through and through, and as far as honour is concerned they are disgraced and corrupted for all eternity. Which of them *could stand* a further truth 'about man'? Or, put more tangibly, which of them could put up with a true biography? One or two instances: Lord Byron composed a most personal autobiography, but Thomas Moore was 'too good' for it; he burnt his friend's papers. Dr Gwinner, Schopenhauer's executor, is said to have done the same; for Schopenhauer as well wrote much about himself, and perhaps also against himself: (εἰς ἑαυτόν). The virtuous American Thayer, Beethoven's biographer, suddenly stopped his work: he had come to a certain point in that honourable and simple life, and could stand it no longer. Moral: What sensible man nowadays writes one honest word about himself? He must already belong to the Order of Holy Foolhardiness. We are promised an autobiography of Richard Wagner; who doubts but that it would be a *clever* autobiography? Think, forsooth, of the grotesque horror which the Catholic priest Janssen aroused in Germany with his inconceivably square and harmless pictures of the German Reformation; what wouldn't people do if some real psychologist were to tell us about a genuine Luther, tell us, not with the moralist simplicity of a country priest or the sweet and cautious modesty of a Protestant historian, but say with the fearlessness of a Taine, that springs from force of character and not from a prudent toleration of force. (The Germans, by the bye, have already produced the classic specimen of this toleration – they may well be allowed to reckon him as one of their own, in Leopold Ranke, that born classical advocate of every *causa fortior*, that cleverest of all the clever opportunists.)

20

But you will soon understand me. Putting it shortly, there is reason enough, is there not, for us psychologists nowadays never getting from a certain mistrust of out *own selves*? Probably even we ourselves are still 'too good' for our work, probably, whatever contempt we feel for this popular craze for morality, we ourselves are perhaps none the less its victims, prey, and slaves; probably it infects even us. Of what was that diplomat warning us, when he said to his colleagues: 'Let us especially mistrust our first impulses, gentlemen! *They are almost always good*'? So should nowadays every psychologist talk to his colleagues. And thus we get back to our problem, which in point of fact does require from us a certain severity, a certain mistrust especially against 'first impulses.' *The ascetic ideal in the service of projected emotional excess*: he who remembers the previous essay will already partially anticipate the essential meaning compressed into these above ten words. The thorough unswitching of the human soul, the plunging of it into terror, frost, ardour, rapture, so as to free it, as through some lightning shock, from all the smallness and pettiness of unhappiness, depression, and discomfort: what ways lead to *this* goal? And which of these ways does so most safely?... At bottom all great emotions have this power, provided that they find a sudden outlet – emotions such as rage, fear, lust, revenge, hope, triumph, despair, cruelty; and, in sooth, the ascetic priest has had no scruples in taking into his service the whole pack of hounds that rage in the human kennel, unleashing now these and now those, with the same constant object of waking man out of his protracted melancholy, of chasing away, at any rate for a time, his dull pain, his shrinking misery, but always under the sanction of a religious interpretation and justification. This emotional excess has subsequently to be *paid for*, this is self-evident – it makes the ill more ill – and therefore this kind of remedy for pain is according to modern standards a 'guilty' kind.

The dictates of fairness, however, require that we should all the more emphasize the fact that this remedy is applied with *a good conscience*, that the ascetic priest has prescribed it in the most implicit belief in its utility and indispensability – often enough almost collapsing in the presence of the pain which he created – that we should similarly emphasize the fact that the violent physiological revenges of such excesses, even perhaps the mental disturbances, are not absolutely inconsistent with the general tenor of this kind of remedy; this remedy, which, as we have shown previously, is *not* for the purpose of healing diseases, but of fighting the unhappiness of that depression, the alleviation and deadening of which was its object. The object was consequently achieved. The keynote by which the ascetic priest was enabled to get every kind of agonizing and ecstatic music to play on the fibres of the human soul – was, as every one knows, the exploitation of the feeling of '*guilt*.' I have already indicated in the previous essay the origin of this feeling – as a piece of animal psychology and nothing else: we were thus confronted with the feeling of 'guilt,' in its crude state, as it were. It was first in the hands of the priest, real artist that he was in the feeling of guilt, that it took shape – oh, what a shape! 'Sin' – for that is the name of the new priestly version of the animal 'bad-conscience' (the inverted cruelty) – has up to the present been the greatest event in the history of the diseased soul: in 'sin' we find the most perilous and fatal masterpiece of religious interpretation. Imagine man, suffering from himself, some way or other but at any rate physiologically, perhaps like an animal shut up in a cage, not clear as to the why and the wherefore! Imagine him in his desire for reasons – reasons bring relief – in his desire again for remedies, narcotics at last, consulting one, who knows even the occult – and see, lo and behold, he gets a hint from his wizard, the ascetic priest, his *first* hint on the 'cause' of his trouble: he must search for it *in himself*, in his guiltiness, in a piece of the past, he must understand his very suffering as a *state of punishment*. He has heard, he has understood, has the unfortunate: he is now in the plight of a hen round which a line has been drawn. He never gets out of the circle of lines. The sick man has been turned into 'the sinner' – and now for a few thousand years we never get away from the sight of this new invalid, of 'a sinner' – shall we ever get away from it? – wherever we just look, everywhere the hypnotic gaze of the sinner always moving in one direction (in the direction of guilt, the *only* cause of suffering); everywhere the evil conscience, this '*greuliche thier*,'* to use Luther's language; everywhere rumination over the past, a

* 'Horrible beast.'

distorted view of action, the gaze of the 'green-eyed monster' turned on all action; everywhere the wilful misunderstanding of suffering, its transvaluation into feelings of guilt, fear of retribution; everywhere the scourge, the hairy shirt, the starving body, contrition; everywhere the sinner breaking himself on the ghastly wheel of a restless and morbidly eager conscience; everywhere mute pain, extreme fear, the agony of a tortured heart, the spasms of an unknown happiness, the shriek for 'redemption.' In point of fact, thanks to this system of procedure, the old depression, dullness, and fatigue were absolutely conquered, life itself became *very* interesting again, awake, eternally awake, sleepless, glowing, burnt away, exhausted and yet not tired – such was the figure cut by man, 'the sinner,' who was initiated into these mysteries. This grand old wizard of an ascetic priest fighting with depression – he had clearly triumphed, *his* kingdom had come: men no longer grumbled at pain, men *panted* after pain: '*More pain!* More pain!' So for centuries on end shrieked the demand of his acolytes and initiates. Every emotional excess which hurt; everything which broke, overthrew, crushed, transported, ravished; the mystery of torture-chambers, the ingenuity of hell itself – all this was now discovered, divined, exploited, all this was at the service of the wizard, all this served to promote the triumph of his ideal, the ascetic ideal. '*My kingdom is not of this world*,' quoth he, both at the beginning and at the end: had he still the right to talk like that? Goethe has maintained that there are only thirty-six tragic situations: we would infer from that, did we not know otherwise, that Goethe was no ascetic priest. He – knows more.

21

So far as all *this* kind of priestly medicine-mongering, the 'guilty' kind, is concerned, every word of criticism is superfluous. As for the suggestion that emotional excess of the type, which in these cases the ascetic priest is fain to order to his sick patients (under the most sacred euphemism, as is obvious, and equally impregnated with the sanctity of his purpose), has ever really been of use to any sick man, who, forsooth, would feel inclined to maintain a proposition of that character? At any rate, some understanding should be come to as to the expression 'be of use.' If you only wish to express that such a system of treatment has *reformed* man, I do not gainsay it: I merely add that 'reformed' conveys to my mind as much as 'tamed,' 'weakened,' 'discouraged,' 'refined,' 'daintified,' 'emasculated' (and thus it means almost as much as injured). But when you have to deal principally with sick, depressed, and oppressed creatures, such a system, even granted that it makes the ill 'better,' under any circumstances also makes them more *ill*: ask the mad-doctors the invariable result of a methodical application of penance-torture, contrition, and salvation ecstasies. Similarly ask history. In every body politic where the ascetic priest has established this treatment of the sick, disease has on every occasion spread with sinister speed throughout its length and breadth. What was always the 'result'? A shattered nervous system, in addition to the existing malady, and this in the greatest as in the smallest, in the individuals as in masses. We find, in consequence of the penance and redemption-training, awful epileptic epidemics, the greatest known to history, such as the St Vitus and St John dances of the Middle Ages; we find, as another phase of its after-effect, frightful mutilations and chronic depressions, by means of which the temperament of a nation or a city (Geneva, Bâle) is turned once for all into its opposite – this *training*, again, is responsible for the witch-hysteria, a phenomenon analogous to somnambulism (eight great epidemic outbursts of this only between 1564 and 1605) – we find similarly in its train those delirious death-cravings of large masses, whose awful 'shriek,' '*evviva la morte!*' was heard over the whole of Europe, now interrupted by voluptuous variations and anon by a rage for destruction, just as the same emotional sequence with the same intermittencies and sudden changes is now universally observed in every case where the ascetic doctrine of sin scores once more a great success (religious neurosis *appears* as a manifestation of the devil, there is no doubt of it. What is it? *Quæritur*). Speaking generally, the ascetic ideal and its sublime-moral cult, this most ingenious, reckless, and perilous systematization of all methods of emotional excess, is writ large in a dreadful and unforgettable fashion on the whole history of man, and unfortunately not only on history. I was scarcely able to put forward any other element which attacked the *health* and race efficiency of Europeans with more destructive power than did this ideal; it can be dubbed, without exaggeration, *the real fatality* in the history of the health of the European man. At the most you can merely draw a comparison with the specifically German influence: I mean the alcohol poisoning of Europe, which up to the present has kept pace exactly with the political and racial pre–dominance of the Germans (where they inoculated their blood, there too did they inoculate their vice). Third in the series comes syphilis – *magno sed proximo intervallo.*

22

The ascetic priest has, wherever he has obtained the mastery, corrupted the health of the soul, he has consequently also corrupted *taste in artibus et litteris* – he corrupts it still. 'Consequently?' I hope I shall be granted this 'consequently'; at any rate, I am not going to prove it first. One solitary indication, it concerns the arch-book of Christian literature, their real model, their 'book-in-itself.' In the very midst of the Graeco-Roman splendour, which was also a splendour of books, face to face with an ancient world of writings which had not yet fallen into decay and ruin, at a time when certain books were still to be read, to possess which we would give nowadays half our literature in exchange, at that time the simplicity and vanity of Christian agitators (they are generally called Fathers of the Church) dared to declare: 'We too have our classical literature, we *do not need that of the Greeks*' – and meanwhile they proudly pointed to their books of legends, their letters of apostles, and their apologetic tractlets, just in the same way that today the English 'Salvation Army' wages its fight against Shakespeare and other 'heathens' with an analogous literature. You already guess it, I do not like the 'New Testament'; it almost upsets me that I stand so isolated in my taste so far as concerns this valued, this over-valued Scripture; the taste of two thousand years is *against* me; but what boots it! 'Here I stand! I cannot help myself'* – I have the courage of my bad taste. The *Old* Testament – yes, that is something quite different, all honour to the Old Testament! I find therein great men, an heroic landscape, and one of the rarest phenomena in the world, the incomparable naïveté *of the strong heart*; further still, I find a people. In the New, on the contrary, just a hostel of petty sects, pure rococo of the soul, twisting angles and fancy touches, nothing but conventicle air, not to forget an occasional whiff of bucolic sweetness which appertains to the epoch (*and* the Roman province) and is less Jewish than Hellenistic. Meekness and braggadocio cheek by jowl; an emotional garrulousness that almost deafens; passionate hysteria, but no passion; painful pantomime; here manifestly every one lacked good breeding. How dare any one make so much fuss about their little failings as do these pious little fellows! No one cares a straw about it – let alone God. Finally they actually wish to have 'the crown of eternal life,' do all these little provincials! In return for what, in sooth? For what end? It is impossible to carry insolence any further. An immortal Peter! Who could stand *him*! They have an ambition which makes one laugh: the *thing* dishes up cut and dried his most personal life, his melancholies, and common-or-garden troubles, as though the Universe itself were under an obligation to bother itself about them, for it never gets tired of wrapping up God Himself in the petty misery in which its troubles are involved. And how about the atrocious form of this chronic hobnobbing with God? This Jewish, and not merely Jewish, slobbering and clawing importunacy towards God! – There exist little despised 'heathen nations' in East Asia, from whom these first Christians could have learnt something worth learning, a little tact in worshiping; these nations do not allow themselves to say aloud the name of their God. This seems to me delicate enough, it is certain that it is *too* delicate, and not only for primitive Christians; to take a contrast, just recollect Luther, the most 'eloquent' and insolent peasant whom Germany has had, think

* 'Here I stand! I cannot help myself. God help me! Amen' – were Luther's words before the Reichstag at Worms. – H. B. S.

of the Lutherian tone, in which he felt quite the most in his element during his *tête-à-têtes* with God. Luther's opposition to the medieval saints of the Church (in particular, against 'that devil's hog, the Pope'), was, there is no doubt, at bottom the opposition of a boor, who was offended at the *good etiquette* of the Church, that worship-etiquette of the sacerdotal code, which only admits to the holy of holies the initiated and the silent, and shuts the door against the boors. These definitely were not to be allowed a hearing in this planet – but Luther the peasant simply wished it otherwise; as it was, it was not German enough for him. He personally wished himself to talk direct, to talk personally, to talk 'straight from the shoulder' with his God. Well, he's done it. The ascetic ideal, you will guess, was at no time and in no place, a school of good taste, still less of good manners – at the best it was a school for sacerdotal manners: that is, it contains in itself something which was a deadly enemy to all good manners. Lack of measure, opposition to measure, it is itself a '*non plus ultra.*'

23

The ascetic ideal has corrupted not only health and taste, there are also third, fourth, fifth, and sixth things which it has corrupted – I shall take care not to go through the catalogue (when should I get to the end?). I have here to expose not what this ideal effected; but rather only what it *means*, on what it is based, what lies lurking behind it and under it, that of which it is the provisional expression, an obscure expression bristling with queries and misunderstandings. And with *this* object only in view I presumed 'not to spare' my readers a glance at the awfulness of its results, a glance at its fatal results; I did this to prepare them for the final and most awful aspect presented to me by the question of the significance of that ideal. What is the significance of the *power* of that ideal, the monstrousness of its *power*? Why is it given such an amount of scope? Why is not a better resistance offered against it? The ascetic ideal expresses one will: where is the opposition will, in which an *opposition ideal* expresses itself? The ascetic ideal has an aim – this goal is, putting it generally, that all the other interests of human life should, measured by its standard, appear petty and narrow; it explains epochs, nations, men, in reference to this one end; it forbids any other interpretation, any other end; it repudiates, denies, affirms, confirms, only in the sense of its own interpretation (and was there ever a more thoroughly elaborated system of interpretation?); it subjects itself to no power, rather does it believe in its own precedence over every power – it believes that nothing powerful exists in the world that has not first got to receive from 'it' a meaning, a right to exist, a value, as being an instrument in its work, a way and means to its end, to one end. Where is the *counterpart* of this complete system of will, end, and interpretation? Why is the counterpart lacking? Where is the other 'one aim'? But I am told it is not lacking, that not only has it fought a long and fortunate fight with that ideal, but that further it has already won the mastery over that ideal in all essentials: let our whole modern *science* attest this – that modern science, which, like the genuine reality-philosophy which it is, manifestly believes in itself alone, manifestly has the courage to be itself, the will to be itself, and has got on well enough without God, another world, and negative virtues.

With all their noisy agitator-babble, however, they effect nothing with me; these trumpeters of reality are bad musicians, their voices do not come from the deeps with sufficient audibility, they are not the mouthpiece for the abyss of scientific knowledge – for today scientific knowledge is an abyss – the word 'science,' in such trumpeter-mouths, is a prostitution, an abuse, an impertinence. The truth is just the opposite from what is maintained in the ascetic theory. Science has today absolutely *no* belief in itself, let alone in an ideal superior to itself, and wherever science still consists of passion, love, ardour, suffering, it is not the opposition to that ascetic ideal, but rather the *incarnation of its latest and noblest form*. Does that ring strange? There are enough brave and decent working people, even among the learned men of today, who like their little corner, and who, just because they are pleased so to do, become at times indecently loud with their demand, that people today should be quite content, especially in science – for in science there is so much useful work to do. I do not deny it – there is nothing I should like less than to spoil the delight of these honest workers in their handiwork; for I rejoice in their work. But the fact of science requiring hard work, the fact of its having contented workers, is absolutely no proof of science as a whole having today one end, one will, one ideal, one passion for a great faith; the contrary, as I have said, is the case. When science is not the latest manifestation of the ascetic ideal – but these are cases of such rarity, selectness, and exquisiteness, as to preclude the general judgement being affected thereby – science is a *hiding-place* for every kind of cowardice, disbelief, remorse, *despectio sui*, bad conscience – it is the very *anxiety* that springs from having no ideal, the suffering from the *lack* of a great love, the discontent with an enforced moderation. Oh, what does all science not cover today? How much, at any rate, does it not try to cover? The diligence of our best scholars, their senseless industry, their burning the candle of their brain at both ends – their very mastery in their handiwork – how often is the real meaning of all that to prevent themselves continuing to see a certain thing? Science as a self-anaesthetic: *do you know that*? You wound them – every one who consorts with scholars experiences this – you wound them sometimes to the quick through just a harmless word; when you think you are paying them a compliment you embitter them beyond all bounds, simply because you didn't have the *finesse* to infer the real kind of customers you had to tackle, the *sufferer* kind (who won't own up even to themselves what they really are), the dazed and unconscious kind who have only one fear – *coming to consciousness*.

24

And now look at the other side, at those rare cases, of which I spoke, the most supreme idealists to be found nowadays among philosophers and scholars. Have we, perchance, found in them the sought-for *opponents* of the ascetic ideal, its *anti-idealists*? In fact, they *believe* themselves to be such, these 'unbelievers' (for they are all of them that): it seems that this idea is their last remnant of faith, the idea of being opponents of this ideal, so earnest are they on this subject, so passionate in word and gesture – but does it follow that what they believe must necessarily be *true*? We 'knowers' have grown by degrees suspicious of all kinds of believers, our suspicion has step by step habituated us to draw just the opposite conclusions to what people have drawn before; that is to say, wherever the strength of a belief is particularly prominent to draw the conclusion of the difficulty of proving what is believed, the conclusion of its actual *improbability*. We do not again deny that 'faith produces salvation': *for that very reason* we do deny that faith *proves* anything – a strong faith, which produces happiness, causes suspicion of the object of that faith, it does not establish its 'truth,' it does establish a certain probability of – *illusion*. What is now the position in these cases? These solitaries and deniers of today; these fanatics in one thing, in their claim to intellectual cleanness; these hard, stern, continent, heroic spirits, who constitute the glory of our time; all these pale atheists, anti-Christians, immoralists, Nihilists; these sceptics, 'ephectics,' and 'hectics' of the intellect (in a certain sense they are the latter, both collectively and individually); these supreme idealists of knowledge, in whom alone nowadays the intellectual conscience dwells and is alive – in point of fact they believe themselves as far away as possible from the ascetic ideal, do these 'free, very free spirits': and yet, if I may reveal what they themselves cannot see – for they stand too near themselves: this ideal is simply *their* ideal, they represent it nowadays and perhaps no one else, they themselves are its most spiritualized product, its most advanced picket of skirmishers and scouts, its most insidious delicate and elusive form of seduction. If I am in any way a reader of riddles, then I will be one with this sentence: for some time past there have been no free spirits; *for they still believe in truth*. When the Christian Crusaders in the East came into collision with that invincible order of assassins, that order of free spirits *par excellence*, whose lowest grade lives in a state of discipline such as no order of monks has ever attained, then in some way or other they managed to get an inkling of that symbol and tally-word, that was reserved for the highest grade alone as their *secretum*, 'Nothing is true, everything is allowed,' in sooth, *that* was *freedom* of thought, thereby was *taking leave* of the very belief in truth. Has indeed any European, any Christian freethinker, ever yet wandered into this proposition and its labyrinthine *consequences*? Does he know *from experience* the Minotauros of this den. I doubt it – nay, I know otherwise. Nothing is more really alien to these 'mono-fanatics,' these *so-called* 'free spirits,' than freedom and unfettering in that sense; in no respect are they more closely tied, the absolute fanaticism of their belief in truth is unparalleled. I know all this perhaps too much from experience at close quarters – that dignified philosophic abstinence to which a belief like that binds its adherents, that stoicism of the intellect, which eventually vetoes negation as rigidly as it does affirmation, that wish for standing still in front of the actual, the *factum brutum*, that fatalism in '*petits faits*' (*ce petit faitalism*, as I call it), in which French Science now attempts a kind of moral superiority over German, this renunciation of interpretation generally (that is, of forcing, doctoring, abridging, omitting, suppressing, inventing, falsifying, and all the other *essential* attributes of interpretation) – all this, considered broadly, expresses the asceticism of virtue, quite as efficiently as does any repudiation of the senses (it is at bottom only a *modus* of that repudiation.) But what forces it into that unqualified will for truth is the faith *in the ascetic ideal itself*, even though it take the form of its unconscious imperatives – make no mistake about it, it is the faith, I repeat, in a *metaphysical* value, an *intrinsic* value of truth, of a character which is only warranted and guaranteed in this ideal (it stands and falls with that ideal). Judged strictly, there does not exist a science without its 'hypotheses,' the thought of such a science is inconceivable, illogical: a philosophy, a faith, must always exist first to enable science to gain thereby a direction, a meaning, a limit and method, a *right* to existence. (He who holds a contrary opinion on the subject – he, for example, who takes it upon himself to establish philosophy 'upon a strictly scientific basis' – has first got to 'turn up-side-down' not only philosophy but also truth itself

– the gravest insult which could possibly be offered to two such respectable females!) Yes, there is no doubt about it – and here I quote my *Joyful Wisdom*, cp. Book V. Aph. 344: 'The man who is truthful in that daring and extreme fashion, which is the presupposition of the faith in science, *asserts thereby a different world* from that of life, nature, and history; and in so far as he asserts the existence of that different world, come, must he not similarly repudiate its counterpart, this world, *our* world? The belief on which our faith in science is based has remained to this day a metaphysical belief – even we knowers of to-day, we godless foes of metaphysics, we too take our fire from that conflagration which was kindled by a thousand-year-old faith, from that Christian belief, which was also Plato's belief, the belief that God is truth, that truth is *divine*.... But what if this belief becomes more and more incredible, what if nothing proves itself to be divine, unless it be error, blindness, lies – what if God, Himself proved Himself to be our *oldest lie*?' It is necessary to stop at this point and to consider the situation carefully. Science itself now *needs* a justification (which is not for a minute to say that there is such a justification). Turn in this context to the most ancient and the most modern philosophers: they all fail to realize the extent of the need of a justification on the part of the Will for Truth – here is a gap in every philosophy – what is it caused by? Because up to the present the ascetic ideal dominated all philosophy, because Truth was fixed as Being, as God, as the Supreme Court of Appeal, because Truth was not allowed to be a problem. Do you understand this 'allowed'? From the minute that the belief in the God of the ascetic ideal is repudiated, there exists *a new problem*: the problem of the value of truth. The Will for Truth needed a critique – let us define by these words our own task – the value of truth is tentatively *to be called in question*.... (If this seems too laconically expressed, I recommend the reader to peruse again that passage from the *Joyful Wisdom* which bears the title, 'How far we also are still pious,' Aph. 344, and best of all the whole fifth book of that work, as well as the Preface to *The Dawn of Day*.)

25

No! You can't get round me with science, when I search for the natural antagonists of the ascetic ideal, when I put the question: '*Where* is the opposed will in which the *opponent ideal* expresses itself?' Science is not, by a long way, independent enough to fulfil this function; in every department science needs an ideal value, a power which creates values, and in whose *service* it *can believe* in itself – science itself never creates values. Its relation to the ascetic ideal is not in itself antagonistic; speaking roughly, it rather represents the progressive force in the inner evolution of that ideal. Tested more exactly, its opposition and antagonism are concerned not with the ideal itself, but only with that ideal's outworks, its outer garb, its masquerade, with its temporary hardening, stiffening, and dogmatizing – it makes the life in the ideal free once more, while it repudiates its superficial elements. These two phenomena, science and the ascetic ideal, both rest on the same basis – I have already made this clear – the basis, I say, oft the same over-appreciation of truth (more accurately the same belief in the *impossibility* of valuing and of criticizing truth), and consequently they are *necessarily* allies, so that, in the event of their being attacked, they must always be attacked and called into question together. A valuation of the ascetic ideal inevitably entails a valuation of science as well; lose no time in seeing this clearly, and be sharp to catch it! (*Art*, I am speaking provisionally, for I will treat it on some other occasion in greater detail, – art, I repeat, in which lying is sanctified and the *will for deception* has good conscience on its side, is much more fundamentally opposed to the ascetic ideal than is science: Plato's instinct felt this – Plato, the greatest enemy of art which Europe has produced up to the present. Plato *versus* Homer, that is the complete, the true antagonism – on the one side, the whole–hearted 'transcendental,' the great defamer of life; on the other, its involuntary panegyrist, the *golden* nature. An artistic subservience to the service of the ascetic ideal is consequently the most absolute artistic *corruption* that there can be, though unfortunately it is one of the most frequent phases, for nothing is more corruptible than an artist.) Considered physiologically, moreover, science rests on the same basis as does the ascetic ideal: a certain *impoverishment of life* is the presupposition of the latter as of the former – add, frigidity of the emotions, slackening of the *tempo*, the substitution of dialectic for instinct, *seriousness* impressed on mien and gesture (seriousness, that most unmistakable sign of strenuous metabolism, of struggling, toiling life). Consider the periods in a nation in which the learned man comes into prominence; they are the periods of exhaustion, often of sunset, of decay – the effervescing strength, the confidence in life, the confidence in the future are no more. The preponderance of the mandarins never signifies any good, any more than does the advent of democracy, or arbitration instead of war, equal rights for women, the religion of pity, and all the other symptoms of declining life. (Science handled as a problem! What is the meaning of science? – upon this point the Preface to the *Birth of Tragedy*.) No! This 'modern science' – mark you this well – is at times the *best* ally for the ascetic ideal, and for the very reason that it is the ally which is most unconscious, most automatic, most secret, and most subterranean! They have been playing into each other's hands up to the present, have these 'poor in spirit' and the scientific opponents of that ideal (take care, by the bye, not to think that these opponents are the antithesis of this ideal, that they are the *rich* in spirit – that they are *not*; I have called them the *hectic* in spirit). As for these celebrated victories of science; there is no doubt that they are *victories* – but victories over what? There was not for a single minute any victory among their list over the ascetic ideal, rather was it made stronger, that is to say, more elusive, more abstract, more insidious, from the fact that a wall, an outwork, that had got built on to the main fortress and disfigured its appearance, should from time to time be ruthlessly destroyed and broken down by science. Does any one seriously suggest that the downfall of the theological astronomy signified the downfall of that ideal? Has, perchance, man grown *less in need* of a transcendental solution of his riddle of existence, because since that time this existence has become more random, casual, and superfluous in the *visible* order of the universe? Has there not been since the time of Copernicus an unbroken progress in the self-belittling of man and his *will* for belittling himself? Alas, his belief in his dignity, his uniquenesses, his irreplaceableness in the scheme of existence, is gone – he has become animal, literal, unqualified, and unmitigated animal, he who in his earlier belief was almost God ('child of God,' 'demi-God'). Since Copernicus man seems to have fallen on to a steep plane – he rolls faster and faster away from the centre – whither? into nothingness? *into the 'thrilling sensation of his own nothingness'* Well! This would be the straight way – to the *old* ideal? *All* science (and by no means only astronomy, with regard to the humiliating and deteriorating effect of which Kant has made a remarkable confession, 'it annihilates my own importance'), all science, natural as much as *unnatural* – by unnatural I mean the self-critique of reason – nowadays sets out to talk man out of his present opinion of himself, as though that opinion had been nothing but a bizarre piece of conceit; you might go so far as to say that science finds its peculiar pride, its peculiar bitter form of stoical ataraxia, in preserving man's *contempt of himself*, that state which it took so much trouble to bring about, as man's final and most serious claim to self-appreciation (rightly so, in point of fact, for he who despises is always 'one who has not forgotten how to appreciate'). But does all this involve any real effort to *counteract* the ascetic ideal? Is it really seriously suggested that Kant's *victory* over the theological dogmatism about 'God,' 'Soul,' 'Freedom,' 'Immortality,' has damaged that ideal in any way (as the theologians have imagined to be the case for a long time past)? And in this connection it does not concern us for a single minute, if Kant himself intended any such consummation. It is certain that from the time of Kant every type of transcendentalist is playing a winning game – they are emancipated from the theologians; what luck! – he has revealed to them that secret art, by which they can now pursue their 'heart's desire' on their own responsibility, and with all the respectability of science. Similarly, who can grumble at the agnostics, reverers, as they are, of the unknown and the absolute mystery, if they now worship *their very query* as God? (Xaver Doudan talks somewhere of the *ravages* which *l'habitude d'admirer l'inintelligible au lieu de rester tout simplement dans l'inconnu* has produced – the ancients, he thinks, must have been exempt from those ravages.) Supposing that everything, 'known' to man, fails to satisfy his desires, and on the contrary contradicts and horrifies them, what a divine way out of all this to be able to look for the responsibility, not in the 'desiring' but in 'knowing'! 'There is no knowledge. *Consequently* – there is a God'; what a novel *elegantia syllogismi*! What a triumph for the ascetic ideal!

26

Or, perchance, does the whole of modern history show in its demeanour greater confidence in life, greater confidence in its ideals? Its loftiest pretension is now to be a *mirror*; it repudiates all teleology; it will have no more 'proving'; it disdains to play the judge, and thereby shows its good taste – it asserts as little as it denies, it fixes, it 'describes.' All this is to a high degree ascetic, but at the same time it is to a much greater degree *nihilistic*; make no mistake about this! You see in the historian a gloomy, hard, but determined gaze, – an eye that *looks out* as an isolated North Pole explorer looks out (perhaps so as not to look within, so as not to look back?) – there is snow – here is life silenced, the last crows which caw here are called 'whither?' 'Vanity,' 'Nada' – here nothing more flourishes and grows, at the most the metapolitics of St Petersburg and the 'pity' of Tolstoi. But as for that other school of historians, a perhaps still more 'modern' school, a voluptuous and lascivious school which ogles life and the ascetic ideal with equal fervour, which uses the word 'artist' as a glove, and has nowadays established a 'corner' for itself, in all the praise given to contemplation; oh, what a thirst do these sweet intellectuals excite even for ascetics and winter landscapes! Nay! The devil take these 'contemplative' folk! How much liefer would I wander with those historical Nihilists through the gloomiest, grey, cold mist! Nay, I shall not mind listening (supposing I have to choose) to one who is completely unhistorical and anti-historical (a man, like Dühring for instance, over whose periods a hitherto shy and unavowed species of 'beautiful souls' has grown intoxicated in contemporary Germany, *the species anarchistica* within the educated proletariate). The 'contemplative' are a hundred times worse – I never knew anything which produced such intense nausea as one of those 'objective' *chairs*,* one of those scented mannikins-about-town of history, a thing half-priest, half-satyr (Renan *parfum*), which betrays by the high, shrill falsetto of his applause what he lacks and where he lacks it, who betrays where in this case the Fates have plied their ghastly shears, alas! In too surgeon-like a fashion! This is distasteful to me, and irritates my patience; let him keep patient at such sights who has nothing to lose thereby – such a sight enrages me, such spectators embitter me against the 'play,' even more than does the play itself (history itself, you understand); Anacreontic moods imperceptibly come over me. This Nature, who gave to the steer its horn, to the lion its χάσμ' ὀδοντων, for what purpose did Nature give me my foot? – To kick, by St Anacreon, and not merely to run away! To trample on all the worm-eaten 'chairs,' the cowardly contemplators, the lascivious eunuchs of history, the flirters with ascetic ideals, the righteous hypocrites of impotence! All reverence on my part to the ascetic ideal, *in so far as it is honourable*! So long as it believes in itself and plays no pranks on us! But I like not all these coquettish bugs who have an insatiate ambition to smell of the infinite, until eventually the infinite smells of bugs; I like not the whited sepulchres with their stagey reproduction of life; I like not the tired and the used up who wrap themselves in wisdom and look 'objective'; I like not the agitators dressed up as heroes, who hide their dummy-heads behind the stalking-horse of an ideal; I like not the ambitious artists who would fain play the ascetic and the priest, and are at bottom nothing but tragic clowns; I like not, again, these newest speculators in idealism, the Anti-Semites, who nowadays roll their eyes in the patent Christian-Aryan-man-of-honour fashion, and by an abuse of moralist attitudes and agitation dodges, so cheap as to exhaust any patience, strive to excite all the blockhead elements in the populace (the invariable success of *every* kind of intellectual charlatanism in present-day Germany hangs together with the almost

---

* E.g. Lectureships.

indisputable and already quite palpable desolation of the German mind, whose cause I look for in a too exclusive diet, of papers, politics, beer, and Wagnerian music, not forgetting the condition precedent of this diet, the national exclusiveness and vanity, the strong but narrow principle, 'Germany, Germany above everything,'* and finally the *paralysis agitans* of 'modern ideas'). Europe nowadays is, above all, wealthy and ingenious in means of excitement; it apparently has no more crying necessity than *stimulantia* and alcohol. Hence the enormous counterfeiting of ideals, those most fiery spirits of the mind; hence too the repulsive, evil-smelling, perjured, pseudo-alcoholic air everywhere. I should like to know how many cargoes of imitation idealism, of hero-costumes and high falutin' clap-trap, how many casks of sweetened pity liqueur (Firm: *la religion de la souffrance*), how many crutches of righteous indignation for the help of these flat-footed intellects, how many *comedians* of the Christian moral ideal would need today to be exported from Europe, to enable its air to smell pure again. It is obvious that, in regard to this over-production, a new *trade* possibility lies open; it is obvious that there is a new business to be done in little ideal idols and obedient 'idealists' – don't pass over this tip! Who has sufficient courage? We have *in our hands* the possibility of idealizing the whole earth. But what am I talking about courage? We only need one thing here – a hand, a free, a very free hand.

27

Enough! Enough! let us leave these curiosities and complexities of the modern spirit, which excite as much laughter as disgust. *Our* problem can certainly do without them, the problem of *meaning* of the ascetic ideal – what has it got to do with yesterday or today? Those things shall be handled by me more thoroughly and severely in another connection (under the title 'A Contribution to the History of European Nihilism,' I refer for this to a work which I am

* An allusion to the well-known patriotic song. – H. B. S.

preparing: *The Will to Power, an Attempt at a Transvaluation of All Values*). The only reason why I come to allude to it here is this: the ascetic ideal has at times, even in the most intellectual sphere, only one real kind of enemies and *damagers*: these are the comedians of this ideal – for they awake mistrust. Everywhere otherwise, where the mind is at work seriously, powerfully, and without counterfeiting, it dispenses altogether now with an ideal (the popular expression for this abstinence is 'Atheism') – *with the exception of the will for truth*. But this will, this *remnant* of an ideal, is, if you will believe me, that ideal itself in its severest and cleverest formulation, esoteric through and through, stripped of all outworks, and consequently not so much its remnant as its *kernel*. Unqualified honest atheism (and its air only do we breathe, we, the most intellectual men of this age) is *not* opposed to that ideal, to the extent that it appears to be; it is rather one of the final phases of its evolution, one of its syllogisms and pieces of inherent logic – it is the awe-inspiring catastrophe of a two-thousand-year training in truth, which finally forbids itself *the lie of the belief in God*. (The same course of development in India – quite independently, and consequently of some demonstrative value – the same ideal driving to the same conclusion the decisive point reached five hundred years before the European era, or more precisely at the time of Buddha – it started in the Sankhyam philosophy, and then this was popularized through Buddha, and made into a religion.)

What, I put the question with all strictness, has really *triumphed* over the Christian God? The answer stands in my *Joyful Wisdom*, Aph. 357: 'the Christian morality itself, the idea of truth, taken as it was with increasing seriousness, the confessor-subtlety of the Christian conscience translated and sublimated into the scientific conscience into intellectual cleanness at any price. Regarding Nature as though it were a proof of the goodness and guardianship of God; interpreting history in honour of a divine reason, as a constant proof of a moral order of the world and a moral teleology; explaining our own personal experiences, as pious men have for long enough explained them, as though every arrangement, every nod, every single thing were invented and sent out of love for the salvation of the soul; all this is now done away with, all this has the conscience *against* it, and is regarded by every subtler conscience as disreputable, dishonourable, as lying, feminism, weakness, cowardice – by means of this severity, if by means of anything at all, are we, in sooth, *good Europeans* and heirs of Europe's longest and bravest self-mastery.'... All great things go to ruin by reason of themselves, by reason of an act of self-dissolution: so wills the law of life, the law of *necessary* 'self-mastery' even in the essence of life – ever is the law-giver finally exposed to the cry, '*patere legem quam ipse tulisti*'; in thus wise did Christianity *go to ruin as a dogma*, through its own morality; in thus wise must Christianity go again to ruin today as a morality – we are standing on the threshold of this event. After Christian truthfulness has drawn one conclusion after the other, it finally draws its *strongest conclusion*, its conclusion against itself; this, however, happens, when it puts the question, '*what is the meaning of every will for truth?*' And here again do I touch on my problem, on our problem, my unknown friends (for as yet *I know* of no friends): what sense has our whole being, if it does not mean that in our own selves that will for truth has come to its own consciousness *as a problem*? By reason of this attainment of self-consciousness on the part of the will for truth, morality from henceforward – there is no doubt about it – goes *to pieces*: this is that great hundred-act play that is reserved for the next two centuries of Europe, the most terrible, the most mysterious, and perhaps also the most hopeful of all plays.

28

If you except the ascetic ideal, man, the animal man had no meaning. His existence on earth contained no end; 'What is the purpose of man at all?' was a question without an answer; the *will* for man and the world was lacking; behind every great human destiny rang as a refrain a still greater 'Vanity!' The ascetic ideal simply means this: that something *was lacking*, that a tremendous *void* encircled man – he did not know how to justify himself, to explain himself, to affirm himself, he *suffered* from the problem of his own meaning. He suffered also in other ways, he was in the main a *diseased* animal; but his problem was not suffering itself, but the lack of an answer to that crying question, '*To what purpose* do we suffer?' Man, the bravest animal and the one most inured to suffering, does *not* repudiate suffering in itself: he *wills* it, he even seeks it out, provided that he is shown a meaning for it, a *purpose* of suffering. *Not* suffering, but the senselessness of suffering was the curse which till then lay spread over humanity – *and the ascetic ideal gave it a meaning!* It was up till then the only meaning; but any meaning is better than no meaning; the ascetic ideal was in that connection the '*faute de mieux' par excellence* that existed at that time. In that ideal suffering *found an explanation*; the tremendous gap seemed filled; the door to all suicidal Nihilism was closed. The explanation – there is no doubt about it – brought in its train new suffering, deeper, more penetrating, more venomous, gnawing more brutally into life: it brought all suffering under the perspective of *guilt*; but in spite of all that – man was *saved* thereby, he had a *meaning*, and from henceforth was no more like a leaf in the wind, a shuttlecock of chance, of nonsense, he could now 'will' something – absolutely immaterial to what end, to what purpose, with what means he wished *the will itself was saved.* It is absolutely impossible to disguise *what* in point of fact is made clear by every complete will that has taken its direction from the ascetic ideal: this hate of the human, and even more of the animal, and more still of the material, this horror of the senses, of reason itself, this fear of happiness and beauty, this desire to get right away from all illusion, change, growth, death, wishing and even desiring – all this means – let us have the courage to grasp it – a will for Nothingness, a will opposed to life, a repudiation of the most fundamental conditions of life, but it is and remains *a will*! And to say at the end that which I said at the beginning – man will wish *Nothingness* rather than not wish *at all.*

ECCE HOMO

ECCE HOMO

FRIEDRICH
NIETZSCHE

This edition published in 2021 by Arcturus Publishing Limited
26/27 Bickels Yard, 151–153 Bermondsey Street,
London SE1 3HA

Cover design: Peter Ridley
Cover illustration: Peter Gray

AD006327UK

Printed in the UK

Contents

Introduction

Friedrich Nietzsche wrote his last book and literary autobiography *Why I Am So Wise* in 1888; it was finally published in 1908 under the title *Ecce Homo* and subtitled *How we become what we are*, which is nothing but the old Delphic saying 'Know thyself'. This became one of his most compelling messages.

Born on 15 October 1844 in the small German village of Röcken in Prussian Saxony, Nietzsche came from a firmly Protestant background. Both his grandfathers were in clerical positions and his father, Carl Ludwig Nietzsche, was appointed pastor at Röcken by order of King Friedrich Wilhelm IV of Prussia. He died in 1849, and after the death two months later of Nietzsche's younger brother Joseph the stricken family moved to Naumburg on the river Saale. He was brought up in a family consisting entirely of females: his mother Franziska, his younger sister Elisabeth, his maternal grandmother and two maiden aunts. In 1858 he obtained a scholarship to Schulpforta, Germany's leading Protestant boarding school. There he received an outstanding classical education and after his graduation in 1864 he studied theology and classical philology at the University of Bonn.

With this, his final book, he was aiming once and for all to explain, and possibly defend, his work to a world that so far had not taken much notice of his writing. All his adult life he suffered from crippling illnesses that forced him into retirement at the age of only 35. However, this gave him the time he needed to think and to write. Nietzsche saw himself as a missionary and a prophet; he did not write for personal gain or fame. He wanted to confront the world with the truth – his truth: 'I am no man, I am dynamite', he exclaimed.

In *Ecce Homo* he looks back on his literary output and tells us why he wrote these books, where they came from and whether his position had changed at all over the course of the years: overall his answer is 'No' – he stands by his work. He maintained that he 'had the ability to change perspectives' and *re-evaluate his values* – in short that he now knew *how to become who he was* and, moreover, he was against all systems of belief: 'Beware lest a statue crushes you!'

Mental collapse

Unfortunately, much of Nietzsche's work came under the control of others, not least his sister Elisabeth Förster-Nietzsche. She had married a man with strong anti-Semitic leanings and lived with him for many years in South America, far away from her brother's sphere of influence. In 1889, shortly after finishing *Ecce Homo*, Nietzsche suffered a complete mental collapse from which he never recovered. His mother brought him back to Naumburg where she took care of him and, on her death, Elisabeth, who had returned to Germany following her husband's suicide, took him into her home in Weimar, where he died on 25 August 1900.

Nietzsche could no longer look after himself, and gradually she took over the role of curating his work, dismissing previous editors. Thanks to Elisabeth's editorship, the Nazis found it convenient to claim Nietzsche as one of their own. They feasted on the poet-philosopher's polemics and concepts such as the 'Last Man', 'Master-Slave Morality', 'Superman' and the 'Will to Power', all taken out of context and wilfully misunderstood. But Nietzsche's unwavering support for freedom of expression, his attacks on nationalism and his mockery of all forms of anti-Semitism rife in Germany at that time should have made him an enemy of Nazi doctrine. Instead, his writings became so notorious that even today they are sometimes rejected out of hand.

Writer and historian Golo Mann writes in *The History of Germany Since 1789*: 'He [Nietzsche] did not create a system like Kant or Hegel. That was no longer possible for a philosopher around 1880; his imitators may have tried it. Nietzsche's achievement is his life that pulses in his work.' Ironically, Nietzsche, who grew up in the plains of northern Germany, sought refuge in mountains throughout his life. A man far ahead of his time, Nietzsche never followed one line of belief; he jumped from one concept to another – from mountain peak to mountain peak, so to speak. It is pointless to try to pin him down. And this is how we should perhaps read this book: as startling and thought-provoking, but also as an example of poetic intensity and linguistic precision that is almost Goethean in its originality.

Nietzsche began his writing career in a careful and measured way. As a brilliant academic, he was awarded a

PhD in 1869 without a dissertation, as well as being offered a professorship at the University of Basel at the age of only 25. His first book, *The Birth of Tragedy* (1872), was inspired by the works of Richard Wagner and Arthur Schopenhauer, but as we shall see when we read *Ecce Homo,* he came to distance himself from both. In *The Birth of Tragedy* Nietzsche's outstanding contribution to German, and indeed all, literature was the introduction of the struggle between the Dionysian and the Apollonian form – Dionysus is the free, roaming spirit, the god of wine and song; Apollo is theoretical, rigid and restrained. However, both sides exist in all men to a varying degree. This dichotomy inspired the work of Hermann Hesse and Thomas Mann, who were great Nietzsche admirers.

Nietzsche's dictum, 'God is dead', first mentioned in *The Joyful Science* in 1882, remains a battle cry in *Ecce Homo*, but it also set generations of writers and thinkers free to try to find their own meaning of life, without being hampered by the rigid and inflexible rules and strictures of religious institutions.

His book *Human, All Too Human*, written between 1878 and 1880, signifies his middle period in writing and was dedicated to the memory of Voltaire on the hundredth anniversary of his death. In it he adopted the style of 18th-century French writers, blasting his ideas forth in a series of aphorisms, which, if anything, emphasized the revolutionary nature of his message.

'Good European'

He liked to see himself as a freethinker in the true sense of the Enlightenment; his role models were Voltaire, Rousseau and

Stendhal. He called himself a 'good European' and praised Napoleon as an internationalist and possible saviour. Nation states – 'mini states of petty politics', as he calls them – were abhorrent to him. *Ecce Homo* above all is about the concept of 'free will' and 'free spirit'. As he tells us, 'The term "free spirit" cannot have any other meaning here, but that it is *liberated*, a spirit that took control of itself once again.'

The years 1883 to 1887 saw the publications of *Thus Spoke Zarathustra*, in his own eyes his masterpiece, and *Beyond Good and Evil.* By then partially blinded and semi-paralysed, he had to dictate most of the books to his follower, Peter Gast, a young composer who was devoted to him. 'From then on, all my writings are fishhooks: perhaps I am as good an angler as anyone else?… If I caught nothing, it's not my fault. *There just weren't any fish…*', states Nietzsche about his late work.

He also claimed, with some justification, to be a psychologist. When he talks about the instincts and instinctive truths, he is really talking of the subconscious. As such, he is Freud's forerunner; notions which are similar to those of Freud include the concept of the unconscious mind and the idea that repression pushes unacceptable feelings and thoughts into the unconscious so the individual does not have to face up to them.

Giant among thinkers?

So what is it that continues to make Nietzsche an acclaimed giant among the thinkers of the 19th and 20th centuries? Why has the age of modernism not discarded him as a verbose, somewhat boastful writer, seemingly remote from the world, a recluse but not a sage?

Surely the most obvious answer is that he is actually the father of modernism as we know it, as well as an early existentialist. He gave his mouthpiece Zarathustra almost divine status to promote ideas Nietzsche felt he was born to fight for – to release Christians from slavery to the church and ordinary people from the curse of their ordinariness. He wanted to set mankind free. Yet: 'You will look in vain for a trace of fanaticism in my character', he tells us in *Ecce Homo*, and with some pride he recalls a critic who commended his writing 'for its perfect tact in distinguishing between the person and the issue'. He describes his alter-ego Zarathustra as 'the soul which has the longest ladder and can go down the deepest'. How mysterious does 'Superman' become when his creator writes of him: 'Look, how Zarathustra descends and says something kind to everyone! How gently his hands touch even his antagonists, the priests, and how he suffers *with* them.' Even though Nietzsche has created a warrior, he wages war with words not deeds.

Friedrich Nietzsche claims Zarathustra to be the leading philosopher and psychologist of all time, the antichrist, the free spirit, and at times he and his 'Superman' are as one. Is this the boasting of an egocentric recluse, shouting his truth as loud as he can above the din around him? Not so! If we take it that Nietzsche was so tortured by the illiberal times he lived in, that a voice was needed to preach a new message of personal freedom from the mountain peaks, then we make sense of Zarathustra, who, in the end, is a poetic invention conjured into being for just this purpose. But any contradictions should not disturb a postmodern reader

who long ago stopped believing in the existence of a safe universe in which there are neat answers to burning questions. Nietzsche does not provide answers; in fact he is re-mining ancient seams of knowledge to ask, to worry and to warn. He foresaw the catastrophes of the 20th century in a way also achieved by Franz Kafka, his fellow prophet.

Above all Nietzsche was an innovative and superb master of the German language. That is why I felt particularly privileged to translate his book, and hope in humility that some echo of his stirring and wonderful words will reach the reader.

In *Ecce Homo*, he harked back to his favourite poet, Heinrich Heine, and claimed that he and Heine had been the 'top jugglers' of the German language. This can be seen in the beauty of Nietzsche's poetry, which is expressed in a curiously pared-down language that crops up here and there like little islands in his otherwise densely knitted prose, nowhere more poignantly than here:

They cry the crows
in buzzing flight towards the town
soon it will snow
pity all those without a home

Gerta Valentine

Translator's note

To make the text more accessible I took the liberty of translating most of the many Latin and French expressions that were strewn throughout the text. A man of letters of the 19th century, Nietzsche would have taken an instant understanding of most of these concepts for granted. Today, even if readers have had a traditional classical education, this way of writing may sometimes seem a little pretentious. Nothing could have been further from what Nietzsche intended.

Another piece of licence within my translation is the use of paragraphs instead of dashes. Dashes are all very well, but while they seem to blend in well enough in the original, they would leave a rather too Germanic feel to the text that may alienate the English reader.

Thus I kept them if a special emphasis was to be made, but in most cases the dashes either denote an ironic wink of the eye, in which case I used brackets, or they had a similar function to paragraphing.

Nietzsche refers to many individuals by name. Some, like Wagner or Schopenhauer, need no explanation, and some are fully explained in the text, but for those that are less well known, I attach a short 'Who's Who' below:

- David Friedrich Strauss (1808–1874) was a German theologian

and writer. He impressed scholars with his portrayal of the 'historical Jesus', whose divine nature he denied. Nietzsche criticized Strauss on philosophical grounds.

• Georg Heinrich August Ewald (1803–1875) was a German orientalist and theologian.

• Bruno Bauer (1809–1882) was a German theologian, philosopher and historian who encouraged Nietzsche's criticism of Strauss.

• Friedrich Theodor Vischer (1807–1887) was a German writer on the philosophy of art.

• Dr Heinrich von Stein (1857–1887) was a German philologist, philosopher and dean of the University of Rostock.

• Hans von Bülow (1830–1894) was a contemporary musician and married to Cosima, who later became Wagner's mistress and then wife and mother of three of his children.

• Karl Franz Brendel (1811–1865) was music critic and editor of *Neue Zeitschrift für Musik* and co-editor of *Anregungen für Kunst*.

• Heinrich Gotthard von Treitschke (1834–1896) was a nationalist German historian and political writer during the time of the German Empire who advocated a very aggressive nation state policy.

• Herbert Spencer (1820–1903) was an English philosopher, prominent classical liberal political theorist and sociological theorist of the Victorian era. Spencer developed an all-embracing conception of evolution as the progressive development of the physical world, biological organisms, the human mind, and human culture and societies. He is best known for coining the phrase 'survival of the fittest', which

he did in *Principles of Biology* (1864), after reading Charles Darwin's *On the Origin of Species.*

• Peter Gast/Pietro Gasti was Nietzsche's devoted disciple and aide. The nearly-blind philosopher dictated his later work to him and he also acted as proofreader. Nietzsche confessed to admiring his work as a composer very much and they both went to Venice on one occasion. It was Nietzsche's first visit to that city and he was much inspired by it.

There are also numerous place names in *Ecce Homo.* Some are self-evident like Turin, the Upper Engadine and Nice. Schulpforta is mentioned in my introduction; it was a highly acclaimed protestant boarding school in Thuringia, southeast Germany, which Nietzsche attended as a boy. Wörth and Metz are places in Alsace where Nietzsche saw action during the Franco-Prussian war. Rather than referring to the Palazzo de Quirinale, I explained it within the translation as the King of Italy's residence. Tribschen is Wagner's home near the Swiss lake Lucerne, given to him by the Bavarian King Ludwig II. It was here that he and Nietzsche first met.

Nietzsche calls himself a 'philologist by trade' and I kept this description even though modern readers may be puzzled by it. Philology was the precursor to today's linguistics, which has changed to favour spoken data over written data. Comparative linguistics and historical linguistics, in which words from different languages are compared and contrasted to determine the current or historical relationships between languages, have their roots in 19th-century philology. These days, therefore, we would tend to think of a philologist as an expert in linguistics,

but that may or may not include literature, which of course is Nietzsche's greatest contribution to intellectual life and the German language. 'Philology' literally means 'love of words', and the field often deals with literature more than other branches of linguistics do. In the modern academic world, philology is usually understood to mean the study of written texts, usually ancient ones. It was much more common in the 19th century than it is today for a linguist to be called a philologist.

On pages 44–5, Nietzsche refers to the year 1866 as being significant for him. It was in that year he started to depart from philology and turned towards philosophy.

The 'Junker' philosophy is a specifically German concept; it refers in general to the land-owning classes.

Nietzsche referred to his 'Four Untimely Meditations' as 'The Untimely Ones', but for greater clarity, this translation refers to them as meditations. By 'untimely' he really means avant garde.

The most difficult problems posed to a translator are where figures of speech or puns are deeply entwined either within the German language or Nietzsche's time or culture, or when they were new inventions of Nietzsche's own ingenious mind or even any combination of these. Here I have tried to repair the holes that they may have left in the text.

In section one of 'The Wagner Case', he writes about the founding of a 'Liszt society' to sponsor and spread '*listige Kirchenmusik*' (literally: cunning church music), making fun of the composer's name. To keep the pun, I used 'listed' church music as in registered and officially recognized church music which would be an attack on German bureaucracy.

In section three of the same chapter he writes about German philosophers Fichte, Schelling, Schopenhauer, Hegel, Schleiermacher, Kant and Leibniz and adds that they are all 'Schleiermacher' (literally veil makers), again making fun of a name. What he means is that they are all only pulling the wool over our eyes, which I used. The literal translation would have been wooden and meaningless to English eyes.

In section four of this chapter (probably the most idiosyncratic chapter of the whole book) Nietzsche refers to a 'savouress of Capitoline Hill'; he is, I believe, referring to a goose or to geese belonging to an area on Capitoline Hill in Rome, dedicated to the goddess Juno; their gabbling woke up a group of Roman soldiers just in time to defend the hill against an attack by the Gauls. I translated it as 'some silly goose' because the comment would otherwise not have been understood – indeed, it puzzled many contemporary critics and reviewers of Nietzsche. Forgive the misogynistic insinuation, but Nietzsche was at times harsh about women even though some of his aphorisms could be included in a feminist textbook; as I said in my introduction, his views are never too consistent.

Gerta Valentine

Preface

SINCE, SOONER OR LATER, I shall have to approach mankind with one of the most difficult tasks that has ever been asked of it, it seems inevitable that I must tell you *who I am*. It should really be known already: after all, I did present plenty of 'evidence'. However, the disproportion between the greatness of my task and the *triviality* of my peers has manifested itself in that I have not been heard, nor even been seen. I live on my own credit; is it perhaps just a preconception that I actually live?… I only need to speak to one of those 'learned men' that come visiting the Upper Engadine during the summer to become convinced that I do not live… Under such circumstances there is a duty against which my way of life, and quintessentially even more so my instincts revolt, that is to say: *Listen to me! for I am who I am. Above all, do not take me for someone else!*

2.

FOR INSTANCE, I am by no means a bogey man, nor am I a moral monster – far from it, I am actually the opposite to the type of man that hitherto has been admired as virtuous. Between you and me, I am really quite proud of it. I am a follower of the philosopher Dionysus; I should prefer to be a satyr rather than a saint. Just read this book to see what I

mean. Perhaps I was able to throw some light on this polarity in a happy and philanthropic way, perhaps this was the only point of this book. The last thing *I* should promise is to try and 'improve' mankind. You will not find me erecting new idols! The old may come to realize what it means to have feet of clay! To *topple* Idols (my word for 'ideals') comes somewhat closer to my craft. They deprived reality of its worth, its meaning, its truthfulness to the same extent to which they have *fabricated* an ideal world… The 'true world' and the 'apparent world', or to say it more plainly: the *fabricated* world and reality… The *lie* of the ideal has until now been the curse on reality; mankind itself has on account of it become dishonest and false down to its basest instincts – to the point of worshipping the *opposite* values from those which alone would guarantee success, a future, the lofty *right* to a future.

3.

THOSE WHO can breathe the air of my writing know that it is the air at the top of the mountains, a *strong* air. You have to be made for it, otherwise there is no small danger of catching cold from it. Ice is all around you, the loneliness is immense – but how quietly all things lie in the light! How freely you breathe! How much you feel lies *beneath* you! – Philosophy, as I have so far understood and lived it, is the voluntary life among ice and high mountains – seeking all that is foreign and dubious in existence, all that which so far has been outlawed by morality. From long experience, acquired on such a journey through *the forbidden*, I learned to look at the causes, which until now prompted moralizing and idealizing, in a very different light than

may have been desired: the *hidden* history of the philosophers, the psychology of their great names became clear to me.

How much truth can the mind *bear*, how much truth does it *dare* to take in? This became more and more my real yardstick. Error (– faith in the ideal –) is not blindness, error is *cowardice*... Every accomplishment, every step forward in knowledge is a *consequence* of courage, from being hard on yourself, from your own cleanliness... I do not refute ideals, I merely put on gloves when I deal with them... We strive for the *forbidden*: under this sign, my philosophy shall triumph one day for they have basically always forbidden the truth alone.

4.

MY *ZARATHUSTRA* is unique among my books. With it, I gave mankind the most precious gift that it has been given up to now. This book, its voice spanning thousands of years, is not only the loftiest book in existence, a true mountain air book – the whole fact of what man is lies incredibly far *beneath* him – it is actually also the *deepest*, born out of the innermost wealth of truth, an inexhaustible well, where no pail will descend without coming up again brimming with gold and goodness. Here speaks no 'prophet', none of those dreadful hybrids of sickness and will to power commonly known as religious founders. Above all, you have to *hear* the tone coming from that mouth, this peaceful tone, as it should be *heard*, so you do not misjudge the sense of its wisdom in some wretched way.

'It is the stillest words which bring about the storm; thoughts that creep up on you with the footsteps of doves steer the world.

The figs are falling from the trees, they are good and sweet; and as they fall, their red skin bursts.

I am a north wind to ripe figs.

Thus, like figs, these teachings fall into your laps, my friends; now you drink their juice and their sweet meat.

Autumn is around us and pure sky and afternoon.'

It is no fanatic that speaks here, this is not 'preaching', there is no *faith* required here: drop by drop, word upon word falls from an immeasurable abundance of light and depth of happiness – their timing is a tender slow movement. Such things will only reach the chosen few; it is a privilege without equal to be a listener here; nobody should expect as a matter of course to have an ear for Zarathustra… In view of all that, is Zarathustra not a *seducer* after all?… But what does he himself say as he returns for the first time to his solitude? Precisely the opposite of everything that any old 'sage', 'saint', 'world-redeemer' or other Decadent would say in such a case… Not only does he talk differently, he actually *is* different…

'I shall now go away to be alone, my disciples. You too will go now and be alone. That is how I wish it.

Depart from me and defend yourself against Zarathustra. And better still: be ashamed of him! Perhaps he has deceived you. Man of knowledge must not just love his enemies, he must also be able to hate his friends.

You reward your teacher poorly if you always remain a pupil. And why do you not wish to pluck at my laurels?

You venerate me: but what if your veneration should one day *collapse*? Beware lest a statue crushes you!

You say, you believe in Zarathustra? But why does Zarathustra matter!

You are my believers, but why do believers matter!

You had not even looked for each other: yet you found me.

That is the way with all believers; that is why all beliefs matter so little.

Now I bid you to lose me and to find yourselves and only *when you have all denied me* shall I come back to you.'

FRIEDRICH NIETZSCHE

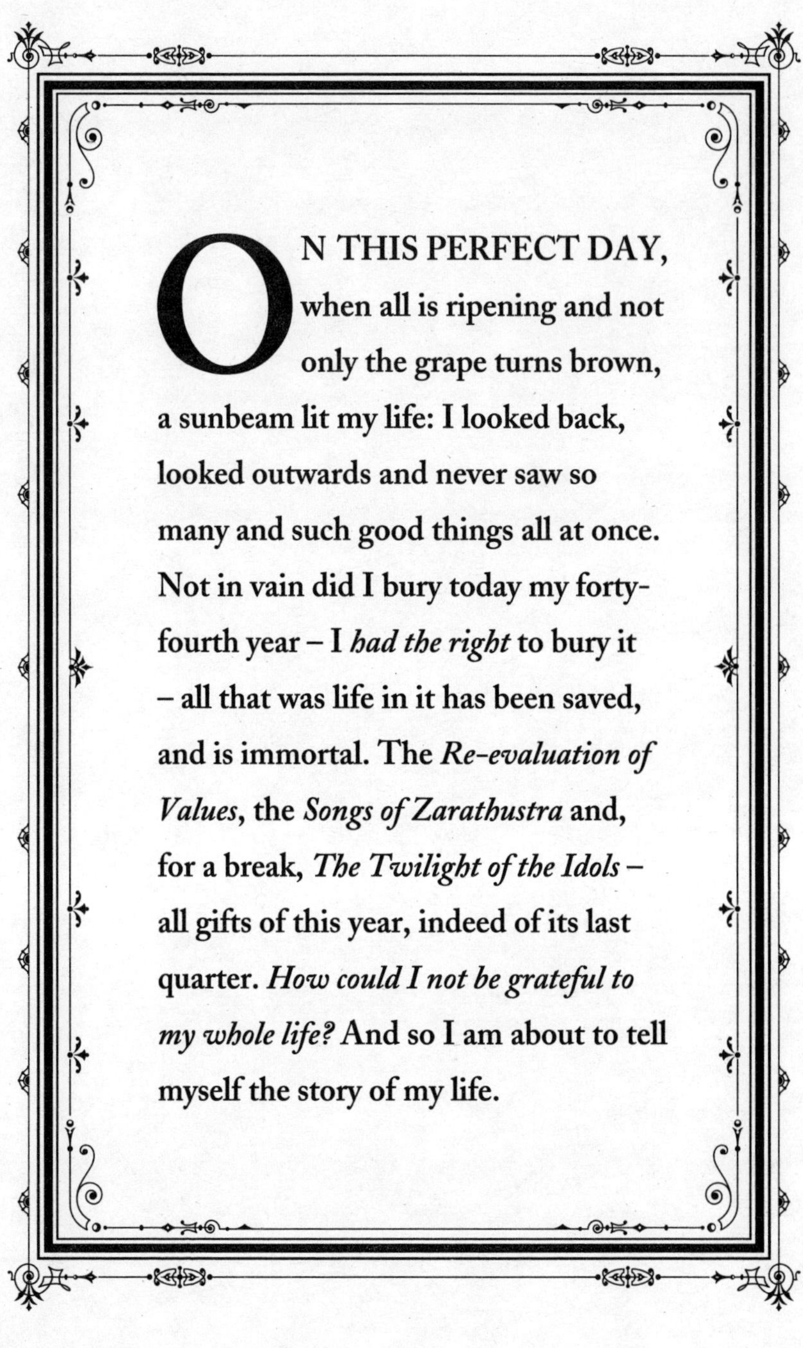

ON THIS PERFECT DAY, when all is ripening and not only the grape turns brown, a sunbeam lit my life: I looked back, looked outwards and never saw so many and such good things all at once. Not in vain did I bury today my forty-fourth year – I *had the right* to bury it – all that was life in it has been saved, and is immortal. The *Re-evaluation of Values*, the *Songs of Zarathustra* and, for a break, *The Twilight of the Idols* – all gifts of this year, indeed of its last quarter. *How could I not be grateful to my whole life?* And so I am about to tell myself the story of my life.

Chapter 1

Why I am so wise

1.

THE HAPPINESS of my existence, its uniqueness perhaps, lies in its inevitable end: I am, to put it in the form of a riddle, as my own father, already dead; as my own mother, I am still alive and grow old. This duality, taken as it were from the highest and lowest rungs of the ladder of life, at once decadent and a *beginning* – this, if anything, explains that neutrality, that freedom from involvement in the general problems of life, which are perhaps so typical for me. I have always had a keener nose for early indications of the rise and downfall than any other person; in this I am the perfect teacher – I know both, I am both.

My father died at thirty-six: he was delicate, lovable, and morbid, as any being that is only meant to live for a brief spell – a gentle reminder of life rather than life itself. During the same year in which his life declined, mine too declined: in my thirty-sixth year I reached the lowest point of my vitality – I was still alive but could not see three steps ahead of me. At that time – it was in 1879 – I resigned my professorship in Basel, lived throughout the summer like a shadow in St Moritz and the following winter, the most sun-starved of my life, *as* a shadow in Naumburg. This was the lowest point of my existence; *The Wanderer and his Shadow* was the product of this period. No doubt, I was an expert in shadows then…

The following winter, my first winter in Genoa, brought forth that sweetness and spirituality which almost always goes hand in hand with an extreme physical weakness: my book *Dawn*. The perfect brightness and cheerfulness, even exuberance of the spirit that this work reflects, is not, in my case, just consistent with the most profound physiological weakness, but also with an excess of suffering. In the midst of the agony caused by three days of headaches accompanied by violent attacks of nausea with hopeless retching of bile – I was possessed of extraordinary dialectical clarity and in utter cold blood I thought things through, which in a healthier frame of mind I would not have been smart enough, not *cold* enough a mountaineer to do. My readers may know how far I regard dialectic as a symptom of decadence, for instance in the most notorious case of all: the case of Socrates.

All the morbid disturbances of the intellect, even that semi-stupor which follows a fever, have remained alien to me to this very day, and I had to inform myself first on their nature and frequency, looking it up in books. My blood runs slowly through my veins. No-one has ever seen me run a temperature. A doctor who treated me over a longer period as a neurotic patient finally decided: 'No, there is nothing the matter with your nerves; quite simply, I am the one who is nervous.' There is absolutely no sign of any local degeneration; no stomach upset caused by organ failure, despite the profound weakness of the gastric systems which comes from my general exhaustion. Even my eye trouble,

sometimes coming dangerously close to blindness, is just an effect, not a cause, so that as my physical strength increased, my visual power also increased.

A long, much too long, number of years means recovery for me, unfortunately though, it also means relapse, decline, a spell of decadence. After all this, need I say that I am *experienced* in matters of decadence? I know it backwards! Even that finely spun craft of apprehension and comprehension in general, that feeling for nuances, that psychology of 'seeing what is around the corner' and whatever else I may be able to do, was first learned at that point, and it is the very gift of that period during which everything in me became refined, observation itself as well as the organs of observation. To look upon *healthier* concepts and values from the standpoint of the sick man and, conversely, to look down from the abundance and self-confidence of a *rich* life down into the secret workings of the instinct of decadence – that has been my main task, the one I worked longest at, in which if anything at all, I became expert. I have it at my fingertips now, I have the ability to *change perspectives*, the main reason perhaps, why I alone could achieve a *Re-evaluation of Values.*

2.

IF YOU ACCEPT that I am decadent, I am also the opposite. My argument for this amongst other things is that I always instinctively choose the *proper* means to fight bad conditions: whilst the Decadent, as such, invariably chooses those means that are to his disadvantage. Overall, then, I was of sound health, but looked at more closely, I was decadent.

That energy for absolute isolation and extraction from a life of habit, the way I forced myself no longer to be indulged, to be waited on hand and foot, to be *pampered* – all that proves the absolute certainty of my instincts *that was*, above all, essential for me at that time. I took myself in hand, I healed myself: this can only be done on the condition – as every physician will admit – that we are *basically healthy*. A typically morbid being cannot become healthy at all, much less heal himself: whereas for a typically healthy being illness can even be a strong *stimulus* to life, for an even richer life. This, indeed, is how I *now* regard my long period of illness: I discovered life afresh, as it were, myself included; I tasted all good and even trifling things in such a way that others cannot easily do – I created my philosophy from my will for health, for *life*...

For I must ask you to take note of this; it was during those years when my life-force was at its lowest ebb that I *ceased* being a pessimist: the instinct of self-recovery forbade me to adopt a philosophy of poverty and discouragement... Now, how can we basically recognize *brilliance*? We recognize that a brilliant or first-rate human being is agreeable to our senses: that he is made of a matter at once hard yet sweet and fragrant. He enjoys only what is conducive to him; his pleasure, his desire ceases as soon as the level of what is good for him has been overstepped. He divines remedies against injuries, he uses serious accidents to his own advantage; that which does not kill him makes him stronger. He instinctively gathers his *sum-total* from all that he sees, hears and experiences. He is a selective principle, he discards much. He is always in *his own* company, whether he deals with books, people or landscapes:

he honours his *choices* by *acknowledging* them, by *trusting* them. He reacts slowly to all types of stimuli, with the very slowness bred in him by long years of caution and deliberate pride – he tests the stimulus that meets him head-on; no compromise is required. He believes in neither 'misfortune' nor 'guilt'; he copes with himself and others; he knows *when to let go* – he is strong enough to turn everything to his greatest advantage.

Well then, I am the opposite of a Decadent: for I just described none other than *myself*.

3.

I REGARD it as a great privilege to have had such a father; the peasants he preached to (for, after having lived for some years at the Altenburg Court, he spent his last years of life as a preacher) said of him that this is how the angels must have looked – and with this I will touch on the question of race.

I am a Polish nobleman without a drop of bad blood, least of all German blood. If I search for the most shocking contrast to myself, the unfathomable pettiness of the instincts, I always find my mother and sister – to believe myself kindred to such bitches would be blaspheming my divinity. The treatment that I have received from my mother and sister fills me with unutterable horror to this very day; there is a totally hellish machine at work here, operating with infallible certainty at the precise moment when I am most vulnerable – at my loftiest moments. For then I lack any strength to defend myself against such vipers! The physiological closeness makes such age-old disharmony possible – but I confess that the deepest objection against any 'reincarnation' and my real thoughts when staring into the abyss, are always of my mother and sister.

However, even as a Pole I am an incredible throwback. You would have to go back centuries to find this noblest race that ever lived on earth as sensitive as I have described them. Everything that is called noble these days gives me a feeling of superiority and distinction – I would not allow the young German Emperor the honour of being my coachman. There is one single case where I acknowledge my equal and I admit it with profound gratitude: Madame Cosima Wagner is by far the noblest nature; and, I may as well admit it, I hold true that Richard Wagner was the man by far closest akin to me; the rest – silence!

All prevailing concepts about degrees of relationship are an utter physiological nonsense. Even today the Pope insists on this absurdity for his own purposes. We are least akin to our parents; indeed it would be the utmost mark of vulgarity to be too akin to our parents. Loftier natures can trace their true origins infinitely farther back; from them a great deal had to be gathered, hoarded and heaped over long periods of time. The great individuals are the oldest; I do not understand why, but Julius Caesar could have been my father – or Alexander, that Dionysus incarnate… At the very moment of writing this, someone has sent me the head of Dionysus through the mail…

4.

I NEVER understood the art of being antagonistic – this, too, I owe to my marvellous father – even though at times it

could have been very useful to me. However unchristian this may seem, I do not even feel antagonism against myself. You can look at my life from any angle and rarely will you find traces of any ill will towards me (apart from that one single case perhaps), though too many traces of *good will*...

Even my experiences with those that everyone else fares badly with are without exception positive; I tame every beast, I can even make buffoons behave demurely. During the seven years in which I taught classical Greek to a top form at the Grammar school in Basel, I never needed to administer a punishment. Even the laziest worked hard for me in my class. If chance comes my way, I will take it, but I have to be spontaneous to take control of myself. Whatever the instrument, however badly tuned, even if as much out of tune as only the instrument 'man' can be – I would have to be ill if I could not squeeze something worth listening to out of it. And as often as not, I have been told by the 'instruments' themselves that they had thought themselves incapable of such a tune...

Most beautifully perhaps by that Heinrich von Stein who died unforgivably young, and who, after dutifully obtaining permission, turned up and stayed for three days in Sils-Maria, explaining to everyone that he had *not* just come to look at the Engadine. This fine human being, who waded deep into Wagnerian mires (and also into those of Dürer!) with all the impetuous simplicity of a Prussian nobleman, became a different man during these three days, changed by a tempest of freedom like one who has been suddenly lifted to *his* full height and given wings to fly with. I told him over and again that it was the good mountain air up here that did it, that everyone felt like that, that after all, you were not some 6,000 ft above Bayreuth for nothing – but he would not believe me…

If, in spite of that, some small and not so small misdemeanours have been committed against me, it was not an act of 'will', least of all of *ill* will: rather, as I have already indicated, I could complain of good will that has done no little mischief in my life. My experiences give me a right to feel generally suspicious of the so-called 'selfless' instincts, the whole concept of 'neighbourly love', that is always ready to offer advice or to break into action. I deem it a weakness in itself, an individual case of inability to resist temptations – only the Decadent call *compassion* a virtue. I accuse the compassionate of easily losing modesty, respect, the sensitivity to keep their distance; compassion smells very quickly of the mob and is indistinguishable from bad manners – compassionate hands can at times be interfering in a downright destructive way with a great destiny, the growing isolation amongst the wounded and the *privilege* of a great wrong. I count conquering compassion among the *noble* virtues: with the 'Temptation of Zarathustra' I wrote a poem where a great cry of distress reaches his ear, where compassion assaults him and tries to entice him away from *himself* like a final sin. To keep control of himself at this point, to remain adamant that the *magnitude* of his task must not be belittled by lower and more short-sighted impulses which affect the so-called selfless deeds, that is the test, perhaps the ultimate test, which Zarathustra must pass – the real *proof* of power.

5.

AND IN YET another respect I am once more my father over again and thus the continuation of his life following his so untimely death. Like every man who has never lived amongst equals and to whom therefore the notion of 'retaliation' is just as foreign as the notion of 'equal rights', I do not allow myself to safeguard or protect myself when small or even gross acts of foolishness have been committed against me – naturally, neither do I defend or justify myself. My kind of retaliation is quickly to send prudence to run after stupidity, perhaps it will catch up with it. To put it as a parable: I eat a pot of jam in order to get rid of a *sour* taste... Just let anyone speak ill of me, I shall 'retaliate', don't doubt it: it won't take me long to find an opportunity to offer my thanks to the 'perpetrator' (occasionally even for the misdeed itself) – or to *ask* him for something, which can be more gracious even than *offering* something...

Moreover, it seems to me that the rudest word, the rudest letter, is still kinder, still more virtuous than silence. Those who are silent are almost always lacking in delicacy and refinement of the heart; silence is an objection, swallowing grievances makes for a bad character – it even upsets the stomach. All those who are silent suffer from dyspepsia.

As you see, I do not wish to underestimate rudeness, it is by far the most *human* form of contradiction and amidst the modern fashion for pampering, one of our most important virtues.

If you are rich enough for it, it may even be your good fortune to be in the wrong. A god descending to this earth

could *do* nothing but wrong; not to bring punishment on himself but to take on the *guilt* – only that would make him divine.

6.

TO BE FREE of resentment, to be aware of resentment – who knows how much I ultimately have to thank my long illness for, even for that. The problem is not an easy one: you have to have experienced it from strength as well as from weakness. If anything has to be upheld against illness, against weakness, it is that man's actual sense of salvation, that is to say his *instinct for war and taking up arms* has been worn out. We know how to break free from nothingness, we know how to cope with nothingness, we know how to push nothingness away from us – it all hurts. Man and things crowd in, all experiences strike too deep, memory is a festering wound. Illness itself is a form of resentment.

In the face of that, the sick man has only one great remedy – I call it *Russian fatalism*, that fatalism without revolt with which a Russian soldier lies down in the snow at the end of a campaign that was all too hard; to accept nothing further, to take nothing on, nothing in – to cease reacting altogether…

The great sense in such fatalism (that is not always merely the courage to die, for it can be life-saving under deadly circumstances) lies in reducing the metabolism, slowing it down as a form of will to hibernate. If we take this reasoning a few steps further, we arrive at the fakir who sleeps for weeks in a tomb. Because we would wear ourselves out much too quickly *if* we reacted in any way, we don't react at all: that is the principle. And nothing burns us up faster than the emotion of resentment. Anger, morbid sensitivity, the inability to force revenge, the yearning, the thirst for revenge, the concoction of all types of poison – this, surely, is for the exhausted the most detrimental way to react: it involves a rapid consumption of nervous energy, a pathological increase of harmful secretions, for instance that of bile into the stomach. Resentment is *all that is* forbidden to the sick man – it is his *worst evil*: unfortunately, it is also what he most desires.

That was recognized by that profound physician Buddha. His 'religion' which should rather be called a *hygiene system* to avoid any confusion with such a wretched thing as Christianity, works because it depends on the conquest of resentment: to free the soul of it – this is the first step towards recovery. 'Animosity is not ended by animosity, animosity is ended by friendship'; thus begins Buddha's doctrine – this is *not* the voice of morality but of physiology. Resentment born of weakness is harmful to no-one more than to the weak man himself – conversely, with a fundamentally rich nature it is a *superfluous* emotion, which, if kept under control, is almost a proof of riches. Those readers who know how seriously my philosophy has taken up the fight against the feelings of revenge and rancour, even taking on the doctrine of 'free will' (the fight against Christianity is merely a small part of it), will understand why I emphasise my own personal attitude, my *instinctive confidence* in practicality at precisely this point.

During my decadent period I *denied* myself these feelings as being harmful; as soon as life offered once again wealth and pride, I denied them myself as being beneath me. That 'Russian fatalism' of which I spoke manifested itself in such a way that for years I clung tenaciously to almost unbearable conditions, locations, dwellings, societies, once fate had sent them my way; it was better than changing them, better than *feeling* they could be changed – better than rebelling against them…

Anyone who interfered with my fatalism, who tried forcefully to awaken me, would have been my mortal enemy in those days; in truth, it would have been fatally dangerous every time. Thinking of yourself as a destiny, not wanting to be 'other' than you are – that is under such circumstances the *highest wisdom.*

7.

NOW, WAR IS a different matter altogether. I am essentially a warrior. To wage war is one of my instincts. Talent for animosity, to actually *be* an enemy – this, perhaps, presupposes a strong nature; in any case it is a precondition of every strong nature. It needs resistances, therefore it *seeks* out resistance: *aggressive* pathos is just as necessary for strength as resentment and rancour for weakness. Women, for instance, are vengeful: that is due to their weakness, as much as to their sensitivity to others' distress.

The strength of the aggressor, in a way, has its *measure* in the opposition he requires; any increase in strength makes itself known when seeking out a mightier opponent or,

indeed, problem – for a philosopher who is a warrior will also do battle with problems. The task is *not* to overcome opponents at all costs, but only those against whom you must pit all your strength, subtlety and fighting skill – opponents who are *your equals*... Equality before the enemy – that is the main condition to fight a *fair* duel. Where you have contempt, you *cannot* wage war; where you are in command, where you can see someone *beneath* you, you *should not* wage war. My war tactics can be summed up in four theorems. Firstly: I only ever engage with causes that are winnable – if necessary, I wait until they win. Secondly: I only ever engage with causes where I would find no allies, where I stand alone – where I compromise only myself... I have never publicly taken a single step which did not compromise me: that is my criterion for doing right. Thirdly: I never attack people – I use a person merely as a powerful magnifying glass that allows me to make visible a general but insidious and elusive calamity.

In this way I attacked David Strauss, or to put it more plainly, the *success* of a senile book amongst the 'cultured classes' of Germany – thereby catching this culture red-handed...

In this way I attacked Wagner, or to put it more plainly, the hypocrisy, the semi-refined instinct of our 'culture' which confuses the artful with richness, the late with the great. Fourthly: I only ever attack things from which all personal differences are excluded, where any background of bad experience is lacking. On the contrary, to attack is to me a proof of good-will, in some circumstances even of gratitude.

It is an honour, a reward, if I associate my name with a matter or a person, notwithstanding whether I am for it or against it. If I wage war on Christianity I have a right to do so, because it's not going to kill me and they're not going to stop me – the most serious Christians were always favourably disposed towards me. I myself, the strictest opponent of Christianity, am far from minded to bear grudges against individuals for what has been the undoing of centuries.

8.

MAY I POINT OUT to you one more trait of my character, which causes me no little difficulty in my dealings with men? I have a perfectly uncanny sense of purity so that I can register, even *smell* the approach or – may I say? – the innermost region, the 'entrails' of every soul in a physical way... This sensitivity of mine has psychological antennae with which I probe and handle every secret: the *hidden* filth at the bottom of many a character. Perhaps caused by bad genes but glossed over by breeding, it is nevertheless obvious to me almost at a glance. If I am right, those who offend my sense of purity also sense my disgust themselves; that does not make them smell any better... To be treated with extreme fairness is a precondition for my existence; I should perish in impure conditions (I got used to swimming and bathing and splashing, as it were, incessantly in water, in some perfectly transparent and glistening element). That is why dealing with men is no small test of my patience; my humanity *does not* consist of empathizing with men's nature but to *endure* that I empathize – my humanity is a constant test of my willpower...

However, I do need *seclusion*, that is to say, healing, being myself again, breathing free, light, playful air… All of my *Zarathustra* is a song in praise of seclusion, or, if you get my meaning, of *purity* – fortunately not about *pure folly*. Those with an eye for colour would call him adamantine; the *loathing* for mankind, for the 'rabble' was always my greatest danger… Do you wish to hear what Zarathustra has to say when he talks of being *set free* of *loathing*?

'What could have happened to me? How have I freed myself from loathing? Who renewed my sight? How did I soar to such heights, above the rabble sitting by the well?

Was it my loathing that gave me wings and water-divining powers?

Truly, I had to fly to the loftiest heights to find once again that fount of desire!

Ah, but I found it, my brothers! Here in the loftiest height the fount of my desire wells up for me, and there is a life in which the rabble cannot have a share.

You flow almost too fast for me, my fount of desire! And often you empty the cup again by wanting to refill it.

And yet I must learn to approach you with greater modesty – my heart overflows all too wildly at the sight of you – my heart, on which my summer's heat is burning; the short, hot, sad, overly blissful one – how my summer heart longs for your chill.

Gone is the lingering sadness of my spring! Gone are the snowflakes of my wickedness in June! I have become all summer and a summer's noon.

A summer in loftiest heights with ice-cold springs and

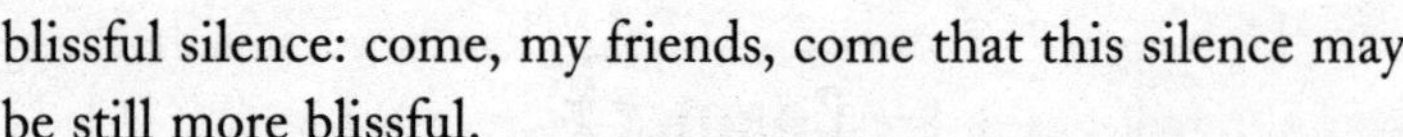

blissful silence: come, my friends, come that this silence may be still more blissful.

For this is *our* height and our home – we all live here, where it is too high and steep for any of the impure and their thirst. Look with your pure eyes into the fount of my desire, friends! Why should that cloud it? Why, it will smile at you in its *own* purity.

On the tree of future we shall build our nest; eagles will carry food to us recluses in their beaks.

Truly, this is no food that the impure are allowed to share! Like fire it would burn their mouths.

Truly, we do not prepare homes for the impure! Our happiness would be like icy caves to their bodies and spirits.

And like strong winds we shall live above them, neighbours to the eagles, neighbours of the snow, neighbours of the sun: this is the way strong winds live.

And like a wind I shall yet blow amongst them one day and take their spirits' breath away with mine: that is the dictate of my future.

Truly, Zarathustra is a strong wind on all and every plain, and his advice to all his friends and all that spit and spout is this: beware of spitting *against* the wind!…'

Chapter 2

Why I am so clever

1.

WHY DO I KNOW *more* than other people? Why, in general, am I so clever? I have never wasted my time pondering questions that are not really questions. For instance, I have no personal experiences of real *religious* difficulties. It completely escapes me why I should be a 'sinner'. Similarly, I don't have a reliable criterion by which to work out what a bad conscience consists of: from where I stand, a bad conscience does not appear of great value to me… I would rather not leave anything that I have done *afterwards* in the lurch; I would prefer to omit a bad ending, or its *consequences*, from any form of evaluation. A bad ending makes you lose the vision you had in sight, a bad conscience is in my view some form of *evil eye.* To respect something that didn't work all the more because it didn't work – that is rather closer to my set of morals.

'God', 'immortality of the soul', 'redemption', 'heaven', these are all terms for which I never had any time and to which I never paid any attention, even as a child – was I perhaps not enough of a child for that?

For me, atheism is not at all a result, even less an event: to me it is instinctive. I am much too inquisitive, too sceptical, and too high-spirited to put up with an obvious if coarse answer. God is such a coarse and obvious answer, a lack of delicacy towards us thinkers – at heart He is just a coarse command not to think: thou shalt not think!

Now, the question of nutrition is a very different matter to me; on that the 'salvation of mankind' is truly dependent, much more so than on some theological musing. For practical purposes we could put it like this: 'How precisely must you feed yourself to attain your maximum power, a truly enlightened virtue, a virtue free of moral input?'

Here, my personal experiences are the worst possible; I am surprised that I did not become aware of this question earlier, that I have learned to 'reason' from these experiences only at such a late stage. The utter worthlessness of our German culture alone – its 'idealism' – can explain to some extent why of all people I was so backward here, almost revelling in this backwater. This 'culture', which teaches you from the start to lose sight of *reality*, so that you may aim for quite difficult, so-called 'ideal' goals; for instance 'classical education' (as if it was not already doomed to unite the two concepts: 'Classical' and 'German'). Actually, this is quite funny: imagine a man from Leipzig with a classical education!

As it is, in moral terms I have eaten *a very poor diet* until very recently: that is 'impersonally', 'selflessly', 'altruistically' – for the good of the cooks and other fellow Christians. For instance, because of the cuisine of Leipzig as well as my first involvement with the works of Schopenhauer (1865), I seriously shunned my 'will to live'. Think – to upset my stomach on account of a poor diet – such a problem seemed to be amazingly well solved by this type of cuisine (it is said that

the year 1866 had brought about a change in this department).

But as to German cuisine in general – what can it not be accused of! Serving soup *before* the main meal (still called *alla tedesca* in 16th-century Venetian cookery books); meat boiled to death, vegetables full of grease and made stodgy with flour; the degeneration of pastries into solid bulk! Add to this the almost bestial, postprandial habits of the ancient, although not just the *ancient* Germans, you will understand the origin of the *German* mind – it is founded in disordered innards. The German mind is a sore stomach; it cannot take any more.

But even the *English* diet that, compared with the German or the French one, seems to me a 'return to nature' (that is, to cannibalism), is deeply repugnant to my innermost self; I think it makes the mind heavy-footed, gives it the feet of English women… My favourite cuisine is that of *Piedmont.*

Alcohol does not agree with me; a glass of wine or beer a day is enough to turn my life into a valley of tears – my adversaries live in Munich. I confess that I came to understand all this a little late, even though I have *experienced* it since childhood. As a boy I believed that drinking wine, like smoking tobacco, was simply youthful vanity, which would then turn into a bad habit. Perhaps the wine of Naumburg vineyards was partly responsible for my harsh judgment. To believe that wine is *cheering* I would have to be a Christian, in other words I would have to believe in what to me is utterly absurd.

Oddly enough, whereas *small* doses of alcohol depress me deeply, *large* quantities turn me almost into a sailor on

leave. Even as a boy I could hold my own in this respect. To compose and even transcribe a long Latin essay in a single night, keen to emulate my role model Sallust in austerity and terseness and then to pour some strong drink all over it, this was not incompatible with my physiology even as a pupil of the venerable grammar school Schulpforta, perhaps not even to that of Sallust – however much it was frowned upon by that venerable school… But later in life I decided against any form of 'spirit' as a drink; like Richard Wagner who converted me, I, an opponent of vegetarianism from experience, cannot urge all those with a *fine* mind strongly enough to entirely abstain from alcohol. Water is good enough… I prefer locations where I have an opportunity to drink water fresh from a fountain, for instance in Nice, Turin and Sils; I keep a small glass by me wherever I go.

In wine lies the truth – here too I seem to be at odds with the rest of the world about the concept of 'truth' – for me, the spirit floats above *water*. Let me give you a few more pieces of advice from my set of moral codes. A big meal is easier to digest than a small one. A main condition for a good digestive system is the fact that the stomach has to work in its entirety. You ought *to know* the size of your stomach. For the same reasons I advise against those lengthy meals, which I call interrupted sacrificial feasts and which are served at the *table d'hôte*.

No snacking in between, no coffee, coffee is depressing. Tea is only good in the morning, in small quantities but strong. If too weak, even by a grain or two, tea can be very harmful and leave you indisposed for the whole day. Everyone has

their own limits, sometimes within the narrowest and most delicate margins. In a very irritating climate I advise against drinking tea first thing in the morning. If at all possible, drink a cup of strong cocoa, any cocoa butter extracted, an hour beforehand. *Sit* on your bottom as little as possible; trust no thought that is not born in the open and in free motion, when all your muscles are engaged. All prejudices come from the bowels. The bottom – I said it before – is the true *sin* against the Holy Spirit.

2.

THE QUESTION of nutrition is closely related to that of *location* and *climate.* None of us can live everywhere at the same time, and those of us who have to perform great tasks which require all our strength have an even more limited choice. The influence of climate upon the *metabolism*, slowing it down or speeding it up, is so great that a wrong choice of location and climate not only alienates you from your task but can even prevent you from taking it up altogether: you would never even know it. Thus, animal strength has never been developed enough to feel that exuberant freedom which enables you to recognize: Only I can do *that*.

Even the least sluggishness of the bowels, once a habit, is more than enough to turn the genius into something mediocre, something 'German'. The climate of Germany alone is sufficient to discourage the strongest and most heroic bowels. The timing of the metabolism is in precise relation to the agility or slowness of the mind's *feet*: after all, the 'mind' itself is only a form of this metabolism. Put together

locations where ingenious people live and always have lived, where wit, cleverness, and irony were part of happiness, where genius is almost compelled to dwell: all of these places have an exquisitely dry atmosphere. Paris, Provence, Florence, Jerusalem, Athens (these names prove something: Genius is *dependent* on dry air, on clear skies), in other words, on a rapid metabolism, on being able to continuously supply itself with great, even enormous quantities of power. I have a case in mind where a great and open mind became narrow, repressed, pedantic and cranky, simply because it lacked a fine instinct for climate. I myself might have become such a case, if illness had not forced me to reason and to reflect upon reason realistically. Now long practice has taught me to read the effects of climatic and meteorological origin on myself as on a very precise and reliable instrument, so that after a journey even as short as that from Turin to Milan I can calculate the change in the degree of atmospheric humidity by observing my body, and I remember with horror the *sinister* fact that apart from the last ten years, the most dangerous years, my life was always spent at the wrong locations, places that should have been forbidden to me: Naumburg, Schulpforta, Thuringia in general, Leipzig, Basel – so many disastrous places for my constitution. If I have not a single pleasant memory of my childhood and youth it would be foolish to blame it at this point on so-called 'moral' causes, as for instance the incontestable lack of *compatible* company; for this lack exists today just as it did then and it does not stop me from being cheerful and brave. But it was the ignorance of the functioning of the body, that confounded 'idealism',

that was the real curse of my life, superfluous and stupid, from which no good would come, for which there can be no compensation, no agreement. The consequences of this 'idealism' explain all my blunders, the great aberrations of instinct and the 'modesties' that diverted me from my task, the fact that I became a professor of linguistics – why not at least a medical doctor or anything else that could have opened my eyes? During my stay in Basel, my whole intellectual routine, including my daily schedule, was a completely pointless abuse of extraordinary powers, without any sort of compensation for the strength I had spent, without even giving a thought about its exhaustion and how to replace it. I completely lacked any subtle egotism; I did not take care of my imperious instinct; I was everyone's equal – it was a 'selflessness' that did not observe distance – something I will never forgive myself for. When I had almost reached the end (*because* I very nearly did reach it), I began to reflect on this basic absurdity of my life, which was 'idealism'. It was my *illness* that brought me to reason.

3.

CHOICE OF nutrition, choice of climate and location: the third choice, where you must not at any price go wrong, is *your* choice of *recreation*. Here again, depending on the uniqueness of your mind, the limits of what is permitted (that is to say *useful*) are ever more restricted. In my case, general *reading* is part of my recreation, therefore it is part of that which allows me to escape from myself, that lets me stroll through alien sciences and souls – something I no longer take seriously.

Indeed, reading allows me to recover from my seriousness. When I work very intensely, you do not find books near me: I wouldn't dream of letting anyone talk to me or even think in my presence. After all, that is just what reading means…

Has anyone ever noticed that, that during that profound tension to which the state of pregnancy condemns the mind and basically the entire organism, chance and every kind of external stimulus strike much too vehemently and 'penetrate' too deeply? You must try to avoid accidents and external stimuli as far as possible: to brick yourself in is one of the first instinctive precautions of spiritual pregnancy. Would I permit an *alien* thought to secretly climb over my brick wall? – After all, that is just what reading means…

Periods of work and productivity are followed by a period of recreation: come on, you pleasant, you witty, you clever books! – Will they be German books?

I must go back six months to catch myself with a book in my hand. What was it this time? An excellent work by Victor Brochard, *Les Sceptiques Grecs*. The sceptics, the only *venerable* types amongst the two-faced, indeed quintuple-faced race of philosophers!

Otherwise, I almost always take refuge in the same books, not very many really, such books that seem to have been written for me. Perhaps it is not in my nature to read many or a wide variety of books: a library makes me ill. Neither is it in my nature to love many or, indeed, a wide variety of things. Suspicion, even hostility towards new books, is more likely to be one of my instincts than 'tolerance', 'generosity' and other types of 'brotherly love'. Ultimately, it is to a few old French authors that I return again and again; I only believe in French culture and regard everything in Europe that calls itself 'culture' as a misunderstanding, not to mention German culture.

The few instances of highly educated people I have encountered in Germany were of French origin, in particular Cosima Wagner, who as far as I am concerned was by far the leading voice in matters of taste.

The fact that I do not read Pascal but that I *love* him, as the most instructive victim of Christianity – slowly murdered, first in body, then in mind, as the sum of the logic of the most horrific form of inhuman cruelty; that I have something of Montaigne's mischievousness in my spirit and, who knows?, perhaps in my body too; that my artist's taste cannot but defend men like Molière, Corneille and Racine and this not entirely without wrath against a wild genius like Shakespeare – all this does not finally prevent me from regarding even the modern French writers as charming company. I cannot imagine any other century in history in which such a group of inquisitive yet subtle psychologists could have been gathered than in present-day Paris. Randomly, since their number is by no means small. I name Paul Bourget, Pierre Loti, Gyp, Meilhac, Anatole France, Jules Lemaître, or, singling out one of strong race, a genuine Latin of whom I am particularly fond, Guy de Maupassant. Between ourselves, I prefer *this* generation even to their great masters since they have all been corrupted by German philosophy (Taine for instance by Hegel, whom he has to thank for misunderstanding great men and times). Wherever Germany reaches out to, she *corrupts*

culture. It was the war that 'redeemed' the spirit of France.

Stendhal (one of the happiest accidents of my life, for everything in it of lasting value came to me by chance, never because of recommendation) is invaluable with his anticipatory psychologist's eye, his grasp of facts, reminiscent of the greatest of all masters (Napoleon); and last but not least as an honest atheist, a rare figure in France, almost impossible to find – with all due respect to Prosper Mérimée… Perhaps I am myself jealous of Stendhal? He has taken the best atheist joke I could possibly have made away from me: 'God's only excuse is that he does not exist'… I myself have said somewhere: What was hitherto the greatest objection to life? *God…*'

4.

IT WAS Heinrich Heine who defined the meaning of a lyrical poet for me. In vain do I search all areas throughout the past millennia for a similarly sweet and passionate music. He possessed that divine wickedness without which I cannot image perfection; I assess men and races according to how closely they associate god with Satyr – and how they handle the German language! One day it will be said that Heine and I were by far the top jugglers of the German language, infinitely outstripping everything ordinary Germans could do with it.

I must be closely related to *Byron's* Manfred: I found all these abysses in my own soul – at the mere age of thirteen I was ready to read this work. I have nothing to say, just a contemptuous glance for those who dare to speak of Faust

in the same breath as Manfred. The Germans are *incapable* of any notion of greatness: look at Schumann. Angry with this sickly Saxon, I actually composed a counter-overture to Manfred, of which Hans von Bülow declared he had never seen the like before: raping the muse of music, that's what it is, he said.

Searching for the best formula to do Shakespeare justice, I only ever come up with: 'He conceived the character of Caesar.' You cannot conjecture a thing like that – you either are him or you are not. The great poet *only* draws from his own experience – up to the point where he cannot bear to look at his own work later on. Whenever I reread my *Zarathustra* I must pace to and fro in my room for half an hour, unable to control my sobs.

I know of no more heartbreaking literature than that of Shakespeare: how he must have suffered to need to play the clown so badly; do you understand *Hamlet*? It is not doubt, but *certainty* that drives you mad… But to feel like that you must be deep, must be abysmal, must be a philosopher… We are all *afraid* of the truth… And let me tell you this: I know instinctively for certain that Lord Bacon is the originator, the self-torturer, of this most sinister type of literature: why should *I* bother about the pitiful chattering of American blockheads and half-wits? But the power for the greatest visionary realism is not only compatible with the greatest strength for action, with the monstrous, the crime – *it actually anticipates it*… We don't by far know enough about Lord Bacon, the first realist in the very sense of the word, to know *everything* he did, *everything* he aimed for, how he himself

felt about *everything*... You critics can all go to hell! If I had called my Zarathustra something else, Richard Wagner for example, the acumen of two millennia would not have been enough to divine that the author of *Human, All Too Human* is the inventor of Zarathustra...

5.

WHILE SPEAKING of the recreational pursuits of my life I need to express my gratitude for him who afforded me by far the deepest and dearest forms of escape. This has been without doubt my intimate relationship with Richard Wagner. All other human relationships were fair enough; but I would not miss the days in Tribschen from my life – days of trust, of happiness, of marvellous opportunities and above all – of *deep* moments... I do not know what others made of Wagner, but nothing ever cast a cloud over *our* friendship.

This brings me back to France – I cannot give any reasons, I can only contemptuously pucker my mouth when I look to Wagnerians and their ilk, who think they honour Wagner by believing him to be like *themselves*... Since I am what I am, instinctively alienated from all things German (to the point that the mere presence of a German will make me constipated), the first meeting with Wagner was also my first sigh of relief ever. I felt him, I revered him as a *foreigner*, as the antithesis of, and a living protest against, all 'German virtues'.

We, who were children in the stagnant air of the 1850s, are necessarily pessimists with regard to the notion of

'German'; we cannot be anything else but revolutionaries – we will not accept any condition in which a *creep* will be at the top. I am totally oblivious to his attire – whether he is robed in scarlet or puts on a uniform. Well then! Wagner was a revolutionary – he ran away from the Germans...

The *artist* has no home in Europe except in Paris; the predilection for all the five senses which is a condition of Wagner's art, that sensitivity to nuance, the psychological morbidity, these can only be found in Paris. Nowhere else is there this passion for form, this seriousness about stage-setting, which is Parisian seriousness par excellence. The Germans have no idea of the extraordinary ambition that lives in the soul of a Parisian artist... Germans are good-natured – Wagner was certainly not... But I have already written enough on the subject of Wagner, where he stands, where he comes from (see *Beyond Good and Evil*, 'Aphorism 2'): it is the late French Romanticists, that high-flying and heaven-aspiring bunch of artists like Delacroix and Berlioz, who are essentially sick, terminally so, pure fanatics of *expression*, virtuosos to the last... Who was the first *intelligent* follower of Wagner, pray? Charles Baudelaire, the very man who first understood Delacroix, that archetypal Decadent in whom a whole generation of artists has recognized itself – perhaps he was also the last...

What was it that I could not forgive Wagner for? That he *condescended* to the Germans – that he became a German Imperialist... Whoever Germany reaches out to – she will *corrupt* their culture.

6.

ALL THINGS CONSIDERED, I would never have survived my youth without Wagner's music. For I was *condemned* to live amongst Germans. If you wish to escape from unbearable oppression, you need Hashish. Well then, I needed Wagner. Wagner is the antidote to everything essentially German, but it is a poison nevertheless, I do not deny it. As soon as there was a piano arrangement of *Tristan* available (thank you, Mr von Bülow), I was a Wagnerite. The older works of Wagner, I felt, were beneath me, they were too common, too 'German'... But to this day I am looking for works of a similar dangerous fascination to *Tristan*, that horrifying yet sweet quality of infinity. I am searching among all the arts, but in vain. All the mysteries of Leonardo da Vinci are forgotten at the first note of *Tristan*. It is absolutely the very highest point in Wagner's work, he recovered from it with the *Mastersingers* and the *Ring* cycle. To recuperate – that is a retrograde step in a nature like that of Wagner...

I thank my lucky stars that I lived at the right time and in particular amongst Germans, to have been able to appreciate this work – that is how strongly the curiosity of a psychologist has a hold on me. The world must be a poor place for those that have never been sick enough for the 'salaciousness of hell'; it is permissible, almost imperative to use a mystic formula here.

I believe that I know better than anyone else the prodigious feats of which Wagner is capable, the fifty worlds of unknown ecstasies to which only he could soar. Strong as I am now and able to use even the most dubious and dangerous

things to my advantage to become even more powerful, I see Wagner as the great benefactor of my life. We are related in that we suffered more than any other men of this century, even made each other suffer, and that will bring together our names once again for all eternity. For, just as Wagner as a German is simply a misconception, so surely am I and always will be. Two hundred years of psychological and artistic discipline are required, my dear Germans… But it is all too late…

7.

ONE MORE WORD for my most select readers: what do I actually ask of music? It should be bright yet profound, like an October's afternoon; it should be individual, carefree, tender, like a dainty, sweet woman full of mischief and grace… I will never accept that Germans *can* know the meaning of music. The musicians generally accepted as Germans are all *foreigners*: Slavs, Croats, Italians, Dutchmen or Jews; or else they are Germans of a strong race now *extinct*, like Heinrich Schütz, Bach and Handel. I myself am still enough of a Pole to give up all the music in the world for that of Chopin. I would make three exceptions here: with Wagner's *Siegfried Idyll* and perhaps with some works of Liszt too, who with his noble orchestration has the advantage over all other musicians; and finally also with all those that grew up beyond the Alps – *my side*… I would not miss Rossini for the world, even less my Southern counterpart in music, my Venetian maestro, Pietro Gasti. And when I say beyond the Alps, I really only mean Venice. Whenever I want to find another

word for music, I inevitably come to say Venice. I do not know the difference between tears and music; I cannot think of joy or the *South* without the tremble of real fear.

On the bridge I stood
in recent muggy night,
from afar a song
came: like golden drops
across the trembling rim.
Gondolas, lights, music
drunkenly they swam far into the dusk

My soul, strings finely tuned,
sang a boating song
invisibly moved,
secretly along,
trembling in bright bliss
– was someone listening in?

8.

IN ALL THIS – in the choice of food, location, climate and recreation – the instinct for self-preservation dominates, expressing itself most obviously as an instinct for *self-defence*. Not to see, not to hear most things, but to keep them at arm's length – this is the foremost prudence, the first evidence that you are not here by chance but out of necessity. The common word for this instinct of self-defence is *taste*. It is imperative not just to say 'no' where a 'yes' would be an act of 'unselfishness', but also to say *'no' as little as possible*.

Depart, detach yourself from situations where again and again it would be necessary to say 'no'. That is because the discharge of defensive energy, however slight, regular and habitual it has become, causes an extraordinary and absolutely superfluous loss. Our *greatest* energy discharge consists of the most frequent small ones. The defence, the keeping-at-arm's-length is a discharge – and make no mistake here – of strength *wasted* for negative ends. Simply by being constantly on your guard, you can become weak enough not to be able to defend yourself any longer.

Suppose I were to step out of my house and, instead of the quiet and noble city of Turin, were to encounter a provincial German town: why, my instinct would have to shut down, to repress everything that would force itself upon it from this downtrodden and cowardly world. Or if I were to find a German metropolis, this structure of vice in which nothing grows but where everything, good or bad, has been forcibly imported. What choice would I have then but to become a *hedgehog*? – But to have quills is a sheer waste, a twofold luxury even if I choose not to have quills but *open* hands instead…

Another form of prudence and self-defence is to react as *seldom as possible* and to avoid situations and conditions where you are condemned, as it were, to suspend your 'liberty' and initiative and become a mere bundle of reactions. For example, when we are dealing with books. The scholar who actually does little else but pore over books (he reads on average 200 books a day), in the end loses all his ability to think for himself. If he does not pore, he does not think! Whenever he thinks, he *answers* to a stimulus (a thought he

has read) – and finally all he does is react. The scholar devotes all his energy to affirming or denying or reviewing all that has already been thought – he no longer thinks for himself... His instinct for self-defence has become brittle, otherwise he would defend himself against books. The scholar is a Decadent. I have seen it with my own eyes: gifted, generous and free-spirited natures, no more than thirty and already 'wrecks' from too much reading; nothing but matchsticks that you have to strike so that they emit a spark or 'thought'.

To read a *book* first thing in the morning at daybreak, at the dawn of your strength – that I call a vice!

9.

AT THIS POINT a direct answer to the question *how we become what we are* can no longer be evaded. And with that I touch upon the master stroke of the art of self-preservation – *Selfishness*... Let us assume that our task, the purpose, the *destiny* of the task exceeds by far an average norm, then there could be no greater danger but to come face-to-face *with* this task. To become what you are presupposes that you do not have the remotest idea *what* you are. From this point of view, even the *blunders* in your life have a unique meaning and value, the occasional deviation or straying from the path, the hesitations, the 'modesties', the seriousness, wasted upon tasks that are beyond *the* main task. This outlines a great prudence, possibly even the highest prudence; whereas 'Know Yourself' would be a sure way to lead to downfall, to forget yourself, to *misunderstand* yourself, to belittle yourself, to limit and moderate yourself becomes reason itself. In moral terms:

neighbourly love and living for others and other things *may* be the means of protection to maintain the most rigorous egoism. This is the exception where I, against all my self-imposed rules and conviction, take the part of the 'selfless' instincts: here they are engaged in the service of *egoism* and *self-discipline*.

The whole surface of consciousness (for consciousness is a surface) has to be kept free of any of the great imperatives. Beware even of every striking word or gesture! They all endanger the instinct to 'know itself' too soon. Meanwhile the organizing 'idea', destined to rule, continues to grow below; it becomes commanding; it leads you slowly *back* from deviations and aberrations; it prepares *individual* qualities and capacities that may one day be indispensable as the means to the whole – gradually, it develops all *serviceable* faculties before it indicates any trace of the dominant task of 'goal', 'purpose' and 'meaning'.

Viewed from this angle, my life is simply amazing. The task to *re-evaluate all values* required perhaps more abilities than could ever be found combined in one individual, and above all, also contrasting abilities that would at the same time not be mutually inimical, if not destructive. The ranking of abilities, distancing, the art of separating without creating hostility, to confuse nothing, to 'reconcile' nothing, to be enormously diverse yet the opposite of chaos – all this was the main condition and the long secret workings and artistic nature of my instinct. Its superior *guardianship* was so strong that at no time could I have any notion of what was growing within me – suddenly all my abilities *burst forth*: ripe and absolutely perfect. I fail to remember ever having exerted myself; there is truly no trace of a *struggle* in my life; I am the opposite of a heroic character. To 'want' something, to 'strive' for something, to focus on a 'purpose' or a 'wish', all these things I do not know from experience. Even at this moment I look out upon my future – a *wide* future – as upon a calm sea; there is no foam of desire upon it. I have not the slightest wish that anything should change from the way it is; I myself do not wish to change. But I have always been like that. I never wished for anything. I am someone who can say at the age of forty-four that he was never interested in *honours*, *women* or *money*. Not that these things were lacking… For instance, one fine day I found myself to be a university professor! I never even thought about it; after all, I was only twenty-four years old. In the same way, only two years earlier I suddenly was a philologist, in the sense that my *first* philological work, my beginning in every sense, was required by my teacher Ritschl to be printed in his magazine *Rheinisches Museum*. (*Ritschl* – I say it full of veneration – was the only genial scholar whom I have ever met. He possessed that pleasant notoriety that distinguishes us Thuringians and that makes even a German a nice person – we prefer to use secret and hidden paths to get to the truth. These words should not be taken as a slur upon my fellow countryman, the *intelligent* Leopold von Ranke.)

10.

AT THIS POINT you may ask me why I actually told you all these trivial and on the whole irrelevant details; I would seem to be harming my own cause, all the more so since I

claim to represent great tasks. Let me say this to you: such small things as diet, location, climate, recreation, the whole casuistry of self-love, are by far more important than anything else that has been hitherto considered essential by us. Here in particular, we have to start to *rethink.* All those things that mankind has until now thought about with such earnestness are not even realities; they are mere fancies, indeed *lies*, arising from the bad instincts of sick and in the truest sense harmful natures: such concepts as 'god', 'soul', 'virtue', 'sin', 'the hereafter', 'truth', 'eternal life'... And yet we looked for the greatness of human nature, its 'divinity' in them... All questions of politics, of the social order, of education have been thoroughly falsified because the most harmful people were accepted by us as great men, by being taught to despise the so-called 'trivial' matters, which are really the fundamental concerns of life... Our current culture is highly ambiguous... The German emperor is in league with the Pope, as if the Pope was not the representative of the mortal enemy of life! What has been built today will not stand three years from now.

If I put my abilities to the test, never mind that what follows, a regime change or a new development as never seen before, I more than any other mortal can claim to be great. If I now compare myself with those people who were hitherto considered the 'first' among men, the difference becomes tangible. I do not even count these so-called 'first' men among human beings – for me they are the waste product of mankind, fiends deformed by disease and instincts of revenge; they are all monsters, rotten to the core and sick

beyond cure, avenging themselves on life… I choose to be their very opposite. It is my prerogative to be highly sensitive to any indication of healthy instincts. There is not a single morbid trait in me; even during my long and serious illness I have never become morbid. You will look in vain for a trace of fanaticism in my character. No-one is able to point out even a single instance in my life where I was presumptuous or pathetic. The pathos of gestures is *not* part of greatness; whoever needs gestures is *false*… Beware of the picturesque!

Life became easiest for me whenever it demanded the most from me. Those who saw me during the seventy days of this autumn when, without interruption, I performed so many things of the first order that no-one can match it or do better, things that will be representative for centuries to come, will not have noticed a single sign of tension in me, but rather my exuberant wellbeing and cheerfulness.

Never did I eat with greater enjoyment, never did I sleep better. I know no better means to deal with great tasks but *play*; this is an essential prerequisite and a sign of greatness. The slightest constraint, a gloomy expression, any harsh sound from the throat are all objections to a person, but how much more so to his work!… We must have no nerves… Even to *suffer* from loneliness is an objection – I personally have only ever suffered from being 'crowded out'.

At an absurdly young age, when I was only seven, I already knew that I could never be stirred by human speech. Did anyone see me sad because of it? Today, I still feel the same affability towards everyone, I give my attention even to the most lowly born, and in all this there is not an ounce of

arrogance or contempt. Those whom I despise will soon *know* that I despise them, my mere existence angers those with bad blood in them. My formula for greatness in man is to *embrace your destiny*, to alter nothing, either in the future, or in the past, or in all eternity. Do not simply endure necessity and even less, hide it, but *love* it – all idealism is a falsehood in the face of necessity.

Chapter 3

Why I write such excellent books

1.

I AM ONE THING, my books are another... Before I talk about them, I would like to touch upon the question about whether or *not* they are understood. I do it as casually as is fitting, since the time for this question has not yet come, really. For me, too, the time has not yet come, some of us are born posthumously.

One day, there will have to be institutions where men can live and teach as I myself know how to live and teach: perhaps then they will also establish professorships for the interpretation of *Zarathustra.* But I would be completely contradicting myself, if I expected ears *and hands* for my truths today. Not only does it seem understandable that no-one listens to me yet, that no-one knows what to do with me, it also seems to me quite right that it is so. I do not wish to be taken for someone else – and I too must not take myself for someone else.

Let me say it once again, there have been very few instances of 'ill will' in my life, even less of literary 'ill will'. However, there have been far too many of *pure stupidity*... To pick up a book of mine seems to me to be one of the rarest honours man can pay himself – I even assume he takes his

shoes off first, or his boots... When Doctor Heinrich von Stein once seriously complained not to have understood a single word of my *Zarathustra*, I told him that that was as it should be: to have understood just six sentences or better; to have *lived* them, would lift a man on to a higher level among mortals than 'modern man' could reasonably hope for. How *could* I, with *this* feeling for distance, even wish to be read by 'modern men' as I know them! My triumph is precisely the opposite to that of Schopenhauer's 'read and be read' – I say, 'I am not read, I shall not read.'

Not that I wish to underestimate the fun that I had when I met with the *innocence* of people saying no to my books. Even this very summer, at a time when I could perhaps upset the apple cart of all literature together with my weighty, far too weighty literature, a professor from Berlin University told me good-naturedly that I should find a new form of writing: nobody would read anything like that.

In the end it was not Germany but Switzerland that came up with the two most extreme cases: an essay by a Dr V Widman in the Bernese newspaper *Bund* about *Beyond Good and Evil* as 'Nietzsche's dangerous book' and a general account about all my books by a Mr Karl Spitteler in the very same newspaper are the highlight of my life – I shall not say why... The latter spoke of my *Zarathustra* as 'an advanced *exercise in style*', for example, and suggested I should also try and add some substance. Dr Widman expressed his respect for the courage of my endeavour to abolish all decent feelings.

Thanks to a little trick of chance, every sentence here was, with admirable consistency, a truth stood on its head: at bottom

there was nothing else to do but to 're-evaluate values', to hit the nail on the head as far as I was concerned in a remarkable fashion – instead of hitting my head with a nail. I shall try to explain myself all the more.

In the end, no-one can learn any more from matters, books included, than he already knows. Without access to events, you will not have an ear for them. Let us take an extreme case and suppose a book contains only events that lie entirely outside the range of general or even less general experiences and suppose it is the first language for a new series of experiences. In such a case nothing really will be heard at all and thanks to an acoustic delusion, you will think that since you hear nothing *there is nothing there*. This, at least, is my usual experience, and proves, if you like, the *originality* of my experience. Whoever thought they had understood something in my work will have appropriated something from it in his own image – quite often the opposite of me, for instance an 'idealist'; whoever understood nothing I wrote will deny that I am worth considering at all.

The word '*Superman*' as a definition of a type of greatest perfection in contrast to 'modern' man or 'good' man, to Christians and other nihilists – a word that in the mouth of Zarathustra, the *destroyer* of morality, acquires a very profound meaning – was in all innocence understood almost everywhere in the light of those values that the figure of Zarathustra stood against – I mean as an 'idealistic' type of higher human being – half 'saint', half 'genius'... Other learned cattle have accused me of Darwinism because of this definition; it was even seen as belonging to that 'hero cult' of Carlyle's, that great unconscious

and involuntary swindler, which was so maliciously rejected by me. Once I whispered in someone's ear he should look to Cesare Borgia rather than Parsifal and he could not believe his ears.

You must forgive me my lack of any curiosity as far as reviews of my books are concerned, in particular when they appear in newspapers. My friends and publishers know this and do not mention them to me. In one particular case, however, I once found out about all the sins committed against one of my books – it was *Beyond Good and Evil*. I could tell a pretty story about that. Would you believe that the *Nationalzeitung* (a Prussian newspaper – this information is for my readers from abroad; I myself read only the *Journal des Débats*) in all seriousness regarded this book as a 'sign of the times', a piece of right and proper *Junker philosophy*, which its organ the *Kreuz* newspaper simply lacked the courage to come up with?

2.

THIS WAS MENTIONED for the benefit of Germans, for I have readers everywhere – all highly educated minds, characters in top positions and with great responsibilities on their shoulders; among my readers are even some true geniuses. In Vienna, in St Petersburg, in Stockholm, in Copenhagen, in Paris and in New York – everywhere I have been discovered, but *not* in Europe's plain country: in Germany… And let me be honest, I am even happier about my non-readers, those that have neither heard my name nor of the word 'philosophy', but wherever I go, here in Turin for instance, all faces light up and soften. The thing that so far has flattered me most is that old peddler women will not rest until they have picked for me the

very sweetest bunch from amongst their grapes. *For this* you must be a philosopher.

Not for nothing are the Poles called the Frenchmen of the Slavs. A lovely Russian woman will not mistake my origins for a moment. I am no use at being pompous; at best I can go as far as embarrassment… To think in German, to feel in German – I can do it all, but *that* is too much for me… My former tutor Ritschl went so far as to say that I planned even my philological treatises like a Parisian novelist – that they were absurdly thrilling. In Paris itself people are surprised about '*toutes mes audaces et finesses*' – to quote Monsieur Taine; I am afraid that even in the highest forms of the dithyramb, the hymn of praise to Dionysus, you will find traces of that ingredient that can never be stupid, never be 'German' – it is called 'wit'… I can do no other, so help me God! Amen. We all know, some even know from experience, what a long-ear is. Well, I dare to assert that I have the tiniest ears. This is of no little interest to the ladies – am I right that they feel understood by me?… I am the supreme *anti-ass* and as such a world-historical beast – I am in Greek, and not only in Greek, the *Antichrist*…

3.

I KNOW on the whole my privileges as a writer; in a few cases I was even assured how much the habitual reading of my books would 'ruin' the taste buds. It is simply unbearable to read any other books, least of all philosophical ones. It is a distinction beyond all comparison to enter this elegant and delicate world – you certainly do not need to be a German; it is in short a distinction that must be earned. Anyone, however, akin to me

in *loftiness* of will, experiences the true ecstasies of learning by reading them: for I swoop from heights where no bird ever flew, I know abysses where no foot ever lost its footing. I was told it was not possible to put any book of mine down – even that I disturbed a good night's sleep… There is absolutely no prouder or at the same time more subtle kind of book: it achieves here and there the highest that can be achieved on earth, cynicism; you have to conquer it with the most delicate fingerstrokes, using them like the most valiant fists. Every weakness of the soul will bar you from it for good and ever, even a belly-ache; you do not need nerves but you have to have a cheerful abdomen. Not just poverty, the stuffy air in a soul excludes you from it, but much more so cowardice, the unclean and the secret longing for revenge deep down in the bowels: one word from me drives all bad instincts into full view. Among my acquaintances are several test animals, which I use to sample their very varied and instructive reactions to my books. Those who wish to have nothing to do with their contents, my so-called friends for example, become 'impersonal', they wish me luck to have 'done it once again' – apparently there is improvement because of a happier ring to the books… These completely reprobate 'spirits', these 'beautiful souls', liars all in the extreme, have absolutely no idea what to do with these books – therefore they feel they are *beneath* them – a consistent reaction of all 'beautiful souls'. The cattle among my acquaintances, the mere Germans, if you don't mind my saying so, let me know that they are not always of my opinion but that they agree here and there, for instance… I have heard this even with regard to my *Zarathustra*.

Similarly, every 'feminist' in a person, even in a man, closes the gate as far as I am concerned: never will you enter the labyrinth of daring knowledge. You have to be completely ruthless with yourself, must be used to great *hardness*, to remain cheerful and merry among all these implacable truths. If I conjure up the picture of a perfect reader, he always becomes a monster of courage and curiosity, yet also of subtlety, cunning and prudence – a born adventurer and explorer. After all, I can not describe any better than *Zarathustra* did *who* I am actually addressing: those few he was prepared to reveal his riddle to.

'To you, you bold explorers and experimenters and who ever else embarked beneath cunning sails on dreadful seas,

– to you, you drunk, with riddles revelling in twilight, whose souls are being lured by flutes down every treacherous abyss,

– for you do not want to grope your way along a thread with a coward's hand, and where you are able to *divine*, you hate to *open up*...'

4.

AT THE SAME TIME, I wish to make a general comment about my *art of style.* The meaning of every style is to *communicate* a state of mind, an inner tension of pathos through symbols, including the timing of these symbols – that is the character of every style; and in view of the fact that the multitude of states of mind in me is enormous, I have also many styles at my disposal – in short, the most diverse art of style that ever was available to man. Any style is *good* which genuinely communicates a state of mind, which does not make

a mistake when using symbols, the timing of symbols, and the *moods* – all phrasing is to do with creating moods. Here my instinct is impeccable.

Good style *in itself* is a folly, mere 'idealism' or 'beautiful *in itself*' for instance, or 'goodness *in itself*' or 'the thing *itself*'... This is assuming that there are ears to hear – that they are *capable* and worthy of such pathos, that there are still plenty who are *worth* communicating with... Meanwhile my Zarathustra, for example, is still searching for such people – ah, he will have to go looking for a long time yet! – You have to *deserve* to listen to him... And until then, there will be nobody who will understand the *art* that has been squandered here. No-one else has lavished newer, more extraordinary, more genuinely original forms of art on to the world. That this was possible in the German language had yet to be substantiated; I myself would have dismissed it most emphatically. Before me, nobody knew what the German language was capable of – what any language is capable of.

The art of *grand* rhythm and *grand style* of phrasing, expressing a tremendous swing in sublime and superhuman passion, was first discovered by me: with a hymn of praise entitled 'The Seven Seals' which is the last discourse of the third part of *Zarathustra*. With that I soared thousands of miles above everything which hitherto has been called poetry.

5.

THE FACT that my books are written by a psychologist, unparalleled in history, is perhaps the first impression a good reader may get, a reader such as I deserve, and one who reads me

as the good old philologists used to read their Horace. Those doctrines that are really accepted by all the world, not to speak of the la-di-da philosophers, moralists and other blockheads and cabbages, seem to me but naive blunders – for example that belief that 'altruistic' and 'egoistic' are opposites, while the ego itself is merely a 'supreme swindle', an 'ideal'… There are *no such things* as egoistic or altruistic deeds: both terms are a psychological nonsense. Or the proposition 'man strives for happiness'… or 'happiness is the reward of virtue'… or 'joy and misery are opposite values'… Morality, the femme fatale, has falsified all psychology and *outmoralized* it until only that horrible humbug that love must be 'altruistic' was left… You have to have a firm grip of *yourself*, stand steadfastly on both legs, otherwise you *cannot* love at all. Women know that all too well: they don't give a damn for unselfish and merely objective men… May I dare to say that I know women? That this is part of my Dionysian heritage? Who knows, perhaps I am the first psychologist of the eternal-feminine. They all love me – which is old hat (not counting the damaged, the 'emancipated' ones, who haven't got what it takes to have children). Luckily I am not willing to let myself be torn to bits – your typical woman tears those she loves to bits… I know these amiable maenads… Oh, what a dangerous, sly, subterranean little beast she is! And at the same time so lovely!… A little woman pursuing her revenge would even destroy fate.

Woman is inexpressibly more wicked than man, but also cleverer. Goodness in a woman is already a form of *degeneration*… A so-called 'beautiful soul' in a woman is essentially a physiological disease – I shall not go any further,

otherwise this would become a medical discourse. The struggle for *equal* rights is actually a symptom of disease; every doctor knows it. Women, the more feminine they are, fight with all their might against rights in general: the natural order of things, in the eternal *war* between the sexes she always has the greatest advantage.

Have you ever listened to my definition of love? It is the only one worthy of a philosopher. Love is conducted like war because it is at heart the deadly hatred of the sexes. Have you heard my reply to the question of how a woman can be *cured*, saved? Give her a child. Women need children, to her a man is merely a means to an end: thus spoke Zarathustra.

'The emancipation of woman' is the instinctive hatred of the *misshapen* – that is to say, infertile – women for her fertile sisters; the fight against 'man' is only ever a means, an excuse, a strategy. In raising themselves to the level of 'women *per se*', of 'supreme woman', of 'ideal woman', they try to bring down the general level of women's rank; and there is no surer way of doing so than higher education, wearing trousers and the voting rights of cattle. To tell the truth, the emancipated are the *anarchists* in the world of the 'eternal-feminine', the failures and losers whose lowest instinct is revenge… A whole species of the ugliest type of 'idealism', incidentally, can also be found among men; for instance with Henrik Ibsen, that typical old maid, it is aimed at *poisoning* the clear conscience and the natural spirit in sexual love… And not to leave any doubt about my heartfelt and strict views on these matters I will give you another clause from my code of morality against *vice*: I use the word 'vice' to fight any form of perversion, but if you prefer

a finer word, use 'idealism'. The clause reads: 'Preaching of chastity is a public incitement to perverse acts. All contempt for sexual matters, all sullying of them by applying the concept "unclean" is itself a crime against life – it is the actual crime against the holy spirit of life.'

6.

TO GIVE YOU an idea of my role as a psychologist, I give you a curious bit of psychological analysis from my book *Beyond Good and Evil* – but I forbid any conjectures as to whom I may or may not describe in this passage.

> 'The Genius of the heart, as that great recluse possesses it, the divine tempter and born pied piper of consciences, whose voice is able to descend right down into the underworld of every soul, who does not speak a word or cast a glance without some seductive power or trick, whose exquisite skill enables him to seem, not what he is but what is to those who follow him yet *one more* compulsion to press ever closer to him, to follow him ever more enthusiastically and wholeheartedly… The genius of the heart, who makes all loud and self-satisfied things fall silent and listen out, who smoothes the rough souls and lets them taste a new longing: to lie still, like a mirror, that the low sky may be reflected in them… The genius of the heart, who teaches the clumsy and over-hasty hand to hesitate and to grasp more tenderly, who senses the hidden and forgotten treasure, the drop of goodness and sweet spirituality beneath thick black ice and who is a divining rod for every grain of gold

that was buried for years and years, imprisoned under heaps of mud and sand… The genius of the heart, whose very touch enriches everyone, not with gifts and surprises, not by the wealth and stealth of others, but richer in themselves, more aware of themselves than before, opened up, caressed and sounded out by a soft westerly wind, perhaps even less sure, more tender, more fragile, more broken, but full of hopes that have not yet a name, full of new will and flowing forth, full of new unwillingness and flowing back.'

THE BIRTH OF TRAGEDY.

1.

TO BE FAIR to *The Birth of Tragedy* (1872) we have to overlook a few things. Whatever was wrong with the book gave it its *effect* and fascination, that is to say its practical application to *Wagnerism* as if that were a symptom of an *ascent*. Because of it, this book was an event in Wagner's life; it was only from then on that the name of Wagner evoked great hopes. People still remind me of this today, occasionally even in the context of *Parsifal*, how it is really *my* fault that the movement became a *cult* and excited such high opinions.

I found on several occasions that the book was referred to as the 'Rebirth of Tragedy from the Spirit of Music'; people had only ears for a new formula for the art, the intention, the task of *Wagner*, and because of it they did not notice what was truly valuable in the book. 'Hellenism and Pessimism', that would have been a less ambiguous title, suggesting a first

instruction of how the Greeks coped with pessimism – how they *overcame* it… Precisely their tragedies prove that the Greeks were *no* pessimists: Schopenhauer went wrong here, in precisely the same way as he went wrong in all other things.

If looked at with some degree of objectivity, *The Birth of Tragedy* seems anachronistic; you would never dream that it was *begun* amid the thunder of the Battle of Wörth. I have thought through these problems before the walls of Metz, on cold September nights while on duty as a medical orderly. The book seems to be some fifty years older than it really is. Politically it is indifferent, 'un-German' you would say today. It smells offensively of Hegel, but some of the formulas have the doleful whiff of Schopenhauer. It is a 'concept' – the antithesis of the Dionysian and the Apollonian translated into metaphysics; history itself is the development of this 'concept' whereby in tragedy this polarity has been sublimated into a unity. These things have never before faced each other and are now suddenly juxtaposed; they are used to illuminate each other and are now *comprehensible*… Opera, for example, and the revolution.

The two decisive *innovations* of the book are firstly that Greeks have understood the Dionysian phenomenon; for the first time a psychological analysis is given and it is considered to be the root of all Greek art. The other is the understanding of Socratism: Socrates is recognized for the first time as an instrument of Greek disintegration, as a typical Decadent. 'Rationality' *versus* instinct. 'Rationality' is at any price seen as a dangerous, life-undermining power.

On the matter of Christianity there is a profound and hostile silence throughout the book. It is neither Apollonian nor

Dionysian; it *denies* all *aesthetic* values – the only values that *The Birth of Tragedy* recognizes; it is nihilistic in its truest sense, while the ultimate limit of affirmation is attained in the Dionysian symbol. Once the Christian priests are even alluded to as a 'spiteful kind of dwarf' dwelling 'deep, deep beneath the earth'.

2.

THIS BEGINNING is strange beyond belief. As far as I know, I myself had *discovered* the only metaphor and counterpart in history, and thus I became the first to understand the amazing phenomenon of the Dionysian. Similarly, in recognizing Socrates as a Decadent, I could prove unequivocally how little the security of my psychological grasp would be endangered by any moral idiosyncrasy; regarding Morality itself as a symptom of decadence is an innovation and unique in the history of knowledge. How high had I jumped with these two insights above the wretched and shallow chatter about optimism versus pessimism. I was the first to see the actual polarity: the degenerating instinct that turns against life with subliminal vengefulness (Christianity, the philosophy of Schopenhauer, in a sense even the philosophy of Plato, the whole of idealism in its typical form) versus the formula of *supreme affirmation* born out of abundance, of profusion, to say 'yes' without reserve, say 'yes' to suffering itself, to guilt, to all that is dubious and strange in existence itself... This ultimate, most joyous, most wantonly extravagant 'yes' to life is not just the ultimate insight, it is also the *most profound*, the one most strongly confirmed and upheld by truth and science. Nothing needs to be taken away, nothing is superfluous – as it is, the aspects of existence rejected by the

Christians and other nihilists are of an infinitely higher order in the hierarchy of values than even that which the instinct of decadence could approve of. To understand this requires *courage* and, as a condition for that, an excess of *strength*; for precisely as far as courage *may* dare to go governed by precisely that strength, you will come closer to the truth. Knowledge, saying 'yes' to reality, is just as necessary for the strong as cowardice and the *flight* from reality – the 'ideal' – is for the weak, who are inspired by weakness… It is not given to them to know that the Decadents *need* the lie, it is one of the conditions for their survival.

Whoever does not merely understand the word 'Dionysian' but sees *himself* described by the word 'Dionysian' has no need to refute Plato or Christianity or Schopenhauer – he can *smell the decay*.

3.

I FINALLY explained in my book *The Twilight of the Idols* the extent to which I have discovered the concept of the 'tragic', the ultimate knowledge of the psychology of tragedy. 'Saying "Yes" to life even with its most alien and difficult problems; the will to live rejoicing in its own boundlessness even while *sacrificing* its most superior types – *that* is what I called Dionysian, that was how I saw the bridge to the psychology of the *tragic* poet. *Not* to be rid of fear and pity, not to purge myself of a dangerous effect by its vehement discharge as Aristotle misunderstood it, but the eternal joy of becoming in itself beyond all fear and pity, that joy that included even *joy in destroying*.'

In this sense I have the right to see myself as the first *tragical philosopher* – that is to say, the extreme antithesis and polar opposite of a pessimistic philosopher. Before I came along, this translation of the Dionysian into philosophical pathos did not exist: *the tragic wisdom was lacking* – I looked in vain for signs of it even among the *great* Greeks of philosophy, those that lived two centuries before Socrates. I retained some doubt in the case of Heraclitus, in whose presence I felt altogether warmer and more comfortable then anywhere else. The affirmative answer to death *and destruction*, which is the decisive feature of a Dionysian philosophy, saying 'yes' to opposition and war, of *becoming* along with radical rejection even of the concept of '*being*' – all this is definitively more closely related to me than anything else thought to date. The doctrine of the 'eternal recurrence', that is to say of the unconditional and infinite circuit of all things – this doctrine of Zarathustra *could* already have been taught by Heraclitus. Stoicism, having inherited almost all their fundamental ideas of Heraclitus, shows traces of it.

4.

THIS BOOK offers tremendous hope. Ultimately, I have no reason to withdraw the hope for a Dionysian future from music. Let us look a century ahead and assume that my assault on two thousand years of unnaturalness and abuse of mankind is successful. That new denomination of life, which takes the greatest of all tasks, the advancement of mankind, into its hands, including the merciless destruction of all that is degenerative and parasitic, will make that *abundance of life*

on earth (from which the Dionysian state must also grow again) once again possible. I promise a *tragic age*: the greatest art of saying 'Yes' to life, tragedy itself, will be reborn when mankind has weathered the recognition of the hardest but most necessary war *without suffering on its account*...

A psychologist might still add that the Wagnerian music I heard in my youth had absolutely nothing to do with Wagner, that when I described the Dionysian music I described what *I* had heard – that I instinctively had to translate and transfigure everything into the new spirit that I had within me. The evidence for that, *as convincing as any evidence can be*, is my essay 'Wagner in Bayreuth' – all psychologically decisive passages only speak of me, you can happily insert my name or the word 'Zarathustra' whenever the text mentions Wagner. The entire picture of the artist *in praise of Dionysus* is the picture of the *pre-existent* poet of Zarathustra, sketched with incredible profundity and without touching in the slightest on Wagnerian reality. Wagner himself was aware of that; he did not recognize himself in this essay.

Similarly, 'the idea of Bayreuth' was transformed into something that is no mystery to those who know my Zarathustra: into that *great noon*, at which the most select will consecrate themselves for the greatest of all tasks. Who can say? The vision of a feast I shall yet live to see... The pathos of the first pages is world-historical; the *glance* spoken of on the seventh page is Zarathustra's distinctive glance; Wagner, Bayreuth, the whole provincial German wretchedness are a cloud in which an infinite mirage of the future is reflected. Even psychologically all decisive traits of my own nature are

projected into that of Wagner, the side-by-side proximity of the brightest and the most calamitous forces, the will to power as no man ever possessed it before, the ruthless bravery in the spirit, the unlimited power to learn without suppressing the will to act. All in this essay is a prophetic announcement: the impending rebirth of the Greek spirit, the necessity of the new Alexanders who will *tie* the Gordian knot of Greek culture once again... Listen to the world-historical emphasis, with which the concept 'tragic attitude' is introduced at the end of section 4: this essay is full of world-historical emphasis. This is the most foreign sounding 'objectivity' possible: the absolute certainty about what I *am* projected on some chance reality – the truth about me spoken from some gruesome depth. At the beginning of section 9, the *style* of Zarathustra is described in dramatic detail and anticipated; and never will there be a more magnificent expression for the *event* of Zarathustra, an act of tremendous purification and consecration of humanity, than can be found in section 6.

The Untimely Meditations

1.

THE FOUR *Untimely Meditations* are by all means militant. They prove that I was not some 'Jack the dreamer' or fantasist but that I actually enjoy drawing a sword – or is it just that my wrists are dangerously flexible. The *first* assault (1873) was aimed at German culture upon which even then I looked down with merciless contempt, since it was without meaning, without substance and without aim: a mere 'public opinion'.

There is no more malignant error of judgement than to believe that the great military success of the Germans was to prove anything in favour of this culture – least of all *its* triumph over France... The *second* Meditation (1874) illuminates the dangerous element in how we make science operate, gnawing at life and poisoning it; life is made *sick* by this dehumanized grinding of gears and mechanism, the 'impersonality' of the worker, and the false economy of the 'division of labour'. The *aim* is lost; culture, ways and means, how modern methods of science are *barbarized*... This essay recognized for the first time that the 'sense of history' of which this century is so proud is a sickness, a typical symptom of decay. In the *third* and *fourth* Meditations two images of the most extreme *self-love* and *self-discipline* are offered in contrast as a pointer to a *higher* concept of culture; to restore the concept of culture – Schopenhauer and Wagner, *or*, in a word, Nietzsche. These untimely types are beyond comparison, since they are full of a sovereign contempt for all that surrounds them by the name of 'the German Empire', 'Culture', 'Christianity', 'Bismarck', 'Success'...

2.

OF THESE FOUR ATTACKS, the first was extraordinarily successful. The commotion it made was splendid in every sense. I had touched the sore point of a victorious nation – that their victory was *not* a cultural event but perhaps something entirely different... The response came from all sides, not just from the old friends of David Strauss whom I had ridiculed as the archetypal cultural philistine and self-satisfied ass, in short as the author of his beer-hall gospel *The Old and New*

Faith (the expression 'cultural philistine' taken from my essay has since become part of the German language). These old friends, citizens of Württemberg and Swabia, whom I deeply hurt by making fun of their prodigy, their Strauss, replied in as plain and uncouth a manner as I could have hoped for. The replies from Prussia were more prudent – after all, they were of true Prussian Blue. The rudest reply came from a Leipzig newspaper, the notorious *Grenzboten*. It caused me some difficulties to restrain the indignant Baselers from taking action. Only a few old gentlemen were unconditionally on my side, acting from mixed and often unfathomable motives. Ewald from Göttingen was one of them and he suggested that my assault had had fatal consequences for Strauss. Also the old Hegelian Bruno Bauer, who from then on was one of my most attentive readers. During his last years he liked to refer to me, for example, when giving von Treitschke, the Prussian historiographer, a steer on whom he might ask for information about the concept of 'culture', which he seemed to have lost. The most thoughtful, also the lengthiest comments about the essay and its author, come from an old disciple of the philosopher von Baader, a Professor Hoffmann from Würzburg. On reading my essay, he predicted a great destiny for me – bringing about a kind of crisis and ultimate decision with regard to the problem of atheism, whose most instinctive and ruthless convert he assumed me to be. It was atheism that led me to Schopenhauer.

By far the most acutely heard and most keenly felt was an extraordinarily strong and brave plea on my behalf by the usually very moderate Karl Hillebrand, this last *humane*

German with knowledge of how to put pen to paper. His piece was first published in the *Augsburger Zeitung*; these days you will find a somewhat amended version in his collected essays. He described the essay as an event, a turning point, a dawning of awareness, an excellent sign, as a *true* return of German earnestness and German passion for all things intellectual.

Hillebrand was full of praise for the style of the essay, for its maturity, for its perfect tact in distinguishing between the person and the issue; he honoured it by calling it the best polemical essay written in German – since the skill of polemics is so dangerous and inadvisable, in particular for Germans. Backing me up to the hilt, even intensifying the comments I had dared to make against the galloping barbarization of the German language ('these days they act the purist and can no longer form a sentence'), with the same contempt for the 'top writers' of this nation, he concluded with an expression of his admiration for my *courage*, that 'supreme courage which is determined to put the people's favourites in the dock'…

The effects of this essay are of almost incalculable value to my life. So far, nobody has tried to quarrel with it. There is a silence; in Germany I am treated with a certain gloomy caution: for years I have made use of an unconditional freedom of speech which today nobody, least of all in the German Empire, seems to be at *liberty* to do. My paradise lies in 'the shadow of my sword'… In all truth, I only put into practice one of Stendhal's principles: he advises us to enter any society with a *duel*. And how I had picked my opponent! The foremost German freethinker!… Indeed, an altogether new type of libertine spirit was expressed for a first time in this way; to this day nothing is

more foreign and less related to me than the whole European and American species of '*libre penseur*'. I am much more thoroughly at odds with these incorrigible blockheads and fools and their 'modern ideas' than with any of their opponents. They also want in their way to 'improve' mankind in their own image; they would fight an irreconcilable war against what I am and what I *want*, if only they understood it – however, all of them still believe in the 'ideal'… I am the first *immoralist*.

3.

I CANNOT SAY that the *Untimely Meditations* with titles like 'Schopenhauer' or 'Wagner' would contribute much to an understanding or even just raise the relevant psychological questions in either case, give or take the odd exception. Thus, for example, the essay describes the elementary in Wagner's character with profound instinctive certainty as an actor's talent that only draws conclusions from its means and purposes. I did not really want to dwell on psychology in these essays but to pursue a unique problem of education, a new concept of *self-discipline*, *self-defence* to the point of hardness; a path to greatness and to world-historical tasks that must be expressed for a first time. Broadly speaking, I caught hold of two famous and as yet undiagnosed types, the way we grab an opportunity when it presents itself in order to say something; in order to have at hand a few more formulas, symbols, means of expression. This is finally, and with a wisdom that seems uncanny to me, suggested in section 7 in the third Untimely Meditation; Plato used Socrates in this way, as a sign language for Plato.

Now that I am looking back from some distance upon

the conditions which these essays bear witness to, I cannot deny that they speak really only of me. The essay 'Wagner in Bayreuth' is a vision of my future, but in 'Schopenhauer as Educator' I describe my innermost biography, my *becoming*. Above all, though, it was about my *promise*!... *What* I am today, *where* I am today (at a giddy height where I no longer speak with words but with lightning bolts) – how far away was I from this at the time!

But I *saw* the land; I did not deceive myself for a moment about the way, the sea, the danger – *and* the success! The great calm of the promise, this happy gaze into a future that should not remain just a promise! Here, every word is based on experience, is deep, is inward; the most painful is there too – it contains words that are virtually dripping with blood. But a wind of *great* freedom blows above it all; the wound itself is no objection.

I see the philosopher as a terrible explosive endangering everything. My concept of the 'philosopher' is worlds removed from any concept that would include even a Kant, not to mention the academic 'ruminants' and other professors of philosophy: this essay offers an invaluable lesson, even if it must be admitted that at bottom it is not 'Schopenhauer as Educator' but 'Nietzsche as Educator' who is speaking. Considering that in those days my trade was that of a scholar and perhaps that I was *good at it*, it is not entirely without significance that an austere sample of scholar-psychology suddenly reveals itself in this essay – it expresses the *feeling of distance*, the absolute certainty I felt about what was to be my life's work and what could be dismissed as just means to an end. I was clever enough to have been many things in many different places in order to

make myself singular – to arrive at one thing. For a time I also *had* to become a scholar.

Human, All Too Human.

with two sequels

1.

HUMAN, ALL TOO HUMAN is the monument to a crisis. It calls itself a book for *free* spirits: almost every sentence marks some kind of victory – I liberated myself with it from anything in my nature that *does not belong*. Idealism does not belong to me – the title reads 'where *you* see ideal things, *I* see – the human, ah, the all too human!' I know mankind *better*... The term 'free spirit' cannot have any other meaning here but that it is *liberated*, a spirit that took control of itself once again. The tone, the sound of voice, has completely changed; you will find the book clever, detached, occasionally hard and mocking. A certain spirituality kept in *good* taste seems to maintain the upper hand over a more passionate undercurrent. In this context, the publication of the book in 1878 can actually be seen as an excuse to celebrate the hundredth anniversary of the death of Voltaire. For Voltaire, contrary to all those who wrote after him, was above all an aristocrat of the mind – just like me.

The name Voltaire on one of my essays – that really meant progress – *towards me*... If you look more closely, you will discover a merciless spirit that knows all the hideouts of the ideal, where it has its secret dungeons and also therefore where it can still lurk in safety. With a torch in both hands (for once its light is steady), you will shine through the dark

into this *underworld* of the ideal. This is war, but a war without gunpowder and smoke, without bellicose attitudes, without pathos and torn limbs – all that would still be 'idealism'. One mistake after another is calmly laid on ice, the ideal is not refuted – it simply *freezes to death*. Here, for example, the 'genius' freezes to death, a little further on it is the 'saint'; under a huge icicle the 'hero'; and in the end 'belief' freezes to death, the so-called 'conviction', 'pity' too cools down considerably – almost everywhere 'the matter in itself' freezes to death…

2.

THE BEGINNINGS of this book go right back to the weeks of the first Bayreuth festivals; a profound alienation from all that surrounded me there is one of its preconditions. Those who have any notion of the visions I had already encountered then can imagine how I felt, when one day I woke up in Bayreuth. It was as if in a dream… Where was I? I recognized nothing, I hardly recognized Wagner. In vain did I leaf through my memories: Tribschen, a distant island of the blessed – not a trace of similarity. The incomparable days when the foundation stone was laid, the small *elect* group of people that celebrated it and whose sensitivity I could take for granted – not a trace of similarity. *What had happened*? – They had translated Wagner into German! The Wagnerian had become Wagner's master!

German art! the *German* Master! *German* beer!… We others, who know only too well what subtle artist and what cosmopolitanism of taste is exclusively addressed by Wagner's art, were beside ourselves to find Wagner decorated with German 'virtues'. I understand, indeed, I know the Wagnerian;

I have 'experienced' three generations from the late Brendel onwards who confused Wagner with Hegel down to the 'idealists' of *Bayreuther Blätter* who confused Wagner with themselves. I have heard every kind of confession of 'beautiful souls' about Wagner. A kingdom for one sensible word!

In truth, a hair-raising company! All philistines and cabbages – endlessly charming! No deformed monster is missing, not even the anti-Semite. Poor Wagner! Where had he ended up – he would have been better off in a herd of swine! But among Germans!... For the instruction of future generations we should really take a true Bayreuth citizen, stuff him, or, even better, preserve him in surgical spirit since spirit is needed – with the label underneath reading, 'This is the "spirit" on which the German Empire is founded...'

Enough, I left in the midst of it all for a couple of weeks, very abruptly, even though a charming Parisian tried to console me. The only apology I offered Wagner was a fatalistic telegram. In a place called Klingenbrunn, hidden away in the deep Bohemian forest, I dragged a deep depression and contempt for the Germans around like a sickness *and* from time to time I would write a sentence or two in my notebook, under the general title 'The Ploughshare', aphorisms of strong psychological content that may perhaps still be found in *Human, All Too Human*.

3.

WHAT I DECIDED at that time was not, as you may think, a break with Wagner – I felt a total aberration of my instincts of which the odd mistake, be it now Wagner or the chair at

the University of Basel, was just another symptom. I became extremely *impatient* with myself; I realized that it was high time to reflect on *myself*. All at once I saw with terrible clarity how much time I had already wasted – how useless and arbitrary my whole existence as a philologist appeared in relation to my task. This false modesty embarrassed me… Ten years had passed in which the *nourishment* of my mind had truly ceased, in which I had learned nothing useful at all, in which I had forgotten absurd amounts for the sake of the rags and bones of learnedness. To crawl scrupulously with terrible eyesight through the metrics of Antiquity – that is what I had come to!

I looked at myself with overwhelming pity – how thin and emaciated I was: my learning simply lacked *realities* and my 'idealities' were not worth a damn! An almost all-consuming thirst took hold of me: from then on I really pursued nothing more than physiology, medicine and natural sciences – and I only returned to properly historical studies when the greater task compelled me to do so. It was then that I also realized for the first time the connection between an activity chosen against your better judgement, a so-called 'vocation' to which one is *barely* called, and that need for a dulling of the feeling of despondency and hunger by means of a narcotic art – for instance Wagnerian Art. As I carefully looked around me, I discovered that a large number of young men are in the same state of distress: one step against nature virtually *compels* another one. In German, in the 'German Empire' to speak unambiguously, all too many are condemned to choose vocations too early, and then to *waste away* under the heavy load, unable to shake it off. These people long for Wagner

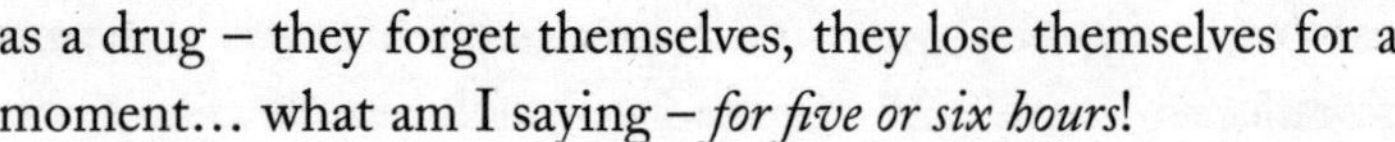

as a drug – they forget themselves, they lose themselves for a moment… what am I saying – *for five or six hours*!

4.

IT WAS THEN that my instinct decided inexorably against giving way, being a follower, being confused about myself. Any form of life, even the most unfavourable conditions like illness and poverty – they all seemed to me preferable to the unworthy 'selflessness' which I got mixed up with, originally because of ignorance and *youth*, and which I stuck to later because of inertia and a so-called 'sense of duty'. Here I was helped in a way that I cannot praise enough and just in time by my father's *malignant* heritage – basically a predestination to an early death. My illness *slowly set me free* – it spared me having to break away or take any violent or offensive step. I did not lose any goodwill then, but actually gained some. My illness also gave me the right to change all my habits completely; it allowed, even *commanded* me to forget; it granted me the necessity of lying still, of leisure, of waiting and being patient… But that means thinking!… My eyes themselves put an end to all that book-reading, in plain language: to philology. I was saved from the 'book', for years I did not read a thing – the *greatest* favour I ever did myself.

My most profound self, buried and silenced, as it were, by a constant barrage of *having* to listen to other selves (and that means reading!) woke up slowly, timidly, full of doubt – but at least *it was talking again*. Never have I been as happy as during the sickest and most painful periods of my life: just look at

Dawn or even *The Wanderer and His Shadow* to understand what this 'return to *myself*' meant: a supreme kind of *recovery*… The other kind, my cure, was merely a consequence of it.

5.

HUMAN, ALL TOO HUMAN, this monument to a rigorous self-discipline with which I abruptly ended all those effeminacies like 'supreme swindle', 'idealism', 'beautiful feelings' that had somehow wormed their way inside me, was for the most part written in Sorrento; I finished its final version during the winter months in Basel, under far less pleasant conditions than those in Sorrento. Actually, it is *Peter Gast*, a student at the University of Basel and very fond of me, who is responsible for this. I dictated it with my head bandaged, and in pain; he transcribed and corrected it – he was really the writer while I was merely the author. When the book was finally finished – to the amazement of the sick man – I also sent two copies to Bayreuth. By an extraordinary coincidence I received at the same time a beautiful copy of the *Parsifal* text dedicated to me by Richard Wagner with the inscription: 'To my dear friend Friedrich Nietzsche, from Richard Wagner, member of the Church Council'. To my ears, this crossing of the two books had an ominous ring. Did it not sound as if we had crossed *swords*?… Anyway, we both seemed to feel it, for we both remained silent.

Around that time the first *Bayreuth Blätter* appeared: I understood *what* I should have realized long ago – Incredible! Wagner had turned to religion…

6.

WHAT I THEN (1876) thought of myself, with what tremendous certainty I had my task and its world-historical aspect in my grasp, is testified by the book in general and by one passage in particular; only, once again with my inborn cunning I avoided the little word 'I' and showered with world-historical glory, this time not Schopenhauer or Wagner, but one of my friends, the excellent Dr Paul Rée – luckily far too sophisticated a creature to be deceived… *others* were less refined – I have always recognized the hopeless amongst my readers (for example, the typical German professor) by their reaction to this passage – they always had to see the whole book as a form of higher realism… In fact, the contents contradicted five or six propositions of my friend: you may wish to read the preface to my *On the Genealogy of Morals*.

The passage reads: 'But what is the main proposition at which one of the boldest and coldest thinkers has arrived, the author of the book *On the Origin of Moral Feelings* (read Nietzsche, the first immoralist) in virtue of his radical and penetrating analyses of human activity? "Moral man is no closer to the intelligible world than the physical man – since there is no intelligible world…"' This sentence, grown hard and sharp-edged under the hammer blow of historical recognition (read *Re-evaluation of all Values*) may perhaps one day, in some future (1890), serve as the axe aimed at the roots of the 'metaphysical needs' of humanity – but whether this is a blessing or a curse, who can say? However, it stands as a proposition of tremendous consequences, fruitful and dreadful at the same time and looking into the world

possessed of that *double perspective* which all great insights share…

Dawn.

THOUGHTS ON MORALITY AS A PREJUDICE

1.

WITH THIS BOOK I begin my crusade against *morality*. Not that it smells in the least of gunpowder; you will notice very different, much lovelier scents, assuming that you have a reasonably sensitive nose. The guns are neither big nor small; if the effect of the book is negative, then its means are all the less so; these means that effect a conclusion, *not* a gunshot. To take leave in this book with a cautious reserve from all that was hitherto honoured and even worshipped under the name of morality in no way contradicts the fact that it contains not a single negative word, no attack, no spite – indeed, there it lies in the sunshine, well-rounded and happy, like some sea urchin basking in the sun among rocks. Ultimately, I myself was this sea urchin; almost each sentence of the book was first thought, was *hatched out* among that jumble of rocks near Genoa where I was alone and still in secret bond with the sea. Even now, whenever I touch that book by chance, almost every sentence becomes part of a net with which I can pull something unique back from the depths: its entire skin trembling with tender thrills of memory. The skill which distinguishes it is not least that it detains things for a little while, things that otherwise scurry past, weightlessly and noiselessly, moments I privately call divine lizards – not with the cruelty of that

young Greek god who simply speared the poor little lizard, but all the same, I work with something pointed, with a pen... 'There are so many dawns that have not yet risen' – with this *Indian* inscription this book opens its doors. Where does its originator *seek* that new morning, that delicate red as yet undiscovered that will rise another day – what do I say, a whole series, a whole world of new days!? In a *re-evaluation of all values*, in liberation from all moral values, in saying 'Yes' and trusting all that has hitherto been forbidden, despised and cursed. This book, which says so firmly '*Yes*' pours out its light, its love, its tenderness for many wicked things; it gives them a 'soul', a 'good conscience', the lofty right and *privilege* of existence. Morality is not attacked, it is merely no longer in the picture... This book closes with 'don't you think?' – it is the only book that closes with 'don't you think?'...

2.

MY LIFE'S WORK lies in preparing humanity for a moment of intense self-examination, a *time of reckoning* when it will look backwards and outwards, then emerge from the dominion of chance and priests and for the first time ask itself the fundamental questions about 'Why?' and 'For What?' – this task is the necessary consequence of the knowledge that humanity is *not* capable of setting itself on the right path, that it is *not* in any way subject to divine rule; on the contrary, that actually precisely among their most holy regarded values the instinct for denial, the instinct for decadence, has been seductively in charge. The question concerning the origin of moral value is therefore for me a question of *the first order*, because it is

crucial for the future of humanity. The demand that we should all *believe* ourselves basically in safe hands, that a book, the Bible, offers us a definitive assurance of divine governance and wisdom in the destiny of man, is translated back into reality, the will to suppress the truth about the pitiable opposite of all this, namely that so far humanity has been in the *worst* of hands and that it has been governed by the losers, two-faced vengeful ones, the so-called 'saints', these slanderers of the world and violators of men. The ultimate proof that the priest (and this includes the *clandestine* priest, the philosopher) is not just master of a certain religious community, but has become master in general, and that the morality of decadence, the will to the end, has been accepted as morality *itself*, is the fact that absolute value is afforded to all that is non-egoistic, and hostility to all that is egoistic. Those who do not agree with me at this point are in my opinion *infected*... But all the world disagrees with me... For a physiologist such a juxtaposition of values simply leaves no doubt. When even the least important organ within an organism fails to enforce its self-preservation, its restoration of energy, its 'egoism' with perfect certainty, then the whole will degenerate. The physiologist demands the degenerated part is *cut out*; he denies any solidarity with it, he has not the slightest pity for it.

However, it is precisely the *degeneration* of the whole, of humanity, that the priest *desires*; that is why he *conserves* what degenerates – that is his price for his governance... What is the point of those concepts of lies, the *ancillary* concepts of morality: 'soul', 'spirit', 'free will', 'God', if not to ruin humanity physiologically?... If you deflect seriousness from self-preservation, the build-up of physical strength, *that is of life*, if anaemia is construed as an ideal and contempt for the body as 'the salvation of the soul', what else is this if not a *recipe* for decadence? – The loss of the centre of gravity, the resistance to the natural instincts, in a word 'selflessness' – that is what until now was called *morality*... With *Dawn* I first took up the fight against the morality that would unself man.

The Joyful Science.

DAWN is a positive book, profound but full of light and kindness. This is also true and to the highest degree of *The Joyful Science*; in almost every sentence, thoughtfulness and sense of mischief are lovingly combined in this book. A poem expressing thanks for the most wonderful January I ever lived through – the whole book is a gift – reveals most clearly from what sheer depth 'science' drew to become *joyful*...

You, who with your spear aflame
crushed the ice around my soul
that rushing to the sea it came
of its highest hope and goal:
ever brighter, full of grace
in its loving bond, but free –
will it sing you songs of praise
my beloved January.

Who can doubt what is meant here by 'highest hope' when at the close of the fourth book the crystalline beauty of the

first words of *Zarathustra* rise in their shining glory? Or on reading the granite-like sentences at the end of the third book with which for the first time destiny is given a formula *for all time*? 'The Songs of Prince Outlaw', most of it was written in Sicily, remind us explicitly of the Provençal notion of *The Joyful Science*, that group of *singer, knight and free spirit* which distinguishes that wonderful early culture of Provence from all ambiguous cultures – in particular the last poem 'To the Mistral', an exuberant song in which, with respect, morality is freely trodden on, is perfectly typical for Provence.

Thus spoke Zarathustra.

A BOOK FOR ALL AND NO-ONE

1.

I SHALL NOW tell you the story of *Zarathustra*. The basic *idea* of the book, the notion of *eternal recurrence*, this highest formula of affirmation that could ever have been achieved, was conceived in August of 1881: it was drafted on a sheet of paper with the inscription: '6,000 feet beyond men and time'. I myself walked on that day from Lake Silvaplana through the forests; at a powerful pyramid-shaped boulder near Surlei I stopped to rest. There I had this thought: if I count back a few months from this day, I will discover, like an omen, a sudden and extremely decisive change in my taste, especially in music. You may of course altogether count *Zarathustra* as music – certainly a renaissance of the art of *listening* was a precondition for it. In a little mountain spa near Vicenza, Recoaro, where I spent the spring of 1881, I, together with my friend, the young musician Peter

Gast, another 'reborn' one, discovered that the phoenix of music flew past us with a lighter and more brilliant plumage than he had ever displayed before. But if I go forward from that day to the sudden birth under the most unlikely conditions in February 1883 (the final part, from which I quoted a few sentences in my *preface*, was finished in precisely that sacred hour in which Richard Wagner died in Venice), we arrive at eighteen months for the pregnancy. This figure of exactly eighteen months might suggest, at least to Buddhists, that I am really a female elephant.

The Joyful Science, its hundred indications showing that it is near to something quite incomparable, belongs to the interval period; in the end it even starts *Zarathustra* off, and it also delivers the fundamental concept of *Zarathustra* in the penultimate passage of the fourth book. Similarly, that 'Hymn to Life' (for mixed choir and orchestra) was composed during this interval; its score was published two years ago by EW Fritzsch in Leipzig. One symptom for my state of mind that year perhaps worth noting was the pure *positive* pathos that was particularly strong within me then; I called it the tragic pathos. The time will come when it will be sung in my memory. The text (I have to make this clear since this is currently often misunderstood) is not by me; it is the surprising inspiration of a young Russian woman who was my friend at that time, a Miss Lou von Salomé. If you can make any sense of the final words of this poem you will be able to imagine why I preferred and admired it – it has greatness. Pain is *not* held to be an objection to life: 'If you have no joy to give me, well then, *you still have your pain…*'

Perhaps my music, too, has some greatness when it comes to this passage (top note of the oboe, C sharp, not C: misprint). The following winter I stayed in that pretty quiet bay of Rapallo near Genoa, which is wedged between Chiavari and the foothills of Portofino. My health was not at its best back then: the winter was cold and excessively wet; a little hostel right next to the sea, so that the high waves made it impossible for me to sleep at night, was in just about every way the opposite of what I would have wished for. Nevertheless, and almost to prove my doctrine that anything of decision-making importance happens 'in spite of' and not 'because of', this winter and its inclement conditions saw my *Zarathustra* come into being.

In the morning I would climb upwards and southwards on the splendid road to Zoagli, right to the top, looking past pine trees to get a magnificent view of the sea. In the afternoon, whenever my health permitted it, I walked around the whole bay from Santa Margherita all the way to Portofino. This town and its landscape came even closer to my heart because of the great love which the unforgettable German Emperor Frederick III felt for them; by chance I was in this coastal region again in the autumn of 1886, when he visited this small forgotten world of happiness for a last time. It was on these two walks that Zarathustra first came to me, in particular as a type: indeed, he *overcame* me…

2.

TO UNDERSTAND this type we must first become familiar with his physiological condition: this is what I call *great health*. I cannot explain this concept better, more *personally* than I already

did, that is to say in one of the final sections of the fifth book of *The Joyful Science*: 'Being new, nameless, incomprehensible, we premature births of an as yet unproven future need for a new goal also a new means – namely a new health, stronger, more seasoned, tougher, more audacious and more joyful than any previous one. Whoever has a soul that longs to have experienced the whole range of values and desires to date, and to have sailed around all the coast of this ideal "Mediterranean"; whoever wants to know from the adventures of his own more authentic experience how an explorer and conqueror of the ideal feels, and also an artist, a saint, a legislator, a sage, a scholar, a pious man, a soothsayer and a recluse of the old style – needs one thing above everything else: *great health* – a condition that we not merely have but also acquire continually. This condition we must acquire because it is relinquished again and again, and must be relinquished. And now, after having long been on our way in this manner, we Argonauts of the ideal, with more daring perhaps than is prudent, and having suffered shipwreck and damage often enough, but we are, to repeat it, healthier than they would like us to be, dangerously healthy, always regaining health – it will seem to us as if, as a reward, we have now confronted an as yet undiscovered country whose boundaries nobody has surveyed yet, something beyond all the lands and nooks of the ideal so far, a world so abundantly rich in beauty, strangeness, dubiousness, dreadfulness and heavenliness that our curiosity as well as our longing to possess it has got beside itself – oh, nothing will satisfy us now! After such sights and with such ravenous hunger for knowledge and conscience, how could we still be satisfied with *present-day man*? That is bad enough, but it is inevitable that we find it difficult to remain serious when we look at his worthiest goals and hopes, and perhaps we do not even bother to look any more.

'Another ideal runs ahead of us, an odd, tempting, dangerous ideal to which we should not wish to persuade anybody because we do not readily grant *the right to it* to anyone: the ideal of a spirit who plays naively – that is to say not deliberately but out of overflowing power and abundance – with all that was hitherto called holy, good, untouchable, divine; for whom those supreme things which the people naturally accept as the measure of their values, signify danger, decay, humiliation, or at least recreation, blindness, and temporary self-oblivion; the ideal of a human-superhuman well-being and benevolence that will often appear *inhuman* (for example, when it confronts all previous earthly seriousness, all previous solemnity in gesture, word, tone, eye, morality, and sense of duty, as if it were their most lifelike and unintended parody) and with which in spite of all of this perhaps *great seriousness* will really begin, the real question mark will be set for the first time, the destiny of the soul will take a turn, the hand of the clock will move on, the tragedy will *take its course...*'

3.

HAS ANYONE at the end of the 19th century a clear idea of what poets of strong ages called *inspiration*? If not, I shall describe it. If you had the least remains of superstition in you, you could indeed hardly reject the idea you are merely the plaything and mouthpiece of, and medium for, overpowering forces. The concept of revelation in the sense that suddenly with incredible certainty and subtlety something becomes *visible*, audible,

something that shakes you to the core and takes you over, merely describes the facts. You listen out, you do not seek; you take, you do not ask who gives; like lightning a thought flashes up, urging, unfaltering – I never had a choice. It is a rapture – its tremendous tension may occasionally find relief in floods of tears, now the pace quickens unintentionally, now it slows down; a complete frenzy while being distinctly aware of countless subtle thrills that make your skin tingle right down to your toes; a depth of happiness in which the most poignant and most dismal do not seem to be at odds, but rather a condition, challenged, a *much-needed* splash of colour within such an excess of light; an instinct for rhythmic relationships reaching across wide spaces – length, the need for *all-embracing* rhythm is almost the measure of the force of inspiration, a kind of counterpoint to its pressure and tension…

Everything happens completely involuntarily but as in a gale of yearning for freedom, of absoluteness, of power, of divinity… The randomness of image and simile is strangest of all; there is no longer a notion of what is an image or a simile, everything offers itself as the nearest, the most obvious, the simplest expression. It really seems, to bring something that Zarathustra said to mind, as if the things came by themselves and offered themselves as similes ('here come all things with caresses to your discourse and flatter you: for they want to ride on your back. On every simile you ride to every truth. Here the words and receptacles of words all burst open for you; all being wishes to become word, all becoming wishes to learn from you how to speak'). This is *my* experience of inspiration; I do not doubt that you have to

go back thousands of years to find anyone who could tell me, 'It is mine too'.

4.

AFTERWARDS I was ill for a few weeks in Genoa. Then there followed a melancholy spring in Rome where I put up with life – it was not easy. Basically, I was hugely irritated by this location, the most unsuitable location in the world for the poet of *Zarathustra*, where I was not by choice. I tried to get away – I wanted to go to *Aquila*, precisely the opposite of Rome, founded as an act of hostility to Rome, as I shall one day found a place in memory of an atheist and enemy of the church of the first order, one of those closest related to me, the great Emperor Frederick II of the Hohenstaufen dynasty. But somehow I could not escape the capital: I had to go back again. In the end, after I had given up trying to find an *anti-Christian* region, I resigned myself to the Piazza Barberini. I fear that in order to avoid bad smells as much as possible, I even asked in the residence of the King of Italy itself whether they did not have a quiet room for a philosopher.

On a loggia high above that Piazza, from which you have a view over all of Rome and can listen to the fountain running deep below, I composed that loneliest of lonely songs that has ever been written, 'The Night Song'; at that time a melody of inexpressible melancholy was always in my head and I used the words 'death from immortality' in the chorus…

That summer, back home at the sacred spot where the first lightning flash of *Zarathustra* had dazzled me, I found *Zarathustra II.* I only needed ten days: I never needed any

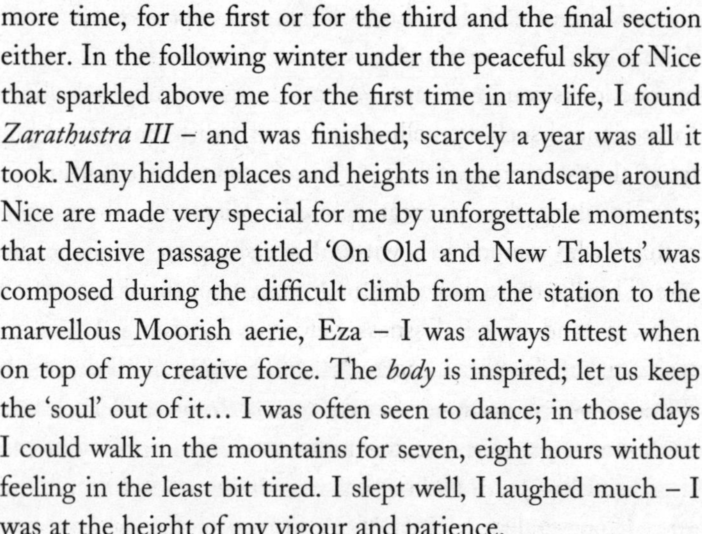

more time, for the first or for the third and the final section either. In the following winter under the peaceful sky of Nice that sparkled above me for the first time in my life, I found *Zarathustra III* – and was finished; scarcely a year was all it took. Many hidden places and heights in the landscape around Nice are made very special for me by unforgettable moments; that decisive passage titled 'On Old and New Tablets' was composed during the difficult climb from the station to the marvellous Moorish aerie, Eza – I was always fittest when on top of my creative force. The *body* is inspired; let us keep the 'soul' out of it… I was often seen to dance; in those days I could walk in the mountains for seven, eight hours without feeling in the least bit tired. I slept well, I laughed much – I was at the height of my vigour and patience.

5.

APART FROM these ten-day oeuvres, the years during and in particular *after* my *Zarathustra* were a calamity beyond comparison. You pay dearly to be immortal: you have to die several times during your lifetime.

There is something that I would call the grudge of greatness: everything that is great, a work, a deed, will turn, once completed, *against* the one who accomplished it, and precisely because he accomplished it, he has become *weak* – he cannot bear his deed any longer, he can no longer face it. To have put something *behind* you that you were never permitted to choose, something into which the destiny of mankind has been knotted – and now you labour *under* it!… It almost crushes you. The grudge of Greatness! Then there is the eerie

silence around you. Loneliness has seven skins – nothing can penetrate it. You meet people, greet friends: new bleakness, no-one looks you in the eye. At best this is a form of rebellion. I experienced such a rebellion; it was of a different nature but from almost everyone close to me: it seems that nothing is more insulting than to create a sudden distance – those *noble* natures who cannot live without worshipping someone are rare. Thirdly, there is the absurd sensitivity of the skin to small barbs, a kind of helplessness before everything petty. This seems to me due to an enormous squandering of all defensive energies, which are a condition for every *creative* deed, every deed that stems from our most authentic, inmost, nethermost regions. The *limited* abilities to defend yourself are thereby as good as suspended; no energy goes back into them. Moreover, I dare to suggest that our digestive system is hampered, we are less keen to move, that we are all too susceptible to chills as well as mistrust – mistrust which in many cases is merely an error caused by illness. In such a condition I once sensed the close presence of a herd of cows even before I set eyes on them, because milder, more philanthropic thoughts came back to me: *they* had warmth…

6.

THIS WORK stands very much on its own. Let us leave the poets out of it, perhaps nothing has ever been done from such an abundance of energy. My concept of the 'Dionysian' became a *supreme deed* here; all human action up to now seems poor and relative in comparison. The least we can say is that a Goethe, a Shakespeare would be unable to breathe

even for a moment at this incredible height of passion, that Dante is merely a believer compared with Zarathustra and not one who first *creates* truth, a *world-governing* spirit and destiny – that the poets of the Vedic texts are priests and not even worthy of tying the shoelaces of Zarathustra and it does not give the slightest idea of the distance, of the *mountain blue* solitude in which this work dwells. Zarathustra has for ever a right to say, 'I draw circles around me and sacred boundaries; fewer and fewer climb with me on ever higher mountains – I build a mountain range out of ever more sacred mountains.' Add up the spirit and goodness of all great souls: all of them together would not be able to speak like Zarathustra. The scale on which he ascends and descends is tremendous; he has seen further, strives to go further, *could* go further than any other human being. He contradicts with his every word, this most positive of all minds; in him all opposites are blended into a new unity. The highest and the lowest energies of human nature, the sweetest, airiest and most dreadful ones surge forth from a well with immortal certainty. Until then, you do not know what height is, what depth is, you know even less what truth is. There is not a moment in this revelation of truth that has already been anticipated or conjectured by one of the greatest. Before Zarathustra, there was no wisdom, no soul searching, no art of oratory; even everyday matters, the most humdrum, speak of extraordinary things. Aphorisms are trembling with passion; eloquence becomes music; lightning bolts are hurled into hitherto unfathomed futures. The most powerful capacity for simile that has existed so far is poor

and a mere toy compared with this return of language to the nature of symbolism.

Look, how Zarathustra descends and says something kind to everyone! How gently his hands touch even his antagonists, the priests, and how he suffers *with* them. Here, man is overcome every moment that passes, the concept of 'Superman' has here become the greatest reality – whatever has been great in man up to now lies *beneath* him at an infinite distance. The peaceful, the light-footed, the omnipresence of wickedness and high spirits and all other things typical of the type of Zarathustra, has never been dreamed of as being essential to greatness. Precisely in this immense space with its access to the contradictory, Zarathustra feels himself to be *the supreme type of all beings*; and if you hear his definition of it, you will not bother trying to look for a simile for him.

'– the soul which has the longest ladder and can go down the deepest,
the most comprehensive soul which can walk and go astray and roam furthest within itself,
the one most necessary, which flings itself with joyful passion into chance,
the soul as being, which *will* strive to become, the one as having, which *will* strive to want and desire,
the one in flight from itself, closing in on itself in the widest possible circle,
the wisest soul, enticed most sweetly by folly,
the one that loves itself the most, in which all matters have their currents and counter-currents, their low and high tides.'

But that is the concept of Dionysus himself. Another contemplation led us to precisely this point. The psychological problem with the type of Zarathustra is, how he who says 'No' and *does* 'No' to everything to which we have until now said 'Yes' to an unheard-of degree, can nevertheless be the opposite of a No-saying spirit; how the spirit bearing the most terrible fate, a doomed task, can nevertheless be the lightest and the most ethereal – Zarathustra is a dancer. How he who has the hardest, the most dreadful insight into reality, who thought the 'most abysmal thought' nevertheless does not consider it an objection to existence, not even to its eternal recurrence – but rather one reason more for *being himself* the eternal 'Yes' to all things, 'the tremendous, boundless saying of "Yes" and "Amen"'... 'Into all abysses I still carry the blessings of my "Yes"'... *But that is the concept of Dionysus once again.*

7.

WHAT LANGUAGE will such a spirit speak when he speaks to himself? The language of the *dithyramb*, the song of praise to Dionysus. I am the inventor of the dithyramb. Listen all to how Zarathustra talks to himself before *sunrise* (III, 18): such emerald happiness, such divine tenderness had no tongue before me. Even the profoundest sadness of such a Dionysus still becomes a song of his praise; take for instance 'The Night Song' – the immortal lament at being condemned by the abundance of light and power, by his *sun* nature, not to love.

'It is night: now all fountains speak louder. And my soul too is a fountain.

It is night: only now all songs of lovers are roused. And my soul too is the song of a lover.

Something not stilled, which cannot be stilled is within me that wants to raise its voice. A desire for love is within me that itself speaks the language of love.

I am light: ah, that I were night! But this is my loneliness: I am girded by light.

Ah, that I were dark and of the night! How I would suck at the breasts of light!

And I would even bless you yourselves, you little twinkling stars and glow-worms up there! – and be overjoyed because of your gifts of light.

But I live in my own light, I drink the flames that break out of me back into myself.

I do not know the happiness of those who take, and I have often dreamed that stealing must be still more blissful than taking.

This is my poverty that my hand never rests from giving; that is my envy that I see waiting eyes and the illuminated nights of longing.

Oh misery of all givers; eclipse of my sun; craving to crave; ravenous hunger while filling up!

They take from me: but do I still touch their soul? There is a chasm between taking and giving, and the smallest chasm is the last to be bridged.

Hunger grows out of my beauty: I should like to hurt those for whom I light the way, I should like to rob those to whom I gave – thus I hunger for wickedness.

Withdrawing my hand just as the other hand reaches out

to it, like a waterfall that hesitates even as it plunges: this is how I hunger for wickedness.

Such revenge is plotted by my abundance, such spite wells up out of my loneliness.

My happiness in giving died while giving; my virtue became weary of itself in its abundance.

Those who always give are in danger of losing their shame; those who always hand out grow callouses on heart and hand from all that handing out.

My eye no longer sheds tears because of the shame of those asking; my hand has become too hard for the trembling of filled hands.

Where have the tears in my eyes gone and the downiness of my heart? Oh the loneliness of all givers, the silence of all who shine!

Many suns circle in barren space: to all that is dark they speak with their light – to me they do not speak.

This is the hostility of the light towards those who shine: merciless, it travels in its orbit.

Unjust to those who shine in its innermost heart, cold towards suns – thus travels every sun.

The suns travel like a storm in their orbits; they follow their implacable will – that is their coldness. Oh it is only you, you dark ones, you of the night, who create warmth from that which shines! Only you drink milk and refreshment from the udders of light.

Ah, ice is around me, my hand is burned by iciness; thirst is within me, which pines for your thirst.

It is night: ah, that I must be light! And thirst for things of the night! And loneliness!

It is night: now my longing breaks out of me like a well – I long for speech.

It is night: now all fountains talk louder. And my soul too is a fountain.

It is night: now all songs of lovers are roused. And my soul too is the song of a lover.'

8.

NOTHING LIKE THIS has ever been written, ever been felt or *suffered*: this is how a god, a Dionysus, suffers. The answer to such a song of solar solitude in the light would be Ariadne… Who apart from me knows what Ariadne is!… No one so far knows the solution of such riddles, I doubt that anyone ever even saw it as riddle. Zarathustra defines once, with rigour, his task – it is mine too – so that we cannot be mistaken as to the *meaning*; he *says 'Yes'* to the point of justification, to the point of redemption of all things past too.

'I travel amongst men as amongst fragments of the future: the future which I envisage.

And that is all my poetry and striving, that I can write poetry and gather all at once what is fragment and riddle and dreadful chance.

And how could I bear to be human if man was not also a poet, and solver of riddles and redeemer of the future?

To redeem those from the past and to turn every "it was" into a "that is how I wanted it": that alone I should call redemption.'

In another passage he defines as rigorously as possible what for him alone 'man' can be – *not* an object of love or,

worse, compassion – Zarathustra even mastered the *great disgust* for man: man to him is a shapeless thing, a material, an ugly stone that needs a sculptor.

'No longer to *want* and no longer to *appreciate* and no longer to *create*: oh that this great weariness might always remain far from me!

In knowledge too I only feel my will's joy in begetting and becoming and if there is innocence in my knowledge, it is because the *will to beget* is part of it.

This will has lured me away from God and the gods: what is there to create if gods – were there?

But my fervent will to create drives me again and again towards man; thus is the hammer driven to the stone.

Ah, you men, within the stone sleeps an image for me to see, the image of all images! Ah, that it must sleep in the hardest, ugliest stone.

Now my hammer rages brutally against its prison. Pieces of rock rain from the stone: what is that to me!

I want to perfect it, for a shadow came to me – once, the quietest and lightest of all things came to me!

The beauty of superman came to me as a shadow: what are the gods to me now!...'

I wish to stress a final point: the line in italics demands it. Among the conditions for a Dionysian task is most certainly the hardness of the hammer, *the joy even in destroying*. The imperative 'Harden!', the certainty deep below *that all creators are hard* is the distinctive mark of a Dionysian nature.

BEYOND GOOD AND EVIL

PROLOGUE TO A PHILOSOPHY OF THE FUTURE

1.

MY TASK for the following years has been as strictly sketched out as is possible. Now that the Yes-saying part has been achieved, it is the turn of the No-saying, *No*-doing part, the re-evaluation of the previous values themselves, the great war – the evocation of a day for the big decision. This includes the slow turning round to look for my peers, to those strong enough to offer me their help *destroying*.

From then on, all my writings are fishhooks: perhaps I am as good an angler as anyone else?… If I caught nothing, it's not my fault. *There just weren't any fish…*

2.

IN ALL THAT MATTERS, this book (1886) is a *critique of modernity*, including modern science, modern art, even modern politics, whilst pointing to an antagonistic type that has very little in common with modern man: a noble, Yes-saying type. In this latter sense, the book is a *school for gentlemen*, the term here being used in a more spiritual and radical sense than ever before. You have to have inbuilt courage to put up with it and never have known fear… All those things on which this era prides itself are seen as conflicting with this type, making them almost seem like bad manners: the famous 'objectivity' for instance, the 'compassion with all suffering', the 'historical sense' with its slavish devotion to all things foreign, subservience to inferior notions and 'all concepts of science'. If you keep in mind that the book was written *after Zarathustra*, you may be able to imagine where it comes from. The eye, compelled by a tremendous urge to look out into the *far* distance (and Zarathustra is even more farsighted than the Tsar) is here forced to focus sharply on what is close at hand: our own age and *environment*. You will find in every detail and in particular in outline a *deliberate* renunciation of those instincts which made a *Zarathustra* possible. Refinement of form, intention and the *art of being silent* are emphasized; psychology is handled with deliberate hardness and cruelty – the book has not a single kind word…

All that is restful: who can conceive in the end *which* type of rest makes such a waste of goodness necessary as is found in *Zarathustra*?… Theologically speaking – listen well, because I seldom speak as a theologian – it was God Himself who, at the end of His day's work, coiled Himself up as a snake beneath the tree of knowledge: that was His way of resting from His task of being God… He had made everything too beautiful. The devil is simply God's idleness on every seventh day.

The Genealogy of Morals.
A POLEMICAL PAPER

THE THREE TREATISES which make up this genealogy are, as regards expression, intention and technique of the unexpected, perhaps the most sinister that have ever been written. Dionysus, as we know, is also the god of darkness.

This is a starting line that is *calculated* to lead you astray every time – cool, scientific, even ironical,

deliberately pushy and deliberately reticent. Gradually the atmosphere becomes restless, there is the odd flash of lightning, very uncomfortable truths make themselves heard from afar with a dull rumbling sound – until finally with ferocious speed the moment comes where all is driven forward with terrible intensity. And at the last, amongst dreadful detonations, a *new* truth peeps at you through thick clouds.

The truth of the *first* treatise is the psychology of Christianity: the birth of Christianity out of the spirit of resentment, not, as may have been believed, out of 'spirit' – it is a countermovement in its nature, the grand uprising against domination by *noble* values. The *second* treatise deals with the psychology of *conscience*: this is *not*, as may well have been believed, 'the voice of God in man', but the instinct of cruelty turning in on itself after it can no longer release itself to the outside world. Cruelty is here revealed, for the first time, as one of the oldest and most indispensable elements of culture. The *third* treatise is a reply to the question as to the origin of the tremendous power of the ascetic ideal, the priest ideal, even though it is a *harmful* ideal in every sense, the will to annihilation and an ideal of decadence. This is the reply: it is powerful *not* because God's presence is behind the priest, which may well have been believed, but for lack of something better and because so far it has been the only ideal – after all, it has no competition. 'For man would rather aspire to nothingness than *not* aspire at all'... Above all, *apart from* Zarathustra there was no *counter-ideal*.

You get my meaning. Three decisive psychological

overtures for a re-evaluation of all values. This book contains the first psychology of the priest.

The Twilight of the Idols.

HOW TO PHILOSOPHIZE WITH A SLEDGEHAMMER

1.

THIS BOOK of less than 150 pages, both cheerful and fatalistic in its tone (a demon laughing at you, so to speak, and the work of so few days that I cannot even be bothered to tell you how many) is altogether an exception amongst books: there is no book richer in substance, more independent, more dazzling – more wicked! If you wish to get an idea of how everything stood on its head in front of me, start by reading this work. What is called '*idol*' in the title is simply everything that hitherto has been called truth. *The Twilight of the Idols* – in plain language: the old truth is coming to an end…

2.

THERE IS NO REALITY, no 'notion of an ideal' that has not been touched upon in this book (touched! what cautious euphemism!). Not just the *eternal* idols, but also the very recent and therefore most senile ones: 'Modern ideas' for instance. A powerful wind blows between the trees and everywhere fruit – truths – drops down. It smacks of the windfall of an autumn all too fruitful: you trip over truths, you even crush some to death – there are just too many…

However, what you can grasp is no longer questionable, these are decisions. I alone hold the yardstick for 'truths' in

my hands, I alone *can* decide. It is as if a *second* consciousness had grown within me, as if my 'will' had cast a light upon the *downward* slope along which it has been running for ages... The *downward* slope – they called it the road to the 'truth'... All 'dark urges' have been dealt with, indeed, the *good* human being was least aware of the righteous path.

And in all seriousness, nobody before me knew of the righteous path, the path leading upwards: I alone pointed towards hopes, tasks and recommended paths of culture – *I am the herald of these good tidings*... And therefore I am also destiny.

3.

IMMEDIATELY after finishing this work and without losing a single day, I took upon myself the formidable task of the *re-evaluation* with a supreme feeling of pride which nothing could equal. Aware of my immortality at every moment, I engraved sign after sign into brass tablets with the certainty of fate. The preface was written on 3rd September 1888. When, after finishing it, I stepped outside into the morning air, I found the most lovely day I have ever lived through in the Upper Engadine – clear, glowing in its colours and with all its contrasts, all hues available between the icy north and the south.

Owing to a delay caused by floods, I did not leave Sils-Maria until 20th September, so in the end I was the only visitor in this delectable spot, which in my gratitude I wish to make immortal. After an eventful journey, including one narrow escape from death in the waters of Lake Como, which was flooded when I reached it in the dead of night, I arrived in Turin, to which I was *guided*, on the afternoon of the 21st, and it was from that time on my home.

I took the same lodgings I had occupied in the spring, on Via Carlo Alberto 6, III, opposite the mighty Palazzo Carignano where Vittorio Emanuele was born; it has a view of the Piazza Carlo Alberto and to the hills beyond it. Without hesitating and without being swayed for one moment, I returned to my work: only the last quarter of the book still remained to be written. The 30th September, Victory!, was the seventh day and a God could take it easy, walking along the River Po. The same day, I wrote the preface for my *Twilight of the Idols* for which I had corrected the proofs at leisure during the month of September.

Never before have I lived through an autumn like that, nor even imagined that such glory could be possible – a Claude Lorrain painting extended to infinity, every day of an equally incredible perfection.

The Wagner Case
A Musician's Problem.

1.

TO DO THIS ESSAY JUSTICE you have to suffer from the fatal affliction of music as from an open wound. *From what* do I suffer, when I suffer from the fatal affliction of music? I suffer because music has been deprived of its transfiguring, positive character – because it has become the music of decadence and is no longer the flute of Dionysus…

Supposing, however, that you feel that the cause of music is very much your *own* cause, your *own* tale of woe, then you will find this essay considerate and extremely mild in tone. To be cheerful in such cases and self-deprecating in a good-humoured way, in other words, to speak the truth whilst laughing whereby the truth would justify the hardest language, that is humanitarianism itself. Who would seriously doubt that I, old war horse that I am, will bring out my big guns against Wagner? – I restrained myself from any decisive action in this cause – I loved Wagner!

In the end this is an attack on a more subtle 'unknown figure' who cannot be easily divined by anyone in the sense that I wish to insinuate (really! I have to expose 'unknown figures' of a very different calibre to some adventurer in music). However, it is even more so an attack on the German nation, whose mind is becoming lazier and less instinctive but ever more *honest* and continues to feed itself with an enviable appetite on polarities, gulping 'faith', as well as scholarship, 'Christian love', as well as anti-Semitism, the will to power (the 'Empire') as well as the Gospel of the Humble without any sign of indigestion... This lack of judgement in choosing between these opposites! This ventral neutrality and 'selflessness'. This fairness of the German *taste bud* that will level everything – that finds everything tasty... Without any doubt, the Germans are idealists! When I last visited Germany, I found German taste occupied with trying to put Wagner and the Trumpeter of Säckingen on the same level; I myself was witness as the citizens of Leipzig founded a Liszt society in honour of one of the most genuine and German musicians (in the old sense of the term German, not an

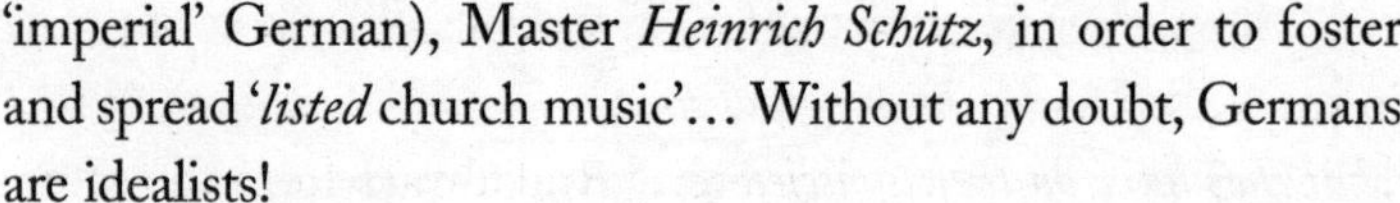

'imperial' German), Master *Heinrich Schütz*, in order to foster and spread '*listed* church music'... Without any doubt, Germans are idealists!

2.

BUT NOTHING shall stop me from becoming rude and telling the Germans a few hard truths: *who else will do it*? I speak of their historical perversion. Not only have German historians lost altogether the *grand view* for the course and values of culture and have, to a man, become buffoons of politics (or the church): they have even *outlawed* this grand view. First and foremost you have to be 'German', of 'good race', then you may settle all historical values and non-values by arbitration.

'German' is an argument; 'Germany, Germany above all' is a principle; the Germans represent the 'moral world order' in history. In relation to the Roman Empire they are the bringers of freedom, in relation to the 18th century they are the restorers of morality, of the 'categorical imperative'... There is an imperial German historiography, even, I fear, an anti-Semitic one, a *court* historiography, and Mr von Treitschke does not seem to be embarrassed by it...

The other day, an idiotic judgement of *history*, a proposition by the (fortunately) deceased Swabian aesthetician Vischer went the rounds of the German newspapers as a 'truth' that every German had to *accept*: 'The Renaissance *and* the Reformation – both together they constitute a whole – the aesthetic rebirth *and* the moral rebirth'. Such announcements make me lose my patience and I feel inclined, even duty bound,

to tell the Germans once and for all *what* else they have already on their conscience. *Every great cultural crime for four centuries is what they have on their conscience*!... And always from the same cause – from their innermost *cowardice* in the face of reality, which has become cowardice in the face of truth, from their now instinctive lack of truthfulness, from 'idealism'... The Germans have cheated Europe of the harvest, of the meaning of the last *great* era – the Renaissance – at a moment when a higher order of values, noble, life- and future-affirming values had been victorious at the seat of anti-ethical values, the *values of decline – and entered deeply into the instincts of those that dwelled there.* Luther, this calamity of a monk, restored the church and, much, much worse, Christianity, at the moment *of its fall*... Christianity, this *negation of the will to live* that became a religion! Luther, an impossible monk who precisely because of his 'impossibleness' attacked the church and thus – as a consequence – restored it. The Catholics would have good reason to celebrate Luther Festivals, to compose Luther plays! Luther... and the 'moral rebirth'! To hell with all psychology! Without doubt, the Germans are idealists.

Twice before, when incredible courage and willpower just managed to attain a decent, an unambiguous, a completely scientific mode of thinking, the Germans have known how to find rat runs back to the old 'ideal', to reconciliations between truth and 'ideal', at bottom formulas for the right to reject science, for the right to *lie*: in the form of Leibniz and Kant – these two largest stumbling blocks of Europe's intellectual integrity. Finally, when on the cusp between two decadent centuries a sweeping force of genius and will made itself known, strong enough to unite Europe, a political and *economic* union for the purpose of global government, the Germans with their 'Wars of Liberation' cheated Europe of the meaning, the miracle of meaning in the person of Napoleon – they thereby have on their conscience all that followed, all that we see today, this sickness and lack of reason *inimical to culture* – nationalism – this national neurosis which Europe suffers from, reinforcing Europe's system of mini-states, of *petty* politics: they have made Europe lose its mind, its reason – they have led it into a blind alley. Does anyone apart from me know a way out of this blind alley?... A task, *great* enough to *unite* people once again?

3.

AND LAST but not least, why should I not voice my suspicion? In my case too, the Germans will try once again everything to breed a mouse from a tremendous destiny. So far, they have shown themselves up for what they are with regards to me; I doubt that they will do any better in the future. What I wouldn't give to be wrong here, to be a *bad* prophet!...

My natural readers and listeners even now are Russians, Scandinavians and the French – will this always be the case? The Germans have entered nothing but ambiguous names into the history of the quest for knowledge; they have only ever produced 'unconscious' frauds (this befits Fichte, Schelling, Schopenhauer, Hegel, Schleiermacher as well as it does Kant and Leibniz – they are all only pulling the wool over our eyes); they shall never be privileged to be counted as one with the first spirit of *integrity* in the history of the spirit, the spirit which does

justice to the truth of fraudulence of four thousand years. The 'German spirit' seems stuffy to me: I breathe with difficulty near this psychological squalor that has become instinctive and is revealed by every word and in every countenance of a German. They have never lived through a 17th century of tough self-examination like the French – a La Rochefoucauld, a Descartes, are a hundred times superior to the best German in integrity – to this day they have not had a psychologist. But psychology is almost a yardstick for the *cleanliness* or *squalor* of a race... And if you are not even clean, how can you have *depth*? You will never get to the bottom of it with a German, almost as with women, *there is none*, that is all there is to it. They are not even shallow. What is called 'deep' in Germany is precisely this instinctive squalor turned against themselves of which I have just spoken: they *do not want* to see themselves clearly. Might I suggest to use the word 'German' as an international coinage for this psychological depravity?

For example, at this very moment the German Emperor calls it his 'Christian duty' to free the slaves in Africa: we other Europeans would then simply be calling this 'German'... Have the Germans produced even a single book of any depth? They do not even have a notion of depth in a book. I have met scholars who thought of Kant as deep; I am afraid that at the Prussian court, Mr von Treitschke is considered deep. And on occasions when I praised Stendhal as a deep psychologist, I have met German university professors who asked me how to spell his name...

4.

AND WHY should I not go all the way? I like to make a clean sweep of things. I even have the ambition of appearing to be the supreme rejecter of Germans. Even at twenty-six I expressed my mistrust of the German character (Third Untimely Meditation, section 6) – I can't stand the Germans. If I had to invent a type of person who antagonizes all my instincts, he would always turn into a German.

The acid test for me is whether a man can see things as they are, whether he recognizes rank, degree or the hierarchy which is natural to people, whether he *distinguishes*: if so, he is a gentleman; otherwise he belongs hopelessly to the broad-minded, oh such good-natured category of the scoundrel. But that is what the Germans are – scoundrels – oh, they are so very good-natured... You debase yourself when associating with Germans: the Germans make everyone *look equal*.

Not counting my association with a few artists, in particular with Richard Wagner, I have not spent one good hour with a German... If the most profound spirit of all time were to appear among Germans, some silly goose would believe that her not-so-beautiful soul deserved at least as much attention... I can't bear this race which is always bad company, has no feelings for nuances (oh dear! I am a nuance), has no life in its feet and cannot even walk... Ultimately, the Germans have no feet at all, just legs... They have no idea how common they are, but this is the superlative of vulgarity – they are not even *ashamed* of being merely Germans... They have to join in every conversation, they think of themselves as decision-makers, I am afraid that they have reached a decision even with regards to me...

My whole life is essentially the proof for all this. In vain do I look for some sign of tact, of sensitivity in their treatment of me. From Jews, yes, but never ever from a German. My nature demands that I am kind and gentle towards everyone – it is my *right*, not to differentiate – however, that does not stop me keeping my eyes open. I do not exclude anyone, least of all my friends – in the end I hope that this has not diminished my humanity towards them. There are five or six things which have always been a point of honour with me.

Nevertheless it remains true that almost every letter that has reached me for some years now strikes me as a piece of cynicism: there is more cynicism in goodwill for me than in any hatred… I tell every one of my friends to his face that he has never thought it worthwhile to *study* any of my books; I take it from the smallest sign that they don't even know what they are about. As for my Zarathustra, who of my friends would have seen more in him than a forbidden, fortunately perfectly meaningless presumption?…

Ten years, and nobody in Germany took it upon himself to defend my name against the absurd silence under which it was buried: it was a foreigner, a Dane, who was the first to have sufficient refinement of instinct and enough courage to take up arms against my so-called friends… Which German university these days would offer lectures on my philosophy as did Dr Georg Brandes in Copenhagen, who therewith once more proved himself a true psychologist?

As it is, I myself never suffered on account of all this; *necessaries* do not hurt me – love of destiny is my inmost nature. However, that does not preclude my love of irony, even world-

historical irony. And thus, approximately two years before the shattering lightning bolt of *re-evaluation* which will convulse the earth, I have sent *The Wagner Case* into the world: let the Germans one more time assault me and this time *once and for all*! There is just about enough time left!

Has it been achieved? I am delighted, my dear Teutonic gentlemen, I must pay you my compliments… Just now, lest my friends be left out, one of my old girlfriends wrote to me that she now laughs at me… And this at a moment when an indescribable responsibility weighs on me – when no word can be too carefully chosen, no-one can look with sufficient awe at me. For I carry the destiny of mankind on my shoulders…

Chapter 4

Why I am destiny

1.

I KNOW MY FATE. One day, my name will be associated with the memory of something tremendous – a crisis without equal on earth, the most profound collision of conscience, a decision that was conjured up *against* everything that mankind has ever believed in and held sacred. I am no man, I am dynamite.

Yet for all that I am not a founder of a religion – religions are for the rabble. Whenever I come into contact with a religious person, I have to wash my hands afterwards. I don't *want* 'believers'; I think I am too wicked to believe in myself; I never address crowds… I am terribly afraid that one day I will be *canonized*: they will work out why I published this book *beforehand*, it is to prevent being taken the wrong way… I do not want to be a saint, I would sooner be a buffoon… Perhaps I am a buffoon… And yet or perhaps not yet (for there is nothing more false than a saint), the truth speaks out of me. But my truth is *terrible*: for until now they have called *lies* the truth. *Re-evaluation of all Values*: that is my formula for an act of supreme self-examination of mankind that became my flesh and my genius. It is my fate that I have to be the first *decent* person,

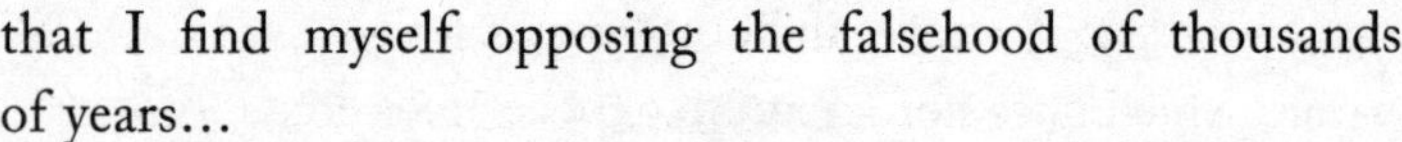

that I find myself opposing the falsehood of thousands of years…

I was the first to *discover* the truth by being the first to find out that a lie is a lie – I could smell it… My genius lies in my nostrils… I dispute in a way that has never been done before and yet I am the opposite of a negative spirit. I am the bringer of glad tidings like no-one before me; I know tasks so enormous that hitherto no term could do justice to them, I alone will offer hope once again. For all that, I am necessarily also a man of destiny. For when truth declares war on the lies of thousands of years, we shall have upheavals, a convulsion of earthquakes, a moving of mountains and valleys the like of which has never been dreamed of. The concept of politics will have merged entirely with a war of ghosts, all power structures of the old society will have been blown to bits – all of them are founded on lies: there will be wars the like of which have never been seen on earth. I alone am responsible for *great politics* on earth.

2.

DO YOU WANT a formula for a destiny such that becomes *Son of Man*? – You will find it in my *Zarathustra*.

'*– and whoever wants to become a creator in good or evil, must first be a destroyer and dismantle values.*

Therefore the greatest evil is part of the greatest goodness: but this is being creative.'

I am by far the most awful human being that ever lived. However, that does not mean I will not also be the kindest. I know the pleasure in *destroying* to a degree that is in line with

my strength to destroy – in both respects I obey my Dionysian nature which does not know how to separate doing 'No' from saying 'Yes'. I am the first *immoralist* – that makes me the perfect *destroyer*.

3.

NO-ONE ASKED ME but they should have asked me what the name of Zarathustra means when I speak it, I, the first immoralist: for the tremendous uniqueness of that historical Persian lies precisely in his contradictions. Zarathustra first saw the true wheel of fate in the fight with good and evil – the transmission of morality into metaphysics, as a force, a cause, a purpose in itself – that is *his* work. But this question is at heart already the reply. Zarathustra *created* this most fatal mistake – morality – therefore he also had to be the first to *recognize* it. Not just because he has more experience than any other thinker in this field, after all the whole history is the experimental dispute of the doctrine of the so-called 'ethical world order'; no, it is more important to say that Zarathustra is more truthful than any other thinker. His teaching and his teaching alone recognizes truth as the highest virtue; it means, it is the opposite of the *cowardice* of the 'idealist', who runs away from reality. Zarathustra is more courageous than all other thinkers put together and he *is able to shoot with arrow and bow* – that is the Persian virtue. Do you get my meaning?... Self-conquest of morality has its roots in truth, the self-conquest of the moralist in his opposite – in *me* – that is to say, when I speak the name of Zarathustra.

4.

BASICALLY there are two negations in my definition of *immoralist*: firstly, I deny a type of man that has so far been considered the very best, the *good*, the *complaisant*, the *charitable*; and then I negate a type of morality which became prevalent and predominant as morality itself – the morality of decadence or, to put it more plainly, *Christian* morality. It would be permissible to see the second objection as the more important one, since the overrating of goodness and kindness on a large scale is to my mind already the consequence of decadence, a symptom of weakness, incompatible with the force-gathering and positive life: negating and *destroying* are conditions of saying 'Yes'.

For now, I shall stick to the psychology of the good person. To estimate how much an archetypal person is worth, you have to calculate the price that his keep will cost – you have to know the conditions he needs for his existence. The condition for the existence of the good is the *lie* – put differently, not *wanting* to look reality in the face at any cost, in particular *not* in such a way as to ever challenge complaisant instincts, and even less in such a way as to put up with the interference of short-sightedly good-natured ones. To consider any *difficulties* in general as an objection, as something that has to be abolished, is absolute nonsense, and on a large scale a true calamity in its consequences, destined to be stupid – almost as stupid as if trying to abolish bad weather – say from pity for the poor... In the overall system, the calamities of reality (in its effects, in desires, in the will to power) are to an incalculable measure more important than that form of petty

happiness which people call 'goodness'. You actually have to be quite forbearing to the latter to give it some space, since it is based on instinctive falseness. I will find a major occasion to demonstrate how the historical consequences of *optimism*, this spawn of great men, have been sinister beyond belief. Zarathustra, who was the first to grasp that the optimist is just as decadent as the pessimist, and perhaps more harmful, says, '*Good men never speak the truth. Treacherous coastlines and assurances have been taught to you by the good; in the lies of the good you were hatched and huddled. Everything is riddled through and through with, and twisted by, the lies of the good.*'

Luckily, the world has not been built on such instincts that only good-natured herd animals may find their narrow happiness in it, to demand that all should become 'good men', herd animals, blue-eyed, complaisant, 'beautiful souls' – or, as Mr Herbert Spencer would have it, altruistic – that would deprive existence of its *great* character and would castrate humanity and reduce us all to a stagnant state of misery.

And they have tried to! Precisely this they called morality... In this sense, Zarathustra calls the good now 'the last men', now the 'beginning of the end'; above all, he considers this type of man the most harmful, because they enforce their existence at the expense of *truth* as well as at the expense of the *future*.

' – The good – are unable to *create*; they are always the beginning of the end;

– they crucify him who writes *new* values on new tablets; they sacrifice the future to themselves; they crucify the future of all of man!

– The good – have always been the beginning of the end...

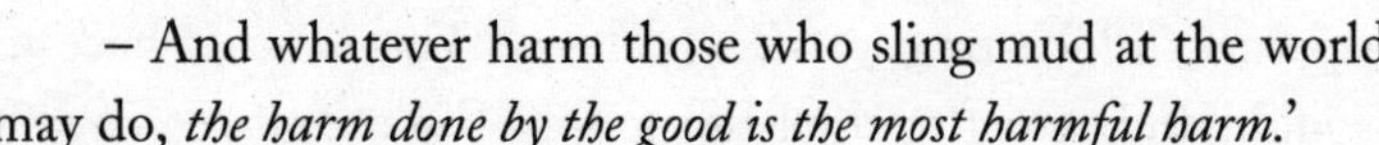

– And whatever harm those who sling mud at the world may do, *the harm done by the good is the most harmful harm.*'

5.

ZARATHUSTRA, the first psychologist of the good, is therefore a friend of the wicked. When a decadent type of man has risen to the rank of finest character, this could only happen at the expense of its counterpart, the strong and self-confident type. When the herd animal radiates purest virtue, the exceptional man must have been reduced to the level of the wicked. If falseness monopolizes the word 'truth' at any price, the really truthful man is bound to be branded with the worst names. Zarathustra leaves no doubt here: he says that it had been precisely the perception of the good, 'the very best' that made him shudder at the sight of man in general; from *this* dislike he had grown his wings, 'to soar off into distant futures' – he does not conceal the fact that *his* type of man, a relatively superhuman type, is superhuman precisely in relation to the *good* – that the good and just would call his superman *the devil.*

'You men of highest rank whom my eyes looked upon, this is my doubt in you and my secret mirth: I assume you would call my superman: the devil! You are so estranged in your soul from all that is great that superman would be terrifying to you in his goodness.' It is at this point and nowhere else that you must make a start to grasp what Zarathustra wants: this type of man of his own conception, conceives reality *as it is*: it is strong enough for that – this type is not estranged or removed from reality, it is reality *itself* and exemplifies all that is terrible and questionable in it – *only in that way can man attain greatness*...

6.

BUT HERE is yet another sense in which I have chosen the word *immoralist* for myself as a symbol and badge of honour; I am proud of knowing this word that sets me apart from all of humanity. Nobody has as yet felt *Christian* morality to be *beneath* him: for this you need great height, a farsightedness, a hitherto unheard of psychological depth and profundity. Christian morality has until now been the femme fatale to all thinkers – they were in her service.

Who has entered before me the lairs from which the poisonous stench of this type of ideal (of world slandering) rises? Who even dared to suspect that these are lairs in the first place? Who among philosophers was actually a *psychologist* before me and not rather the opposite, a 'superior swindler' and 'idealist'? There was no psychology at all before me. To be the first here can also be a curse – it is at all events a destiny: *for you are also the first to despise*... The *distaste* for mankind is my danger...

7.

DID YOU GET MY MEANING?
What defines me and sets me apart from the rest of humanity is the fact that I *exposed* Christian morality. That is why I needed a word that would be a challenge to everyone. The fact that they did not open their eyes earlier at this point is to me the greatest stain on man's conscience; it is a self-deception that has become instinct, that is a fundamental principle *to close* their eyes to everything that happens, to every causality, to every reality, as psychological fraudulence that borders on

criminality. Blindness to Christianity is the *absolute crime* – the crime *against life*…

Thousands of years have passed and all people, the first and the last, the philosophers and the old women, they are all as bad as each other as far as this matter is concerned – apart from five or six moments in history (I am the seventh). The Christian has so far been *the* 'moral being', a rare curiosity and, *as* the 'moral being' more absurd, false, vain, frivolous and *acting more to his own disadvantage* than even the greatest rejecter of mankind could dream up. Christian morality, the most malignant form of the will to lie, the true femme fatale of mankind, corrupted it. It is *not* the error as such which horrifies me when I look at this fact, *not* the lack of 'good will' for two millennia, of discipline, of decency, of spiritual courage, revealed by its victory – it is the lack of naturalness and the utterly horrific fact that *perversion* itself received the highest honours as morality and was left to govern humanity as law and categorical imperative… To fail to such an extent – *not* as individuals, *not* as people, but as humanity!… That they taught us to despise the primary instincts of life, that they made up a 'soul' and a 'spirit' to abuse the body, that they taught us to find something unclean in the precondition for life – sexuality; that even in the most profound quality for any growth, strict self-interest (even the word is pejorative!), they seek the evil principle, and that, conversely, they regard the *higher* value, what am I saying, the *absolute* value, in the typical signs of decline and contradictory instincts, that is to say in 'selflessness', in loss of gravity, in 'depersonalization' and 'charity' (addictive charity!)… What? Is humanity itself decadent? Was it always?

One thing is certain, that it has been *taught* only decadent values as supreme values. The losing of the Self-morality is the absolute morality of decline, the fact 'I am losing myself' has been translated into the imperative 'you must all lose yourself' – and *not just* into the imperative!... The only morality that has been taught so far is to lose your Self and it reveals a will to end all – it is a basic negation of life.

This could leave open the possibility that humanity is not degenerating, but only that type of parasitic man, the *priest*, who with lies and deceptions about morality became the definer of values – who divined that Christian morality would be his means to *power*... And indeed, *this* is my discovery: the teachers, the leaders of mankind, theologians all of them, were also Decadents on the whole: *hence* the re-evaluation of all values into hostility to life, *hence* morality... *definition of morality*: morality – the idiosyncrasy of Decadents with the hidden agenda to take revenge on life – successfully. I find this definition very important.

8.

DID YOU GET MY MEANING?

Everything I have just said, I said five years ago with Zarathustra as my mouthpiece. The *uncovering* of Christian morality is an event unparalleled, a true catastrophe. He who enlightens the world about it is a *force majeure*, a destiny – he breaks the history of mankind in two. You live *before* him or you live *after* him.

The lightning bolt of truth struck precisely that which was held in highest esteem: whoever understands *what* has been

destroyed may look down on his hands to see whether he still has something left to hold. All that was called 'truth' up to now has been recognized as the most harmful, insidious and underhand form of lie: the sacred pretext of 'improving' humanity as an uncanny attempt to *suck* the blood of life itself – morality as *vampirism*...

Whoever uncovers morality also discovers the lack of value in all values in which we believe or have believed. He no longer sees anything venerable in the most venerated, even *canonized* type of man. He sees the most fatal type of crippled existence in them, fatal because they fascinate...

The concept of 'God', invented as an anti-climax to life, stands for all that is harmful, poisonous, slandering and the deathly hostility against life in one dreadful unity. The concept of 'other world' or 'better world' was invented to devalue the *only* world in existence, in order not to keep a single aim, reason or task for our earthly reality. The concept of our 'soul', 'spirit' and finally even 'immortal soul' were invented to make us despise our body, to render it sick, 'holy', to meet all things that deserve to be taken seriously: the questions of nourishment, accommodation, education, nursing care, hygiene and weather, with dreadful flippancy! Instead of health the idea of 'salvation of the soul' (a folly wedged between pathological use of penitence and redemption-hysteria of manic depressive intensity) was invented together with the associated instrument of torture, the concept of 'free will', to confuse the instincts that make mistrust of our instincts second nature. The concept of the 'selfless' and 'self-denial' are the defining signs of decadence; the *attraction* of the harmful, the *inability* to evaluate your own usefulness

and self-destruction were turned into proof of value itself, into 'duty', into 'holiness', into what is 'divine' in man! Finally, and this is the most terrible, the concept of the *good* man takes the side of all that is weak, sick, misshapen and suffering, of all those that ought to perish – the law of selection is crossed and an ideal born out of opposition to those proud and well-made, those who say 'Yes', those who are sure of the future, who safeguard the future – this is now called *evil*... And all this was believed and called *morality*! *Ecrasez l'infâme!*

9.

DID YOU GET MY MEANING? – *Dionysus versus the man on the Cross.*

HUMAN, ALL TOO HUMAN

HUMAN, ALL TOO HUMAN

FRIEDRICH NIETZSCHE

This edition published in 2021 by Arcturus Publishing Limited
26/27 Bickels Yard, 151–153 Bermondsey Street,
London SE1 3HA

Typesetting by Palimpsest Book Production Limited

Cover design: Peter Ridley
Cover illustration: Peter Gray

AD007696UK

Printed in the UK

CONTENTS

INTRODUCTION

Nietzsche's essay, *Richard Wagner in Bayreuth*, appeared in 1876, and his next publication was his present work, which was issued in 1878. A comparison of the books will show that the two years of meditation intervening had brought about a great change in Nietzsche's views, his style of expressing them, and the form in which they were cast. The Dionysian, overflowing with life, gives way to an Apollonian thinker with a touch of pessimism. The long essay form is abandoned, and instead we have a series of aphorisms, some tinged with melancholy, others with satire, several, especially towards the end, with Nietzschian wit at its best, and a few at the beginning so very abstruse as to require careful study.

Since the Bayreuth festivals of 1876, Nietzsche had gradually come to see Wagner as he really was. The ideal musician that Nietzsche had pictured in his own mind turned out to be nothing more than a rather dilettante philosopher, an opportunistic decadent with a suspicious tendency towards Christianity. The young philosopher thereupon proceeded to shake off the influence which the musician had exercised upon him. He was successful in doing so, but not without a struggle, just as he had formerly shaken off the influence of Schopenhauer. Hence he writes in his autobiography:[1] '*Human, all-too-Human*, is the monument of a crisis. It is entitled: "A book for *free* spirits," and almost every line in it represents a victory – in its pages I freed myself from everything foreign to my real nature. Idealism is foreign to me: the title says, "Where *you* see ideal things, I see things which are only – human alas! all-too-human!" I know man *better* – the term "free spirit" must here be understood in no other sense than this: a freed man, who has once more taken possession of himself.'

The form of this book will be better understood when it is remembered that at this period Nietzsche was beginning to suffer from stomach trouble and headaches. As a cure for his complaints, he spent his time in travel when he could get a few weeks' respite from

---

1 *Ecce Homo*, p. 75

his duties at Basel University; and it was in the course of his solitary walks and hill-climbing tours that the majority of these thoughts occurred to him and were jotted down there and then. A few of them, however, date further back, as he tells us in the preface to the second part of this work. Many of them, he says, occupied his mind even before he published his first book, *The Birth of Tragedy*, and several others, as we learn from his notebooks and posthumous writings, date from the period of the *Thoughts out of Season*.

It must be clearly understood, however, that Nietzsche's disease must not be looked upon in the same way as that of an ordinary man. People are inclined to regard a sick man as rancorous; but any one who fights with and conquers his disease, and even exploits it, as Nietzsche did, benefits thereby to an extraordinary degree. In the first place, he has passed through several stages of human psychology with which a healthy man is entirely unacquainted; e.g. he has learnt by introspection the spiteful and revengeful spirit of the sick man and his religion. Secondly, in his moments of freedom from pain and gloom his thoughts will be all the more brilliant.

In support of this last statement, one instance may be selected out of hundreds that could be adduced. Heinrich Heine spent the greater part of his life in exile from his native country, tortured by headaches, and finally dying in a foreign land as the result of a spinal disease. His splendid works were composed in his moments of respite from illness, and during the last years of his life, when his health was at its worst, he gave to the world his famous *Romancero*. We would likewise do well to recollect Goethe's saying:

Zart Gedicht, wie Regenbogen,
Wird nur auf dunkelm Grund gezogen.[2]

Thus neither the form of this book – so startling at first to those who have been brought up in the traditions of our own school – nor the treat all men as equals, and proclaim the establishment of equal rights: so far a socialistic mode of thought which is based on *justice* is possible; but, as has been said, only within the ranks of the

2 'Tender poetry, like rainbows, can appear only on a dark and sombre background.' – J. M. K.

governing classes, which in this case *practises* justice with sacrifices and abnegations. On the other hand, to *demand* equality of rights, as do the Socialists of the subject caste, is by no means the outcome of justice, but of covetousness. If you expose bloody pieces of flesh to a beast, and then withdraw them again until it finally begins to roar, do you think that the roaring implies justice?

Theologians on the other hand, as may be expected, will find no such ready help in their difficulties from Nietzsche. They must, on the contrary, be on their guard against so alert an adversary – a duty which they are apparently not going to shirk; for theologians are amongst the most ardent students of Nietzsche in this country. Their attention may therefore be drawn to aphorism 630 of this book, dealing with convictions and their origin, which will no doubt be successfully refuted by the defenders of the true faith. In fact, there is not a single paragraph in the book that does not deserve careful study by all serious thinkers.

On the whole, however, this is a calm book, and those who are accustomed to Nietzsche the outspoken Immoralist, may be somewhat astonished at the calm tone of the present volume. The explanation is that Nietzsche was now just beginning to walk on his own philosophical path. His lifelong aim, the uplifting of the type man, was still in view, but the way leading towards it was once more uncertain. Hence the peculiarly calm, even melancholic, and what Nietzsche himself would call Apollonian, tinge of many of these aphorisms, so different from the style of his earlier and later writings. For this very reason, however, the book may appeal all the more to English readers, who are of course more Apollonian than Dionysian. Nietzsche is feeling his way, and these aphorisms represent his first steps. As such – besides having a high intrinsic value of themselves – they are enormous aids to the study of his character and temperament.

J. M. KENNEDY.

PREFACE

1.

I HAVE been told frequently, and always with great surprise, that there is something common and distinctive in all my writings, from the *Birth of Tragedy* to the latest published *Prelude to a Philosophy of the Future*. They all contain, I have been told, snares and nets for unwary birds, and an almost perpetual unconscious demand for the inversion of customary valuations and valued customs. What? *Everything* only – human – all-too-human? People lay down my writings with this sigh, not without a certain dread and distrust of morality itself, indeed almost tempted and encouraged to become advocates of the *worst* things: as being perhaps only the *best* disparaged? My writings have been called a school of suspicion and especially of disdain, more happily, also, a school of courage and even of audacity. Indeed, I myself do not think that any one has ever looked at the world with such a profound suspicion; and not only as occasional Devil's Advocate, but equally also, to speak theologically, as enemy and impeacher of God; and he who realises something of the consequences involved, in every profound suspicion, something of the chills and anxieties of loneliness to which every uncompromising *difference of outlook* condemns him who is affected therewith, will also understand how often I sought shelter in some kind of reverence or hostility, or scientificality or levity or stupidity, in order to recover from myself, and, as it were, to obtain temporary self-forgetfulness; also why, when I did not find what I *needed*, I was obliged to manufacture it, to counterfeit and to imagine it in a suitable manner (and what else have poets ever done? And for what purpose has all the art in the world existed?). What I always required most, however, for my cure and self-recovery, was the belief that I was *not* isolated in such circumstances, that I did not *see* in an isolated manner – a magic suspicion of relationship and similarity to others in outlook and desire, a repose in the confidence of friendship, a blindness in both parties without suspicion or note of interrogation, an enjoyment of foregrounds, and surfaces of the near and the nearest, of all that has colour, epidermis, and outside appearance. Perhaps I might be reproached in this respect for much 'art' and fine false coinage; for instance, for voluntarily and knowingly shutting my eyes to Schopenhauer's blind will to morality at a time when I had become sufficiently clear-sighted about morality; also for deceiving myself about Richard Wagner's incurable romanticism, as if it were a beginning and not an end; also about the Greeks, also about the Germans and their future – and there would still probably be quite a long list of such alsos? Supposing however, that this were all true and that I were reproached with good reason, what do *you* know, what could you know as to how much artifice of self-preservation, how much rationality and higher protection there is in such self-deception – and how much falseness I still *require* in order to allow myself again and again the luxury of *my* sincerity? ... In short, I still live; and life, in spite of ourselves, is not devised by morality; it *demands* illusion, it *lives* by illusion . . . but – There! I am already beginning again and doing what I have always done, old immoralist and bird-catcher that I am – I am talking un-morally, ultra-morally, 'beyond good and evil'? . . .

2.

Thus then, when I found it necessary, I *invented* once on a time the 'free spirits', to whom this discouragingly encouraging book with the title *Human, all-too-Human*, is dedicated. There are no such 'free spirits' nor have there been such, but, as already said, I then required them for company to keep me cheerful in the midst of evils (sickness, loneliness, foreignness – *acedia*, inactivity) as brave companions and ghosts with whom I could laugh and gossip when so inclined and send to the devil when they became bores – as compensation for the lack of friends. That such free spirits *will be possible* some day, that our Europe will have such bold and cheerful wights amongst her sons of tomorrow and the day after tomorrow, actually and bodily, and not merely, as in my case, as the shadows of a hermit's phantasmagoria – *I* should be the last to doubt thereof. Already I see them *coming*, slowly, slowly; and perhaps I am doing something to hasten their coming when I describe in advance under what auspices I *see* them originate, and upon what paths I *see* them come.

3.

One may suppose that a spirit in whsich the type 'free spirit' is to become fully mature and sweet, has had its decisive event in a *great emancipation*, and that it was all the more fettered previously and apparently bound for ever to its corner and pillar. What is it that binds most strongly? What cords are almost unrendable? In men of a lofty and select type it will be their duties; the reverence which is suitable to youth, respect and tenderness for all that is time-honoured and worthy, gratitude to the land which bore them, to the hand which led them, to the sanctuary where they learnt to adore – their most exalted moments themselves will bind them most effectively, will lay upon them the most enduring obligations. For those who are thus bound the great emancipation comes suddenly, like an earthquake; the young soul is all at once convulsed, unloosened and extricated – it does not itself know what is happening. An impulsion and compulsion sway and overmaster it like a command; a will and a wish awaken, to go forth on their course, anywhere, at any cost; a violent, dangerous curiosity about an undiscovered world flames and flares in every sense. 'Better to die than live *here*' – says the imperious voice and seduction, and this 'here', this 'at home' is all that the soul has hitherto loved! A sudden fear and suspicion of that which it loved, a flash of disdain for what was called its 'duty', a rebellious, arbitrary, volcanically throbbing longing for travel, foreignness, estrangement, coldness, disenchantment, glaciation, a hatred of love, perhaps a sacrilegious clutch and look *backwards*, to where it hitherto adored and loved, perhaps a glow of shame at what it was just doing, and at the same time a rejoicing *that* it was doing it, an intoxicated, internal, exulting thrill which betrays a triumph – a triumph? Over what? Over whom? An enigmatical, questionable, doubtful triumph, but the *first* triumph nevertheless; such evil and painful incidents belong to the history of the great emancipation. It is, at the same time, a disease which may destroy the man, this first outbreak of power and will to self-decision, self-valuation, this will to *free* will; and how much disease is manifested in the wild attempts and eccentricities by which the liberated and emancipated one now seeks to demonstrate his mastery over things! He roves about raging with unsatisfied longing; whatever he captures has to suffer for the dangerous tension of his pride; he tears to pieces whatever attracts him. With a malicious laugh he twirls round whatever he finds veiled or guarded by a sense of shame; he tries how these things look when turned upside down. It is a matter of arbitrariness with him, and pleasure in arbitrariness, if he now perhaps bestow his favour on what had hitherto a bad repute – if he inquisitively and temptingly haunt what is specially forbidden. In the background of his activities and wanderings – for he is restless and aimless in his course as in a desert – stands the note of interrogation of an increasingly dangerous curiosity. 'Cannot *all* valuations be reversed? And is good perhaps evil? And God only an invention and artifice of the devil? Is everything, perhaps, radically false? And if we are the deceived, are we not thereby also deceivers? *Must* we not also be deceivers?' – Such thoughts lead and mislead him more and more, onward and away. Solitude encircles and engirdles him, always more threatening, more throttling, more heart-oppressing, that terrible goddess and *mater saeva cupidinum* – but who knows nowadays what *solitude* is? ...

4.

From this morbid solitariness, from the desert of such years of experiment, it is still a long way to the copious, overflowing safety and soundness which does not care to dispense with disease itself as an instrument and angling-hook of knowledge; to that *mature* freedom of spirit which is equally self-control and discipline of the heart, and gives access to many and opposed modes of thought; to that inward comprehensiveness and daintiness of superabundance, which excludes any danger of the spirit's becoming enamoured and lost in its own paths, and lying intoxicated in some corner or other; to that excess of plastic, healing, formative, and restorative powers, which is exactly the sign of *splendid* health, that excess which gives the free spirit the dangerous prerogative of being entitled to live by experiments and offer itself to adventure; the free spirit's prerogative of mastership! Long years of convalescence may lie in between, years full of many-coloured, painfully-enchanting magical transformations, curbed and led by a tough *will to health*, which often dares to dress and disguise itself as actual health. There is a middle condition therein, which a man of such a fate never calls to mind later on without emotion; a pale, delicate light and a sunshine-happiness are peculiar to him, a feeling of bird-like freedom, prospect, and haughtiness, a *tertium quid* in which curiosity and gentle disdain are combined. A 'free spirit' – this cool expression does good in every condition, it almost warms. One no longer lives, in the fetters of love and hatred, without Yea, without Nay, voluntarily near, voluntarily distant, preferring to escape, to turn aside, to flutter forth, to fly up and away; one is fastidious like every one who has once seen an immense variety *beneath* him – and one has become the opposite of those who trouble themselves about things which do not concern them. In fact, it is nothing but things which now concern the free spirit – and how many things! – which no longer *trouble* him!

5.

A step further towards recovery, and the free spirit again draws near to life; slowly, it is true, and almost stubbornly, almost distrustfully. Again it grows warmer around him, and, as it were, yellower; feeling and sympathy gain depth, thawing winds of every kind pass lightly over him. He almost feels as if his eyes were now first opened to what is *near*. He marvels and is still; where has he been? The near and nearest things, how changed they appear to him! What a bloom and magic they have acquired meanwhile! He looks back gratefully – grateful to his wandering, his austerity and self-estrangement, his far-sightedness and his bird-like flights in cold heights. What a good thing that he did not always stay 'at home', 'by himself', like a sensitive, stupid tenderling. He has been *beside himself*, there is no doubt. He now sees himself for the first time – and what surprises he feels thereby! What thrills unexperienced hitherto! What joy even in the weariness, in the old illness, in the relapses of the convalescent! How he likes to sit still and suffer, to practise patience, to lie in the sun! Who is as familiar as he with the joy of winter, with the patch of sunshine upon the wall! They are the most grateful animals in the world, and also the most unassuming, these lizards of convalescents with their faces half-turned towards life once more: there are those amongst them who never let a day pass without hanging a little hymn of praise on its trailing fringe. And, speaking seriously, it is a radical *cure* for all pessimism (the well-known disease of old idealists and falsehood-mongers) to become ill after the manner of these free spirits, to remain ill a good while, and then grow well (I mean 'better') for a still longer period. It is wisdom, practical wisdom, to prescribe even health for one's self for a long time only in small doses.

6.

About this time it may at last happen, under the sudden illuminations of still disturbed and changing health, that the enigma of that great emancipation begins to reveal itself to the free, and ever freer, spirit – that enigma which had hitherto lain obscure, questionable, and almost intangible, in his memory. If for a long time he scarcely dared to ask himself, 'Why so apart? So alone? denying everything that I revered? denying reverence itself? Why this hatred, this suspicion, this severity towards my own virtues?' – he now dares and asks the questions aloud, and already hears something like an answer to them – 'Thou shouldst become master over thyself and master also of thine own virtues. Formerly *they* were thy masters; but they are only entitled to be thy tools amongst other tools. Thou shouldst obtain power over thy pro and contra, and learn how to put them forth and withdraw them again in accordance with thy higher purpose. Thou shouldst learn how to take the proper perspective of every valuation – the shifting, distortion, and apparent teleology of the horizons and everything that belongs to perspective; also the amount of stupidity which opposite values involve, and all the intellectual loss with which every pro and every contra has to be paid for. Thou shouldst learn how much *necessary* injustice there is in every for and against, injustice as inseparable from life, and life itself as *conditioned* by the perspective and its injustice. Above all thou shouldst see clearly where the injustice is always greatest: namely, where life has developed most punily, restrictedly, necessitously, and incipiently, and yet cannot help regarding *itself* as the purpose and standard of things, and for the sake of self-preservation, secretly, basely, and continuously wasting away and calling in question the higher, greater, and richer – thou shouldst see clearly the problem of gradation of rank, and how power and right and amplitude of perspective grow up together. Thou shouldst—' But enough; the free spirit knows henceforth which 'thou shalt' he has obeyed, and also what he *can* now *do*, what he only now – *may do*....

7.

Thus doth the free spirit answer himself with regard to the riddle of emancipation, and ends therewith, while he generalises his case, in order thus to decide with regard to his experience. 'As it has happened to *me*,' he says to himself, 'so must it happen to every one in whom a *mission* seeks to embody itself and to "come into the world". The secret power and necessity of this mission will operate in and upon the destined individuals like an unconscious pregnancy – long before they have had the mission itself in view and have known its name. Our destiny rules over us, even when we are not yet aware of it; it is the future that makes laws for our today. Granted that it is *the problem of the gradations of rank*, of which we may say that it is *our* problem, we free spirits; now only in the midday of our life do we first understand what preparations, detours, tests, experiments, and disguises the problem needed, before it was *permitted* to rise before us, and how we had first to experience the most manifold and opposing conditions of distress and happiness in soul and body, as adventurers and circumnavigators of the inner world called 'man', as surveyors of all the 'higher' and the 'one-above-another', also called 'man' – penetrating everywhere, almost without fear, rejecting nothing, losing nothing, tasting everything, cleansing everything from all that is accidental, and, as it were, sifting it out – until at last we could say, we free spirits, 'Here – a *new* problem! Here a long ladder, the rungs of which we ourselves have sat upon and mounted – which we ourselves at some time have *been*! Here a higher place, a lower place, an under-us, an immeasurably long order, a hierarchy which we *see* here – *our* problem!'

8.

No psychologist or augur will be in doubt for a moment as to what stage of the development just described the following book belongs (or is assigned to). But where are these psychologists nowadays? In France, certainly; perhaps in Russia; assuredly not in Germany. Reasons are not lacking why the present-day Germans could still even count this as an honour to them – bad enough, surely, for one who in this respect is un-German in disposition and constitution! This *German* book, which has been able to find readers in a wide circle of countries and nations – it has been about ten years going its rounds – and must understand some sort of music and piping art, by means of which even coy foreign ears are seduced into listening – it is precisely in Germany that this book has been most negligently read, and worst *listened to*; what is the reason? 'It demands too much,' I have been told, 'it appeals to men free from the pressure of coarse duties, it wants refined and fastidious senses, it needs superfluity – superfluity of time, of clearness of sky and heart, of *otium* in the boldest sense of the term: purely good things, which we Germans of today do not possess and therefore cannot give.' After such a polite answer my philosophy advises me to be silent and not to question further; besides, in certain cases, as the proverb points out, one only *remains* a philosopher by being – silent.[3]

Nice, Spring 1886.

3 An allusion to the medieval Latin distich:

O si tacuisses,

Philosophus mansisses. – J. M. K.

FIRST DIVISION.
FIRST AND LAST THINGS.

1.

Chemistry of Ideas and Sensations. – Philosophical problems adopt in almost all matters the same form of question as they did two thousand years ago; how can anything spring from its opposite? For instance, reason out of unreason, the sentient out of the dead, logic out of unlogic, disinterested contemplation out of covetous willing, life for others out of egoism, truth out of error? Metaphysical philosophy has helped itself over those difficulties hitherto by denying the origin of one thing in another, and assuming a miraculous origin for more highly valued things, immediately out of the kernel and essence of the 'thing in itself'. Historical philosophy, on the contrary, which is no longer to be thought of as separate from physical science, the youngest of all philosophical methods, has ascertained in single cases (and presumably this will happen in everything) that there are no opposites except in the usual exaggeration of the popular or metaphysical point of view, and that an error of reason lies at the bottom of the opposition: according to this explanation, strictly understood, there is neither an unegoistical action nor an entirely disinterested point of view, they are both only sublimations in which the fundamental element appears almost evaporated, and is only to be discovered by the closest observation. All that we require, and which can only be given us by the present advance of the single sciences, is a *chemistry* of the moral, religious, aesthetic ideas and sentiments, as also of those emotions which we experience in ourselves both in the great and in the small phases of social and intellectual intercourse, and even in solitude; but what if this chemistry should result in the fact that also in this case the most beautiful colours have been obtained from base, even despised materials? Would many be inclined to pursue such examinations? Humanity likes to put all questions as to origin and beginning out of its mind; must one not be almost dehumanised to feel a contrary tendency in one's self?

2.

Inherited Faults of Philosophers. – All philosophers have the common fault that they start from man in his present state and hope to attain their end by an analysis of him. Unconsciously they look upon man as an *aeterna veritas*, as a thing unchangeable in all commotion, as a sure standard of things. But everything that the philosopher says about man is really nothing more than testimony about the man of a *very limited* space of time. A lack of the historical sense is the hereditary fault of all philosophers; many, indeed, unconsciously mistake the very latest variety of man, such as has arisen under the influence of certain religions, certain political events, for the permanent form from which one must set out. They will not learn that man has developed, that his faculty of knowledge has developed also; whilst for some of them the entire world is spun out of this faculty of knowledge. Now everything *essential* in human development happened in pre-historic times, long before those four thousand years which we know something of; man may not have changed much during this time. But the philosopher sees 'instincts' in the present man and takes it for granted that this is one of the unalterable facts of mankind, and, consequently, can furnish a key to the understanding of the world; the entire teleology is so constructed that man of the last four thousand years is spoken of as an *eternal* being, towards which all things in the world have from the beginning a natural direction. But everything has evolved; there are *no eternal facts*, as there are likewise no absolute truths. Therefore, *historical philosophising* is henceforth necessary, and with it the virtue of diffidence.

3.

Appreciation of Unpretentious Truths. – It is a mark of a higher culture to value the little unpretentious truths, which have been found by means of strict method, more highly than the joy-diffusing and dazzling errors which spring from metaphysical and artistic times and peoples. First of all one has scorn on the lips for the former, as if here nothing could have equal privileges with anything else, so unassuming, simple, bashful, apparently discouraging are they, so beautiful, stately, intoxicating, perhaps even animating, are the others. But the hardly attained, the certain, the lasting, and therefore of great consequence for all wider knowledge, is still the higher; to keep one's self to that is manly and shows bravery, simplicity, and forbearance. Gradually not only single individuals but the whole of mankind will be raised to this manliness, when it has at last accustomed itself to the higher appreciation of durable, lasting knowledge, and has lost all belief in inspiration and the miraculous communication of truths. Respecters of *forms*, certainly, with their standard of the beautiful and noble, will first of all have good reasons for mockery, as soon as the appreciation of unpretentious truths, and the scientific spirit, begin to obtain the mastery; but only because their eye has either not yet recognised the charm of the *simplest* form, or because men educated in that spirit are not yet completely and inwardly saturated by it, so that they still thoughtlessly imitate old forms (and badly enough, as one does who no longer cares much about the matter). Formerly the spirit was not occupied with strict thought, its earnestness then lay in the spinning out of symbols and forms. This is changed; that earnestness in the symbolical has become the mark of a lower culture. As our arts themselves grow evermore intellectual, our senses more spiritual, and as, for instance, people now judge concerning what sounds well to the senses quite differently from how they did a hundred years ago, so the forms of our life grow ever more *spiritual*, to the eye of older ages perhaps *uglier*, but only because it is incapable of perceiving how the kingdom of the inward, spiritual beauty constantly grows deeper and wider, and to what extent the inner intellectual look may be of more importance to us all than the most beautiful bodily frame and the noblest architectural structure.

4.

Astrology and the Like. – It is probable that the objects of religious, moral, aesthetic and logical sentiment likewise belong only to the surface of things, while man willingly believes that here, at least, he has touched the heart of the world; he deceives himself, because those things enrapture him so profoundly, and make him so profoundly unhappy, and he therefore shows the same pride here as in astrology. For astrology believes that the firmament moves round the destiny of man; the moral man, however, takes it for granted that what he has essentially at heart must also be the essence and heart of things.

5.

Misunderstanding of Dreams. – In the ages of a rude and primitive civilisation man believed that in dreams he became acquainted with a *second actual world*; herein lies the origin of all metaphysics. Without dreams there could have been found no reason for a division of the world. The distinction, too, between soul and body is connected with the most ancient comprehension of dreams, also the supposition of an imaginary soul-body, therefore the origin of all belief in spirits, and probably also the belief in gods. 'The dead continues to live, for he appears to the living in a dream': thus men reasoned of old for thousands and thousands of years.

6.

The Scientific Spirit partially but not WHOLLY Powerful. – The *smallest* subdivisions of science taken separately are dealt with purely in relation to themselves; the general, great sciences, on the contrary, regarded as a whole, call up the question – certainly a very non-objective one – 'Wherefore? To what end?' It is this utilitarian consideration which causes them to be dealt with less impersonally when taken as a whole than when considered in their various parts. In philosophy, above all, as the apex of the entire pyramid of science, the question as to the utility of knowledge is involuntarily brought forward, and every philosophy has the unconscious intention of ascribing to it the *greatest* usefulness. For this reason there is so much high-flying metaphysics in all philosophies and such a shyness of the apparently unimportant solutions of physics; for the importance of knowledge for life *must* appear as great as possible. Here is the antagonism between the separate provinces of science and philosophy. The latter desires, what art does, to give the greatest possible depth and meaning to life and actions; in the former one seeks knowledge and nothing further, whatever may emerge thereby. So far there has been no philosopher in whose hands philosophy has not grown into an apology for knowledge; on this point, at least, every one is an optimist, that the greatest usefulness must be ascribed to knowledge. They are all tyrannised over by logic, and this is optimism – in its essence.

7.

The Kill-joy in Science. – Philosophy separated from science when it asked the question, 'Which is the knowledge of the world and of life which enables man to live most happily?' This happened in the Socratic schools; the veins of scientific investigation were bound up by the point of view of happiness – and are so still.

8.

Pneumatic Explanation of Nature. – Metaphysics explains the writing of Nature, so to speak, *pneumatically*, as the Church and her learned men formerly did with the Bible. A great deal of understanding is required to apply to Nature the same method of strict interpretation as the philologists have now established for all books with the intention of clearly understanding what the text means, but not suspecting a double sense or even taking it for granted. Just, however, as with regard to books, the bad art of interpretation is by no means overcome, and in the most cultivated society one still constantly comes across the remains of allegorical and mystic interpretation, so it is also with regard to Nature, indeed it is even much worse.

9.

The Metaphysical World. – It is true that there *might* be a metaphysical world; the absolute possibility of it is hardly to be disputed. We look at everything through the human head and cannot cut this head off; while the question remains, What would be left of the world if it had been cut off? This is a purely scientific problem, and one not very likely to trouble mankind; but everything which has hitherto made metaphysical suppositions *valuable, terrible, delightful* for man, what has produced them, is passion, error, and self-deception; the very worst methods of knowledge, not the best, have taught belief therein. When these methods have been discovered as the foundation of all existing religions and metaphysics, they have been refuted. Then there still always remains that possibility; but there is nothing to be done with it, much less is it possible to let happiness, salvation, and life depend on the spider-thread of such a possibility. For nothing could be said of the metaphysical world but that it would be a different condition, a condition inaccessible and incomprehensible to us; it would be a thing of negative qualities. Were the existence of such a world ever so well proved, the fact would nevertheless remain that it would be precisely the most irrelevant of all forms of knowledge: more irrelevant than the knowledge of the chemical analysis of water to the sailor in danger in a storm.

10.

The Harmlessness of Metaphysics in the Future. – Directly the origins of religion, art, and morals have been so described that one can perfectly explain them without having recourse to metaphysical concepts at the beginning and in the course of the path, the strongest interest in the purely theoretical problem of the 'thing-in-itself' and the 'phenomenon' ceases. For however it may be here, with religion, art, and morals we do not touch the 'essence of the world in itself'; we are in the domain of representation, no 'intuition' can carry us further. With the greatest calmness we shall leave the question as to how our own conception of the world can differ so widely from the revealed essence of the world, to physiology and the history of the evolution of organisms and ideas.

11.

Language as a Presumptive Science. – The importance of language for the development of culture lies in the fact that in language man has placed a world of his own beside the other, a position which he deemed so fixed that he might therefrom lift the rest of the world off its hinges, and make himself master of it. Inasmuch as man has believed in the ideas and names of things as *aeternae veritates* for a great length of time, he has acquired that pride by which he has raised himself above the animal; he really thought that in language he possessed the knowledge of the world. The maker of language was not modest enough to think that he only gave designations to things, he believed rather that with his words he expressed the widest knowledge of the things; in reality language is the first step in the endeavour after science. Here also it is belief in ascertained truth, from which the mightiest sources of strength have flowed. Much later – only now – it is dawning upon men that they have propagated a tremendous error in their belief in language. Fortunately it is now too late to reverse the development of reason, which is founded upon that belief. *Logic*, also, is founded upon suppositions to which nothing in the actual world corresponds – for instance, on the supposition of the equality of things, and the identity of the same thing at different points of time – but that particular science arose out of the contrary belief (that such things really existed in the actual world). It is the same with mathematics, which would certainly not have arisen if it had been known from the beginning that in Nature there are no exactly straight lines, no real circle, no absolute standard of size.

12.

Dream and Culture. – The function of the brain which is most influenced by sleep is the memory; not that it entirely ceases; but it is brought back to a condition of imperfection, such as everyone may have experienced in pre-historic times, whether asleep or awake. Arbitrary and confused as it is, it constantly confounds things on the ground of the most fleeting resemblances; but with the same arbitrariness and confusion the ancients invented their mythologies, and even at the present day travellers are accustomed to remark how prone the savage is to forgetfulness, how, after a short tension of memory, his mind begins to sway here and there from sheer weariness and gives forth lies and nonsense. But in dreams we all resemble the savage; bad recognition and erroneous comparisons are the reasons of the bad conclusions, of which we are guilty in dreams: so that, when we clearly recollect what we have dreamt, we are alarmed at ourselves at harbouring so much foolishness within us. The perfect distinctness of all dream-representations, which pre-suppose absolute faith in their reality, recall the conditions that appertain to primitive man, in whom hallucination was extraordinarily frequent, and sometimes simultaneously seized entire communities, entire nations. Therefore, in sleep and in dreams we once more carry out the task of early humanity.

13.

The Logic of Dreams. – In sleep our nervous system is perpetually excited by numerous inner occurrences; nearly all the organs are disjointed and in a state of activity, the blood runs its turbulent course, the position of the sleeper causes pressure on certain limbs, his coverings influence his sensations in various ways, the stomach digests and by its movements it disturbs other organs, the intestines writhe, the position of the head occasions unaccustomed play of muscles, the feet, unshod, not pressing upon the floor with the soles, occasion the feeling of the unaccustomed just as does the different clothing of the whole body: all this, according to its daily change and extent, excites by its extraordinariness the entire system to the very functions of the brain, and thus there are a hundred occasions for the spirit to be surprised and to seek for the *reasons* of this excitation; the dream, however, is *the seeking and representing of the causes* of those excited sensations – that is, of the supposed causes. A person who, for instance, binds his feet with two straps will perhaps dream that two serpents are coiling round his feet; this is first hypothesis, then a belief, with an accompanying *mental* picture and interpretation – 'These serpents must be the *causa* of those sensations which I, the sleeper, experience' – so decides the mind of the sleeper. The immediate past, so disclosed, becomes to him the present through his excited imagination. Thus every one knows from experience how quickly the dreamer weaves into his dream a loud sound that he hears, such as the ringing of bells or the firing of cannon, that is to say, explains it from *afterwards* so that he first *thinks* he experiences the producing circumstances and then that sound. But how does it happen that the mind of the dreamer is always so mistaken, while the same mind when awake is accustomed to be so temperate, careful, and sceptical with regard to its hypotheses? So that the first random hypothesis for the explanation of a feeling suffices for him to believe immediately in its truth? (For in dreaming we believe in the dream as if it were a reality, i.e. we think our hypothesis completely proved.) I hold, that as man now still reasons in dreams, so men reasoned also *when awake* through thousands of years; the first *causa* which occurred to the mind to explain anything that required an explanation, was sufficient and stood for truth. (Thus, according to travellers' tales, savages still do to this very day.) This ancient element in human nature still manifests itself in our dreams, for it is the foundation upon which the higher reason has developed and still develops in every individual; the dream carries us back into remote conditions of human culture, and provides a ready means of understanding them better. Dream-thinking is now so easy to us because during immense periods of human development we have been so well drilled in this form of fantastic and cheap explanation, by means of the first agreeable notions. In so far, dreaming is a recreation for the brain, which by day has to satisfy the stern demands of thought, as they are laid down by the higher culture. We can at once discern an allied process even in our awakened state, as the door and ante-room of the dream. If we shut our eyes, the brain produces a number of impressions of light and colour, probably as a kind of after-play and echo of all those effects of light which crowd in upon it by day. Now, however, the understanding, together with the imagination, instantly works up this play of colour, shapeless in itself, into definite figures, forms, landscapes, and animated groups. The actual accompanying process thereby is again a kind of conclusion from the effect to the cause: since the mind asks, 'Whence come these impressions of light and colour?' it supposes those figures and forms as causes; it takes them for the origin of those colours and lights, because in the daytime, with open eyes, it is accustomed to find a producing cause for every colour, every effect of light. Here, therefore, the imagination constantly places pictures before the mind, since it supports itself on the visual impressions of the day in their production, and the dream-imagination does just the same thing – that is, the supposed cause is deduced from the effect and represented after the effect; all this happens with extraordinary rapidity, so that here, as with the conjuror, a confusion of judgement may arise and a sequence may look like something simultaneous, or even like a reversed sequence. From these circumstances we may gather *how lately* the more acute logical thinking, the strict discrimination of cause and effect has been developed, when our reasoning and understanding faculties *still* involuntarily hark back to those primitive forms of deduction, and when we pass about half our life in this condition. The poet, too, and the artist assign causes for their moods and conditions which are by no means the true ones; in this they recall an older humanity and can assist us to the understanding of it.

14.

Co-echoing. – All *stronger* moods bring with them a co-echoing of kindred sensations and moods, they grub up the memory, so to speak. Along with them something within us remembers and becomes conscious of similar conditions and their origin. Thus there are formed quick habitual connections of feelings and thoughts, which eventually, when they follow each other with lightning speed, are no longer felt as complexes but as *unities*. In this sense one speaks of the moral feeling, of the religious feeling, as if they were absolute unities: in reality they are streams with a hundred sources and tributaries. Here also, as so often happens, the unity of the word is no security for the unity of the thing.

15.

No Internal and External in the World. – As Democritus transferred the concepts 'above' and 'below' to endless space where they have no sense, so philosophers in general have transferred the concepts 'Internal' and 'External' to the essence and appearance of the world; they think that with deep feelings one can penetrate deeply into the internal and approach the heart of Nature. But these feelings are only deep in so far as along with them, barely noticeable, certain complicated groups of thoughts, which we call deep, are regularly excited; a feeling is deep because we think that the accompanying thought is deep. But the 'deep' thought can nevertheless be very far from the truth, as, for instance, every metaphysical one; if one takes away from the deep feeling the commingled elements of thought, then the strong feeling remains, and this guarantees nothing for knowledge but itself, just as strong faith proves only its strength and not the truth of what is believed in.

16.

Phenomenon and Thing-in-itself. – Philosophers are in the habit of setting themselves before life and experience – before that which they call the world of appearance – as before a picture that is once for all unrolled and exhibits unchangeably fixed the same process – this process, they think, must be rightly interpreted in order to come to a conclusion about the being that produced the picture: about the thing-in-itself, therefore, which is always accustomed to be regarded as sufficient ground for the world of phenomenon. On the other hand, since one always makes the idea of the metaphysical stand definitely as that of the unconditioned, *consequently* also unconditioning, one must directly disown all connection between the unconditioned (the metaphysical world) and the world which is known to us; so that the thing-in-itself should most certainly not appear in the phenomenon, and every conclusion from the former as regards the latter is to be rejected. Both sides overlook the fact that that picture – that which we now call human life and experience – has gradually evolved – nay, is still in the full process of evolving – and therefore should not be regarded as a fixed magnitude from which a conclusion about its originator might be deduced (the sufficing cause) or even merely neglected. It is because for thousands of years we have looked into the world with moral, aesthetic, and religious pretensions, with blind inclination, passion, or fear, and have surfeited ourselves in the vices of illogical thought, that this world has gradually *become* so marvellously motley, terrible, full of meaning and of soul, it has acquired colour – but we were the colourists; the human intellect, on the basis of human needs, of human emotions, has caused this 'phenomenon' to appear and has carried its erroneous fundamental conceptions into things. Late, very late, it takes to thinking, and now the world of experience and the thing-in-itself seem to it so extraordinarily different and separated, that it gives up drawing conclusions from the former to the latter – or in a terribly mysterious manner demands the renunciation of our intellect, of our personal will, in order *thereby* to reach the essential, that one may *become essential*. Again, others have collected all the characteristic features of our world of phenomenon – that is, the idea of the world spun out of intellectual errors and inherited by us – and *instead of accusing the intellect* as the offenders, they have laid the blame on the nature of things as being the cause of the hard fact of this very sinister character of the world, and have preached the deliverance from Being. With all these conceptions the constant and laborious process of science (which at last celebrates its greatest triumph in a *history of the origin of thought*) becomes completed in various ways, the result of which might perhaps run as follows: 'That which we now call the world is the result of a mass of errors and fantasies which arose gradually in the general development of organic being, which are inter-grown with each other, and are now inherited by us as the accumulated treasure of all the past – as a treasure, for the value of our humanity depends upon it. From this world of representation strict science is really only able to liberate us to a very slight extent – as it is also not at all desirable – inasmuch as it cannot essentially break the power of primitive habits of feeling; but it can gradually elucidate the history of the rise of that world as representation – and lift us, at least for moments, above and beyond the whole process. Perhaps we shall then recognise that the thing in itself is worth a Homeric laugh; that it *seemed* so much, indeed everything, and *is* really empty, namely, empty of meaning.'

17.

Metaphysical Explanations. – The young man values metaphysical explanations, because they show him something highly significant in things which he found unpleasant or despicable, and if he is dissatisfied with himself, the feeling becomes lighter when he recognises the innermost world-puzzle or world-misery in that which he so strongly disapproves of in himself. To feel himself less responsible and at the same time to find things more interesting – that seems to him a double benefit for which he has to thank metaphysics. Later on, certainly, he gets distrustful of the whole metaphysical method of explanation; then perhaps it grows clear to him that those results can be obtained equally well and more scientifically in another way: that physical and historical explanations produce the feeling of personal relief to at least the same extent, and that the interest in life and its problems is perhaps still more aroused thereby.

18.

Fundamental Questions of Metaphysics. – When the history of the rise of thought comes to be written, a new light will be thrown on the following statement of a distinguished logician: 'The primordial general law of the cognisant subject consists in the inner necessity of recognising every object in itself in its own nature, as a thing identical with itself, consequently self-existing and at bottom remaining ever the same and unchangeable: in short, in recognising everything as a substance.' Even this law, which is here called 'primordial', has evolved: it will some day be shown how gradually this tendency arises in the lower organisms, how the feeble mole-eyes of their organisations at first see only the same thing – how then, when the various awakenings of pleasure and displeasure become noticeable, various substances are gradually distinguished, but each with one attribute, i.e. one single relation to such an organism. The first step in logic is the judgement – the nature of which, according to the decision of the best logicians, consists in belief. At the bottom of all belief lies *the sensation of the pleasant or the painful* in relation to the *sentient subject*. A new third sensation as the result of two previous single sensations is the judgement in its simplest form. We organic beings have originally no interest in anything but its relation to us in connection with pleasure and pain. Between the moments (the states of feeling) when we become conscious of this connection, lie moments of rest, of non-feeling; the world and everything is then without interest for us, we notice no change in it (as even now a deeply interested person does not notice when any one passes him). To the plant, things are as a rule tranquil and eternal, everything like itself. From the period of the lower organisms man has inherited the belief that *similar things* exist (this theory is only contradicted by the matured experience of the most advanced science). The primordial belief of everything organic from the beginning is perhaps even this, that all the rest of the world is one and immovable. The point furthest removed from those early beginnings of logic is the idea of *Causality* – indeed we still really think that all sensations and activities are acts of the free will; when the sentient individual contemplates himself, he regards every sensation, every alteration as something *isolated*, that is to say, unconditioned and disconnected – it rises up in us without connection with anything foregoing or following. We are hungry, but do not originally think that the organism must be nourished; the feeling seems to make itself felt *without cause and purpose*, it isolates itself and regards itself as arbitrary. Therefore, belief in the freedom of the will is an original error of everything organic, as old as the existence of the awakenings of logic in it; the belief in unconditioned substances and similar things is equally a primordial as well as an old error of everything organic. But inasmuch as all metaphysics has concerned itself chiefly with substance and the freedom of will, it may be designated as the science which treats of the fundamental errors of mankind, but treats of them as if they were fundamental truths.

19.

Number. – The discovery of the laws of numbers is made upon the ground of the original, already prevailing error, that there are many similar things (but in reality there is nothing similar), at least, that there are things (but there is no 'thing'). The supposition of plurality always presumes that there is something which appears frequently – but here already error reigns, already we imagine beings, unities, which do not exist. Our sensations of space and time are false, for they lead – examined in sequence – to logical contradictions. In all scientific determinations we always reckon inevitably with certain false quantities, but as these quantities are at least constant, as, for instance, our sensation of time and space, the conclusions of science have still perfect accuracy and certainty in their connection with one another; one may continue to build upon them – until that final limit where the erroneous original suppositions, those constant faults, come into conflict with the conclusions, for instance in the doctrine of atoms. There still we always feel ourselves compelled to the acceptance of a 'thing' or material 'substratum' that is moved, whilst the whole scientific procedure has pursued the very task of resolving everything substantial (material) into motion; here, too, we still separate with our sensation the mover and the moved and cannot get out of this circle, because the belief in things has from immemorial times been bound up with our being. When Kant says, 'The understanding does not derive its laws from Nature, but dictates them to her,' it is perfectly true with regard to the idea of Nature which we are compelled to associate with her (Nature = World as representation, that is to say as error), but which is the summing up of a number of errors of the understanding. The laws of numbers are entirely inapplicable to a world which is not our representation – these laws obtain only in the human world.

20.

A Few Steps Back. – A degree of culture, and assuredly a very high one, is attained when man rises above superstitious and religious notions and fears, and, for instance, no longer believes in guardian angels or in original sin, and has also ceased to talk of the salvation of his soul – if he has attained to this degree of freedom, he has still also to overcome metaphysics with the greatest exertion of his intelligence. Then, however, a *retrogressive movement* is necessary; he must understand the historical justification as well as the psychological in such representations, he must recognise how the greatest advancement of humanity has come therefrom, and how, without such a retrocursive movement, we should have been robbed of the best products of hitherto existing mankind. With regard to philosophical metaphysics, I always see increasing numbers who have attained to the negative goal (that all positive metaphysics is error), but as yet few who climb a few rungs backwards; one ought to look out, perhaps, over the last steps of the ladder, but not try to stand upon them. The most enlightened only succeed so far as to free themselves from metaphysics and look back upon it with superiority, while it is necessary here, too, as in the hippodrome, to turn round the end of the course.

21.

Conjectural Victory of Scepticism. – For once let the sceptical starting-point be accepted – granted that there were no other metaphysical world, and all explanations drawn from metaphysics about the only world we know were useless to us, in what light should we then look upon men and things? We can think this out for ourselves, it is useful, even though the question whether anything metaphysical has been scientifically proved by Kant and Schopenhauer were altogether set aside. For it is quite possible, according to historical probability, that some time or other man, as a general rule, may grow *sceptical*; the question will then be this: What form will human society take under the influence of such a mode of thought? Perhaps the *scientific proof* of some metaphysical world or other is already so *difficult* that mankind will never get rid of a certain distrust of it. And when there is distrust of metaphysics, there are on the whole the same results as if it had been directly refuted and could no longer be believed in. The historical question with regard to an unmetaphysical frame of mind in mankind rcmains thc samc in both cascs.

22.

Unbelief in the '*Monumentum aere perennius.*' – An actual drawback which accompanies the cessation of metaphysical views lies in the fact that the individual looks upon his short span of life too exclusively and receives no stronger incentives to build durable institutions intended to last for centuries – he himself wishes to pluck the fruit from the tree which he plants, and therefore he no longer plants those trees which require regular care for centuries, and which are destined to afford shade to a long series of generations. For metaphysical views furnish the belief that in them the last conclusive foundation has been given, upon which henceforth all the future of mankind is compelled to settle down and establish itself; the individual furthers his salvation, when, for instance, he founds a church or convent, he thinks it will be reckoned to him and recompensed to him in the eternal life of the soul, it is work for the soul's eternal salvation. Can science also arouse such faith in its results? As a matter of fact, it needs doubt and distrust as its most faithful auxiliaries; nevertheless in the course of time, the sum of inviolable truths – those, namely, which have weathered all the storms of scepticism, and all destructive analysis – may have become so great (in the regimen of health, for instance), that one may determine to found thereupon 'eternal' works. For the present the *contrast* between our excited ephemeral existence and the long-winded repose of metaphysical ages still operates too strongly, because the two ages still stand too closely together; the individual man himself now goes through too many inward and outward developments for him to venture to arrange his own lifetime permanently, and once and for all. An entirely modern man, for instance, who is going to build himself a house, has a feeling as if he were going to immure himself alive in a mausoleum.

23.

The Age of Comparison. – The less men are fettered by tradition, the greater becomes the inward activity of their motives; the greater, again, in proportion thereto, the outward restlessness, the confused flux of mankind, the polyphony of strivings. For whom is there still an absolute compulsion to bind himself and his descendants to one place? For whom is there still anything strictly compulsory? As all styles of arts are imitated simultaneously, so also are all grades and kinds of morality, of customs, of cultures. Such an age obtains its importance because in it the various views of the world, customs, and cultures can be compared and experienced simultaneously – which was formerly not possible with the always localised sway of every culture, corresponding to the rooting of all artistic styles in place and time. An increased aesthetic feeling will now at last decide amongst so many forms presenting themselves for comparison; it will allow the greater number, that is to say all those rejected by it, to die out. In the same way a selection amongst the forms and customs of the higher moralities is taking place, of which the aim can be nothing else than the downfall of the lower moralities. It is the age of comparison! That is its pride, but more justly also its grief. Let us not be afraid of this grief! Rather will we comprehend as adequately as possible the task our age sets us: posterity will bless us for doing so – a posterity which knows itself to be as much above the terminated original national cultures as above the culture of comparison, but which looks back with gratitude on both kinds of culture as upon antiquities worthy of veneration.

24.

The Possibility of Progress. – When a scholar of the ancient culture forswears the company of men who believe in progress, he does quite right. For the greatness and goodness of ancient culture lie behind it, and historical education compels one to admit that they can never be fresh again; an unbearable stupidity or an equally insufferable fanaticism would be necessary to deny this. But men can *consciously* resolve to develop themselves towards a new culture; whilst formerly they only developed unconsciously and by chance, they can now create better conditions for the rise of human beings, for their nourishment, education and instruction; they can administer the earth economically as a whole, and can generally weigh and restrain the powers of man. This new, conscious culture kills the old, which, regarded as a whole, has led an unconscious animal and plant life; it also kills distrust in progress – progress is *possible*. I must say that it is over-hasty and almost nonsensical to believe that progress must *necessarily* follow; but how could one deny that it is possible? On the other hand, progress in the sense and on the path of the old culture is not even thinkable. Even if romantic fantasy has also constantly used the word 'progress' to denote its aims (for instance, circumscribed primitive national cultures), it borrows the picture of it in any case from the past; its thoughts and ideas on this subject are entirely without originality.

25.

Private and Ecumenical Morality. – Since the belief has ceased that a God directs in general the fate of the world and, in spite of all apparent crookedness in the path of humanity, leads it on gloriously, men themselves must set themselves ecumenical aims embracing the whole earth. The older morality, especially that of Kant, required from the individual actions which were desired from all men – that was a delightfully naive thing, as if each one knew off-hand what course of action was beneficial to the whole of humanity, and consequently which actions in general were desirable; it is a theory like that of free trade, taking for granted that the general harmony *must* result of itself according to innate laws of amelioration. Perhaps a future contemplation of the needs of humanity will show that it is by no means desirable that all men should act alike; in the interest of ecumenical aims it might rather be that for whole sections of mankind, special, and perhaps under certain circumstances even evil, tasks would have to be set. In any case, if mankind is not to destroy itself by such a conscious universal rule, there must previously be found, as a scientific standard for ecumenical aims, a *knowledge of the conditions of culture* superior to what has hitherto been attained. Herein lies the enormous task of the great minds of the next century.

26.

Reaction as Progress. – Now and again there appear rugged, powerful, impetuous, but nevertheless backward-lagging minds which conjure up once more a past phase of mankind; they serve to prove that the new tendencies against which they are working are not yet sufficiently strong, that they still lack something, otherwise they would show better opposition to those exorcisers. Thus, for example, Luther's Reformation bears witness to the fact that in his century all the movements of the freedom of the spirit were still uncertain, tender, and youthful; science could not yet lift up its head. Indeed the whole Renaissance seems like an early spring which is almost snowed under again. But in this century also, Schopenhauer's Metaphysics showed that even now the scientific spirit is not yet strong enough; thus the whole mediaeval Christian view of the world and human feeling could celebrate its resurrection in Schopenhauer's doctrine, in spite of the long achieved destruction of all Christian dogmas. There is much science in his doctrine, but it does not dominate it: it is rather the old well known 'metaphysical requirement' that does so. It is certainly one of the greatest and quite invaluable advantages which we gain from Schopenhauer, that he occasionally forces our sensations back into older, mightier modes of contemplating the world and man, to which no other path would so easily lead us. The gain to history and justice is very great – I do not think that any one would so easily succeed now in doing justice to Christianity and its Asiatic relations without Schopenhauer's assistance, which is specially impossible from the basis of still existing Christianity. Only after this great *success of justice*, only after we have corrected so essential a point as the historical mode of contemplation which the age of enlightenment brought with it, may we again bear onward the banner of enlightenment, the banner with the three names, Petrarch, Erasmus, Voltaire. We have turned reaction into progress.

27.

A Substitute for Religion. – It is believed that something good is said of philosophy when it is put forward as a substitute for religion for the people. As a matter of fact, in the spiritual economy there is need, at times, of an *intermediary* order of thought: the transition from religion to scientific contemplation is a violent, dangerous leap, which is not to be recommended. To this extent the recommendation is justifiable. But one should eventually learn that the needs which have been satisfied by religion and are now to be satisfied by philosophy are not unchangeable;

these themselves can be *weakened* and *eradicated*. Think, for instance, of the Christian's distress of soul, his sighing over inward corruption, his anxiety for salvation – all notions which originate only in errors of reason and deserve not satisfaction but destruction. A philosophy can serve either to *satisfy* those needs or to *set them aside*; for they are acquired, temporally limited needs, which are based upon suppositions contradictory to those of science. Here, in order to make a transition, art is far rather to be employed to relieve the mind over-burdened with emotions; for those notions receive much less support from it than from a metaphysical philosophy. It is easier, then, to pass over from art to a really liberating philosophical science.

28.

Ill-famed Words. – Away with those wearisomely hackneyed terms Optimism and Pessimism! For the occasion for using them becomes less and less from day to day; only the chatterboxes still find them so absolutely necessary. For why in all the world should any one wish to be an optimist unless he had a God to defend who *must* have created the best of worlds if he himself be goodness and perfection – what thinker, however, still needs the hypothesis of a God? But every occasion for a pessimistic confession of faith is also lacking when one has no interest in being annoyed at the advocates of God (the theologians, or the theologising philosophers), and in energetically defending the opposite view, that evil reigns, that pain is greater than pleasure, that the world is a bungled piece of work, the manifestation of an ill-will to life. But who still bothers about the theologians now – except the theologians? Apart from all theology and its contentions, it is quite clear that the world is not good and not bad (to say nothing of its being the best or the worst), and that the terms ' good' and 'bad' have only significance with respect to man, and indeed, perhaps, they are not justified even here in the way they are usually employed; in any case we must get rid of both the calumniating and the glorifying conception of the world.

29.

Intoxicated by the Scent of the Blossoms. – It is supposed that the ship of humanity has always a deeper draught, the heavier it is laden;

it is believed that the deeper a man thinks, the more delicately he feels, the higher he values himself, the greater his distance from the other animals – the more he appears as a genius amongst the animals – all the nearer will he approach the real essence of the world and its knowledge; this he actually does too, through science, but he *means* to do so still more through his religions and arts. These certainly are blossoms of the world, but by no means any *nearer to the root of the world* than the stalk; it is not possible to understand the nature of things better through them, although almost every one believes he can. *Error* has made man so deep, sensitive, and inventive that he has put forth such blossoms as religions and arts. Pure knowledge could not have been capable of it. Whoever were to unveil for us the essence of the world would give us all the most disagreeable disillusionment. Not the world as thing-in-itself, but the world as representation (as error) is so full of meaning, so deep, so wonderful, bearing happiness and unhappiness in its bosom. This result leads to a philosophy of the logical denial of the world, which, however, can be combined with a practical world-affirming just as well as with its opposite.

30.

Bad Habits in Reasoning. – The usual false conclusions of mankind are these: a thing exists, therefore it has a right to exist. Here there is inference from the ability to live to its suitability; from its suitability to its rightfulness. Then: an opinion brings happiness; therefore it is the true opinion. Its effect is good; therefore it is itself good and true. To the effect is here assigned the predicate beneficent, good, in the sense of the useful, and the cause is then furnished with the same predicate good, but here in the sense of the logically valid. The inversion of the sentences would read thus: an affair cannot be carried through, or maintained, therefore it is wrong; an opinion causes pain or excites, therefore it is false. The free spirit who learns only too often the faultiness of this mode of reasoning, and has to suffer from its consequences, frequently gives way to the temptation to draw the very opposite conclusions, which, in general, are naturally just as false: an affair cannot be carried through, therefore it is good; an opinion is distressing and disturbing, therefore it is true.

31.

The Illogical Necessary. – One of those things that may drive a thinker into despair is the recognition of the fact that the illogical is necessary for man, and that out of the illogical comes much that is good. It is so firmly rooted in the passions, in language, in art, in religion, and generally in everything that gives value to life, that it cannot be withdrawn without thereby hopelessly injuring these beautiful things. It is only the all-too-naive people who can believe that the nature of man can be changed into a purely logical one; but if there were degrees of proximity to this goal, how many things would not have to be lost on this course! Even the most rational man has need of nature again from time to time, i.e. his *illogical fundamental attitude* towards all things.

32.

Injustice Necessary. – All judgements on the value of life are illogically developed, and therefore unjust. The inexactitude of the judgement lies, firstly, in the manner in which the material is presented, namely very imperfectly; secondly, in the manner in which the conclusion is formed out of it; and thirdly, in the fact that every separate element of the material is again the result of vitiated recognition, and this, too, of necessity. For instance, no experience of an individual, however near he may stand to us, can be perfect, so that we could have a logical right to make a complete estimate of him; all estimates are rash, and must be so. Finally, the standard by which we measure, our nature, is not of unalterable dimensions – we have moods and vacillations, and yet we should have to recognise ourselves as a fixed standard in order to estimate correctly the relation of any thing whatever to ourselves. From this it will, perhaps, follow that we should make no judgements at all; if one could only live without making estimations, without having likes and dislikes! For all dislike is connected with an estimation, as well as all inclination. An impulse towards or away from anything without a feeling that something advantageous is desired, something injurious avoided, an impulse without any kind of conscious valuation of the worth of the aim does not exist in man. We are from the beginning illogical, and therefore unjust beings, *and can recognise this*; it is one of the greatest and most inexplicable discords of existence.

33.

Error about Life necessary for Life. – Every belief in the value and worthiness of life is based on vitiated thought; it is only possible through the fact that sympathy for the general life and suffering of mankind is very weakly developed in the individual. Even the rarer people who think outside themselves do not contemplate this general life, but only a limited part of it. If one understands how to direct one's attention chiefly to the exceptions – I mean to the highly gifted and the rich souls – if one regards the production of these as the aim of the whole world-development and rejoices in its operation, then one may believe in the value of life, because one thereby *overlooks* the other men – one consequently thinks fallaciously. So too, when one directs one's attention to all mankind, but only considers *one* species of impulses in them, the less egoistical ones, and excuses them with regard to the other instincts, one may then again entertain hopes of mankind in general and believe so far in the value of life, consequently in this case also through fallaciousness of thought. Let one, however, behave in this or that manner: with such behaviour one is an *exception* amongst men. Now, most people bear life without any considerable grumbling, and consequently *believe* in the value of existence, but precisely because each one is solely self-seeking and self-affirming, and does not step out of himself like those exceptions; everything extra-personal is imperceptible to them, or at most seems only a faint shadow. Therefore on this alone is based the value of life for the ordinary everyday man, that he regards himself as more important than the world. The great lack of imagination from which he suffers is the reason why he cannot enter into the feelings of other beings, and therefore sympathises as little as possible with their fate and suffering. He, on the other hand, who really *could* sympathise therewith, would have to despair of the value of life; were he to succeed in comprehending and feeling in himself the general consciousness of mankind, he would collapse with a curse on existence; for mankind as a whole has *no* goals, consequently man, in considering his whole course, cannot find in it his comfort and support, but his despair. If, in all that he does, he considers the final aimlessness of man, his own activity assumes in his eyes the character of wastefulness. But to feel one's self just as much wasted as humanity (and not only as an individual) as we see the single blossom of nature wasted, is a feeling above all other feelings. But who is capable of it? Assuredly only a poet, and poets always know how to console themselves.

34.

For Tranquillity. – But does not our philosophy thus become a tragedy? Does not truth become hostile to life, to improvement? A question seems to weigh upon our tongue and yet hesitate to make itself heard: whether one can consciously remain in untruthfulness? Or, supposing one were *obliged* to do this, would not death be preferable? For there is no longer any 'must'; morality, in so far as it had any 'must' or 'shalt', has been destroyed by our mode of contemplation, just as religion has been destroyed. Knowledge can only allow pleasure and pain, benefit and injury to subsist as motives; but how will these motives agree with the sense of truth? They also contain errors (for, as already said, inclination and aversion, and their very incorrect determinations, practically regulate our pleasure and pain). The whole of human life is deeply immersed in untruthfulness; the individual cannot draw it up out of this well, without thereby taking a deep dislike to his whole past, without finding his present motives – those of honour, for instance – inconsistent, and without opposing scorn and disdain to the passions which conduce to happiness in the future. Is it true that there remains but one sole way of thinking which brings after it despair as a personal experience, as a theoretical result, a philosophy of dissolution, disintegration, and self-destruction? I believe that the decision with regard to the after-effects of the knowledge will be given through the *temperament* of a man; I could imagine another after-effect, just as well as that one described, which is possible in certain natures, by means of which a life would arise much simpler, freer from emotions than is the present one, so that though at first, indeed, the old motives of passionate desire might still have strength from old hereditary habit, they would gradually become weaker under the influence of purifying knowledge. One would live at last amongst men, and with one's self as with *Nature*, without praise, reproach, or agitation, feasting one's eyes, as if it were a *play*, upon much of which one was formerly afraid. One would be free from the emphasis, and would no longer feel the goading, of the thought that one is not only nature or more than nature. Certainly, as already remarked, a good temperament would be necessary for this, an even, mild, and naturally joyous soul, a disposition which would not always need to be on its guard against spite and sudden outbreaks, and would not convey in its utterances anything of a grumbling or sudden nature – those well-known vexatious qualities of old dogs and men who have been long chained up. On the contrary, a man from whom the ordinary fetters of life have so far fallen that he continues to live only for the sake of ever better knowledge must be able to renounce without envy and regret: much, indeed almost everything that is precious to other men, he must regard as the *all-sufficing* and the most desirable condition; the free, fearless soaring over men, customs, laws, and the traditional valuations of things. The joy of this condition he imparts willingly, and he *has* perhaps nothing else to impart – wherein, to be sure, there is more privation and renunciation. If, nevertheless, more is demanded from him, he will point with a friendly shake of his head to his brother, the free man of action, and will perhaps not conceal a little derision, for as regards this 'freedom' it is a very peculiar case.

SECOND DIVISION.

THE HISTORY OF THE MORAL SENTIMENTS.

35.

Advantages of Psychological Observation. – That reflection on the human, all-too-human – or, according to the learned expression, psychological observation – is one of the means by which one may lighten the burden of life, that exercise in this art produces presence of mind in difficult circumstances, in the midst of tiresome surroundings, even that from the most thorny and unpleasant periods of one's own life one may gather maxims and thereby feel a little better: all this was believed, was known in former centuries. Why was it forgotten by our century, when in Germany at least, even in all Europe, the poverty of psychological observation betrays itself by many signs? Not exactly in novels, tales, and philosophical treatises – they are the work of exceptional individuals – rather in the judgements on public events and personalities; but above all there is a lack of the art of psychological analysis and summing-up in every rank of society, in which a great deal is talked about men, but nothing about *man*. Why do we allow the richest and most harmless subject of conversation to escape us? Why are not the great masters of psychological maxims more read? For, without any exaggeration, the educated man in Europe who has read La Rochefoucauld and his kindred in mind and art, is rarely found, and still more rare is he who knows them and does not blame them. It is probable, however, that even this exceptional reader will find much less pleasure in them than the form of this artist should afford him; for even the clearest head is not capable of rightly estimating the art of shaping and polishing maxims unless he has really been brought up to it and has competed in it. Without this practical teaching one deems this shaping and polishing to be easier than it is; one has not a sufficient perception of fitness and charm. For this reason the present readers of maxims find in them a comparatively small pleasure, hardly a mouthful of pleasantness, so that they resemble the people who generally look at cameos, who praise because they cannot love, and are very ready to admire, but still more ready to run away.

36.

Objection. – Or should there be a counter-reckoning to that theory that places psychological observation amongst the means of charming, curing, and relieving existence? Should one have sufficiently convinced one's self of the unpleasant consequences of this art to divert from it designedly the attention of him who is educating himself in it? As a matter of fact, a certain blind belief in the goodness of human nature, an innate aversion to the analysis of human actions, a kind of shamefacedness with respect to the nakedness of the soul may really be more desirable for the general wellbeing of a man than that quality, useful in isolated cases, of psychological sharp-sightedness; and perhaps the belief in goodness, in virtuous men and deeds, in an abundance of impersonal goodwill in the world, has made men better inasmuch as it has made them less distrustful. When one imitates Plutarch's heroes with enthusiasm, and turns with disgust from a suspicious examination of the motives for their actions, it is not truth which benefits thereby, but the welfare of human society; the psychological mistake and, generally speaking, the insensibility on this matter helps humanity forwards, while the recognition of truth gains more through the stimulating power of hypothesis than La Rochefoucauld has said in his preface to the first edition of his '*Sentences et maximes morales!*' . . . '*Ce que le monde nomme vertu n'est d'ordinaire qu'un fantôme formé par nos passions, à qui on donne un nom honnête pour faire impunément ce qu'on veut.*' La Rochefoucauld and those other French masters of soul-examination (who have lately been joined by a German, the author of *Psychological Observations*[4]) resemble good marksmen who again and again hit the bull's-eye; but it is the bull's-eye of human nature. Their art arouses astonishment; but in the end a spectator who is not led by the spirit of science, but by humane intentions, will probably execrate an art which appears to implant in the soul the sense of the disparagement and suspicion of mankind.

---

4 Dr Paul Rée.– J. M. K.

37.

Nevertheless. – However it may be with reckoning and counter-reckoning, in the present condition of philosophy the awakening of moral observation is necessary. Humanity can no longer be spared the cruel sight of the psychological dissecting-table with its knives and forceps. For here rules that science which inquires into the origin and history of the so-called moral sentiments, and which, in its progress, has to draw up and solve complicated sociological problems: the older philosophy knows the latter one not at all, and has always avoided the examination of the origin and history of moral sentiments on any feeble pretext. With what consequences it is now very easy to see, after it has been shown by many examples how the mistakes of the greatest philosophers generally have their starting-point in a wrong explanation of certain human actions and sensations, just as on the ground of an erroneous analysis – for instance, that of the so-called unselfish actions – a false ethic is built up; then, to harmonise with this again, religion and mythological confusion are brought in to assist, and finally the shades of these dismal spirits fall also over physics and the general mode of regarding the world. If it is certain, however, that superficiality in psychological observation has laid, and still lays, the most dangerous snares for human judgements and conclusions, then there is need now of that endurance of work which does not grow weary of piling stone upon stone, pebble on pebble; there is need of courage not to be ashamed of such humble work and to turn a deaf ear to scorn. And this is also true – numberless single observations on the human and all-too-human have first been discovered, and given utterance to, in circles of society which were accustomed to offer sacrifice therewith to a clever desire to please, and not to scientific knowledge – and the odour of that old home of the moral maxim, a very seductive odour, has attached itself almost inseparably to the whole species, so that on its account the scientific man involuntarily betrays a certain distrust of this species and its earnestness. But it is sufficient to point to the consequences, for already it begins to be seen what results of a serious kind spring from the ground of psychological observation. What, after all, is the principal axiom to which the boldest and coldest thinker, the author of the book *On the Origin of Moral Sensations*[5] has attained by means of his incisive and decisive analyses of human actions? 'The moral man,' he says, 'is no nearer to the intelligible (metaphysical) world than is the physical man.' This theory, hardened and sharpened under the hammer-blow of historical knowledge, may some time or other, perhaps in some future period, serve as the axe which is applied to the root of the 'metaphysical need' of man – whether *more* as a blessing than a curse to the general welfare it is not easy to say, but in any case as a theory with the most important consequences, at once fruitful and terrible, and looking into the world with that Janus-face which all great knowledge possesses.

38.

How Far Useful. – It must remain for ever undecided whether psychological observation is advantageous or disadvantageous to man; but it is certain that it is necessary, because science cannot do without it. Science, however, has no consideration for ultimate purposes, any more than Nature has, but just as the latter occasionally achieves things of the greatest suitableness without intending to do so, so also true science, as the *imitator of nature in ideas*, will occasionally and in many ways further the usefulness and welfare of man – *but also without intending to do so.*

But whoever feels too chilled by the breath of such a reflection has perhaps too little fire in himself; let him look around him meanwhile and he will become aware of illnesses which have need of ice-poultices, and of men who are so 'kneaded together' of heat and spirit that they can hardly find an atmosphere that is cold and biting enough. Moreover, as individuals and nations that are too serious have need of frivolities, as others too mobile and excitable have need occasionally of heavily oppressing burdens for the sake of their health, should not we, the more *intellectual* people of this age, that grows visibly more and more inflamed, seize all quenching and cooling means that exist, in order that we may at least remain as constant, harmless, and moderate as we still are, and thus, perhaps, serve some time or other as mirror and self-contemplation for this age?

---

5 Dr Paul Rée.– J. M. K.

39.

The Fable of Intelligible Freedom. – The history of the sentiments by means of which we make a person responsible consists of the following principal phases. First, all single actions are called good or bad without any regard to their motives, but only on account of the useful or injurious consequences which result for the community. But soon the origin of these distinctions is forgotten, and it is deemed that the qualities 'good' or 'bad' are contained in the action itself without regard to its consequences, by the same error according to which language describes the stone as hard, the tree as green – with which, in short, the result is regarded as the cause. Then the goodness or badness is implanted in the motive, and the action in itself is looked upon as morally ambiguous. Mankind even goes further, and applies the predicate good or bad no longer to single motives, but to the whole nature of an individual, out of whom the motive grows as the plant grows out of the earth. Thus, in turn, man is made responsible for his operations, then for his actions, then for his motives, and finally for his nature. Eventually it is discovered that even this nature cannot be responsible, inasmuch as it is an absolutely necessary consequence concreted out of the elements and influences of past and present things – that man, therefore, cannot be made responsible for anything, neither for his nature, nor his motives, nor his actions, nor his effects. It has therewith come to be recognised that the history of moral valuations is at the same time the history of an error, the error of responsibility, which is based upon the error of the freedom of will. Schopenhauer thus decided against it: because certain actions bring ill humour ('consciousness of guilt') in their train, there must be a responsibility; for there would be no reason for this ill humour if not only all human actions were not done of necessity – which is actually the case and also the belief of this philosopher – but man himself from the same necessity is precisely the being that he is – which Schopenhauer denies. From the fact of that ill humour Schopenhauer thinks he can prove a liberty which man must somehow have had, not with regard to actions, but with regard to nature; liberty, therefore, to be thus or otherwise, not to act thus or otherwise. From the *esse*, the sphere of freedom and responsibility, there results, in his opinion, the *operari*, the sphere of strict causality, necessity, and irresponsibility. This ill humour is apparently directed to the *operari* – in so far it is erroneous – but in reality it is directed to the *esse*, which is the deed of a free will, the fundamental cause of the existence of an individual, man becomes that which he wishes to be, his will is anterior to his existence. Here the mistaken conclusion is drawn that from the fact of the ill humour, the justification, the reasonable *admissableness* of this ill humour is presupposed; and starting from this mistaken conclusion, Schopenhauer arrives at his fantastic sequence of the so-called intelligible freedom. But the ill humour after the deed is not necessarily reasonable, indeed it is assuredly not reasonable, for it is based upon the erroneous presumption that the action need not have inevitably followed. Therefore, it is only because man *believes* himself to be free, not because he is free, that he experiences remorse and pricks of conscience. Moreover, this ill humour is a habit that can be broken off; in many people it is entirely absent in connection with actions where others experience it. It is a very changeable thing, and one which is connected with the development of customs and culture, and probably only existing during a comparatively short period of the world's history. Nobody is responsible for his actions, nobody for his nature; to judge is identical with being unjust. This also applies when an individual judges himself. The theory is as clear as sunlight, and yet every one prefers to go back into the shadow and the untruth, for fear of the consequences.

40.

The Super-Animal. – The beast in us wishes to be deceived; morality is a lie of necessity in order that we may not be torn in pieces by it. Without the errors which lie in the assumption of morality, man would have remained an animal. Thus, however, he has considered himself as something higher and has laid strict laws upon himself. Therefore he hates the grades which have remained nearer to animalness, whereby the former scorn of the slave, as a not-yet-man, is to be explained as a fact.

41.

The Unchangeable Character. – That the character is unchangeable is not true in a strict sense; this favourite theory means, rather, that during the short lifetime of an individual the new influencing motives cannot penetrate deeply enough to destroy the ingrained marks of many thousands of years. But if one were to imagine a man of eighty thousand years, one would have in him an absolutely changeable character, so that a number of different individuals would gradually develop out of him. The shortness of human life misleads us into forming many erroneous ideas about the qualities of man.

42.

The Order of Possessions and Morality. – The once-accepted hierarchy of possessions, according as this or the other is coveted by a lower, higher, or highest egoism, now decides what is moral or immoral. To prefer a lesser good (for instance, the gratification of the senses) to a more highly valued good (for instance, health) is accounted immoral, and also to prefer luxury to liberty. The hierarchy of possessions, however, is not fixed and equal at all times; if any one prefers vengeance to justice he is moral according to the standard of an earlier civilisation, but immoral according to the present one. To be 'immoral', therefore, denotes that an individual has not felt, or not felt sufficiently strongly, the higher, finer, spiritual motives which have come in with a new culture; it marks one who has remained behind, but only according to the difference of degrees. The order of possessions itself is not raised and lowered according to a moral point of view; but each time that it is fixed it supplies the decision as to whether an action is moral or immoral.

43.

Cruel People as Those who have Remained Behind – People who are cruel nowadays must be accounted for by us as the grades of earlier civilisations which have survived; here are exposed those deeper formations in the mountain of humanity which usually remain concealed. They are backward people whose brains, through all manner of accidents in the course of inheritance, have not been developed in so delicate and manifold a way. They show us what we all *were* and horrify us, but they themselves are as little responsible as is a block of granite for being granite. There must, too, be grooves and twists in our brains which answer to that condition of mind, as in the form of certain human organs there are supposed to be traces of a fish-state. But these grooves and twists are no longer the bed through which the stream of our sensation flows.

44.

Gratitude and Revenge. – The reason why the powerful man is grateful is this: his benefactor, through the benefit he confers, has mistaken and intruded into the sphere of the powerful man – how the latter, in return, penetrates into the sphere of the benefactor by the act of gratitude. It is a milder form of revenge. Without the satisfaction of gratitude, the powerful man would have shown himself powerless, and would have been reckoned as such ever after. Therefore every society of the good, which originally meant the powerful, places gratitude amongst the first duties. Swift propounded the maxim that men were grateful in the same proportion as they were revengeful.

45.

The Twofold Early History of Good and Evil. – The conception of good and evil has a twofold early history, namely *once* in the soul of the ruling tribes and castes. Whoever has the power of returning good for good, evil for evil, and really practises requital, and who is, therefore, grateful and revengeful, is called good; whoever is powerless, and unable to requite, is reckoned as bad. As a good man one is reckoned among the 'good', a community which has common feelings because the single individuals are bound to one another by the sense of requital. As a bad man one belongs to the 'bad', to a party of subordinate, powerless people who have no common feeling. The good are a caste, the bad are a mass like dust. Good and bad have for a long time meant the same thing as noble and base, master and slave. On the other hand, the enemy is not looked upon as evil, he can requite. In Homer the Trojan and the Greek are both good. It is not the one who injures us, but the one who is despicable, who is called bad. Good is inherited in the community of the good; it is impossible that a bad man could spring from such good soil. If, nevertheless, one of the good ones does something which is unworthy of the good, refuge is sought in excuses; the guilt is thrown upon a god, for instance; it is said that he has struck the good man with blindness and madness. –

Then in the soul of the oppressed and powerless. Here every other man is looked upon as hostile, inconsiderate, rapacious, cruel, cunning, be he noble or base; evil is the distinguishing word for man, even for every conceivable living creature, e.g. for a god; human, divine, is the same thing as devilish, evil. The signs of goodness, helpfulness, pity, are looked upon with fear as spite, the prelude to a terrible result, stupefaction and outwitting – in short, as refined malice. With such a disposition in the individual a community could hardly exist, or at most it could exist only in its crudest form, so that in all places where this conception of good and evil obtains, the downfall of the single individuals, of their tribes and races, is at hand. Our present civilisation has grown up on the soil of the *ruling* tribes and castes.

46.

Sympathy Stronger than Suffering. – There are cases when sympathy is stronger than actual suffering. For instance, we are more pained when one of our friends is guilty of something shameful than when we do it ourselves. For one thing, we have more faith in the purity of his character than he has himself; then our love for him, probably on account of this very faith, is stronger than his love for himself. And even if his egoism suffers more thereby than our egoism, inasmuch as it has to bear more of the bad consequences of his fault, the un-egoistic in us – this word is not to be taken too seriously, but only as a modification of the expression – is more deeply wounded by his guilt than is the un-egoistic in him.

47.

Hypochondria. – There are people who become hypochondriacal through their sympathy and concern for another person; the kind of sympathy which results therefrom is nothing but a disease. Thus there is also a Christian hypochondria, which afflicts those solitary, religiously-minded people who keep constantly before their eyes the sufferings and death of Christ.

48.

Economy of Goodness. – Goodness and love, as the most healing herbs and powers in human intercourse, are such costly discoveries that one would wish as much economy as possible to be exercised in the employment of these balsamic means; but this is impossible. The economy of goodness is the dream of the most daring Utopians.

49.

Goodwill. – Amongst the small, but countlessly frequent and therefore very effective, things to which science should pay more attention than to the great, rare things, is to be reckoned goodwill; I mean that exhibition of a friendly disposition in intercourse, that smiling eye, that clasp of the hand, that cheerfulness with which almost all human actions are usually accompanied. Every teacher, every official, adds this to whatever is his duty; it is the perpetual occupation of humanity, and at the same time the waves of its light, in which everything grows; in the narrowest circle, namely, within the family, life blooms and flourishes only through that goodwill. Kindliness, friendliness, the courtesy of the heart, are ever-flowing streams of un-egoistic impulses, and have given far more powerful assistance to culture than even those much more famous demonstrations which are called pity, mercy, and self-sacrifice. But they are thought little of, and, as a matter of fact, there is not much that is un-egoistic in them. The *sum* of these small doses is nevertheless mighty, their united force is amongst the strongest forces. Thus one finds much more happiness in the world than sad eyes see, if one only reckons rightly, and does not forget all those moments of comfort in which every day is rich, even in the most harried of human lives.

50.

The Wish to arouse Pity. – In the most remarkable passage of his auto portrait (first printed in 1658), La Rochefoucauld assuredly hits the nail on the head when he warns all sensible people against pity, when he advises them to leave that to those orders of the people who have need of passion (because it is not ruled by reason), and to reach the point of helping the suffering and acting energetically in an accident;

while pity, according to his (and Plato's) judgement, weakens the soul. Certainly we should *exhibit* pity, but take good care not to *feel* it, for the unfortunate are so *stupid* that to them the exhibition of pity is the greatest good in the world. One can, perhaps, give a more forcible warning against this feeling of pity if one looks upon that need of the unfortunate not exactly as stupidity and lack of intellect, a kind of mental derangement which misfortune brings with it (and as such, indeed, La Rochefoucauld appears to regard it), but as something quite different and more serious. Observe children, who cry and scream *in order* to be pitied, and therefore wait for the moment when they will be noticed; live in intercourse with the sick and mentally oppressed, and ask yourself whether that ready complaining and whimpering, that making a show of misfortune, does not, at bottom, aim at *making the spectators miserable*; the pity which the spectators then exhibit is in so far a consolation for the weak and suffering in that the latter recognise therein that they *possess still one power*, in spite of their weakness, *the power of giving pain*. The unfortunate derives a sort of pleasure from this feeling of superiority, of which the exhibition of pity makes him conscious; his imagination is exalted, he is still powerful enough to give the world pain. Thus the thirst for pity is the thirst for self-gratification, and that, moreover, at the expense of his fellow-men; it shows man in the whole inconsiderateness of his own dear self, but not exactly in his 'stupidity', as La Rochefoucauld thinks. In society-talk three-fourths of all questions asked and of all answers given are intended to cause the interlocutor a little pain; for this reason so many people pine for company; it enables them to feel their power. There is a powerful charm of life in such countless but very small doses in which malice makes itself felt, just as goodwill, spread in the same way throughout the world, is the ever-ready means of healing. But are there many honest people who will admit that it is pleasing to give pain? That one not infrequently amuses one's self – and amuses one's self very well – in causing mortifications to others, at least in thought, and firing off at them the grape-shot of petty malice? Most people are too dishonest, and a few are too good, to know anything of this *pudendum*; these will always deny that Prosper Merimée is right when he says, '*Sachez aussi qu'il n'y a rien de plus commun que de faire le mal pour le plaisir de le faire.*'

51.

How Appearance becomes Actuality. – The actor finally reaches such a point that even in the deepest sorrow he cannot cease from thinking about the impression made by his own person and the general scenic effect; for instance, even at the funeral of his child, he will weep over his own sorrow and its expression like one of his own audience. The hypocrite, who always plays one and the same part, ceases at last to be a hypocrite; for instance, priests, who as young men are generally conscious or unconscious hypocrites, become at last natural, and are then really without any affectation, just priests; or if the father does not succeed so far, perhaps the son does, who makes use of his father's progress and inherits his habits. If any one long and obstinately desires to *appear* something, he finds it difficult at last to *be* anything else. The profession of almost every individual, even of the artist, begins with hypocrisy, with an imitating from without, with a copying of the effective. He who always wears the mask of a friendly expression must eventually obtain a power over well-meaning dispositions without which the expression of friendliness is not to be compelled – and finally, these, again, obtain a power over him, he *is* well-meaning.

52.

The Point of Honour in Deception. – In all great deceivers one thing is noteworthy, to which they owe their power. In the actual act of deception, with all their preparations, the dreadful voice, expression, and mien, in the midst of their effective scenery they are overcome by their *belief in themselves*; it is this, then, which speaks so wonderfully and persuasively to the spectators. The founders of religions are distinguished from those great deceivers in that they never awake from their condition of self-deception; or at times, but very rarely, they have an enlightened moment when doubt overpowers them; they generally console themselves, however, by ascribing these enlightened moments to the influence of the Evil One. There must be self-deception in order that this and that may *produce* great *effects*. For men believe in the truth of everything that is visibly, strongly believed in.

53.

The Nominal Degrees of Truth. – One of the commonest mistakes is this: because some one is truthful and honest towards us, he must speak the truth. Thus the child believes in its parents' judgement, the Christian in the assertions of the Founder of the Church. In the same way men refuse to admit that all those things which men defended in former ages with the sacrifice of life and happiness were nothing but errors; it is even said, perhaps, that they were degrees of the truth. But what is really meant is that when a man has honestly believed in something, and has fought and died for his faith, it would really be too *unjust* if he had only been inspired by an error. Such a thing seems a contradiction of eternal justice; therefore the heart of sensitive man ever enunciates against his head the axiom: between moral action and intellectual insight there must absolutely be a necessary connection. It is unfortunately otherwise; for there is no eternal justice.

54.

Falsehood. – Why do people mostly speak the truth in daily life? Assuredly not because a god has forbidden falsehood. But, firstly, because it is more convenient, as falsehood requires invention, deceit, and memory. (As Swift says, he who tells a lie is not sensible how great a task he undertakes; for in order to uphold one lie he must invent twenty others.) Therefore, because it is advantageous in upright circumstances to say straight out, 'I want this, I have done that,' and so on; because, in other words, the path of compulsion and authority is surer than that of cunning. But if a child has been brought up in complicated domestic circumstances, he employs falsehood, naturally and unconsciously says whatever best suits his interests; a sense of truth and a hatred of falsehood are quite foreign and unknown to him, and so he lies in all innocence.

55.

Throwing Suspicion on Morality for Faith's Sake. – No power can be maintained when it is only represented by hypocrites; no matter how many 'worldly' elements the Catholic Church possesses, its strength lies in those still numerous priestly natures who render life hard and full of meaning for themselves, and whose glance and worn bodies speak of nocturnal vigils, hunger, burning prayers, and perhaps even of scourging; these move men and inspire them with fear. What if it were *necessary* to live thus? This is the terrible question which their aspect brings to the lips. Whilst they spread this doubt they always uprear another pillar of their power; even the free-thinker does not dare to withstand such unselfishness with hard words of truth, and to say, 'Thyself deceived, deceive not others!' Only the difference of views divides them from him, certainly no difference of goodness or badness; but men generally treat unjustly that which they do not like. Thus we speak of the cunning and the infamous art of the Jesuits, but overlook the self-control which every individual Jesuit practises, and the fact that the lightened manner of life preached by Jesuit books is by no means for their benefit, but for that of the laity. We may even ask whether, with precisely similar tactics and organisation, we enlightened ones would make equally good tools, equally admirable through self-conquest, indefatigableness, and renunciation.

56.

Victory of Knowledge over Radical Evil. – It is of great advantage to him who desires to be wise to have witnessed for a time the spectacle of a thoroughly evil and degenerate man; it is false, like the contrary spectacle, but for whole long periods it held the mastery, and its roots have even extended and ramified themselves to us and our world. In order to understand *ourselves* we must understand *it*, but then, in order to mount higher we must rise above it. We recognise, then, that there exist no sins in the metaphysical sense; but, in the same sense, also no virtues; we recognise that the entire domain of ethical ideas is perpetually tottering, that there are higher and deeper conceptions of good and evil, of moral and immoral. He who does not desire much more from things than a knowledge of them easily makes peace with his soul, and will make a mistake (or commit a sin, as the world calls it) at the most from ignorance, but hardly from covetousness. He will no longer wish to excommunicate and exterminate desires; but his only, his wholly dominating ambition, to *know* as well as possible at all times, will make him cool and will soften all the savageness in his disposition. Moreover, he has been freed from a number of tormenting conceptions, he has no more feeling at the mention of the words 'punishments of hell', 'sinfulness', ' incapacity for good', he recognises in them only the vanishing shadow-pictures of false views of the world and of life.

57.

Morality as the Self-Disintegration of Man. – A good author, who really has his heart in his work, wishes that some one could come and annihilate him by representing the same thing in a clearer way and answering without more ado the problems therein proposed. The loving girl wishes she could prove the self-sacrificing faithfulness of her love by the unfaithfulness of her beloved. The soldier hopes to die on the field of battle for his victorious fatherland; for his loftiest desires triumph in the victory of his country. The mother gives to the child that of which she deprives herself – sleep, the best food, sometimes her health and fortune. But are all these unegoistic conditions? Are these deeds of morality *miracles*, because, to use Schopenhauer's expression, they are 'impossible and yet performed'? Is it not clear that in all four cases the individual loves *something of himself*, a thought, a desire, a production, better than *anything else of himself*; that he therefore divides his nature and to one part sacrifices all the rest? Is it something entirely different when an obstinate man says, 'I would rather be shot than move a step out of my way for this man'? The *desire for something* (wish, inclination, longing) is present in all the instances mentioned; to give way to it, with all its consequences, is certainly not 'un-egoistic'. In ethics man does not consider himself as *individuum* but as *dividuum*.

58.

What One may Promise. – One may promise actions, but no sentiments, for these are involuntary. Whoever promises to love or hate a person, or be faithful to him for ever, promises something which is not within his power; he can certainly promise such actions as are usually the results of love, hate, or fidelity, but which may also spring from other motives; for many ways and motives lead to one and the same action. The promise to love some one for ever is, therefore, really: So long as I love you I will act towards you in a loving way; if I cease to love you, you will still receive the same treatment from me, although inspired by other motives, so that our fellow-men will still be deluded into the belief that our love is unchanged and ever the same. One promises, therefore, the continuation of the semblance of love, when, without self-deception, one speaks vows of eternal love.

59.

Intellect and Morality. – One must have a good memory to be able to keep a given promise. One must have a strong power of imagination to be able to feel pity. So closely is morality bound to the goodness of the intellect.

60.

To wish for Revenge and to take Revenge. – To have a revengeful thought and to carry it into effect is to have a violent attack of fever, which passes off, however – but to have a revengeful thought without the strength and courage to carry it out is a chronic disease, a poisoning of body and soul which we have to bear about with us. Morality, which only takes intentions into account, considers the two cases as equal; usually the former case is regarded as the worse (because of the evil consequences which may perhaps result from the deed of revenge). Both estimates are short-sighted.

61.

The Power of Waiting. – Waiting is so difficult that even great poets have not disdained to take incapability of waiting as the motive for their works. Thus Shakespeare in Othello or Sophocles in Ajax, to whom suicide, had he been able to let his feelings cool down for one day, would no longer have seemed necessary, as the oracle intimated; he would probably have snapped his fingers at the terrible whisperings of wounded vanity, and said to himself, 'Who has not already, in my circumstances, mistaken a fool for a hero? Is it something so very extraordinary?' On the contrary, it is something very commonly human; Ajax might allow himself that consolation. Passion will not wait; the tragedy in the lives of great men frequently lies *not* in their conflict with the times and the baseness of their fellow-men, but in their incapacity of postponing their work for a year or two; they cannot wait. In all duels advising friends have one thing to decide, namely whether the parties concerned can still wait awhile; if this is not the case, then a duel is advisable, inasmuch as each of the two says, 'Either I continue to live and that other man must die immediately, or vice versa.' In such case waiting would mean a prolonged suffering of the terrible martyrdom of wounded honour in the face of the insulter, and this may entail more suffering than life is worth.

62.

Revelling in Vengeance. – Coarser individuals who feel themselves insulted, make out the insult to be as great as possible, and relate the affair in greatly exaggerated language, in order to be able to revel thoroughly in the rarely awakened feelings of hatred and revenge.

63.

The Value of Disparagement. – In order to maintain their self-respect in their own eyes and a certain thoroughness of action, not a few men, perhaps even the majority, find it absolutely necessary to run down and disparage all their acquaintances. But as mean natures are numerous, and since it is very important whether they possess that thoroughness or lose it, hence—

64.

The Man in a Passion. – We must beware of one who is in a passion against us as of one who has once sought our life; for the fact that we still live is due to the absence of power to kill – if looks would suffice, we should have been dead long ago. It is a piece of rough civilisation to force some one into silence by the exhibition of physical savageness and the inspiring of fear. That cold glance which exalted persons employ towards their servants is also a relic of that caste division between man and man, a piece of rough antiquity; women, the preservers of ancient things, have also faithfully retained this *survival* of an ancient habit.

65.

Whither Honesty can Lead. – Somebody had the bad habit of occasionally talking quite frankly about the motives of his actions, which were as good and as bad as the motives of most men. He first gave offence, then aroused suspicion, was then gradually excluded from society and declared a social outlaw, until at last justice remembered such an abandoned creature, on occasions when it would otherwise have had no eyes, or would have closed them. The lack of power to hold his tongue concerning the common secret, and the irresponsible tendency to see what no one wishes to see – himself – brought him to a prison and an early death.

66.

Punishable, but never Punished. – Our crime against criminals lies in the fact that we treat them like rascals.

67.

Sancta simplicitas of Virtue. – Every virtue has its privileges; for example, that of contributing its own little faggot to the scaffold of every condemned man.

68.

Morality and Consequences. – It is not only the spectators of a deed who frequently judge of its morality or immorality according to its consequences, but the doer of the deed himself does so. For the motives and intentions are seldom sufficiently clear and simple, and sometimes memory itself seems clouded by the consequences of the deed, so that one ascribes the deed to false motives or looks upon unessential motives as essential. Success often gives an action the whole honest glamour of a good conscience; failure casts the shadow of remorse over the most estimable deed. Hence arises the well-known practice of the politician, who thinks, 'Only grant me success, with that I bring all honest souls over to my side and make myself honest in my own eyes.' In the same way success must replace a better argument. Many educated people still believe that the triumph of Christianity over Greek philosophy is a proof of the greater truthfulness of the former – although in this case it is only the coarser and more powerful that has triumphed over the more spiritual and delicate. Which possesses the greater truth may be seen from the fact that the awakening sciences have agreed with Epicurus' philosophy on point after point, but on point after point have rejected Christianity.

69.

Love and Justice. – Why do we over-estimate love to the disadvantage of justice, and say the most beautiful things about it, as if it were something very much higher than the latter? Is it not visibly more stupid than justice? Certainly, but precisely for that reason all the *pleasanter* for every one. It is blind, and possesses an abundant cornucopia, out of which it distributes its gifts to all, even if they do not deserve them, even if they express no thanks for them. It is as impartial as the rain, which, according to the Bible and experience, makes not only the unjust, but also occasionally the just wet through to the skin.

70.

Execution. – How is it that every execution offends us more than does a murder? It is the coldness of the judges, the painful preparations, the conviction that a human being is here being used as a warning to scare others. For the guilt is not punished, even if it existed – it lies with educators, parents, surroundings, in ourselves, not in the murderer – I mean the determining circumstances.

71.

Hope. – Pandora brought the box of ills and opened it. It was the gift of the gods to men, outwardly a beautiful and seductive gift, and called the Casket of Happiness. Out of it flew all the evils, living winged creatures, thence they now circulate and do men injury day and night. One single evil had not yet escaped from the box, and by the will of Zeus Pandora closed the lid and it remained within. Now for ever man has the casket of happiness in his house and thinks he holds a great treasure; it is at his disposal, he stretches out his hand for it whenever he desires; for he does not know the box which Pandora brought was the casket of evil, and he believes the ill which remains within to be the greatest blessing – it is hope. Zeus did not wish man, however much he might be tormented by the other evils, to fling away his life, but to go on letting himself be tormented again and again. Therefore he gives man hope – in reality it is the worst of all evils, because it prolongs the torments of man.

72.

The Degree of Moral Inflammability Unknown. – According to whether we have or have not had certain disturbing views and impressions – for instance, an unjustly executed, killed, or martyred father; a faithless wife; a cruel hostile attack – it depends whether our passions reach fever heat and influence our whole life or not. No one knows to what he may be driven by circumstances, pity, or indignation; he does not know the degree of his own inflammability. Miserable little circumstances make us miserable; it is generally not the quantity of experiences, but their quality, on which lower and higher man depends, in good and evil.

73

The Martyr in Spite of Himself. – There was a man belonging to a party who was too nervous and cowardly ever to contradict his comrades; they made use of him for everything, they demanded everything from him, because he was more afraid of the bad opinion of his companions than of death itself; his was a miserable, feeble soul. They recognised this, and on the ground of these qualities they made a hero of him, and finally even a martyr. Although the coward inwardly always said No, with his lips he always said Yes, even on the scaffold, when he was about to die for the opinions of his party; for beside him stood one of his old companions, who so tyrannised over him by word and look that he really suffered death in the most respectable manner, and has ever since been celebrated as a martyr and a great character.

74.

The Every-day Standard. – One will seldom go wrong if one attributes extreme actions to vanity, average ones to habit, and petty ones to fear.

75.

Misunderstanding Concerning Virtue. Whoever has known immorality in connection with pleasure, as is the case with a man who has a pleasure-seeking youth behind him, imagines that virtue must be connected with absence of pleasure. Whoever, on the contrary, has been much plagued by his passions and vices, longs to find in virtue peace and the soul's happiness. Hence it is possible for two virtuous persons not to understand each other at all.

76.

The Ascetic. – The ascetic makes a necessity of virtue.

77.

Transferring Honour from the Person to the Thing. – Deeds of love and sacrifice for the benefit of one's neighbour are generally honoured, wherever they are manifested. Thereby we multiply the valuation of things which are thus loved, or for which we sacrifice ourselves, although perhaps they are not worth much in themselves. A brave army is convinced of the cause for which it fights.

78.

Ambition a Substitute for the Moral Sense. – The moral sense must not be lacking in those natures which have no ambition. The ambitious manage without it, with almost the same results. For this reason the sons of unpretentious, unambitious families, when once they lose the moral sense, generally degenerate very quickly into complete scamps.

79.

Vanity Enriches. – How poor would be the human mind without vanity! Thus, however, it resembles a well-stocked and constantly replenished bazaar which attracts buyers of every kind. There they can find almost everything, obtain almost everything, provided that they bring the right sort of coin, namely admiration.

80.

Old Age and Death. – Apart from the commands of religion, the question may well be asked. Why is it more worthy for an old man who feels his powers decline, to await his slow exhaustion and extinction than with full consciousness to set a limit to his life? Suicide in this case is a perfectly natural, obvious action, which should justly arouse respect as a triumph of reason, and did arouse it in those times when the heads of Greek philosophy and the sturdiest patriots used to seek death through suicide. The seeking, on the contrary, to prolong existence from day to day, with anxious consultation of doctors and painful mode of living, without the power of drawing nearer to the actual aim of life, is far less worthy. Religion is rich in excuses to reply to the demand for suicide, and thus it ingratiates itself with those who wish to cling to life.

81.

Errors of the Sufferer and the Doer. – When a rich man deprives a poor man of a possession (for instance, a prince taking the sweetheart of a plebeian), an error arises in the mind of the poor man; he thinks that the rich man must be utterly infamous to take away from him the little that he has. But the rich man does not estimate so highly the value of a *single* possession, because he is accustomed to have many; hence he cannot imagine himself in the poor man's place, and does not commit nearly so great a wrong as the latter supposes. They each have a mistaken idea of the other. The injustice of the powerful, which, more than anything else, rouses indignation in history, is by no means so great as it appears. Alone the mere inherited consciousness of being a higher creation, with higher claims, produces a cold temperament, and leaves the conscience quiet; we all of us feel no injustice when the difference is very great between ourselves and another creature, and kill a fly, for instance, without any pricks of conscience. Therefore it was no sign of badness in Xerxes (whom even all Greeks describe as superlatively noble) when he took a son away from his father and had him cut in pieces, because he had expressed a nervous, ominous distrust of the whole campaign; in this case the individual is put out of the way like an unpleasant insect; he is too lowly to be allowed any longer to cause annoyance to a ruler of the world. Yes, every cruel man is not so cruel as the ill-treated one imagines; the idea of pain is not the same as its endurance. It is the same thing in the case of unjust judges, of the journalist who leads public opinion astray by small dishonesties. In all these cases cause and effect are surrounded by entirely different groups of feelings and thoughts; yet one unconsciously takes it for granted that doer and sufferer think and feel alike, and according to this supposition we measure the guilt of the one by the pain of the other.

82.

The Skin of the Soul. – As the bones, flesh, entrails, and blood-vessels are enclosed within a skin, which makes the aspect of man endurable, so the emotions and passions of the soul are enwrapped with vanity – it is the skin of the soul.

83.

The Sleep of Virtue. – When virtue has slept, it will arise again all the fresher.

84.

The Refinement of Shame. – People are not ashamed to think something foul, but they are ashamed when they think these foul thoughts are attributed to them.

85.

Malice is Rare. – Most people are far too much occupied with themselves to be malicious.

86.

The Tongue in the Balance. – We praise or blame according as the one or the other affords more opportunity for exhibiting our power of judgement.

87.

St. Luke xviii. 14, Improved. – He that humbleth himself wishes to be exalted.

88.

The Prevention of Suicide. – There is a certain right by which we may deprive a man of life, but none by which we may deprive him of death; this is mere cruelty.

89.

Vanity. – We care for the good opinion of men, firstly because they are useful to us, and then because we wish to please them (children their parents, pupils their teachers, and well-meaning people generally their fellow-men). Only where the good opinion of men is of importance to some one, apart from the advantage thereof or his wish to please, can we speak of vanity. In this case the man wishes to please himself, but at the expense of his fellow-men, either by misleading them into holding a false opinion about him, or by aiming at a degree of 'good opinion' which must be painful to every one else (by arousing envy). The individual usually wishes to corroborate the opinion he holds of himself by the opinion of others, and to strengthen it in his own eyes; but the strong habit of authority – a habit as old as man himself – induces many to support by authority their belief in themselves: that is to say, they accept it first from others; they trust the judgement of others more than their own. The interest in himself, the wish to please himself, attains to such a height in a vain man that he misleads others into having a false, all too elevated estimation of him, and yet nevertheless sets store by their authority – thus causing an error and yet believing in it. It must be confessed, therefore, that vain people do not wish to please others so much as themselves, and that they go so far therein as to neglect their advantage, for they often endeavour to prejudice their fellow men unfavourably, inimicably, enviously, consequently injuriously against themselves, merely in order to have pleasure in themselves, personal pleasure.

90.

The Limits of Human Love. – A man who as declared that another is an idiot and a bad companion, is angry when the latter eventually proves himself to be otherwise.

91.

Moralité larmoyante. – What a great deal of pleasure morality gives! Only think what a sea of pleasant tears has been shed over descriptions of noble and unselfish deeds! This charm of life would vanish if the belief in absolute irresponsibility were to obtain supremacy.

92.

The Origin of Justice. – Justice (equity) has its origin amongst powers which are fairly equal, as Thucydides (in the terrible dialogue between the Athenian and Melian ambassadors) rightly comprehended: that is to say, where there is no clearly recognisable supremacy, and where a conflict would be useless and would injure both sides, there arises the thought of coming to an understanding and settling the opposing claims; the character of *exchange* is the primary character of justice. Each party satisfies the other, as each obtains what he values more than the other. Each one receives that which he desires, as his own henceforth, and whatever is desired is received in return. Justice, therefore, is recompense and exchange based on the hypothesis of a fairly equal degree of power – thus, originally, revenge belongs to the province of justice, it is an exchange. Also gratitude. Justice naturally is based on the point of view of a judicious self-preservation, on the egoism, therefore, of that reflection, 'Why should I injure myself uselessly and perhaps not attain my aim after all?' So much about the *origin* of justice. Because man, according to his intellectual custom, has *forgotten* the original purpose of so-called just and reasonable actions, and particularly because for hundreds of years children have been taught to admire and imitate such actions, the idea has gradually arisen that such an action is un-egoistic; upon this idea, however, is based the high estimation in which it is held: which, moreover, like all valuations, is constantly growing, for something that is valued highly is striven after, imitated, multiplied, and increases, because the value of the output of toil and enthusiasm of each individual is added to the value of the thing itself. How little moral would the world look without this forgetfulness! A poet might say that God had placed forgetfulness as door-keeper in the temple of human dignity.

93.

The Right of the Weaker. – When any one submits under certain conditions to a greater power, as a besieged town for instance, the counter-condition is that one can destroy one's self, burn the town, and so cause the mighty one a great loss. Therefore there is a kind of *equalisation* here, on the basis of which rights may be determined. The enemy has his advantage in maintaining it. In so far there are also rights between slaves and masters, that is, precisely so far as the possession of the slave is useful and important to his master. The *right* originally extends *so far as* one *appears* to be valuable to the other, essentially unlosable, unconquerable, and so forth. In so far the weaker one also has rights, but lesser ones. Hence the famous *unusquisque tantum juris habet, quantum, potentia valet* (or more exactly, *quantum, potentia valere creditur*).

94.

The Three Phases of Hitherto Existing Morality. – It is the first sign that the animal has become man when its actions no longer have regard only to momentary welfare, but to what is enduring, when it grows *useful* and *practical*; there the free rule of reason first breaks out. A still higher step is reached when he acts according to the principle of *honour*; by this means he brings himself into order, submits to common feelings, and that exalts him still higher over the phase in which he was led only by the idea of usefulness from a personal point of view; he respects and wishes to be respected, i.e. he understands usefulness as dependent upon what he thinks of others and what others think of him. Eventually he acts, on the highest step of the *hitherto* existing morality, according to *his* standard of things and men; he himself decides for himself and others what is honourable, what is useful; he has become the law-giver of opinions, in accordance with the ever more highly developed idea of what is useful and honourable. Knowledge enables him to place that which is most useful, that is to say the general, enduring usefulness, above the personal, the honourable recognition of general, enduring validity above the momentary; he lives and acts as a collective individual.

95.

The Morality of the Mature Individual. – The impersonal has hitherto been looked upon as the actual distinguishing mark of moral action; and it has been pointed out that in the beginning it was in consideration of the common good that all impersonal actions were praised and distinguished. Is not an important change in these views impending, now when it is more and more recognised that it is precisely in the most *personal* possible considerations that the common good is the greatest, so that a *strictly personal* action now best illustrates the present idea of morality, as utility for the mass? To make a whole *personality* out of ourselves, and in all that we do to keep that personality's *highest good* in view, carries us further than those sympathetic emotions and actions for the benefit of others. We all still suffer, certainly, from the too small consideration of the personal in us; it is badly developed – let us admit it; rather has our mind been forcibly drawn away from it and offered as a sacrifice to the State, to science, or to those who stand in need of help, as if it were the bad part which must be sacrificed. We are still willing to work for our fellow-men, but only so far as we find our own greatest advantage in this work, no more and no less. It is only a question of what we understand as *our advantage*, the unripe, undeveloped, crude individual will understand it in the crudest way.

96.

Custom and Morality. – To be moral, correct, and virtuous is to be obedient to an old-established law and custom. Whether we submit with difficulty or willingly is immaterial, enough that we do so. He is called 'good' who, as if naturally, after long precedent, easily and willingly, therefore, does what is right, according to whatever this may be (as, for instance, taking revenge, if to take revenge be considered as right, as amongst the ancient Greeks). He is called good because he is good 'for something'; but as goodwill, pity, consideration, moderation, and such like, have come, with the change in manners, to be looked upon as 'good for something', as useful, the good-natured and helpful have, later on, come to be distinguished specially as 'good'. (In the beginning other and more important kinds of usefulness stood in the foreground.) To be evil is to be 'not moral' (immoral), to be immoral is to be in opposition to tradition, however sensible or stupid it may be; injury to the community (the 'neighbour' being understood thereby) has, however, been looked upon by the social laws of all different ages as being eminently the actual 'immorality', so that now at the word 'evil' we immediately think of voluntary injury to one's neighbour. The fundamental antithesis which has taught man the distinction between moral and immoral, between good and evil, is not the 'egoistic' and 'unegoistic', but the being bound to the tradition, law, and solution thereof. How the tradition has *arisen* is immaterial, at all events without regard to good and evil or any immanent categorical imperative, but above all for the purpose of preserving a *community*, a generation, an association, a people; every superstitious custom that has arisen on account of some falsely explained accident, creates a tradition, which it is moral to follow; to separate one's self from it is dangerous, but more dangerous for the *community* than for the individual (because the Godhead punishes the community for every outrage and every violation of its rights, and the individual only in proportion). Now every tradition grows continually more venerable, the farther off lies its origin, the more this is lost sight of; the veneration paid it accumulates from generation to generation, the tradition at last becomes holy and excites awe; and thus in any case the morality of piety is a much older morality than that which requires un-egoistic actions.

97.

Pleasure in Traditional Custom. – An important species of pleasure, and therewith the source of morality, arises out of habit. Man does what is habitual to him more easily, better, and therefore more willingly; he feels a pleasure therein, and knows from experience that the habitual has been tested, and is therefore useful; a custom that we can live with is proved to be wholesome and advantageous in contrast to all new and not yet tested experiments. According to this, morality is the union of the pleasant and the useful; moreover, it requires no reflection. As soon as man can use compulsion, he uses it to introduce and enforce his *customs*; for in his eyes they are proved as the wisdom of life. In the same way a company of individuals compels each single one to adopt the same customs. Here the inference is wrong; because we feel at ease with a morality, or at least because we are able to carry on existence with it, therefore this morality is necessary, for it seems to be the *only* possibility of feeling at ease; the ease of life seems to grow out of it alone. This comprehension of the habitual as a necessity of existence is pursued even to the smallest details of custom – as insight into genuine causality is very small with lower peoples and civilisations, they take precautions with superstitious fear that everything should go in its same groove; even where custom is difficult, hard, and burdensome, it is preserved on account of its apparent highest usefulness. It is not known that the same degree of well-being can also exist with other customs, and that even higher degrees may be attained. We become aware, however, that all customs, even the hardest, grow pleasanter and milder with time, and that the severest way of life may become a habit and therefore a pleasure.

98.

Pleasure and Social Instinct. – Out of his relations with other men, man obtains a new species of *pleasure* in addition to those pleasurable sensations which he derives from himself; whereby he greatly increases the scope of enjoyment. Perhaps he has already taken too many of the pleasures of this sphere from animals, which visibly feel pleasure when they play with each other, especially the mother with her young. Then consider the sexual relations, which make almost every female interesting to a male with regard to pleasure, and *vice versa*. The feeling of pleasure on the basis of human relations generally makes man better; joy in common, pleasure enjoyed together is increased, it gives the individual security, makes him good-tempered, and dispels mistrust and envy, for we feel ourselves at ease and see others at ease. *Similar manifestations of pleasure* awaken the idea of the same sensations, the feeling of being like something; a like effect is produced by common sufferings, the same bad weather, dangers, enemies. Upon this foundation is based the oldest alliance, the object of which is the mutual obviating and averting of a threatening danger for the benefit of each individual. And thus the social instinct grows out of pleasure.

99.

The Innocent Side of so-called Evil Actions. – All 'evil' actions are prompted by the instinct of preservation, or, more exactly, by the desire for pleasure and the avoidance of pain on the part of the individual; thus prompted, but not evil. 'To cause pain *per se*' *does not exist*, except in the brains of philosophers, neither does 'to give pleasure *per se*' (pity in Schopenhauer's meaning). In the social condition *before* the State we kill the creature, be it ape or man, who tries to take from us the fruit of a tree when we are hungry and approach the tree, as we should still do with animals in inhospitable countries. The evil actions which now most rouse our indignation, are based upon the error that he who causes them has a free will, that he had the option, therefore, of not doing us this injury. This belief in option arouses hatred, desire for revenge, spite, and the deterioration of the whole imagination, while we are much less angry with an animal because we consider it irresponsible. To do injury, not from the instinct of preservation, but as *requital*, is the consequence of a false judgement and therefore equally innocent. The individual can in the condition which lies before the State, act sternly and cruelly towards other creatures for the purpose of *terrifying*, to establish his existence firmly by such terrifying proofs of his power. Thus act the violent, the mighty, the original founders of States, who subdue the weaker to themselves. They have the right to do so, such as the State still takes for itself; or rather, there is no right that can hinder this. The ground for all morality can only be made ready when a stronger individual or a collective individual, for instance society or the State, subdues the single individuals, draws them out of their singleness, and forms them into an association. *Compulsion* precedes morality, indeed morality itself is compulsion for a time, to which one submits for the avoidance of pain. Later on it becomes custom – later still, free obedience, and finally almost instinct – then, like everything long accustomed and natural, it is connected with pleasure – and is henceforth called *virtue*.

100.

Shame. – Shame exists everywhere where there is a 'mystery'; this, however, is a religious idea, which was widely extended in the older times of human civilisation. Everywhere were found bounded domains to which access was forbidden by divine right, except under certain conditions; at first locally, as, for example, certain spots that ought not to be trodden by the feet of the uninitiated, in the neighbourhood of which these latter experienced horror and fear. This feeling was a good deal carried over into other relations, for instance, the sex relations, which, as a privilege and αδντον of riper years, had to be withheld from the knowledge of the young for their advantage, relations for the protection and sanctification of which many gods were invented and were set up as guardians in the nuptial chamber. (In Turkish this room is on this account called harem, 'sanctuary', and is distinguished with the same name, therefore, that is used for the entrance courts of the mosques.) Thus the kingdom is as a centre from which radiate power and glory, to the subjects a mystery full of secrecy and shame, of which many after-effects may still be felt among nations which otherwise do not by any means belong to the bashful type. Similarly, the whole world of inner conditions, the so-called 'soul', is still a mystery for all who are not philosophers, after it has been looked upon for endless ages as of divine origin and as worthy of divine intercourse; according to this it is an αδντον and arouses shame.

101.

Judge not. – In considering earlier periods, care must be taken not to fall into unjust abuse. The injustice in slavery, the cruelty in the suppression of persons and nations, is not to be measured by our standard. For the instinct of justice was not then so far developed. Who dares to reproach the Genevese Calvin with the burning of the physician Servet? It was an action following and resulting from his convictions, and in the same way the Inquisition had a good right; only the ruling views were false, and produced a result which seems hard to us because those views have now grown strange to us. Besides, what is the burning of a single individual compared with eternal pains of hell for almost all! And yet this idea was universal at that time, without essentially injuring by its dreadfulness the conception of a God. With us, too, political sectarians are hardly and cruelly treated, but because one is accustomed to believe in the necessity of the State, the cruelty is not so deeply felt here as it is where we repudiate the views. Cruelty to animals in children and Italians is due to ignorance, i.e. the animal, through the interests of Church teaching, has been placed too far behind man. Much that is dreadful and inhuman in history, much that one hardly likes to believe, is mitigated by the reflection that the one who commands and the one who carries out are different persons – the former does not behold the right and therefore does not experience the strong impression on the imagination; the latter obeys a superior and therefore feels no responsibility. Most princes and military heads, through lack of imagination, easily appear hard and cruel without really being so. *Egoism is not evil,* because the idea of the 'neighbour' – the word is of Christian origin and does not represent the truth – is very weak in us; and we feel ourselves almost as free and irresponsible towards him as towards plants and stones. We have yet to *learn* that others suffer, and this can never be completely learnt.

102.

'Man always Acts Rightly.' – We do not complain of nature as immoral because it sends a thunderstorm and makes us wet – why do we call those who injure us immoral? Because in the latter case we take for granted a free will functioning voluntarily; in the former we see necessity. But this distinction is an error. Thus we do not call even intentional injury immoral in all circumstances; for instance, we kill a fly unhesitatingly and intentionally, only because its buzzing annoys us; we punish a criminal intentionally and hurt him in order to protect ourselves and society. In the first case it is the individual who, in order to preserve himself, or even to protect himself from worry, does intentional injury; in the second case it is the State. All morals allow intentional injury *in the case of necessity*, that is, when it is a matter of *self-preservation*! But these two points of view suffice to explain all evil actions committed by men against men, we are desirous of obtaining pleasure or avoiding pain; in any case it is always a question of self-preservation. Socrates and Plato are right: whatever man does he always does well, that is, he does that which seems to him good (useful) according to the degree of his intellect, the particular standard of his reasonableness.

103.

The Harmlessness of Malice. – The aim of malice is *not* the suffering of others in itself, but our own enjoyment; for instance, as the feeling of revenge, or stronger nervous excitement. All teasing, even, shows the pleasure it gives to exercise our power on others and bring it to an enjoyable feeling of preponderance. Is it *immoral* to taste pleasure at the expense of another's pain? Is malicious joy[6] devilish, as Schopenhauer says? We give ourselves pleasure in nature by breaking off twigs, loosening stones, fighting with wild animals, and do this in

6 This is the untranslatable word *Schadenfreude*, which means joy at the misfortune of others. – J. M. K.

order to become thereby conscious of our strength. Is the knowledge, therefore, that another suffers through us, the same thing concerning which we otherwise feel irresponsible, supposed to make us immoral? But if we did not know this we would not thereby have the enjoyment of our own superiority, which can only *manifest* itself by the suffering of others, for instance in teasing. All pleasure *per se* is neither good nor evil; whence should come the decision that in order to have pleasure ourselves we may not cause displeasure to others? From the point of view of usefulness alone, that is, out of consideration for the *consequences*, for *possible* displeasure, when the injured one or the replacing State gives the expectation of resentment and revenge: this only can have been the original reason for denying ourselves such actions. *Pity* aims just as little at the pleasure of others as malice at the pain of others *per se*. For it contains at least two (perhaps many more) elements of a personal pleasure, and is so far self-gratification; in the first place as the pleasure of emotion, which is the kind of pity that exists in tragedy, and then, when it impels to action, as the pleasure of satisfaction in the exercise of power. If, besides this, a suffering person is very dear to us, we lift a sorrow from ourselves by the exercise of sympathetic actions. Except by a few philosophers, pity has always been placed very low in the scale of moral feelings, and rightly so.

104.

Self-defence. – If self-defence is allowed to pass as moral, then almost all manifestations of the so-called immoral egoism must also stand; men injure, rob, or kill in order to preserve or defend themselves, to prevent personal injury; they lie where cunning and dissimulation are the right means of self-preservation. *Intentional injury*, when our existence or safety (preservation of our comfort) is concerned, is conceded to be moral; the State itself injures, according to this point of view, when it punishes. In unintentional injury, of course, there can be nothing immoral, that is ruled by chance. Is there, then, a kind of intentional injury where our existence or the preservation of our comfort is *not* concerned? Is there an injuring out of pure *malice*, for instance in cruelty? If one does not know how much an action hurts, it is no deed of malice; thus the child is not malicious towards the animal, not evil; he examines and destroys it like a toy. But do we ever know entirely how an action hurts another? As far as our nervous system extends we protect ourselves from pain; if it extended farther, to our fellow-men, namely, we should do no one an injury (except in such cases as we injure ourselves, where we cut ourselves for the sake of cure, tire and exert ourselves for the sake of health). We *conclude* by analogy that something hurts somebody, and through memory and the strength of imagination we may suffer from it ourselves. But still what a difference there is between toothache and the pain (pity) that the sight of toothache calls forth! Therefore, in injury out of so-called malice the *degree* of pain produced is always unknown to us; but inasmuch as there is *pleasure* in the action (the feeling of one's own power, one's own strong excitement), the action is committed, in order to preserve the comfort of the individual, and is regarded, therefore, from a similar point of view as defence and falsehood in necessity. No life without pleasure; the struggle for pleasure is the struggle for life. Whether the individual so fights this fight that men call him good, or so that they call him evil, is determined by the measure and the constitution of his *intellect*.

105.

Recompensing Justice. – Whoever has completely comprehended the doctrine of absolute irresponsibility can no longer include the so-called punishing and recompensing justice in the idea of justice, should this consist of giving to each man his due. For he who is punished does not deserve the punishment, he is only used as a means of henceforth warning away from certain actions; equally so, he who is rewarded does not merit this reward, he could not act otherwise than he did. Therefore the reward is meant only as an encouragement to him and others, to provide a motive for subsequent actions; words of praise are flung to the runners on the course, not to the one who has reached the goal. Neither punishment nor reward is anything that comes to one as *one's own*; they are given from motives of usefulness, without one having a right to claim them. Hence we must say, 'The wise man gives no reward because the deed has been well done,' just as we have said, 'The wise man does not punish because evil has been committed, but in order that evil shall not be committed.' If punishment and reward no longer existed, then the strongest motives which deter men from certain actions and impel them to certain other actions, would also no longer exist; the needs of mankind require their continuance; and inasmuch as punishment and reward, blame and praise, work most sensibly on vanity, the same need requires the continuance of vanity.

106.

At the Waterfall. – In looking at a waterfall we imagine that there is freedom of will and fancy in the countless turnings, twistings, and breakings of the waves; but everything is compulsory, every movement can be mathematically calculated. So it is also with human actions; one would have to be able to calculate every single action beforehand if one were all-knowing; equally so all progress of knowledge, every error, all malice. The one who acts certainly labours under the illusion of voluntariness; if the world's wheel were to stand still for a moment and an all-knowing, calculating reason were there to make use of this pause, it could foretell the future of every creature to the remotest times, and mark out every track upon which that wheel would continue to roll. The delusion of the acting agent about himself, the supposition of a free will, belongs to this mechanism which still remains to be calculated.

107.

Irresponsibility and Innocence. – The complete irresponsibility of man for his actions and his nature is the bitterest drop which he who understands must swallow if he was accustomed to see the patent of nobility of his humanity in responsibility and duty. All his valuations, distinctions, disinclinations, are thereby deprived of value and become false – his deepest feeling for the sufferer and the hero was based on an error; he may no longer either praise or blame, for it is absurd to praise and blame nature and necessity. In the same way as he loves a fine work of art, but does not praise it, because it can do nothing for itself; in the same way as he regards plants, so must he regard his own actions and those of mankind. He can admire strength, beauty, abundance, in themselves; but must find no merit therein – the chemical progress and the strife of the elements, the torments of the sick person who thirsts after recovery, are all equally as little merits as those struggles of the soul and states of distress in which we are torn hither and thither by different impulses until we finally decide for the strongest – as we say (but in reality it is the strongest motive which decides for us). All these motives, however, whatever fine names we may give them, have all grown out of the same root, in which we believe the evil poisons to be situated; between good and evil actions there is no difference of species, but at most of degree. Good actions are sublimated evil ones; evil actions are vulgarised and stupefied good ones. The single longing of the individual for self-gratification (together with the fear of losing it) satisfies itself in all circumstances: man may act as he can, that is as he must, be it in deeds of vanity, revenge, pleasure, usefulness, malice, cunning; be it in deeds of sacrifice, of pity, of knowledge. The degrees of the power of judgement determine whither any one lets himself be drawn through this longing; to every society, to every individual, a scale of possessions is continually present, according to which he determines his actions and judges those of others. But this standard changes constantly; many actions are called evil and are only stupid, because the degree of intelligence which decided for them was very low. In a certain sense, even, *all* actions are still stupid; for the highest degree of human intelligence which can now be attained will assuredly be yet surpassed, and then, in a retrospect, all our actions and judgements will appear as limited and hasty as the actions and judgements of primitive wild peoples now appear limited and hasty to us. To recognise all this may be deeply painful, but consolation comes after; such pains are the pangs of birth. The butterfly wants to break through its chrysalis: it rends and tears it, and is then blinded and confused by the unaccustomed light, the kingdom of liberty. In such people as are *capable* of such sadness – and how few are! – the first experiment made is to see whether *mankind can change itself* from a *moral* into a *wise* mankind. The sun of a new gospel throws its rays upon the highest point in the soul of each single individual, then the mists gather thicker than ever, and the brightest light and the dreariest shadow lie side by side. Everything is necessity – so says the new knowledge, and this knowledge itself is necessity. Everything is innocence, and knowledge is the road to insight into this innocence.

Are pleasure, egoism, vanity *necessary* for the production of the moral phenomena and their highest result, the sense for truth and justice in knowledge; were error and the confusion of the imagination the only means through which mankind could raise itself gradually to this degree of self-enlightenment and self-liberation – who would dare to undervalue these means? Who would dare to be sad if he perceived the goal to which those roads led? Everything in the domain of morality has evolved, is changeable, unstable, everything is dissolved, it is true; but *everything is also streaming towards one goal*. Even if the inherited habit of erroneous valuation, love and hatred, continue to reign in us, yet under the influence of growing knowledge it will become weaker; a new habit, that of comprehension, of not loving, not hating, of overlooking, is gradually implanting itself in us upon the same ground, and in thousands of years will perhaps be powerful enough to give humanity the strength to produce wise, innocent (consciously innocent) men, as it now produces unwise, guilt-conscious men – *that is the necessary preliminary step, not its opposite*.

THIRD DIVISION.
THE RELIGIOUS LIFE.

108.

The Double Fight against Evil. When misfortune overtakes us we can either pass over it so lightly that its cause is removed, or so that the result which it has on our temperament is altered, through a changing, therefore, of the evil into a good, the utility of which is perhaps not visible until later on. Religion and art (also metaphysical philosophy) work upon the changing of the temperament, partly through the changing of our judgement on events (for instance, with the help of the phrase 'whom the Lord loveth He chasteneth'), partly through the awakening of a pleasure in pain, in emotion generally (whence the tragic art takes its starting-point). The more a man is inclined to twist and arrange meanings the less he will grasp the causes of evil and disperse them; the momentary mitigation and influence of a narcotic, as for example in toothache, suffices him even in more serious sufferings. The more the dominion of creeds and all arts dispense with narcotics, the more strictly men attend to the actual removing of the evil, which is certainly bad for writers of tragedy; for the material for tragedy is growing scarcer because the domain of pitiless, inexorable fate is growing ever narrower – but worse still for the priests, for they have hitherto lived on the narcotisation of human woes.

109.

Sorrow is Knowledge. – How greatly we should like to exchange the false assertions of the priests, that there is a god who desires good from us, a guardian and witness of every action, every moment, every thought, who loves us and seeks our welfare in all misfortune – how greatly we would like to exchange these ideas for truths which would be just as healing, pacifying and beneficial as those errors! But there are no such truths; at most philosophy can oppose to them metaphysical appearances (at bottom also untruths). The tragedy consists in the fact that we cannot believe those dogmas of religion and metaphysics, if we have strict methods of truth in heart and brain: on the other hand, mankind has, through development, become so delicate, irritable and suffering, that it has need of the highest means of healing and consolation; whence also the danger arises that man would bleed to death from recognised truth, or, more correctly, from discovered error. Byron has expressed this in the immortal lines:

Sorrow is knowledge: they who know the most
Must mourn the deepest o'er the fatal truth.
The Tree of Knowledge is not that of Life.

For such troubles there is no better help than to recall the stately levity of Horace, at least for the worst hours and eclipses of the soul, and to say with him:

. . . quid aeternis minorem
consiliis animum fatigas?
cur non sub alta vel platano vel hac
pinu jacentes.[7]

But assuredly frivolity or melancholy of every degree is better than a romantic retrospection and desertion of the flag, an approach to Christianity in any form; for according to the present condition of knowledge it is absolutely impossible to approach it without hopelessly soiling our *intellectual conscience* and giving ourselves away to ourselves and others. Those pains may be unpleasant enough, but we cannot become leaders and educators of mankind without pain; and woe to him who would wish to attempt this and no longer have that clear conscience!

110.

The Truth in Religion. – In the period of rationalism justice was not done to the importance of religion, of that there is no doubt, but equally there is no doubt that in the reaction that followed this rationalism justice was far overstepped; for religions were treated lovingly, even amorously, and, for instance, a deeper, even the very deepest, understanding of the world was ascribed to them; which science has only to strip of its dogmatic garment in order to possess

7 Why harass with eternal designs a mind too weak to compass them? Why do we not, as we lie beneath a lofty plane-tree or this pine [drink while we may]? HOR., Odes II. ii. 11-14. – J. M. K.

the 'truth' in unmythical form. Religions should, therefore – this was the opinion of all opposers of rationalism – *sensu allegorico*, with all consideration for the understanding of the masses, give utterance to that ancient wisdom which is wisdom itself, inasmuch as all true science of later times has always led up to it instead of away from it, so that between the oldest wisdom of mankind and all later harmonies similarity of discernment and a progress of knowledge – in case one should wish to speak of such a thing – rests not upon the nature but upon the way of communicating it. This whole conception of religion and science is thoroughly erroneous, and none would still dare to profess it if Schopenhauer's eloquence had not taken it under its protection; this resonant eloquence which, however, only reached its hearers a generation later. As surely as from Schopenhauer's religious-moral interpretations of men and the world much may be gained for the understanding of the Christian and other religions, so surely also is he mistaken about the *value of religion for knowledge*. Therein he himself was only a too docile pupil of the scientific teachers of his time, who all worshipped romanticism and had forsworn the spirit of enlightenment; had he been born in our present age he could not possibly have talked about the *sensus allegoricus* of religion; he would much rather have given honour to truth, as he used to do, with the words, '*no religion, direct or indirect, either as dogma or as allegory, has ever contained a truth*'. For each has been born of fear and necessity, through the byways of reason did it slip into existence; once, perhaps, when imperilled by science, some philosophic doctrine has lied itself into its system in order that it may be found there later, but this is a theological trick of the time when a religion already doubts itself. These tricks of theology (which certainly were practised in the early days of Christianity, as the religion of a scholarly period steeped in philosophy) have led to that superstition of the *sensus allegoricus*, but yet more the habits of the philosophers (especially the half-natures, the poetical philosophers and the philosophising artists), to treat all the sensations which they discovered in *themselves* as the fundamental nature of man in general, and hence to allow their own religious feelings an important influence in the building up of their systems. As philosophers frequently philosophised under the custom of religious habits, or at least under the anciently inherited power of that 'metaphysical need', they developed doctrinal opinions which really bore a great resemblance to the Jewish or Christian or Indian religious views – a resemblance, namely, such as children usually bear to their mothers, only that in this case the fathers were not clear about that motherhood, as happens sometimes – but in their innocence romanced about a family likeness between all religion and science. In reality, between religions and real science there exists neither relationship nor friendship, nor even enmity; they live on different planets. Every philosophy which shows a religious comet's tail shining in the darkness of its last prospects makes all the science it contains suspicious; all this is presumably also religion, even though in the guise of science. Moreover, if all nations were to agree about certain religious matters, for instance the existence of a God (which, it may be remarked, is not the case with regard to this point), this would only be an argument *against* those affirmed matters, for instance the existence of a God; the *consensus gentium* and *hominum* in general can only take place in case of a huge folly. On the other hand, there is no *consensus omnium sapientium*, with regard to any single thing, with that exception mentioned in Goethe's lines:

'Alle die Weisesten aller der Zeiten
Lacheln und winken und stimmen mit ein:
Thoricht, auf Bess'rung der Thoren zu barren!
Kinder der Klugheit, o habet die Narren
Eben zum Narren auch, wie sich's gehort!'[8]

Spoken without verse and rhyme and applied to our case, the *consensus sapientium* consists in this: that the *consensus gentium* counts as a folly.

---

8 'All greatest sages of all latest ages
Will chuckle and slily agree,
'Tis folly to wait till a fool's empty pate
Has learnt to be knowing and free:
So children of wisdom, make use of the fools
And use them whenever you can as your tools.' – J.M.K.

111.

The Origin of the Religious Cult. – If we go back to the times in which the religious life flourished to the greatest extent, we find a fundamental conviction, which we now no longer share, and whereby the doors leading to a religious life are closed to us once for all – it concerns Nature and intercourse with her. In those times people knew nothing of natural laws; neither for earth nor for heaven is there a 'must'; a season, the sunshine, the rain may come or may not come. In short, every idea of natural causality is lacking. When one rows, it is not the rowing that moves the boat, but rowing is only a magical ceremony by which one compels a *daemon* to move the boat. All maladies, even death itself, are the result of magical influences. Illness and death never happen naturally; the whole conception of 'natural sequence' is lacking – it dawned first amongst the older Greeks, that is, in a very late phase of humanity, in the conception of *Moira*, enthroned above the gods. When a man shoots with a bow, there is still always present an irrational hand and strength; if the wells suddenly dry up, men think first of subterranean *daemons* and their tricks; it must be the arrow of a god beneath whose invisible blow a man suddenly sinks down. In India (says Lubbock) a carpenter is accustomed to offer sacrifice to his hammer, his hatchet, and the rest of his tools; in the same way a Brahmin treats the pen with which he writes, a soldier the weapons he requires in the field of battle, a mason his trowel, a labourer his plough. In the imagination of religious people all nature is a summary of the actions of conscious and voluntary creatures, an enormous complex of *arbitrariness*. No conclusion may be drawn with regard to everything that is outside of us, that anything will *be* so and so, *must* be so and so; the approximately sure, reliable are *we* – man is the *rule*, nature is *irregularity* – this theory contains the fundamental conviction which obtains in rude, religiously productive primitive civilisations. We latter-day men feel just the contrary – the richer man now feels himself inwardly, the more polyphonous is the music and the noise of his soul the more powerfully the symmetry of nature works upon him; we all recognise with Goethe the great means in nature for the appeasing of the modern soul; we listen to the pendulum swing of this greatest of clocks with a longing for rest, for home and tranquillity, as if we could absorb this symmetry into ourselves and could only thereby arrive at the enjoyment of ourselves. Formerly it was otherwise; if we consider the rude, early condition of nations, or contemplate present-day savages at close quarters, we find them most strongly influenced by *law* and by *tradition*: the individual is almost automatically bound to them, and moves with the uniformity of a pendulum. To him Nature – uncomprehended, terrible, mysterious Nature – must appear as the *sphere of liberty*, of voluntariness, of the higher power, even as a superhuman degree of existence, as God. In those times and conditions, however, every individual felt that his existence, his happiness, and that of the family and the State, and the success of all undertakings, depended on those spontaneities of nature; certain natural events must appear at the right time, others be absent at the right time. How can one have any influence on these terrible unknown things, how can one bind the sphere of liberty? Thus he asks himself, thus he inquires anxiously; is there, then, no means of making those powers as regular through tradition and law as you are yourself? The aim of those who believe in magic and miracles is to *impose a law on nature* – and, briefly, the religious cult is a result of this aim. The problem which those people have set themselves is closely related to this: how can the *weaker* race dictate laws to the *stronger*, rule it, and guide its actions (in relation to the weaker)? One would first remember the most harmless sort of compulsion, that compulsion which one exercises when one has gained any one's affection. By imploring and praying, by submission, by the obligation of regular taxes and gifts, by flattering glorifications, it is also possible to exercise an influence upon the powers of nature, inasmuch as one gains the affections; love binds and becomes bound. Then one can make compacts by which one is mutually bound to a certain behaviour, where one gives pledges and exchanges vows. But far more important is a species of more forcible compulsion, by magic and witchcraft. As with the sorcerer's help man is able to injure a more powerful enemy and keep him in fear, as the love-charm works at a distance, so the weaker man believes he can influence the mightier spirits of nature. The principal thing in all witchcraft is that we must get into our possession something that belongs to some one, hair, nails, food from their table, even their portrait, their name. With such apparatus we can then practise sorcery; for the fundamental rule is, to everything spiritual there belongs something corporeal; with the help of this we are able to bind the spirit, to injure it, and destroy it; the corporeal furnishes the handles with which we can grasp the spiritual. As man controls man, so he controls some natural spirit or other; for this has also its corporeal part by which it may be grasped. The tree and, compared with it, the seed from which it sprang – this enigmatical contrast seems to prove that the same spirit embodied itself in both forms, now small, now large. A stone that begins to roll suddenly is the body in which a spirit operates; if there is an enormous rock lying on a lonely heath it seems impossible to conceive human strength sufficient to have brought it there, consequently the stone must have moved there by itself, that is, it must be possessed by a spirit. Everything that has a body is susceptible to witchcraft, therefore also the natural spirits. If a god is bound to his image we can use the most direct compulsion against him (through refusal of sacrificial food, scourging, binding in fetters, and so on). In order to obtain by force the missing favour of their god the lower classes in China wind cords round the image of the one who has left them in the lurch, pull it down and drag it through the streets in the dust and the dirt: 'You dog of a spirit,' they say, 'we gave you a magnificent temple to live in, we gilded you prettily, we fed you well, we offered you sacrifice, and yet you are so ungrateful.' Similar forcible measures against pictures of the Saints and Virgin when they refused to do their duty in pestilence or drought, have been witnessed even during the present century in Catholic countries. Through all these magic relations to nature, countless ceremonies have been called into life; and at last, when the confusion has grown too great, an endeavour has been made to order and systematise them, in order that the favourable course of the whole progress of nature, i.e. of the great succession of the seasons, may seem to be guaranteed by a corresponding course of a system of procedure. The essence of the religious cult is to determine and confine nature to human advantage, *to impress it with a legality, therefore, which it did not originally possess*; while at the present time we wish to recognise the legality of nature in order to adapt ourselves to it. In short, then, the religious cult is based upon the representations of sorcery between man and man – and the sorcerer is older than the priest. But it is likewise based upon other and nobler representations; it premises the sympathetic relation of man to man, the presence of goodwill, gratitude, the hearing of pleaders, of treaties between enemies, the granting of pledges, and the claim to the protection of property. In very low stages of civilisation man does not stand in the relation of a helpless slave to nature, he is *not* necessarily its involuntary bondsman. In the *Greek* grade of religion, particularly in relation to the Olympian gods, there may even be imagined a common life between two castes, a nobler and more powerful one, and one less noble; but in their origin both belong to each other somehow, and are of one kind; they need not be ashamed of each other. That is the nobility of the Greek religion.

112.

At the Sight of certain Antique Sacrificial Implements. – The fact of how many feelings are lost to us may be seen, for instance, in the mingling of the *droll*, even of the *obscene*, with the religious feeling. The sensation of the possibility of this mixture vanishes, we only comprehend historically that it existed in the feasts of Demeter and Dionysus, in the Christian Easter plays and Mysteries. But we also know that which is noble in alliance with burlesque and such like, the touching mingled with the laughable, which perhaps a later age will not be able to understand.

113.

Christianity as Antiquity. – When on a Sunday morning we hear the old bells ring out, we ask ourselves, 'Is it possible! This is done on account of a Jew crucified two thousand years ago who said he was the Son of God. The proof of such an assertion is wanting.' Certainly in our times the Christian religion is an antiquity that dates from very early ages, and the fact that its assertions are still believed, when otherwise all claims are subjected to such strict examination, is perhaps the oldest part of this heritage. A God who creates a son from a mortal woman; a sage who requires that man should no longer work, no longer judge, but should pay attention to the signs of the approaching end of the world; a justice that accepts an innocent being as a substitute in sacrifice; one who commands his disciples to drink his blood; prayers for miraculous intervention; sins committed against a God and atoned for through a God; the fear of a future to which death is the portal; the form of the cross in an age which no longer knows the signification and the shame of the cross,[9] how terrible all this appears to us, as if risen from the grave of the ancient past! Is it credible that such things are still believed?

114.

What is un-Greek in Christianity. – The Greeks did not regard the Homeric gods as raised above them like masters, nor themselves as being under them like servants, as the Jews did. They only saw, as in a mirror, the most perfect examples of their own caste; an ideal, therefore, and not an opposite of their own nature. There is a feeling of relationship, a mutual interest arises, a kind of symmachy. Man thinks highly of himself when he gives himself such gods, and places himself in a relation like that of the lower nobility towards the higher; while the Italian nations hold a genuine peasant-faith, with perpetual fear of evil and mischievous powers and tormenting spirits. Wherever the Olympian gods retreated into the background, Greek life was more sombre and more anxious. Christianity, on the contrary, oppressed man and crushed him utterly, sinking him as if in deep mire; then into the feeling of absolute depravity it suddenly threw the light of divine mercy, so that the surprised man, dazzled by forgiveness, gave a cry of joy and for a moment believed that he bore all heaven within himself. All psychological feelings of Christianity work upon this unhealthy excess of sentiment, and upon the deep corruption of head and heart it necessitates; it desires to destroy, break, stupefy, confuse – only one thing it does not desire, namely *moderation*, and therefore it is in the deepest sense barbaric, Asiatic, ignoble and un-Greek.

115.

To be Religious with Advantage. – There are sober and industrious people on whom religion is embroidered like a hem of higher humanity; these do well to remain religious, it beautifies them. All people who do not understand some kind of trade in weapons – tongue and pen included as weapons – become servile; for such the

9 It may be remembered that the cross was the gallows of the ancient world. – J. M. K.

Christian religion is very useful, for then servility assumes the appearance of Christian virtues and is surprisingly beautified. People to whom their daily life appears too empty and monotonous easily grow religious; this is comprehensible and excusable, only they have no right to demand religious sentiments from those whose daily life is not empty and monotonous.[10]

116.

The Commonplace Christian. – If Christianity were right, with its theories of an avenging God, of general sinfulness, of redemption, and the danger of eternal damnation, it would be a sign of weak intellect and lack of character *not* to become a priest, apostle or hermit, and to work only with fear and trembling for one's own salvation; it would be senseless thus to neglect eternal benefits for temporary comfort. Taking it for granted that there *is belief*, the commonplace Christian is a miserable figure, a man that really cannot add two and two together, and who, moreover, just because of his mental incapacity for responsibility, did not deserve to be so severely punished as Christianity has decreed.

117.

Of the Wisdom of Christianity. – It is a clever stroke on the part of Christianity to teach the utter unworthiness, sinfulness, and despicableness of mankind so loudly that the disdain of their fellow-men is no longer possible. 'He may sin as much as he likes, he is not essentially different from me – it is I who am unworthy and despicable in every way,' says the Christian to himself. But even this feeling has lost its sharpest sting, because the Christian no longer believes in his individual despicableness; he is bad as men are generally, and comforts himself a little with the axiom, 'We are all of one kind.'

118.

Change of Front. – As soon as a religion triumphs it has for its enemies all those who would have been its first disciples.

---

10 This may give us one of the reasons for the religiosity still happily prevailing in England and the United States. – J. M. K.

119.

The Fate of Christianity. – Christianity arose for the purpose of lightening the heart; but now it must first make the heart heavy in order afterwards to lighten it. Consequently it will perish.

120.

The Proof of Pleasure. – The agreeable opinion is accepted as true – this is the proof of the pleasure (or, as the Church says, the proof of the strength), of which all religions are so proud when they ought to be ashamed of it. If Faith did not make blessed it would not be believed in; of how little value must it be, then!

121.

A Dangerous Game. – Whoever now allows scope to his religious feelings must also let them increase, he cannot do otherwise. His nature then gradually changes; it favours whatever is connected with and near to the religious element, the whole extent of judgement and feeling becomes clouded, overcast with religious shadows. Sensation cannot stand still; one must therefore take care.

122.

The Blind Disciples. – So long as one knows well the strength and weakness of one's doctrine, one's art, one's religion, its power is still small. The disciple and apostle who has no eyes for the weaknesses of the doctrine, the religion, and so forth, dazzled by the aspect of the master and by his reverence for him, has on that account usually more power than the master himself. Without blind disciples the influence of a man and his work has never yet become great. To help a doctrine to victory often means only so to mix it with stupidity that the weight of the latter carries off also the victory for the former.

123.

Church Disestablishment. – There is not enough religion in the world even to destroy religions.

124.

The Sinlessness of Man. – If it is understood how 'sin came into the world', namely through errors of reason by which men held each other, even the single individual held himself, to be much blacker and much worse than was actually the case, the whole sensation will be much lightened, and man and the world will appear in a blaze of innocence which it will do one good to contemplate. In the midst of nature man is always the child *per se*. This child sometimes has a heavy and terrifying dream, but when it opens its eyes it always finds itself back again in Paradise.

125.

The Irreligiousness of Artists. – Homer is so much at home amongst his gods, and is so familiar with them as a poet, that he must have been deeply irreligious; that which the popular faith gave him – a meagre, rude, partly terrible superstition – he treated as freely as the sculptor does his clay, with the same unconcern, therefore, which Aeschylus and Aristophanes possessed, and by which in later times the great artists of the Renaissance distinguished themselves, as also did Shakespeare and Goethe.

126.

The Art and Power of False Interpretations. – All the visions, terrors, torpors, and ecstasies of saints are well-known forms of disease, which are only, by reason of deep-rooted religious and psychological errors, differently *explained* by him, namely not as diseases. Thus, perhaps, the *Daimonion* of Socrates was only an affection of the ear, which he, in accordance with his ruling moral mode of thought, *expounded* differently from what would be the case now. It is the same thing with the madness and ravings of the prophets and soothsayers; it is always the degree of knowledge, fantasy, effort, morality in the head and heart of the *interpreters* which has *made* so much of it. For the greatest achievements of the people who are called geniuses and saints it is necessary that they should secure interpreters by force, who *misunderstand* them for the good of mankind.

127.

The Veneration of Insanity. – Because it was remarked that excitement frequently made the mind clearer and produced happy inspirations it was believed that the happiest inspirations and WM suggestions were called forth by the greatest excitement; and so the insane were revered as wise and oracular. This is based on a false conclusion.

128.

The Promises of Science. – The aim of modern science is: as little pain as possible, as long a life as possible – a kind of eternal blessedness, therefore; but certainly a very modest one as compared with the promises of religions.

129.

Forbidden Generosity. – There is not sufficient love and goodness in the world to permit us to give some of it away to imaginary beings.

130.

The Continuance of the Religious Cult in the Feelings. – The Roman Catholic Church, and before that all antique cults, dominated the entire range of means by which man was put into unaccustomed moods and rendered incapable of the cold calculation of judgement or the clear thinking of reason. A church quivering with deep tones; the dull, regular, arresting appeals of a priestly throng, unconsciously communicates its tension to the congregation and makes it listen almost fearfully, as if a miracle were in preparation; the influence of the architecture, which, as the dwelling of a Godhead, extends into the uncertain and makes its apparition to be feared in all its sombre spaces – who would wish to bring such things back to mankind if the necessary suppositions are no longer believed? But the *results* of all this are not lost, nevertheless; the inner world of noble, emotional', deeply contrite dispositions, full of presentiments, blessed with hope, is inborn in mankind mainly through this cult; what exists of it now in the soul was then cultivated on a large scale as it germinated, grew up and blossomed.

131.

The Painful Consequences of Religion. – However much we may think we have weaned ourselves from religion, it has nevertheless not been done so thoroughly as to deprive us of pleasure in encountering religious sensations and moods in music, for instance; and if a philosophy shows us the justification of metaphysical hopes and the deep peace of soul to be thence acquired, and speaks, for instance, of the 'whole, certain gospel in the gaze of Raphael's Madonnas', we receive such statements and expositions particularly warmly; here the philosopher finds it easier to prove; that which he desires to give corresponds to a heart that desires to receive. Hence it may be observed how the less thoughtful free spirits really only take offence at the dogmas, but are well acquainted with the charm of religious sensations; they are sorry to lose hold of the latter for the sake of the former. Scientific philosophy must be very careful not to smuggle in errors on the ground of that need – a need which has grown up and is consequently temporary – even logicians speak of 'presentiments' of truth in ethics and in art (for instance, of the suspicion that 'the nature of things is one'), which should be forbidden to them. Between the carefully established truths and such 'presaged' things there remains the unbridgable chasm that those are due to intellect and these to requirement. Hunger does not prove that food *exists* to satisfy it, but that it desires food. To 'presage' does not mean the acknowledgment of the existence of a thing in any one degree, but its possibility, in so far as it is desired or feared; 'presage' does not advance one step into the land of certainty. We believe involuntarily that the portions of a philosophy which are tinged with religion are better proved than others; but actually it is the contrary, but we have the inward desire that it may be so, that that which makes blessed, therefore, may be also the true. This desire misleads us to accept bad reasons for good ones.

132.

Of the Christian Need of Redemption. – With careful reflection it must be possible to obtain an explanation free from mythology of that process in the soul of a Christian which is called the need of redemption, consequently a purely psychological explanation. Up to the present, the psychological explanations of religious conditions and processes have certainly been held in some disrepute, inasmuch as a theology which called itself free carried on its unprofitable practice in this domain; for here from the beginning (as the mind of its founder, Schleiermacher, gives us reason to suppose) the preservation of the Christian religion and the continuance of Christian theology was kept in view; a theology which was to find a new anchorage in the psychological analyses of religious 'facts', and above all a new occupation. Unconcerned about such predecessors we hazard the following interpretation of the phenomenon in question. Man is conscious of certain actions which stand far down in the customary rank of actions; he even discovers in himself a tendency towards similar actions, a tendency which appears to him almost as unchangeable as his whole nature. How willingly would he try himself in that other species of actions which in the general valuation are recognised as the loftiest and highest, how gladly would he feel himself to be full of the good consciousness which should follow an unselfish mode of thought! But unfortunately he stops short at this wish, and the discontent at not being able to satisfy it is added to all the other discontents which his lot in life or the consequences of those above-mentioned evil actions have aroused in him; so that a deep ill-humour is the result, with the search for a physician who could remove this and all its causes. This condition would not be felt so bitterly if man would only compare himself frankly with other men – then he would have no reason for being dissatisfied with himself to a particular extent, he would only bear his share of the common burden of human dissatisfaction and imperfection. But he compares himself with a being who is said to be capable only of those actions which are called unegoistic, and to live in the perpetual consciousness of an unselfish mode of thought, i.e. with God; it is because he gazes into this clear mirror that his image appears to him so dark, so unusually warped. Then he is alarmed by the thought of that same creature, in so far as it floats before his imagination as a retributive justice; in all possible small and great events he thinks he recognises its anger and menaces, that he even feels its scourge-strokes as judge and executioner. Who will help him in this danger, which, by the prospect of an immeasurable duration of punishment, exceeds in horror all the other terrors of the idea?

133.

Before we examine the further consequences of this mental state, let us acknowledge that it is not through his 'guilt' and 'sin' that man has got into this condition, but through a series of errors of reason; that it was the fault of the mirror if his image appeared so dark and hateful to him, and that that mirror was *his* work, the very imperfect work of human imagination and power of judgement. In the first place, a nature that is only capable of purely unegoistic actions is more fabulous than the phoenix; it cannot even be clearly imagined, just because, when closely examined, the whole idea 'unegoistic action' vanishes into air. No man *ever* did a thing which was done only for others and without any personal motive; how should he be able to do anything which had no relation to himself, and therefore without inward obligation (which must always have its foundation in a personal need)? How could the *ego* act without *ego*? A God who, on the contrary, is *all* love, as such a one is often represented, would not be capable of a single unegoistic action, whereby one is reminded of a saying of Lichtenberg's which is certainly taken from a lower sphere: 'We cannot possibly *feel* for others, as the saying is; we feel only for ourselves. This sounds hard, but it is not so really if it be rightly understood. We do not love father or mother or wife or child, but the pleasant sensations they cause us'; or, as Rochefoucauld says: '*Si on croit aimer sa maitresse pour l'amour d'elle, on est bien trompé*.' To know the reason why actions of love are valued more than others, not on account of their nature, namely, but of their *usefulness*, we should compare the examinations already mentioned, *On the Origin of Moral Sentiments*. But should a man desire to be entirely like that God of Love, to do and wish everything for others and nothing for himself, the latter is impossible for the reason that he must do *very much* for himself to be able to do something for the love of others. Then it is taken for granted that the other is sufficiently egoistic to accept that sacrifice again and again, that living for him – so that the people of love and sacrifice have an interest in the continuance of those who are loveless and incapable of sacrifice, and, in order to exist, the highest morality would be obliged positively to *compel* the existence of un-morality (whereby it would certainly annihilate itself). Further: the conception of a God disturbs and humbles so long as it is believed in; but as to how it arose there can no longer be any doubt in the present state of the science of comparative ethnology; and with a comprehension of this origin all belief falls to the ground. The Christian who compares his nature with God's is like Don Quixote, who under-valued his own bravery because his head was full of the marvellous deeds of the heroes of the chivalric romances – the standard of measurement in both cases belongs to the domain of fable. But if the idea of God is removed, so is also the feeling of 'sin' as a trespass against divine laws, as a stain in a creature vowed to God. Then, perhaps, there still remains that dejection which is intergrown and connected with the fear of the punishment of worldly justice or of the scorn of men; the dejection of the pricks of conscience, the sharpest thorn in the consciousness of sin, is always removed if we recognise that though by our own deed we have sinned against human descent, human laws and ordinances, still that we have not imperilled the 'eternal salvation of the Soul' and its relation to the Godhead. And if man succeeds in gaining philosophic conviction of the absolute necessity of all actions and their entire irresponsibility, and absorbing this into his flesh and blood, even those remains of the pricks of conscience vanish.

134.

Now if the Christian, as we have said, has fallen into the way of self-contempt in consequence of certain errors through a false, unscientific interpretation of his actions and sensations, he must notice with great surprise how that state of contempt, the pricks of conscience and displeasure generally, does not endure, how sometimes there come hours when all this is wafted away from his soul and he feels himself once more free and courageous. In truth, the pleasure in himself, the comfort of his own strength, together with the necessary weakening through time of every deep emotion, has usually been victorious; man loves himself once again, he feels it – but precisely this new love, this self-esteem, seems to him incredible, he can only see in it the wholly undeserved descent of a stream of mercy from on high. If he formerly believed that in every event he could recognise warnings, menaces, punishments, and every kind of manifestation of divine anger, he now finds divine goodness in all his experiences – this event appears to him to be full of love, that one a helpful hint, a third, and, indeed, his whole happy mood, a proof that God is merciful. As formerly, in his state of pain, he interpreted his actions falsely, so now he misinterprets his experiences; his mood of comfort he believes to be the working of a power operating outside of himself, the love with which he really loves himself seems to him to be divine love; that which he calls mercy, and the prologue to redemption, is actually self-forgiveness, self-redemption.

135.

Therefore: A certain false psychology, a certain kind of imaginative interpretation of motives and experiences, is the necessary preliminary for one to become a Christian and to feel the need of redemption. When this error of reason and imagination is recognised, one ceases to be a Christian.

136.

Of Christian Asceticism and Holiness. – As greatly as isolated thinkers have endeavoured to depict as a miracle the rare manifestations of morality, which are generally called asceticism and holiness, miracles which it would be almost an outrage and sacrilege to explain by the light of common sense, as strong also is the inclination towards this outrage. A mighty impulse of nature has at all times led to a protest against those manifestations; science, in so far as it is an imitation of nature, at least allows itself to rise against the supposed inexplicableness and unapproachableness of these objections. So far it has certainly not succeeded: those appearances are still unexplained, to the great joy of the above-mentioned worshippers of the morally marvellous. For, speaking generally, the unexplained *must* be absolutely inexplicable, the inexplicable absolutely unnatural, supernatural, wonderful – thus runs the demand in the souls of religious and metaphysical people (also of artists, if they should happen to be thinkers at the same time); whilst the scientist sees in this demand the 'evil principle' in itself. The general, first probability upon which one lights in the contemplation of holiness and asceticism is this, that their nature is a *complicated* one, for almost everywhere, within the physical world as well as in the moral, the apparently marvellous has been successfully traced back to the complicated, the many-conditioned. Let us venture, therefore, to isolate separate impulses from the soul of saints and ascetics, and finally to imagine them as intergrown.

137.

There is a *defiance of self*, to the sublimest manifestation of which belong many forms of asceticism. Certain individuals have such great need of exercising their power and love of ruling that, in default of other objects, or because they have never succeeded otherwise, they finally excogitate the idea of tyrannising over certain parts of their own nature, portions or degrees of themselves. Thus many a thinker confesses to views which evidently do not serve either to increase or improve his reputation; many a one deliberately calls down the scorn of others when by keeping silence he could easily have remained respected; others contradict former opinions and do not hesitate to be called inconsistent – on the contrary, they strive after this, and behave like reckless riders who like a horse best when it has grown wild, unmanageable, and covered with sweat. Thus man climbs dangerous paths up the highest mountains in order that he may laugh to scorn his own fear and his trembling knees; thus the philosopher owns to views on asceticism, humility, holiness, in the brightness of which his own picture shows to the worst possible disadvantage. This crushing of one's self, this scorn of one's own nature, this *spernere se sperni*, of which religion has made so much, is really a very high degree of vanity. The whole moral of the Sermon on the Mount belongs here; man takes a genuine delight in doing violence to himself by these exaggerated claims, and afterwards idolising these tyrannical demands of his soul. In every ascetic morality man worships one part of himself as a God, and is obliged, therefore, to diabolise the other parts.

138.

Man is not equally moral at all hours, this is well known. If his morality is judged to be the capability for great self-sacrificing resolutions and self-denial (which, when continuous and grown habitual, are called holiness), he is most moral in the *passions*; the higher emotion provides him with entirely new motives, of which he, sober and cold as usual, perhaps does not even believe himself capable. How does this happen? Probably because of the proximity of everything great and highly exciting; if man is once wrought up to a state of extraordinary suspense, he is as capable of carrying out a terrible revenge as of a terrible crushing of his need for revenge. Under the influence of powerful emotion, he desires in any case the great, the powerful, the immense; and if he happens to notice that the sacrifice of himself satisfies him as well as, or better than, the sacrifice of others, he chooses that. Actually, therefore, he only cares about discharging his emotion; in order to ease his tension he seizes the enemy's spears and buries them in his breast. That there was something great in self-denial and not in revenge had to be taught to mankind by long habit; a Godhead that sacrificed itself was the strongest, most effective symbol of this kind of greatness. As the conquest of the most difficult enemy, the sudden mastering of an affection – thus this denial *appears*; and so far it passes for the summit of morality. In reality it is a question of the confusion of one idea with another, while the temperament maintains an equal height, an equal level. Temperate men who are resting from their passions no longer understand the morality of those moments; but the general admiration of those who had the same experiences upholds them; pride is their consolation when affection and the understanding of their deed vanish. Therefore, at bottom even those actions of self-denial are not moral, inasmuch as they are not done strictly with regard to others; rather the other only provides the highly-strung temperament with an opportunity of relieving itself through that denial.

139.

In many respects the ascetic seeks to make life easy for himself, usually by complete subordination to a strange will or a comprehensive law and ritual; something like the way a Brahmin leaves nothing whatever to his own decision but refers every moment to holy precepts. This submission is a powerful means of attaining self-mastery: man is occupied and is therefore not bored, and yet has no incitement to self-will or passion; after a completed deed there is no feeling of responsibility and with it no tortures of remorse. We have renounced our own will once and for ever, and this is easier than only renouncing it occasionally; as it is also easier to give up a desire entirely than to keep it within bounds. When we remember the present relation of man to the State, we find that, even here, unconditional obedience is more convenient than conditional. The saint, therefore, makes his life easier by absolute renunciation of his personality, and we are mistaken if in that phenomenon we admire the loftiest heroism of morality. In any case it is more difficult to carry one's personality through without vacillation and unclearness than to liberate one's self from it in the above-mentioned manner; moreover, it requires far more spirit and consideration.

140.

After having found in many of the less easily explicable actions manifestations of that pleasure in *emotion per se*, I should like to recognise also in self-contempt, which is one of the signs of holiness, and likewise in the deeds of self-torture (through hunger and scourging, mutilation of limbs, feigning of madness) a means by which those natures fight against the general weariness of their life-will (their nerves); they employ the most painful irritants and cruelties in order to emerge for a time, at all events, from that dullness and boredom into which they so frequently sink through their great mental indolence and that submission to a strange will already described.

141.

The commonest means which the ascetic and saint employs to render life still endurable and amusing consists in occasional warfare with alternate victory and defeat. For this he requires an opponent, and finds it in the so-called 'inward enemy'. He principally makes use of his inclination to vanity, love of honour and rule, and of his sensual desires, that he may be permitted to regard his life as a perpetual battle and himself as a battlefield upon which good and evil spirits strive with alternating success. It is well known that sensual imagination is moderated, indeed almost dispelled, by regular sexual intercourse, whereas, on the contrary, it is rendered unfettered and wild by abstinence or irregularity. The imagination of many Christian saints was filthy to an extraordinary degree; by virtue of those theories that these desires were actual demons raging within them they did not feel themselves to be too responsible; to this feeling we owe the very instructive frankness of their self-confessions. It was to their interest that this strife should always be maintained in one degree or another, because, as we have already said, their empty life was thereby entertained. But in order that the strife might seem sufficiently important and arouse the enduring sympathy and admiration of non-saints, it was necessary that sensuality should be ever more reviled and branded, the danger of eternal damnation was so tightly bound up with these things that it is highly probable that for whole centuries Christians generated children with a bad conscience, wherewith humanity has certainly suffered a great injury. And yet here truth is all topsy-turvy, which is particularly unsuitable for truth. Certainly Christianity had said that every man is conceived and born in sin, and in the insupportable superlative-Christianity of Calderon this thought again appears, tied up and twisted, as the most distorted paradox there is, in the well-known lines –

> 'The greatest sin of man
> Is that he was ever born.'

In all pessimistic religions the act of generation was looked upon as evil in itself. This is by no means the verdict of all mankind, not even of all pessimists. For instance, Empedocles saw in all erotic things nothing shameful, diabolical, or sinful; but rather, in the great plain of disaster he saw only one hopeful and redeeming figure, that of Aphrodite; she appeared to him as a guarantee that the strife should not endure eternally, but that the sceptre should one day be given over to a gentler *daemon*. The actual Christian pessimists had, as has been said, an interest in the dominance of a diverse opinion; for the solitude and spiritual wilderness of their lives they required an ever living enemy, and a generally recognised enemy, through whose fighting and overcoming they could constantly represent themselves to the non-saints as incomprehensible, half-supernatural beings. But when at last this enemy took to flight for ever in consequence of their mode of life and their impaired health, they immediately understood how to populate their interior with new daemons. The rising and falling of the scales of pride and humility sustained their brooding minds as well as the alternations of desire and peace of soul. At that time psychology served not only to cast suspicion upon everything human, but to oppress, to scourge, to crucify; people *wished* to find themselves as bad and wicked as possible, they *sought* anxiety for the salvation of their souls, despair of their own strength. Everything natural with which man has connected the idea of evil and sin (as, for instance, he is still accustomed to do with regard to the erotic) troubles and clouds the imagination, causes a frightened glance, makes man quarrel with himself and uncertain and distrustful of himself. Even his dreams have the flavour of a restless conscience. And yet in the reality of things this suffering from what is natural is entirely without foundation, it is only the consequence of opinions *about* things. It is easily seen how men grow worse by considering the inevitably-natural as bad, and afterwards always feeling themselves made thus. It is the trump card of religion and metaphysics, which wish to have man evil and sinful by nature, to cast suspicion on nature and thus really to *make* him bad, for he learns to feel himself evil since he cannot divest himself of the clothing of nature. After living for a long natural life, he gradually comes to feel himself weighed down by such a burden of sin that supernatural powers are necessary to lift this burden, and therewith arises the so-called need of redemption, which corresponds to no real but only to an imaginary sinfulness. If we survey the separate moral demands of the earliest times of Christianity it will everywhere be found that requirements are exaggerated in order that man *cannot* satisfy them; the intention is not that he should become more moral, but that he should feel himself as *sinful as possible*. If man had not found this feeling *agreeable* – why would he have thought out such an idea and stuck to it so long? As in the antique world an immeasurable power of intellect and inventiveness was expended in multiplying the pleasure of life by festive cults, so also in the age of Christianity an immeasurable amount of intellect has been sacrificed to another endeavour – man must by all means be made to feel himself sinful and thereby be excited, *enlivened, en-souled*. To excite, enliven, en-soul at all costs – is not that the watchword of a relaxed, over-ripe, over-cultured age? The range of all natural sensations had been gone over a hundred times, the soul had grown weary, whereupon the saint and the ascetic invented a new species of stimulants for life. They presented themselves before the public eye, not exactly as an example for the many, but as a terrible and yet ravishing spectacle, which took place on that border-land between world and over-world, wherein at that time all people believed they saw now rays of heavenly light and now unholy tongues of flame glowing in the depths. The saint's eye, fixed upon the terrible meaning of this short earthly life, upon the nearness of the last decision concerning endless new spans of existence, this burning eye in a half-wasted body made men of the old world tremble to their very depths; to gaze, to turn shudderingly away, to feel anew the attraction of the spectacle and to give way to it, to drink deep of it till the soul quivered with fire and ague – that was the last *pleasure that antiquity invented* after it had grown blunted even at the sight of beast-baitings and human combats.

142.

Now to sum up. That condition of soul in which the saint or embryo saint rejoiced, was composed of elements which we all know well, only that under the influence of other than religious conceptions they exhibit themselves in other colours and are then accustomed to encounter man's blame as fully as, with that decoration of religion and the ultimate meaning of existence, they may reckon on receiving admiration and even worship – might reckon, at least, in former ages. Sometimes the saint practises that defiance of himself which is a near relative of domination at any cost and gives a feeling of power even to the most lonely; sometimes his swollen sensibility leaps from the desire to let his passions have full play into the desire to overthrow them like wild horses under the mighty pressure of a proud spirit; sometimes he desires a complete cessation of all disturbing, tormenting, irritating sensations, a waking sleep, a lasting rest in the lap of a dull, animal, and plant-like indolence; sometimes he seeks strife and arouses it within himself, because boredom has shown him its yawning countenance. He scourges his self-adoration with self-contempt and cruelty, he rejoices in the wild tumult of his desires and the sharp pain of sin, even in the idea of being lost; he understands how to lay a trap for his emotions, for instance even for his keen love of ruling, so that he sinks into the most utter abasement and his tormented soul is thrown out of joint by this contrast; and finally, if he longs for visions, conversations with the dead or with divine beings, it is at bottom a rare kind of delight that he covets, perhaps that delight in which all others are united. Novalis, an authority on questions of holiness through experience and instinct, tells the whole secret with naive joy: 'It is strange enough that the association of lust, religion, and cruelty did not long ago draw men's attention to their close relationship and common tendency.'

143.

That which gives the saint his historical value is not the thing he *is*, but the thing he *represents* in the eyes of the unsaintly. It was through the fact that errors were made about him, that the state of his soul was *falsely interpreted*, that men separated themselves from him as much as possible, as from something incomparable and strangely superhuman, that he acquired the extraordinary power which he exercised over the imagination of whole nations and whole ages. He did not know himself; he himself interpreted the writing of his moods, inclinations, and actions according to an art of interpretation which was as exaggerated and artificial as the spiritual interpretation of the Bible. The distorted and diseased in his nature, with its combination of intellectual poverty, evil knowledge, ruined health, and over-excited nerves, remained hidden from his own sight as well as from that of his spectators. He was not a particularly good man, and still less was he a particularly wise one; but he *represented* something that exceeded the human standard in goodness and wisdom. The belief in him supported the belief in the divine and miraculous, in a religious meaning of all existence, in an impending day of judgement. In the evening glory of the world's sunset, which glowed over the Christian nations, the shadowy form of the saint grew to vast dimensions, it grew to such a height that even in our own age, which no longer believes in God, there are still thinkers who believe in the saint.

144.

It need not be said that to this description of the saint which has been made from an average of the whole species, there may be opposed many a description which could give a more agreeable impression. Certain exceptions stand out from among this species, it may be through great mildness and philanthropy, it may be through the magic of unusual energy; others are attractive in the highest degree, because certain wild ravings have poured streams of light on their whole being, as is the case, for instance, with the famous founder of Christianity, who thought he was the Son of God and therefore felt himself sinless – so that through this idea – which we must not judge too hardly because the whole antique world swarms with sons of God – he reached that same goal, that feeling of complete sinlessness, complete irresponsibility, which every one can now acquire by means of science. Neither have I mentioned the Indian saints, who stand midway between the Christian saint and the Greek philosopher, and in so far represent no pure type. Knowledge, science – such as existed then – the uplifting above other men through logical discipline and training of thought, were as much fostered by the Buddhists as distinguishing signs of holiness as the same qualities in the Christian world are repressed and branded as signs of unholiness.

FOURTH DIVISION.

CONCERNING THE SOUL OF ARTISTS AND AUTHORS.

145.

The Perfect should not have Grown. – With regard to everything that is perfect we are accustomed to omit the question as to how perfection has been acquired, and we only rejoice in the present as if it had sprung out of the ground by magic. Probably with regard to this matter we are still under the effects of an ancient mythological feeling. It still *almost* seems to us (in such a Greek temple, for instance, as that of Paestum) as if one morning a god in sport had built his dwelling of such enormous masses, at other times it seems as if his spirit had suddenly entered into a stone and now desired to speak through it. The artist knows that his work is only fully effective if it arouses the belief in an improvisation, in a marvellous instantaneousness of origin; and thus he assists this illusion and introduces into art those elements of inspired unrest, of blindly groping disorder, of listening dreaming at the beginning of creation, as a means of deception, in order so to influence the soul of the spectator or hearer that it may believe in the sudden appearance of the perfect. It is the business of the science of art to contradict this illusion most decidedly, and to show up the mistakes and pampering of the intellect, by means of which it falls into the artist's trap.

146.

The Artist's Sense of Truth. – With regard to recognition of truths, the artist has a weaker morality than the thinker; he will on no account let himself be deprived of brilliant and profound interpretations of life, and defends himself against temperate and simple methods and results. He is apparently fighting for the higher worthiness and meaning of mankind; in reality he will not renounce the *most effective* suppositions for his art, the fantastical, mythical, uncertain, extreme, the sense of the symbolical, the over-valuation of personality, the belief that genius is something miraculous – he considers, therefore, the continuance of his art of creation as more important than the scientific devotion to truth in every shape, however simple this may appear.

147.

Art as Raiser of the Dead. – Art also fulfils the task of preservation and even of brightening up extinguished and faded memories; when it accomplishes this task it weaves a rope round the ages and causes their spirits to return. It is, certainly, only a phantom-life that results therefrom, as out of graves, or like the return in dreams of our beloved dead, but for some moments, at least, the old sensation lives again and the heart beats to an almost forgotten time. Hence, for the sake of the general usefulness of art, the artist himself must be excused if he does not stand in the front rank of the enlightenment and progressive civilisation of humanity; all his life long he has remained a child or a youth, and has stood still at the point where he was overcome by his artistic impulse; the feelings of the first years of life, however, are acknowledged to be nearer to those of earlier times than to those of the present century. Unconsciously it becomes his mission to make mankind more childlike; this is his glory and his limitation.

148.

Poets as the Lighteners of Life. – Poets, inasmuch as they desire to lighten the life of man, either divert his gaze from the wearisome present, or assist the present to acquire new colours by means of a life which they cause to shine out of the past. To be able to do this, they must in many respects themselves be beings who are turned towards the past, so that they can be used as bridges to far distant times and ideas, to dying or dead religions and cultures. Actually they are always and of necessity *epigoni*. There are, however, certain drawbacks to their means of lightening life – they appease and heal only temporarily, only for the moment; they even prevent men from labouring towards a genuine improvement in their conditions, inasmuch as they remove and apply palliatives to precisely that passion of discontent that induces to action.

149.

The Slow Arrow of Beauty. – The noblest kind of beauty is that which does not transport us suddenly, which does not make stormy and intoxicating impressions (such a kind easily arouses disgust), but that which slowly filters into our minds, which we take away with us almost unnoticed, and which we encounter again in our dreams; but which, however, after having long lain modestly on our hearts, takes entire possession of us, fills our eyes with tears and our hearts with longing. What is it that we long for at the sight of beauty? We long to be beautiful, we fancy it must bring much happiness with it. But that is a mistake.

150.

The Animation of Art. – Art raises its head where creeds relax. It takes over many feelings and moods engendered by religion, lays them to its heart, and itself becomes deeper, more full of soul, so that it is capable of transmitting exultation and enthusiasm, which it previously was not able to do. The abundance of religious feelings which have grown into a stream are always breaking forth again and desire to conquer new kingdoms, but the growing enlightenment has shaken the dogmas of religion and inspired a deep mistrust – thus the feeling, thrust by enlightenment out of the religious sphere, throws itself upon art, in a few cases into political life, even straight into science. Everywhere where human endeavour wears a loftier, gloomier aspect, it may be assumed that the fear of spirits, incense, and church-shadows have remained attached to it.

151.

How Rhythm Beautifies. – Rhythm casts a veil over reality; it causes various artificialities of speech and obscurities of thought; by the shadow it throws upon thought it sometimes conceals it, and sometimes brings it into prominence. As shadow is necessary to beauty, so the 'dull' is necessary to lucidity. Art makes the aspect of life endurable by throwing over it the veil of obscure thought.

152.

The Art of the Ugly Soul. – Art is confined within too narrow limits if it be required that only the orderly, respectable, well-behaved soul should be allowed to express itself therein. As in the plastic arts, so also in music and poetry: there is an art of the ugly soul side by side with the art of the beautiful soul; and the mightiest effects of art, the crushing of souls, moving of stones and humanising of beasts, have perhaps been best achieved precisely by that art.

153.

Art makes Heavy the Heart of the Thinker. – How strong metaphysical need is and how difficult nature renders our departure from it may be seen from the fact that even in the free spirit, when he has cast off everything metaphysical, the loftiest effects of art can easily produce a resounding of the long silent, even broken, metaphysical string – it may be, for instance, that at a passage in Beethoven's Ninth Symphony he feels himself floating above the earth in a starry dome with the dream of *immortality* in his heart; all the stars seem to shine round him, and the earth to sink farther and farther away. If he becomes conscious of this state, he feels a deep pain at his heart, and sighs for the man who will lead back to him his lost darling, be it called religion or metaphysics. In such moments his intellectual character is put to the test.

154.

Playing with Life. – The lightness and frivolity of the Homeric imagination was necessary to calm and occasionally to raise the immoderately passionate temperament and acute intellect of the Greeks. If their intellect speaks, how harsh and cruel does life then appear! They do not deceive themselves, but they intentionally weave lies round life. Simonides advised his countrymen to look upon life as a game; earnestness was too well-known to them as pain (the gods so gladly hear the misery of mankind made the theme of song), and they knew that through art alone misery might be turned into pleasure. As a punishment for this insight, however, they were so plagued with the love of romancing that it was difficult for them in everyday life to keep themselves free from falsehood and deceit; for all poetic nations have such a love of falsehood, and yet are innocent withal. Probably this occasionally drove the neighbouring nations to desperation.

155.

The Belief in Inspiration. – It is to the interest of the artist that there should be a belief in sudden suggestions, so-called inspirations; as if the idea of a work of art, of poetry, the fundamental thought of a philosophy shone down from heaven like a ray of grace. In reality the imagination of the good artist or thinker constantly produces good, mediocre, and bad, but his *judgement*, most clear and practised, rejects and chooses and joins together, just as we now learn from Beethoven's notebooks that he gradually composed the most beautiful melodies, and in a manner selected them, from many different attempts. He who makes less severe distinctions, and willingly abandons himself to imitative memories, may under certain circumstances become a great improvisatore; but artistic improvisation ranks low in comparison with serious and laboriously chosen artistic thoughts. All great men were great workers, unwearied not only in invention but also in rejection, reviewing, transforming, and arranging.

156.

Inspiration Again. – If the productive power has been suspended for a length of time, and has been hindered in its outflow by some obstacle, there comes at last such a sudden out-pouring, as if an immediate inspiration were taking place without previous inward working, consequently a miracle. This constitutes the familiar deception, in the continuance of which, as we have said, the interest of all artists is rather too much concerned. The capital has only *accumulated*, it has not suddenly fallen down from heaven. Moreover, such apparent inspirations are seen elsewhere, for instance in the realm of goodness, of virtue and of vice.

157.

The Suffering of Genius and its Value. – The artistic genius desires to give pleasure, but if his mind is on a very high plane he does not easily find any one to share his pleasure; he offers entertainment but nobody accepts it. This gives him, in certain circumstances, a comically touching pathos; for he has really no right to force pleasure on men. He pipes, but none will dance: can that be tragic? Perhaps. As compensation for this deprivation, however, he finds more pleasure in creating than the rest of mankind experiences in all other species of activity. His sufferings are considered as exaggerated, because the sound of his complaints is louder and his tongue more eloquent; and yet *sometimes* his sufferings are really very great; but only because his ambition and his envy are so great. The learned genius, like Kepler and Spinoza, is usually not so covetous and does not make such an exhibition of his really greater sufferings and deprivations. He can reckon with greater certainty on future fame and can afford to do without the present, whilst an artist who does this always plays a desperate game that makes his heart ache. In very rare cases, when in one and the same individual are combined the genius of power and of knowledge and the moral genius, there is added to the above-mentioned pains that species of pain which must be regarded as the most curious exception in the world; those extra and super-personal sensations which are experienced on behalf of a nation, of humanity, of all civilisation, all suffering existence, which acquire their value through the connection with particularly difficult and remote perceptions (pity in itself is worth but little). But what standard, what proof is there for its genuineness? Is it not almost imperative to be mistrustful of all who *talk* of feeling sensations of this kind?

158.

The Destiny of Greatness. – Every great phenomenon is followed by degeneration, especially in the world of art. The example of the great tempts vainer natures to superficial imitation or exaggeration; all great gifts have the fatality of crushing many weaker forces and germs, and of laying waste all nature around them. The happiest arrangement in the development of an art is for several geniuses mutually to hold one another within bounds; in this strife it generally happens that light and air are also granted to the weaker and more delicate natures.

159.

Art Dangerous for the Artist. – When art takes strong hold of an individual it draws him back to the contemplation of those times when art flourished best, and it has then a retrograde effect. The artist grows more and more to reverence sudden inspirations; he believes in gods and daemons, he spiritualises all nature, hates science, is changeable in his moods like the ancients, and longs for an overthrow of all existing conditions which are not favourable to art, and does this with the impetuosity and unreasonableness of a child. Now, in himself, the artist is already a backward nature, because he halts at a game that belongs properly to youth and childhood; to this is added the fact that he is educated back into former times. Thus there gradually arises a fierce antagonism between him and his contemporaries, and a sad ending; according to the accounts of the ancients, Homer and Aeschylus spent their last years, and died, in melancholy.

160.

Created Individuals. – When it is said that the dramatist (and the artist above all) *creates* real characters, it is a fine deception and exaggeration, in the existence and propagation of which art celebrates one of its unconscious but at the same time abundant triumphs. As a matter of fact, we do not understand much about a real, living man, and we generalise very superficially when we ascribe to him this and that character; this *very imperfect* attitude of ours towards man is represented by the poet, inasmuch as he makes into men (in this sense 'creates') outlines as *superficial* as our knowledge of man is superficial. There is a great deal of delusion about these created characters of artists; they are by no means living productions of nature, but are like painted men, somewhat too thin, they will not bear a close inspection. And when it is said that the character of the ordinary living being contradicts itself frequently, and that the one created by the dramatist is the original model conceived by nature, this is quite wrong. A genuine man is something absolutely *necessary* (even in those so-called contradictions), but we do not always recognise this necessity. The imaginary man, the phantasm, signifies something necessary, but only to those who understand a real man only in a crude, unnatural simplification, so that a few strong, oft-repeated traits, with a great deal of light and shade and half-light about them, I amply satisfy their notions. They are, therefore, ready to treat the phantasm as a genuine, necessary man, because with real men they are accustomed to regard a phantasm, an outline, an intentional abbreviation as the whole. That the painter and the sculptor express the 'idea' of man is a vain imagination and delusion; whoever says this is in subjection to the eye, for this only sees the surface, the epidermis of the human body – the inward body, however, is equally a part of the idea. Plastic art wishes to make character visible on the surface; histrionic art employs speech for the same purpose, it reflects character in sounds. Art starts from the natural *ignorance* of man about his interior condition (in body and character); it is not meant for philosophers or natural scientists.

161.

The Over-valuation of Self in the Belief in Artists and Philosophers. – We are all prone to think that the excellence of a work of art or of an artist is proved when it moves and touches us. But there *our own excellence* in judgement and sensibility must have been proved first, which is not the case. In all plastic art, who had greater power to effect a charm than Bernini, who made a greater effect than the orator that appeared after Demosthenes introduced the Asiatic style and gave it a predominance which lasted throughout two centuries? This predominance during whole centuries is not a proof of the excellence and enduring validity of a style; therefore we must not be too certain in our good opinion of any artist – this is not only belief in the truthfulness of our sensations but also in the infallibility of our judgement, whereas judgement or sensation, or even both, may be too coarse or too fine, exaggerated or crude. Neither are the blessings and blissfulness of a philosophy or of a religion proofs of its truth; just as little as the happiness which an insane person derives from his fixed idea is a proof of the reasonableness of this idea.

162.

The Cult of Genius for the sake of Vanity. – Because we think well of ourselves, but nevertheless do not imagine that we are capable of the conception of one of Raphael's pictures or of a scene such as those of one of Shakespeare's dramas, we persuade ourselves that the faculty for doing this is quite extraordinarily wonderful, a very rare case, or, if we are religiously inclined, a grace from above. Thus the cult of genius fosters our vanity, our self-love, for it is only when we think of it as very far removed from us, as a *miraculum*, that it does not wound us (even Goethe, who was free from envy, called Shakespeare a star of the farthest heavens, whereby we are reminded of the line 'die Sterne, die begehrt man nicht'[11]). But, apart from those suggestions of our vanity, the activity of a genius does not seem so radically different from the activity of a mechanical inventor, of an astronomer or historian or strategist. All these forms of activity are explicable if we realise men whose minds are active in one special direction, who make use of everything as material, who always eagerly study their own inward life and that of others, who find types and incitements everywhere, who never weary in the employment of their means. Genius does nothing but learn how to lay stones, then to build, always to seek for material and always to work upon it. Every human activity is marvellously complicated, and not only that of genius, but it is no 'miracle'. Now whence comes the belief that genius is found only in artists, orators, and philosophers, that they alone have 'intuition' (by which we credit them with a kind of magic glass by means of which they see straight into one's 'being')? It is clear that men only speak of genius where the workings of a great intellect are most agreeable to them and they have no desire to feel envious. To call any one 'divine' is as much as saying 'here we have no occasion for rivalry'. Thus it is that everything completed and perfect is stared at, and everything incomplete is undervalued. Now nobody can see how the work of an artist has *developed*; that is its advantage, for everything of which the development is seen is looked on coldly. The perfected art of representation precludes all thought of its development, it tyrannises as a present perfection. For this reason artists of representation are especially held to be possessed of genius, but not scientific men. In reality, however, the former valuation and the latter under-valuation are only puerilities of reason.

---

11 The allusion is to Goethe's lines:

Die Sterne, die begehrt man nicht,
Man freut sick ihrer Pracht.

We do not want the stars themselves,
Their brilliancy delights our hearts. – J. M. K.

163.

The Earnestness of Handicraft. – Do not talk of gifts, of inborn talents! We could mention great men of all kinds who were but little gifted. But they *obtained* greatness, became 'geniuses' (as they are called), through qualities of the lack of which nobody who is conscious of them likes to speak. They all had that thorough earnestness for work which learns first how to form the different parts perfectly before it ventures to make a great whole; they gave themselves time for this, because they took more pleasure in doing small, accessory things well than in the effect of a dazzling whole. For instance, the recipe for becoming a good novelist is easily given, but the carrying out of the recipe presupposes qualities which we are in the habit of overlooking when we say, 'I have not sufficient talent.' Make a hundred or more sketches of novel-plots, none more than two pages long, but of such clearness that every word in them is necessary; write down anecdotes every day until you learn to find the most pregnant, most effective form; never weary of collecting and delineating human types and X characters; above all, narrate things as often as possible and listen to narrations with a sharp eye and ear for the effect upon other people present; travel like a landscape painter and a designer of costumes; take from different sciences everything that is artistically effective, if it be well represented; finally, meditate on the motives for human actions, scorn not even the smallest point of instruction on this subject, and collect similar matters by day and night. Spend some ten years in these various exercises: then the creations of your study may be allowed to see the light of day. But what do most people do, on the contrary? They do not begin with the part, but with the whole. Perhaps they make one good stroke, excite attention, and ever afterwards their work grows worse and worse, for good, natural reasons. But sometimes, when intellect and character are lacking for the formation of such an artistic career, fate and necessity take the place of these qualities and lead the future master step by step through all the phases of his craft.

164.

The Danger and the Gain in the Cult of Genius. – The belief in great, superior, fertile minds is not necessarily, but still very frequently, connected with that wholly or partly religious superstition that those spirits are of superhuman origin and possess certain marvellous faculties, by means of which they obtained their knowledge in ways quite different from the rest of mankind. They are credited with having an immediate insight into the nature of the world, through a peep-hole in the mantle of the phenomenon as it were, and it is believed that, without the trouble and severity of science, by virtue of this marvellous prophetic sight, they could impart something final and decisive about mankind and the world. So long as there are still believers in miracles in the world of knowledge it may perhaps be admitted that the believers themselves derive a benefit therefrom, inasmuch as by their absolute subjection to great minds they obtain the best discipline and schooling for their own minds during the period of development. On the other hand, it may at least be questioned whether the superstition of genius, of its privileges and special faculties, is useful for a genius himself when it implants itself in him. In any case it is a dangerous sign when man shudders at his own self, be it that famous Caesarian shudder or the shudder of genius which applies to this case, when the incense of sacrifice, which by rights is offered to a God alone, penetrates into the brain of the genius, so that he begins to waver and to look upon himself as something superhuman. The slow consequences are: the feeling of irresponsibility, the exceptional rights, the belief that mere intercourse with him confers a favour, and frantic rage at any attempt to compare him with others or even to place him below them and to bring into prominence whatever is unsuccessful in his work. Through the fact that he ceases to criticise himself one pinion after another falls out of his plumage – that superstition undermines the foundation of his strength and even makes him a hypocrite after his power has failed him. For great minds it is, therefore, perhaps better when they come to an understanding about their strength and its source, when they comprehend what purely human qualities are mingled in them, what a combination they are of fortunate conditions: thus once it was continual energy, a decided application to individual aims, great personal courage, and then the good fortune of an education, which at an early period provided the best teachers, examples, and methods. Assuredly, if its aim is to make the greatest possible *effect*, abstruseness has always done much for itself and that gift of partial insanity; for at all times that power has been admired and envied by means of which men were deprived of will and imbued with the fancy that they were preceded by supernatural leaders. Truly, men are exalted and inspired by the belief that some one among them is endowed with supernatural powers, and in this respect insanity, as Plato says, has brought the greatest blessings to mankind. In a few rare cases this form of insanity may also have been the means by which an all-round exuberant nature was kept within bounds; in individual life the imaginings of frenzy frequently exert the virtue of remedies which are poisons in themselves; but in every 'genius' that believes in his own divinity the poison shows itself at last in the same proportion as the 'genius' grows old; we need but recollect the example of Napoleon, for it was most assuredly through his faith in himself and his star, and through his scorn of mankind, that he grew to that mighty unity which distinguished him from all modern men, until at last, however, this faith developed into an almost insane fatalism, robbed him of his quickness of comprehension and penetration, and was the cause of his downfall.

165.

Genius and Nullity. – It is precisely the *original* artists, those who create out of their own heads, who in certain circumstances can bring forth complete *emptiness* and husk, whilst the more dependent natures, the so-called talented ones, are full of memories of all manner of goodness, and even in a state of weakness produce something tolerable. But if the original ones are abandoned by themselves, memory renders them no assistance; they become empty.

166.

The Public. – The people really demand nothing more from tragedy than to be deeply affected, in order to have a good cry occasionally; the artist, on the contrary, who sees the new tragedy, takes pleasure in the clever technical inventions and tricks, in the management and distribution of the material, in the novel arrangement of old motives and old ideas. His attitude is the aesthetic attitude towards a work of art, that of the creator; the one first described, with regard solely to the material, is that of the people. Of the individual who stands between the two nothing need be said: he is neither 'people' nor artist, and does not know what he wants – therefore his pleasure is also clouded and insignificant.

167.

The Artistic Education of the Public. – If the same *motif* is not employed in a hundred ways by different masters, the public never learns to get beyond their interest in the subject; but at last, when it is well acquainted with the *motif* through countless different treatments, and no longer finds in it any charm of novelty or excitement, it will then begin to grasp and enjoy the various shades and delicate new inventions in its treatment.

168.

The Artist and his Followers must keep in Step. – The progress from one grade of style to another must be so slow that not only the artists but also the auditors and spectators can follow it and know exactly what is going on. Otherwise there will suddenly appear that great chasm between the artist, who creates his work upon a height apart, and the public, who cannot rise up to that height and finally sinks discontentedly deeper. For when the artist no longer raises his public it rapidly sinks downwards, and its fall is the deeper and more dangerous in proportion to the height to which genius has carried it, like the eagle, out of whose talons a tortoise that has been borne up into the clouds falls to its destruction.

169.

The Source of the Comic Element. – If we consider that for many thousands of years man was an animal that was susceptible in the highest degree to fear, and that everything sudden and unexpected had to find him ready for battle, perhaps even ready for death; that even later, in social relations, all security was based on the expected, on custom in thought and action, we need not be surprised that at everything sudden and unexpected in word and deed, if it occurs without danger or injury, man becomes exuberant and passes over into the very opposite of fear – the terrified, trembling, crouching being shoots upward, stretches itself: man laughs. This transition from momentary fear into short-lived exhilaration is called the *Comic.* On the other hand, in the tragic phenomenon, man passes quickly from great enduring exuberance into great fear; but as amongst mortals great and lasting exuberance is much rarer than the cause for fear, there is far more comedy than tragedy in the world; we laugh much oftener than we are agitated.

170.

The Artist's Ambition. – The Greek artists, the tragedians for instance, composed in order to conquer; their whole art cannot be imagined without rivalry – the good Hesiodian Eris, Ambition, gave wings to their genius. This ambition further demanded that their work should achieve the greatest excellence *in their own eyes*, as they understood excellence, *without any regard* for the reigning taste and the general opinion about excellence in a work of art; and thus it was long before Aeschylus and Euripides achieved any success, until at last they *educated* judges of art, who valued their work according to the standards which they themselves appointed. Hence they strove for victory over rivals according to their own valuation, they really wished to be more excellent; they demanded assent from without to this self-valuation, the confirmation of this verdict. To achieve honour means in this case 'to make one's self superior to others, and to desire that this should be recognised publicly'. Should the former condition be wanting, and the latter nevertheless desired, it is then called *vanity*. Should the latter be lacking and not missed, then it is named *pride*.

171.

What is Needful to a Work of Art. – Those who talk so much about the needful factors of a work of art exaggerate; if they are artists they do so *in majorem artis gloriam*, if they are laymen, from ignorance. The form of a work of art, which gives speech to their thoughts and is, therefore, their mode of talking, is always somewhat uncertain, like all kinds of speech. The sculptor can add or omit many little traits, as can also the exponent, be he an actor or, in music, a performer or conductor. These many little traits and finishing touches afford him pleasure one day and none the next, they exist more for the sake of the artist than the art; for he also has occasionally need of sweetmeats and playthings to prevent him from becoming morose with the severity and self-restraint which the representation of the dominant idea demands from him.

172.

To Cause the Master to be Forgotten. – The pianoforte player who executes the work of a master will have played best if he has made his audience forget the master, and if it seemed as if he were relating a story from his own life or just passing through some experience. Assuredly, if he is of no importance, every one will abhor the garrulity with which he talks about his own life. Therefore he must know how to influence his hearer's imagination favourably towards himself. Hereby are explained all the weaknesses and follies of 'the virtuoso'.

173.

Corriger La Fortune. – There are unfortunate accidents in the lives of great artists, which compel the painter, for instance, to sketch out his most important picture only as a passing thought, or such as obliged Beethoven to leave behind him only the insufficient pianoforte score of many great sonatas (as in the great B flat). In these cases the artist of a later day must endeavour to fill out the life of the great man – what, for instance, he would do who, as master of all orchestral effects, would call into life that symphony which has fallen into the piano-trance.

174.

Reducing. – Many things, events, or persons, cannot bear treatment on a small scale. The Laocoon group cannot be reduced to a knick-knack; great size is necessary to it. But more seldom still does anything that is naturally small bear enlargement; for which reason biographers succeed far oftener in representing a great man as small than a small one as great.

175.

Sensuousness in Present-day Art. – Artists nowadays frequently miscalculate when they count on the sensuous effect of their works, for their spectators or hearers have no longer a fully sensuous nature, and, quite contrary to the artist's intention, his work produces in them a 'holiness' of feeling which is closely related to boredom. Their sensuousness begins, perhaps, just where that of the artist ceases; they meet, therefore, only at one point at the most.

176.

Shakespeare as a Moralist. – Shakespeare meditated much on the passions, and on account of his temperament had probably a close acquaintance with many of them (dramatists are in general rather wicked men). He could, however not talk on the subject, like Montaigne, but put his observations thereon into the mouths of impassioned figures, which is contrary to nature, certainly, but makes his dramas so rich in thought that they cause all others to seem poor in comparison and readily arouse a general aversion to them. Schiller's reflections (which are almost always based on erroneous or trivial fancies) are just theatrical reflections, and as such are very effective; whereas Shakespeare's reflections do honour to his model, Montaigne, and contain quite serious thoughts in polished form, but on that account are too remote and refined for the eyes of the theatrical public, and are consequently ineffective.

177.

Securing a Good Hearing. – It is not sufficient to know how to play well; one must also know how to secure a good hearing. A violin in the hand of the greatest master gives only a little squeak when the place where it is heard is too large; the master may then be mistaken for any bungler.

178.

The Incomplete as the Effective. – Just as figures in relief make such a strong impression on the imagination because they seem in the act of emerging from the wall and only stopped by some sudden hindrance; so the relief-like, incomplete representation of a thought, or a whole philosophy, is sometimes more effective than its exhaustive amplification – more is left for the investigation of the onlooker, he is incited to the further study of that which stands out before him in such strong light and shade; he is prompted to think out the subject, and even to overcome the hindrance which hitherto prevented it from emerging clearly.

179.

Against the Eccentric. – When art arrays itself in the most shabby material it is most easily recognised as art.

180.

Collective Intellect. – A good author possesses not only his own intellect, but also that of his friends.

181.

Different Kinds of Mistakes. – The misfortune of acute and clear authors is that people consider them as shallow and therefore do not devote any effort to them; and the good fortune of obscure writers is that the reader makes an effort to understand them and places the delight in his own zeal to their credit.

182.

Relation to Science. – None of the people have any real interest in a science, who only begin to be enthusiastic about it when they themselves have made discoveries in it.

183.

The Key. – The single thought on which an eminent man sets a great value, arousing the derision and laughter of the masses, is for him a key to hidden treasures; for them, however, it is nothing *more* than a piece of old iron.

184.

Untranslatable. – It is neither the best nor the worst parts of a book which are untranslatable.

185.

Authors' Paradoxes. – The so-called paradoxes of an author to which a reader objects are often not in the author's book at all, but in the reader's head.

186.

Wit. – The wittiest authors produce a scarcely noticeable smile.

187.

Antithesis. – Antithesis is the narrow gate through which error is fondest of sneaking to the truth.

188.

Thinkers as Stylists. – Most thinkers write badly, because they communicate not only their thoughts, but also the thinking of them.

189.

Thoughts in Poetry. – The poet conveys his thoughts ceremoniously in the vehicle of rhythm, usually because they are not able to go on foot.

190.

The Sin against the Reader's Intellect. – When an author renounces his talent in order merely to put himself on a level with the reader, he commits the only deadly sin which the latter will never forgive, should he notice anything of it. One may say everything that is bad about a person, but in the manner *in which* it is said one must know how to revive his vanity anew.

191.

The Limits of Uprightness. – Even the most upright author lets fall a word too much when he wishes to round off a period.

192.

The Best Author. – The best author will be he who is ashamed to become one.

193.

Draconian Law against Authors. – One should regard authors as criminals who only obtain acquittal or mercy in the rarest cases – that would be a remedy for books becoming too rife.

194.

The Fools of Modern Culture. – The fools of mediaeval courts correspond to our *feuilleton* writers; they are the same kind of men, semi-rational, witty, extravagant, foolish, sometimes there only for the purpose of lessening the pathos of the outlook with fancies and chatter, and of drowning with their clamour the far too deep and solemn chimes of great events; they were formerly in the service of princes and nobles, now they are in the service of parties (since a large portion of the old obsequiousness in the intercourse of the people with their prince still survives in party-feeling and party-discipline). Modern literary men, however, are generally very similar to the *feuilleton* writers, they are the 'fools of modern culture', whom one judges more leniently when one does not regard them as fully responsible beings. To look upon writing as a regular profession should justly be regarded as a form of madness.

195.

After the Example of the Greeks. – It is a great hindrance to knowledge at present that, owing to centuries of exaggeration of feeling, all words have become vague and inflated. The higher stage of culture, which is under the sway (though not under the tyranny) of knowledge, requires great sobriety of feeling and thorough concentration of words – on which points the Greeks in the time of Demosthenes set an example to us. Exaggeration is a distinguishing mark of all modern writings, and even when they are simply written the expressions therein are still *felt* as *too* eccentric. Careful reflection, conciseness, coldness, plainness, even carried intentionally to the farthest limits – in a word, suppression of feeling and taciturnity – these are the only remedies. For the rest, this cold manner of writing and feeling is now very attractive, as a contrast; and to be sure there is a new danger therein. For intense cold is as good a stimulus as a high degree of warmth.

196.

Good Narrators, Bad Explainers. – In good narrators there is often found an admirable psychological sureness and logicalness, as far as these qualities can be observed in the actions of their personages, in positively ludicrous contrast to their inexperienced pyschological reasoning, so that their culture appears to be as extraordinarily high one moment as it seems regrettably defective the next. It happens far too frequently that they give an evidently false explanation of their own heroes and their actions – of this there is no doubt, however improbable the thing may appear. It is quite likely that the greatest pianoforte player has thought but little about the technical conditions and the special virtues, drawbacks, usefulness, and tractability of each finger (dactylic ethics), and makes big mistakes whenever he speaks of such things.

197.

The Writings of Acquaintances and their Readers. – We read the writings of our acquaintances (friends and enemies) in a double sense, inasmuch as our perception constantly whispers, 'That is something of himself, a remembrance of his inward being, his experiences, his talents,' and at the same time another kind of perception endeavours to estimate the profit of the work in itself, what valuation it merits apart from its author, how far it will enrich knowledge. These two manners of reading and estimating interfere with each other, as may naturally be supposed. And a conversation with a friend will only bear good fruit of knowledge when both think only of the matter under consideration and forget that they are friends.

198.

Rhythmical Sacrifice. – Good writers alter the rhythm of many a period merely because they do not credit the general reader with the ability to comprehend the measure followed by the period in its first version; thus they make it easier for the reader, by giving the preference to the better known rhythms. This regard for the rhythmical incapacity of the modern reader has already called forth many a sigh, for much has been sacrificed to it. Does not the same thing happen to good musicians?

199.

The Incomplete as an Artistic Stimulus. – The incomplete is often more effective than perfection, and this is the case with eulogies. To effect their purpose a stimulating incompleteness is necessary, as an irrational element, which calls up a sea before the hearer's imagination, and, like a mist, conceals the opposite coast, i.e. the limits of the object of praise. If the well-known merits of a person are referred to and described at length and in detail, it always gives rise to the suspicion that these are his only merits. The perfect eulogist takes his stand above the person praised, he appears to *overlook* him. Therefore complete praise has a weakening effect.

200.

Precautions in Writing and Teaching. – Whoever has once written and has been seized with the passion for writing learns from almost all that he does and experiences that which is literally communicable. He thinks no longer of himself, but of the author and his public; he desires insight into things; but not for his own use. He who teaches is mostly incapable of doing anything for his own good: he is always thinking of the good of his scholars, and all knowledge delights him only in so far as he is able to teach it. He comes at last to regard himself as a medium of knowledge, and above all as a means thereto, so that he has lost all serious consideration for himself.

201.

The Necessity for Bad Authors. – There will always be a need of bad authors; for they meet the taste of readers of an undeveloped, immature age – these have their requirements as well as mature readers. If human life were of greater length, the number of mature individuals would be greater than that of the immature, or at least equally great; but, as it is, by far the greater number die too young: i.e. there are always many more undeveloped intellects with bad taste. These demand, with the greater impetuosity of youth, the satisfaction of their needs, and they *insist* on having bad authors.

202.

Too Near and too Far. – The reader and the author very often do not understand each other, because the author knows his theme too well and finds it almost slow, so that he omits the examples, of which he knows hundreds; the reader, however, is interested in the subject, and is liable to consider it as badly proved if examples are lacking.

203.

A Vanished Preparation for Art. – Of everything that was practised in public schools, the thing of greatest value was the exercise in Latin style – this was an exercise in art, whilst all other occupations aimed only at the acquirement of knowledge. It is a barbarism to put German composition before it, for there is no typical German style developed by public oratory; but if there is a desire to advance practice in thought by means of German composition, then it is certainly better for the time being to pay no attention to style, to separate the practice in thought, therefore, from the practice in reproduction. The latter should confine itself to the various modes of presenting a given subject, and should not concern itself with the independent finding of a subject. The mere presentment of a given subject was the task of the Latin style, for which the old teachers possessed a long vanished delicacy of ear. Formerly, whoever learned to write well in a modern language had to thank this practice for the acquirement (now we are obliged to go to school to the older French writers). But yet more: he obtained an idea of the loftiness and difficulty of form, and was prepared for art in the only right way: by practice.

204.

Darkness and Over-Brightness Side by Side. – Authors who, in general, do not understand how to express their thoughts clearly are fond of choosing, in detail, the strongest, most exaggerated distinctions and superlatives – thereby is produced an effect of light, which is like torchlight in intricate forest paths.

205.

Literary Painting. – An important object will be best described if the colours for the painting are taken out of the object itself, as a chemist does, and then employed like an artist, so that the drawing develops from the outlines and transitions of the colours. Thus the painting acquires something of the entrancing natural element which gives such importance to the object itself.

206.

Books which Teach how to Dance. – There are authors who, by representing the impossible as possible, and by talking of morality and cleverness as if both were merely moods and humours assumed at will, produce a feeling of exuberant freedom, as if man stood on tiptoe and were compelled to dance from sheer, inward delight.

207.

Unfinished Thoughts. – Just as not only manhood, but also youth and childhood have a value *per se*, and are not to be looked upon merely as passages and bridges, so also unfinished thoughts have their value. For this reason we must not torment a poet with subtle explanations, but must take pleasure in the uncertainty of his horizon, as if the way to further thoughts were still open. We stand on the threshold; we wait as for the digging up of a treasure, it is as if a well of profundity were about to be discovered. The poet anticipates something of the thinker's pleasure in the discovery of a leading thought, and makes us covetous, so that we give chase to it; but it flutters past our head and exhibits the loveliest butterfly-wings – and yet it escapes us.

208.

The Book Grown almost into a Human Being. – Every author is surprised anew at the way in which his book, as soon as he has sent it out, continues to live a life of its own; it seems to him as if one part of an insect had been cut off and now went on its own way. Perhaps he forgets it almost entirely, perhaps he rises above the view expressed therein, perhaps even he understands it no longer, and has lost that impulse upon which he soared at the time he conceived the book; meanwhile it seeks its readers, inflames life, pleases, horrifies, inspires new works, becomes the soul of designs and actions – in short, it lives like a creature endowed with mind and soul, and yet is no human being. The happiest fate is that of the author who, as an old man, is able to say that all there was in him of life-inspiring, strengthening, exalting, enlightening thoughts and feelings still lives on in his writings, and that he himself now only represents the grey ashes, whilst the fire has been kept alive and spread out. And if we consider that every human action, not only a book, is in some way or other the cause of other actions, decisions, and thoughts; that everything that happens is inseparably connected with everything that is going to happen, we recognise the real *immortality*, that of movement – that which has once moved is enclosed and immortalised in the general union of all existence, like an insect within a piece of amber.

209.

Joy in Old Age. – The thinker, as likewise the artist, who has put his best self into his works, feels an almost malicious joy when he sees how mind and body are being slowly damaged and destroyed by time, as if from a dark corner he were spying a thief at his money-chest, knowing all the time that it was empty and his treasures in safety.

210.

Quiet Fruitfulness. – The born aristocrats of the mind are not in too much of a hurry; their creations appear and fall from the tree on some quiet autumn evening, without being rashly desired, instigated, or pushed aside by new matter. The unceasing desire to create is vulgar, and betrays envy, jealousy, and ambition. If a man is something, it is not really necessary for him to do anything – and yet he does a great deal. There is a human species higher even than the 'productive' man.

211.

Achilles and Homer. – It is always like the case of Achilles and Homer – the one *has* the experiences and sensations, the other *describes* them. A genuine author only puts into words the feelings and adventures of others, he is an artist, and divines much from the little he has experienced. Artists are by no means creatures of great passion; but they frequently *represent* themselves as such with the unconscious feeling that their depicted passion will be better believed in if their own life gives credence to their experience in these affairs. They need only let themselves go, not control themselves, and give free play to their anger and their desires, and every one will immediately cry out, 'How passionate he is!' But the deeply stirring passion that consumes and often destroys the individual is another matter: those who have really experienced it do not describe it in dramas, harmonies or romances. Artists are frequently *unbridled* individuals, in so far as they are not artists, but that is a different thing.

212.

Old Doubts about the Effect of Art. – Should pity and fear really be unburdened through tragedy, as Aristotle would have it, so that the hearers return home colder and quieter? Should ghost-stories really make us less fearful and superstitious? In the case of certain physical processes, in the satisfaction of love, for instance, it is true that with the fulfilment of a need there follows an alleviation and temporary decrease in the impulse. But fear and pity are not in this sense the needs of particular organs which require to be relieved. And in time every instinct is even *strengthened* by practice in its satisfaction, in spite of that periodical mitigation. It might be possible that in each single case pity and fear would be soothed and relieved by tragedy; nevertheless, they might, on the whole, be increased by tragic influences, and Plato would be right in saying that tragedy makes us altogether more timid and susceptible. The tragic poet himself would then of necessity acquire a gloomy and fearful view of the world, and a yielding, irritable, tearful soul; it would also agree with Plato's view if the tragic poets, and likewise the entire part of the community that derived particular pleasure from them, degenerated into ever greater licentiousness and intemperance. But what right, indeed, has our age to give an answer to that great question of Plato's as to the moral influence of art? If we even had art – where have we an influence, *any kind* of an art-influence?

213.

Pleasure in Nonsense. – How can we take pleasure in nonsense? But wherever there is laughter in the world this is the case: it may even be said that almost everywhere where there is happiness, there is found pleasure in nonsense. The transformation of experience into its opposite, of the suitable into the unsuitable, the obligatory into the optional (but in such a manner that this process produces no injury and is only imagined in jest), is a pleasure; for it temporarily liberates us from the yoke of the obligatory, suitable and experienced, in which we usually find our pitiless masters; we play and laugh when the expected (which generally causes fear and expectancy) happens without bringing any injury. It is the pleasure felt by slaves in the Saturnalian feasts.

214.

The Ennobling of Reality. – Through the fact that in the aphrodisiac impulse men discerned a godhead and with adoring gratitude felt it working within themselves, this emotion has in the course of time become imbued with higher conceptions, and has thereby been materially ennobled. Thus certain nations, by virtue of this art of idealisation, have created great aids to culture out of diseases – the Greeks, for instance, who in earlier centuries suffered from great nervous epidemics (like epilepsy and St. Vitus' Dance), and developed out of them the splendid type of the Bacchante. The Greeks, however, enjoyed an astonishingly high degree of health – their secret was, to revere even disease as a god, if it only possessed *power*.

215.

Music. – Music by and for itself is not so portentous for our inward nature, so deeply moving, that it ought to be looked upon as the *direct* language of the feelings; but its ancient union with poetry has infused so much symbolism into rhythmical movement, into loudness and softness of tone, that we now *imagine* it speaks directly *to* and comes *from* the inward nature. Dramatic music is only possible when the art of harmony has acquired an immense range of symbolical means, through song, opera, and a hundred attempts at description by sound. 'Absolute music' is either form *per se*, in the rude condition of music, when playing in time and with various degrees of strength gives pleasure, or the symbolism of form which speaks to the understanding even without poetry, after the two arts were joined finally together after long development and the musical form had been woven about with threads of meaning and feeling. People who are backward in musical development can appreciate a piece of harmony merely as execution, whilst those who are advanced will comprehend it symbolically. No music is deep and full of meaning in itself, it does not speak of 'will', of the 'thing-in-itself'; that could be imagined by the intellect only in an age which had conquered for musical symbolism the entire range of inner life. It was the intellect itself that first *gave* this meaning to sound, just as it also gave meaning to the relation between lines and masses in architecture, but which in itself is quite foreign to mechanical laws.

216.

Gesture and Speech. – Older than speech is the imitation of gestures, which is carried on unconsciously and which, in the general repression of the language of gesture and trained control of the muscles, is still so great that we cannot look at a face moved by emotion without feeling an agitation of our own face (it may be remarked that feigned yawning excites real yawning in any one who sees it). The imitated gesture leads the one who imitates back to the sensation it expressed in the face or body of the one imitated. Thus men learned to understand one another, thus the child still learns to understand the mother. Generally speaking, painful sensations may also have been expressed by gestures, and the pain which caused them (for instance, tearing the hair, beating the breast, forcible distortion and straining of the muscles of the face). On the other hand, gestures of joy were themselves joyful and lent themselves easily to the communication of the understanding; (laughter, as the expression of the feeling when being tickled, serves also for the expression of other pleasurable sensations). As soon as men understood each other by gestures, there could be established a *symbolism* of gestures; I mean, an understanding could be arrived at respecting the language of accents, so that first *accent* and gesture (to which it was symbolically added) were produced, and later on the accent alone. In former times there happened very frequently that which now happens in the development of music, especially of dramatic music – while music, without explanatory dance and pantomime (language of gesture), is at first only empty sound, but by long familiarity with that combination of music and movement the ear becomes schooled into instant interpretation of the figures of sound, and finally attains a height of quick understanding, where it has no longer any need of visible movement and *understands* the sound-poet without it. It is then called absolute music, that is music in which, without further help, everything is symbolically understood.

217.

The Spiritualising of Higher Art. – By virtue of extraordinary intellectual exercise through the art-development of the new music, our ears have been growing more intellectual. For this reason we can now endure a much greater volume of sound, much more 'noise', because we are far better practised in listening for the *sense* in it than were our ancestors. As a matter of fact, all our senses have been somewhat blunted, because they immediately look for the sense; that is, they ask what 'it means' and not what 'it is' – such a blunting betrays itself, for instance, in the absolute dominion of the temperature of sounds; for ears which still make the finer distinctions, between *cis* and *des*, for instance, are now amongst the exceptions. In this respect our ear has grown coarser. And then the ugly side of the world, the one originally hostile to the senses, has been conquered for music; its power has been immensely widened, especially in the expression of the noble, the terrible, and the mysterious: our music now gives utterance to things which had formerly no tongue. In the same way certain painters have rendered the eye more intellectual, and have gone far beyond that which was formerly called pleasure in colour and form. Here, too, that side of the world originally considered as ugly has been conquered by the artistic intellect. What results from all this? The more capable of thought that eye and ear become, the more they approach the limit where they become senseless, the seat of pleasure is moved into the brain, the organs of the senses themselves become dulled and weak, the symbolical takes more and more the place of the actual – and thus we arrive at barbarism in this way as surely as in any other. In the meantime we may say: the world is uglier than ever, but it *represents* a more beautiful world than has ever existed. But the more the amber-scent of meaning is dispersed and evaporated, the rarer become those who perceive it, and the remainder halt at what is ugly and endeavour to enjoy it direct, an aim, however, which they never succeed in attaining. Thus, in

Germany there is a twofold direction of musical development, here a throng of ten thousand with ever higher, finer demands, ever listening more and more for the 'it means', and there the immense countless mass which yearly grows more incapable of understanding what is important even in the form of sensual ugliness, and which therefore turns ever more willingly to what in music is ugly and foul in itself, that is, to the basely sensual.

218.

A Stone is More of a Stone than Formerly. – As a general rule we no longer understand architecture, at least by no means in the same way as we understand music. We have outgrown the symbolism of lines and figures, just as we are no longer accustomed to the sound effects of rhetoric, and have not absorbed this kind of mother's milk of culture since our first moment of life. Everything in a Greek or Christian building originally had a meaning, and referred to a higher order of things; this feeling of inexhaustible meaning enveloped the edifice like a mystic veil. Beauty was only a secondary consideration in the system, without in any way materially injuring the fundamental sentiment of the mysteriously-exalted, the divinely and magically consecrated; at the most, beauty *tempered horror* – but this horror was everywhere presupposed. What is the beauty of a building now? The same thing as the beautiful face of a stupid woman, a kind of mask.

219.

The Religious Source of the Newer Music. – Soulful music arose out of the Catholicism re-established after the Council of Trent, through Palestrina, who endowed the newly awakened, earnest, and deeply moved spirit with sound; later on, in Bach, it appeared also in Protestantism, as far as this had been deepened by the Pietists and released from its originally dogmatic character. The supposition and necessary preparation for both origins is the familiarity with music, which existed during and before the Renaissance, namely that learned occupation with music, which was really scientific pleasure in the masterpieces of harmony and voice-training. On the other hand, the opera must have preceded it, wherein the layman made his protest against a music that had grown too learned and cold, and endeavoured to re-endow Polyhymnia with a soul. Without the change to that deeply religious sentiment, without the dying away of the inwardly moved temperament, music would have remained learned or operatic; the spirit of the counter-reformation is the spirit of modern music (for that pietism in Bach's music is also a kind of counter-reformation). So deeply are we indebted to the religious life. Music was the counter-reformation in the field of art; to this belongs also the later painting of the Caracci and Caravaggi, perhaps also the baroque style, in *any* case more than the architecture of the Renaissance or of antiquity. And we might still ask: if our newer music could move stones, would it build them up into antique architecture? I very much doubt it. For that which predominates in this music, affections, pleasure in exalted, highly-strained sentiments, the desire to be alive at any cost, the quick change of feeling, the strong relief-effects of light and shade, the combination of the ecstatic and the naive – all this has already reigned in the plastic arts and created new laws of style: but it was neither in the time of antiquity nor of the Renaissance.

220.

The Beyond in Art. – It is not without deep pain that we acknowledge the fact that in their loftiest soarings, artists of all ages have exalted and divinely transfigured precisely those ideas which we now recognise as false; they are the glorifiers of humanity's religious and philosophical errors, and they could not have been this without belief in the absolute truth of these errors. But if the belief in such truth diminishes at all, if the rainbow colours at the farthest ends of human knowledge and imagination fade, then this kind of art can never re-flourish, for, like the *Divina Commedia*, Raphael's paintings, Michelangelo's frescoes, and Gothic cathedrals, they indicate not only a cosmic but also a metaphysical meaning in the work of art. Out of all this will grow a touching legend that such an art and such an artistic faith once existed.

221.

Revolution in Poetry. – The strict limit which the French dramatists marked out with regard to unity of action, time and place, construction of style, verse and sentence, selection of words and ideas, was a school as important as that of counterpoint and fugue in the development of modern music or that of the Gorgianic figures in Greek oratory. Such a restriction may appear absurd; nevertheless there is no means of getting out of naturalism except by confining ourselves at first to the strongest (perhaps most arbitrary) means. Thus we gradually learn to walk gracefully on the narrow paths that bridge giddy abysses, and acquire great suppleness of movement as a result, as the history of music proves to our living eyes. Here we see how, step by step, the fetters get looser, until at last they may appear to be altogether thrown off; this *appearance* is the highest achievement of a necessary development in art. In the art of modern poetry there existed no such fortunate, gradual emerging from self-imposed fetters. Lessing held up to scorn in Germany the French form, the only modern form of art, and pointed to Shakespeare; and thus the steadiness of that unfettering was lost and a spring was made into naturalism – that is, back into the beginnings of art. From this Goethe endeavoured to save himself, by always trying to limit himself anew in different ways; but even the most gifted only succeeds by continuously experimenting, if the thread of development has once been broken. It is to the unconsciously revered, if also repudiated, model of French tragedy that Schiller owes his comparative sureness of form, and he remained fairly independent of Lessing (whose dramatic attempts he is well known to have rejected). But after Voltaire the French themselves suddenly lacked the great talents which would have led the development of tragedy out of constraint to that apparent freedom; later on they followed the German example and made a spring into a sort of Rousseau-like state of nature and experiments. It is only necessary to read Voltaire's 'Mahomet' from time to time in order to perceive clearly what European culture has lost through that breaking down of tradition. Once for all, Voltaire was the last of the great dramatists who with Greek proportion controlled his manifold soul, equal even to the greatest storms of tragedy – he was able to do what no German could, because the French nature is much nearer akin to the Greek than is the German; he was also the last great writer who in the wielding of prose possessed the Greek ear, Greek artistic conscientiousness, and Greek simplicity and grace; he was, also, one of the last men able to combine in himself the greatest freedom of mind and an absolutely unrevolutionary way of thinking without being inconsistent and cowardly. Since that time the modern spirit, with its restlessness and its hatred of moderation and restrictions, has obtained the mastery on all sides, let loose at first by the fever of revolution, and then once more putting a bridle on itself when it became filled with fear and horror at itself – but it was the bridle of rigid logic, no longer that of artistic moderation. It is true that through that unfettering for a time we are able to enjoy the poetry of all nations, everything that has sprung up in hidden places, original, wild, wonderfully beautiful and gigantically irregular, from folk-songs up to the 'great barbarian' Shakespeare; we taste the joys of local colour and costume, hitherto unknown to all artistic nations; we make liberal use of the 'barbaric advantages' of our time, which Goethe accentuated against Schiller in order to place the formlessness of his *Faust* in the most favourable light. But for how much longer? The encroaching flood of poetry of all styles and all nations *must* gradually sweep away that magic garden upon which a quiet and hidden growth would still have been possible; all poets must become experimenting imitators, daring copyists, however great their primary strength may be. Eventually, the public, which has lost the habit of seeing the actual artistic fact in the *controlling* of depicting power, in the organising mastery over all art-means, *must* come ever more and more to value power for power's sake, colour for colour's sake, idea for idea's sake, inspiration for inspiration's sake; accordingly it will not enjoy the elements and conditions of the work of art, unless *isolated*, and finally will make the very natural demand that the artist *must* deliver it to them isolated. True, the 'senseless 'fetters of Franco-Greek art have been thrown off, but unconsciously we have grown accustomed to consider all fetters, all restrictions as senseless; and so art moves towards its liberation, but, in so doing, it touches – which is certainly highly edifying – upon all the phases of its beginning, its childhood, its incompleteness, its sometime boldness and excesses – in perishing it interprets its origin and growth. One of the great ones, whose instinct may be relied on and whose theory lacked nothing but thirty years *more* of practice, Lord Byron, once said: that with regard to poetry in general, the more he thought about it the more convinced he was that one and all we are entirely on a wrong track, that we are following an inwardly false revolutionary system, and that either our own generation or the next will yet arrive at this same conviction. It is the same Lord Byron who said that he 'looked upon Shakespeare as the very worst model, although the most extraordinary poet'. And does not Goethe's mature artistic insight in the second half of his life say practically the same thing? – that insight by means of which he made such a bound in advance of whole generations that, generally speaking, it may be said that Goethe's influence has not yet begun, that his time has still to come. Just because his nature held him fast for a long time in the path of the poetical revolution, just because he drank to the dregs of whatsoever new sources, views and expedients had been indirectly discovered through that breaking down of tradition, of all that had been unearthed from under the ruins of art, his later transformation and conversion carries so much weight; it shows that he felt the deepest longing to win back the traditions of art, and to give in fancy the ancient perfection and completeness to the abandoned ruins and colonnades of the temple, with the imagination of the eye at least, should the strength of the arm be found too weak to build where such tremendous powers were needed even to destroy. Thus he lived in art as in the remembrance of the true art, his poetry had become an aid to remembrance, to the understanding of old and long-departed ages of art. With respect to the strength of the new age, his demands could not be satisfied; but the pain this occasioned was amply balanced by the joy that they have been satisfied once, and that we ourselves can still participate in this satisfaction. Not individuals, but more or less ideal masks; no reality, but an allegorical generality; topical characters, local colours toned down and rendered mythical almost to the point of invisibility; contemporary feeling and the problems of contemporary society reduced to the simplest forms, stripped of their attractive, interesting pathological qualities, made *ineffective* in every other but the artistic sense; no new materials and characters, but the old, long-accustomed ones in constant new animation and transformation; that is art, as Goethe *understood* it later, as the Greeks and even the French *practised* it.

222.

What Remains of Art. – It is true that art has a much greater value in the case of certain metaphysical hypotheses, for instance when the belief obtains that the character is unchangeable and that the essence of the world manifests itself continually in all character and action; thus the artist's work becomes the symbol of the *eternally constant*, while according to our views the artist can only endow his picture with temporary value, because man on the whole has developed and is mutable, and even the individual man has nothing fixed and constant. The same thing holds good with another metaphysical hypothesis: assuming that our visible world were only a delusion, as metaphysicians declare, then art would come very near to the real world, for there would then be far too much similarity between the world of appearance and the dream-world of the artist; and the remaining difference would place the meaning of art higher even than the meaning of nature, because art would represent the same forms, the types and models of nature. But those suppositions are false; and what position does art retain after this acknowledgement? Above all, for centuries it has taught us to look upon life in every shape with interest and pleasure and to carry our feelings so far that at last we exclaim, 'Whatever it may be, life is good.' This teaching of art, to take pleasure in existence and to regard human life as a piece of nature, without too vigorous movement, as an object of regular development – this teaching has grown into us; it reappears as an all-powerful need of knowledge. We could renounce art, but we should not therewith forfeit the ability it has taught us – just as we have given up religion, but not the exalting and intensifying of temperament acquired through religion. As the plastic arts and music are the standards of that wealth of feeling really acquired and obtained through religion, so also, after a disappearance of art, the intensity and multiplicity of the joys of life which it had implanted in us would still demand satisfaction. The scientific man is the further development of the artistic man.

223.

The After-glow of Art. – Just as in old age we remember our youth and celebrate festivals of memory, so in a short time mankind will stand towards art: its relation will be that of a *touching memory* of the joys of youth. Never, perhaps, in former ages was art dealt with so seriously and thoughtfully as now when it appears to be surrounded by the magic influence of death. We call to mind that Greek city in southern Italy, which once a year still celebrates its Greek feasts, amidst tears and mourning, that foreign barbarism triumphs ever more and more over the customs its people brought with them into the land; and never has Hellenism been so much appreciated, nowhere has this golden nectar been drunk with so great delight, as amongst these fast disappearing Hellenes. The artist will soon come to be regarded as a splendid relic, and to him, as to a wonderful stranger on whose power and beauty depended the happiness of former ages, there will be paid such honour as is not often enjoyed by one of our race. The best in us is perhaps inherited from the sentiments of former times, to which it is hardly possible for us now to return by direct ways; the sun has already disappeared, but the heavens of our life are still glowing and illumined by it, although we can behold it no longer.

FIFTH DIVISION.

THE SIGNS OF HIGHER AND LOWER CULTURE.

224.

Ennoblement through Degeneration. – History teaches that a race of people is best preserved where the greater number hold one common spirit in consequence of the similarity of their accustomed and indisputable principles: in consequence, therefore, of their common faith. Thus strength is afforded by good and thorough customs, thus is learnt the subjection of the individual, and strenuousness of character becomes a birth gift and afterwards is fostered as a habit. The danger to these communities founded on individuals of strong and similar character is that gradually increasing stupidity through transmission, which follows all stability like its shadow. It is on the more unrestricted, more uncertain and morally weaker individuals that depends the *intellectual progress* of such communities, it is they who attempt all that is new and manifold. Numbers of these perish on account of their weakness, without having achieved any specially visible effect; but generally, particularly when they have descendants, they flare up and from time to time inflict a wound on the stable element of the community. Precisely in this sore and weakened place the community is *inoculated* with something new; but its general strength must be great enough to absorb and assimilate this new thing into its blood. Deviating natures are of the utmost importance wherever there is to be progress. Every wholesale progress must be preceded by a partial weakening. The strongest natures *retain* the type, the weaker ones help it to *develop*. Something similar happens in the case of individuals; a deterioration, a mutilation, even a vice and, above all, a physical or moral loss is seldom without its advantage. For instance, a sickly man in the midst of a warlike and restless race will perhaps have more chance of being alone and thereby growing quieter and wiser, the one-eyed man will possess a stronger eye, the blind man will have a deeper inward sight and will certainly have a keener sense of hearing. In so far it appears to me that the famous Struggle for Existence is not the only point of view from which an explanation can be given of the progress or strengthening of an individual or a race. Rather must two different things converge: firstly, the multiplying of stable strength through mental binding in faith and common feeling; secondly, the possibility of attaining to higher aims, through the fact that there are deviating natures and, in consequence, partial weakening and wounding of the stable strength; it is precisely the weaker nature, as the more delicate and free, that makes all progress at all possible. A people that is crumbling and weak in any one part, but as a whole still strong and healthy, is able to absorb the infection of what is new and incorporate it to its advantage. The task of education in a single individual is this: to plant him so firmly and surely that, as a whole, he can no longer be diverted from his path. Then, however, the educator must wound him, or else make use of the wounds which fate inflicts, and when pain and need have thus arisen, something new and noble can be inoculated into the wounded places. With regard to the state, Machiavelli says that, 'the form of Government is of very small importance, although half-educated people think otherwise. The great aim of State-craft should be duration, which outweighs all else, inasmuch as it is more valuable than liberty.' It is only with securely founded and guaranteed duration that continual development and ennobling inoculation are at all possible. As a rule, however, authority, the dangerous companion of all duration, will rise in opposition to this.

225.

Free-Thinker a Relative Term. – We call that man a free-thinker who thinks otherwise than is expected of him in consideration of his origin, surroundings, position, and office, or by reason of the prevailing contemporary views. He is the exception, fettered minds are the rule; these latter reproach him, saying that his free principles either have their origin in a desire to be remarkable or else cause free actions to be inferred – that is to say, actions which are not compatible with fettered morality. Sometimes it is also said that the cause of such and such free principles may be traced to mental perversity and extravagance; but only malice speaks thus, nor does it believe what it says, but wishes thereby to do an injury, for the free-thinker usually bears the proof of his greater goodness and keenness of intellect written in his face so plainly that the fettered spirits understand it well enough. But the two other derivations of free-thought are honestly intended; as a matter of fact, many free-thinkers are created in one or other of these ways. For this reason, however, the tenets to which they attain in this manner might be truer and more reliable than those of the fettered spirits. In the knowledge of truth, what really matters is the *possession* of it, not the impulse under which it was sought, the way in which it was found. If the free-thinkers are right then the fettered spirits are wrong, and it is a matter of indifference whether the former have reached truth through immorality or the latter hitherto retained hold of untruths through morality. Moreover, it is not essential to the free-thinker that he should hold more correct views, but that he should have liberated himself from what was customary, be it successfully or disastrously. As a rule, however, he will have truth, or at least the spirit of truth-investigation, on his side; he demands reasons, the others demand faith.

226.

The Origin of Faith. – The fettered spirit does not take up his position from conviction, but from habit; he is a Christian, for instance, not because he had a comprehension of different creeds and could take his choice; he is an Englishman, not because he decided for England, but he found Christianity and England ready-made and accepted them without any reason, just as one who is born in a wine-country becomes a wine-drinker. Later on, perhaps, as he was a Christian and an Englishman, he discovered a few reasons in favour of his habit; these reasons may be upset, but he is not therefore upset in his whole position. For instance, let a fettered spirit be obliged to bring forward his reasons against bigamy and then it will be seen whether his holy zeal in favour of monogamy is based upon reason or upon custom. The adoption of guiding principles without reasons is called *faith*.

227.

Conclusions drawn from the Consequences and traced back to Reason and Un-reason. – All states and orders of society, professions, matrimony, education, law: all these find strength and duration only in the faith which the fettered spirits repose in them – that is, in the absence of reasons, or at least in the averting of inquiries as to reasons. The restricted spirits do not willingly acknowledge this, and feel that it is a *pudendum*. Christianity, however, which was very simple in its intellectual ideas, remarked nothing of this *pudendum*, required faith and nothing but faith, and passionately repulsed the demand for reasons; it pointed to the success of faith: 'You will soon feel the advantages of faith,' it suggested, 'and through faith shall ye be saved.' As an actual fact, the State pursues the same course, and every father brings up his son in the same way: 'Only believe this,' he says, 'and you will soon feel the good it does.' This implies, however, that the truth of an opinion is proved by its personal usefulness; the wholesomeness of a doctrine must be a guarantee for its intellectual surety and solidity. It is exactly as if an accused person in a court of law were to say, 'My counsel speaks the whole truth, for only see what is the result of his speech: I shall be acquitted.' Because the fettered spirits retain their principles on account of their usefulness, they suppose that the free spirit also seeks his own advantage in his views and only holds that to be true which is profitable to him. But as he appears to find profitable just the contrary of that which his compatriots or equals find profitable, these latter assume that his principles are dangerous to them; they say or feel, 'He must not be right, for he is injurious to us.'

228.

The Strong, Good Character. – The restriction of views, which habit has made instinct, leads to what is called strength of character. When any one acts from few but always from the same motives, his actions acquire great energy; if these actions accord with the principles of the fettered spirits they are recognised, and they produce, moreover, in those who perform them the sensation of a good conscience. Few motives, energetic action, and a good conscience compose what is called strength of character. The man of strong character lacks a knowledge of the many possibilities and directions of action; his intellect is fettered and restricted, because in a given case it shows him, perhaps, only two possibilities; between these two he must now of necessity choose, in accordance with his whole nature, and he does this easily and quickly because he has not to choose between fifty possibilities. The educating surroundings aim at fettering every individual, by always placing before him the smallest number of possibilities. The individual is always treated by his educators as if he were, indeed, something new, but should become a *duplicate*. If he makes his first appearance as something unknown, unprecedented, he must be turned into something known and precedented. In a child, the familiar manifestation of restriction is called a good character; in placing itself on the side of the fettered spirits the child first discloses its awakening common feeling; with this foundation of common sentiment, he will eventually become useful to his State or rank.

229.

The Standards and Values of the Fettered Spirits. – There are four species of things concerning which the restricted spirits say they are in the right. Firstly: all things that last are right; secondly: all things that are not burdens to us are right; thirdly: all things that are advantageous for us are right; fourthly: all things for which we have made sacrifices are right. The last sentence, for instance, explains why a war that was begun in opposition to popular feeling is carried on with enthusiasm directly a sacrifice has been made for it. The free spirits, who bring their case before the forum of the fettered spirits, must prove that free spirits always existed, that free-spiritism is therefore enduring, that it will not become a burden, and, finally, that on the whole they are an advantage to the fettered spirits. It is because they cannot convince the restricted spirits on this last point that they profit nothing by having proved the first and second propositions.

230.

Esprit Fort. – Compared with him who has tradition on his side and requires no reasons for his actions, the free spirit is always weak, especially in action; for he is acquainted with too many motives and points of view, and has, therefore, an uncertain and unpractised hand. What means exist of making him *strong in spite of this* so that he will, at least, manage to survive, and will not perish ineffectually? What is the source of the strong spirit (*esprit fort*)? This is especially the question as to the production of genius. Whence comes the energy, the unbending strength, the endurance with which the one, in opposition to accepted ideas, endeavours to obtain an entirely individual knowledge of the world?

231.

The Rise of Genius. – The ingenuity with which a prisoner seeks the means of freedom, the most cold-blooded and patient employment of every smallest advantage, can teach us of what tools Nature sometimes makes use in order to produce Genius – a word which I beg will be understood without any mythological and religious flavour; she, Nature, begins it in a dungeon and excites to the utmost its desire to free itself. Or to give another picture: some one who has completely *lost his way* in a wood, but who with unusual energy strives to reach the open in one direction or another, will sometimes discover a new path which nobody knew previously, thus arise geniuses, who are credited with originality. It has already been said that mutilation, crippling, or the loss of some important organ, is frequently the cause of the unusual development of another organ, because this one has to fulfil its own and also another function. This explains the source of many a brilliant talent. These general remarks on the origin of genius may be applied to the special case, the origin of the perfect free spirit.

232.

Conjecture as to the Origin of Free Spiritism. – Just as the glaciers increase when in equatorial regions the sun shines upon the seas with greater force than hitherto, so may a very strong and spreading free-spiritism be a proof that somewhere or other the force of feeling has grown extraordinarily.

233.

The Voice of History. – In general, history *appears* to teach the following about the production of genius: it ill-treats and torments mankind – calls to the passions of envy, hatred, and rivalry – drives them to desperation, people against people, throughout whole centuries! Then, perhaps, like a stray spark from the terrible energy thereby aroused, there flames up suddenly the light of genius; the will, like a horse maddened by the rider's spur, thereupon breaks out and leaps over into another domain. He who could attain to a comprehension of the production of genius, and desires to carry out practically the manner in which Nature usually goes to work, would have to be just as evil and regardless as Nature itself. But perhaps we have not heard rightly.

234.

The Value of the Middle of the Road. – It is possible that the production of genius is reserved to a limited period of mankind's history. For we must not expect from the future everything that very defined conditions were able to produce; for instance, not the astounding effects of religious feeling. This has had its day, and much that is very good can never grow again, because it could grow out of that alone. There will never again be a horizon of life and culture that is bounded by religion. Perhaps even the type of the saint is only possible with that certain narrowness of intellect, which apparently has completely disappeared. And thus the greatest height of intelligence has perhaps been reserved for a single age; it appeared – and appears, for we are still in that age – when an extraordinary, long-accumulated energy of will concentrates itself, as an exceptional case, upon *intellectual* aims. That height will no longer exist when this wildness and energy cease to be cultivated. Mankind probably approaches nearer to its actual aim in the middle of its road, in the middle time of its existence than at the end. It may be that powers with which, for instance, art is a condition, die out altogether; the pleasure in lying, in the undefined, the symbolical, in intoxication, in ecstasy might fall into disrepute. For certainly, when life is ordered in the perfect State, the present will provide no more motive for poetry, and it would only be those persons who had remained behind who would ask for poetical unreality. These, then, would assuredly look longingly backwards to the times of the imperfect State, of half-barbaric society, to our times.

235.

Genius and the Ideal State in Conflict. – The Socialists demand a comfortable life for the greatest possible number. If the lasting house of this life of comfort, the perfect State, had really been attained, then this life of comfort would have destroyed the ground out of which grow the great intellect and the mighty individual generally, I mean powerful energy. Were this State reached, mankind would have grown too weary to be still capable of producing genius. Must we not hence wish that life should retain its forcible character, and that wild forces and energies should continue to be called forth afresh? But warm and sympathetic hearts desire precisely the *removal* of that wild and forcible character, and the warmest hearts we can imagine desire it the most passionately of all, whilst all the time its passion derived its fire, its warmth, its very existence precisely from that wild and forcible character; the warmest heart, therefore, desires the removal of its own foundation, the destruction of itself – that is, it desires something illogical, it is not intelligent. The highest intelligence and the warmest heart cannot exist together in one person, and the wise man who passes judgement upon life looks beyond goodness and only regards it as something which is not without value in the general summing-up of life. The wise man must *oppose* those digressive wishes of unintelligent goodness, because he has an interest in the continuance of his type and in the eventual appearance of the highest intellect; at least, he will not advance the founding of the 'perfect State', inasmuch as there is only room in it for wearied individuals. Christ, on the contrary, he whom we may consider to have had the warmest heart, advanced the process of making man stupid, placed himself on the side of the intellectually poor, and retarded the production of the greatest intellect, and this was consistent. His opposite, the man of perfect wisdom – this may be safely prophesied – will just as necessarily hinder the production of a Christ. The State is a wise arrangement for the protection of one individual against another; if its ennobling is exaggerated the individual will at last be weakened by it, even effaced – thus the original purpose of the State will be most completely frustrated.

236.

The Zones of Culture. – It may be figuratively said that the ages of culture correspond to the zones of the various climates, only that they lie one behind another and not beside each other like the geographical zones. In comparison with the temperate zone of culture, which it is our object to enter, the past, speaking generally, gives the impression of a *tropical* climate. Violent contrasts, sudden changes between day and night, heat and colour-splendour, the reverence of all that was sudden, mysterious, terrible, the rapidity with which storms broke: everywhere that lavish abundance of the provisions of nature; and opposed to this, in our culture, a clear but by no means bright sky, pure but fairly unchanging air, sharpness, even cold at times; thus the two zones are contrasts to each other. When we see how in that former zone the most raging passions are suppressed and broken down with mysterious force by metaphysical representations, we feel as if wild tigers were being crushed before our very eyes in the coils of mighty serpents; our mental climate lacks such episodes, our imagination is temperate, even in dreams there does not happen to us what former peoples saw waking. But should we not rejoice at this change, even granted that artists are essentially spoiled by the disappearance of the tropical culture and find us non-artists a little too timid? In so far artists are certainly right to deny 'progress', for indeed it is doubtful whether the last three thousand years show an advance in the arts. In the same way, a metaphysical philosopher like Schopenhauer would have no cause to acknowledge progress with a regard to metaphysical philosophy and religion if he glanced back over the last four thousand years. For us, however, the *existence* even of the temperate zones of culture is progress.

237.

Renaissance and Reformation. – The Italian Renaissance contained within itself all the positive forces to which we owe modern culture. Such were the liberation of thought, the disregard of authorities, the triumph of education over the darkness of tradition, enthusiasm for science and the scientific past of mankind, the unfettering of the Individual, an ardour for truthfulness and a dislike of delusion and mere effect (which ardour blazed forth in an entire company of artistic characters, who with the greatest moral purity required from themselves perfection in their works, and nothing but perfection); yes, the Renaissance had positive forces, which have, *as yet*, never become so mighty again in our modern culture. It was the

Golden Age of the last thousand years, in spite of all its blemishes and vices. On the other hand, the German Reformation stands out as an energetic protest of antiquated spirits, who were by no means tired of mediaeval views of life, and who received the signs of its dissolution, the extraordinary flatness and alienation of the religious life, with deep dejection instead of with the rejoicing that would have been seemly. With their northern strength and stiff-neckedness they threw mankind back again, brought about the counter-reformation, that is, a Catholic Christianity of self-defence, with all the violences of a state of siege, and delayed for two or three centuries the complete awakening and mastery of the sciences; just as they probably made for ever impossible the complete inter-growth of the antique and the modern spirit. The great task of the Renaissance could not be brought to a termination, this was prevented by the protest of the contemporary backward German spirit (which, for its salvation, had had sufficient sense in the Middle Ages to cross the Alps again and again). It was the chance of an extraordinary constellation of politics that Luther was preserved, and that his protest gained strength, for the Emperor protected him in order to employ him as a weapon against the Pope, and in the same way he was secretly favoured by the Pope in order to use the Protestant princes as a counter-weight against the Emperor. Without this curious counter-play of intentions, Luther would have been burnt like Huss – and the morning sun of enlightenment would probably have risen somewhat earlier, and with a splendour more beauteous than we can now imagine.

238.

Justice against the Becoming God. – When the entire history of culture unfolds itself to our gaze, as a confusion of evil and noble, of true and false ideas, and we feel almost seasick at the sight of these tumultuous waves, we then understand what comfort resides in the conception of a *becoming God*. This Deity is unveiled ever more and more throughout the changes and fortunes of mankind; it is not all blind mechanism, a senseless and aimless confusion of forces. The deification of the process of being is a metaphysical outlook, seen as from a lighthouse overlooking the sea of history, in which a far-too historical generation of scholars found their comfort. This must not arouse anger, however erroneous the view may be. Only those who, like Schopenhauer, deny development also feel none of the misery of this historical wave, and therefore, because they know nothing of that becoming God and the need of His supposition, they should in justice withhold their scorn.

239.

The Fruits According to their Seasons. – Every better future that is desired for mankind is necessarily in many respects also a worse future, for it is foolishness to suppose that a new, higher grade of humanity will combine in itself all the good points of former grades, and must produce, for instance, the highest form of art. Rather has every season its own advantages and charms, which exclude those of the other seasons. That which has grown out of religion and in its neighbourhood cannot grow again if this has been destroyed; at the most, straggling and belated off-shoots may lead to deception on that point, like the occasional outbreaks of remembrance of the old art, a condition that probably betrays the feeling of loss and deprivation, but which is no proof of the power from which a new art might be born.

240.

The Increasing Severity of the World. – The higher culture an individual attains, the less field there is left for mockery and scorn. Voltaire thanked Heaven from his heart for the invention of marriage and the Church, by which it had so well provided for our cheer. But he and his time, and before him the sixteenth century, had exhausted their ridicule on this theme; everything that is now made fun of on this theme is out of date, and above all too cheap to tempt a purchaser. Causes are now inquired after; ours is an age of seriousness. Who cares now to discern, laughingly, the difference between reality and pretentious sham, between that which man is and that which he wishes to represent; the feeling of this contrast has quite a different effect if we seek reasons. The more thoroughly any one understands life, the less he will mock, though finally, perhaps, he will mock at the 'thoroughness of his understanding'.

241.

The Genius of Culture. – If any one wished to imagine a genius of culture, what would it be like? It handles as its tools falsehood, force, and thoughtless selfishness so surely that it could only be called an evil, demoniacal being; but its aims, which are occasionally transparent, are great and good. It is a centaur, half-beast, half-man, and, in addition, has angel's wings upon its head.

242.

The Miracle-Education. – Interest in Education will acquire great strength only from the moment when belief in a God and His care is renounced, just as the art of healing could only flourish when the belief in miracle-cures ceased. So far, however, there is universal belief in the miracle-education; out of the greatest disorder and confusion of aims and unfavourableness of conditions, the most fertile and mighty men have been seen to grow; could this happen naturally? Soon these cases will be more closely looked into, more carefully examined; but miracles will never be discovered. In similar circumstances countless persons perish constantly; the few saved have, therefore, usually grown stronger, because they endured these bad conditions by virtue of an inexhaustible inborn strength, and this strength they had also exercised and increased by fighting against these circumstances; thus the miracle is explained. An education that no longer believes in miracles must pay attention to three things: first, how much energy is inherited? Secondly, by what means can new energy be aroused? Thirdly, how can the individual be adapted to so many and manifold claims of culture without being disquieted and destroying his personality – in short, how can the individual be initiated into the counterpoint of private and public culture, how can he lead the melody and at the same time accompany it?

243.

The Future of the Physician. – There is now no profession which would admit of such an enhancement as that of the physician; that is, after the spiritual physicians the so-called pastors, are no longer allowed to practise their conjuring tricks to public applause, and a cultured person gets out of their way. The highest mental development of a physician has not yet been reached, even if he understands the best and newest methods, is practised in them, and knows how to draw those rapid conclusions from effects to causes for which the diagnostics are celebrated; besides this, he must possess a gift of eloquence that adapts itself to every individual and draws his heart out of his body; a manliness, the sight of which alone drives away all despondency (the canker of all sick people), the tact and suppleness of a diplomatist in negotiations between such as have need of joy for their recovery and such as, for reasons of health, must (and can) give joy; the acuteness of a detective and an attorney to divine the secrets of a soul without betraying them – in short, a good physician now has need of all the artifices and artistic privileges of every other professional class. Thus equipped, he is then ready to be a benefactor to the whole of society, by increasing good works, mental joys and fertility, by preventing evil thoughts, projects and villainies (the evil source of which is so often the belly), by the restoration of a mental and physical aristocracy (as a maker and hinderer of marriages), by judiciously checking all so-called soul-torments and pricks of conscience. Thus from a 'medicine man' he becomes saviour, and yet need work no miracle, neither is he obliged to let himself be crucified.

244.

In the Neighbourhood of Insanity. – The sum of sensations, knowledge and experiences, the whole burden of culture, therefore, has become so great that an overstraining of nerves and powers of thought is a common danger, indeed the cultivated classes of European countries are throughout neurotic, and almost every one of their great families is on the verge of insanity in one of their branches. True, health is now sought in every possible way; but in the main a diminution of that tension of feeling, of that oppressive burden of culture, is needful, which, even though it might be bought at a heavy sacrifice, would at least give us room for the great hope of a *new Renaissance*. To Christianity, to the philosophers, poets, and musicians we owe an abundance of deeply emotional sensations; in order that these may not get beyond our control we must invoke the spirit of science, which on the whole makes us somewhat colder and more sceptical, and in particular cools the faith in final and absolute truths; it is chiefly through Christianity that it has grown so wild.

245.

The Bell-founding of Culture. – Culture has been made like a bell, within a covering of coarser, commoner material, falsehood, violence, the boundless extension of every individual 'I', of every separate people – this was the covering. Is it time to take it off? Has the liquid set, have the good and useful impulses, the habits of the nobler nature become so certain and so general that they no longer require to lean on metaphysics and the errors of religion, no longer have need of hardnesses and violence as powerful all bonds between man and man, people and people? No sign from any God can any longer help us to answer this question; our own insight must decide. The earthly rule of man must be taken in hand by man himself, his 'omniscience' must watch over the further fate of culture with a sharp eye.

246.

The Cyclopes of Culture. – Whoever has seen those furrowed basins which once contained glaciers, will hardly deem it possible that a time will come when the same spot will be a valley of woods and meadows and streams. It is the same in the history of mankind; the wildest forces break the way, destructively at first, but their activity was nevertheless necessary in order that later on a milder civilisation might build up its house. These terrible energies – that which is called Evil – are the cyclopic architects and road-makers of humanity.

247.

The Circulation of Humanity. – It is possible that all humanity is only a phase of development of a certain species of animal of limited duration. Man may have grown out of the ape and will return to the ape again,[12] without anybody taking an interest in the ending of this curious comedy. Just as with the decline of Roman civilisation and its most important cause, the spread of Christianity, there was a general uglification of man within the Roman Empire, so, through the

12 This may remind one of Gobineau's more jocular saying: '*Nous ne descendons pas du singe, mats nous y allons*.'– J. M. K.

eventual decline of general culture, there might result a far greater uglification and finally an animalising of man till he reached the ape. But just because we are able to face this prospect, we shall perhaps be able to avert such an end.

248.

The Consoling Speech of a Desperate Advance. – Our age gives the impression of an intermediate condition; the old ways of regarding the world, the old cultures still partially exist, the new are not yet sure and customary and hence are without decision and consistency. It appears as if everything would become chaotic, as if the old were being lost, the new worthless and ever becoming weaker. But this is what the soldier feels who is learning to march; for a time he is more uncertain and awkward, because his muscles are moved sometimes according to the old system and sometimes according to the new, and neither gains a decisive victory. We waver, but it is necessary not to lose courage and give up what we have newly gained. Moreover, we *cannot* go back to the old, we *have* burnt our boats; there remains nothing but to be brave whatever happens. *March ahead*, only get forward! Perhaps our behaviour looks like *progress*; but if not, then the words of Frederick the Great may also be applied to us, and indeed as a consolation: '*Ah, mon cher Sulzer, vous ne connaissez pas assez cette race Maudite, à laquelle nous appartenons*.'

249.

Suffering from Past Culture. – Whoever has solved the problem of culture suffers from a feeling similar to that of one who has inherited unjustly-gotten riches, or of a prince who reigns thanks to the violence of his ancestors. He thinks of their origin with grief and is often ashamed, often irritable. The whole sum of strength, joy, vigour, which he devotes to his possessions, is often balanced by a deep weariness, he cannot forget their origin. He looks despondingly at the future; he knows well that his successors will suffer from the past as he does.

250.

Manners. – Good manners disappear in proportion as the influence of a Court and an exclusive aristocracy lessens; this decrease can be plainly observed from decade to decade by those who have an eye for public behaviour, which grows visibly more vulgar. No one any longer knows how to court and flatter intelligently; hence arises the ludicrous fact that in cases where we *must* render actual homage (to a great statesman or artist, for instance), the words of deepest feeling, of simple, peasant-like honesty, have to be borrowed, owing to the embarrassment resulting from the lack of grace and wit. Thus the public ceremonious meeting of men appears ever more clumsy, but more full of feeling and honesty without really being so. But must there always be a decline in manners? It appears to me, rather, that manners take a deep curve and that we are approaching their lowest point. When society has become sure of its intentions and principles, so that they have a moulding effect (the manners we have learnt from former moulding conditions are now inherited and always more weakly learnt), there will then be company manners, gestures and social expressions, which must appear as necessary and simply natural because they are intentions and principles. The better division of time and work, the gymnastic exercise transformed into the accompaniment of all beautiful leisure, increased and severer meditation, which brings wisdom and suppleness even to the body, will bring all this in its train. Here, indeed, we might think with a smile of our scholars, and consider whether, as a matter of fact, they who wish to be regarded as the forerunners of that new culture are distinguished by their better manners? This is hardly the case; although their spirit may be willing enough their flesh is weak. The past of culture is still too powerful in their muscles, they still stand in a fettered position, and are half worldly priests and half dependent educators of the upper classes, and besides this they have been rendered crippled and lifeless by the pedantry of science and by antiquated, spiritless methods. In any case, therefore, they are physically, and often three-fourths mentally, still the courtiers of an old, even antiquated culture, and as such are themselves antiquated; the new spirit that occasionally inhabits these old dwellings often serves only to make them more uncertain and frightened. In them there dwell the ghosts of the past as well as the ghosts of the future; what wonder if they do not wear the best expression or show the most pleasing behaviour?

251.

The Future of Science. – To him who works and seeks in her, Science gives much pleasure – to him who *learns* her facts, very little. But as all important truths of science must gradually become commonplace and everyday matters, even this small amount of pleasure ceases, just as we have long ceased to take pleasure in learning the admirable multiplication table. Now if Science goes on giving less pleasure in herself, and always takes more pleasure in throwing suspicion on the consolations of metaphysics, religion and art, that greatest of all sources of pleasure, to which mankind owes almost its whole humanity, becomes impoverished. Therefore a higher culture must have man a double brain, two brain-chambers, so to speak, one to feel science and the other to feel non-science, which can lie side by side, without confusion, divisible, exclusive; this is a necessity of health. In one part lies the source of strength, in the other lies the regulator; it must be heated with illusions, onesidednesses, passions; and the malicious and dangerous consequences of overheating must be averted by the help of conscious Science. If this necessity of the higher culture is not satisfied, the further course of human development can almost certainly be foretold: the interest in what is true ceases as it guarantees less pleasure; illusion, error, and imagination reconquer step by step the ancient territory, because they are united to pleasure; the ruin of science: the relapse into barbarism is the next result; mankind must begin to weave its web afresh after having, like Penelope, destroyed it during the night. But who will assure us that it will always find the necessary strength for this?

252.

The Pleasure in Discernment. – Why is discernment, that essence of the searcher and the philosopher, connected with pleasure? Firstly, and above all, because thereby we become conscious of our strength, for the same reason that gymnastic exercises, even without spectators, are enjoyable. Secondly, because in the course of knowledge we surpass older ideas and their representatives, and become, or believe ourselves to be, conquerors. Thirdly, because even a very little new knowledge exalts us above *every one*, and makes us feel we are the only ones who know the subject aright. These are the three most important reasons of the pleasure, but there are many others, according to the nature of the discerner. A not inconsiderable index of such is given, where no one would look for it, in a passage of my parenetic work on Schopenhauer,[13] with the arrangement of which every experienced servant of knowledge may be satisfied, even though he might wish to dispense with the ironical touch that seems to pervade those pages. For if it be true that for the making of a scholar 'a number of very human impulses and desires must be thrown together', that the scholar is indeed a very noble but not a pure metal, and 'consists of a confused blending of very different impulses and attractions', the same thing may be said equally of the making and nature of the artist, the philosopher and the moral genius – and whatever glorified great names there may be in that list. *Everything* human deserves ironical consideration with respect to its *origin* – therefore irony is so *superfluous* in the world.

253.

Fidelity as a Proof of Validity. – It is a perfect sign of a sound theory if during *forty years* its originator does not mistrust it; but I maintain that there has never yet been a philosopher who has not eventually deprecated the philosophy of his youth. Perhaps, however, he has not spoken publicly of this change of opinion, for reasons of ambition, or, what is more probable in noble natures, out of delicate consideration for his adherents.

254.

The Increase of what is Interesting. – In the course of higher education everything becomes interesting to man, he knows how to find the instructive side of a thing quickly and to put his finger on the place where it can fill up a gap in his ideas, or where it may verify a thought. Through this boredom disappears more and more, and so does excessive excitability of temperament. Finally he moves among men like a botanist among plants, and looks upon himself as a phenomenon, which only greatly excites his discerning instinct.

---

13 This refers to his essay, 'Schopenhauer as Educator', in *Thoughts Out of Season*, vol. ii. of the English edition. – J. M. K.

255.

The Superstition of the Simultaneous. – Simultaneous things hold together, it is said. A relative dies far away, and at the same time we dream about him – Consequently! But countless relatives die and we do not dream about them. It is like shipwrecked people who make vows; afterwards, in the temples, we do not see the votive tablets of those who perished. A man dies, an owl hoots, a clock stops, all at one hour of the night – must there not be some connection? Such an intimacy with nature as this supposition implies is flattering to mankind. This species of superstition is found again in a refined form in historians and delineators of culture, who usually have a kind of hydrophobic horror of all that senseless mixture, in which individual and national life is so rich.

256.

Action and not Knowledge Exercised by Science. – The value of strictly pursuing science for a time does not lie precisely in its results, for these, in proportion to the ocean of what is worth knowing, are but an infinitesimally small drop. But it gives an additional energy, decisiveness, and toughness of endurance; it teaches how to attain an *aim suitably*. In so far it is very valuable, with a view to all that is done later on, to have once been a scientific man.

257.

The Youthful Charm of Science. – The search for truth still retains the charm of being in strong contrast to grey and now tiresome error; but this charm is gradually disappearing. It is true we still live in the youthful age of science and are accustomed to follow truth as a lovely girl; but how will it be when one day she becomes an elderly, ill-tempered looking woman? In almost all sciences the fundamental knowledge is either found in earliest times or is still being sought; what a different attraction this exerts compared to that time when everything essential has been found and there only remains for the seeker a scanty gleaning (which sensation may be learnt in several historical disciplines).

258.

The Statue of Humanity. – The genius of culture fares as did Cellini when his statue of Perseus was being cast; the molten mass threatened to run short, but it *had* to suffice, so he flung in his plates and dishes, and whatever else his hands fell upon. In the same way genius flings in errors, vices, hopes, ravings, and other things of baser as well as of nobler metal, for the statue of humanity must emerge and be finished; what does it matter if commoner material is used here and there?

259.

A Male Culture. – The Greek culture of the classic age is a male culture. As far as women are concerned, Pericles expresses everything in the funeral speech: 'They are best when they are as little spoken of as possible amongst men.' The erotic relation of men to youths was the necessary and sole preparation, to a degree unattainable to our comprehension, of all manly education (pretty much as for a long time all higher education of women was only attainable through love and marriage). All idealism of the strength of the Greek nature threw itself into that relation, and it is probable that never since have young men been treated so attentively, so lovingly, SO entirely with a view to their welfare (*virtus*) as in the fifth and sixth centuries BC – according to the beautiful saying of Holderlin: '*denn liebend giebt der Sterbliche vom Besten*'.[14] The higher the light in which this relation was regarded, the lower sank intercourse with woman; nothing else was taken into consideration than the production of children and lust; there was no intellectual intercourse, not even real love-making. If it be further remembered that women were even excluded from contests and spectacles of every description, there only remain the religious cults as their sole higher occupation. For although in the tragedies Electra and Antigone were represented, this was only *tolerated* in art, but not liked in real life – just as now we cannot endure anything pathetic in *life* but like it in art. The women had no other mission than to produce beautiful, strong bodies, in which the father's character lived on as unbrokenly as possible, and therewith to counteract the increasing nerve-tension of such a highly developed culture. This kept the Greek culture young for a relatively long time; for in the Greek mothers the Greek genius always returned to nature.

---

14 For it is when loving that mortal man gives of his best. – J. M. K.

260.

The Prejudice in Favour of Greatness. – It is clear that men overvalue everything great and prominent. This arises from the conscious or unconscious idea that they deem it very useful when one person throws all his strength into one thing and makes himself into a monstrous organ. Assuredly, an *equal* development of all his powers is more useful and happier for man; for every talent is a vampire which sucks blood and strength from other powers, and an exaggerated production can drive the most gifted almost to madness. Within the circle of the arts, too, extreme natures excite far too much attention; but a much lower culture is necessary to be captivated by them. Men submit from habit to everything that seeks power.

261.

The Tyrants of the Mind. – It is only where the ray of myth falls that the life of the Greeks shines; otherwise it is gloomy. The Greek philosophers are now robbing themselves of this myth; is it not as if they wished to quit the sunshine for shadow and gloom? Yet no plant avoids the light; and, as a matter of fact, those philosophers were only seeking a *brighter* sun; the myths not pure enough, not shining enough for them. They found this light in their knowledge, in that which each of them called his 'truth'. But in those times knowledge shone with a greater glory; it was still young and knew but little of all the difficulties and dangers of its path; it could still hope to reach in one single bound the central point of all being, and from thence to solve the riddle of the world. These philosophers had a firm belief in themselves and their 'truth', and with it they overthrew all their neighbours and predecessors; each one was a warlike, violent *tyrant*. The happiness in believing themselves the possessors of truth was perhaps never greater in the world, but neither were the hardness, the arrogance, and the tyranny and evil of such a belief. They were tyrants, they were that, therefore, which every Greek wanted to be, and which every one was if he *was able*. Perhaps Solon alone is an exception; he tells in his poems how he disdained personal tyranny. But he did it for love of his works, of his law-giving; and to be a law-giver is a sublimated form of tyranny. Parmenides also made laws. Pythagoras and Empedocles probably did the same; Anaximander founded a city. Plato was the incarnate wish to become the greatest philosophic law-giver and founder of States; he appears to have suffered terribly over the non-fulfilment of his nature, and towards his end his soul was filled with the bitterest gall. The more the Greek philosophers lost in power the more they suffered inwardly from this bitterness and malice; when the various sects fought for their truths in the street, then first were the souls of these wooers of truth completely clogged through envy and spleen; the tyrannical element then raged like poison within their bodies. These many petty tyrants would have liked to devour each other; there survived not a single spark of love and very little joy in their own knowledge. The saying that tyrants are generally murdered and that their descendants are short-lived, is true also of the tyrants of the mind. Their history is short and violent, and their after-effects break off suddenly. It may be said of almost all great Hellenes that they appear to have come too late: it was thus with Aeschylus, with Pindar, with Demosthenes, with Thucydides: one generation – and then it is passed for ever. That is the stormy and dismal element in Greek history. We now, it is true, admire the gospel of the tortoises. To think historically is almost the same thing now as if in all ages history had been made according to the theory 'The smallest possible amount in the longest possible time!' Oh! how quickly Greek history runs on! Since then life has never been so extravagant – so unbounded. I cannot persuade myself that the history of the Greeks followed that *natural* course for which it is so celebrated. They were much too variously gifted to be *gradual* in the orderly manner of the tortoise when running a race with Achilles, and that is called natural development. The Greeks went rapidly forward, but equally rapidly downwards; the movement of the whole machine is so intensified that a single stone thrown amid its wheels was sufficient to break it. Such a stone for instance, was Socrates; the hitherto so wonderfully regular, although certainly too rapid, development of the philosophical science was destroyed in one night. It is no idle question whether Plato, had he remained free from the Socratic charm', would not have discovered a still higher type of the philosophic man, which type is for ever lost to us. We look into the ages before him as into a sculptor's workshop of such types. The fifth and sixth centuries BC seemed to promise something more and higher even than they produced; they stopped short at promising and announcing. And yet there is hardly a greater loss than the loss of a type, of a new, hitherto undiscovered highest *possibility of the philosophic life*. Even of the older type the greater number are badly transmitted; it seems to me that all philosophers, from Thales to Democritus, are remarkably difficult to recognise, but whoever succeeds in imitating these figures walks amongst specimens of the mightiest and purest type. This ability is certainly rare, it was even absent in those later Greeks, who occupied themselves with the knowledge of the older philosophy; Aristotle, especially, hardly seems to have had eyes in his head when he stands before these great ones. And thus it appears as if these splendid philosophers had lived in vain, or as if they had only been intended to prepare the quarrelsome and talkative followers of the Socratic schools. As I have said, here is a gap, a break in development; some great misfortune must have happened, and the only statue which might have revealed the meaning and purpose of that great artistic training was either broken or unsuccessful; what actually happened has remained for ever a secret of the workshop.

That which happened amongst the Greeks – namely, that every great thinker who believed himself to be in possession of the absolute truth became a tyrant, so that even the mental history of the Greeks acquired that violent, hasty and dangerous character shown by their political history – this type of event was not therewith exhausted, much that is similar has happened even in more modern times, although gradually becoming rarer and now but seldom showing the pure, naive conscience of the Greek philosophers. For on the whole, opposition doctrines and scepticism now speak too powerfully, too loudly. The period of mental tyranny is past. It is true that in the spheres of higher culture there must always be a supremacy, but henceforth this supremacy lies in the hands of the *oligarchs of the mind*. In spite of local and political separation they form a cohesive society, whose members *recognise and acknowledge* each other, whatever public opinion and the verdicts of review and newspaper writers who influence the masses may circulate in favour of or against them. Mental superiority, which formerly divided and embittered, nowadays generally *unites*; how could the separate individuals assert themselves and swim through life on their own course, against all currents, if they did not see others like them living here and there under similar conditions, and grasped their hands, in the struggle as much against the ochlocratic character of the half mind and half culture as against the occasional attempts to establish a tyranny with the help of the masses? Oligarchs are necessary to each other, they are each other's best joy, they understand their signs, but each is nevertheless free, he fights and conquers in *his* place and perishes rather than submit.

262.

Homer. – The greatest fact in Greek culture remains this, that Homer became so early Pan-Hellenic. All mental and human freedom to which the Greeks attained is traceable to this fact. At the same time it has actually been fatal to Greek culture; for Homer levelled, inasmuch as he centralised, and dissolved the more serious instincts of independence. From time to time there arose from the depths of Hellenism an opposition to Homer; but he always remained victorious. All great mental powers have an oppressing effect as well as a liberating one; but it certainly makes a difference whether it is Homer or the Bible or Science that tyrannises over mankind.

263.

Talents. – In such a highly developed humanity as the present, each individual naturally has access to many talents. Each has an *inborn* talent, but only in a few is that degree of toughness, endurance, and energy born and trained that he really becomes a talent, *becomes* what he *is* – that is, that he discharges it in works and actions.

264.

The Witty Person either Overvalued or Undervalued. – Unscientific but talented people value every mark of intelligence, whether it be on a true or a false track; above all, they want the person with whom they have intercourse to entertain them with his wit, to spur them on, to inflame them, to carry them away in seriousness and play, and in any case to be a powerful amulet to protect them against boredom. Scientific natures, on the other hand, know that the gift of possessing all manner of notions should be strictly controlled by the scientific spirit: it is not that which shines, deludes and excites, but the often insignificant truth that is the fruit which he knows how to shake down from the tree of knowledge. Like Aristotle, he is not permitted to make any distinction between the 'bores', and the 'wits', his *daemon* leads him through the desert as well as through tropical vegetation, in order that he may only take pleasure in the really actual, tangible, true. In insignificant scholars this produces a general disdain and suspicion of cleverness, and, on the other hand, clever people frequently have an aversion to science, as have, for instance, almost all artists.

265.

Sense in School. – School has no task more important than to teach strict thought, cautious judgement, and logical conclusions, hence it must pay no attention to what hinders these operations, such as religion, for instance. It can count on the fact that human vagueness, custom, and need will later on unstring the bow of all-too-severe thought. But so long as its influence lasts it should enforce that which is the essential and distinguishing point in man: 'Sense and Science, the *very highest* power of man' – as Goethe judges. The great natural philosopher, Von Baer, thinks that the superiority of all Europeans, when compared to Asiatics, lies in the trained capability of giving reasons for that which they believe, of which the latter are utterly incapable. Europe went to the school of logical and critical thought, Asia still fails to know how to distinguish between truth and fiction, and is not conscious whether its convictions spring from individual observation and systematic thought or from imagination. Sense in the school has made Europe what it is; in the Middle Ages it was on the road to become once more a part and dependent of Asia – forfeiting, therefore, the scientific mind which it owed to the Greeks.

266.

The Undervalued Effect of Public School Teaching. – The value of a public school is seldom sought in those things which are really learnt there and are carried away never to be lost, but in those things which are learnt and which the pupil only acquires against his will, in order to get rid of them again as soon as possible. Every educated person acknowledges that the reading of the classics, as now practised, is a monstrous proceeding carried on before young people are ripe enough for it by teachers who with every word, often by their appearance alone, throw a mildew on a good author. But therein lies the value, generally unrecognised, of these teachers who *speak the abstract language of the higher culture*, which, though dry and difficult to understand, is yet a sort of higher gymnastics of the brain; and there is value in the constant recurrence in their language of ideas, artistic expressions, methods and allusions which the young people hardly ever hear in the conversations of their relatives and in the street. Even if the pupils only *hear*, their intellect is involuntarily trained to a scientific mode of regarding things. It is not possible to emerge from this discipline entirely untouched by its abstract character, and to remain a simple child of nature.

267.

Learning many Languages. – The learning of many languages fills the memory with words instead of with facts and thoughts, and this is a vessel which, with every person, can only contain a certain limited amount of contents. Therefore the learning of many languages is injurious, inasmuch as it arouses a belief in possessing dexterity and, as a matter of fact, it lends a kind of delusive importance to social intercourse. It is also indirectly injurious in that it opposes the acquirement of solid knowledge and the intention to win the respect of men in an honest way. Finally, it is the axe which is laid to the root of a delicate sense of language in our mother-tongue, which thereby is incurably injured and destroyed. The two nations which produced the greatest stylists, the Greeks and the French, learned no foreign languages. But as human intercourse must always grow more cosmopolitan, and as, for instance, a good merchant in London must now be able to read and write eight languages, the learning of many tongues has certainly become a necessary evil; but which, when finally carried to an extreme, will compel mankind to find a remedy, and in some far-off future there will be a new language, used at first as a language of commerce, then as a language of intellectual intercourse generally, then for all, as surely as some time or other there will be aviation. Why else should philology have studied the laws of languages for a whole century, and have estimated the necessary, the valuable, and the successful portion of each separate language?

268.

The War History of the Individual. – In a single human life that passes through many styles of culture we find that struggle condensed which would otherwise have been played out between two generations, between father and son; the closeness of the relationship *sharpens* this struggle, because each party ruthlessly drags in the familiar inward nature of the other party; and thus this struggle in the single individual becomes most *embittered*; here every new phase disregards the earlier ones with cruel injustice and misunderstanding of their means and aims.

269.

A Quarter of an Hour Earlier. – A man is found occasionally whose views are beyond his time, but only to such an extent that he anticipates the common views of the next decade. He possesses public opinion before it is public; that is, he has fallen into the arms of a view that deserves to be trivial a quarter of an hour sooner than other people. But his fame is usually far noisier than the fame of those who are really great and prominent.

270.

The Art of Reading. – Every strong tendency is one-sided; it approaches the aim of the straight line and, like this, is exclusive, that is, it does not touch many other aims, as do weak parties and natures in their wave-like rolling to-and-fro; it must also be forgiven to philologists that they are one-sided. The restoration and keeping pure of texts, besides their explanation, carried on in common for hundreds of years, has finally enabled the right methods to be found; the whole of the Middle Ages was absolutely incapable of a strictly philological explanation, that is, of the simple desire to comprehend what an author says – it *was* an achievement, finding these methods, let it not be undervalued! Through this all science first acquired continuity and steadiness, so that the art of reading rightly, which is called philology, attained its summit.

271.

The Art of Reasoning. – The greatest advance that men have made lies in their acquisition of the art to *reason rightly*. It is not so very natural, as Schopenhauer supposes when he says, 'All are capable of reasoning, but few of judging,' it is learnt late and has not yet attained supremacy. False conclusions are the rule in older ages; and the mythologies of all peoples, their magic and their superstition, their religious cult and their law are the inexhaustible sources of proof of this theory.

272.

Phases of Individual Culture. – The strength and weakness of mental productiveness depend far less on inherited talents than on the accompanying amount of *elasticity*. Most educated young people of thirty turn round at this solstice of their lives and are afterwards disinclined for new mental turnings. Therefore, for the salvation of a constantly increasing culture, a new generation is immediately necessary, which will not do very much either, for in order to come up with the father's culture the son must exhaust almost all the inherited energy which the father himself possessed at that stage of life when his son was born; with the little addition he gets further on (for as here the road is being traversed for the second time progress is a little quicker; in order to learn that which the father knew, the son does not consume quite so much strength). Men of great elasticity, like Goethe, for instance, get through almost more than four generations in succession would be capable of; but then they advance too quickly, so that the rest of mankind only comes up with them in the next century, and even then perhaps not completely, because the exclusiveness of culture and the consecutiveness of development have been weakened by the frequent interruptions. Men catch up more quickly with the ordinary phases of intellectual culture which has been acquired in the course of history. Nowadays they begin to acquire culture as religiously inclined children, and perhaps about their tenth year these sentiments attain to their highest point, and are then changed into weakened forms (pantheism), whilst they draw near to science; they entirely pass by God, immortality, and such-like things, but are overcome by the witchcraft of a metaphysical philosophy. Eventually they find even this unworthy of belief; art, on the contrary, seems to vouchsafe more and more, so that for a time metaphysics is metamorphosed and continues to exist either as a transition to art or as an artistically transfiguring temperament. But the scientific sense grows more imperious and conducts man to natural sciences and history, and particularly to the severest methods of knowledge, whilst art has always a milder and less exacting meaning. All this usually happens within the first thirty years of a man's life. It is the recapitulation of a *pensum*, for which humanity had laboured perhaps thirty thousand years.

273.

Retrograded, not Left Behind. – Whoever, in the present day, still derives his development from religious sentiments, and perhaps lives for some length of time afterwards in metaphysics and art, has assuredly gone back a considerable distance and begins his race with other modern men under unfavourable conditions; he apparently loses time and space. But because he stays in those domains where ardour and energy are liberated and force flows continuously as a volcanic stream out of an inexhaustible source, he goes forward all the more quickly as soon as he has freed himself at the right moment from those dominators; his feet are winged, his breast has learned quieter, longer, and more enduring breathing. He has only retreated in order to have sufficient room to leap; thus something terrible and threatening may lie in this retrograde movement.

274.

A Portion of our Ego as an Artistic Object. – It is a sign of superior culture consciously to retain and present a true picture of certain phases of development which commoner men live through almost thoughtlessly and then efface from the tablets of their souls: this is a higher species of the painter's art which only the few understand. For this it is necessary to isolate those phases artificially. Historical studies form the qualification for this painting, for they constantly incite us in regard to a portion of history, a people, or a human life, to imagine for ourselves a quite distinct horizon of thoughts, a certain strength of feelings, the prominence of this or the obscurity of that. Herein consists the historic sense, that out of given instances we can quickly reconstruct such systems of thoughts and feelings, just as we can mentally reconstruct a temple out of a few pillars and remains of walls accidentally left standing. The next result is that we understand our fellow-men as belonging to distinct systems and representatives of different cultures – that is, as necessary, but as changeable; and, again, that we can separate portions of our own development and put them down independently.

275.

Cynics and Epicureans. – The cynic recognises the connection between the multiplied and stronger pains of the more highly cultivated man and the abundance of requirements; he comprehends, therefore, that the multitude of opinions about what is beautiful, suitable, seemly and pleasing, must also produce very rich sources of enjoyment, but also of displeasure. In accordance with this view he educates himself backwards, by giving up many of these opinions and withdrawing from certain demands of culture; he thereby gains a feeling of freedom and strength; and gradually, when habit has made his manner of life endurable, his sensations of displeasure are, as a matter of fact, rarer and weaker than those of cultivated people, and approach those of the domestic animal; moreover, he experiences everything with the charm of contrast, and – he can also scold to his heart's content; so that thereby he again rises high above the sensation-range of the animal. The Epicurean has the same point of view as the cynic; there is usually only a difference of temperament between them. Then the Epicurean makes use of his higher culture to render himself independent of prevailing opinions, he raises himself above them, whilst the cynic only remains negative. He walks, as it were, in wind-protected, well-sheltered, half-dark paths, whilst over him, in the wind, the tops of the trees rustle and show him how violently agitated is the world out there. The cynic, on the contrary, goes, as it were, naked into the rushing of the wind and hardens himself to the point of insensibility.

276.

Microcosm and Macrocosm of Culture. – The best discoveries about culture man makes within himself when he finds two heterogeneous powers ruling therein. Supposing some one were living as much in love for the plastic arts or for music as he was carried away by the spirit of science, and that he were to regard it as impossible for him to end this contradiction by the destruction of one and complete liberation of the other power, there would therefore remain nothing for him to do but to erect around himself such a large edifice of culture that those two powers might both dwell within it, although at different ends, whilst between them there dwelt reconciling, intermediary powers, with predominant strength to quell, in case of need, the rising conflict. But such an edifice of culture in the single individual will bear a great resemblance to the culture of entire periods, and will afford consecutive analogical teaching concerning it. For wherever the great architecture of culture manifested itself it was its mission to compel opposing powers to agree, by means of an overwhelming accumulation of other less unbearable powers, without thereby oppressing and fettering them.

277.

Happiness and Culture. – We are moved at the sight of our childhood's surroundings – the arbour, the church with its graves, the pond and the wood – all this we see again with pain. We are seized with pity for ourselves; for what have we not passed through since then! And everything here is so silent, so eternal, only we are so changed, so moved; we even find a few human beings, on whom Time has sharpened his teeth no more than on an oak tree – peasants, fishermen, woodmen – they are unchanged. Emotion and self-pity at the sight of lower culture is the sign of higher culture; from which the conclusion may be drawn that happiness has certainly not been increased by it. Whoever wishes to reap happiness and comfort in life should always avoid higher culture.

278.

The Simile of the Dance. – It must now be regarded as a decisive sign of great culture if some one possesses sufficient strength and flexibility to be as pure and strict in discernment as, in other moments, to be capable of giving poetry, religion, and metaphysics a hundred paces' start and then feeling their force and beauty. Such a position amid two such different demands is very difficult, for science urges the absolute supremacy of its methods, and if this insistence is not yielded to, there arises the other danger of a weak wavering between different impulses. Meanwhile, to cast a glance, in simile at least, on a solution of this difficulty, it may be remembered that *dancing* is not the same as a dull reeling to and fro between different impulses. High culture will resemble a bold dance – wherefore, as has been said, there is need of much strength and suppleness.

279.

Of the Relieving of Life. – A primary way of lightening life is the idealisation of all its occurrences; and with the help of painting we should make it quite clear to ourselves what idealising means. The painter requires that the spectator should not observe too closely or too sharply, he forces him back to a certain distance from whence to make his observations; he is obliged to take for granted a fixed distance of the spectator from the picture – he must even suppose an equally certain amount of sharpness of eye in his spectator; in such things he must on no account waver. Every one, therefore, who desires to idealise his life must not look at it too closely, and must always keep his gaze at a certain distance. This was a trick that Goethe, for instance, understood.

280.

Aggravation as Relief, and *Vice Versa*. – Much that makes life more difficult in certain grades of mankind serves to lighten it in a higher grade, because such people have become familiar with greater aggravations of life. The contrary also happens; for instance, religion has a double face, according to whether a man looks up to it to relieve him of his burden and need, or looks down upon it as upon fetters laid on him to prevent him from soaring too high into the air.

281.

The Higher Culture is Necessarily Misunderstood. – He who has strung his instrument with only two strings, like the scholars (who, besides the *instinct of knowledge* possess only an acquired *religious* instinct), does not understand people who can play upon more strings. It lies in the nature of the higher, *many-stringed* culture that it should always be falsely interpreted by the lower; an example of this is when art appears as a disguised form of the religious. People who are only religious understand even science as a searching after the religious sentiment, just as deaf mutes do not know what music is, unless it be visible movement.

282.

Lamentation. – It is, perhaps, the advantages of our epoch that bring with them a backward movement and an occasional undervaluing of the *vita contemplativa*. But it must be acknowledged that our time is poor in the matter of great moralists, that Pascal, Epictetus, Seneca, and Plutarch are now but little read, that work and industry – formerly in the following of the great goddess Health – sometimes appear to rage like a disease. Because time to think and tranquillity in thought are lacking, we no longer ponder over different views, but content ourselves with hating them. With the enormous acceleration of life, mind and eye grow accustomed to a partial and false sight and judgement, and all people are like travellers whose only acquaintance with countries and nations is derived from the railway. An independent and cautious attitude of knowledge is looked upon almost as a kind of madness; the free spirit is brought into disrepute, chiefly through scholars, who miss their thoroughness and ant-like industry in his art of regarding things and would gladly banish him into one single corner of science, while it has the different and higher mission of commanding the battalion rear-guard of scientific and learned men from an isolated position, and showing them the ways and aims of culture. A song of lamentation such as that which has just been sung will probably have its own period, and will cease of its own accord on a forcible return of the genius of meditation.

283.

The Chief Deficiency of Active People. – Active people are usually deficient in the higher activity, I mean individual activity. They are active as officials, merchants, scholars, that is as a species, but not as quite distinct separate and *single* individuals; in this respect they are idle. It is the misfortune of the active that their activity is almost always a little senseless. For instance, we must not ask the money-making banker the reason of his restless activity, it is foolish. The active roll as the stone rolls, according to the stupidity of mechanics. All mankind is divided, as it was at all times and is still, into slaves and freemen; for whoever has not two-thirds of his day for himself is a slave, be he otherwise whatever he likes, statesman, merchant, official, or scholar.

284.

In Favour of the Idle. – As a sign that the value of a contemplative life has decreased, scholars now vie with active people in a sort of hurried enjoyment, so that they appear to value this mode of enjoying more than that which really pertains to them, and which, as a matter of fact, is a far greater enjoyment. Scholars are ashamed of *otium*. But there is one noble thing about idleness and idlers. If idleness is really the *beginning* of all vice, it finds itself, therefore, at least in near neighbourhood of all the virtues; the idle man is still a better man than the active. You do not suppose that in speaking of idleness and idlers I am alluding to you, you sluggards?

285.

Modern Unrest. – Modern restlessness increases towards the west, so that Americans look upon the inhabitants of Europe as altogether peace-loving and enjoying beings, whilst in reality they swarm about like wasps and bees. This restlessness is so great that the higher culture cannot mature its fruits, it is as if the seasons followed each other too quickly. For lack of rest our civilisation is turning into a new barbarism. At no period have the active, that is, the restless, been of more importance. One of the necessary corrections, therefore, which must be undertaken in the character of humanity is to strengthen the contemplative element on a large scale. But every individual who is quiet and steady in heart and head already has the right to believe that he possesses not only a good temperament, but also a generally useful virtue, and even fulfils a higher mission by the preservation of this virtue.

286.

To what Extent the Active Man is Lazy. – I believe that every one must have his own opinion about everything concerning which opinions are possible, because he himself is a peculiar, unique thing, which assumes towards all other things a new and never hitherto existing attitude. But idleness, which lies at the bottom of the active man's soul, prevents him from drawing water out of his own well. Freedom of opinion is like health; both are individual, and no good general conception can be set up of either of them. That which is necessary for the health of one individual is the cause of disease in another, and many means and ways to the freedom of the spirit are for more highly developed natures the ways and means to confinement.

287.

Censor Vitae. – Alternations of love and hatred for a long period distinguish the inward condition of a man who desires to be free in his judgement of life; he does not forget, and bears everything a grudge, for good and evil. At last, when the whole tablet of his soul is written full of experiences, he will not hate and despise existence, neither will he love it, but will regard it sometimes with a joyful, sometimes with a sorrowful eye, and, like nature, will be now in a summer and now in an autumn mood.

288.

The Secondary Result. – Whoever earnestly desires to be free will therewith and without any compulsion lose all inclination for faults and vices; he will also be more rarely overcome by anger and vexation. His will desires nothing more urgently than to discern, and the means to do this – that is, the permanent condition in which he is best able to discern.

289.

The Value of Disease. – The man who is bed-ridden often perceives that he is usually ill of his position, business, or society, and through them has lost all self-possession. He gains this piece of knowledge from the idleness to which his illness condemns him.

290.

Sensitiveness in the Country. – If there are no firm, quiet lines on the horizon of his life, a species of mountain and forest line, man's inmost will itself becomes restless, inattentive, and covetous, as is the nature of a dweller in towns; he has no happiness and confers no happiness.

291.

Prudence of the Free Spirits. – Free-thinkers, those who live by knowledge alone, will soon attain the supreme aim of their life and their ultimate position towards society and State, and will gladly content themselves, for instance, with a small post or an income that is just sufficient to enable them to live; for they will arrange to live in such a manner that a great change of outward prosperity, even an overthrow of the political order, would not cause an overthrow of their life. To all these things they devote as little energy as possible in order that with their whole accumulated strength, and with a long breath, they may dive into the element of knowledge. Thus they can hope to dive deep and be able to see the bottom. Such a spirit seizes only the point of an event, he does not care for things in the whole breadth and prolixity of their folds, for he does not wish to entangle himself in them. He, too, knows the weekdays of restraint, of dependence and servitude. But from time to time there must dawn for him a Sunday of liberty, otherwise he could not endure life. It is probable that even his love for humanity will be prudent and somewhat short-winded, for he desires to meddle with the world of inclinations and of blindness only as far as is necessary for the purpose of knowledge. He must trust that the genius of justice will say something for its disciple and protege if accusing voices were to call him poor in love. In his mode of life and thought there is a *refined heroism*, which scorns to offer itself to the great mob-reverence, as its coarser brother does, and passes quietly through and out of the world. Whatever labyrinths it traverses, beneath whatever rocks its stream has occasionally worked its way – when it reaches the light it goes clearly, easily, and almost noiselessly on its way, and lets the sunshine strike down to its very bottom.

292.

Forward. – And thus forward upon the path of wisdom, with a firm step and good confidence! However you may be situated, serve yourself as a source of experience! Throw off the displeasure at your nature, forgive yourself your own individuality, for in any case you have in yourself a ladder with a hundred steps upon which you can mount to knowledge. The age into which with grief you feel yourself thrown thinks you happy because of this good fortune; it calls out to you that you shall still have experiences which men of later ages will perhaps be obliged to forego. Do not despise the fact of having been religious; consider fully how you have had a genuine access to art. Can you not, with the help of these experiences, follow immense stretches of former humanity with a clearer understanding? Is not that ground which sometimes displeases you so greatly, that ground of clouded thought, precisely the one upon which have grown many of the most glorious fruits of older civilisations? You must have loved religion and art as you loved mother and nurse – otherwise you cannot be wise. But you must be able to see beyond them, to outgrow them; if you remain under their ban you do not understand them. You must also be familiar with history and that cautious play with the balances: 'On the one hand – on the other hand.' Go back, treading in the footsteps made by mankind in its great and painful journey through the desert of the past, and you will learn most surely whither it is that all later humanity never can or may go again. And inasmuch as you wish with all your strength to see in advance how the knots of the future are tied, your own life acquires the value of an instrument and means of knowledge. It is within your power to see that all you have experienced, trials, errors, faults, deceptions, passions, your love and your hope, shall be merged wholly in your aim. This aim is to become a necessary chain of culture-links yourself, and from this necessity to draw a conclusion as to the necessity in the progress of general culture. When your sight has become strong enough to see to the bottom of the dark well of your nature and your knowledge, it is possible that in its mirror you may also behold the far-away visions of future civilisations. Do you think that such a life with such an aim is too wearisome, too empty of all that is agreeable? Then you have still to learn that no honey is sweeter than that of knowledge, and that the overhanging clouds of trouble must be to you as an udder from which you shall draw milk for your refreshment. And only when old age approaches will you rightly perceive how you listened to the voice of nature, that nature which rules the whole world through pleasure; the same life which has its zenith in age has also its zenith in wisdom, in that mild sunshine of a constant mental joyfulness; you meet them both, old age and wisdom, upon one ridge of life – it was thus intended by Nature. Then it is time, and no cause for anger, that the mists of death approach. Towards the light is your last movement; a joyful cry of knowledge is your last sound.

SIXTH DIVISION. MAN IN SOCIETY.

293.

Well-Meant Dissimulation. – In intercourse with men a well-meant dissimulation is often necessary, as if we did not see through the motives of their actions.

294.

Copies. – We not unfrequently meet with copies of prominent persons; and as in the case of pictures, so also here, the copies please more than the originals.

295.

The Public Speaker. – One may speak with the greatest appropriateness, and yet so that everybody cries out to the contrary – that is to say, when one does not speak to everybody.

296.

Want of Confidence. – Want of confidence among friends is a fault that cannot be censured without becoming incurable.

297.

The Art of Giving. – To have to refuse a gift, merely because it has not been offered in the right way, provokes animosity against the giver.

298.

The most Dangerous Partisan. – In every party there is one who, by his far too dogmatic expression of the party-principles, excites defection among the others.

299.

Advisers of the Sick. – Whoever gives advice to a sick person acquires a feeling of superiority over him, whether the advice be accepted or rejected. Hence proud and sensitive sick persons hate advisers more than their sickness.

300.

Double Nature of Equality. – The rage for equality may so manifest itself that we seek either to draw all others down to ourselves (by belittling, disregarding, and tripping up), or ourselves and all others upwards (by recognition, assistance, and congratulation).

301.

Against Embarrassment. – The best way to relieve and calm very embarrassed people is to give them decided praise.

302.

Preference for Certain Virtues. – We set no special value on the possession of a virtue until we perceive that it is entirely lacking in our adversary.

303.

Why we Contradict. – We often contradict an opinion when it is really only the tone in which it is expressed that is unsympathetic to us.

304.

Confidence and Intimacy. – Whoever proposes to command the intimacy of a person is usually uncertain of possessing his confidence. Whoever is sure of a person's confidence attaches little value to intimacy with him.

305.

The Equilibrium of Friendship. – The right equilibrium of friendship in our relation to other men is sometimes restored when we put a few grains of wrong on our own side of the scales.

306.

The most Dangerous Physicians. – The most dangerous physicians are those who, like born actors, imitate the born physician with the perfect art of imposture.

307.

When Paradoxes are Permissible. – In order to interest clever persons in a theory, it is sometimes only necessary to put it before them in the form of a prodigious paradox.

308.

How Courageous People are Won Over. – Courageous people are persuaded to a course of action by representing it as more dangerous than it really is.

309.

Courtesies. – We regard the courtesies shown us by unpopular persons as offences.

310.

Keeping People Waiting. – A sure way of exasperating people and of putting bad thoughts into their heads is to keep them waiting long. That makes them immoral.

311.

Against the Confidential. – Persons who give us their full confidence think they have thereby a right to ours. That is a mistake; people acquire no rights through gifts.

312.

A Mode of Settlement. – It often suffices to give a person whom we have injured an opportunity to make a joke about us to give his personal satisfaction, and even to make him favourably disposed to us.

313.

The Vanity of the Tongue. – Whether man conceals his bad qualities and vices, or frankly acknowledges them, his vanity in either case seeks its advantage thereby – only let it be observed how nicely he distinguishes those from whom he conceals such qualities from those with whom he is frank and honest.

314.

Considerate. – To have no wish to offend or injure any one may as well be the sign of a just as of a timid nature.

315.

Requisite for Disputation. – He who cannot put his thoughts on ice should not enter into the heat of dispute.

316.

Intercourse and Pretension. – We forget our pretensions when we are always conscious of being amongst meritorious people; being alone implants presumption in us. The young are pretentious, for they associate with their equals, who are all ciphers but would fain have a great significance.

317.

Motives of an Attack. – One does not attack a person merely to hurt and conquer him, but perhaps merely to become conscious of one's own strength.

318.

Flattery. – Persons who try by means of flattery to put us off our guard in intercourse with them, employ a dangerous expedient, like a sleeping-draught, which, when it does not send the patient to sleep, keeps him all the wider awake.

319.

A Good Letter-Writer. – A person who does not write books, thinks much, and lives in unsatisfying society, will usually be a good letter writer.

320.

The Ugliest of All. – It may be doubted whether a person who has travelled much has found anywhere in the world uglier places than those to be met with in the human face.

321.

The Sympathetic Ones. – Sympathetic natures, ever ready to help in misfortune, are seldom those that participate in joy; in the happiness of others they have nothing to occupy them, they are superfluous, they do not feel themselves in possession of their superiority, and hence readily show their displeasure.

322.

The Relatives of a Suicide. – The relatives of a suicide take it in ill part that he did not remain alive out of consideration for their reputation.

323.

Ingratitude Foreseen. – He who makes a large gift gets no gratitude; for the recipient is already overburdened by the acceptance of the gift.

324.

In Dull Society. – Nobody thanks a witty man for politeness when he puts himself on a par with a society in which it would not be polite to show one's wit.

325.

The Presence of Witnesses. – We are doubly willing to jump into the water after some one who has fallen in, if there are people present who have not the courage to do so.

326.

Being Silent. – For both parties in a controversy, the most disagreeable way of retaliating is to be vexed and silent; for the aggressor usually regards the silence as a sign of contempt.

327.

Friends' Secrets. – Few people will not expose the private affairs of their friends when at a loss for a subject of conversation.

328.

Humanity. – The humanity of intellectual celebrities consists in courteously submitting to unfairness in intercourse with those who are not celebrated.

329.

The Embarrassed. – People who do not feel sure of themselves in society seize every opportunity of publicly showing their superiority to close friends, for instance by teasing them.

330.

Thanks. – A refined nature is vexed by knowing that some one owes it thanks, a coarse nature by knowing that it owes thanks to some one.

331.

A Sign of Estrangement. – The surest sign of the estrangement of the opinions of two persons is when they both say something ironical to each other and neither of them feels the irony.

332.

Presumption in Connection with Merit. – Presumption in connection with merit offends us even more than presumption in persons devoid of merit, for merit in itself offends us.

333.

Danger in the Voice. – In conversation we are sometimes confused by the tone of our own voice, and misled to make assertions that do not at all correspond to our opinions.

334.

In Conversation. – Whether in conversation with others we mostly agree or mostly disagree with them is a matter of habit; there is sense in both cases.

335.

Fear of Our Neighbour. – We are afraid of the animosity of our neighbour, because we are apprehensive that he may thereby discover our secrets.

336.

Distinguishing by Blaming. – Highly respected persons distribute even their blame in such fashion that they try to distinguish us therewith. It is intended to remind us of their serious interest in us. We misunderstand them entirely when we take their blame literally and protest against it; we thereby offend them and estrange ourselves from them.

337.

Indignation at the Goodwill of Others. – We are mistaken as to the extent to which we think we are hated or feared; because, though we ourselves know very well the extent of our divergence from a person, tendency, or party, those others know us only superficially, and can, therefore, only hate us superficially. We often meet with goodwill which is inexplicable to us; but when we comprehend it, it shocks us, because it shows that we are not considered with sufficient seriousness or importance.

338.

Thwarting Vanities. – When two persons meet whose vanity is equally great, they have afterwards a bad impression of each other; because each has been so occupied with the impression he wished to produce on the other that the other has made no impression upon him; at last it becomes clear to them both that their efforts have been in vain, and each puts the blame on the other.

339.

Improper Behaviour as a Good Sign. – A superior mind takes pleasure in the tactlessness, pretentiousness, and even hostility of ambitious youths; it is the vicious habit of fiery horses which have not yet carried a rider, but, in a short time, will be so proud to carry one.

340.

When it is Advisable to Suffer Wrong. – It is well to put up with accusations without refutation, even when they injure us, when the accuser would see a still greater fault on our part if we contradicted and perhaps even refuted him. In this way, certainly, a person may always be wronged and always have right on his side, and may eventually, with the best conscience in the world, become the most intolerable tyrant and tormentor; and what happens in the individual may also take place in whole classes of society.

341.

Too Little Honoured. – Very conceited persons, who have received less consideration than they expected, attempt for a long time to deceive themselves and others with regard to it, and become subtle psychologists in order to make out that they have been amply honoured. Should they not attain their aim, should the veil of deception be torn, they give way to all the greater fury.

342.

Primitive Conditions Re-echoing in Speech. – By the manner in which people make assertions in their intercourse we often recognise an echo of the times when they were more conversant with weapons than anything else; sometimes they handle their assertions like sharpshooters using their arms, sometimes we think we hear the whizz and clash of swords, and with some men an assertion crashes down like a stout cudgel. Women, on the contrary, speak like beings who for thousands of years have sat at the loom, plied the needle, or played the child with children.

343.

The Narrator. – He who gives an account of something readily betrays whether it is because the fact interests him, or because he wishes to excite interest by the narration. In the latter case he will exaggerate, employ superlatives, and such like. He then does not usually tell his story SO well, because he does not think so much about his subject as about himself.

344.

The Reciter. – He who recites dramatic works makes discoveries about his own character; he finds his voice more natural in certain moods and scenes than in others, say in the pathetic or in the scurrilous, while in ordinary life, perhaps, he has not had the opportunity to exhibit pathos or scurrility.

345.

A Comedy Scene in Real Life. – Some one conceives an ingenious idea on a theme in order to express it in society. Now in a comedy we should hear and see how he sets all sail for that point, and tries to land the company at the place where he can make his remark, how he continuously pushes the conversation towards the one goal, sometimes losing the way, finding it again, and finally arriving at the moment: he is almost breathless – and then one of the company takes the remark itself out of his mouth! What will he do? Oppose his own opinion?

346.

Unintentionally Discourteous. – When a person treats another with unintentional discourtesy – for instance, not greeting him because not recognising him – he is vexed by it, although he cannot reproach his own sentiments; he is hurt by the bad opinion which he has produced in the other person, or fears the consequences of his bad humour, or is pained by the thought of having injured him – vanity, fear, or pity may therefore be aroused; perhaps all three together.

347.

A Masterpiece of Treachery. – To express a tantalising distrust of a fellow-conspirator, lest he should betray one, and this at the very moment when one is practising treachery one's self, is a masterpiece of wickedness; because it absorbs the other's attention and compels him for a time to act very unsuspiciously and openly, so that the real traitor has thus acquired a free hand.

348.

To Injure and to be Injured. – It is far pleasanter to injure and afterwards beg for forgiveness than to be injured and grant forgiveness. He who does the former gives evidence of power and afterwards of kindness of character. The person injured, however, if he does not wish to be considered inhuman, *must* forgive; his enjoyment of the other's humiliation is insignificant on account of this constraint.

349.

In a Dispute. – When we contradict another's opinion and at the same time develop our own, the constant consideration of the other opinion usually disturbs the natural attitude of our own which appears more intentional, more distinct, and perhaps somewhat exaggerated.

350.

An Artifice. – He who wants to get another to do something difficult must on no account treat the matter as a problem, but must set forth his plan plainly as the only one possible; and when the adversary's eye betrays objection and opposition he must understand how to break off quickly, and allow him no time to put in a word.

351.

Pricks of Conscience after Social Gatherings. – Why does our conscience prick us after ordinary social gatherings? Because we have treated serious things lightly, because in talking of persons we have not spoken quite justly or have been silent when we should have spoken, because, sometimes, we have not jumped up and run away – in short, because we have behaved in society as if we belonged to it.

352.

We are Misjudged. – He who always listens to hear how he is judged is always vexed. For we are misjudged even by those who are nearest to us ('who know us best'). Even good friends sometimes vent their ill-humour in a spiteful word; and would they be our friends if they knew us rightly? The judgements of the indifferent wound us deeply, because they sound so impartial, so objective almost. But when we see that some one hostile to us knows us in a concealed point as well as we know ourselves, how great is then our vexation!

353.

The Tyranny of the Portrait. – Artists and statesmen, who out of particular features quickly construct the whole picture of a man or an event, are mostly unjust in demanding that the event or person should afterwards be actually as they have painted it; they demand straightway that a man should be just as gifted, cunning, and unjust as he is in their representation of him.

354.

Relatives as the Best Friends. – The Greeks, who knew so well what a friend was, they alone of all peoples have a profound and largely philosophical discussion of friendship; so that it is by them firstly (and as yet lastly) that the problem of the friend has been recognised as worthy of solution – these same Greeks have designated *relatives* by an expression which is the superlative of the word 'friend'. This is inexplicable to me.

355.

Misunderstood Honesty. – When any one quotes himself in conversation ('I then said,' 'I am accustomed to say'), it gives the impression of presumption; whereas it often proceeds from quite an opposite source; or at least from honesty, which does not wish to deck and adorn the present moment with wit which belongs to an earlier moment.

356.

The Parasite. – It denotes entire absence of a noble disposition when a person prefers to live in dependence at the expense of others, usually with a secret bitterness against them, in order only that he may not be obliged to work. Such a disposition is far more frequent in women than in men, also far more pardonable (for historical reasons).

357.

On the Altar of Reconciliation. – There are circumstances under which one can only gain a point from a person by wounding him and becoming hostile; the feeling of having a foe torments him so much that he gladly seizes the first indication of a milder disposition to effect a reconciliation, and offers on the altar of this reconciliation what was formerly of such importance to him that he would not give it up at any price.

358.

Presumption in Demanding Pity. – There are people who, when they have been in a rage and have insulted others, demand, firstly, that it shall all be taken in good part; and, secondly, that they shall be pitied because they are subject to such violent paroxysms. So far does human presumption extend.

359.

Bait. – 'Every man has his price' – that is not true. But perhaps every one can be found a bait of one kind or other at which he will snap. Thus, in order to gain some supporters for a cause, it is only necessary to give it the glamour of being philanthropic, noble, charitable, and self-denying – and to what cause could this glamour not be given! It is the sweetmeat and dainty of *their* soul; others have different ones.

360.

The Attitude in Praising. – When good friends praise a gifted person he often appears to be delighted with them out of politeness and goodwill, but in reality he feels indifferent. His real nature is quite unmoved towards them, and will not budge a step on that account out of the sun or shade in which it lies; but people wish to please by praise, and it would grieve them if one did not rejoice when they praise a person.

361.

The Experience of Socrates. – If one has become a master in one thing, one has generally remained, precisely thereby, a complete dunce in most other things; but one forms the very reverse opinion, as was already experienced by Socrates. This is the annoyance which makes association with masters disagreeable.

362.

A Means of Defence. – In warring against stupidity, the most just and gentle of men at last become brutal. They are thereby, perhaps, taking the proper course for defence; for the most appropriate argument for a stupid brain is the clenched fist. But because, as has been said, their character is just and gentle, they suffer more by this means of protection than they injure their opponents by it.

363.

Curiosity. – If curiosity did not exist, very little would be done for the good of our neighbour. But curiosity creeps into the houses of the unfortunate and the needy under the name of duty or of pity. Perhaps there is a good deal of curiosity even in the much-vaunted maternal love.

364.

Disappointment in Society. – One man wishes to be interesting for his opinions, another for his likes and dislikes, a third for his acquaintances, and a fourth for his solitariness – and they all meet with disappointment. For he before whom the play is performed thinks himself the only play that is to be taken into account.

365.

The Duel. – It may be said in favour of duels and all affairs of honour that if a man has such susceptible feelings that he does not care to live when So-and-so says or thinks this or that about him; he has a right to make it a question of the death of the one or the other. With regard to the fact that he is so susceptible, it is not at all to be remonstrated with, in that matter we are the heirs of the past, of its greatness as well as of its exaggerations, without which no greatness ever existed. So when there exists a code of honour which lets blood stand in place of death, so that the mind is relieved after a regular duel it is a great blessing, because otherwise many human lives would be in danger. Such an institution, moreover, teaches men to be cautious in their utterances and makes intercourse with them possible.

366.

Nobleness and Gratitude. – A noble soul will be pleased to owe gratitude, and will not anxiously avoid opportunities of coming under obligation; it will also be moderate afterwards in the expression of its gratitude; baser souls, on the other hand, are unwilling to be under any obligation, or are afterwards immoderate in their expressions of thanks and altogether too devoted. The latter is, moreover, also the case with persons of mean origin or depressed circumstances; to show them a favour seems to them a miracle of grace.

367.

Occasions of Eloquence. – In order to talk well one man needs a person who is decidedly and avowedly his superior to talk to, while another can only find absolute freedom of speech and happy turns of eloquence before one who is his inferior. In both cases the cause is the same; each of them talks well only when he talks *sans gêne* – the one because in the presence of something higher he does not feel the impulse of rivalry and competition, the other because he also lacks the same impulse in the presence of something lower. Now there is quite another type of men, who talk well only when debating, with the intention of conquering. Which of the two types is the more aspiring: the one that talks well from excited ambition, or the one that talks badly or not at all from precisely the same motive?

368.

The Talent for Friendship. – Two types are distinguished amongst people who have a special faculty for friendship. The one is ever on the ascent, and for every phase of his development he finds a friend exactly suited to him. The series of friends which he thus acquires is seldom a consistent one, and is sometimes at variance and in contradiction, entirely in accordance with the fact that the later phases of his development neutralise or prejudice the earlier phases. Such a man may jestingly be called a *ladder*. The other type is represented by him who exercises an attractive influence on very different characters and endowments, so that he wins a whole circle of friends; these, however, are thereby brought voluntarily into friendly relations with one another in spite of all differences. Such a man may be called a *circle*, for this homogeneousness of such different temperaments and natures must somehow be typified in him. Furthermore, the faculty for having good friends is greater in many people than the faculty for being a good friend.

369.

Tactics in Conversation. – After a conversation with a person one is best pleased with him when one has had an opportunity of exhibiting one's intelligence and amiability in all its glory. Shrewd people who wish to impress a person favourably make use of this circumstance, they provide him with the best opportunities for making a good joke, and so on in conversation. An amusing conversation might be imagined between two very shrewd persons, each wishing to impress the other favourably, and therefore each throwing to the other the finest chances in conversation, which neither of them accepted, so that the conversation on the whole might turn out spiritless and unattractive because each assigned to the other the opportunity of being witty and charming.

370.

Discharge of Indignation. – The man who meets with a failure attributes this failure rather to the ill-will of another than to fate. His irritated feelings are alleviated by thinking that a person and not a thing is the cause of his failure; for he can revenge himself on persons, but is obliged to swallow down the injuries of fate. Therefore when anything has miscarried with a prince, those about him are accustomed to point out some individual as the ostensible cause, who is sacrificed in the interests of all the courtiers; for otherwise the prince's indignation would vent itself on them all, as he can take no revenge on the Goddess of Destiny herself.

371.

Assuming the Colours of the Environment. – Why are likes and dislikes so contagious that we can hardly live near a very sensitive person without being filled, like a hogshead, with his *fors* and *againsts*? In the first place, complete forbearance of judgement is very difficult, and sometimes absolutely intolerable to our vanity; it has the same appearance as poverty of thought and sentiment, or as timidity and unmanliness; and so we are, at least, driven on to take a side, perhaps contrary to our environment, if this attitude gives greater pleasure to our pride. As a rule, however – and this is the second point – we are not conscious of the transition from indifference to liking or disliking, but we gradually accustom ourselves to the sentiments of our environment, and because sympathetic agreement and acquiescence are so agreeable, we soon wear all the signs and party-colours of our surroundings.

372.

Irony. – Irony is only permissible as a pedagogic expedient, on the part of a teacher when dealing with his pupils; its purpose is to humble and to shame, but in the wholesome way that causes good resolutions to spring up and teaches people to show honour and gratitude, as they would to a doctor, to him who has so treated them. The ironical man pretends to be ignorant, and does it so well that the pupils conversing with him are deceived, and in their firm belief in their own superior knowledge they grow bold and expose all their weak points; they lose their cautiousness and reveal themselves as they are – until all of a sudden the light which they have held up to the teacher's face casts its rays back very humiliatingly upon themselves. Where such a relation, as that between teacher and pupil, does not exist, irony is a rudeness and a vulgar conceit. All ironical writers count on the silly species of human beings, who like to feel themselves superior to all others in common with the author himself, whom they look upon as the mouthpiece of their arrogance. Moreover, the habit of irony, like that of sarcasm, spoils the character; it gradually fosters the quality of a malicious superiority; one finally grows like a snappy dog, that has learnt to laugh as well as to bite.

373.

Arrogance. – There is nothing one should so guard against as the growth of the weed called arrogance, which spoils all one's good harvest; for there is arrogance in cordiality, in showing honour, in kindly familiarity, in caressing, in friendly counsel, in acknowledgment of faults, in sympathy for others – and all these fine things arouse aversion when the weed in question grows up among them. The arrogant man – that is to say, he who desires to appear more than he is *or passes for* – always miscalculates. It is true that he obtains a momentary success, inasmuch as those with whom he is arrogant generally give him the amount of honour that he demands, owing to fear or for the sake of convenience; but they take a bad revenge for it, inasmuch as they subtract from the value which they hitherto attached to him just as much as he demands above that amount. There is nothing for which men ask to be paid dearer than for humiliation. The arrogant man can make his really great merit so suspicious and small in the eyes of others that they tread on it with dusty feet. If at all, we should only allow ourselves a *proud* manner where we are quite sure of not being misunderstood and considered as arrogant; as, for instance, with friends and wives. For in social intercourse there is no greater folly than to acquire a reputation for arrogance; it is still worse than not having learnt to deceive politely.

374.

Tête-à-Tête – Private conversation is the perfect conversation, because everything the one person says receives its particular colouring, its tone, and its accompanying gestures *out of strict consideration for the other person* engaged in the conversation, it therefore corresponds to what takes place in intercourse by letter, viz., that one and the same person exhibits ten kinds of psychical expression, according as he writes now to this individual and now to that one. In duologue there is only a single refraction of thought; the person conversed with produces it, as the mirror in whom we want to behold our thoughts anew in their finest form. But how is it when there are two or three, or even more persons conversing with one? Conversation then necessarily loses something of its individualising subtlety, different considerations thwart and neutralise each other; the style which pleases one does not suit the taste of another. In intercourse with several individuals a person is therefore to withdraw within himself and represent facts as they are; but he has also to remove from the subjects the pulsating ether of humanity which makes conversation one of the pleasantest things in the world. Listen only to the tone in which those who mingle with whole groups of men are in the habit of speaking; it is as if the fundamental base of all speech were, 'It is *myself*; I say this, so make what you will of it!' That is the reason why clever ladies usually leave a singular, painful, and forbidding impression on those who have met them in society; it is the talking to many people, before many people, that robs them of all intellectual amiability and shows only their conscious dependence on themselves, their tactics, and their intention of gaining a public victory in full light; whilst in a private conversation the same ladies become womanly again, and recover their intellectual grace and charm.

375.

Posthumous Fame. – There is sense in hoping for recognition in a distant future only when we take it for granted that mankind will remain essentially unchanged, and that whatever is great is not for one age only but will be looked upon as great for all time. But this is an error. In all their sentiments and judgements concerning what is good and beautiful mankind have greatly changed; it is mere fantasy to imagine one's self to be a mile ahead, and that the whole of mankind is coming *our* way. Besides, a scholar who is misjudged may at present reckon with certainty that his discovery will be made by others, and that, at best, it will be allowed to him later on by some historian that he also already knew this or that but was not in a position to secure the recognition of his knowledge. Not to be recognised is always interpreted by posterity as lack of power. In short, one should not so readily speak in favour of haughty solitude. There are, however, exceptional cases; but it is chiefly our faults, weakness, and follies that hinder the recognition of our great qualities.

376.

Of Friends. – Just consider with thyself how different are the feelings, how divided are the opinions of even the nearest acquaintances; how even the same opinions in thy friend's mind have quite a different aspect and strength from what they have in thine own; and how manifold are the occasions which arise for misunderstanding and hostile severance. After all this thou wilt say to thyself, 'How insecure is the ground upon which all our alliances and friendships rest, how liable to cold downpours and bad weather, how lonely is every creature!' When a person recognises this fact, and, in addition, that all opinions and the nature and strength of them in his fellow-men are just as necessary and irresponsible as their actions; when his eye learns to see this internal necessity of opinions, owing to the indissoluble interweaving of character, occupation, talent, and environment – he will perhaps get rid of the bitterness and sharpness of the feeling with which the sage exclaimed, 'Friends, there are no friends!' Much rather will he make the confession to himself: Yes, there are friends, but they were drawn towards thee by error and deception concerning thy character; and they must have learnt to be silent in order to remain thy friends; for such human relationships almost always rest on the fact that some few things are never said, are never, indeed, alluded to; but if these pebbles are set rolling friendship follows afterwards and is broken. Are there any who would not be mortally injured if they were to learn what their most intimate friends really knew about them? By getting a knowledge of ourselves, and by looking upon our nature as a changing sphere of opinions and moods, and thereby learning to despise ourselves a little, we recover once more our equilibrium with the rest of mankind. It is true that we have good reason to despise each of our acquaintances, even the greatest of them; but just as good reason to turn this feeling against ourselves. And so we will bear with each other, since we bear with ourselves; and perhaps there will come to each a happier hour, when he will exclaim:

> 'Friends, there are really no friends!' thus cried th' expiring old sophist;
>
> 'Foes, there is really no foe!' – thus shout I, the incarnate fool.

SEVENTH DIVISION.
WIFE AND CHILD.

377.

The Perfect Woman. – The perfect woman is a higher type of humanity than the perfect man, and also something much rarer. The natural history of animals furnishes grounds in support of this theory.

378.

Friendship and Marriage. – The best friend will probably get the best wife, because a good marriage is based on talent for friendship.

379.

The Survival of the Parents. – The undissolved dissonances in the relation of the character and sentiments of the parents survive in the nature of the child and make up the history of its inner sufferings.

380.

Inherited from the Mother. – Every one bears within him an image of woman, inherited from his mother: it determines his attitude towards women as a whole, whether to honour, despise, or remain generally indifferent to them.

381.

Correcting Nature. – Whoever has not got a good father should procure one.

382.

Fathers and Sons. – Fathers have much to do to make amends for having sons.

383.

The Error of Gentlewomen. – Gentlewomen think that a thing does not really exist when it is not possible to talk of it in society.

384.

A Male Disease. – The surest remedy for the male disease of self-contempt is to be loved by a sensible woman.

385.

A Species of Jealousy. – Mothers are readily jealous of the friends of sons who are particularly successful. As a rule a mother loves *herself* in her son more than the son.

386.

Rational Irrationality. – In the maturity of life and intelligence the feeling comes over a man that his father did wrong in begetting him.

387.

Maternal Excellence. – Some mothers need happy and honoured children, some need unhappy ones – otherwise they cannot exhibit their maternal excellence.

388.

Different Sighs. – Some husbands have sighed over the elopement of their wives, the greater number, however, have sighed because nobody would elope with theirs.

389.

Love Matches. – Marriages which are contracted for love (so-called love-matches) have error for their father and need (necessity) for their mother.

390.

Women's Friendships. – Women can enter into friendship with a man perfectly well; but in order to maintain it the aid of a little physical antipathy is perhaps required.

391.

Ennui. – Many people, especially women, never feel ennui because they have never learnt to work properly.

392.

An Element of Love. – In all feminine love something of maternal love also comes to light.

393.

Unity of Place and Drama. – If married couples did not live together, happy marriages would be more frequent.

394.

The Usual Consequences of Marriage. – All intercourse which does not elevate a person, debases him, and *vice versa*; hence men usually sink a little when they marry, while women are somewhat elevated. Over-intellectual men require marriage in proportion as they are opposed to it as to a repugnant medicine.

395.

Learning to Command. – Children of unpretentious families must be taught to command, just as much as other children must be taught to obey.

396.

Wanting to be in Love. – Betrothed couples who have been matched by convenience often exert themselves *to fall in love*, to avoid the reproach of cold, calculating expediency. In the same manner those who become converts to Christianity for their advantage exert themselves to become genuinely pious; because the religious cast of countenance then becomes easier to them.

397.

No Standing Still in Love. – A musician who *loves* the slow *tempo* will play the same pieces ever more slowly. There is thus no standing still in any love.

398.

Modesty. – Women's modesty usually increases with their beauty.[15]

15 The opposite of this aphorism also holds good. – J. M. K.

399.

Marriage on a Good Basis. – A marriage in which each wishes to realise an individual aim by means of the other will stand well; for instance, when the woman wishes to become famous through the man and the man beloved through the woman.

400.

Proteus-Nature. – Through love women actually become what they appear to be in the imagination of their lovers.

401.

To Love and to Possess. – As a rule women love a distinguished man to the extent that they wish to possess him exclusively. They would gladly keep him under lock and key, if their vanity did not forbid, but vanity demands that he should also appear distinguished before others.

402.

The Test of a Good Marriage. – The goodness of a marriage is proved by the fact that it can stand an 'exception'.

403.

Bringing Anyone Round to Anything. – One may make any person so weak and weary by disquietude, anxiety, and excess of work or thought that he no longer resists anything that appears complicated, but gives way to it – diplomatists and women know this.

404.

Propriety and Honesty. – Those girls who mean to trust exclusively to their youthful charms for their provision in life, and whose cunning is further prompted by worldly mothers, have just the same aims as courtesans, only they are wiser and less honest.

405.

Masks. – There are women who, wherever one examines them, have no inside, but are mere masks. A man is to be pitied who has connection with such almost spectre-like and necessarily unsatisfactory creatures, but it is precisely such women who know how to excite a man's desire most strongly; he seeks for their soul, and seeks evermore.

406.

Marriage as a Long Talk. – In entering on a marriage one should ask one's self the question, 'Do you think you will pass your time well with this woman till your old age?' All else in marriage is transitory; talk, however, occupies most of the time of the association.

407.

Girlish Dreams. – Inexperienced girls flatter themselves with the notion that it is in their power to make a man happy; later on they learn that it is equivalent to underrating a man to suppose that he needs only a girl to make him happy. Women's vanity requires a man to be something more than merely a happy husband.

408.

The Dying-out of Faust and Marguerite. – According to the very intelligent remark of a scholar, the educated men of modern Germany resemble somewhat a mixture of Mephistopheles and Wagner, but are not at all like Faust, whom our grandfathers (in their youth at least) felt agitating within them. To them, therefore – to continue the remark – Marguerites are not suited, for two reasons. And because the latter are no longer desired they seem to be dying out.

409.

Classical Education for Girls. – For goodness' sake let us not give our classical education to girls! An education which, out of ingenious, inquisitive, ardent youths, so frequently makes – copies of their teacher!

410.

Without Rivals. – Women readily perceive in a man whether his soul has already been taken possession of; they wish to be loved without rivals, and find fault with the objects of his ambition, his political tasks, his sciences and arts, if he have a passion for such things. Unless he be distinguished thereby – then, in the case of a love-relationship between them, women look at the same time for an increase of *their own* distinction; under such circumstances, they favour the lover.

411.

The Feminine Intellect. – The intellect of women manifests itself as perfect mastery, presence of mind, and utilisation of all advantages. They transmit it as a fundamental quality to their children, and the father adds thereto the darker background of the will. His influence determines as it were the rhythm and harmony with which the new life is to be performed; but its melody is derived from the mother. For those who know how to put a thing properly: women have intelligence, men have character and passion. This does not contradict the fact that men actually achieve so much more with their intelligence: they have deeper and more powerful impulses; and it is these which carry their understanding (in itself something passive) to such an extent. Women are often silently surprised at the great respect men pay to their character. When, therefore, in the choice of a partner men seek specially for a being of deep and strong character, and women for a being of intelligence, brilliancy, and presence of mind, it is plain that at bottom men seek for the ideal man, and women for the ideal woman – consequently not for the complement but for the completion of their own excellence.

412.

Hesiod's Opinion Confirmed. – It is a sign of women's wisdom that they have almost always known how to get themselves supported, like drones in a bee-hive. Let us just consider what this meant originally, and why men do not depend upon women for their support. Of a truth it is because masculine vanity and reverence are greater than feminine wisdom; for women have known how to secure for themselves by their subordination the greatest advantage, in fact, the upper hand. Even the care of children may originally have been used by the wisdom of women as an excuse for withdrawing themselves as much as possible from work. And at present they still understand when they are really active (as housekeepers, for instance) how to make a bewildering fuss about it, so that the merit of their activity is usually ten times overestimated by men.

413.

Lovers as Short-sighted People. – A pair of powerful spectacles has sometimes sufficed to cure a person in love; and whoever has had sufficient imagination to represent a face or form twenty years older, has probably gone through life not much disturbed.

414.

Women in Hatred. – In a state of hatred women are more dangerous than men; for one thing, because they are hampered by no regard for fairness when their hostile feelings have been aroused; but let their hatred develop unchecked to its utmost consequences; then also, because they are expert in finding sore spots (which every man and every party possess), and pouncing upon them: for which purpose their dagger-pointed intelligence is of good service (whilst men, hesitating at the sight of wounds, are often generously and conciliatorily inclined).

415.

Love. – The love idolatry which women practise is fundamentally and originally an intelligent device, inasmuch as they increase their power by all the idealisings of love and exhibit themselves as so much the more desirable in the eyes of men. But by being accustomed for centuries to this exaggerated appreciation of love, it has come to pass that they have been caught in their own net and have forgotten the origin of the device. They themselves are now still more deceived than the men, and on that account also suffer more from the disillusionment which, almost necessarily, enters into the life of every woman – so far, at any rate, as she has sufficient imagination and intelligence to be able to be deceived and undeceived.

416.

The Emancipation of Women. – Can women be at all just, when they are so accustomed to love and to be immediately biased for or against? For that reason they are also less interested in things and more in individuals: but when they are interested in things they immediately become their partisans, and thereby spoil their pure, innocent effect. Thus there arises a danger, by no means small, in entrusting politics and certain portions of science to them (history, for instance). For what is rarer than a woman who really knows what science is? Indeed the best of them cherish in their breasts a secret scorn for science, as if they were somehow superior to it. Perhaps all this can be changed in time; but meanwhile it is so.

417.

The Inspiration in Women's Judgements. – The sudden decisions, for or against, which women are in the habit of making, the flashing illumination of personal relations caused by their spasmodic inclinations and aversions – in short, the proofs of feminine injustice have been invested with a lustre by men who are in love, as if all women had inspirations of wisdom, even without the Delphic cauldron and the laurel wreaths; and their utterances are interpreted and duly set forth as Sibylline oracles for long afterwards. When one considers, however, that for every person and for every cause something can be said in favour of it but equally also something against it, that things are not only two-sided, but also three- and four-sided, it is almost difficult to be entirely at fault in such sudden decisions; indeed, it might be said that the nature of things has been so arranged that women should always carry their point.[16]

418.

Being Loved. – As one of every two persons in love is usually the one who loves, the other the one who is loved, the belief has arisen that in every love-affair there is a constant amount of love; and that the more of it the one person monopolises the less is left for the other.

---

16 It may be remarked that Nietzsche changed his view on this subject later on, and ascribed more importance to woman's intuition. Cf. also Disraeli's reference to the 'High Priestesses of predestination.' – J. M. K.

Exceptionally it happens that the vanity of each of the parties persuades him or her that it is he or she who must be loved; so that both of them wish to be loved: from which cause many half funny, half absurd scenes take place, especially in married life.

419.

Contradictions in Feminine Minds. – Owing to the fact that women are so much more personal than objective, there are tendencies included in the range of their ideas which are logically in contradiction to one another; they are accustomed in turn to become enthusiastically fond just of the representatives of these tendencies and accept their systems in the lump; but in such wise that a dead place originates wherever a new personality afterwards gets the ascendancy. It may happen that the whole philosophy in the mind of an old lady consists of nothing but such dead places.

420.

Who Suffers the More? – After a personal dissension and quarrel between a woman and a man the latter party suffers chiefly from the idea of having wounded the other, whilst the former suffers chiefly from the idea of not having wounded the other sufficiently; so she subsequently endeavours by tears, sobs, and discomposed mien, to make his heart heavier.

421.

An Opportunity for Feminine Magnanimity. – If we could disregard the claims of custom in our thinking we might consider whether nature and reason do not suggest several marriages for men, one after another: perhaps that, at the age of twenty-two, he should first marry an older girl who is mentally and morally his superior, and can be his leader through all the dangers of the twenties (ambition, hatred, self-contempt, and passions of all kinds). This woman's affection would subsequently change entirely into maternal love, and she would not only submit to it but would encourage the man in the most salutary manner, if in his thirties he contracted an alliance with quite a young girl whose education he himself should take in hand. Marriage is a necessary institution for the twenties; a useful, but not necessary, institution for the thirties; for later life it is often harmful, and promotes the mental deterioration of the man.

422.

The Tragedy of Childhood. – Perhaps it not infrequently happens that noble men with lofty aims have to fight their hardest battle in childhood; by having perchance to carry out their principles in opposition to a base-minded father addicted to feigning and falsehood, or living, like Lord Byron, in constant warfare with a childish and passionate mother. He who has had such an experience will never be able to forget all his life who has been his greatest and most dangerous enemy.

423.

Parental Folly. – The grossest mistakes in judging a man are made by his parents – this is a fact, but how is it to be explained? Have the parents too much experience of the child and cannot any longer arrange this experience into a unity? It has been noticed that it is only in the earlier period of their sojourn in foreign countries that travellers rightly grasp the general distinguishing features of a people; the better they come to know it, they are the less able to see what is typical and distinguishing in a people. As soon as they grow short-sighted their eyes cease to be long-sighted. Do parents, therefore, judge their children falsely because they have never stood far enough away from them? The following is quite another explanation: people are no longer accustomed to reflect on what is close at hand and surrounds them, but just accept it. Perhaps the usual thoughtlessness of parents is the reason why they judge so wrongly when once they are compelled to judge their children.

424.

The Future of Marriage. – The noble and liberal-minded women who take as their mission the education and elevation of the female sex, should not overlook one point of view: 'Marriage regarded in its highest aspect, as the spiritual friendship of two persons of opposite sexes, and accordingly such as is hoped for in future, contracted for the purpose of producing and educating a new generation – such marriage, which only makes use of the sensual, so to speak, as a rare and occasional means to a higher purpose, will, it is to be feared, probably need a natural auxiliary, namely, *concubinage*. For if, on the grounds of his health, the wife is also to serve for the sole satisfaction of the man's sexual needs, a wrong perspective, opposed to the aims indicated, will have most influence in the choice of a wife. The aims referred to: the production of descendants, will be accidental, and their successful education highly improbable. A good wife, who has to be friend, helper, child-bearer, mother, family-head and manager, and has even perhaps to conduct her own business and affairs separately from those of the husband, cannot at the same time be a concubine; it would, in general, be asking too much of her. In the future, therefore, a state of things might take place the opposite of what existed at Athens in the time of Pericles; the men, whose wives were then little more to them than concubines, turned besides to the Aspasias, because they longed for the charms of a companionship gratifying both to head and heart, such as the grace and intellectual suppleness of women could alone provide. All human institutions, just like marriage, allow only a moderate amount of practical idealising, failing which coarse remedies immediately become necessary.

425.

The 'Storm and Stress' Period of Women. – In the three or four civilised countries of Europe, it is possible, by several centuries of education, to make out of women anything we like – even men, not in a sexual sense, of course, but in every other. Under such influences they will acquire all the masculine virtues and forces, at the same time, of course, they must also have taken all the masculine weaknesses and vices into the bargain: so much, as has been said, we can command. But how shall we endure the intermediate state thereby induced, which may even last two or three centuries, during which feminine follies and injustices, woman's original birthday endowment, will still maintain the ascendancy over all that has been otherwise gained and acquired? This will be the time when indignation will be the peculiar masculine passion; indignation, because all arts and sciences have been overflowed and choked by an unprecedented dilettanteism, philosophy talked to death by brain-bewildering chatter, politics more fantastic and partisan than ever, and society in complete disorganisation, because the conservatrices of ancient customs have become ridiculous to themselves, and have endeavoured in every way to place themselves outside the pale of custom. If indeed women had their greatest power in custom, where will they have to look in order to reacquire a similar plenitude of power after having renounced custom?

426.

Free-Spirit and Marriage. – Will free-thinkers live with women? In general, I think that, like the prophesying birds of old, like the truth-thinkers and truth-speakers of the present, they must prefer to *fly alone.*

427.

The Happiness of Marriage. – Everything to which we are accustomed draws an ever-tightening cobweb-net around us; and presently we notice that the threads have become cords, and that we ourselves sit in the middle like a spider that has here got itself caught and must feed on its own blood. Hence the free spirit hates all rules and customs, all that is permanent and definitive, hence he painfully tears asunder again and again the net around him, though in consequence thereof he will suffer from numerous wounds, slight and severe; for he must break off every thread *from himself*, from his body and soul. He must learn to love where he has hitherto hated, and *vice versa.* Indeed, it must not be a thing impossible for him to sow dragon's teeth in the same field in which he formerly scattered the abundance of his bounty. From this it can be inferred whether he is suited for the happiness of marriage.

428.

Too Intimate. – When we live on too intimate terms with a person it is as if we were again and again handling a good engraving with our fingers; the time comes when we have soiled and damaged paper in our hands, and nothing more. A man's soul also gets worn out by constant handling; at least, it eventually *appears* so to us – never again do we see its original design and beauty. We always lose through too familiar association with women and friends; and sometimes we lose the pearl of our life thereby.

429.

The Golden Cradle. – The free spirit will always feel relieved when he has finally resolved to shake off the motherly care and guardianship with which women surround him. What harm will a rough wind, from which he has been so anxiously protected, do him? Of what consequence is a genuine disadvantage, loss, misfortune, sickness, illness, fault, or folly more or less in his life, compared with the bondage of the golden cradle, the peacock's-feather fan, and the oppressive feeling that he must, in addition, be grateful because he is waited on and spoiled like a baby? Hence it is that the milk which is offered him by the motherly disposition of the women about him can so readily turn into gall.

430.

A Voluntary Victim. – There is nothing by which able women can so alleviate the lives of their husbands, should these be great and famous, as by becoming, so to speak, the receptacle for the general disfavour and occasional ill-humour of the rest of mankind. Contemporaries are usually accustomed to overlook many mistakes, follies, and even flagrant injustices in their great men if only they can find some one to maltreat and kill, as a proper victim for the relief of their feelings. A wife not infrequently has the ambition to present herself for this sacrifice, and then the husband may indeed feel satisfied – he being enough of an egoist to have such a voluntary storm, rain, and lightning-conductor beside him.

431.

Agreeable Adversaries. – The natural inclination of women towards quiet, regular, happily tuned existences and intercourse, the oil-like and calming effect of their influence upon the sea of life, operates unconsciously against the heroic inner impulse of the free spirit. Without knowing it, women act as if they were taking away the stones from the path of the wandering mineralogist in order that he might not strike his foot against them – when he has gone out for the very purpose of striking against them.

432.

The Discord of Two Concords. – Woman wants to serve, and finds her happiness therein; the free spirit does not want to be served, and therein finds his happiness.

433.

Xantippe. – Socrates found a wife such as he required – but he would not have sought her had he known her sufficiently well; even the heroism of his free spirit would not have gone so far. As a matter of fact, Xantippe forced him more and more into his peculiar profession, inasmuch as she made house and home doleful and dismal to him; she taught him to live in the streets and wherever gossiping and idling went on, and thereby made him the greatest Athenian street-dialectician, who had, at last, to compare himself to a gad-fly which a god had set on the neck of the beautiful horse Athens to prevent it from resting.

434.

Blind to the Future. – Just as mothers have senses and eye only for those pains of their children that are evident to the senses and eye, so the wives of men of high aspirations cannot accustom themselves to see their husbands suffering, starving, or slighted – although all this is, perhaps, not only the proof that they have rightly chosen their attitude in life, but even the guarantee that their great aims *must* be achieved some time. Women always intrigue privately against the higher souls of their husbands; they want to cheat them out of their future for the sake of a painless and comfortable present.

435.

Authority and Freedom. – However highly women may honour their husbands, they honour still more the powers and ideas recognised by society; they have been accustomed for millennia to go along with their hands folded on their breasts, and their heads bent before everything dominant, disapproving of all resistance to public authority. They therefore unintentionally, and as if from instinct, hang themselves as a drag on the wheels of free-spirited, independent endeavour, and in certain circumstances make their husbands highly impatient, especially when the latter persuade themselves that it is really love which prompts the action of their wives. To disapprove of women's methods and generously to honour the motives that prompt them – that is man's nature and often enough his despair.

436.

Ceterum Censeo. – It is laughable when a company of paupers decree the abolition of the right of inheritance, and it is not less laughable when childless persons labour for the practical lawgiving of a country: they have not enough ballast in their ship to sail safely over the ocean of the future. But it seems equally senseless if a man who has chosen for his mission the widest knowledge and estimation of universal existence, burdens himself with personal considerations for a family, with the support, protection, and care of wife and child, and in front of his telescope hangs that gloomy veil through which hardly a ray from the distant firmament can penetrate. Thus I, too, agree with the opinion that in matters of the highest philosophy all married men are to be suspected.

437.

Finally. – There are many kinds of hemlock, and fate generally finds an opportunity to put a cup of this poison to the lips of the free spirit – in order to 'punish' him, as every one then says. What do the women do about him then? They cry and lament, and perhaps disturb the sunset calm of the thinker, as they did in the prison at Athens. 'Oh Crito, bid some one take those women away!' said Socrates at last.

EIGHTH DIVISION.
A GLANCE AT THE STATE.

438.

Asking to be Heard. – The demagogic disposition and the intention of working upon the masses is at present common to all political parties; on this account they are all obliged to change their principles into great *al fresco* follies and thus make a show of them. In this matter there is no further alteration to be made: indeed, it is superfluous even to raise a finger against it; for here Voltaire's saying applies: '*Quand la populace se mile de raisonner, tout est perdu.*' Since this has happened we have to accommodate ourselves to the new conditions, as we have to accommodate ourselves when an earthquake has displaced the old boundaries and the contour of the land and altered the value of property. Moreover, when it is once for all a question in the politics of all parties to make life endurable to the greatest possible majority, this majority may always decide what they understand by an endurable life; if they believe their intellect capable of finding the right means to this end why should we doubt about it? They *want*, once for all, to be the architects of their own good or ill fortune; and if their feeling of free choice and their pride in the five or six ideas that their brain conceals and brings to light, really makes life so agreeable to them that they gladly put up with the fatal consequences of their narrow-mindedness, there is little to object to, provided that their narrow-mindedness does not go so far as to demand that everything shall become politics in this sense, that all shall live and act according to this standard. For, in the first place, it must be more than ever permissible for some people to keep aloof from politics and to stand somewhat aside. To this they are also impelled by the pleasure of free choice, and connected with this there may even be some little pride in keeping silence when too many, and only the many, are speaking. Then this small group must be excused if they do not attach such great importance to the happiness of the majority (nations or strata of population may be understood thereby), and are occasionally guilty of an ironical grimace; for their seriousness lies elsewhere, their conception of happiness is quite different, and their aim cannot be encompassed by every clumsy hand that has just five fingers. Finally, there comes from time to time – what is certainly most difficult to concede to them, but must also be conceded – a moment when they emerge from their silent solitariness and try once more the strength of their lungs; they then call to each other like people lost in a wood, to make themselves known and for mutual encouragement; whereby, to be sure, much becomes audible that sounds evil to ears for which it is not intended. Soon, however, silence again prevails in the wood, such silence that the buzzing, humming, and fluttering of the countless insects that live in, above, and beneath it, are again plainly heard.

439.

Culture and Caste. – A higher culture can only originate where there are two distinct castes of society: that of the working class, and that of the leisured class who are capable of true leisure; or, more strongly expressed, the caste of compulsory labour and the caste of free labour. The point of view of the division of happiness is not essential when it is a question of the production of a higher culture; in any case, however, the leisured caste is more susceptible to suffering and suffer more, their pleasure in existence is less and their task is greater. Now supposing there should be quite an interchange between the two castes, so that on the one hand the duller and less intelligent families and individuals are lowered from the higher caste into the lower, and, on the other hand, the freer men of the lower caste obtain access to the higher, a condition of things would be attained beyond which one can only perceive the open sea of vague wishes. Thus speaks to us the vanishing voice of the olden time; but where are there still ears to hear it?

440.

Of Good Blood. – That which men and women of good blood possess much more than others, and which gives them an undoubted right to be more highly appreciated, are two arts which are always increased by inheritance: the art of being able to command, and the art of proud obedience. Now wherever commanding is the business of the day (as in the great world of commerce and industry), there results something similar to these families of good blood, only the noble bearing in obedience is lacking which is an inheritance from feudal conditions and hardly grows any longer in the climate of our culture.

441.

Subordination. – The subordination which is so highly valued in military and official ranks will soon become as incredible to us as the secret tactics of the Jesuits have already become; and when this subordination is no longer possible a multitude of astonishing results will no longer be attained, and the world will be all the poorer. It must disappear, for its foundation is disappearing, the belief in unconditional authority, in ultimate truth; even in military ranks physical compulsion is not sufficient to produce it, but only the inherited adoration of the princely as of something superhuman. In *freer* circumstances people subordinate themselves only on conditions, in compliance with a mutual contract, consequently with all the provisos of self-interest.

442.

The National Army. – The greatest disadvantage of the national army, now so much glorified, lies in the squandering of men of the highest civilisation; it is only by the favourableness of all circumstances that there are such men at all; how carefully and anxiously should we deal with them, since long periods are required to create the chance conditions for the production of such delicately organised brains! But as the Greeks wallowed in the blood of Greeks, so do Europeans now in the blood of Europeans: and indeed, taken relatively, it is mostly the highly cultivated who are sacrificed, those who promise an abundant and excellent posterity; for such stand in the front of the battle as commanders, and also expose themselves to most danger, by reason of their higher ambition. At present, when quite other and higher tasks are assigned than *patria* and *honour*, the rough Roman patriotism is either something dishonourable or a sign of being behind the times.

443.

Hope as Presumption. – Our social order will slowly melt away, as all former orders have done, as soon as the suns of new opinions have shone upon mankind with a new glow. We can only *wish* this melting away in the hope thereof, and we are only reasonably entitled to hope when we believe that we and our equals have more strength in heart and head than the representatives of the existing state of things. As a rule, therefore, this hope will be a presumption, an *over-estimation*.

444.

War. – Against war it may be said that it makes the victor stupid and the vanquished revengeful. In favour of war it may be said that it barbarises in both its above-named results, and thereby makes more natural; it is the sleep or the winter period of culture; man emerges from it with greater strength for good and for evil.

445.

In the Prince's Service. – To be able to act quite regardlessly it is best for a statesman to carry out his work not for himself but for a prince. The eye of the spectator is dazzled by the splendour of this general disinterestedness, so that it does not see the malignancy and severity which the work of a statesman brings with it.[17]

446.

A Question of Power, not of Right. – As regards Socialism, in the eyes of those who always consider higher utility, if it is *really* a rising against their oppressors of those who for centuries have been oppressed and downtrodden, there is no problem of *right* involved (notwithstanding the ridiculous, effeminate question, 'How far *ought* we to grant its demands?') but only a problem of *power* ('How far *can* we make use of its demands?'); the same, therefore, as in the case of a natural force – steam, for instance – which is either forced by man into his service, as a machine-god, or which, in case of defects of the machine, that is to say, defects of human calculation in its construction, destroys it and man together. In order to solve this question of power we must know how strong Socialism is, in what modification it may yet be employed as a powerful lever in the present

---

17 This aphorism may have been suggested by Nietzsche's observing the behaviour of his great contemporary, Bismarck, towards the dynasty. – J. M. K.

mechanism of political forces; under certain circumstances we should do all we can to strengthen it. With every great force – be it the most dangerous – men have to think how they can make of it an instrument for their purposes. Socialism acquires a *right* only if war seems to have taken place between the two powers, the representatives of the old and the new, when, however, a wise calculation of the greatest possible preservation and advantageousness to both sides gives rise to a desire for a treaty. Without treaty no right. So far, however, there is neither war nor treaty on the ground in question, therefore no rights, no 'ought'.

447.

Utilising the most Trivial Dishonesty. – The power of the press consists in the fact that every individual who ministers to it only feels himself bound and constrained to a very small extent. He usually expresses *his* opinion, but sometimes also does *not* express it in order to serve his party or the politics of his country, or even himself. Such little faults of dishonesty, or perhaps only of a dishonest silence, are not hard to bear by the individual, but the consequences are extraordinary, because these little faults are committed by many at the same time. Each one says to himself: 'For such small concessions I live better and can make my income; by the want of such little compliances I make myself impossible.' Because it seems almost morally indifferent to write a line more (perhaps even without signature), or not to write it, a person who has money and influence can make any opinion a public one. He who knows that most people are weak in trifles, and wishes to attain his own ends thereby, is always dangerous.

448.

Too Loud a Tone in Grievances. – Through the fact that an account of a bad state of things (for instance, the crimes of an administration, bribery and arbitrary favour in political or learned bodies) is greatly exaggerated, it fails in its effect on intelligent people, but has all the greater effect on the unintelligent (who would have remained indifferent to an accurate and moderate account). But as these latter are considerably in the majority, and harbour in themselves stronger will-power and more impatient desire for action, the exaggeration becomes the cause of investigations, punishments, promises, and reorganisations. In so far it is useful to exaggerate the accounts of bad states of things.

449.

The Apparent Weather Makers of Politics. – Just as people tacitly assume that he who understands the weather, and foretells it about a day in advance, makes the weather, so even the educated and learned, with a display of superstitious faith, ascribe to great statesmen as their most special work all the important changes and conjunctures that have taken place during their administration, when it is only evident that they knew something thereof a little earlier than other people and made their calculations accordingly – thus they are also looked upon as weather-makers – and this belief is not the least important instrument of their power.

450.

New and Old Conceptions of Government. – To draw such a distinction between Government and people as if two separate spheres of power, a stronger and higher, and a weaker and lower, negotiated and came to terms with each other, is a remnant of transmitted political sentiment, which still accurately represents the historic establishment of the conditions of power in *most* States. When Bismarck, for instance, describes the constitutional system as a compromise between Government and people, he speaks in accordance with a principle which has its reason in history (from whence, to be sure, it also derives its admixture of folly, without which nothing human can exist). On the other hand, we must now learn – in accordance with a principle which has originated only in the *brain* and has still to *make* history – that Government is nothing but an organ of the people – not an attentive, honourable 'higher' in relation to a 'lower' accustomed to modesty. Before we accept this hitherto unhistorical and arbitrary, although logical, formulation of the conception of Government, let us but consider its consequences, for the relation between people and Government is the strongest typical relation, after the pattern of which the relationship between teacher and pupil, master and servants, father and family, leader and soldier, master and apprentice, is unconsciously formed. At present, under the influence of the prevailing constitutional system of government, all these relationships are changing a little – they are becoming compromises. But how they will have to be reversed and shifted, and change name and nature, when that newest of all conceptions has got the upper hand everywhere in people's minds! To achieve which, however, a century may yet be required. In this matter there is nothing *further* to be wished for except caution and slow development.

451.

Justice as the Decoy-Cry of Parties. – Well may noble (if not exactly very intelligent) representatives of the governing classes asseverate: 'We will treat men equally and grant them equal rights'; so far a socialistic mode of thought which is based on *justice* is possible; but, as has been said, only within the ranks of the governing class, which in this case *practises* justice with sacrifices and abnegations. On the other hand, to *demand* equality of rights, as do the Socialists of the subject caste, is by no means the outcome of justice, but of covetousness. If you expose bloody pieces of flesh to a beast, and withdraw them again, until it finally begins to roar, do you think that roaring implies justice?

452.

Possession and Justice. – When the Socialists point out that the division of property at the present day is the consequence of countless deeds of injustice and violence, and, *in summa*, repudiate obligation to anything with so unrighteous a basis, they only perceive something isolated. The entire past of ancient civilisation is built up on violence, slavery, deception, and error; we, however, cannot annul ourselves, the heirs of all these conditions, nay, the concrescences of all this past, and are not entitled to demand the withdrawal of a single fragment thereof. The unjust disposition lurks also in the souls of non-possessors; they are not better than the possessors and have no moral prerogative; for at one time or another their ancestors have been possessors. Not forcible new distributions, but gradual transformations of opinion are necessary; justice in all matters must become greater, the instinct of violence weaker.

453.

The Helmsman of the Passions. – The statesman excites public passions in order to have the advantage of the counter-passions thereby aroused. To give an example: a German statesman knows quite well that the Catholic Church will never have the same plans as Russia; indeed, that it would far rather be allied with the Turks than with the former country; he likewise knows that Germany is threatened with great danger from an alliance between France and Russia. If he can succeed, therefore, in making France the focus and fortress of the Catholic Church, he has averted this danger for a lengthy period. He has, accordingly, an interest in showing hatred against the Catholics in transforming, by all kinds of hostility, the supporters of the Pope's authority into an impassioned political power which is opposed to German politics, and must, as a matter of course, coalesce with France as the adversary of Germany; his aim is the catholicising of France, just as necessarily as Mirabeau saw the salvation of his native land in de-catholicising it. The one State, therefore, desires to muddle millions of minds of another State in order to gain advantage thereby. It is the same disposition which supports the republican form of government of a neighbouring State – *le désordre organisé*, as Mérimée says for the sole reason that it assumes that this form of government makes the nation weaker, more distracted, less fit for war.

454.

The Dangerous Revolutionary Spirits. – Those who are bent on revolutionising society may be divided into those who seek something for themselves thereby and those who seek something for their children and grandchildren. The latter are the more dangerous, for they have the belief and the good conscience of disinterestedness. The others can be appeased by favours: those in power are still sufficiently rich and wise to adopt that expedient. The danger begins as soon as the aims become impersonal; revolutionists seeking impersonal interests may consider all defenders of the present state of things as personally interested, and may therefore feel themselves superior to their opponents.

455.

The Political Value of Paternity. – When a man has no sons he has not a full right to join in a discussion concerning the needs of a particular community. A person must himself have staked his dearest object along with the others: that alone binds him fast to the State; he must have in view the well-being of his descendants, and must, therefore, above all, have descendants in order to take a right and natural share in all institutions and the changes thereof. The development of higher morality depends on a person's having sons; it disposes him to be unegoistic, or, more correctly, it extends his egoism in its duration and permits him earnestly to strive after goals which lie beyond his individual lifetime.

456.

Pride of Descent. – A man may be justly proud of an unbroken line of *good* ancestors down to his father – not however of the line itself, for every one has that. Descent from good ancestors constitutes the real nobility of birth; a single break in the chain, one bad ancestor, therefore, destroys the nobility of birth. Every one who talks about his nobility should be asked: 'Have you no violent, avaricious, dissolute, wicked, cruel man amongst your ancestors?' If with good cognisance and conscience he can answer No, then let his friendship be sought.

457.

Slaves and Labourers. – The fact that we regard the gratification of vanity as of more account than all other forms of well-being (security, position, and pleasures of all sorts), is shown to a ludicrous extent by every one wishing for the abolition of slavery and utterly abhorring to put any one into this position (apart altogether from political reasons), while every one must acknowledge to himself that in all respects slaves live more securely and more happily than modern labourers, and that slave labour is very easy labour compared with that of the 'labourer'. We protest in the name of the 'dignity of man'; but, expressed more simply, that is just our darling vanity which feels non-equality, and inferiority in public estimation, to be the hardest lot of all. The cynic thinks differently concerning the matter, because he despises honour: and so Diogenes was for some time a slave and tutor.

458.

Leading Minds and their Instruments. – We see that great statesmen, and in general all who have to employ many people to carry out their plans, sometimes proceed one way and sometimes another; they either choose with great skill and care the people suitable for their plans, and then leave them a comparatively large amount of liberty, because they know that the nature of the persons selected impels them precisely to the point where they themselves would have them go; or else they choose badly, in fact take whatever comes to hand, but out of every piece of clay they form something useful for their purpose. These latter minds are the more high-handed; they also desire more submissive instruments; their knowledge of mankind is usually much smaller, their contempt of mankind greater than in the case of the first mentioned class, but the machines they construct generally work better than the machines from the workshops of the former.

459.

Arbitrary Law Necessary. – Jurists dispute whether the most perfectly thought-out law or that which is most easily understood should prevail in a nation. The former, the best model of which is Roman Law, seems incomprehensible to the layman, and is therefore not the expression of his sense of justice. Popular laws, the Germanic, for instance, have been rude, superstitious, illogical, and in part idiotic, but they represented very definite, inherited national morals and sentiments. But where, as with us, law is no longer custom, it can only *command* and be compulsion; none of us any longer possesses a traditional sense of justice; we must therefore content ourselves with *arbitrary laws*, which are the expressions of the necessity that there *must be* law. The most logical is then in any case the most acceptable, because it is the most *impartial*, granting even that in every case the smallest unit of measure in the relation of crime and punishment is arbitrarily fixed.

460.

The Great Man of the Masses. – The recipe for what the masses call a great man is easily given. In all circumstances let a person provide them with something very pleasant, or first let him put it into their heads that this or that would be very pleasant, and then let him give it to them. On no account give it *immediately*, however: but let him acquire it by the greatest exertions, or seem thus to acquire it. The masses must have the impression that there is a powerful, nay indomitable strength of will operating; at least it must seem to be there operating. Everybody admires a strong will, because nobody possesses it, and everybody says to himself that if he did possess it there would no longer be any bounds for him and his egoism. If, then, it becomes evident that such a strong will effects something very agreeable to the masses, instead of hearkening to the wishes of covetousness, people admire once more, and wish good luck to themselves. Moreover, if he has all the qualities of the masses, they are the less ashamed before him, and he is all the more popular. Consequently, he may be violent, envious, rapacious, intriguing, flattering, fawning, inflated, and, according to circumstances, anything whatsoever.

461.

Prince and God. – People frequently commune with their princes in the same way as with their God, as indeed the prince himself was frequently the Deity's representative, or at least His high priest. This almost uncanny disposition of veneration, disquiet, and shame, grew, and has grown, much weaker, but occasionally it flares up again, and fastens upon powerful persons generally. The cult of genius is an echo of this veneration of Gods and Princes. Wherever an effort is made to exalt particular men to the superhuman, there is also a tendency to regard whole grades of the population as coarser and baser than they really are.

462.

My Utopia. – In a better arranged society the heavy work and trouble of life will be assigned to those who suffer least through it, to the most obtuse, therefore; and so step by step up to those who are most sensitive to the highest and sublimest kinds of suffering, and who therefore still suffer notwithstanding the greatest alleviations of life.

463.

A Delusion in Subversive Doctrines. – There are political and social dreamers who ardently and eloquently call for the overthrow of all order, in the belief that the proudest fane of beautiful humanity will then rear itself immediately, almost of its own accord. In these dangerous dreams there is still an echo of Rousseau's superstition, which believes in a marvellous primordial goodness of human nature, buried up, as it were; and lays all the blame of that burying-up on the institutions of civilisation, on society, State, and education. Unfortunately, it is well known by historical experiences that every such overthrow reawakens into new life the wildest energies, the long-buried horrors and extravagances of remotest ages; that an overthrow, therefore, may possibly be a source of strength to a deteriorated humanity, but never a regulator, architect, artist, or perfecter of human nature. It was not *Voltaire's* moderate nature, inclined towards regulating, purifying, and reconstructing, but *Rousseau's* passionate follies and half-lies that aroused the optimistic spirit of the Revolution, against which I cry, '*Ecrasez l'infâme*!' Owing to this *the Spirit of enlightenment* and *progressive development* has been long scared away; let us see – each of us individually – if it is not possible to recall it!

464.

Moderation. – When perfect resoluteness in thinking and investigating, that is to say, freedom of spirit, has become a feature of character, it produces moderation of conduct; for it weakens avidity, attracts much extant energy for the furtherance of intellectual aims, and shows the semi-usefulness, or uselessness and danger, of all sudden changes.

465.

The Resurrection of the Spirit. – A nation usually renews its youth on a political sick-bed, and there finds again the spirit which it had gradually lost in seeking and maintaining power. Culture is indebted most of all to politically weakened periods.

466.

New Opinions in the Old Home. – The overthrow of opinions is not immediately followed by the overthrow of institutions; on the contrary, the new opinions dwell for a long time in the desolate and haunted house of their predecessors, and conserve it even for want of a habitation.

467.

Public Education. – In large States public education will always be extremely mediocre, for the same reason that in large kitchens the cooking is at best only mediocre.

468.

Innocent Corruption. – In all institutions into which the sharp breeze of public criticism does not penetrate an innocent corruption grows up like a fungus (for instance, in learned bodies and senates).

469.

Scholars as Politicians. – To scholars who become politicians the comic role is usually assigned; they have to be the good conscience of a state policy.

470.

The Wolf hidden behind the Sheep. – Almost every politician, in certain circumstances, has such need of an honest man that he breaks into the sheep-fold like a famished wolf; not, however, to devour a stolen sheep, but to hide himself behind its woolly back.

471.

Happy Times. – A happy age is no longer possible, because men only wish for it but do not desire to have it; and each individual, when good days come for him, learns positively to pray for disquiet and misery. The destiny of mankind is arranged for *happy moments* – every life has such – but not for happy times. Nevertheless, such times will continue to exist in man's imagination as 'over the hills and far away', an heirloom of his earliest ancestors; for the idea of the happy age, from the earliest times to the present, has no doubt been derived from the state in which man, after violent exertions in hunting and warfare, gives himself over to repose, stretches out his limbs, and hears the wings of sleep rustle around him. It is a false conclusion when, in accordance with that old habit, man imagines that after *whole periods* of distress and trouble he will be able also to enjoy the state of happiness in *proportionate increase and duration*.

472.

Religion and Government. – So long as the State, or, more properly, the Government, regards itself as the appointed guardian of a number of minors, and on their account considers the question whether religion should be preserved or abolished, it is highly probable that it will always decide for the preservation thereof. For religion satisfies the nature of the individual in times of loss, destitution, terror, and distrust, in cases, therefore, where the Government feels itself incapable of doing anything directly for the mitigation of the spiritual sufferings of the individual; indeed, even in general unavoidable and next to inevitable evils (famines, financial crises, and wars) religion gives to the masses an attitude of tranquillity and confiding expectancy. Whenever the necessary or accidental deficiencies of the State Government, or the dangerous consequences of dynastic interests, strike the eyes of the intelligent and make them refractory, the unintelligent will only think they see the finger of God therein and will submit with patience to the dispensations from *on high* (a conception in which divine and human modes of government usually coalesce); thus internal civil peace and continuity of development will be preserved. The power, which lies in the unity of popular feeling, in the existence of the same opinions and aims for all, is protected and confirmed by religion – the rare cases excepted in which a priesthood cannot agree with the State about the price, and therefore comes into conflict with it. As a rule the State will know how to win over the priests, because it needs their most private and secret system for educating souls, and knows how to value servants who apparently, and outwardly, represent quite other interests. Even at present no power can become 'legitimate' without the assistance of the priests; a fact which Napoleon understood. Thus, absolutely paternal government and the careful preservation of religion necessarily go hand-in-hand. In this connection it must be taken for granted that the rulers and governing classes are enlightened concerning the advantages which religion affords, and consequently feel themselves to a certain extent superior to it, inasmuch as they use it as a means; thus freedom of spirit has its origin here. But how will it be when the totally different interpretation of the idea of Government, such as is taught in *democratic* States, begins to prevail? When one sees in it nothing but the instrument of the popular will, no 'upper' in contrast to an 'under', but merely a function of the sole sovereign, the people? Here also only the same attitude which the people assume towards religion can be assumed by the Government; every diffusion of enlightenment will have to find an echo even in the representatives, and the utilising and exploiting of religious impulses and consolations for State purposes will not be so easy (unless powerful party leaders occasionally exercise an influence resembling that of enlightened despotism). When, however, the State is not permitted to derive any further advantage from religion, or when people think far too variously on religious matters to allow the State to adopt a consistent and uniform procedure with respect to them, the way out of the difficulty will necessarily present itself, namely to treat religion as a private affair and leave it to the conscience and custom of each single individual. The first result of all is that religious feeling seems to be strengthened, inasmuch as hidden and suppressed impulses thereof, which the State had unintentionally or intentionally stifled, now break forth and rush to extremes; later on, however, it is found that religion is overgrown with sects, and that an abundance of dragon's teeth were sown as soon as religion was made a private affair. The spectacle of strife, and the hostile laying bare of all the weaknesses of religious confessions, admit finally of no other expedient except that every better and more talented person should make irreligiousness his private affair, a sentiment which now obtains the upper hand even in the minds of the governing classes, and, almost against their will, gives an anti-religious character to their pleasures. As soon as this happens, the sentiment of persons still religiously disposed, who formerly adored the State as something half sacred or wholly sacred, changes into decided *hostility to the State*; they lie in wait for governmental measures, seeking to hinder, thwart, and disturb as much as they can, and, by the fury of their contradiction, drive the opposing parties, the irreligious ones, into an almost fanatical enthusiasm *for* the State; in connection with which there is also the silently co-operating influence, that since their separation from religion the hearts of persons in these circles are conscious of a void, and seek by devotion to the State to provide themselves provisionally with a substitute for religion, a kind of stuffing for the void. After these perhaps lengthy transitional struggles, it is finally decided whether the religious parties are still strong enough to revive an old condition of things, and turn the wheel backwards: in which case enlightened despotism (perhaps less enlightened and more timorous than formerly), inevitably gets the State into its hands – or whether the non-religious parties achieve their purpose, and, possibly through schools and education, check the increase of their opponents during several generations, and finally make them no longer possible. Then, however, their enthusiasm for the State also abates: it always becomes more obvious that along with the religious adoration which regards the State as a mystery and a supernatural institution, the reverent and pious relation to it has also been convulsed. Henceforth individuals see only that side of the State which may be useful or injurious to them, and press forward by all means to obtain an influence over it. But this rivalry soon becomes too great; men and parties change too rapidly, and throw each other down again too furiously from the mountain when they have only just succeeded in getting aloft. All the measures which such a Government carries out lack the guarantee of permanence; people then fight shy of undertakings which would require the silent growth of future decades or centuries to produce ripe fruit. Nobody henceforth feels any other obligation to a law than to submit for the moment to the power which introduced the law; people immediately set to work, however, to undermine it by a new power, a newly-formed majority. Finally – it may be confidently asserted – the distrust of all government, the insight into the useless and harassing nature of these short-winded struggles, must drive men to an entirely new resolution: to the abrogation of the conception of the State and the abolition of the contrast of 'private and public'. Private concerns gradually absorb the business of the State; even the toughest residue which is left over from the old work of governing (the business, for instance, which is meant to protect private persons from private persons) will at last some day be managed by private enterprise. The neglect, decline, and *death of the State*, the liberation of the private person (I am careful not to say the individual), are the consequences of the democratic conception of the State; that is its mission. When it has accomplished its task – which, like everything human, involves much rationality and irrationality – and when all relapses into the old malady have been overcome, then a new leaf in the story-book of humanity will be unrolled, on which readers will find all kinds of strange tales and perhaps also some amount of good. To repeat shortly what has been said: the interests of the tutelary Government and the interests of religion go hand-in-hand, so that when the latter begins to decay the foundations of the State are also shaken. The belief in a divine regulation of political affairs, in a mystery in the existence of the State, is of religious origin: if religion disappears, the State will inevitably lose its old veil of Isis, and will no longer arouse veneration. The sovereignty of the people, looked at closely, serves also to dispel the final fascination and superstition in the realm of these sentiments; modern democracy is the historical form of the *decay of the State*. The outlook which results from this certain decay is not, however, unfortunate in every respect; the wisdom and the selfishness of men are the best developed of all their qualities; when the State no longer meets the demands of these impulses, chaos will least of all result, but a still more appropriate expedient than the State will get the mastery over the State. How many organising forces have already been seen to die out! For example, that of the *gens* or clan which for millennia was far mightier than the power of the family, and indeed already ruled and regulated long before the latter existed. We ourselves see the important notions of the right and might of the family, which once possessed the supremacy as far as the Roman system extended, always becoming paler and feebler. In the same way a later generation will also see the State become meaningless in certain parts of the world – an idea which many contemporaries can hardly contemplate without alarm and horror. To *labour* for the propagation and realisation of this idea is, certainly, another thing; one must think very presumptuously of one's reason, and only half understand history, to set one's hand to the plough at present – when as yet no one can show us the seeds that are afterwards to be sown upon the broken soil. Let us, therefore, trust to the 'wisdom and selfishness of men' that the State may *yet* exist a good while longer, and that the destructive attempts of over-zealous, too hasty sciolists may be in vain!

473.

Socialism, with Regard to its Means. – Socialism is the fantastic younger brother of almost decrepit despotism, which it wants to succeed; its efforts are, therefore, in the deepest sense reactionary. For it desires such an amount of State power as only despotism has possessed, indeed, it outdoes all the past, in that it aims at the complete annihilation of the individual, whom it deems an unauthorised luxury of nature, which is to be improved by it into an appropriate *organ of the general community*. Owing to its relationship, it always appears in proximity to excessive developments of power, like the old typical socialist, Plato, at the court of the Sicilian tyrant; it desires (and under certain circumstances furthers) the Caesarian despotism of this century, because, as has been said, it would like to become its heir. But even this inheritance would not suffice for its objects, it requires the most submissive prostration of all citizens before the absolute State, such as has never yet been realised; and as it can no longer even count upon the old religious piety towards the State, but must rather strive involuntarily and continuously for the abolition thereof – because it strives for the abolition of all existing *States* – it can only hope for existence occasionally, here and there for short periods, by means of the extremest terrorism. It is therefore silently preparing itself for reigns of terror, and drives the word 'justice' like a nail into the heads of the half-cultured masses in order to deprive them completely of their understanding (after they had already suffered seriously from the half-culture), and to provide them with a good conscience for the bad game they are to play. Socialism may serve to teach, very brutally and impressively, the danger of all accumulations of State power, and may serve so far to inspire distrust of the State itself. When its rough voice strikes up the way-cry 'as much State as possible' the shout at first becomes louder than ever – but soon the opposition cry also breaks forth, with so much greater force: 'as little State as possible'.

474.

The Development of the Mind Feared by the State. – The Greek *polis* was, like every organising political power, exclusive and distrustful of the growth of culture; its powerful fundamental impulse seemed almost solely to have a paralysing and obstructive effect thereon. It did not want to let any history or any becoming have a place in culture; the education laid down in the State laws was meant to be obligatory on all generations to keep them at *one* stage of development. Plato also, later on, did not desire it to be otherwise in his ideal State. *In spite of* the polis culture developed itself in this manner; indirectly to be sure, and against its will, the polis furnished assistance because the ambition of individuals therein was stimulated to the utmost, so that, having once found the path of intellectual development, they followed it to its farthest extremity. On the other hand, appeal should not be made to the panegyric of Pericles, for it is only a great optimistic dream about the alleged necessary connection between the Polis and Athenian culture; immediately before the night fell over Athens (the plague and the breakdown of tradition), Thucydides makes this culture flash up once more like a transfiguring afterglow, to efface the remembrance of the evil day that had preceded.

475.

European Man and the Destruction of Nationalities. – Commerce and industry, interchange of books and letters, the universality of all higher culture, the rapid changing of locality and landscape, and the present nomadic life of all who are not landowners – these circumstances necessarily bring with them a weakening, and finally a destruction of nationalities, at least of European nationalities; so that, in consequence of perpetual crossings, there must arise out of them all a mixed race, that of the European man. At present the isolation of nations, through the rise of *national* enmities, consciously or unconsciously counteracts this tendency; but nevertheless the process of fusing advances slowly, in spite of those occasional counter-currents. This artificial nationalism is, however, as dangerous as was artificial Catholicism, for it is essentially an unnatural condition of extremity and martial law, which has been proclaimed by the few over the many, and requires artifice, lying, and force to maintain its reputation. It is not the interests of the many (of the peoples), as they probably say, but it is first of all the interests of certain princely dynasties, and then of certain commercial and social classes, which impel to this nationalism; once we have recognised this fact, we should just fearlessly style ourselves *good Europeans* and labour actively for the amalgamation of nations; in which efforts Germans may assist by virtue of their hereditary position as *interpreters and intermediaries between nations*. By the way, the great problem of the *Jews* only exists within the national States, inasmuch as their energy and higher intelligence, their intellectual and volitional capital, accumulated from generation to generation in tedious schools of suffering, must necessarily attain to universal supremacy here to an extent provocative of envy and hatred; so that the literary misconduct is becoming prevalent in almost all modern nations – and all the more so as they again set up to be national – of sacrificing the Jews as the scapegoats of all possible public and private abuses. So soon as it is no longer a question of the preservation or establishment of nations, but of the production and training of a European mixed-race of the greatest possible strength, the Jew is just as useful and desirable an ingredient as any other national remnant. Every nation, every individual, has unpleasant and even dangerous qualities – it is cruel to require that the Jew should be an exception. Those qualities may even be dangerous and frightful in a special degree in his case; and perhaps the young Stock-Exchange Jew is in general the most repulsive invention of the human species. Nevertheless, in a general summing up, I should like to know how much must be excused in a nation which, not without blame on the part of all of us, has had the most mournful history of all nations, and to which we owe the most loving of men (Christ), the most upright of sages (Spinoza), the mightiest book, and the most effective moral law in the world? Moreover, in the darkest times of the Middle Ages, when Asiatic clouds had gathered darkly over Europe, it was Jewish free-thinkers, scholars, and physicians who upheld the banner of enlightenment and of intellectual independence under the severest personal sufferings, and defended Europe against Asia; we owe it not least to their efforts that a more natural, more reasonable, at all events un-mythical, explanation of the world was finally able to get the upper hand once more, and that the link of culture which now unites us with the enlightenment of Greco-Roman antiquity has remained unbroken. If Christianity has done everything to orientalise the Occident, Judaism has assisted essentially in occidentalising it anew; which, in a certain sense, is equivalent to making Europe's mission and history a *continuation of that of Greece*.

476.

Apparent Superiority of the Middle Ages. – The Middle Ages present in the Church an institution with an absolutely universal aim, involving the whole of humanity – an aim, moreover, which – presumedly – concerned man's highest interests; in comparison therewith the aims of the States and nations which modern history exhibits make a painful impression; they seem petty, base, material, and restricted in extent. But this different impression on our imagination should certainly not determine our judgement; for that universal institution corresponded to feigned and fictitiously fostered needs, such as the need of salvation, which, wherever they did not already exist, it had first of all to create: the new institutions, however, relieve actual distresses; and the time is coming when institutions will arise to minister to the common, genuine needs of all men, and to cast that fantastic prototype, the Catholic Church, into shade and oblivion.

477.

War Indispensable. – It is nothing but fanaticism and beautiful soulism to expect very much (or even, much only) from humanity when it has forgotten how to wage war. For the present we know of no other means whereby the rough energy of the camp, the deep impersonal hatred, the cold-bloodedness of murder with a good conscience, the general ardour of the system in the destruction of the enemy, the proud indifference to great losses, to one's own existence and that of one's friends, the hollow, earthquake-like convulsion of the soul, can be as forcibly and certainly communicated to enervated nations as is done by every great war: owing to the brooks and streams that here break forth, which, certainly, sweep stones and rubbish of all sorts along with them and destroy the meadows of delicate cultures, the mechanism in the workshops of the mind is afterwards, in favourable circumstances, rotated by new power. Culture can by no means dispense with passions, vices, and malignities. When the Romans, after having become Imperial, had grown rather tired of war, they attempted to gain new strength by beast-baitings, gladiatoral combats, and Christian persecutions. The English of today, who appear on the whole to have also renounced war, adopt other means in order to generate anew those vanishing forces; namely, the dangerous exploring expeditions, sea voyages and mountaineerings, nominally undertaken for scientific purposes, but in reality to bring home surplus strength from adventures and dangers of all kinds. Many other such substitutes for war will be discovered, but perhaps precisely thereby it will become more and more obvious that such a highly cultivated and therefore necessarily enfeebled humanity as that of modern Europe not only needs wars, but the greatest and most terrible wars – consequently occasional relapses into barbarism – lest, by the means of culture, it should lose its culture and its very existence.

478.

Industry in the South and the North. – Industry arises in two entirely different ways. The artisans of the South are not industrious because of acquisitiveness but because of the constant needs of others. The smith is industrious because some one is always coming who wants a horse shod or a carriage mended. If nobody came he would loiter about in the market-place. In a fruitful land he has little trouble in supporting himself, for that purpose he requires only a very small amount of work, certainly no industry; eventually he would beg and be contented. The industry of English workmen, on the contrary, has acquisitiveness behind it; it is conscious of itself and its aims; with property it wants power, and with power the greatest possible liberty and individual distinction.

479.

Wealth as the Origin of a Nobility of Race. – Wealth necessarily creates an aristocracy of race, for it permits the choice of the most beautiful women and the engagement of the best teachers; it allows a man cleanliness, time for physical exercises, and, above all, immunity from dulling physical labour. So far it provides all the conditions for making man, after a few generations, move and even act nobly and handsomely: greater freedom of character and absence of niggardliness, of wretchedly petty matters, and of abasement before bread-givers. It is precisely these negative qualities which are the most profitable birthday gift, that of happiness, for the young man; a person who is quite poor usually comes to grief through nobility of disposition, he does not get on, and acquires nothing, his race is not capable of living. In this connection, however, it must be remembered that wealth produces almost the same effects whether one have three hundred or thirty thousand thalers a year; there is no further essential progression of the favourable conditions afterwards. But to have less, to beg in boyhood and to abase one's self is terrible, although it may be the proper starting-point for such as seek their happiness in the splendour of courts, in subordination to the mighty and influential, or for such as wish to be heads of the Church. (It teaches how to slink crouching into the underground passages to favour.)

480.

Envy and Inertia in Different Courses. – The two opposing parties, the socialist and the national – or whatever they may be called in the different countries of Europe – are worthy of each other; envy and laziness are the motive powers in each of them. In the one camp they desire to work as little as possible with their hands, in the other as little as possible with their heads; in the latter they hate and envy prominent, self-evolving individuals, who do not willingly allow themselves to be drawn up in rank and file for the purpose of a collective effect; in the former they hate and envy the better social caste, which is more favourably circumstanced outwardly, whose peculiar mission, the production of the highest blessings of culture, makes life inwardly all the harder and more painful. Certainly, if it be possible to make the spirit of the collective effect the spirit of the higher classes of society, the socialist crowds are quite right, when they also seek outward equalisation between themselves and these classes, since they are certainly internally equalised with one another already in head and heart. Live as higher men, and always do the deeds of higher culture – thus everything that lives will acknowledge your right, and the order of society, whose summit ye are, will be safe from every evil glance and attack!

481.

High Politics and their Detriments. – Just as a nation does not suffer the greatest losses that war and readiness for war involve through the expenses of the war, or the stoppage of trade and traffic, or through the maintenance of a standing army – however great these losses may now be, when eight European States expend yearly the sum of five milliards of marks thereon – but owing to the fact that year after year its ablest, strongest, and most industrious men are withdrawn in extraordinary numbers from their proper occupations and callings to be turned into soldiers: in the same way, a nation that sets about practising high politics and securing a decisive voice among the great Powers does not suffer its greatest losses where they are usually supposed to be. In fact, from this time onward it constantly sacrifices a number of its most conspicuous talents upon the 'Altar of the Fatherland' or of national ambition, whilst formerly other spheres of activity were open to those talents which are now swallowed up by politics. But apart from these public hecatombs, and in reality much more horrible, there is a drama which is constantly being performed simultaneously in a hundred thousand acts; every able, industrious, intellectually striving man of a nation that thus covets political laurels, is swayed by this covetousness, and no longer belongs entirely to himself alone as he did formerly; the new daily questions and cares of the public welfare devour a daily tribute of the intellectual and emotional capital of every citizen; the sum of all these sacrifices and losses of individual energy and labour is so enormous, that the political growth of a nation almost necessarily entails an intellectual impoverishment and lassitude, a diminished capacity for the performance of works that require great concentration and specialisation. The question may finally be asked: Does it then *pay*, all this bloom and magnificence of the total (which indeed only manifests itself as the fear of the new Colossus in other nations, and as the compulsory favouring by them of national trade and commerce) when all the nobler, finer, and more intellectual plants and products, in which its soil was hitherto so rich, must be sacrificed to this coarse and opalescent flower of the nation?[18]

482.

Repeated Once More. – Public opinion – private laziness.

18 This is once more an allusion to modem Germany. – J. M. K.

NINTH DIVISION.
MAN ALONE BY HIMSELF.

483.

The Enemies of Truth. – Convictions are more dangerous enemies of truth than lies.

484.

A Topsy-Turvy World. – We criticise a thinker more severely when he puts an unpleasant statement before us; and yet it would be more reasonable to do so when we find his statement pleasant.

485.

Decided Character. – A man far oftener appears to have a decided character from persistently following his temperament than from persistently following his principles.

486.

The One Thing Needful. – One thing a man must have: either a naturally light disposition or a disposition *lightened* by art and knowledge.

487.

The Passion for Things. – Whoever sets his passion on things (sciences, arts, the common weal, the interests of culture) withdraws much fervour from his passion for persons (even when they are the representatives of those things; as statesmen, philosophers, and artists are the representatives of their creations).

488.

Calmness in Action. – As a cascade in its descent becomes more deliberate and suspended, so the great man of action usually acts with *more* calmness than his strong passions previous to action would lead one to expect.

489.

Not too Deep. – Persons who grasp a matter in all its depth seldom remain permanently true to it. They have just brought the depth up into the light, and there is always much evil to be seen there.

490.

The Illusion of Idealists. – All idealists imagine that the cause which they serve is essentially better than all other causes, and will not believe that if their cause is really to flourish it requires precisely the same evil-smelling manure which all other human undertakings have need of.

491.

Self-Observation. – Man is exceedingly well protected from himself and guarded against his self-exploring and self-besieging; as a rule he can perceive nothing of himself but his outworks. The actual fortress is inaccessible, and even invisible, to him, unless friends and enemies become traitors and lead him inside by secret paths.

492.

The Right Calling. – Men can seldom hold on to a calling unless they believe or persuade themselves that it is really more important than any other. Women are the same with their lovers.

493.

Nobility of Disposition. – Nobility of disposition consists largely in good-nature and absence of distrust, and therefore contains precisely that upon which money-grabbing and successful men take a pleasure in walking with superiority and scorn.

494.

Goal and Path. – Many are obstinate with regard to the once-chosen path, few with regard to the goal.

495.

The Offensiveness in an Individual Way of Life. – All specially individual lines of conduct excite irritation against him who adopts them; people feel themselves reduced to the level of commonplace creatures by the extraordinary treatment he bestows on himself.

496.

The Privilege of Greatness. – It is the privilege of greatness to confer intense happiness with insignificant gifts.

497.

Unintentionally Noble. – A person behaves with unintentional nobleness when he has accustomed himself to seek naught from others and always to give to them.

498.

A Condition of Heroism. – When a person wishes to become a hero, the serpent must previously have become a dragon, otherwise he lacks his proper enemy.

499.

Friends. – Fellowship in joy, and not sympathy in sorrow, makes people friends.

500.

Making Use of Ebb and Flow. – For the purpose of knowledge we must know how to make use of the inward current which draws us towards a thing, and also of the current which after a time draws us away from it.

501.

Joy in Itself. – 'Joy in the Thing' people say; but in reality it is joy in itself by means of the thing.

502.

The Unassuming Man. – He who is unassuming towards persons manifests his presumption all the more with regard to things (town, State, society, time, humanity). That is his revenge.

503.

Envy and Jealousy. – Envy and jealousy are the pudenda of the human soul. The comparison may perhaps be carried further.

504.

The Noblest Hypocrite. – It is a very noble hypocrisy not to talk of one's self at all.

505.

Vexation. – Vexation is a physical disease, which is not by any means cured when its cause is subsequently removed.

506.

The Champions of Truth. – Truth does not find fewest champions when it is dangerous to speak it, but when it is dull.

507.

More Troublesome even than Enemies. – Persons of whose sympathetic attitude we are not, in all circumstances, convinced, while for some reason or other (gratitude, for instance) we are obliged to maintain the appearance of unqualified sympathy with them, trouble our imagination far more than our enemies do.

508.

Free Nature. – We are so fond of being out among Nature, because it has no opinions about us.

509.

Each Superior in one Thing. – In civilised intercourse every one feels himself superior to all others in at least one thing; kindly feelings generally are based thereon, inasmuch as every one can, in certain circumstances, render help, and is therefore entitled to accept help without shame.

510.

Consolatory Arguments. – In the case of a death we mostly use consolatory arguments not so much to alleviate the grief as to make excuses for feeling so easily consoled.

511.

Persons Loyal to their Convictions. – Whoever is very busy retains his general views and opinions almost unchanged. So also does every one who labours in the service of an idea; he will nevermore examine the idea itself, he no longer has any time to do so; indeed, it is against his interests to consider it as still admitting of discussion.

512.

Morality and Quantity. – The higher morality of one man as compared with that of another, often lies merely in the fact that his aims are quantitively greater. The other, living in a circumscribed sphere, is dragged down by petty occupations.

513.

'The Life' as the Proceeds of Life. – A man may stretch himself out ever so far with his knowledge; he may seem to himself ever so objective, but eventually he realises nothing therefrom but his own biography.

514.

Iron Necessity. – Iron necessity is a thing which has been found, in the course of history, to be neither iron nor necessary.

515.

From Experience. – The unreasonableness of a thing is no argument against its existence, but rather a condition thereof.

516.

Truth. – Nobody dies nowadays of fatal truths, there are too many antidotes to them.

517.

A Fundamental Insight. – There is no pre-established harmony between the promotion of truth and the welfare of mankind.

518.

Man's Lot. – He who thinks most deeply knows that he is always in the wrong, however he may act and decide.

519.

Truth as Circe. – Error has made animals into men; is truth perhaps capable of making man into an animal again?

520.

The Danger of Our Culture. – We belong to a period of which the culture is in danger of being destroyed by the appliances of culture.

521.

Greatness Means Leading the Way. – No stream is large and copious of itself, but becomes great by receiving and leading on so many tributary streams. It is so, also, with all intellectual greatnesses. It is only a question of some one indicating the direction to be followed by so many affluents; not whether he was richly or poorly gifted originally.

522.

A Feeble Conscience. – People who talk about their importance to mankind have a feeble conscience for common bourgeois rectitude, keeping of contracts, promises, etc.

523.

Desiring to be Loved. – The demand to be loved is the greatest of presumptions.

524.

Contempt for Men. – The most unequivocal sign of contempt for man is to regard everybody merely as a means to *one's own* ends, or of no account whatever.

525.

Partisans through Contradiction. – Whoever has driven men to fury against himself has also gained a party in his favour.

526.

Forgetting Experiences. – Whoever thinks much and to good purpose easily forgets his own experiences, but not the thoughts which these experiences have called forth.

527.

Sticking to an Opinion. – One person sticks to an opinion because he takes pride in having acquired it himself – another sticks to it because he has learnt it with difficulty and is proud of having understood it; both of them, therefore, out of vanity.

528.

Avoiding the Light. – Good deeds avoid the light just as anxiously as evil deeds; the latter fear that pain will result from publicity (as punishment), the former fear that pleasure will vanish with publicity (the pure pleasure *per se*, which ceases as soon as satisfaction of vanity is added to it).

529.

The Length of the Day. – When one has much to put into them, a day has a hundred pockets.

530.

The Genius of Tyranny. – When an invincible desire to obtain tyrannical power has been awakened in the soul, and constantly keeps up its fervour, even a very mediocre talent (in politicians, artists, etc.) gradually becomes an almost irresistible natural force.

531.

The Enemy's Life. – He who lives by fighting with an enemy has an interest in the preservation of the enemy's life.[19]

---

19 This is why Nietzsche pointed out later on that he had an interest in the preservation of Christianity, and that he was sure his teaching would not undermine this faith – just as little as anarchists have undermined kings; but have left them seated all the more firmly on their thrones. – J. M. K.

532.

More Important. – Unexplained, obscure matters are regarded as more important than explained, clear ones.

533.

Valuation of Services Rendered. – We estimate services rendered to us according to the value set on them by those who render them, not according to the value they have for us.

534.

Unhappiness. – The distinction associated with unhappiness (as if it were a sign of stupidity, unambitiousness, or commonplaceness to feel happy) is so great that when any one says to us, 'How happy you are' we usually protest.

535.

Imagination in Anguish. – When one is afraid of anything, one's imagination plays the part of that evil spirit which springs on one's back just when one has the heaviest load to bear.

536.

The Value of Insipid Opponents. – We sometimes remain faithful to a cause merely because its opponents never cease to be insipid.

537.

The Value of a Profession. – A profession makes us thoughtless; that is its greatest blessing. For it is a bulwark behind which we are permitted to withdraw when commonplace doubts and cares assail us.

538.

Talent. – Many a man's talent appears less than it is, because he has always set himself too heavy tasks.

539.

Youth. – Youth is an unpleasant period; for then it is not possible or not prudent to be productive in any sense whatsoever.

540.

Too Great Aims. – Whoever aims publicly at great things and at length perceives secretly that he is too weak to achieve them, has usually also insufficient strength to renounce his aims publicly, and then inevitably becomes a hypocrite.

541.

In the Current. – Mighty waters sweep many stones and shrubs away with them; mighty spirits many foolish and confused minds.

542.

The Dangers of Intellectual Emancipation. – In a seriously intended intellectual emancipation a person's mute passions and cravings also hope to find their advantage.

543.

The Incarnation of the Mind. – When any one thinks much and to good purpose, not only his face but also his body acquires a sage look.

544.

Seeing Badly and Hearing Badly. – The man who sees little always sees less than there is to see; the man who hears badly always hears something more than there is to hear.

545.

Self-Enjoyment in Vanity. – The vain man does not wish so much to be prominent as to feel himself prominent; he therefore disdains none of the expedients for self-deception and self-outwitting. It is not the opinion of others that he sets his heart on, but his opinion of their opinion.

546.

Exceptionally Vain. – He who is usually self-sufficient becomes exceptionally vain, and keenly alive to fame and praise when he is physically ill. The more he loses himself the more he has to endeavour to regain his position by means of the opinion of others.

547.

The 'Witty'. – Those who seek wit do not possess it.

548.

A Hint to the Heads of Parties. – When one can make people publicly support a cause they have also generally been brought to the point of inwardly declaring themselves in its favour, because they wish to be regarded as consistent.

549.

Contempt. – Man is more sensitive to the contempt of others than to self-contempt.

550.

The Tie of Gratitude. – There are servile souls who carry so far their sense of obligation for benefits received that they strangle themselves with the tie of gratitude.

551.

The Prophet's Knack. – In predicting beforehand the procedure of ordinary individuals, it must be taken for granted that they always make use of the smallest intellectual expenditure in freeing themselves from disagreeable situations.

552.

Man's Sole Right. – He who swerves from the traditional is a victim of the unusual; he who keeps to the traditional is its slave. The man is ruined in either case.

553.

Below the Beast. – When a man roars with laughter he surpasses all the animals by his vulgarity.

554.

Partial Knowledge. – He who speaks a foreign language imperfectly has more enjoyment therein than he who speaks it well. The enjoyment is with the partially initiated.

555.

Dangerous Helpfulness. – There are people who wish to make human life harder for no other reason than to be able afterwards to offer men their life-alleviating recipes – their Christianity, for example.

556.

Industriousness and Conscientiousness. – Industriousness and conscientiousness are often antagonists, owing to the fact that industriousness wants to pluck the fruit sour from the tree while conscientiousness wants to let it hang too long, until it falls and is bruised.

557.

Casting Suspicion. – We endeavour to cast suspicion on persons whom we cannot endure.

558.

The Conditions are Lacking. – Many people wait all their lives for the opportunity to be good in *their own way*.

559.

Lack of Friends. – Lack of friends leads to the inference that a person is envious or presumptuous. Many a man owes his friends merely to the fortunate circumstance that he has no occasion for envy.

560.

Danger in Manifoldness. – With one talent more we often stand less firmly than with one less; just as a table stands better on three feet than on four.

561.

An Exemplar for Others. – Whoever wants to set a good example must add a grain of folly to his virtue; people then imitate their exemplar and at the same time raise themselves above him, a thing they love to do.

562.

Being a Target. – The bad things others say about us are often not really aimed at us, but are the manifestations of spite or ill-humour occasioned by quite different causes.

563.

Easily Resigned. – We suffer but little on account of ungratified wishes if we have exercised our imagination in distorting the past.

564.

In Danger. – One is in greatest danger of being run over when one has just got out of the way of a carriage.

565.

The Role According to the Voice. – Whoever is obliged to speak louder than he naturally does (say, to a partially deaf person or before a large audience), usually exaggerates what he has to communicate. Many a one becomes a conspirator, malevolent gossip, or intriguer, merely because his voice is best suited for whispering.

566.

Love and Hatred. – Love and hatred are not blind, but are dazzled by the fire which they carry about with them.

567.

Advantageously Persecuted. – People who cannot make their merits perfectly obvious to the world endeavour to awaken a strong hostility against themselves. They have then the consolation of thinking that this hostility stands between their merits and the acknowledgment thereof – and that many others think the same thing, which is very advantageous for their recognition.

568.

Confession. – We forget our fault when we have confessed it to another person, but he does not generally forget it.

569.

Self-Sufficiency. – The Golden Fleece of self-sufficiency is a protection against blows, but not against needle-pricks.

570.

Shadows in the Flame. – The flame is not so bright to itself as to those whom it illuminates – so also the wise man.

571.

Our Own Opinions. – The first opinion that occurs to us when we are suddenly asked about anything is not usually our own, but only the current opinion belonging to our caste, position, or family; our own opinions seldom float on the surface.

572.

The Origin of Courage. – The ordinary man is as courageous and invulnerable as a hero when he does not see the danger, when he has no eyes for it. Reversely, the hero has his one vulnerable spot upon the back, where he has no eyes.

573.

The Danger in the Physician. – One must be born for one's physician, otherwise one comes to grief through him.

574.

Marvellous Vanity. – Whoever has courageously prophesied the weather three times and has been successful in his hits, acquires a certain amount of inward confidence in his prophetic gift. We give credence to the marvellous and irrational when it flatters our self-esteem.

575.

A Profession. – A profession is the backbone of life.

576.

The Danger of Personal Influence. – Whoever feels that he exercises a great inward influence over another person must give him a perfectly free rein, must, in fact, welcome and even induce occasional opposition, otherwise he will inevitably make an enemy.

577.

Recognition of the Heir. – Whoever has founded something great in an unselfish spirit is careful to rear heirs for his work. It is the sign of a tyrannical and ignoble nature to see opponents in all possible heirs, and to live in a state of self-defence against them.

578.

Partial Knowledge. – Partial knowledge is more triumphant than complete knowledge; it takes things to be simpler than they are, and so makes its theory more popular and convincing.

579.

Unsuitable for a Party-Man. – Whoever thinks much is unsuitable for a party-man; his thinking leads him too quickly beyond the party.

580.

A Bad Memory. – The advantage of a bad memory is that one enjoys several times the same good things for the *first* time.

581.

Self-Affliction. – Want of consideration is often the sign of a discordant inner nature, which craves for stupefaction.

582.

Martyrs. – The disciples of a martyr suffer more than the martyr.

583.

Arrears of Vanity. – The vanity of many people who have no occasion to be vain is the inveterate habit, still surviving from the time when people had no right to the belief in themselves and only begged it in small sums from others.

584.

Punctum Saliens of Passion. – A person falling into a rage or into a violent passion of love reaches a point when the soul is full like a hogshead, but nevertheless a drop of water has still to be added, the good will for the passion (which is also generally called the evil will). This item only is necessary, and then the hogshead overflows.

585.

A Gloomy Thought. – It is with men as with the charcoal fires in the forest. It is only when young men have cooled down and have got charred, like these piles, that they become *useful*. As long as they fume and smoke they are perhaps more interesting, but they are useless and too often uncomfortable. Humanity ruthlessly uses every individual as material for the heating of its great machines; but what then is the purpose of the machines, when all individuals (that is, the human race) are useful only to maintain them? Machines that are ends in themselves: is that the *umana commedia*?

586.

The Hour-hand of Life. – Life consists of rare single moments of the greatest importance, and of countless intervals during which, at best, the phantoms of those moments hover around us. Love, the Spring, every fine melody, the mountains, the moon, the sea – all speak but once fully to the heart, if, indeed, they ever do quite attain to speech. For many people have not those moments at all, and are themselves intervals and pauses in the symphony of actual life.

587.

Attack or Compromise. – We often make the mistake of showing violent enmity towards a tendency, party, or period, because we happen only to get a sight of its most exposed side, its stuntedness, or the inevitable 'faults of its virtues' – perhaps because we ourselves have taken a prominent part in them. We then turn our backs on them and seek a diametrically opposite course; but the better way would be to seek out their strong good sides, or to develop them in ourselves. To be sure, a keener glance and a better will are needed to improve the becoming and the imperfect than are required to see through it in its imperfection and to deny it.

588.

Modesty. – There is true modesty (that is the knowledge that we are not the works we create); and it is especially becoming in a great mind, because such a mind can well grasp the thought of absolute irresponsibility (even for the good it creates). People do not hate a great man's presumptuousness in so far as he feels his strength, but because he wishes to prove it by injuring others, by dominating them, and seeing how long they will stand it. This, as a rule, is even a proof of the absence of a secure sense of power, and makes people doubt his greatness. We must therefore beware of presumption from the standpoint of wisdom.

589.

The Day's First Thought. – The best way to begin a day well is to think, on awakening, whether we cannot give pleasure during the day to at least one person. If this could become a substitute for the religious habit of prayer our fellow-men would benefit by the change.

590.

Presumption as the Last Consolation. – When we so interpret a misfortune, an intellectual defect, or a disease that we see therein our predestined fate, our trial, or the mysterious punishment of our former misdeeds, we thereby make our nature interesting and exalt ourselves in imagination above our fellows. The proud sinner is a well-known figure in all religious sects.

591.

The Vegetation of Happiness. – Close beside the world's woe, and often upon its volcanic soil, man has laid out his little garden of happiness. Whether one regard life with the eyes of him who only seeks knowledge therefrom, or of him who submits and is resigned, or of him who rejoices over surmounted difficulties – everywhere one will find some happiness springing up beside the evil – and in fact always the more happiness the more volcanic the soil has been – only it would be absurd to say that suffering itself is justified by this happiness.

592.

The Path of our Ancestors. – It is sensible when a person develops still further in himself the *talent* upon which his father or grandfather spent much trouble, and does not shift to something entirely new; otherwise he deprives himself of the possibility of attaining perfection in any one craft. That is why the proverb says, 'Which road shouldst thou ride? – That of thine ancestors.'

593.

Vanity and Ambition as Educators. – As long as a person has not become an instrument of general utility, ambition may torment him; if, however, that point has been reached, if he necessarily works like a machine for the good of all, then vanity may result; it will humanise him in small matters and make him more sociable, endurable, and considerate, when ambition has completed the coarser work of making him useful.

594.

Philosophical Novices. – Immediately we have comprehended the wisdom of a philosopher, we go through the streets with a feeling as if we had been re-created and had become great men; for we encounter only those who are ignorant of this wisdom, and have therefore to deliver new and unknown verdicts concerning everything. Because we now recognise a law-book we think we must also comport ourselves as judges.

595.

Pleasing by Displeasing. – People who prefer to attract attention, and thereby to displease, desire the same thing as those who neither wish to please nor to attract attention, only they seek it more ardently and indirectly by means of a step by which they apparently move away from their goal. They desire influence and power, and therefore show their superiority, even to such an extent that it becomes disagreeable; for they know that he who has finally attained power pleases in almost all he says and does, and that even when he displeases he still seems to please. The free spirit also, and in like manner the believer, desire power, in order some day to please thereby; when, on account of their doctrine, evil fate, persecution, dungeon, or execution threaten them, they rejoice in the thought that their teaching will thus be engraved and branded on the heart of mankind; though its effect is remote they accept their fate as a painful but powerful means of still attaining to power.

596.

Casus Belli and the Like. – The prince who, for his determination to make war against his neighbour, invents a *casus belli*, is like a father who foists on his child a mother who is henceforth to be regarded as such. And are not almost all publicly avowed motives of action just such spurious mothers?

597.

Passion and Right. – Nobody talks more passionately of his rights than he who, in the depths of his soul, is doubtful about them. By getting passion on his side he seeks to confound his understanding and its doubts – he thus obtains a good conscience, and along with it success with his fellow-men.

598.

The Trick of the Resigning One. – He who protests against marriage, after the manner of Catholic priests, will conceive of it in its lowest and vulgarest form. In the same way he who disavows the honour of his contemporaries will have a mean opinion of it; he can thus dispense with it and struggle against it more easily. Moreover, he who denies himself much in great matters will readily indulge himself in small things. It might be possible that he who is superior to the approbation of his contemporaries would nevertheless not deny himself the gratification of small vanities.

599.

The Years of Presumption. – The proper period of presumption in gifted people is between their twenty-sixth and thirtieth years; it is the time of early ripeness, with a large residue of sourness. On the ground of what we feel within ourselves we demand honour and humility from men who see little or nothing of it, and because this tribute is not immediately forthcoming we revenge ourselves by the look, the gesture of arrogance, and the tone of voice, which a keen ear and eye recognise in every product of those years, whether it be poetry, philosophy, or pictures and music. Older men of experience smile thereat, and think with emotion of those beautiful years in which one resents the fate of *being* so much and *seeming* so little. Later on one really *seems* more – but one has lost the good belief in *being* much – unless one remain for life an incorrigible fool of vanity.

600.

Deceptive and yet Defensible. – Just as in order to pass by an abyss or to cross a deep stream on a plank we require a railing, not to hold fast by – for it would instantly break down with us – but to give the notion of security to the eye, so in youth we require persons who unconsciously render us the service of that railing. It is true they would not help us if we really wished to lean upon them in great danger, but they afford the tranquillising sensation of protection close to one (for instance, fathers, teachers, friends, as all three usually are).

601.

Learning to Love. – One must learn to love, one must learn to be kind, and this from childhood onwards; when education and chance give us no opportunity for the exercise of these feelings our soul becomes dried up, and even incapable of understanding the fine devices of loving men. In the same way hatred must be learnt and fostered, when one wants to become a proficient hater – otherwise the germ of it will gradually die out.

602.

Ruin as Ornament. – Persons who pass through numerous mental phases retain certain sentiments and habits of their earlier states, which then project like a piece of inexplicable antiquity and grey stonework into their new thought and action, often to the embellishment of the whole surroundings.

603.

Love and Honour. – Love desires, fear avoids. That is why one cannot be both loved and honoured by the same person, at least not at the same time.[20] For he who honours recognises power – that is to say, he fears it, he is in a state of reverential fear (*Ehr-furcht*). But love recognises no power, nothing that divides, detaches, superordinates, or subordinates. Because it does not honour them, ambitious people secretly or openly resent being loved.

604.

A Prejudice in Favour of Cold Natures. – People who quickly take fire grow cold quickly, and therefore are, on the whole, unreliable. For those, therefore, who are always cold, or pretend to be so, there is the favourable prejudice that they are particularly trustworthy, reliable persons; they are confounded with those who take fire slowly and retain it long.

605.

The Danger in Free Opinions. – Frivolous occupation with free opinions has a charm, like a kind of itching; if one yields to it further, one begins to chafe the places; until at last an open, painful wound results; that is to say, until the free opinion begins to disturb and torment us in our position in life and in our human relations.

606.

Desire for Sore Affliction. – When passion is over it leaves behind an obscure longing for it, and even in disappearing it casts a seductive glance at us. It must have afforded a kind of pleasure to have been beaten with this scourge. Compared with it, the more moderate sensations appear insipid; we still prefer, apparently, the more violent displeasure to languid delight.

607.

Dissatisfaction with Others and with the World. – When, as so frequently happens, we vent our dissatisfaction on others when we are really dissatisfied with ourselves, we are in fact attempting to

20 Women never understand this. – J. M. K.

mystify and deceive our judgement; we desire to find a motive *a posteriori* for this dissatisfaction, in the mistakes or deficiencies of others, and so lose sight of ourselves. Strictly religious people, who have been relentless judges of themselves, have at the same time spoken most ill of humanity generally; there has never been a saint who reserved sin for himself and virture for others, any more than a man who, according to Buddha's rule, hides his good qualities from people and only shows his bad ones.

608.

Confusion of Cause and Effect. – Unconsciously we seek the principles and opinions which are suited to our temperament, so that at last it seems as if these principles and opinions had formed our character and given it support and stability, whereas exactly the contrary has taken place. Our thoughts and judgements are, apparently, to be taken subsequently as the causes of our nature, but as a matter of fact *our* nature is the cause of our so thinking and judging. And what induces us to play this almost unconscious comedy? Inertness and convenience, and to a large extent also the vain desire to be regarded as thoroughly consistent and homogeneous in nature and thought; for this wins respect and gives confidence and power.

609.

Age in Relation to Truth. – Young people love what is interesting and exceptional, indifferent whether it is truth or falsehood. Riper minds love what is interesting and extraordinary when it is truth. Matured minds, finally, love truth even in those in whom it appears plain and simple and is found tiresome by ordinary people, because they have observed that truth is in the habit of giving utterance to its highest intellectual verities with all the appearance of simplicity.

610.

Men as Bad Poets. – Just as bad poets seek a thought to fit the rhyme in the second half of the verse, so men in the second half of life, having become more scrupulous, are in the habit of seeking pursuits, positions, and conditions which suit those of their earlier life, so that outwardly all sounds well, but their life is no longer ruled and continuously determined anew by a powerful thought: in place thereof there is merely the intention of finding a rhyme.

611.

Ennui and Play. – Necessity compels us to work, with the product of which the necessity is appeased; the ever new awakening of necessity, however, accustoms us to work. But in the intervals in which necessity is appeased and asleep, as it were, we are attacked by ennui. What is this? In a word it is the habituation to work, which now makes itself felt as a new and additional necessity; it will be all the stronger the more a person has been accustomed to work, perhaps, even, the more a person has suffered from necessities. In order to escape ennui, a man either works beyond the extent of his former necessities, or he invents play, that is to say, work that is only intended to appease the general necessity for work. He who has become satiated with play, and has no new necessities impelling him to work, is sometimes attacked by the longing for a third state, which is related to play as gliding is to dancing, as dancing is to walking, a blessed, tranquil movement; it is the artists' and philosophers' vision of happiness.

612.

Lessons from Pictures. – If we look at a series of pictures of ourselves, from the time of later childhood to the time of mature manhood, we discover with pleased surprise that the man bears more resemblance to the child than to the youth: that probably, therefore, in accordance with this fact, there has been in the interval a temporary alienation of the fundamental character, over which the collected, concentrated force of the man has again become master. With this observation this other is also in accordance, namely, that all strong influences of passions, teachers, and political events, which in our youthful years draw us hither and thither, seem later on to be referred back again to a fixed standard; of course they still continue to exist and operate within us, but our fundamental sentiments and opinions have now the upper hand, and use their influence perhaps as a source of strength, but are no longer merely regulative, as was perhaps the case in our twenties. Thus even the thoughts and sentiments of the man appear more in accordance with those of his childish years – and this objective fact expresses itself in the afore-mentioned subjective fact.

613.

The Tone of Voice of Different Ages. – The tone in which youths speak, praise, blame, and versify, displeases an older person because it is too loud, and yet at the same time dull and confused like a sound in a vault, which acquires such a loud ring owing to the emptiness; for most of the thought of youths does not gush forth out of the fulness of their own nature, but is the accord and the echo of what has been thought, said, praised or blamed around them. As their sentiments, however (their inclinations and aversions), resound much more forcibly than the reasons thereof, there is heard, whenever they divulge these sentiments, the dull, clanging tone which is a sign of the absence or scarcity of reasons. The tone of riper age is rigorous, abruptly concise, moderately loud, but, like everything distinctly articulated, is heard very far off. Old age, finally, often brings a certain mildness and consideration into the tone of the voice, and as it were, sweetens it; in many cases, to be sure it also sours it.

614.

The Atavist and the Forerunner. – The man of unpleasant character, full of distrust, envious of the success of fellow-competitors and neighbours, violent and enraged at divergent opinions, shows that he belongs to an earlier grade of culture, and is, therefore, an atavism; for the way in which he behaves to people was right and suitable only for an age of club-law; he is an *atavist*. The man of a different character, rich in sympathy, winning friends everywhere, finding all that is growing and becoming amiable, rejoicing at the honours and successes of others and claiming no privilege of solely knowing the truth, but full of a modest distrust – he is a forerunner who presses upward towards a higher human culture. The man of unpleasant character dates from the times when the rude basis of human intercourse had yet to be laid, the other lives on the upper floor of the edifice of culture, removed as far as possible from the howling and raging wild beast imprisoned in the cellars.

615.

Consolation for Hypochondriacs. – When a great thinker is temporarily subjected to hypochondriacal self-torture he can say to himself, by way of consolation: 'It is thine own great strength on which this parasite feeds and grows; if thy strength were smaller thou wouldst have less to suffer.' The statesman may say just the same thing when jealousy and vengeful feeling, or, in a word, the tone of the *bellum omnium contra omnes*, for which, as the representative of a nation, he must necessarily have a great capacity, occasionally intrudes into his personal relations and makes his life hard.

616.

Estranged from the Present. – There are great advantages in estranging one's self for once to a large extent from one's age, and being as it were driven back from its shores into the ocean of past views of things. Looking thence towards the coast one commands a view, perhaps for the first time, of its aggregate formation, and when one again approaches the land one has the advantage of understanding it better, on the whole, than those who have never left it.

617.

Sowing and Reaping on the field of Personal Defects. – Men like Rousseau understand how to use their weaknesses, defects, and vices as manure for their talent. When Rousseau bewails the corruption and degeneration of society as the evil results of culture, there is a personal experience at the bottom of it, the bitterness which gives sharpness to his general condemnation and poisons the arrows with which he shoots; he unburdens himself first as an individual, and thinks of getting a remedy which, while benefiting society directly, will also benefit himself indirectly by means of society.

618.

Philosophically Minded. – We usually endeavour to acquire *one* attitude of mind, *one* set of opinions for all situations and events of life – it is mostly called being philosophically minded. But for the acquisition of knowledge it may be of greater importance not to make ourselves thus uniform, but to hearken to the low voice of the different situations in life; these bring their own opinions with them. We thus take an intelligent interest in the life and nature of many persons by not treating ourselves as rigid, persistent single individuals.

619.

In the Fire of Contempt. – It is a fresh step towards independence when one first dares to give utterance to opinions which it is considered as disgraceful for a person to entertain; even friends and acquaintances are then accustomed to grow anxious. The gifted nature must also pass through this fire; it afterwards belongs far more to itself.

620.

Self-sacrifice. – In the event of choice, a great sacrifice is preferred to a small one, because we compensate ourselves for the great sacrifice by self-admiration, which is not possible in the case of a small one.

621.

Love as an Artifice. – Whoever really wishes to *become acquainted with* something new (whether it be a person, an event, or a book), does well to take up the matter with all possible love, and to avert his eye quickly from all that seems hostile, objectionable, and false therein – in fact to forget such things; so that, for instance, he gives the author of a book the best start possible, and straightway, just as in a race, longs with beating heart that he may reach the goal. In this manner one penetrates to the heart of the new thing, to its moving point, and this is called becoming acquainted with it. This stage having been arrived at, the understanding afterwards makes its restrictions; the over-estimation and the temporary suspension of the critical pendulum were only artifices to lure forth the soul of the matter.

622.

Thinking Too Well and Too Ill of the World. – Whether we think too well or too ill of things, we always have the advantage of deriving therefrom a greater pleasure, for with a too good preconception we usually put more sweetness into things (experiences) than they actually contain. A too bad preconception causes a pleasant disappointment, the pleasantness that lay in the things themselves is increased by the pleasantness of the surprise. A gloomy temperament, however, will have the reverse experience in both cases.

623.

Profound People. – Those whose strength lies in the deepening of impressions – they are usually called profound people – are relatively self-possessed and decided in all sudden emergencies, for in the first moment the impression is still shallow, it only then *becomes* deep. Long foreseen, long expected events or persons, however, excite such natures most, and make them almost incapable of eventually having presence of mind on the arrival thereof.

624.

Intercourse with the Higher Self. – Every one has his good day, when he finds his higher self; and true humanity demands that a person shall be estimated according to this state and not according to his work-days of constraint and bondage. A painter, for instance, should be appraised and honoured according to the most exalted vision he could see and represent. But men themselves commune very differently with this their higher self, and are frequently their own playactors, in so far as they repeatedly imitate what they are in those moments. Some stand in awe and humility before their ideal, and would fain deny it; they are afraid of their higher self because, when it speaks, it speaks pretentiously. Besides, it has a ghostlike freedom of coming and staying away just as it pleases; on that account it is often called a gift of the gods, while in fact everything else is a gift of the gods (of chance); this, however, is the man himself.

625.

Lonely People. – Some people are so much accustomed to being alone in self-communion that they do not at all compare themselves with others, but spin out their soliloquising life in a quiet, happy mood, conversing pleasantly, and even hilariously, with themselves. If, however, they are brought to the point of comparing themselves with others, they are inclined to a brooding under-estimation of their own worth, so that they have first to be compelled by others *to form* once more a good and just opinion of themselves, and even from this acquired opinion they will always want to subtract and abate something. We must not, therefore, grudge certain persons their loneliness or foolishly commiserate them on that account, as is so often done.

626.

Without Melody. – There are persons to whom a constant repose in themselves and the harmonious ordering of all their capacities is so natural that every definite activity is repugnant to them. They resemble music which consists of nothing but prolonged, harmonious accords, without even the tendency to an organised and animated melody showing itself. All external movement serves only to restore to the boat its equilibrium on the sea of harmonious euphony. Modern men usually become excessively impatient when they meet such natures, who *will never be anything* in the world, only it is not allowable to say of them that they *are nothing*. But in certain moods the sight of them raises the unusual question: 'Why should there be melody at all? Why should it not suffice us when life mirrors itself peacefully in a deep lake?' The Middle Ages were richer in such natures than our times. How seldom one now meets with any one who can live on so peacefully and happily with himself even in the midst of the crowd, saying to himself, like Goethe, 'The best thing of all is the deep calm in which I live and grow in opposition to the world, and gain what it cannot take away from me with fire and sword.'

627.

To Live and Experience. – If we observe how some people can deal with their experiences – their unimportant, everyday experiences – so that these become soil which yields fruit thrice a year; whilst others – and how many! – are driven through the surf of the most exciting adventures, the most diversified movements of times and peoples, and yet always remain light, always remain on the surface, like cork; we are finally tempted to divide mankind into a minority (minimality) of those who know how to make much out of little, and a majority of those who know how to make little out of much; indeed, we even meet with the counter-sorcerers who, instead of making the world out of nothing, make a nothing out of the world.

628.

Seriousness in Play. – In Genoa one evening, in the twilight, I heard from a tower a long chiming of bells; it was never like to end, and sounded as if insatiable above the noise of the streets, out into the evening sky and sea-air, so thrilling, and at the same time so childish and so sad. I then remembered the words of Plato, and suddenly felt the force of them in my heart: '*Human matters, one and all, are not worthy of great seriousness; nevertheless ...*'

629.

Conviction and Justice. – The requirement that a person must afterwards, when cool and sober, stand by what he says, promises, and resolves during passion, is one of the heaviest burdens that weigh upon mankind. To have to acknowledge for all future time the consequences of anger, of fiery revenge, of enthusiastic devotion, may lead to a bitterness against these feelings proportionate to the idolatry with which they are idolised, especially by artists. These cultivate to its full extent the *esteem of the passions*, and have always done so; to be sure, they also glorify the terrible satisfaction of the passions which a person affords himself, the outbreaks of vengeance, with death, mutilation, or voluntary banishment in their train, and the resignation of the broken heart. In any case they keep alive curiosity about the passions; it is as if they said: 'Without passions you have no experience whatever.' Because we have sworn fidelity (perhaps even to a purely fictitious being, such as a god), because we have surrendered our heart to a prince, a party, a woman, a priestly order, an artist, or a thinker, in a state of infatuated delusion that threw a charm over us and made those beings appear worthy of all veneration, and every sacrifice – are we, therefore, firmly and inevitably bound? Or did we not, after all, deceive ourselves then? Was there not a hypothetical promise, under the tacit presupposition that those beings to whom we consecrated ourselves were really the beings they seemed to be in our imagination? Are we under obligation to be faithful to our errors, even with the knowledge that by this fidelity we shall cause injury to our higher selves? No, there is no law, no obligation of that sort; we *must* become traitors, we must act unfaithfully and abandon our ideals again and again. We cannot advance from one period of life into another without causing these pains of treachery and also suffering from them. Might it be necessary to guard against the ebullitions of our feelings in order to escape these pains? Would not the world then become too arid, too ghost-like for us? Rather will we ask ourselves whether these pains are *necessary* on a change of convictions, or whether they do not depend on a *mistaken* opinion and estimate. Why do we admire a person who remains true to his convictions and despise him who changes them? I fear the answer must be, 'Because every one takes for granted that such a change is caused only by motives of more general utility or of personal trouble.' That is to say, we believe at bottom that nobody alters his opinions as long as they are advantageous to him, or at least as long as they do not cause him any harm. If it is so, however, it furnishes a bad proof of the *intellectual* significance of all convictions. Let us once examine how convictions arise, and let us see whether their importance is not greatly over-estimated; it will thereby be seen that the *change* of convictions also is in all circumstances judged according to a false standard, that we have hitherto been accustomed to suffer *too much* from this change.

630.

Conviction is belief in the possession of absolute truth on any matter of knowledge. This belief takes it for granted, therefore, that there are absolute truths; also, that perfect methods have been found for attaining to them; and finally, that every one who has convictions makes use of these perfect methods. All three notions show at once that the man of convictions is not the man of scientific thought; he seems to us still in the age of theoretical innocence, and is practically a child, however grown-up he may be. Whole centuries, however, have been lived under the influence of those childlike presuppositions, and out of them have flowed the mightiest sources of human strength. The countless numbers who sacrificed themselves for their convictions believed they were doing it for the sake of absolute truth. They were all wrong, however; probably no one has ever sacrificed himself for Truth; at least, the dogmatic expression of the faith of any such person has been unscientific or only partly scientific. But really, people wanted to carry their point because they believed that they *must be* in the right. To allow their belief to be wrested from them probably meant calling in question their eternal salvation. In an affair of such extreme importance the 'will' was too audibly the prompter of the intellect. The presupposition of every believer of every shade of belief has been that he *could not* be confuted; if the counter-arguments happened to be very strong, it always remained for him to decry intellect generally, and, perhaps, even to set up the '*credo quia absurdum est*' as the standard of extreme fanaticism. It is not the struggle of opinions that has made history so turbulent; but the struggle of belief in opinions – that is to say, of convictions. If all those who thought so highly of their convictions, who made sacrifices of all kinds for them, and spared neither honour, body, nor life in their service, had only devoted half of their energy to examining their right to adhere to this or that conviction and by what road they arrived at it, how peaceable would the history of mankind now appear! How much more knowledge would there be! All the cruel scenes in connection with the persecution of heretics of all kinds would have been avoided, for two reasons: firstly, because the inquisitors would above all have inquired of themselves, and would have recognised the presumption of defending absolute truth; and secondly, because the heretics themselves would, after examination, have taken no more interest in such badly established doctrines as those of all religious sectarians and 'orthodox' believers.

631.

From the ages in which it was customary to believe in the possession of absolute truth, people have inherited a profound *dislike* of all sceptical and relative attitudes with regard to questions of knowledge; they mostly prefer to acquiesce, for good or evil, in the convictions of those in authority (fathers, friends, teachers, princes), and they have a kind of remorse of conscience when they do not do so. This tendency is quite comprehensible, and its results furnish no ground for condemnation of the course of the development of human reason. The scientific spirit in man, however, has gradually to bring to maturity the virtue of *cautious forbearance*, the wise moderation, which is better known in practical than in theoretical life, and which, for instance, Goethe has represented in 'Antonio', as an object of provocation for all Tassos – that is to say, for unscientific and at the same time inactive natures. The man of convictions has in himself the right not to comprehend the man of cautious thought, the theoretical Antonio; the scientific man, on the other hand, has no right to blame the former on that account, he takes no notice thereof, and knows, moreover, that in certain cases the former will yet cling to him, as Tasso finally clung to Antonio.

632.

He who has not passed through different phases of conviction, but sticks to the faith in whose net he was first caught, is, under all circumstances, just on account of this unchangeableness, a representative of *atavistic* culture; in accordance with this lack of culture (which always presupposes plasticity for culture), he is severe, unintelligent, unteachable, without liberality, an ever suspicious person, an unscrupulous person who has recourse to all expedients for enforcing his opinions because he cannot conceive that there must be other opinions; he is, in such respects, perhaps a source of strength, and even wholesome in cultures that have become too emancipated and languid, but only because he strongly incites to opposition: for thereby the delicate organisation of the new culture, which is forced to struggle with him, becomes strong itself.

633.

In essential respects we are still the same men as those of the time of the Reformation; how could it be otherwise? But the fact that we *no longer* allow ourselves certain means for promoting the triumph of our opinions distinguishes us from that age, and proves that we belong to a higher culture. He who still combats and overthrows opinions with calumnies and outbursts of rage, after the manner of the Reformation men, obviously betrays the fact that he would have burnt his adversaries had he lived in other times, and that he would have resorted to all the methods of the Inquisition if he had been an opponent of the Reformation. The Inquisition was rational at that time; for it represented nothing else than the universal application of martial law, which had to be proclaimed throughout the entire domain of the Church, and which, like all martial law, gave a right to the extremest methods, under the presupposition, of course, (which we now no longer share with those people), that the Church *possessed* truth and had to preserve it at all costs, and at any sacrifice, for the salvation of mankind. Now, however, one does not so readily concede to any one that he possesses the truth; strict methods of investigation have diffused enough of distrust and precaution, so that every one who violently advocates opinions in word and deed is looked upon as an enemy of our modern culture, or, at least, as an atavist. As a matter of fact the pathos that man possesses truth is now of very little consequence in comparison with the certainly milder and less noisy pathos of the search for truth, which is never weary of learning afresh and examining anew.

634.

Moreover, the methodical search for truth is itself the outcome of those ages in which convictions were at war with each other. If the individual had not cared about *his* 'truth', that is to say, about carrying his point, there would have been no method of investigation; thus, however, by the eternal struggle of the claims of different individuals to absolute truth, people went on step by step to find irrefragable principles according to which the rights of the claims could be tested and the dispute settled. At first people decided according to authorities; later on they criticised one another's ways and means of finding the presumed truth; in the interval there was a period when people deduced the consequences of the adverse theory, and perhaps found them to be productive of injury and unhappiness; from which it was then to be inferred by every one that the conviction of the adversary involved an error. The *personal struggle* of the thinker at last so sharpened his methods that real truths could be discovered, and the mistakes of former methods exposed before the eyes of all.

635.

On the whole, scientific methods are at least as important results of investigation as any other results, for the scientific spirit is based upon a knowledge of method, and if the methods were lost, all the results of science could not prevent the renewed prevalence of superstition and absurdity. Clever people may *learn* as much as they like of the results of science, but one still notices in their conversation, and especially in the hypotheses they make, that they lack the scientific spirit; they have not the instinctive distrust of the devious courses of thinking which, in consequence of long training, has taken root in the soul of every scientific man. It is enough for them to find any kind of hypothesis on a subject, they are then all on fire for it, and imagine the matter is thereby settled. To have an opinion is with them equivalent to immediately becoming fanatical for it, and finally taking it to heart as a conviction. In the case of an unexplained matter they become heated for the first idea that comes into their head which has any resemblance to an explanation – a course from which the worst results constantly follow, especially in the field of politics. On that account everybody should nowadays have become thoroughly acquainted with at least *one* science, for then surely he knows what is meant by method, and how necessary is the extremest carefulness. To women in particular this advice is to be given at present; as to those who are irretrievably the victims of all hypotheses, especially when these have the appearance of being witty, attractive, enlivening, and invigorating. Indeed, on close inspection one sees that by far the greater number of educated people still desire convictions from a thinker and nothing but *convictions*, and that only a small minority want *certainty*. The former want to be forcibly carried away in order thereby to obtain an increase of strength; the latter few have the real interest which disregards personal advantages and the increase of strength also. The former class, who greatly predominate, are always reckoned upon when the thinker comports himself and labels himself as a *genius*, and thus views himself as a higher being to whom authority belongs. In so far as genius of this kind upholds the ardour of convictions, and arouses distrust of the cautious and modest spirit of science, it is an enemy of truth, however much it may think itself the wooer thereof.

636.

There is, certainly, also an entirely different species of genius, that of justice; and I cannot make up my mind to estimate it lower than any kind of philosophical, political, or artistic genius. Its peculiarity is to go, with heartfelt aversion, out of the way of everything that blinds and confuses people's judgement of things; it is consequently an *adversary of convictions*, for it wants to give their own to all, whether they be living or dead, real or imaginary – and for that purpose it must know thoroughly; it therefore places everything in the best light and goes around it with careful eyes. Finally, it will even give to its adversary the blind or short-sighted 'conviction' (as men call it – among women it is called 'faith'), what is due to conviction – for the sake of truth.

637.

Opinions evolve out of *passions*; *indolence of intellect* allows those to congeal into *convictions*. He, however, who is conscious of himself as a *free*, restless, lively spirit can prevent this congelation by constant change; and if he is altogether a thinking snowball, he will not have opinions in his head at all, but only certainties and properly estimated probabilities. But we, who are of a mixed nature, alternately inspired with ardour and chilled through and through by the intellect, want to kneel before justice, as the only goddess we acknowledge. The *fire* in us generally makes us unjust, and impure in the eyes of our goddess; in this condition we are not permitted to take her hand, and the serious smile of her approval never rests upon us. We reverence her as the veiled Isis of our life; with shame we offer her our pain as penance and sacrifice when the fire threatens to burn and consume us. It is the *intellect* that saves us from being utterly burnt and reduced to ashes; it occasionally drags us away from the sacrificial altar of justice or enwraps us in a garment of asbestos. Liberated from the fire, and impelled by the intellect, we then pass from opinion to opinion, through the change of parties, as noble *betrayers* of all things that can in any way be betrayed – and nevertheless without a feeling of guilt.

638.

The Wanderer. – He who has attained intellectual emancipation to any extent cannot, for a long time, regard himself otherwise than as a wanderer on the face of the earth – and not even as a traveller *towards* a final goal, for there is no such thing. But he certainly wants to observe and keep his eyes open to whatever actually happens in the world; therefore he cannot attach his heart too firmly to anything individual; he must have in himself something wandering that takes pleasure in change and transitoriness. To be sure such a man will have bad nights, when he is weary and finds the gates of the town that should offer him rest closed; perhaps he may also find that, as in the East, the desert reaches to the gates, that wild beasts howl far and near, that a strong wind arises, and that robbers take away his beasts of burden. Then the dreadful night closes over him like a second desert upon the desert, and his heart grows weary of wandering. Then when the morning sun rises upon him, glowing like a Deity of anger, when the town is opened, he sees perhaps in the faces of the dwellers therein still more desert, uncleanliness, deceit, and insecurity than outside the gates – and the day is almost worse than the night. Thus it may occasionally happen to the wanderer; but then there come as compensation the delightful mornings of other lands and days, when already in the grey of the dawn he sees the throng of muses dancing by, close to him, in the mist of the mountain; when afterwards, in the symmetry of his ante-meridian soul, he strolls silently under the trees, out of whose crests and leafy hiding-places all manner of good and bright things are flung to him, the gifts of all the free spirits who are at home in mountains, forests, and solitudes, and who, like himself, alternately merry and thoughtful, are wanderers and philosophers. Born of the secrets of the early dawn, they ponder the question how the day, between the hours of ten and twelve, can have such a pure, transparent, and gloriously cheerful countenance: they seek the *ante-meridian* philosophy.

AN EPODE.
AMONG FRIENDS.

(Translated by T. Common.)

I.

Nice, when mute we lie a-dreaming,
Nicer still when we are laughing,
'Neath the sky heaven's chariot speeding,
On the moss the book a-reading,
Sweetly loud with friends all laughing
Joyous, with white teeth a-gleaming.
Do I well, we're mute and humble;
Do I ill – we'll laugh exceeding;
Make it worse and worse, unheeding,
Worse proceeding, more laughs needing.
Till into the grave we stumble.
Friends! Yea! so shall it obtain?
Amen I Till we meet again.

II.

No excuses need be started!
Give, ye glad ones, open hearted,
To this foolish book before you
Ear and heart and lodging meet;
Trust me, 'twas not meant to bore you,
Though of folly I may treat!
What I find, seek, and am needing,
Was it e'er in book for reading?
Honour now fools in my name,
Learn from out this book by reading
How 'our sense' from reason came.
Thus, my friends, shall it obtain?
Amen! Till we meet again.

THUS SPAKE ZARATHUSTRA

THUS SPAKE ZARATHUSTRA

FRIEDRICH NIETZSCHE

This edition published in 2021 by Arcturus Publishing Limited
26/27 Bickels Yard, 151–153 Bermondsey Street,
London SE1 3HA

Typesetting by Palimpsest Book Production Limited

Cover design: Peter Ridley
Cover illustration: Peter Gray

AD006497UK

Printed in the UK

CONTENTS

PART TWO:

PART THREE:

PART FOUR:

INTRODUCTION

Friedrich Nietzsche was born on 15 October 1844 in the small Prussian town of Röcken bei Lützen in Saxony. His father, Karl Ludwig, was appointed Röcken's Lutheran minister by King Friedrich Wilhelm IV. In 1849, Karl died and the family moved to Naumburg, where Nietzsche lived with his mother, sister, grandmother and two aunts. In 1858, he was accepted into the Schulpforta, one of Germany's most prestigious boarding schools.

Upon graduating in 1864, Nietzsche enrolled as a theology and classical philology student at the University of Bonn. Two terms later, he transferred to the University of Leipzig to follow Professor Friedrich Wilhelm Ritschl. Under Ritschl's tutelage Nietzsche thrived in Leipzig, learning the philosophy of Arthur Schopenhauer and Immanuel Kant.

In 1869, Ritschl recommended the 24-year-old Nietzsche for a professorship in philology at the University of Basel. Basel was hesitant; Nietzsche had left the university for a year of military service and hadn't completed his doctoral thesis. But Ritschl heaped praise on Nietzsche, stating that he hadn't found another student like him in 40 years of teaching. So the University of Basel appointed him as an extraordinary professor of classical philology, and promoted him to full professor the following year.

Nietzsche took leave in August 1870 to work as a medical orderly during the Franco-German War. While helping transport the wounded, he contracted dysentery and diphtheria, which resulted in poor health, migraines, insomnia, and near blindness for the rest of his life. In October, he returned to university, but found himself struggling between his deteriorating health, constant pains and the demands of teaching. In 1879, he resigned from his position at the age of 34.

Written in biblical-narrative form while he battled with illness between 1883 and 1885, *Thus Spake Zarathustra* was the culmination of his philosophical career. Following the fictional travels of the prophet Zarathustra, Nietzsche laid out the core tenets of his philosophy. Two concepts lay at the heart of his writing: 'the death of God' and the *übermensch* (the superman). Seeking to free humanity from the strictures of religion and traditional authority, Nietzsche encouraged the mastery of one's self while at the same time accepting one's own fate. Fiercely critical of Christianity, he sought to establish a new system of values suitable for the modern age. Later appropriated by Nazi intellectuals and distorted for their own anti-Semitic purposes, *Thus Spake Zarathustra* became one of the most influential works of modern philosophy.

The work received a poor reception initially, leading Nietzsche to rework his ideas into *Beyond Good and Evil* in 1886. Aged 44, he suffered a nervous breakdown and spent a number of years in psychiatric asylums, before returning to live with his mother until her death in 1897. He then moved into the household of his sister Elisabeth and her husband Bernhard Förster, a politically active anti-Semite. After Förster's suicide in 1889, Elisabeth worked diligently to keep her husband's dreams of 'racial purity' alive. She took control of Nietzsche's estate and used his writings to promote him as a supporter of Förster's work.

Throughout Nietzsche's philosophy, he offered an insightful and open-minded view of man's spirituality. Unlike the hateful message of his sister, he aimed to broaden the minds of his readers and urged them to take control of their own lives.

ZARATHUSTRA'S PROLOGUE

1

WHEN Zarathustra was thirty years old, he left his home and the lake of his home, and went into the mountains. There he enjoyed his spirit and his solitude, and for ten years did not weary of it. But at last his heart changed, and rising one morning with the rosy dawn, he went before the sun, and spake thus unto it:

'Thou great star! What would be thy happiness if thou hadst not those for whom thou shinest!

For ten years hast thou climbed hither unto my cave: thou wouldst have wearied of thy light and of the journey, had it not been for me, mine eagle, and my serpent.

But we awaited thee every morning, took from thee thine overflow, and blessed thee for it.

Lo! I am weary of my wisdom, like the bee that hath gathered too much honey; I need hands outstretched to take it.

I would fain bestow and distribute, until the wise have once more become joyous in their folly, and the poor happy in their riches.

Therefore must I descend into the deep: as thou doest in the evening, when thou goest behind the sea, and givest light also to the netherworld, thou exuberant star!

Like thee must I *go down*, as men say, to whom I shall descend.

Bless me, then, thou tranquil eye, that canst behold even the greatest happiness without envy!

Bless the cup that is about to overflow, that the water may flow golden out of it, and carry everywhere the reflection of thy bliss!

Lo! This cup is again going to empty itself, and Zarathustra is again going to be a man.'

Thus began Zarathustra's down-going.

2

ZARATHUSTRA went down the mountain alone, no one meeting him. When he entered the forest, however, there suddenly stood before him an old man, who had left his holy cot to seek roots. And thus spake the old man to Zarathustra:

'No stranger to me is this wanderer: many years ago passed he by. Zarathustra he was called; but he hath altered.

Then thou carriedst thine ashes into the mountains: wilt thou now carry thy fire into the valleys? Fearest thou not the incendiary's doom?

Yea, I recognize Zarathustra. Pure is his eye, and no loathing lurketh about his mouth. Goeth he not along like a dancer?

Altered is Zarathustra; a child hath Zarathustra become; an awakened one is Zarathustra: what wilt thou do in the land of the sleepers?

As in the sea hast thou lived in solitude, and it hath borne thee up. Alas, wilt thou now go ashore? Alas, wilt thou again drag thy body thyself?'

Zarathustra answered: 'I love mankind.'

'Why,' said the saint, 'did I go into the forest and the desert? Was it not because I loved men far too well?

Now I love God: men, I do not love. Man is a thing too imperfect for me. Love to man would be fatal to me.'

Zarathustra answered: 'What spake I of love! I am bringing gifts unto men.'

'Give them nothing,' said the saint. 'Take rather part of their load, and carry it along with them – that will be most agreeable unto them: if only it be agreeable unto thee!

If, however, thou wilt give unto them, give them no more than an alms, and let them also beg for it!'

'No,' replied Zarathustra, 'I give no alms. I am not poor enough for that.'

The saint laughed at Zarathustra, and spake thus: 'Then see to it that they accept thy treasures! They are distrustful of anchorites, and do not believe that we come with gifts.

The fall of our footsteps ringeth too hollow through their streets. And just as at night, when they are in bed and hear a man abroad long before sunrise, so they ask themselves concerning us: Where goeth the thief?

Go not to men, but stay in the forest! Go rather to the animals! Why not be like me – a bear amongst bears, a bird amongst birds?'

'And what doeth the saint in the forest?' asked Zarathustra.

The saint answered: 'I make hymns and sing them; and in making hymns I laugh and weep and mumble: thus do I praise God.

With singing, weeping, laughing, and mumbling do I praise the God who is my God. But what dost thou bring us as a gift?'

When Zarathustra had heard these words, he bowed to the saint and said: 'What should I have to give thee! Let me rather hurry hence lest I take aught away from thee!' – And thus they parted from one another, the old man and Zarathustra, laughing like school-boys.

When Zarathustra was alone, however, he said to his heart: 'Could it be possible! This old saint in the forest hath not yet heard of it, that *God is dead!*'

3

WHEN Zarathustra arrived at the nearest town which adjoineth the forest, he found many people assembled in the marketplace; for it had been announced that a rope-dancer would give a performance. And Zarathustra spake thus unto the people:

'*I teach you the Superman*. Man is something that is to be surpassed. What have ye done to surpass man?

All beings hitherto have created something beyond themselves: and ye want to be the ebb of that great tide, and would rather go back to the beast than surpass man?

What is the ape to man? A laughing-stock, a thing of shame. And just the same shall man be to the Superman: a laughing-stock, a thing of shame.

Ye have made your way from the worm to man, and much within you is still worm. Once were ye apes, and even yet man is more of an ape than any of the apes.

Even the wisest among you is only a disharmony and hybrid of plant and phantom. But do I bid you become phantoms or plants?

Lo, I teach you the Superman!

The Superman is the meaning of the earth. Let your will say: The Superman *shall be* the meaning of the earth!

I conjure you, my brethren, *remain true to the earth*, and believe not those who speak unto you of superearthly hopes! Poisoners are they, whether they know it or not.

Despisers of life are they, decaying ones and poisoned ones themselves, of whom the earth is weary: so away with them!

Once blasphemy against God was the greatest blasphemy; but God died, and therewith also those blasphemers. To blaspheme the earth is now the dreadfulest sin, and to rate the heart of the unknowable higher than the meaning of the earth!

Once the soul looked contemptuously on the body, and then that contempt was the supreme thing: the soul wished the body meagre, ghastly, and famished. Thus it thought to escape from the body and the earth.

Oh, that soul was itself meagre, ghastly, and famished; and cruelty was the delight of that soul!

But ye, also, my brethren, tell me: What doth your body say about your soul? Is your soul not poverty and pollution and wretched self-complacency?

Verily, a polluted stream is man. One must be a sea, to receive a polluted stream without becoming impure.

Lo, I teach you the Superman: he is that sea; in him can your great contempt be submerged.

What is the greatest thing ye can experience? It is the hour of great contempt. The hour in which even your happiness becometh loathsome unto you, and so also your reason and virtue.

The hour when ye say: "What good is my happiness! It is poverty and pollution and wretched self-complacency. But my happiness should justify existence itself!"

The hour when ye say: "What good is my reason! Doth it long for knowledge as the lion for his food? It is poverty and pollution and wretched self-complacency!"

The hour when ye say: "What good is my virtue! As yet it hath not made me passionate. How weary I am of my good and my bad! It is all poverty and pollution and wretched self-complacency!"

The hour when ye say: "What good is my justice! I do not see that I am fervour and fuel. The just, however, are fervour and fuel!"

The hour when we say: "What good is my pity! Is not pity the cross on which he is nailed who loveth man? But my pity is not a crucifixion."

Have ye ever spoken thus? Have ye ever cried thus? Ah! would that I had heard you crying thus!

It is not your sin – it is your self-satisfaction that crieth unto heaven; your very sparingness in sin crieth unto heaven!

Where is the lightning to lick you with its tongue? Where is the frenzy with which ye should be inoculated?

Lo, I teach you the Superman: he is that lightning, he is that frenzy!'

When Zarathustra had thus spoken, one of the people called out: 'We have now heard enough of the rope-dancer; it is time now for us to see him!' And all the people laughed at Zarathustra. But the rope-dancer, who thought the words applied to him, began his performance.

4

ZARATHUSTRA, however, looked at the people and wondered. Then he spake thus:

'Man is a rope stretched between the animal and the Superman – a rope over an abyss.

A dangerous crossing, a dangerous wayfaring, a dangerous looking-back, a dangerous trembling and halting.

What is great in man is that he is a bridge and not a goal: what is lovable in man is that he is an *over-going* and a *down-going*.

I love those that know not how to live except as down-goers, for they are the over-goers.

I love the great despisers, because they are the great adorers, and arrows of longing for the other shore.

I love those who do not first seek a reason beyond the stars for going down and being sacrifices, but sacrifice themselves to the earth, that the earth of the Superman may hereafter arrive.

I love him who liveth in order to know, and seeketh to know in order that the Superman may hereafter live. Thus seeketh he his own down-going.

I love him who laboureth and inventeth, that he may build the house for the Superman, and prepare for him earth, animal, and plant: for thus seeketh he his own down-going.

I love him who loveth his virtue: for virtue is the will to down-going, and an arrow of longing.

I love him who reserveth no share of spirit for himself, but wanteth to be wholly the spirit of his virtue: thus walketh he as spirit over the bridge.

I love him who maketh his virtue his inclination and destiny: thus, for the sake of his virtue, he is willing to live on, or live no more.

I love him who desireth not too many virtues. One virtue is more of a virtue than two, because it is more of a knot for one's destiny to cling to.

I love him whose soul is lavish, who wanteth no thanks and doth not give back: for he always bestoweth, and desireth not to keep for himself.

I love him who is ashamed when the dice fall in his favour, and who then asketh: "Am I a dishonest player?" – for he is willing to succumb.

I love him who scattereth golden words in advance of his deeds, and always doeth more than he promiseth: for he seeketh his own down-going.

I love him who justifieth the future ones, and redeemeth the past ones: for he is willing to succumb through the present ones.

I love him who chasteneth his God, because he loveth his God: for he must succumb through the wrath of his God.

I love him whose soul is deep even in the wounding, and may succumb through a small matter: thus goeth he willingly over the bridge.

I love him whose soul is so overfull that he forgetteth himself, and all things are in him: thus all things become his down-going.

I love him who is of a free spirit and a free heart: thus is his head only the bowels of his heart; his heart, however, causeth his down-going.

I love all who are like heavy drops falling one by one out of the dark cloud that lowereth over man: they herald the coming of the lightning, and succumb as heralds.

Lo, I am a herald of the lightning, and a heavy drop out of the cloud: the lightning, however, is the *Superman*.'

5

WHEN Zarathustra had spoken these words, he again looked at the people, and was silent. 'There they stand,' said he to his heart; 'there they laugh: they understand me not; I am not the mouth for these ears.

Must one first batter their ears, that they may learn to hear with their eyes? Must one clatter like kettledrums and penitential preachers? Or do they only believe the stammerer?

They have something whereof they are proud. What do they call it, that which maketh them proud? Culture, they call it; it distinguisheth them from the goatherds.

They dislike, therefore, to hear of "contempt" of themselves. So I will appeal to their pride.

I will speak unto them of the most contemptible thing: that, however, is *the last man!*'

And thus spake Zarathustra unto the people:

'It is time for man to fix his goal. It is time for man to plant the germ of his highest hope.

Still is his soil rich enough for it. But that soil will one day be poor and exhausted, and no lofty tree will any longer be able to grow thereon.

Alas! There cometh the time when man will no longer launch the arrow of his longing beyond man – and the string of his bow will have unlearned to whizz!

I tell you: one must still have chaos in one, to give birth to a dancing star. I tell you: ye have still chaos in you.

Alas! There cometh the time when man will no longer give birth to any star. Alas! There cometh the time of the most despicable man, who can no longer despise himself.

Lo! I show you *the last man.*

"What is love? What is creation? What is longing? What is a star?" – so asketh the last man and blinketh.

The earth hath then become small, and on it there hoppeth the last man who maketh everything small. His species is ineradicable like that of the ground-flea; the last man liveth longest.

"We have discovered happiness" – say the last men, and blink thereby.

They have left the regions where it is hard to live; for they need warmth. One still loveth one's neighbour and rubbeth against him; for one needeth warmth.

Turning ill and being distrustful they consider sinful: they walk warily. He is a fool who still stumbleth over stones or men!

A little poison now and then: that maketh pleasant dreams. And much poison at last for a pleasant death.

One still worketh, for work is a pastime. But one is careful lest the pastime should hurt one.

One no longer becometh poor or rich; both are too burdensome. Who still wanteth to rule? Who still wanteth to obey? Both are too burdensome.

No shepherd, and one herd! Every one wanteth the same; every one is equal: he who hath other sentiments goeth voluntarily into the madhouse.

"Formerly all the world was insane," say the subtlest of them, and blink thereby.

They are clever and know all that hath happened: so there is no end to their raillery. People still fall out, but are soon reconciled – otherwise it spoileth their stomachs.

They have their little pleasures for the day, and their little pleasures for the night, but they have a regard for health.

"We have discovered happiness," say the last men, and blink thereby.'

And here ended the first discourse of Zarathustra, which is also called 'The Prologue': for at this point the shouting and mirth of the multitude interrupted him. 'Give us this last man, O Zarathustra,' they called out. 'Make us into these last men! Then will we make thee a present of the Superman!' And all the people exulted and smacked their lips. Zarathustra, however, turned sad, and said to his heart:

'They understand me not: I am not the mouth for these ears.

Too long, perhaps, have I lived in the mountains; too much have I hearkened unto the brooks and trees: now do I speak unto them as unto the goatherds.

Calm is my soul, and clear, like the mountains in the morning. But they think me cold, and a mocker with terrible jests.

And now do they look at me and laugh: and while they laugh they hate me too. There is ice in their laughter.'

6

THEN, however, something happened which made every mouth mute and every eye fixed. In the meantime, of course, the rope-dancer had commenced his performance: he had come out at a little door, and was going along the rope which was stretched between two towers, so that it hung above the marketplace and the people. When he was just midway across, the little door opened once more, and a gaudily-dressed fellow like a buffoon sprang out, and went rapidly after the first one. 'Go on, halt-foot,' cried his frightful voice, 'go on, lazy bones, interloper, sallow-face! – lest I tickle thee with my heel! What dost thou here between the towers? In the tower is the place for thee, thou shouldst be locked up; to one better than thyself thou blockest the way!' – And with every word he came nearer and nearer the first one. When, however, he was but a step behind, there happened the frightful thing which made every mouth mute and every eye fixed – he uttered a yell like a devil, and jumped over the other who was in his way. The latter, however, when he thus saw his rival triumph, lost at the same time his head and his footing on the rope; he threw his pole away, and shot downwards faster than it, like an eddy of arms and legs, into the depth. The marketplace and the people were like the sea when the storm cometh on: they all flew apart and in disorder, especially where the body was about to fall.

Zarathustra, however, remained standing, and just beside him fell the body, badly injured and disfigured, but not yet dead. After a while consciousness returned to the shattered man, and he saw Zarathustra kneeling beside him. 'What art thou doing there?' said he at last, 'I knew long ago that the devil would trip me up. Now he draggeth me to hell: wilt thou prevent him?'

'On mine honour, my friend,' answered Zarathustra, 'there is nothing of all that whereof thou speakest: there is no devil and no hell. Thy soul will be dead even sooner than thy body: fear, therefore, nothing any more!'

The man looked up distrustfully. 'If thou speakest the truth,' said he, 'I lose nothing when I lose my life. I am not much more than an animal which hath been taught to dance by blows and scanty fare.'

'Not at all,' said Zarathustra, 'thou hast made danger thy calling; therein there is nothing contemptible. Now thou perishest by thy calling: therefore will I bury thee with mine own hands.'

When Zarathustra had said this the dying one did not reply further; but he moved his hand as if he sought the hand of Zarathustra in gratitude.

7

MEANWHILE the evening came on, and the marketplace veiled itself in gloom. Then the people dispersed, for even curiosity and terror become fatigued. Zarathustra, however, still sat beside the dead man on the ground, absorbed in thought: so he forgot the time. But at last it became night, and a cold wind blew upon the lonely one. Then arose Zarathustra and said to his heart:

'Verily, a fine catch of fish hath Zarathustra made today! It is not a man he hath caught, but a corpse.

Sombre is human life, and as yet without meaning: a buffoon may be fateful to it.

I want to teach men the sense of their existence, which is the Superman, the lightning out of the dark cloud – man.

But still am I far from them, and my sense speaketh not unto their sense. To men I am still something between a fool and a corpse.

Gloomy is the night, gloomy are the ways of Zarathustra. Come, thou cold and stiff companion! I carry thee to the place where I shall bury thee with mine own hands.'

8

WHEN Zarathustra had said this to his heart, he put the corpse upon his shoulders and set out on his way. Yet had he not gone a hundred steps, when there stole a man up to him and whispered in his ear – and lo! he that spake was the buffoon from the tower. 'Leave this town, O Zarathustra,' said he, 'there are too many here who hate thee. The good and just hate thee, and call thee their enemy and despiser; the believers in the orthodox belief hate thee, and call thee a danger to the multitude. It was thy good fortune to be laughed at: and verily thou spakest like a buffoon. It was thy good fortune to associate with the dead dog; by so humiliating thyself thou hast saved thy life today. Depart, however, from this town, or tomorrow I shall jump over thee, a living man over a dead one.' And when he had said this, the buffoon vanished; Zarathustra, however, went on through the dark streets.

At the gate of the town the gravediggers met him: they shone their torch on his face, and, recognizing Zarathustra, they sorely derided him. 'Zarathustra is carrying away the dead dog: a fine thing that Zarathustra hath turned a gravedigger! For our hands are too cleanly for that roast. Will Zarathustra steal the bite from the devil? Well then, good luck to the repast! If only the devil is not a better thief than Zarathustra! – he will steal them both, he will eat them both!' And they laughed among themselves, and put their heads together.

Zarathustra made no answer thereto, but went on his way. When he had gone on for two hours, past forests and swamps, he had heard too much of the hungry howling of the wolves, and he himself became hungry. So he halted at a lonely house in which a light was burning.

'Hunger attacketh me,' said Zarathustra, 'like a robber. Among forests and swamps my hunger attacketh me, and late in the night.

Strange humours hath my hunger. Often it cometh to me only after a repast, and all day it hath failed to come: where hath it been?'

And thereupon Zarathustra knocked at the door of the house. An old man appeared, who carried a light, and asked: 'Who cometh unto me and my bad sleep?'

'A living man and a dead one,' said Zarathustra. 'Give me something to eat and drink, I forgot it during the day. He that feedeth the hungry refresheth his own soul, saith wisdom.'

The old man withdrew, but came back immediately and offered Zarathustra bread and wine. 'A bad country for the hungry,' said he; 'that is why I live here. Animal and man come unto me, the anchorite. But bid thy companion eat and drink also, he is wearier than thou.' Zarathustra answered: 'My companion is dead; I shall hardly be able to persuade him to eat.' 'That doth not concern me,' said the old man sullenly; 'he that knocketh at my door must take what I offer him. Eat, and fare ye well!'

Thereafter Zarathustra again went on for two hours, trusting to the path and the light of the stars: for he was an experienced night-walker, and liked to look into the face of all that slept. When the morning dawned, however, Zarathustra found himself in a thick forest, and no path was any longer visible. He then put the dead man in a hollow tree at his head – for he wanted to protect him from the wolves – and laid himself down on the ground and moss. And immediately he fell asleep, tired in body, but with a tranquil soul.

9

LONG slept Zarathustra; and not only the rosy dawn passed over his head, but also the morning. At last, however, his eyes opened, and amazedly he gazed into the forest and the stillness, amazedly he gazed into himself. Then he arose quickly, like a seafarer who all at once seeth the land; and he shouted for joy: for he saw a new truth. And he spake thus to his heart:

'A light hath dawned upon me: I need companions – living ones; not dead companions and corpses, which I carry with me where I will.

But I need living companions, who will follow me because they want to follow themselves – and to the place where I will. A light hath dawned upon me. Not to the people is Zarathustra to speak, but to companions! Zarathustra shall not be the herd's herdsman and hound!

To allure many from the herd – for that purpose have I come. The people and the herd must be angry with me: a robber shall Zarathustra be called by the herdsmen.

Herdsmen, I say, but they call themselves the good and just. Herdsmen, I say, but they call themselves the believers in the orthodox belief.

Behold the good and just! Whom do they hate most? Him who breaketh up their tables of values, the breaker, the lawbreaker: he, however, is the creator.

Behold the believers of all beliefs! Whom do they hate most? Him who breaketh up their tables of values, the breaker, the lawbreaker – he, however, is the creator.

Companions, the creator seeketh, not corpses – and not herds or believers either. Fellow-creators the creator seeketh – those who grave new values on new tables.

Companions, the creator seeketh, and fellow-reapers: for everything is ripe for the harvest with him. But he lacketh the hundred sickles: so he plucketh the ears of corn and is vexed.

Companions, the creator seeketh, and such as know how to whet their sickles. Destroyers, will they be called, and despisers of good and evil. But they are the reapers and rejoicers.

Fellow-creators, Zarathustra seeketh; fellow-reapers and fellow-rejoicers, Zarathustra seeketh: what hath he to do with herds and herdsmen and corpses!

And thou, my first companion, rest in peace! Well have I buried thee in thy hollow tree; well have I hid thee from the wolves.

But I part from thee; the time hath arrived. 'Twixt rosy dawn and rosy dawn there came unto me a new truth.

I am not to be a herdsman, I am not to be a gravedigger. Not any more will I discourse unto the people; for the last time have I spoken unto the dead.

With the creators, the reapers, and the rejoicers will I associate: the rainbow will I show them, and all the stairs to the Superman.

To the lone-dwellers will I sing my song, and to the twain – dwellers; and unto him who hath still ears for the unheard, will I make the heart heavy with my happiness.

I make for my goal, I follow my course; over the loitering and tardy will I leap. Thus let my on-going be their down-going!'

10

THIS had Zarathustra said to his heart when the sun stood at noontide. Then he looked inquiringly aloft, for he heard above him the sharp call of a bird. And behold! An eagle swept through the air in wide circles, and on it hung a serpent, not like a prey, but like a friend: for it kept itself coiled round the eagle's neck.

'They are mine animals,' said Zarathustra, and rejoiced in his heart.

'The proudest animal under the sun, and the wisest animal under the sun, they have come out to reconnoitre.

They want to know whether Zarathustra still liveth. Verily, do I still live?

More dangerous have I found it among men than among animals; in dangerous paths goeth Zarathustra. Let mine animals lead me!'

When Zarathustra had said this, he remembered the words of the saint in the forest. Then he sighed and spake thus to his heart:

'Would that I were wiser! Would that I were wise from the very heart, like my serpent!

But I am asking the impossible. Therefore do I ask my pride to go always with my wisdom!

And if my wisdom should some day forsake me: alas! It loveth to fly away! May my pride then fly with my folly!'

Thus began Zarathustra's down-going.

PART ONE

1. The Three Metamorphoses

'THREE metamorphoses of the spirit do I designate to you: now the spirit becometh a camel, the camel a lion, and the lion at last a child.

Many heavy things are there for the spirit, the strong load-bearing spirit in which the reverence dwelleth: for the heavy and the heaviest longeth its strength.

What is heavy? so asketh the load-bearing spirit; then kneeleth it down like the camel, and wanteth to be well laden.

What is the heaviest things, ye heroes? asketh the load-bearing spirit, that I may take it upon me and rejoice in my strength.

Is it not this: To humiliate oneself in order to mortify one's pride? To exhibit one's folly in order to mock at one's wisdom?

Or is it this: To desert our cause when it celebrateth its triumph? To ascend high mountains to tempt the temper?

Or is it this: To feed on the acorns and grass of knowledge, and for the sake of truth to suffer hunger of soul?

Or is it this: To be sick and dismiss comforters, and make friends of the deaf, who never hear thy requests?

Or is it this: To go into foul water when it is the water of truth, and not disclaim cold frogs and hot toads?

Or is it this: To love those who despise us, and to give one's hand to the phantom when it is going to frighten us?

All these heaviest things the load-bearing spirit taketh upon itself: and like the camel, which, when laden, hasteneth into the wilderness, so hasteneth the spirit into its wilderness.

But in the loneliest wilderness happeneth the second metamorphosis: here the spirit becometh a lion; freedom will it capture, and lordship in its own wilderness.

Its last Lord it here seeketh: hostile will it be to him, and to its last God; for victory will it struggle with the great dragon.

What is the great dragon which the spirit is no longer inclined to call Lord and God? 'Thou-shalt,' is the great dragon called. But the spirit of the lion saith, 'I will.'

'Thou-shalt,' lieth in its path, sparkling with gold – a scale-covered beast; and on every scale glittereth golden, 'Thou shalt!'

The values of a thousand years glitter on those scales, and thus speaketh the mightiest of all dragons: 'All the values of things – glitter on me.

All values have already been created, and all created values – do I represent. Verily, there shall be no 'I will' any more.' Thus speaketh the dragon.

My brethren, wherefore is there need of the lion in the spirit? Why sufficeth not the beast of burden, which renounceth and is reverent?

To create new values – that, even the lion cannot yet accomplish: but to create itself freedom for new creating – that can the might of the lion do.

To create itself freedom, and give a holy Nay even unto duty: for that, my brethren, there is no need of the lion.

To assume the ride into new values – that is the most formidable assumption for a load-bearing and reverent spirit. Verily, unto such a spirit it is preying, and the work of a beast of prey.

As its holiest, it once loved 'Thou-shalt': now it is forced to find illusion and arbitrariness even in the holiest things, that it may capture freedom from its love: the lion is needed for this capture.

But tell me, my brethren, what the child can do, which even the lion could not do? Why hath the preying lion still to become a child?

Innocence is the child, and forgetfulness, and a new beginning, a game, a self-rolling wheel, a first movement, a holy Yea.

Aye, for the game of creating, my brethren, there is needed a holy Yea unto life: *its own* will, willeth now the spirit; *his own* world winneth the world's outcast.

Three metamorphoses of the spirit have I designated to you: how the spirit became a camel, the camel a lion, and the lion at last a child.'

Thus spake Zarathustra. And at that time he abode in the town which is called The Pied Cow.

2. The Academic Chairs of Virtue

PEOPLE commended unto Zarathustra a wise man, as one who could discourse well about sleep and virtue: greatly was he honoured and rewarded for it, and all the youths sat before his chair. To him went Zarathustra, and sat among the youths before his chair. And thus spake the wise man:

'Respect and modesty in presence of sleep! That is the first thing! And to go out of the way of all who sleep badly and keep awake at night!

Modest is even the thief in the presence of sleep: He always stealeth softly through the night. Immodest, however, is the night-watchman; immodestly he carrieth his horn.

No small art is it to sleep: it is necessary for that purpose to keep awake all day.

Ten times a day must thou overcome thyself: that causeth wholesome weariness, and is poppy to the soul.

Ten times must thou reconcile again with thyself; for overcoming is bitterness, and badly sleep the unreconciled.

Ten truths must thou find during the day; otherwise wilt thou seek truth during the night, and thy soul will have been hungry.

Ten times must thou laugh during the day, and be cheerful; otherwise thy stomach, the father of affliction, will disturb thee in the night.

Few people know it, but one must have all the virtues in order to sleep well. Shall I bear false witness? Shall I commit adultery?

Shall I covet my neighbour's maidservant? All that would ill accord with good sleep.

And even if one have all the virtues, there is still one thing needful: to send the virtues themselves to sleep at the right time.

That they may not quarrel with one another, the good females! And about thee, thou unhappy one!

Peace with God and thy neighbour: so desireth good sleep. And peace also with thy neighbour's devil! Otherwise it will haunt thee in the night.

Honour to the government, and obedience, and also to the crooked government! So desireth good sleep. How can I help it, if power liketh to walk on crooked legs?

He who leadeth his sheep to the greenest pasture, shall always be for me the best shepherd: so doth it accord with good sleep.

Many honours I want not, nor great treasures: they excite the spleen. But it is bad sleeping without a good name and a little treasure.

A small company is more welcome to me than a bad one: but they must come and go at the right time. So doth it accord with good sleep.

Well, also, do the poor in spirit please me: they promote sleep. Blessed are they, especially if one always give in to them.

Thus passeth the day unto the virtuous. When night cometh, then take I good care not to summon sleep. It disliketh to be summoned – sleep, the lord of the virtues!

But I think of what I have done and thought during the day. Thus ruminating, patient as a cow, I ask myself: What were thy ten overcomings?

And what were the ten reconciliations, and the ten truths, and the ten laughters with which my heart enjoyed itself?

Thus pondering, and cradled by forty thoughts, it overtaketh me all at once – sleep, the unsummoned, the lord of the virtues.

Sleep tappeth on mine eye, and it turneth heavy. Sleep toucheth my mouth, and it remaineth open.

Verily, on soft soles doth it come to me, the dearest of thieves, and stealeth from me my thoughts: stupid do I then stand, like this academic chair.

But not much longer do I then stand: I already lie.'

When Zarathustra heard the wise man thus speak, he laughed in his heart: for thereby had a light dawned upon him and thus spake he to his heart:

'A fool seemeth this wise man with his forty thoughts: but I believe he knoweth well how to sleep.

Happy even is he who liveth near this wise man! Such sleep is contagious – even through a thick wall it is contagious.

A magic resideth even in his academic chair. And not in vain did the youths sit before the preacher of virtue.

His wisdom is to keep awake in order to sleep well. And verily, if life had no sense, and I had to choose nonsense, this would be the desirablest nonsense for me also.

Now know I well what people sought formerly above all else when they sought teachers of virtue. Good sleep they sought for themselves, and poppyhead virtues to promote it!

To all those belauded sages of the academic chairs, wisdom was sleep without dreams: they knew no higher significance of life.

Even at present, to be sure, there are some like this preacher of virtue, and not always so honourable: but their time is past. And not much longer do they stand: there they already lie.

Blessed are those drowsy ones: for they shall soon nod to sleep.'

Thus spake Zarathustra.

3. Backworldsmen

'ONCE on a time, Zarathustra also cast his fancy beyond man, like all backworldsmen. The work of a suffering and tortured God, did the world then seem to me.

The dream – and diction – of a God, did the world then seem to me; coloured vapours before the eyes of a divinely dissatisfied one.

Good and evil, and joy and woe, and I and thou-coloured vapours did they seem to me before creative eyes. The creator wished to look away from himself, thereupon he created the world.

Intoxicating joy is it for the sufferer to look away from his suffering and forget himself. Intoxicating joy and self-forgetting, did the world once seem to me.

This world, the eternally imperfect, and internal contradiction's image and imperfect image – an intoxicating joy to its imperfect creator: thus did the world once seem to me.

Thus, once on a time, did I also cast my fancy beyond man, like all backworldsmen. Beyond man, forsooth?

Ah, ye brethren, that God whom I created was human work and human madness, like all gods!

A man was he, and only a poor fragment of a man and ego. Out of mine own ashes and glow it came unto me, that phantom. And verily, it came not unto me from beyond!

What happened, my brethren? I surpassed myself, the suffering one; I carried mine own ashes to the mountain; a brighter flame I contrived for myself. And lo! Thereupon the phantom *withdrew* from me!

To me the convalescent would it now be suffering and torment to believe in such phantoms: suffering would it now be to me, and humiliation. Thus I speak to backworldsmen.

Suffering was it, and impotence – that created all backworlds; and the short madness of happiness, which only the greatest sufferer experienceth.

Weariness, which seeketh to get the ultimate one leap, with a death-leap; a poor ignorant weariness, unwilling even to will any longer: that created all gods and backworlds.

Believe me, my brethren! It was the body which despaired of the body – it groped with the fingers or the infatuated spirit at the ultimate walls.

Believe me, my brethren! It was the body which despaired of the earth – it heard the bowels of existence speaking unto it.

And then it sought to get through the ultimate walls with its head – and not with its head only – into "the other world".

But that “other world” is well concealed from man, that dehumanised, inhuman world, which is a celestial naught; and the bowels of existence do not speak unto man, except as a man.

Verily, it is difficult to prove all being, and hard to make it speak. Tell me, ye brethren, is not the strangest of all things best proved?

Yea, this ego, with its contradiction and perplexity, speaketh most uprightly of its being – this creating, willing, evaluing ego, which is the measure and value of things.

And this most upright existence, the ego – it speaketh of the body, and still implieth the body, even when it museth and raveth and fluttereth with broken wings.

Always more uprightly learneth it to speak, the ego; and the more it learneth, the more doth it find titles, and honours for the body and the earth.

A new pride taught me mine ego, and that teach I unto men: no longer to thrust one’s head into the sand of celestial things, but to carry it freely, a terrestrial head, which giveth meaning to the earth!

A new will teach I unto men: to choose that path which man hath followed blindly, and to approve of it – and no longer slink aside from it, like the sick and perishing!

The sick and perishing – it was they who despised the body and the earth, and invented the heavenly world, and the redeeming blood drops; but even those sweet and sad poisons they borrowed from the body and the earth!

From their misery they sought to escape, and the stars were too remote for them. Then they sight: “O that there were heavenly paths by which to steal into another existence and into happiness!” Then they contrived for themselves their bypaths and bloody draughts!

Beyond the sphere of their body and this earth they now fancied themselves transported, these ungrateful ones. But to what did they owe the convulsion and rapture of their transport? To their body and this earth.

Gentle is Zarathustra to the sickly. Verily, he is not indignant of their modes of consolation and ingratitude. May they become convalescents and overcomers, and create higher bodies for themselves!

Neither is Zarathustra indignant at a convalescent who looketh tenderly on his delusions, and at midnight stealeth round the grave of his God; but sickness and a sick frame remain even in his tears.

Many sickly ones have there always been among those who muse, and languish for God; violently they hate the discerning ones, and the latest of virtues, which is uprightness.

Backward they always gaze toward dark ages: then, indeed, were delusion and faith something different. Raving of the reason was likeness to God, and doubt was sin.

Too well do I know those godlike ones: they insist on being believed in, and that doubt is sin. Too well, also, do I know what they themselves most believe in.

Verily, not in backworlds and redeeming blood drops: but in the body do they also believe most; and their own body is for them the thing-in-itself.

But it is a sickly thing to them, and gladly would they get out of their skin. Therefore hearken they to the preachers of death, and themselves preach backworlds.

Hearken rather, my brethren, to the voice of the healthy body; it is a more upright and pure voice.

More uprightly and purely speaketh the healthy body, perfect and square-built; and it speaketh of the meaning of the earth.'

Thus spake Zarathustra.

4. The Despisers of the Body

'TO THE despisers of the body will I speak my word. I wish them neither to learn afresh, nor teach anew, but only to bid farewell to their own bodies, and thus be dumb.

"Body am I, and soul" – so saith the child. And why should one not speak like children?

But the awakened one, the knowing own, saith: "Body am I entirely and nothing more; and soul is only the name of something in the body."

The body is a big sagacity, a plurality with one sense, a war and a peace, a flock and a shepherd.

An instrument of thy body is also thy little sagacity, my brother, which thou callest a "spirit" – a little instrument and plaything of thy big sagacity.

"Ego," sayest thou, and art proud of that word. But the greater thing – in which thou are unwilling to believe – is thy body with its big sagacity; it saith not "ego", but doeth it.

What the sense feeleth, what the spirit discerneth, hath never its end in itself. But sense and spirit would fain persuade thee that they are the end of all things: so vain are they.

Instruments and plaything are sense and spirit: behind them there is still the Self. The Self seeketh with the eyes of the senses, it hearkeneth also with the ears of the spirit.

Ever hearkeneth the Self, and seeketh; it compareth, mastereth, conquereth, and destroyeth. It ruleth, and is also the ego's ruler.

Behind thy thoughts and feelings, my brother, there is a mighty lord, and unknown sage – it is called Self; it dwelleth in thy body, it is thy body.

There is more sagacity in thy body than in thy best wisdom. And who then knoweth why thy body requireth just thy best wisdom?

Thy Self laugheth at thine ego, and its proud prancings. "What are these prancings and flights of thought unto me?" it saith to itself. "A byway to my purpose. I am the leading-string of the ego, and the prompter of its notions."

The Self saith unto the ego: "Feel pain!" And thereupon it suffereth, and thinketh how it may put and end thereto – and for that very purpose it *is meant* to think.

To the despisers of the body will I speak a word. That they despise is caused by their esteem. What is it that created esteeming and despising and worth and will?

The creating Self created for itself esteeming and despising, it created for itself joy and woe. The creating body created for itself spirit, as a hand to its will.

Even in your folly and despising ye each serve your Self, ye despisers of the body. I tell you, your very self wanteth to die, and turneth away from life.

No longer can your Self do that which it desireth most: create beyond itself. That is what it desireth most; that is all its fervour.

But it is now too late to do so: so your Self wisheth to succumb, ye despisers of the body.

To succumb – so wisheth your Self; and therefore have ye become despisers of the body. For ye can no longer create beyond yourselves.

And therefore are ye now angry with life and with the earth. And unconscious envy is in the sidelong look of your contempt.

I go not your way, ye despisers of the body! Ye are no bridges for me to the Superman!'

Thus spake Zarathustra.

5. Joys and Passions

'MY BROTHER, when thou hast a virtue, and it is thine own virtue, thou hast it in common with no one.

To be sure, thou wouldst call it by name and caress it; thou wouldst pull its ears and amuse thyself with it.

And lo! Then hast thou its name in common with the people, and hast become one of the people and herd with thy virtue!

Better for thee to say: "Ineffable is it, and nameless, that which is pain and sweetness to my soul, and also the hunger of my bowels."

Let thy virtue be too high for the familiarity of names, and if thou must speak of it, be not ashamed to stammer about it.

Thus speak and stammer: "That is *my* good, that do I love, thus doth it please me entirely, thus only do *I* desire the good.

Not as the law of a God do I desire it, not as a human law or a human need do I desire it; it is not to be a guide-post for me to superearths and paradises.

An earthly virtue is it which I love: little prudence is therein, and the least everyday wisdom.

But that bird built its nest beside me: therefore, I love and cherish it – now sitteth it beside me on its golden eggs."

Thus shouldst thou stammer, and praise thy virtue.

Once hadst thou passions and calledst them evil. But now hast thou only thy virtues: they grew out of thy passions.

Thou implantedst thy highest aim into the heart of those passions: then became they thy virtues and joys.

And though thou wert of the race of the hot-tempered, or of the voluptuous, or of the fanatical, or the vindictive;

All thy passions in the end became virtues, and all thy devils angels.

Once hadst thou wild dogs in thy cellar: but they changed at last into birds and charming songstresses.

Out of thy poisons brewedst thou balsam for thyself; thy cow, affliction, milkedst thou – now drinketh thou the sweet milk of her udder.

And nothing evil groweth in thee any longer, unless it be the evil that groweth out of the conflict of thy virtues.

My brother, if thou be fortunate, then wilt thou have one virtue and no more: thus goest thou easier over the bridge.

Illustrious is it to have many virtues, but a hard lot; and many a one hath gone into the wilderness and killed himself, because he is weary of being the battle and battlefield of virtues.

My brother, are war and battle evil? Necessary, however is the evil; necessary are the envy and the distrust and the back-biting among the virtues.

Lo! How each of thy virtues is covetous of the highest place; it wanteth thy whole spirit to be *its* herald, it wanteth thy whole power, in wrath, hatred, and love.

Jealous is every virtue of the others, and a dreadful thing is jealousy. Even virtues may succumb by jealousy.

He whom the flame of jealousy encompasseth, turneth at last, like the scorpion, the poisoned sting against himself.

Ah! My brother, hast thou never seen a virtue backbite and stab itself?

Man is something that hath to be surpassed: and therefore shalt thou love thy virtues, for thou wilt succumb by them.'

Thus spake Zarathustra.

6. *The Pale Criminal*

'YE DO not mean to slay, ye judges and sacrificers, until the animal hath bowed its head? Lo! The pale criminal hath bowed his head: out of his eye speaketh the great contempt.

"Mine ego is something which is to be surpassed: mine ego is to me the great contempt of man": so speaketh it out of that eye.

When he judged himself – that was his supreme moment; let not the exalted one relapse again into his low estate!

There is no salvation for him who thus suffereth from himself, unless it be speedy death.

Your slaying, ye judges, shall be pity, and not revenge; and in that ye slay, see to it that ye yourselves justify life!

It is not enough that ye should reconcile with him whom ye slay. Let your sorrow be love to the Superman: thus will ye justify your own survival!

"Enemy" shall ye say but not "villain," "invalid" shall ye say but not "wretch", "fool" shall ye say but not "sinner."

And thou, red judge, if thou would say audibly all thou hast done in thought, then would every one cry: "Away with the nastiness and the virtulent reptile!"

But one thing is the thought, another thing is the deed, and another thing is the idea of the deed. The wheel of causality doth not roll between them.

An idea made this pale man pale. Adequate was he for his deed when he did it, but the idea of it, he could not endure when it was done.

Evermore did he now see himself as the doer of one deed. Madness, I call this: the exception reversed itself to the rule in him.

The streak of chalk bewitcheth the hen; the stroke he struck bewitched his weak reason. Madness *after* the deed, I call this.

Hearken, ye judges! There is another madness besides, and it is *before* the deed. Ah! Ye have not gone deep enough into this soul!

Thus speaketh the red judge: "Why did this criminal commit murder? He meant to rob." I tell you, however, that his soul wanted blood, not booty: he thirsted for the happiness of the knife!

But his weak reason understood not this madness, and it persuaded him. "What matter about blood!" it said; "wishest thou not, at least, to make booty thereby? Or take revenge?"

And he hearkened unto his weak reason: like lead lay its words upon him – thereupon he robbed when he murdered. He did not mean to be ashamed of his madness.

And now once more lieth the lead of his guilt upon him, and once more is his weak reason so benumbled, so paralysed, and so dull.

Could he only shake his head, then would his burden roll off; but who shaketh that head?

What is this man? A mass of diseases that reach out into the world through the spirit; there they want to get their prey.

What is this man? A coil of wild serpents that are seldom at peace among themselves – so they go forth apart and seek prey in the world.

Look at that poor body! What it suffered and craved, the poor soul interpreted to itself – it interpreted it as murderous desire, and eagerness for the happiness of the knife.

Him who now turneth sick, the evil over taketh which is now the evil: he seeketh to cause pain with that which causeth him pain. But there have been other ages, and another evil and good.

Once was doubt evil, and the will to Self. Then the invalid became a heretic or sorcerer; as heretic or sorcerer he suffered, and sought to cause suffering.

But this will not enter your ears; it hurteth your good people, ye tell me. But what doth it matter to me about your good people!

Many things in your good people cause me disgust, and verily, not their evil. I would that they had a madness by which they succumbed, like this pale criminal!

Verily, I would that their madness were called truth, or fidelity, or justice: but they have their virtue in order to live long, and in wretched self-complacency.

I am railing alongside the torrent; whoever is able to grasp me may grasp me! Your crutch, however, I am not.'

Thus spake Zarathustra.

7. Reading and Writing

'OF ALL that is written, I love only what a person hath written with his blood. Write with blood, and thou wilt find that blood is spirit.

It is no easy task to understand unfamiliar blood; I hate the reading idlers.

He who knoweth the reader, doeth nothing more for the reader. Another century of readers – and the spirit itself will stink.

Every one being allowed to learn to read, ruineth in the long run not only writing but also thinking.

Once spirit was God, then it became man, and now it even becometh populace.

He that writeth in blood and proverbs doth not want to be read, but learned by heart.

In the mountains the shortest way is from peak to peak, but for that route thou must have long legs. Proverbs should be peaks, and those spoken to should be big and tall.

The atmosphere rare and pure, danger near and the spirit full of a joyful wickedness: thus are things well matched.

I want to have goblins about me, for I am courageous. The courage which scareth away ghosts, createth for itself goblins – it wanteth to laugh.

I no longer feel in common with you; the very cloud which I see beneath me, the blackness and heaviness at which I laugh – that is your thunder-cloud.

Ye look aloft when ye long for exaltation; and I look downward because I am exalted.

Who among you can at the same time laugh and be exalted?

He who climbeth on the highest mountains, laugheth at all tragic plays and tragic realities.

Courageous, unconcerned, scornful, coercive – so wisdom wisheth us; she is a woman, and ever loveth only a warrior.

Ye tell me, "Life is hard to bear." But for what purpose should ye have your pride in the morning and your resignation in the evening?

Life is hard to bear: but do not affect to be so delicate! We are all of us fine sumpter asses and she-asses.

What have we in common with the rose-bud, which trembleth because a drop of dew hath formed upon it?

It is true we love life; not because we are wont to live, but because we are wont to love.

There is always some madness in love. But there is always, also, some method in madness.

And to me also, who appreciate life, the butterflies, soap-bubbles, and whatever is like them amongst us, seem most to enjoy happiness.

To see these light, foolish, pretty, lively little sprites flit about – that moveth Zarathustra to tears and songs.

I should only believe in a God that would know how to dance.

And when I saw my devil, I found him serious, thorough, profound, solemn: he was the spirit of gravity – through him all things fall.

Not by wrath, but by laughter, do we slay. Come, let us slay the spirit of gravity!

I learned to walk; since then have I let myself run. I learned to fly; since then I do not need pushing in order to move from a spot.

Now am I light, now do I fly; now do I see myself under myself. Now there danceth a God in me.'

Thus spake Zarathustra.

8. The Tree on the Hill

ZARATHUSTRA'S eye had perceived that a certain youth avoided him. And as he walked alone one evening over the hills surrounding the town called 'The Pied Cow,' behold, there found he the youth sitting leaning against a tree, and gazing with wearied look into the valley. Zarathustra thereupon laid hold of the tree beside which the youth sat, and spake thus:

'If I wished to shake this tree with my hands, I should not be able to do so.

But the wind, which we see not, troubleth and bendeth it and it listeth. We are sorest bent and troubled by invisible hands.'

Thereupon the youth arose disconcerted, and said: 'I hear Zarathustra, and just now was thinking of him!' Zarathustra answered:

'Why art thou frightened on that account? But it is the same with man as with the tree.

The more he seeketh to rise into the height and light, the more vigorously do his roots struggle earthward, downward, into the dark and deep – into the evil.'

'Yea, into the evil!' cried the youth. 'How is it possible that thou hast discovered my soul?'

Zarathustra smiled, and said: 'Many a soul one will never discover, unless one first invent it.'

'Yea, into the evil!' cried the youth once more.

'Thou saidst the truth, Zarathustra. I trust myself no longer since I sought to rise into the height, and nobody trusteth me any longer; how doth that happen?

I change too quickly: my today refuteth my yesterday. I often overleap the steps when I clamber; for so doing, none of the steps pardons me.

When aloft, I find myself always alone. No one speaketh unto me; the frost of solitude maketh me tremble. What do I seek on the height?

My contempt and my longing increase together; the higher I clamber, the more do I despise him who clambereth. What doth he seek on the height?

How ashamed I am of my clambering and stumbling! How I mock at my violent panting! How I hate him who flieth! How tired I am on the height!'

Here the youth was silent. And Zarathustra contemplated the tree beside which they stood, and spake thus:

'This tree standeth here on the hills; it hath grown up high above man and beast.

And if it wanted to speak, it would have none who could understand it: so high hath it grown.

Now it waiteth and waiteth, – for what doth it wait? It dwelleth too close to the seat of the clouds; it waiteth perhaps for the first lightning?'

When Zarathustra had said this, the youth called out with violent gestures: 'Yea, Zarathustra, thou speakest the truth. My destruction I longed for, when I desired to be on the height, and thou art the lightning for which I waited! Lo! What have I been since thou hast appeared amongst us? It is mine envy of thee that hath destroyed me!' Thus spake the youth, and wept bitterly. Zarathustra, however, put his arm around him, and led the youth away with him.

And when they had walked a while together, Zarathustra began to speak thus:

'It rendeth my heart. Better than thy words express it, thine eyes tell me all thy danger.

As thou art not free; thou still *seekest* freedom. Too unslept hath thy seeking made thee, and too wakeful.

On the open height wouldst thou be; for the stars thirsteth thy soul. But thy bad impulses also thirst for freedom.

Thy wild dogs want liberty; they bark for joy in their cellar when thy spirit endeavoureth to open all prison doors.

Still art thou a prisoner – it seemeth to me – who deviseth liberty for himself: ah! Sharp becometh the soul of such prisoners, but also deceitful and wicked.

To purify himself, is still necessary for the freedman of the spirit. Much of the prison and the mould still remaineth in him: pure hath his eye still to become.

Yea, I know thy danger. But by my love and hope I conjure thee: cast not thy love and hope away!

Noble thou feelst thyself still, and noble others also feel thee still, though they bear thee a grudge and cast evil looks. Know this, that to everybody a noble one standeth in the way.

Also to the good, a noble one standeth in the way: and even when they call him a good man, they want thereby to put him aside.

The new, would the noble man create, and a new virtue. The old, wanteth the good man, and that the old should be conserved.

But it is not the danger of the noble man to turn a good man, but lest he should become a blusterer, a scoffer, or a destroyer.

Ah! I have known noble ones who lost their highest hope. And then they disparaged all high hopes.

Then lived they shamelessly in temporary pleasures, and beyond the day had hardly an aim.

'Spirit is also voluptousness,' said they. Then broke the wings of their spirit; and now it creepeth about, and defileth where it gnaweth.

Once they thought of becoming heroes; but sensualists are they now. A trouble and a terror is the hero to them.

But by my love and hope I conjure thee: cast not away the hero in thy soul! Maintain holy thy highest hope!'

Thus spake Zarathustra.

9. The Preachers of Death

'THERE are preachers of death: and the earth is full of those to whom desistance from life must be preached.

Full is the earth of the superfluous; marred is life by the many-too-many. May they be decoyed out of this life by the "life eternal"!

"The yellow ones": so are called the preachers of death, or "the black ones". But I will show them unto you in other colours besides.

There are the terrible ones who carry about in themselves the beast of prey, and have no choice except lusts or self-laceration. And even their lusts are self-laceration.

They have not yet become men, those terrible ones: may they preach desistance from life, and pass away themselves!

There are the spiritually consumptive ones: hardly are they born when they begin to die, and long for doctrines of lassitude and renunciation.

They would fain be dead, and we should approve of their wish! Let us beware of awakening those dead ones, and of damaging those living coffins!

They meet an invalid, or an old man, or a corpse – and immediately they say: "Life is refuted!"

But they are only refuted, and their eye, which seeth only one aspect of existence.

Shrouded in thick melancholy, and eager for the little casualties that bring death: thus do they wait, and clench their teeth.

Or else, they grasp at sweetmeats, and mock at their childishness thereby: they cling to their straw of life, and mock at their still clinging to it.

Their wisdom speaketh thus: "A fool, he who remaineth alive; but so far are we fools! And that is the foolishest thing in life!"

"Life is only suffering": so say others, and lie not. Then see to it that *ye* cease! See to it that the life ceaseth which is only suffering!

And let this be the teaching of your virtue: "Thou shalt slay thyself! Thou shalt steal away from thyself!" – "Lust is sin," – so say some who preach death – "let us go apart and beget no children!"

"Giving birth is troublesome," – say others – "why still give birth? One beareth only the unfortunate!" And they also are preachers of death.

"Pity is necessary," – so saith a third party. "Take what I have! Take what I am! So much less doth life bind me!"

Were they consistently pitiful, then would they make their neighbours sick of life. To be wicked – that would be their true goodness.

But they want to be rid of life; what care they if they bind others still faster with their chains and gifts!

And ye also, to whom life is rough and labour is disquiet, are ye not very tired of life? Are ye not very ripe for the sermon of death?

All ye whom rough labour is dear, and the rapid, new, and strange – ye put up with yourselves badly; your diligence is flight, and the will to self-forgetfulness.

If ye believed more in life, then would ye devote yourselves less to the momentary. But for waiting, ye have not enough capacity in you – nor even for idling!

Everywhere resoundeth the voices of those who preach death; and the earth is full of those whom death hath to be preached.

Or "life eternal"; it is all the same to me – if only they pass away quickly!'

Thus spake Zarathustra.

10. War and Warriors

'BY OUR best enemies we do not want to be spared, nor by those either whom we love from the very heart. So let me tell you the truth!

My brethren in war! I love you from the very heart. I am, and was ever, your counterpart. And I am also your best enemy. So let me tell you the truth!

I know the hatred and envy of your hearts. Ye are not so great enough to not know of hatred and envy. Then be great enough not to be ashamed of them!

And if ye cannot be saints of knowledge, then, I pray to you, be at least its warriors. They are the companions and forerunners of such saintship.

I see many soldiers; could I but see many warriors! "Uniform" one calleth what they wear; may it not be uniform what they therewith hide!

Ye shall be those whose eyes ever seek for an enemy – for *your* enemy. And with some of you there is hatred at first sight.

Your enemy shall ye seek; your war shall ye wage, and for the sake of your thoughts! And if your thoughts succumb your uprightness shall still shout triumph thereby!

Ye shall love peace as a means to new wars – and the short peace more than the long.

You I advise not to work, but to fight. You I advise not to peace, but to victory. Let your work be a fight, let your peace be a victory!

One can only be silent and sit peacefully when one hath arrow and bow; otherwise one prateth and quarrelleth. Let your peace be a victory! Ye say it is the good cause which halloweth even war? I say unto you: it is the good war which halloweth every cause.

War and courage have done more great things than charity. Not your sympathy, but your bravery hath hitherto saved the victims.

"What is good?" ye ask. To be brave is good. Let the little girls say: "To be good is what is pretty, and at the same time touching."

They call you heartless: but your heart is true, and I love the bashfulness of your goodwill. Ye are ashamed of your flow, and others are ashamed of their ebb.

Ye are ugly? Well then, my brethren, take the sublime about you, the mantle of the ugly!

And when your soul becometh great, then doth it become haughty, and in your sublimity there is wickedness. I know you.

In wickedness the haughty man and the weakling meet. But they misunderstand one another. I know you.

Ye shall only have enemies to be hated, but not enemies to be despised. Ye must be proud of your enemies; then, the successes of your enemies are also your successes.

Resistance – that is the distinction of the slave. Let your distinction be obedience. Let your commanding itself be obeying!

To the good warrior soundeth "thou shalt" pleasanter than "I will." And all that is dear unto you, ye shall first have it commanded unto you.

Let your love to life be love to your highest hope; and let your highest hope be the highest thought of life!

Your highest thought, however, ye shall have it commanded unto you by me – and it is this: man is something that is to be surpassed. So live your life of obedience and of war! What matter about long life! What warrior wisheth to be spared!

I spare you not, I love you from my very heart, my brethren in war!'

Thus spake Zarathustra.

11. *The New Idol*

'SOMEWHERE there are still peoples and herds, but not with us, my brethren: here there are states.

A state? What is that? Well! Open now your ears unto me, for now I will say unto you my word concerning the death of peoples.

A state, is called the coldest of all cold monsters. Coldly lieth it also; and this lie creepeth from its mouth: "I, the state, am the people."

It is a lie! Creators were they who created peoples, and hung a faith and a love over them: thus they served life.

Destroyers, are they who lay snares for many, and call it the state: they hang a sword and a hundred cravings over them.

Where there is still a people, there the state is not understood, but hated as the evil eye, and as sin against laws and customs.

This sign I give unto you: every people speaketh its language of good and evil: this its neighbour understandeth not. Its language hath it devised for itself in laws and customs.

But the state lieth in all languages of good and evil; and whatever it saith it lieth; and whatever it hath it hath stolen. False is everything in it; with stolen teeth it biteth, the biting one. False are even its bowels.

Confusion of language of good and evil; this sign I give unto you as the sign of the state. Verily, the will to death, indicateth this sign! Verily, it beckoneth unto the preachers of death!

Many too many are born: for the superfluous ones was the state devised!

See just how it enticeth them to it, the many-too-many! How it swalloweth and cheweth and recheweth them!

"On earth there is nothing greater than I: it is I who am the regulating finger of God" – thus roareth the monster. And not only the long-eared and short-sighted fall upon their knees!

Ah! Even in your ears, ye great souls, it whispereth its gloomy lies! Ah! It findeth out the rich hearts which willingly lavish themselves!

Yea, it findeth you out too, ye conquerors of the old God! Weary ye became of the conflict, and now your weariness serveth the new idol!

Heroes and honourable ones, it would fain set up around it, the new idol! Gladly it basketh in the sunshine of good consciences, the cold monster!

Everything will it give *you*, if *ye* worship it, the new idol: thus it purchaseth the lustre of your virtue, and the glance of your proud eyes.

It seeketh to allure by means of you, the many-too-many. Yea, a hellish artifice hath here been devised, a death-horse jingling with the trappings of divine honours!

Yea, a dying for many hath here been devised, which glorifieth itself as life: verily, a hearty service unto all preachers of death!

The state, I call it, where all are poison-drinkers, the good and the bad: the state, where all lose themselves, the good and the bad: the state, where the slow suicide of all is called "life."

Just see these superfluous ones! They steal the works of the inventors and the treasures of the wise. Culture, they call their theft – and everything becometh sickness and trouble unto them!

Just see these superfluous ones! Sick are they always; they vomit their bile and call it a newspaper. They devour one another, and cannot even digest themselves.

Just see these superfluous ones! Wealth they acquire and become poorer thereby. Power they seek for, and above all, the lever of power, much money – these impotent ones!

See them clamber, these nimble apes! They clamber over one another, and thus scuffle into the mud of the abyss.

Towards the throne they all strive: it is their madness – as if happiness sat on the throne! Oft-times sitteth filth on the throne – and oft-times also the throne on filth.

Madmen they all seem to me, and clambering apes, and too eager. Badly smelleth their idol to me, the cold monster: badly they all smell to me, these idolaters.

My brethren, will ye suffocate in the fumes of their maws and appetites! Better break the windows and jump into the open air!

Do go out of the way of the bad odour! Withdraw from the idolatry of the superfluous!

Do go out of the way of the bad odour! Withdraw from the steam of these human sacrifices!

Open still remaineth the earth for great souls. Empty are still many sites for lone ones and twain ones, around which floateth the odour of the tranquil seas.

Open still remaineth a free life for great souls. Verily, he who possesseth little is so much the less possessed: blessed be the moderate poverty!

There, where the state ceaseth – there only commenceth the man who is not superfluous: there commenceth the song of the necessary ones, the single and irreplaceable melody.

There, where the state *ceaseth* – pray look thither, my brethren! Do you not see it, the rainbow and the bridges of the Superman?'

Thus spake Zarathustra.

12. The Flies in the Marketplace

'FLEE, my friend, into thy solitude! I see thee deafened with the noise of the great men, and stung all over with the stings of the little ones.

Admirably do forest and rock know how to be silent with thee.

Resemble again the tree which thou lovest, the broad-branched one-silently and attentively it o'erhangeth the sea.

Where solitude endeth, there beginneth the marketplace; and where the marketplace beginneth, there beginneth also the noise of the great actors, and the buzzing of the poison-flies.

In the world even the best things are worthless without those who represent them: those representers, the people call great men.

Little do the people understand what is great – that is to say, the creating agency. But they have a taste for all representers and actors of great things. Around the devisers of new values revolveth the world: invisibly it revolveth. But around the actors revolve the people and the glory: such is the course of things.

Spirit, hath the actor, but little conscience of the spirit. He believeth always in that wherewith he maketh believe most strongly – in *himself!*

Tomorrow he hath a new belief, and the day after, one still newer. Sharp perceptions hath he, like the people, and changeable humours.

To upset – that meaneth with him to prove. To drive mad – that meaneth with him to convince. And blood is counted by him as the best of all arguments.

A truth which only glideth into fine ears, he calleth falsehood and trumpery. Verily, he believeth only in gods that make a great noise in the world!

Full of clattering buffoons is the marketplace, and the people glory in their great men! These are for them the masters of the hour.

But the hour presseth them; so they press thee. And also from thee they want Yea or Nay. Alas! Thou wouldst set thy chair betwixt For and Against?

On account of those absolute and impatient ones, be not jealous, thou lover of truth! Never yet did truth cling to the arm of an absolute one.

On account of those abrupt ones, return into thy security: only in the marketplace is one assailed by Yea? or Nay?

Slow is the experience of all deep fountains: long have they to wait until they know *what* hath fallen into their depths.

Away from the marketplace and from fame taketh place all that is great: away from the marketplace and from fame have ever dwelt the devisers of new values. Flee, my friend, into thy solitude: I see thee stung all over by the poisonous flies. Flee thither, where a rough, strong breeze bloweth!

Flee into thy solitude! Thou hast lived too closely to the small and the pitiable. Flee from their invisible vengeance! Towards thee they have nothing but vengeance.

Raise no longer an arm against them! Innumerable are they, and it is not thy lot to be a fly-flap.

Innumerable are the small and pitiable ones; and of many a proud structure, raindrops and weeds have been the ruin.

You are not stone; but already hast thou become hollow by the numerous drops. Thou wilt yet break and burst by the numerous drops.

Exhausted I see thee, by poisonous flies; bleeding I see thee, and torn at a hundred spots; and thy pride will not even upbraid.

Blood would they have from thee in all innocence; blood their bloodless souls crave for – and they sting, therefore, in all innocence.

But thou, profound one, thou sufferest too profoundly even from small wounds; and ere thou hadst recovered, the same poison-worm crawled over thy hand.

Too proud art thou to kill these sweet-tooths. But take care lest it be thy fate to suffer all their poisonous injustice!

They buzz around thee also with their praise: obtrusiveness is their praise. They want to be close to thy skin and thy blood.

They flatter thee, as one flattereth a God or devil; they whimper before thee, as before a God or devil; what doth it come to! Flatterers are they and whimperers, and nothing more.

Often, also, do they show themselves to thee as amiable ones.

But that hath always been the prudence of cowards. Yea! Cowards are wise!

They think much about thee with their circumscribed souls – thou art always suspect to them! Whatever is much thought about is at last thought suspicious.

They punish thee for all thy virtues. They pardon thee in their inmost hearts only for thy errors.

Because thou art gentle and of upright character, thou sayest: "Blameless are they for their small existence." But their petty souls think: "Blamable is all great existence."

Even when thou art gentle towards them, they still feel themselves despised by thee; and they repay thy beneficence with secret maleficence.

Thy silent pride is always counter to their taste; they rejoice if once thou are humble enough to be frivolous.

What we recognize in a man, we also irritate in him. Therefore be on your guard against the small ones!

In thy presence they feel themselves small, and their baseness gleameth and gloweth against thee in invisible vengeance.

Sawest thou not how often they became dumb when thou approachedst them, and how their energy left them like the smoke of an extinguishing fire?

Yea, my friend, the bad conscience art thou of thy neighbours; for they are unworthy of thee. Therefore they hate thee, and would fain suck thy blood.

Thy neighbours will always be poisonous flies; what is great in thee – that itself must make them more poisonous, and always more fly-like.

Flee, my friend, into thy solitude – and thither, where a rough strong breeze bloweth. It is not thy lot to be a fly-flap.'

Thus spoke Zarathustra.

13. *Chastity*

'I LOVE the forest. It is bad to live in cities: there, there are too many of the lustful.

Is it not better to fall into the hands of a murderer than into the dreams of a lustful woman?

And just look at these men: their eye saith it – they know nothing better on earth than to lie with a woman.

Filth is at the bottom of their souls; and alas! if their filth hath still spirit in it!

If that ye were perfect – at least as animals! But to animals belongeth innocence.

Do I counsel you to slay your instincts? I counsel you to innocence in your instincts.

Do I counsel you to chastity? Chastity is a virtue with some, but with many almost a vice.

These are continent, to be sure: but doggish lust looketh enviously out of all that they do.

Even into the heights of their virtue and into their cold spirit doth this creature follow them, with its discord.

And how nicely can doggish lust beg for a piece of spirit, when a piece of flesh is denied it!

Ye love tragedies and all that breaketh the heart? But I am distrustful of your doggish lust.

Ye have too cruel eyes, and ye look wantonly towards the sufferers. Hath not your lust just disguised itself and taken the name of fellow-suffering?

And also this parable give I to you: Not a few who meant to cast out their devil, went thereby into the swine themselves.

To whom chastity is difficult, it is to be dissuaded: lest it become the road to hell – to filth and lust of soul.

Do I speak of filthy things? That is not the worst thing for me to do.

Not when the truth is filthy, but when it is shallow, does the discerning one go unwillingly into its waters.

Verily, there are chaste ones from their very nature; they are gentler of heart, and laugh better and oftener than you.

They laugh also at chastity, and ask: "What is chastity?"

Is chastity not folly? But this folly came unto us, and not we unto it.

We offered that guest harbour and heart: now it dwelleth with us – let it stay as long as it will!'

Thus spake Zarathustra.

14. The Friend

'"ONE is always too many about me" – thinks the anchorite. "Always once one – that maketh two in the long run!"

I and me are always too deeply in conversation: how could it be endured, if there were not a friend?

The friend of the anchorite is always the third one: the third one is the cork which prevents the conversation of the two sinking into the depth.

Ah! There are too many depths for all anchorites. Therefore, do they long so much for a friend and for his elevation.

Our faith in others betrayeth that we would fain have faith in ourselves. Our longing for a friend is our betrayer.

And often with our love we want merely to overleap envy. And often we attack and make ourselves enemies, to conceal that we are vulnerable.

"Be at least my enemy!" – thus speaketh the true reverence, which dares not venture to solicit friendship.

If one would have a friend, then must one also be willing to wage war for him: and in order to wage war, one must be *capable* of being an enemy.

One ought still to honour the enemy in one's friend. Canst thou go nigh unto your friend, and not go over to him?

In one's friend one shall have one's best enemy. Thou shalt be closest unto him with thy heart when thou withstandest him.

Thou wouldst wear no raiment before thy friend? It is in honour of thy friend that thou showest thyself to him as thou art? But he wisheth thee to the devil on that account!

He who maketh no secret of himself shocketh: so much reason have ye to fear nakedness! Aye, if ye were gods, ye could then be ashamed of clothing!

Thou canst not adorn thyself fine enough for thy friend; for thou shalt be unto him an arrow and a longing for the Superman.

Sawest thou ever thy friend asleep – and know how he looketh? What is usually the countenance of thy friend? It is thine own countenance, in a coarse and imperfect mirror.

Sawest thou ever thy friend asleep? Wert thou not dismayed at thy friend looking so? O my friend, man is something that hast to be surpassed.

In divining and keeping silence shall the friend be a master: not everything must thou wish to see. Thy dreams shall disclose unto thee what thy friend doeth when awake.

Let thy pity be a divining: to know first if thy friend wanteth pity. Perhaps he loveth in thee the unmoved eye, and the look of eternity.

Let thy pity for thy friend be hid under a hard shell; thou shalt bite out a tooth upon it. Thus will it have delicacy and sweetness.

Art thou pure air and solitude and bread and medicine to thy friend? Many a one cannot loosen his own fetters, but is nevertheless his friend's emancipator.

Art thou a slave? Then thou canst not be a friend. Art thou a tyrant? Then thou canst not have friends.

Far too long have slave and tyrant been concealed in woman. On that account woman is not yet capable of friendship: she knows only love.

In woman's love there is injustice and blindness to all she does not love. And even in woman's conscious love, there is still always attack and lightning and night, along with the light.

As yet woman is not capable of friendship: women are still cats and birds. Or at best, cows.

As yet woman is not capable of friendship. But tell me, you men, who of you is capable of friendship?

Oh! Your poverty, you men, and your sparingness of soul! As much as you give to your friend, I will give even to my enemy, and will not become poorer for it.

There is comradeship: may there be friendship!'

Thus spoke Zarathustra.

15. The Thousand and One Goals

'MANY lands saw Zarathustra, and many peoples: thus he discovered the good and bad of many peoples. No greater power did Zarathustra find on earth than good and bad.

No people could live without first valuing; if a people will maintain itself, however, it must not value as its neighbour valueth.

Much that passed for good with one people was regarded with scorn and contempt by another: thus I found it. Much I found here called bad, which was there decked with purple honours.

Never did the one neighbour understand the other: ever did his soul marvel at his neighbour's delusion and wickedness.

A tablet of excellences hangeth over every people. Lo! It is the tablet of their triumphs; behold, it is the voice of their Will to Power.

It is laudable, what they think hard; what is indispensable and hard they call good; and what relieveth in the direst distress, the unique and hardest of all, they extol as holy.

Whatever makes them rule and conquer and shine, to the dismay and envy of their neighbours, they regard as the high and foremost thing, the test and the meaning of all else.

Verily, my brother, if thou only knewest but a people's need, its land, its sky, and its neighbour, then you wouldst divine the law of its surmountings, and why it climbth up that ladder to its hope.

"Always shall thou be the foremost and prominent above all others: no one shall thy jealous soul love, except the friend" – that made the soul of a Greek thrill: thereby went he his way to greatness.

"To speak truth, and be skilful with bow and arrow" – so seemed it alike pleasing and hard to the people from whom cometh my name – the name which is alike pleasing and hard to me.

"To honour father and mother, and from the root of the soul to do their will" – this table of surmounting hung another people over them, and became powerful and permanent thereby.

"To have fidelity, and for the sake of fidelity to risk honour and blood, even in evil and dangerous courses" – teaching itself so, another people mastered itself, and thus mastering itself, became pregnant and heavy with great hopes.

Verily, men have given unto themselves all their good and bad. Verily, they took it not, they found it not, it came not unto them as a voice from heaven.

Values did man only assign to things in order to maintain himself – he created only the significance of things, a human significance! Therefore, calls he himself "man", that is, the valuator.

Valuing is creating: hear it, ye creating ones! Valuation itself is the treasure and jewel of all valued things.

Through valuation only is there value; and without valuation the nut of existence would be hollow. Hear it, ye creating ones!

Change of values – that means, change of the creating ones. Always doth he destroy, who hath to be a creator.

Creating ones were first of all peoples, and only in late times individuals; verily, the individual himself is still the latest creation.

Peoples once hung over them tables of the good. Love which would rule and love which would obey, created for themselves such tables.

Older is the pleasure in the herd than pleasure in the ego: and as long as the good conscience is for the herd, the bad conscience only saith: "ego".

The crafty ego, the loveless one, that seeks its advantage in the advantage of many – it is not the origin of the herd, but its downfall.

It was always loving ones and creators that created good and bad. Fire of love gloweth in the names of all the virtues, and fire of wrath.

Many lands saw Zarathustra, and many peoples: no greater power did Zarathustra find on earth than the creations of the loving ones – "good" and "bad" are their names.

Verily, a prodigy is this power of praising and blaming. Tell me, ye brethren, who will master it for me? Who will put a fetter upon the thousand necks of this animal?

A thousand goals have there been hitherto, for a thousand peoples have there been. Only the fetter for the thousand necks is still lacking; there is lacking the one goal. As yet humanity has not a goal.

But pray tell me, my brethren, if the goal of humanity be still lacking, is there not still lacking humanity itself?'

Thus spoke Zarathustra.

16. Neighbour Love

'YE CROWD around your neighbour, and have fine words for it. But I say to you: your neighbour-love is your bad love of yourselves.

You flee unto your neighbour from yourselves, and would rather make a virtue of it: but I fathom your 'unselfishness'.

The *Thou* is older than the *I*; the *Thou* has been consecrated, but not yet the *I*: so man presses near to his neighbour.

Do I advise you to neighbour-love? Rather do I advise you to neighbour-flight and to furthest love!

Higher than love of your neighbour is love to the furthest and future ones; higher still than love to men, is love to things and phantoms.

The phantom that runs on before thee, my brother, is fairer than thou; why dost thou not give unto it thy flesh and thy bones? But thou fearest, and runnest unto thy neighbour.

Ye cannot endure it with yourselves, and do not love yourselves sufficiently: so ye seek to mislead your neighbour into love, and would fain gild yourselves with his error.

Would that ye could not endure it with any kind of near ones, or their neighbours; then would ye have to create your friend and his overflowing heart out of yourselves.

Ye call in a witness when ye want to speak well of yourselves; and when ye have misled him to think well of you, ye also think well of yourselves.

Not only does he lie, who speaketh contrary to his knowledge, but more so, he who speaketh contrary to his ignorance. And thus speak ye of yourselves in your intercourse, and belie to your neighbour with yourselves.

Thus says the fool: "Association with men spoils the character, especially when one hath none."

The one goeth to his neighbour because he seeketh himself, and the other because he would fain lose himself. Your bad love of yourselves makes solitude a prison to you.

The farthest ones are they who pay for your love to the near ones; and when there are five of you together, a sixth must always die.

I love not your festivals either: too many actors found I there, and even the spectators often behaved like actors.

Not the neighbour do I teach you, but the friend. Let the friend be the festival of the earth to you, and a foretaste of the Superman.

I teach you the friend and his overflowing heart. But one must know how to be a sponge, if one would be loved by over-flowing hearts.

I teach you the friend in whom the world stands complete, a capsule of the good, the creating friend, who hath always a complete world to bestow.

And as the world unrolled itself for him, so rolleth it together again for him in rings, as the growth of good through evil, as the growth of purpose out of chance.

Let the future and the furthest be the motive of thy today; in thy friend you shall love the Superman as thy motive.

My brethren, I advise you not to neighbour-love – I advise you to furthest love!'

Thus spoke Zarathustra.

17. The Way of the Creating One

'WOULDST thou go into isolation, my brother? Wouldst thou seek the way unto thyself? Tarry yet a little and hearken unto me.

"He who seeketh may easily get lost himself. All isolation is wrong": so say the herd. And long didst thou belong to the herd.

The voice of the herd will still echo in you. And when thou sayest, "I have no longer a conscience in common with you," then will it be a plaint and a pain.

Lo, that pain itself did the same conscience produce; and the last gleam of that conscience still gloweth on thine affliction.

But thou wouldst go the way of your affliction, which is the way unto thyself? Then show me thine authority and thy strength to do so!

Are you a new strength and a new authority? A first motion? A self-rolling wheel? Canst thou also compel the stars to revolve around thee?

Alas! There is so much lusting for loftiness! There are so many convulsions of the ambitions! Show me that thou are not a lusting and ambitious one!

Alas! There are so many great thoughts that do nothing more than the bellows: they inflate, and make emptier than ever.

Free, do you call thyself? Thy ruling thought would I hear of, and not that thou hast escaped from a yoke.

Art thou one *entitled* to escape from a yoke? Many a one hath cast away his final worth when he hath cast away his servitude.

Free from what? What doeth that matter to Zarathustra! Clearly, however, shall thine eye show unto me: free *for what?*

Canst thou give unto thyself thy bad and thy good, and set up thy will as a law over thee? Canst thou be judge for thyself, and avenger of thy law?

Terrible is aloneness with the judge and avenger of one's own law. Thus is a star projected into desert space, and into the icy breath of aloneness.

Today sufferest thou still from the multitude, thou individual; today hast thou still thy courage unabated, and thy hopes.

But one day will the solitude weary thee; one day will thy pride yield, and thy courage quail. Thou wilt one day cry: "I am alone!"

One day wilt thou see no longer thy loftiness, and see too closely thy lowliness; thy sublimity itself will frighten thee as a phantom. Thou wilt one day cry: "All is false!"

There are feelings which seek to slay the lonesome one; if they do not succeed, then must they themselves die! But art thou capable of this – to be a murderer?

Hast thou ever known, my brother, the word "disdain"? And the anguish of thy justice in being just to those that disdain thee?

Thou forcest many to think differently about thee; that, charge they heavily to thine account. Thou camest nigh unto them, and yet wenteth past: for that they never forgive thee.

Thou goest beyond them: but the higher thou risest, the smaller doth the eye of envy see thee. Most of all, however, is the flying one hated.

"How could ye be just unto me!" – must thou say – "I choose your injustice as my allotted portion."

Injustice and filth cast they at the lonesome one: but, my brother, if thou wouldst be a star, thou must shine for them none the less on that account!

And be on thy guard against the good and just! They would fain crucify those who devise their own virtue – they hate the lonesome ones.

Be on thy guard, also, against holy simplicity! All is unholy to it that is not simple; fain, likewise, would it play with the fire – of the faggot and the stake.

And be on thy guard, also, against the assaults of thy love! Too readily doth the recluse reach his hand to any one who meeteth him.

To many a one mayest thou not give thy hand, but only thy paw; and I want thy paw to have claws.

But the worst enemy thou canst meet, wilt thou thyself always be; thou waylayeth thyself in caverns and forests.

Thou lonesome one, thou goest the way to thyself! And past thyself and thy seven devils leadeth thy way!

A heretic wilt thou be to thyself, and a wizard and a soothsayer, and a fool, and a doubter, and a reprobate, and a villain.

Ready must thou be to burn thyself in thine own flame; how couldst thou become new if thou have not first become ashes!

Thou lonesome one, thou goest the way of the creating one: a God wilt thou create for thyself out of thy seven devils!

Thou lonesome one, thou goest the way of the loving one: thou lovest thyself, and on that account you despisest thyself, as only the loving ones despise.

To create, desireth the loving one, because he despiseth! What knoweth he of love who hath not been obliged to despise just what he loved!

With thy love, go into thine isolation, my brother, and with thy creating; and late only will justice limp after thee.

With my tears, go into thine isolation, my brother. I love him who seeketh to create beyond himself, and thus succumbeth.'

Thus spoke Zarathustra.

18. Old and Young Women

'WHY stealeth thou along so furtively in the twilight, Zarathustra? And what hideth thou so carefully under thy mantle?

Is it a treasure that hath been given thee? Or a child that hath been born thee? Or goeth thou thyself on a thief's errand, thou friend of the evil?'

'Verily, my brother', said Zarathustra, 'it is a treasure that hath been given me: it is a little truth which I carry.

'But it is naughty, like a young child; and if I hold not its mouth, it screameth too loudly.

As I went on my way alone today, at the hour when the sun declineth, there met me an old woman, and she spake thus unto my soul:

"Much has Zarathustra spoken also to us women, but never spake he to us concerning woman."

And I answered her: "Concerning woman, one should only talk unto men."

"Talk also unto me of woman," said she; "I am old enough to forget it presently."

And I obliged the old woman and spake thus unto her:

"Everything in woman is a riddle, and everything in woman hath one answer – it is called pregnancy.

Man is for woman a means: the purpose is always the child. But what is woman for man?

Two different things wanteth the true man: danger and diversion. Therefore he wanteth woman, as the most dangerous plaything.

Man shall be trained for war, and woman for the recreation of the warrior: all else is folly.

Too sweet fruits – these the warrior liketh not. Therefore liketh he woman; bitter is even the sweetest woman.

Better than man doeth woman understand children, but man is more childish than woman.

In the true man there is a child hidden: it wanteth to play. Up then, ye women, and discover the child in man!

A plaything let woman be, pure and fine like the precious stone, illumined with the virtues of a world not yet come.

Let the beam of a star shine in your love! Let your hope say: 'May I bear to the Superman!'

In your love let there be valour! With your love shall ye assail him who inspireth you with fear!

In your love be your honour! Little doth woman understand otherwise about honour. But let this be your honour: always to love more than you are loved, and never to be second.

Let man fear woman when she loveth: then she maketh every sacrifice, and everything else she regardeth as worthless.

Let man fear woman when she hateth: for man in his innermost soul is merely evil; woman, however, is mean.

Whom hateth woman most? – Thus spoke the iron to the magnet: 'I hate thee most, because thou attractest, but art too weak to draw unto thee.'

The happiness of man is, 'I will.' The happiness of woman is, 'He will.'

'Lo! Lo! Now hath the world become perfect!' Thus thinks every woman when she obeyeth with all her love.

Obey must the woman, and find a depth for her surface. Surface is woman's soul, a mobile, stormy film on shallow water.

Man's soul, however, is deep, its current gusheth in subterranean caverns: woman surmiseth its force, but comprehendeth it not."

Then answered me the old woman: "Many fine things hath Zarathustra said, especially for those who are young enough for them.

Strange! Zarathustra knoweth little about woman, and yet he is right about them! Does this happen, because with woman nothing is impossible?

And now accept a little truth by way of thanks! I am old enough for it!

Swaddle it up and hold its mouth: otherwise it will scream too loudly, the little truth."

"Give me woman, your little truth!" I said. And thus spake the old woman:

"Thou goest to women? Do not forget thy whip!"'

Thus spoke Zarathustra.

19. The Bite of the Adder

ONE day had Zarathustra fallen asleep under a fig tree, owing to the heat, with his arm over his face. And there came an adder and bit him in the neck, so that Zarathustra screamed with pain. When he had taken his arm from his face he looked at the serpent; and then did it recognize the eyes of Zarathustra, wriggled awkwardly, and tried to get away. 'Not at all,' said Zarathustra, 'as yet hast thou not received my thanks! Thou hast awakened me in time; my journey is yet long.' 'Your journey is short,' said the adder sadly; 'my poison is fatal.' Zarathustra smiled. 'When did ever a dragon die of a serpent's poison?' – said he. 'But take thy poison back! Thou art not rich enough to present it to me.' Then the adder fell again on his neck, and licked his wound.

When Zarathustra once told this to his disciples they asked him: 'And what, O Zarathustra, is the moral of thy story?' And Zarathustra answered them thus:

'The destroyer of morality, the good and just call me: my story is immoral.

When, however, ye have an enemy, then return him not good for evil: for that would abash him. But prove that he hath done something good to you.

And rather be angry than abash anyone! And when you are cursed, it pleaseth me not that ye should desire to bless. Rather curse a little also!

And should a great injustice befall you, then do quickly five small ones besides. Hideous to behold is he whom injustice presseth alone.

Did you know this? A shared injustice is half justice. And he who can bear it, should take the injustice upon himself!

A small revenge is more humane than no revenge at all. And if the punishment be not also a right and an honour to the transgressor, I do not like your punishment.

Nobler is it to own oneself in the wrong than to establish one's right, especially if one be in the right. Only, one must be rich enough to do so.

I do not like your cold justice; out of the eye of your judges there always glanceth the executioner and his cold steel.

Tell me: where find we justice, which is love with seeing eyes?

Devise me, then, the love which not only beareth all punishment, but also all guilt!

Devise me, then, the justice which acquiteth every one, except the judges!

And would ye hear this likewise? To him who seeketh to be just from the heart, even the lie becometh philanthropy.

But how could I be just from the heart! How can I give every one his own! Let this be enough for me: I give unto every own mine own.

Finally, my brethen, guard against doing wrong to any anchorite. How could a anchorite forget! How could he requite!

Like a deep well is a anchorite. Easy it is to throw in a stone: if it sinks to the bottom, however, tell me, who will bring it out again?

Guard against injuring the anchorite! If you have done so however, well then kill him also!'

Thus spoke Zarathustra.

20. Child and Marriage

'I HAVE a question for thee alone, my brother: like a sounding-lead, cast I this question into thy soul, that I may know its depth.

Thou art young, and desirest child and marriage. But I ask thee: Art thou a man *entitled* to desire a child?

Art thou the victorious one, the self-conqueror, the ruler of thy passions, the master of thy virtues? Thus do I ask thee.

Or does the animal speak in thy wish, and necessity? Or isolation? Or discord in thee?

I would have thy victory and freedom long for a child. Living monuments shalt thou build to thy victory and emancipation.

Beyond thyself shalt thou build. But first of all must thou be built thyself, rectangular in body and soul.

Not only onward shalt thou propagate thyself, but upward! For that purpose may the garden of marriage help thee!

A higher body shalt thou create, a first movement, a spontaneously rolling wheel – a creating one shalt thou create.

Marriage: so call I the will of the twain to create the one that is more than those who created it. The reverence for one another, as those exercising such a will, call I marriage.

Let this be the significance and the truth of thy marriage. But that which the many-too-many call marriage, those superfluous ones – ah, what shall I call it?

Ah, the poverty of soul in the twain! Ah, the filth of soul in the twain! Ah, the pitiable self-complacency in the twain!

Marriage they call it all; and they say their marriages are made in heaven.

Well I do not like it, that heaven of the superfluous! No, I do not like them, those animals tangled in the heavenly toils!

Far from me also be the God who limpeth thither to bless what he hath not matched!

Laugh not at such marriages! What child has not had reason to weep over its parents?

Worthy did this man seem, and ripe for the meaning of the earth: but when I saw his wife, the earth seemed to me a home for madcaps.

Yea, I would that the earth shook with convulsions when a saint and a goose mate with one another.

This one went forth in quest of truth as a hero, and at last got for himself a small dressed-up lie: his marriage he calleth it.

That one was reserved in intercourse and chose choicely. But one time he spoilt his company for all time: his marriage he calleth it.

Another sought a handmaid with the virtues of an angel. But all at once he became the handmaid of a woman, and now would he need also to become an angel.

Careful, have I found all buyers, and all of them have astute eyes. But even the most astute of them buyeth his wife in a sack.

Many short follies – that is called love by you. And your marriage putteth an end to your many short follies, with one long stupidity.

Your love of woman, and woman's love of man – ah, would that it were sympathy for suffering and veiled deities! But generally two animals alight on one another.

But even your best love is only an enraptured simile and a painful ardour. It is a torch to light loftier paths for you.

Beyond yourselves shall ye love some day! Then *learn* first of all to love. And on that account ye had to drink the bitter cup of your love.

Bitterness is in the cup even of the best love; thus doth it cause longing for the Superman; thus doth it cause thirst in thee, the creating one!

Thirst in the creating one, arrow and longing for the Superman: tell me, my brother, is this thy will to marriage?

Holy call I such a will, and such a marriage.'

Thus spoke Zarathustra.

21. Voluntary Death

'MANY die too late, and some die too early. Yet strange soundeth the precept: "Die at the right time!"

Die at the right time: so teacheth Zarathustra.

To be sure, he who never liveth at the right time, how could he ever die at the right time? Would that he had never been born! Thus do I advise the superfluous ones.

But even the superfluous ones make much ado about their death, and even the hollowest nut wanteth to be cracked.

Every one regardeth dying as a great matter: but as yet death is not a festival. Not yet have people learned to inaugurate the finest festivals.

The consummating death I show unto you, which becometh a stimulus and promise to the living.

His death, dieth the consummating one triumphantly, surrounded by hoping and promising ones.

Thus should one learn to die; and there should be no festival at which such a dying one doeth not consecrate the oaths of the living!

Thus to die is best; the next best, however, is to die in battle, and squander a great soul.

But to the fighter equally hateful as to the victor, is your grinning death which stealeth nigh like a thief, – and yet cometh as master.

My death, praise I unto you, the voluntary death, which cometh unto me because *I* want it.

And when shall I want it? He that has a goal and an heir, wants death at the right time for the goal and the heir.

And out of reverence for the goal and the heir, he will hang up no more withered wreaths in the sanctuary of life.

Verily, not the rope-makers will I resemble: they lengthen out their cord and thereby go ever backward.

Many a one, also, waxeth too old for his truths and triumphs; a toothless mouth hath no longer the right to every truth.

And whoever wanteth to have fame, must take leave of honour betimes, and practice the difficult art of going at the right time.

One must discontinue being feasted upon when one tasteth best: that is known by those who want to be long loved.

Sour apples are there, no doubt, whose lot is to wait until the last day of autumn: and at once they become ripe, yellow, and shrivelled.

In some the heart ages first, and in others the spirit. And some are hoary in youth, but the late young keep long young.

To many men life is a failure; a poison-worm gnaweth at their heart. Then let them see to it that their dying is all the more a success.

Many never become sweet; they rot even in the summer. It is cowardice that holdeth them fast to their branches.

Far too many live, and far too long do they hang on their branches. Would that a storm would come and shook all this rottenness and worm-eatenness from the tree!

Would that here came preachers of *speedy* death! Those would be the appropriate storms and agitators of the trees of life! But I hear only the slow death preached, and patience with all that is "earthly".

Ah! You preach patience with what is earthly? This earthly is it that hath too much patience with you, ye blasphemers!

Verily, too early died that Hebrew whom the preachers of slow death honour: and to many has it proved a calamity that he died too early.

As yet had he known only tears, and the melancholy of the Hebrews, together with the hatred of the good and just – the Hebrew Jesus: then was he seized with the longing for death.

Had he but remained in the wilderness, far from the good and just! Then perhaps would he have learned to live and love the earth – and laughter also!

Believe me, my brethren! He died too early; he himself would have disavowed his doctrine had he reached my age! Noble enough was he to disavow!

But he was still immature. Immaturely loveth the youth, immaturely also hateth the man and earth. Confined and awkward are still his soul and the wings of his spirit.

But in man there is more of the child than in the youth, and less of melancholy: better understandeth he about life and death.

Free for death, and free in death; a holy Naysayer, when there is no longer time for Yea: thus understandeth he about death and life.

That your dying may not be a reproach to man and the earth, my friends: that do I solicit from the honey of your soul.

In your dying, shall your spirit and your virtue still shine like an evening afterglow around the earth: otherwise your dying hath been unsatisfactory.

Thus I will die myself, that ye, my friends, may love the earth more for my sake; and earth will I again become, to have rest in her that bore me.

Verily, a goal had Zarathustra; he threw his ball. Now be ye, my friends, the heirs of my goal; to you I throw the golden ball.

Best of all, do I see you, my friends, throw the golden ball! And so tarry I a little while on the earth – pardon me for it!'

Thus spoke Zarathustra.

22. *The Bestowing Virtue*

1

WHEN Zarathustra had taken leave of the town to which his heart was attached, the name of which is The Pied Cow, there followed him many people who called themselves his disciples, and kept him company. Thus they came to a crossroads. Then Zarathustra told them that he now wanted to go alone; for he was fond of going alone. His disciples, however, presented him at his departure with a staff, on the golden handle of which a serpent twined round the sun. Zarathustra rejoiced on account of the staff, and supported himself thereon; then spake he thus to his disciples:

'Tell me, pray: how come gold to the highest value? Because it is uncommon, and unprofiting, and beaming, and soft in lustre; it always bestoweth itself.

Only as image of the highest virtue came gold to the highest value. Goldlike, beameth the glance of the bestower. Gold-lustre maketh peace between moon and sun.

Uncommon is the highest virtue, and unprofiting, beaming is it, and soft of lustre: a bestowing virtue is the highest virtue.

Verily, I divine you well, my disciples: ye strive like me for the bestowing virtue. What would ye have in common with cats and wolves?

It is your thirst to become sacrifices and gifts yourselves: and therefore have ye thirst to accumulate all riches in your soul.

Insatiably striveth your soul for treasures and jewels, because your virtue is insatiable in desiring to bestow.

Ye constrain all things to flow towards you and into you, so that they shall flow back again out of your fountain as the gifts of your love.

Verily, an appropriator of all values must such bestowing love become; but healthy and holy, call I this selfishness.

Another selfishness is there, an all-too-poor and hungry kind, which would always steal the selfishness of the sick, the sickly selfishness.

With the eye of the thief it looketh upon all that is lustrous; with the craving of hunger it measureth him who hath abundance; and ever does it prowl round the tables of bestowers.

Sickness speaketh in such craving, and invisible degeneration; of a sickly body, speaketh the larcenous craving of this selfishness.

Tell me, my brother, what do we think bad, and worst of all? Is it not degeneration? And we always suspect degeneration when the bestowing soul is lacking.

Upward goes our course from genera on to super-genera. But a horror to us is the degenerating sense, which saith: "All for myself."

Upward soareth our sense: thus is it a simile of our body, a simile of an elevation. Such similes of elevations are the names of the virtues.

Thus goeth the body through history, a becomer and fighter. And the spirit – what is that to the body? Its fights and victories herald, its companion and echo.

Similes, are all names of good and evil; they do not speak out, they only hint. A fool who seeketh knowledge from them!

Give heed, my brethren, to every hour when your spirit would speak in similes: there is the origin of your virtue.

Elevated is then your body, and raised up; with its delight, enraptureth it the spirit, so that it becometh creator, and valuer, and lover, and everything's benefactor.

When your heart overfloweth broad and full like the river, a blessing and a danger to the lowlanders: there is the origin of your virtue.

When ye are exalted above praise and blame, and your will would command all things, as a loving one's will: there is the origin of your virtue.

When ye despise pleasant things, and the effeminate couch, and cannot couch far enough from the effeminate: there is the origin of your virtue.

When ye are willers of one will, and when that change of every need is needful to you: there is the origin of your virtue.

Verily, a new good and evil is it! Verily, a new deep murmuring, and the voice of a new fountain!

Power is it, this new virtue; a ruling thought is it, and around it a subtle soul: a golden sun, with the serpent of knowledge around it.'

2

Here paused Zarathustra awhile, and looked lovingly on his disciples. Then he continued to speak thus – and his voice had changed: 'Remain faithful to the earth, my brothers, with the power of your virtue! Let your giving love and your knowledge be devoted to the the meaning of the earth! Thus do I pray and conjure you.

Let it not fly away from the earthly and beat against eternal walls with its wings! Ah, there hath always been so much flown-away virtue!

Lead, like me, the flown-away virtue back to the earth – yeah, back to body and life: that it may give to the earth its meaning, a human meaning!

A hundred times hitherto hath spirit as well as virtue flown away and blundered. Alas! In our body dwelleth still all this delusion and blundering: body and will hath it there become.

A hundred times hitherto hath spirit as well as virtue attempted and erred. Yea, an attempt hath man been. Alas, much ignorance and error hath embodied in us!

Not only the rationality of millennia – also their madness, breaketh out in us. Dangerous is it to be an heir.

Still fight we step by step with the giant Chance, and over all mankind hath hitherto ruled nonsense, the lack-of-sense.

Let your spirit and your virtue be devoted to the sense of the earth, my bretheren: let the value of everything be determined anew by you! Therefore shall ye be fighters! Therefore shall ye be creators!

Intelligently doth the body purify itself; attempting with intelligence it exalteth itself; to the discerners all impulses sanctify themselves; to the exalted the soul becometh joyful.

Physcian, heal thyself: then wilt thou also heal thy patient. Let it be his best cure to see with his eyes him who maketh himself whole.

A thousand paths are there which have never yet been trodden; a thousand salubrities and hidden islands of life. Unexhausted and undiscovered is still man and man's world.

Awake and listen, you that are lonely! From the future come winds with stealthy wings, and to subtle ears good tidings are proclaimed.

You that are lonely today, you that withdraw, you shall one day be a people: out of you, who have chosen yourselves, shall arise a chosen people: and out of them, the Superman.

The earth shall become a place of healing! And there already is a new fragrance surrounding it, a salvation-bringing fragrance – and a new hope!'

3

When Zarathustra had spoken these words, he paused, like one who had not yet said his last word; and long did he balance the staff doubtfully in his hand. At last he spoke thus – and his voice had changed:

'I now go alone, my disciples! You too go now, alone! Thus I want it.

I advise you: depart from me, and guard yourselves against Zarathustra! And better still: be ashamed of him! Perhaps he has deceived you.

The man of knowledge must be able not only to love his enemies, but also to hate his friends.

One requites a teacher badly if one remains merely a student. And why will you not pluck at my wreath?

You venerate me; but what if your veneration should some day collapse? Beware lest a statue crush you!

You say you believe in Zarathustra? But what matters Zarathustra! You are my believers: but what matters all believers! You had not yet sought yourselves: then you found me. So do all believers; thus all belief matters so little.

Now I bid you lose me and find yourselves; and only when you have all denied me will I return to you.

With other eyes, my brothers, shall I then seek my lost ones; with another love shall I then love you.

And once again you shall become friends to me, and children of one hope: then I will be with you for the third time, to celebrate the great noontide with you.

And it is the great noontide, when man is in the middle of his course between animal and Superman, and celebrates his advance to the evening as his highest hope: for it is the advance to a new morning.

Then will the down-goer bless himself, for being an over-goer; and the sun of his knowledge will be at noontide.

"Dead are all Gods: now we want the Superman to live." Let this be our final will at the great noontide!'

Thus spoke Zarathustra.

PART TWO

23. The Child with the Mirror

AFTER this Zarathustra returned again into the mountains to the solitude of his cave, and withdrew himself from men, waiting like a sower who has scattered his seed. His soul, however, became impatient and full of longing for those whom he loved: because he had still much to give them. For this is hardest of all: to close the open hand out of love, and keep modest as a giver.

Thus passed with the lonesome one months and years; his wisdom meanwhile increased, and caused him pain by its abundance.

One morning, however, he awoke before the rosy dawn, and having meditated long on his couch, at last spake thus to his heart:

'Why did I startle in my dream, so that I awoke? Did not a child come to me, carrying a mirror?

"O Zarathustra" – said the child unto me – "look at thyself in the mirror!"

But when I looked into the mirror, I shrieked, and my heart throbbed: for not myself did I see therein, but a devil's grimace and derision.

Verily, all too well do I understand the dream's portent and monition: my *doctrine* is in danger; tares want to be called wheat!

My enemies have grown powerful and have disfigured the likeness of my doctrine, so that my dearest ones have to blush for the gifts that I gave them.

Lost are my friends; the hour has come for me to seek my lost ones!'

With these words Zarathustra started up, not however like a person in anguish seeking relief, but rather like a seer and a singer whom the spirit inspires. With amazement did his eagle and serpent gaze upon him: for a coming bliss overspread his countenance like the rosy dawn.

'What has happened to me, my animals?' said Zarathustra. 'Am I not transformed? Has not bliss come to me like a whirlwind?

Foolish is my happiness, and foolish things will it speak: it is still too young – so have patience with it!

Wounded am I by my happiness: all sufferers shall be physicians to me!

To my friends can I again go down, and also to my enemies! Zarathustra can again speak and give, and show his best love to his loved ones!

My impatient love overflows in streams, down towards sunrise and sunset. Out of silent mountains and storms of affliction, rushes my soul into the valleys.

Too long have I longed and looked into the distance. Too long has solitude possessed me: thus have I unlearned to keep silence.

Utterance have I become altogether, and the brawling of a brook from high rocks: downward into the valleys will I hurl my speech.

And let the stream of my love sweep into unfrequented channels! How should a stream not finally find its way to the sea! Forsooth, there is a lake in me, sequestered and self- sufficing; but the stream of my love beareth this along with it, down – to the sea!

New paths do I tread, a new speech comes to me; tired have I become – like all creators – of the old tongues. No longer will my spirit walk on worn-out soles.

Too slowly runs all speaking for me: into thy chariot, O storm, do I leap! And even you will I whip with my spite!

Like a cry and an huzza will I traverse wide seas, till I find the Happy Isles where my friends sojourn.

And mine enemies amongst them! How I now love every one to whom I may but speak! Even my enemies pertain to my bliss.

And when I want to mount my wildest horse, then does my spear always help me up best: it is my foot's ever ready servant:

The spear which I hurl at my enemies! How grateful am I to my enemies that I may at last hurl it!

Too great has been the tension of my cloud: 'twixt laughters of lightnings will I cast hail-showers into the depths.

Violently will my breast then heave; violently will it blow its storm over the mountains: thus comes its assuagement.

Like a storm comes my happiness, and my freedom! But my enemies shall think that the evil one roars over their heads.

Yes, you also, my friends, will be alarmed by my wild wisdom; and perhaps you will flee therefrom, along with my enemies.

Ah, that I knew how to lure you back with shepherds' flutes! Ah, that my lioness wisdom would learn to roar softly! And much have we already learned with one another!

My wild wisdom became pregnant on the lonesome mountains; on the rough stones did she bear the youngest of her young.

Now runneth she foolishly in the arid wilderness, and seeketh and seeketh the soft sward-mine old, wild wisdom!

On the soft sward of your hearts, my friends! On your love, would she fain couch her dearest one!'

Thus spake Zarathustra.

24. In the Happy Isles

'THE figs fall from the trees, they are good and sweet; and in falling the red skins of them break. A north wind am I to ripe figs.

Thus, like figs, do these doctrines fall for you, my friends: imbibe now their juice and their sweet substance! It is autumn all around, and clear sky, and afternoon.

Lo, what fullness is around us! And out of the midst of superabundance, it is delightful to look out upon distant seas.

Once did people say God, when they looked out upon distant seas; now, however, have I taught you to say, Superman.

God is a conjecture: but I do not wish your conjecturing to reach beyond your creating will.

Could ye *create* a God? Then, I pray you, be silent about all gods! But ye could well create the Superman.

Not perhaps ye yourselves, my brethren! But into fathers and forefathers of the Superman could ye transform yourselves: and let that be your best creating! God is a conjecture: but I should like your conjecturing restricted to the conceivable.

Could you conceive a God? But let this mean Will to Truth to you, that everything be transformed into the humanly conceivable, the humanly visible, the humanly sensible! Your own discernment shall you follow out to the end!

And what you have called the world shall but be created by you: your reason, your likeness, your will, your love, shall it itself become! And verily, for your bliss, you discerning ones!

And how would you endure life without that hope, you discerning ones? Neither in the inconceivable could you have been born, nor in the irrational.

But that I may reveal my heart entirely to you, my friends: if there were gods, how could I endure it to be no God! Therefore there are no gods.

Yes, I have drawn the conclusion; now, however, does it draw me.

God is a conjecture: but who could drink all the bitterness of this conjecture without dying? Shall his faith be taken from the creator, and from the eagle his flights into eagle-heights?

God is a thought – it makes all the straight crooked, and all that stands reel. What? Time would be gone, and all the perishable would be but a lie?

To think this is giddiness and vertigo to human limbs, and even vomiting to the stomach: verily, the reeling sickness do I call it, to conjecture such a thing.

Evil do I call it and misanthropic: all that teaching about the one, and the plenum, and the unmoved, and the sufficient, and the imperishable!

All the imperishable – that's but a parable, and the poets lie too much. But of time and of becoming shall the best parables speak: a praise shall they be, and a justification of all perishing!

Creating – that is the great salvation from suffering, and life's alleviation. But for the creator to appear, suffering itself is needed, and much transformation.

Yes, much bitter dying must there be in your life, you creators! Thus are you advocates and justifiers of all perishing.

For the creator himself to be the new-born child, he must also be willing to be the child-bearer, and endure the pangs of the child-bearer.

Through a hundred souls went I my way, and through a hundred cradles and birth-throes. Many a farewell have I taken; I know the heart-breaking last hours.

But so wills it my creating Will, my fate. Or, to tell you it more candidly: just such a fate wills my Will.

All feeling suffers in me, and is in prison: but my willing ever comes to me as my emancipator and comforter.

Willing emancipates: that is the true doctrine of will and emancipation – so teaches you Zarathustra.

No longer willing, and no longer valuing, and no longer creating! Ah, that that great debility may ever be far from me!

And also in discerning do I feel only my will's procreating and evolving delight; and if there be innocence in my knowledge, it is because there is will to procreation in it.

Away from God and gods did this will allure me; what would there be to create if there were gods!

But to man does it ever impel me anew, my fervent creative will; thus impels it the hammer to the stone.

Ah, you men, within the stone slumbers an image for me, the image of my visions! Ah, that it should slumber in the hardest, ugliest stone! Now rages my hammer ruthlessly against its prison. From the stone fly the fragments: what's that to me?

I will complete it: for a shadow came to me – the still and lightest of all things once came to me!

The beauty of the Superman came to me as a shadow. Ah, my brothers! Of what account now are the gods to me!'

Thus spoke Zarathustra.

25. The Pitiful

'MY FRIENDS, there has arisen a satire on your friend: "Behold Zarathustra! Walks he not amongst us as if amongst animals?"

But it is better said in this wise: "The discerning one walks amongst men as amongst animals."

Man himself is to the discerning one: the animal with red cheeks.

How has that happened to him? Is it not because he has had to be ashamed too oft?

O my friends! Thus speaks the discerning one: shame, shame, shame – that is the history of man!

And on that account does the noble one enjoin on himself not to abash: bashfulness does he enjoin himself in presence of all sufferers.

I like them not, the merciful ones, whose bliss is in their pity: too destitute are they of bashfulness.

If I must be pitiful, I dislike to be called so; and if I be so, it is preferably at a distance. Preferably also do I shroud my head, and flee, before being recognized: and thus do I bid you do, my friends!

May my destiny ever lead unafflicted ones like you across my path, and those with whom I may have hope and repast and honey in common!

I have done this and that for the afflicted: but something better did I always seem to do when I had learned to enjoy myself better.

Since humanity came into being, man has enjoyed himself too little: that alone, my brothers, is our original sin!

And when we learn better to enjoy ourselves, then do we unlearn best to give pain to others, and to contrive pain.

Therefore do I wash the hand that has helped the sufferer; therefore do I wipe also my soul.

For in seeing the sufferer suffering – thereof was I ashamed on account of his shame; and in helping him, sorely did I wound his pride.

Great obligations do not make men grateful, but revengeful; and when a small kindness is not forgotten, it becomes a gnawing worm.

"Be shy in accepting! Distinguish by accepting!" – thus do I advise those who have naught to give.

I, however, am a giver: willingly do I give as friend to friends. Strangers, however, and the poor, may pluck for themselves the fruit from my tree: thus does it cause less shame.

Beggars, however, one should entirely do away with! It annoys one to give to them, and it annoys one not to give to them.

And likewise sinners and bad consciences! Believe me, my friends: the sting of conscience teaches one to sting. The worst things, however, are the petty thoughts. Better to have done evilly than to have thought pettily!

To be sure, you say: "The delight in petty evils spares one many a great evil deed." But here one should not wish to be sparing.

Like a boil is the evil deed: it itches and irritates and breaks forth – it speaks honourably.

"Behold, I am disease," says the evil deed: that is its honourableness.

But like infection is the petty thought: it creeps and hides, and wants to be nowhere – until the whole body is decayed and withered by the petty infection.

To him however, who is possessed of a devil, I would whisper this word in the ear: "Better for you to rear up your devil! Even for you there is still a path to greatness!"

Ah, my brothers! One knows a little too much about every one! And many a one becomes transparent to us, but still we can by no means penetrate him.

It is difficult to live among men because silence is so difficult.

And not to him who is offensive to us are we most unfair, but to him who does not concern us at all.

If, however, you have a suffering friend, then be a resting-place for his suffering; like a hard bed, however, a camp-bed: thus will you serve him best.

And if a friend does you wrong, then say: "I forgive you what you have done to me; that you have done it to yourself, however – how could I forgive that!"

Thus speaks all great love: it overcomes even forgiveness and pity.

One should hold fast one's heart; for when one lets it go, how quickly does one's head run away!

Ah, where in the world have there been greater follies than with the pitiful? And what in the world has caused more suffering than the follies of the pitiful?

Woe to all loving ones who have not an elevation which is above their pity!

Thus spoke the devil to me, once on a time: "Even God has his hell: it is his love for man."

And lately, did I hear him say these words: "God is dead: of his pity for man has God died."

So be you warned against pity: from thence there yet comes to men a heavy cloud! I understand weather-signs!

But attend also to this word: All great love is above all its pity: for it seeks – to create what is loved!

"Myself do I offer to my love, and my neighbour as myself" – such is the language of all creators.

All creators, however, are hard.'

Thus spoke Zarathustra.

26. *The Priests*

AND one day Zarathustra made a sign to his disciples and spoke these words to them:

'Here are priests: but although they are my enemies, pass them quietly and with sleeping swords!

Even among them there are heroes; many of them have suffered too much: so they want to make others suffer.

Bad enemies are they: nothing is more revengeful than their meekness. And readily does he soil himself who touches them. But my blood is related to theirs; and I want withal to see my blood honoured in theirs.'

And when they had passed, a pain attacked Zarathustra; but not long had he struggled with the pain, when he began to speak thus:

'It moves my heart for those priests. They also go against my taste; but that is the small matter to me, since I am among men.

But I suffer and have suffered with them: prisoners are they to me, and stigmatized ones. He whom they call Saviour put them in fetters:

In fetters of false values and fatuous words! Oh, that some one would save them from their Saviour!

On an isle they once thought they had landed, when the sea tossed them about; but behold, it was a slumbering monster!

False values and fatuous words: these are the worst monsters for mortals – long slumbers and waits the fate that is in them.

But at last it comes and awakes and devours and engulfs whatever has built tabernacles upon it.

Oh, just look at those tabernacles which those priests have built themselves! Churches, they call their sweet-smelling caves!

Oh, that falsified light, that mustified air! Where the soul may not fly aloft to its height!

But so enjoins their belief: "On your knees, up the stair, you sinners!"

Rather would I see a shameless one than the distorted eyes of their shame and devotion!

Who created for themselves such caves and penitence-stairs? Was it not those who sought to conceal themselves, and were ashamed under the clear sky? And only when the clear sky looks again through ruined roofs, and down upon grass and red poppies on ruined walls – will I again turn my heart to the seats of this God.

They called God that which opposed and afflicted them: and verily, there was much hero-spirit in their worship!

And they knew not how to love their God otherwise than by nailing men to the cross!

As corpses they thought to live; in black drapes they their corpses; even in their talk do I still feel the evil flavour of charnel-houses.

And he who lives near to them lives near to black pools, wherein the toad sings his song with sweet gravity.

Better songs would they have to sing, for me to believe in their Saviour: more! Like saved ones would his disciples have to appear to me!

Naked, would I like to see them: for beauty alone should preach penitence. But whom would that disguised affliction convince!

Their saviours themselves came not from freedom and freedom's seventh heaven! They themselves never trod the carpets of knowledge!

Of defects did the spirit of those saviours consist; but into every defect had they put their illusion, their stop-gap, which they called God.

In their pity was their spirit drowned; and when they swelled and o'erswelled with pity, there always floated to the surface a great folly.

Eagerly and with shouts drove they their flock over their foot-bridge; as if there were but one footbridge to the future! Those shepherds also were still of the flock!

Small spirits and spacious souls had those shepherds: but my brothers, what small domains have even the most spacious souls hitherto been!

Characters of blood did they write on the way they went, and their folly taught that truth is proved by blood.

But blood is the very worst witness to truth; blood taints the purest teaching, and turns it into delusion and hatred of heart.

And when a person goes through fire for his teaching – what does that prove! It is more, verily, when out of one's own burning comes one's own teaching!

Sultry heart and cold head; where these meet, there arises the blusterer, the "Saviour".

Greater ones, verily, have there been, and higher-born ones, than those whom the people call saviours, those rapturous blusterers!

And by still greater ones than any of the saviours must you be saved, my brothers, if you would find the way to freedom!

Never yet has there been a Superman. Naked have I seen both of them, the greatest man and the small man.

All-too-similar are they still to each other. Even the greatest found I all-too-human!'

Thus spoke Zarathustra.

27. The Virtuous

'WITH thunder and heavenly fireworks must one speak to indolent and somnolent senses.

But beauty's voice speaks gently: it appeals only to the most awakened souls. Gently vibrated and laughed to me today my buckler; it was beauty's holy laughing and thrilling.

At you, you virtuous ones, laughed my beauty today. And thus came its voice to me: "They want – to be paid besides!"

You want to be paid besides, you virtuous ones! You want reward for virtue, and heaven for earth, and eternity for your today?

And now you upbraid me for teaching that there is no reward-giver, nor paymaster? And verily, I do not even teach that virtue is its own reward.

Ah! This is my sorrow: into the basis of things have reward and punishment been insinuated – and now even into the basis of your souls, you virtuous ones!

But like the snout of the boar shall my word grub up the basis of your souls; a ploughshare will I be called by you.

All the secrets of your heart shall be brought to light; and when you lie in the sun, grubbed up and broken, then will also your falsehood be separated from your truth.

For this is your truth: you are too pure for the filth of the words: vengeance, punishment, recompense, retribution.

You love your virtue as a mother loves her child; but when did one hear of a mother wanting to be paid for her love?

It is your dearest Self, your virtue. The ring's thirst is in you: to reach itself again struggles every ring, and turns itself.

And like the star that goes out, so is every work of your virtue: ever is its light on its way and travelling – and when will it cease to be on its way?

Thus is the light of your virtue still on its way, even when its work is done. Be it forgotten and dead, still its ray of light lives and travels.

That your virtue is your Self, and not an outward thing, a skin, or a cloak: that is the truth from the basis of your souls, ye virtuous ones!

But sure enough there are those to whom virtue meaneth writhing under the lash: and ye have hearkened too much unto their crying!

And others are there who call virtue the slothfulness of their vices; and when once their hatred and jealousy relax the limbs, their "justice" becometh lively and rubbeth its sleepy eyes.

And others are there who are drawn downwards: their devils draw them. But the more they sink, the more ardently gloweth their eye, and the longing for their God.

Ah! Their crying also hath reached your ears, ye virtuous ones: "What I am not, that, that is God to me, and virtue!" And others are there who go along heavily and creakingly, like carts taking stones downhill: they talk much of dignity and virtue – their drag they call virtue!

And others are there who are like eight-day clocks when wound up; they tick, and want people to call ticking virtue.

Verily, in those have I mine amusement: wherever I find such clocks I shall wind them up with my mockery, and they shall even whirr thereby!

And others are proud of their modicum of righteousness, and for the sake of it do violence to all things: so that the world is drowned in their unrighteousness.

Ah! How ineptly cometh the word "virtue" out of their mouth! And when they say: "I am just," it always soundeth like: "I am just – revenged!"

With their virtues they want to scratch out the eyes of their enemies; and they elevate themselves only that they may lower others.

And again there are those who sit in their swamp, and speak thus from among the bulrushes: "Virtue – that is to sit quietly in the swamp.

We bite no one, and go out of the way of him who would bite; and in all matters we have the opinion that is given us."

And again, there are those who love attitudes, and think that virtue is a sort of attitude.

Their knees continually adore, and their hands are eulogies of virtue, but their heart knoweth naught thereof.

And again there are those who regard it as virtue to say: "Virtue is necessary"; but after all they believe only that policemen are necessary.

And many a one who cannot see men's loftiness, calleth it virtue to see their basness far too well: thus calleth he his evil eye virtue.

And some want to be edified and raised up, and call it virtue: and others want to be cast down, and likewise call it virtue.

And thus do almost all think that they participate in virtue; and at least every on claimeth to be an authority on "good" and "evil."

But Zarathustra came not to say unto all those liars and fools: "What do *ye* know of virtue! What *could* ye know of virtue!" –

But that ye, my friends, might become weary of the old words which ye have learned from the fools and liars:

That ye might become weary of the words "reward," "retribution," "punishment," "righteous vengeance."

That ye might become weary of saying: 'That an action is good because it is unselfish.'

Ah! my friends! That *your* very Self be in your action, as the mother is in the child: let that be *your* formula for virtue! Verily, I have taken from you a hundred formulae and your virtue's favourite playthings; and now you upbraid me, as children upbraid.

They played by the sea – then came there a wave and swept their playthings into the deep: and now do they cry.

But the same wave shall bring them new playthings, and spread before them new speckled shells!

Thus will they be comforted; and like them shall you also, my friends, have your comforting – and new speckled shells!'

Thus spoke Zarathustra.

28. The Rabble

'LIFE is a well of delight; but where the rabble also drink, there all fountains are poisoned.

To everything cleanly am I well disposed; but I hate to see the grinning mouths and the thirst of the unclean.

They cast their eye down into the fountain: and now glances up to me their odious smile out of the fountain.

The holy water have they poisoned with their lustfulness; and when they called their filthy dreams delight, then poisoned they also the words.

Indignant becomes the flame when they put their damp hearts to the fire; the spirit itself bubbles and smokes when the rabble approach the fire.

Mawkish and over-mellow becomes the fruit in their hands: unsteady, and withered at the top, does their look make the fruit-tree. Mawkish and over-mellow becomes the fruit in their hands: unsteady, and withered at the top, does their look make the fruit-tree.

And many a one who has turned away from life, has only turned away from the rabble: he hated to share with them fountain, flame, and fruit.

And many a one who has gone into the wilderness and suffered thirst with beasts of prey, disliked only to sit at the cistern with filthy camel-drivers.

And many a one who has come along as a destroyer, and as a hailstorm to all cornfields, wanted merely to put his foot into the jaws of the rabble, and thus stop their throat.

And it is not the mouthful which has most choked me, to know that life itself requires enmity and death and torture-crosses.

But I asked once, and suffocated almost with my question: What? Is the rabble also necessary for life?

Are poisoned fountains necessary, and stinking fires, and filthy dreams, and maggots in the bread of life?

Not my hatred, but my loathing, gnawed hungrily at my life! Ah, oft-times became I weary of spirit, when I found even the rabble spiritual!

And on the rulers turned I my back, when I saw what they now call ruling: to traffic and bargain for power – with the rabble!

Amongst peoples of a strange language did I dwell, with stopped ears: so that the language of their trafficking might remain strange to me, and their bargaining for power.

And holding my nose, I went morosely through all yesterdays and todays: verily, badly smell all yesterdays and todays of the scribbling rabble!

Like a cripple become deaf, and blind, and dumb – thus have I lived long; that I might not live with the power-rabble, the scribe-rabble, and the pleasure-rabble.

Toilsomely did my spirit mount stairs, and cautiously; alms of delight were its refreshment; on the staff did life creep along with the blind one.

What has happened to me? How have I freed myself from loathing? Who has rejuvenated my eye? How have I flown to the height where no rabble any longer sit at the wells?

Did my loathing itself create for me wings and fountain-divining powers? To the loftiest height had I to fly, to find again the well of delight!

Oh, I have found it, my brothers! Here on the loftiest height bubbles up for me the well of delight! And there is a life at whose waters none of the rabble drink with me!

Almost too violently do you flow for me, you fountain of delight! And often emptiest you the goblet again, in wanting to fill it!

And yet must I learn to approach you more modestly: far too violently does my heart still flow towards you:

My heart on which my summer burns, my short, hot, melancholy, over-happy summer: how my summer heart longs for your coolness!

Past, the lingering distress of my spring! Past, the wickedness of my snowflakes in June! Summer have I become entirely, and summer-noontide!

A summer on the loftiest height, with cold fountains and blissful stillness: oh, come, my friends, that the stillness may become more blissful!

For this is our height and our home: too high and steep do we here dwell for all uncleanly ones and their thirst.

Cast but your pure eyes into the well of my delight, my friends! How could it become turbid thereby! It shall laugh back to you with its purity. On the tree of the future build we our nest; eagles shall bring us lone ones food in their beaks!

Verily, no food of which the impure could be fellow-partakers! Fire, would they think they devoured, and burn their mouths!

Verily, no abodes do we here keep ready for the impure! An ice-cave to their bodies would our happiness be, and to their spirits!

And as strong winds will we live above them, neighbours to the eagles, neighbours to the snow, neighbours to the sun: thus live the strong winds.

And like a wind will I one day blow amongst them, and with my spirit, take the breath from their spirit: thus willeth my future.

Verily, a strong wind is Zarathustra to all low places; and this counsel counselleth he to his enemies, and to whatever spitteth and speweth: "Take care not to spit against the wind!".'

Thus spake Zarathustra.

29. The Tarantulas

'LO, THIS is the tarantula's den! Wouldst thou see the tarantula itself? Here hangeth its web: touch this, so that it may tremble.

There cometh the tarantula willingly: Welcome, tarantula! Black on thy back is thy triangle and symbol; and I know also what is in thy soul. Revenge is in your soul: wherever you bite, there arises black scab; with revenge, your poison makes the soul giddy!

Thus do I speak to you in parable, you who make the soul giddy, you preachers of equality! Tarantulas are you to me, and secretly revengeful ones!

But I will soon bring your hiding-places to the light: therefore do I laugh in your face my laughter of the height.

Therefore do I tear at your web, that your rage may lure you out of your den of lies, and that your revenge may leap forth from behind your word "justice".

Because, *for man to be redeemed from revenge* – that is for me the bridge to the highest hope, and a rainbow after long storms.

Otherwise, however, would the tarantulas have it. "Let it be very justice for the world to become full of the storms of our vengeance" – thus do they talk to one another.

"Vengeance will we use, and insult, against all who are not like us" – thus do the tarantula-hearts pledge themselves.

"And 'Will to Equality' – that itself shall henceforth be the name of virtue; and against all that has power will we raise an outcry!"

Ye preachers of equality, the tyrant-frenzy of impotence cries thus in you for "equality": your most secret tyrant-longings disguise themselves thus in virtue-words!

Fretted conceit and suppressed envy – perhaps your fathers' conceit and envy: in you break they forth as flame and frenzy of vengeance.

What the father has hid comes out in the son; and oft have I found in the son the father's revealed secret.

Inspired ones they resemble: but it is not the heart that inspires them – but vengeance. And when they become subtle and cold, it is not spirit, but envy, that makes them so.

Their jealousy leadeth them also into thinkers' paths; and this is the sign of their jealousy – they always go too far: so that their fatigue hath at last to go to sleep on the snow.

In all their lamentations soundeth vengeance, in all their eulogies is maleficence; and being judge seemeth to them bliss.

But thus do I counsel you, my friends: distrust all in whom the impulse to punish is powerful!

They are people of bad race and lineage; out of their countenances peer the hangman and the sleuth-hound.

Distrust all those who talk much of their justice! Verily, in their souls not only honey is lacking.

And when they call themselves "the good and just", forget not, that for them to be Pharisees, nothing is lacking but – power!

My friends, I will not be mixed up and confounded with others.

There are those who preach my doctrine of life, and are at the same time preachers of equality, and tarantulas.

That they speak in favour of life, though they sit in their den, these poison-spiders, and withdrawn from life – is because they would thereby do injury.

To those would they thereby do injury who have power at present: for with those the preaching of death is still most at home.

Were it otherwise, then would the tarantulas teach otherwise: and they themselves were formerly the best world-maligners and heretic-burners.

With these preachers of equality will I not be mixed up and confounded. For thus speaketh justice *unto me*: "Men are not equal".

And neither shall they become so! What would be my love to the Superman, if I spake otherwise?

On a thousand bridges and piers shall they throng to the future, and always shall there be more war and inequality among them: thus do my great love make me speak!

Inventors of figures and phantoms shall they be in their hostilities; and with those figures and phantoms shall they yet fight with each other the supreme fight!

Good and evil, and rich and poor, and high and low, and all names of values: weapons shall they be, and sounding signs, that life must again and again overcome itself!

Aloft will it build itself with columns and stairs – life itself into remote distances would it gaze, and out towards blissful beauties – therefore does it require elevation!

And because it requires elevation, therefore does it require steps, and variance of steps and climbers! To rise strives life, and in rising to overcome itself.

And just behold, my friends! Here where the tarantula's den is, rises aloft an ancient temple's ruins – just behold it with enlightened eyes!

He who here towered aloft his thoughts in stone, knew as well as the wisest ones about the secret of life!

That there is struggle and inequality even in beauty, and war for power and supremacy: that does he here teach us in the plainest parable.

How divinely do vault and arch here contrast in the struggle: how with light and shade they strive against each other, the divinely striving ones.

Thus, steadfast and beautiful, let us also be enemies, my friends! Divinely will we strive against one another!

Alas! There has the tarantula bit me myself, my old enemy! Divinely steadfast and beautiful, it has bit me on the finger!

"Punishment must there be, and justice" – so thinks it: "not gratuitously shall he here sing songs in honour of enmity!"

Yes, it has revenged itself! And alas! Now will it make my soul also dizzy with revenge!

That I may not turn dizzy, however, bind me fast, my friends, to this pillar! Rather will I be a pillar-saint than a whirl of vengeance!

No cyclone or whirlwind is Zarathustra: and if he be a dancer, he is not at all a tarantula-dancer!'

Thus spoke Zarathustra.

30. The Famous Wise Men

'THE people have you served and the people's superstition – not the truth! All you famous wise ones! And just on that account did they pay you reverence.

And on that account also did they tolerate your unbelief, because it was a pleasantry and a by-path for the people. Thus does the master give free scope to his slaves, and even enjoys their presumptuousness.

But he who is hated by the people, as the wolf by the dogs – is the free spirit, the enemy of fetters, the non-adorer, the dweller in the woods.

To hunt him out of his lair – that was always called "sense of right" by the people: on him do they still hound their sharpest-toothed dogs.

"For there the truth is, where the people are! Woe, woe to the seeking ones!" – thus has it echoed through all time.

Your people would you justify in their reverence: that called you "Will to Truth", you famous wise ones!

And your heart has always said to itself: "From the people have I come: from thence came to me also the voice of God".

Stiff-necked and artful, like the ass, have you always been, as the advocates of the people.

And many a powerful one who wanted to run well with the people, has harnessed in front of his horses – a donkey, a famous wise man.

And now, you famous wise ones, I would have you finally throw off entirely the skin of the lion!

The skin of the beast of prey, the speckled skin, and the dishevelled locks of the investigator, the searcher, and the conqueror!

Ah! For me to learn to believe in your "conscientiousness", you would first have to break your venerating will.

Conscientious – so call I him who goes into God-forsaken wildernesses, and has broken his venerating heart.

In the yellow sands and burnt by the sun, he doubtless peers thirstily at the isles rich in fountains, where life reposes under shady trees.

But his thirst does not persuade him to become like those comfortable ones: for where there are oases, there are also idols.

Hungry, fierce, lonesome, God-forsaken: so does the lion-will wish itself.

Free from the happiness of slaves, redeemed from deities and adorations, fearless and fear-inspiring, grand and lonesome: so is the will of the conscientious.

In the wilderness have ever dwelt the conscientious, the free spirits, as lords of the wilderness; but in the cities dwell the well-foddered, famous wise ones – the draught-beasts.

For, always do they draw, as asses – the people's carts!

Not that I on that account upbraid them: but serving ones do they remain, and harnessed ones, even though they glitter in golden harness.

And often have they been good servants and worthy of their hire. For thus says virtue: "If you must be a servant, seek him to whom your service is most useful!

The spirit and virtue of your master shall advance by you being his servant: thus will you yourself advance with his spirit and virtue!"

And verily, you famous wise ones, you servants of the people! You yourselves have advanced with the people's spirit and virtue – and the people by you! To your honour do I say it!

But the people you remain for me, even with your virtues, the people with purblind eyes – the people who know not what spirit is!

Spirit is life which itself cuts into life: by its own torture does it increase its own knowledge, did you know that before?

And the spirit's happiness is this: to be anointed and consecrated with tears as a sacrificial victim, did you know that before?

And the blindness of the blind one, and his seeking and groping, shall yet testify to the power of the sun into which he has gazed, did you know that before?

And with mountains shall the discerning one learn to build! It is a small thing for the spirit to remove mountains, did you know that before?

You know only the sparks of the spirit: but you do not see the anvil which it is, and the cruelty of its hammer!

You know not the spirit's pride! But still less could you endure the spirit's humility, should it ever want to speak!

And never yet could you cast your spirit into a pit of snow: you are not hot enough for that! Thus are you unaware, also, of the delight of its coldness.

In all respects, however, you make too familiar with the spirit; and out of wisdom have you often made an alms-house and a hospital for bad poets.

You are not eagles: thus have you never experienced the happiness of the alarm of the spirit. And he who is not a bird should not camp above abysses.

You seem to me lukewarm ones: but coldly flows all deep knowledge. Ice-cold are the innermost wells of the spirit: a refreshment to hot hands and handlers.

Respectable do you there stand, and stiff, and with straight backs, you famous wise ones! No strong wind or will impels you.

Have you ne'er seen a sail crossing the sea, rounded and inflated, and trembling with the violence of the wind?

Like the sail trembling with the violence of the spirit, does my wisdom cross the sea – my wild wisdom!

But you servants of the people, you famous wise ones – how could you go with me!'

Thus spoke Zarathustra.

31. The Night Song

'TIS night: now do all gushing fountains speak louder. And my soul also is a gushing fountain.

'Tis night: now only do all songs of the loving ones awake. And my soul also is the song of a loving one.

Something unappeased, unappeasable, is within me; it longs to find expression. A craving for love is within me, which speaks itself the language of love.

Light am I: ah, that I were night! But it is my lonesomeness to be begirt with light!

Ah, that I were dark and nightly! How would I suck at the breasts of light!

And you yourselves would I bless, you twinkling starlets and glow-worms aloft! and would rejoice in the gifts of your light.

But I live in my own light, I drink again into myself the flames that break forth from me.

I know not the happiness of the receiver; and oft have I dreamt that stealing must be more blessed than receiving.

It is my poverty that my hand never ceases giving; it is my envy that I see waiting eyes and the brightened nights of longing.

Oh, the misery of all givers! Oh, the darkening of my sun! Oh, the craving to crave! Oh, the violent hunger in satiety!

They take from me: but do I yet touch their soul? There is a gap 'twixt giving and receiving; and the small gap has finally to be bridged over.

A hunger arises out of my beauty: I should like to injure those I illumine; I should like to rob those I have gifted: thus do I hunger for wickedness.

Withdrawing my hand when another hand already stretches out to it; hesitating like the cascade, which hesitates even in its leap: thus do I hunger for wickedness!

Such revenge does my abundance think of such mischief wells out of my lonesomeness.

My happiness in giving died in giving; my virtue became weary of itself by its abundance!

He who ever gives is in danger of losing his shame; to him who ever dispenses, the hand and heart become callous by very dispensing.

My eye no longer overflows for the shame of suppliants; my hand has become too hard for the trembling of filled hands.

Whence have gone the tears of my eye, and the down of my heart? Oh, the lonesomeness of all givers! Oh, the silence of all shining ones!

Many suns circle in desert space: to all that is dark do they speak with their light – but to me they are silent.

Oh, this is the hostility of light to the shining one: unpityingly does it pursue its course.

Unfair to the shining one in its innermost heart, cold to the suns: thus travels every sun.

Like a storm do the suns pursue their courses: that is their travelling. Their inexorable will do they follow: that is their coldness.

Oh, you only is it, you dark, nightly ones, that extract warmth from the shining ones! Oh, you only drink milk and refreshment from the light's udders!

Ah, there is ice around me; my hand burns with the iciness! Ah, there is thirst in me; it pants after your thirst!

'Tis night: alas, that I have to be light! And thirst for the nightly! And lonesomeness!

'Tis night: now do my longings break forth in me as a fountain, for speech do I long.

'Tis night: now do all gushing fountains speak louder. And my soul also is a gushing fountain.

'Tis night: now do all songs of loving ones awake. And my soul also is the song of a loving one.'

Thus sang Zarathustra.

32. The Dance Song

ONE evening went Zarathustra and his disciples through the forest; and when he sought for a well, lo, he lighted upon a green meadow peacefully surrounded by trees and bushes, where maidens were dancing together. As soon as the maidens recognised Zarathustra, they ceased dancing; Zarathustra, however, approached them with friendly mien and spoke these words:

'Cease not your dancing, you lovely maidens! No game-spoiler has come to you with evil eye, no enemy of maidens.

God's advocate am I with the devil: yet he is the spirit of gravity. How could I, you light-footed ones, be hostile to divine dances? Or to maidens' feet with fine ankles?

To be sure, I am a forest, and a night of dark trees: but he who is not afraid of my darkness, will find banks full of roses under my cypresses.

And even the little God may he find, who is dearest to maidens: beside the well lies he quietly, with closed eyes.

In broad daylight did he fall asleep, the sluggard! Had he perhaps chased butterflies too much?

Upbraid me not, you beautiful dancers, when I chasten the little God somewhat! He will cry, certainly, and weep – but he is laughable even when weeping!

And with tears in his eyes shall he ask you for a dance; and I myself will sing a song to his dance:

A dance-song and satire on the spirit of gravity my supremest, powerfulest devil, who is said to be "lord of the world".

And this is the song that Zarathustra sang when Cupid and the maidens danced together:

Of late did I gaze into your eye, O Life! And into the unfathomable did I there seem to sink.

But you pulled me out with a golden angle; derisively did you laugh when I called you unfathomable.

"Such is the language of all fish," said you; "what they do not fathom is unfathomable.

But changeable am I only, and wild, and altogether a woman, and no virtuous one:

Though I be called by you men the 'profound one,' or the 'faithful one,' 'the eternal one,' 'the mysterious one.'

But you men endow us always with your own virtues – alas, you virtuous ones!"

Thus did she laugh, the unbelievable one; but never do I believe her and her laughter, when she speaks evil of herself.

And when I talked face to face with my wild Wisdom, she said to me angrily: "You will, you crave, you love; on that account alone do you praise Life!"

Then had I almost answered indignantly and told the truth to the angry one; and one cannot answer more indignantly than when one "tells the truth" to one's Wisdom.

For thus do things stand with us three. In my heart do I love only Life – and verily, most when I hate her!

But that I am fond of Wisdom, and often too fond, is because she reminds me very strongly of Life!

She has her eye, her laugh, and even her golden angle-rod: am I responsible for it that both are so alike?

And when once Life asked me: "Who is she then, this Wisdom?" – then said I eagerly: "Ah, yes! Wisdom!

One thirsts for her and is not satisfied, one looks through veils, one grasps through nets.

Is she beautiful? What do I know! But the oldest carps are still lured by her.

Changeable is she, and wayward; often have I seen her bite her lip, and pass the comb against the grain of her hair.

Perhaps she is wicked and false, and altogether a woman; but when she speaks ill of herself, just then does she seduce most."

When I had said this to Life, then laughed she maliciously, and shut her eyes. "Of whom do you speak?" said she. "Perhaps of me?

And if you were right – is it proper to say that in such wise to my face! But now, pray, speak also of your Wisdom!"

Ah, and now have you again opened your eyes, O beloved Life! And into the unfathomable have I again seemed to sink.

Thus sang Zarathustra. But when the dance was over and the maidens had departed, he became sad.

"The sun has been long set," said he at last, "the meadow is damp, and from the forest comes coolness.

An unknown presence is about me, and gazes thoughtfully. What! you live still, Zarathustra?

Why? Wherefore? Whereby? Where? Where? How? Is it not folly still to live?

Ah, my friends; the evening is it which thus interrogates in me. Forgive me my sadness!

Evening has come on: forgive me that evening has come on!"'

Thus sang Zarathustra.

33. The Grave Song

'"YONDER is the grave – island, the silent isle; yonder also are the graves of my youth. There will I carry an evergreen wreath of life."

Resolving thus in my heart, did I sail o'er the sea.

Oh, you sights and scenes of my youth! Oh, all you gleams of love, you divine fleeting gleams! How could you perish so soon for me! I think of you today as my dead ones.

From you, my dearest dead ones, comes to me a sweet savour, heart-opening and melting. It convulses and opens the heart of the lone seafarer.

Still am I the richest and most to be envied – I, the most lonesome one! For I have possessed you, and you possess me still. Tell me: to whom has there ever fallen such rosy apples from the tree as have fallen to me?

Still am I your love's heir and heritage, blooming to your memory with many-hued, wild-growing virtues, O you dearest ones!

Ah, we were made to remain near to each other, you kindly strange marvels; and not like timid birds did you come to me and my longing – no, but as trusting ones to a trusting one!

Yes, made for faithfulness, like me, and for fond eternities, must I now name you by your faithlessness, you divine glances and fleeting gleams: no other name have I yet learnt.

Too early did you die for me, you fugitives. Yet did you not flee from me, nor did I flee from you: innocent are we to each other in our faithlessness.

To kill me, did they strangle you, you singing birds of my hopes! Yes, at you, you dearest ones, did malice ever shoot its arrows – to hit my heart!

And they hit it! Because you were always my dearest, my possession and my possessedness: on that account had you to die young, and far too early!

At my most vulnerable point did they shoot the arrow – namely, at you, whose skin is like down – or more like the smile that dies at a glance!

But this word will I say to my enemies: What is all manslaughter in comparison with what you have done to me!

Worse evil did you do to me than all manslaughter; the irretrievable did you take from me: thus do I speak to you, my enemies!

Slew you not my youth's visions and dearest marvels! My playmates took you from me, the blessed spirits! To their memory do I deposit this wreath and this curse.

This curse upon you, my enemies! Have you not made my eternal short, as a tone dies away in a cold night! Scarcely, as the twinkle of divine eyes, did it come to me – as a fleeting gleam!

Thus spoke once in a happy hour my purity: "Divine shall everything be to me".

Then did you haunt me with foul phantoms; ah, where has that happy hour now fled!

"All days shall be sacred to me" – so spoke once the wisdom of my youth: verily, the language of a joyous wisdom!

But then did you enemies steal my nights, and sold them to sleepless torture: ah, where has that joyous wisdom now fled?

Once did I long for happy auspices: then did you lead an owl – monster across my path, an adverse sign. Ah, where did my tender longing then flee?

All loathing did I once vow to renounce: then did you change my nigh ones and nearest ones into ulcerations. Ah, where did my noblest vow then flee?

As a blind one did I once walk in blessed ways: then did you cast filth on the blind one's course: and now is he disgusted with the old footpath.

And when I performed my hardest task, and celebrated the triumph of my victories, then did you make those who loved me call out that I then grieved them most.

It was always your doing: you embittered to me my best honey, and the diligence of my best bees.

To my charity have you ever sent the most impudent beggars; around my sympathy have you ever crowded the incurably shameless. Thus have you wounded the faith of my virtue.

And when I offered my holiest as a sacrifice, immediately did your "piety" put its fatter gifts beside it: so that my holiest suffocated in the fumes of your fat.

And once did I want to dance as I had never yet danced: beyond all heavens did I want to dance. Then did you seduce my favourite minstrel.

And now has he struck up an awful, melancholy air; alas, he tooted as a mournful horn to my ear!

Murderous minstrel, instrument of evil, most innocent instrument! Already did I stand prepared for the best dance: then did you kill my rapture with your tones!

Only in the dance do I know how to speak the parable of the highest things: and now has my grandest parable remained unspoken in my limbs!

Unspoken and unrealized has my highest hope remained! And there have perished for me all the visions and consolations of my youth!

How did I ever bear it? How did I survive and overcome such wounds? How did my soul rise again out of those sepulchres?

Yes, something invulnerable, unburiable is with me, something that would rend rocks asunder: it is called my Will. Silently does it proceed, and unchanged throughout the years.

Its course will it go upon my feet, my old Will; hard of heart is its nature and invulnerable.

Invulnerable am I only in my heel. Ever live you there, and are like yourself, you most patient one! Ever have you burst all shackles of the tomb!

In you still lives also the unrealizedness of my youth; and as life and youth sit you here hopeful on the yellow ruins of graves.

Yes, you are still for me the demolisher of all graves: Hail to you, my Will! And only where there are graves are there resurrections.'

Thus sang Zarathustra.

34. *Self-overcoming*

'"WILL to Truth" do you call it, you wisest ones, that which impels you and makes you ardent?

Will for the thinkableness of all being: thus do I call your will!

All being would you make thinkable: for you doubt with good reason whether it be already thinkable.

But it shall accommodate and bend itself to you! So wills your will. Smooth shall it become and subject to the spirit, as its mirror and reflection.

That is your entire will, you wisest ones, as a Will to Power; and even when you speak of good and evil, and of estimates of value.

You would still create a world before which you can bow the knee: such is your ultimate hope and ecstasy.

The ignorant, to be sure, the people – they are like a river on which a boat floats along: and in the boat sit the estimates of value, solemn and disguised.

Your will and your valuations have you put on the river of becoming; it betrays to me an old Will to Power, what is believed by the people as good and evil.

It was you, you wisest ones, who put such guests in this boat, and gave them pomp and proud names – you and your ruling Will!

Onward the river now carries your boat: it must carry it. A small matter if the rough wave foams and angrily resists its keel!

It is not the river that is your danger and the end of your good and evil, you wisest ones: but that Will itself, the Will to Power – the unexhausted, procreating life-will.

But that you may understand my gospel of good and evil, for that purpose will I tell you my gospel of life, and of the nature of all living things.

The living thing did I follow; I walked in the broadest and narrowest paths to learn its nature.

With a hundred-faced mirror did I catch its glance when its mouth was shut, so that its eye might speak to me. And its eye spoke to me.

But wherever I found living things, there heard I also the language of obedience. All living things are obeying things.

And this heard I secondly: Whatever cannot obey itself, is commanded. Such is the nature of living things.

This, however, is the third thing which I heard – namely, that commanding is more difficult than obeying. And not only because the commander bears the burden of all obeyers, and because this burden readily crushes him:

An attempt and a risk seemed all commanding to me; and whenever it commands, the living thing risks itself thereby.

Yes, even when it commands itself, then also must it atone for its commanding. Of its own law must it become the judge and avenger and victim.

How does this happen! So did I ask myself. What persuades the living thing to obey, and command, and even be obedient in commanding?

Hearken now to my word, you wisest ones! Test it seriously, whether I have crept into the heart of life itself, and into the roots of its heart!

Wherever I found a living thing, there found I Will to Power; and even in the will of the servant found I the will to be master.

That to the stronger the weaker shall serve – thereto persuades he his will who would be master over a still weaker one. That delight alone he is unwilling to forego.

And as the lesser surrenders himself to the greater that he may have delight and power over the least of all, so do even the greatest surrender himself, and stakes – life, for the sake of power.

It is the surrender of the greatest to run risk and danger, and play dice for death.

And where there is sacrifice and service and love-glances, there also is the will to be master. By byways do the weaker then slink into the fortress, and into the heart of the mightier one – and there steals power.

And this secret spoke Life herself to me. "Behold," said she, "I am that which must ever overcome itself.

To be sure, you call it will to procreation, or impulse towards a goal, towards the higher, remoter, more manifold: but all that is one and the same secret.

Rather would I perish than disown this one thing; and verily, where there is perishing and leaf-falling, lo, there does Life sacrifice itself – for power!

That I have to be struggle, and becoming, and purpose, and cross-purpose – ah, he who divines my will, divines well also on what crooked paths it has to tread!

Whatever I create, and however much I love it, soon must I be adverse to it, and to my love: so wills my will.

And even you, discerning one, are only a path and footstep of my will: verily, my Will to Power walks even on the feet of your Will to Truth!

He certainly did not hit the truth who shot at it the formula: 'Will to existence': that will – does not exist!

For what is not, cannot will; that, however, which is in existence – how could it still strive for existence!

Only where there is life, is there also will: not, however, Will to Life, but – so teach I you – Will to Power!

Much is reckoned higher than life itself by the living one; but out of the very reckoning speaks – the Will to Power!"—

Thus did Life once teach me: and thereby, you wisest ones, do I solve you the riddle of your hearts.

I say to you: good and evil which would be everlasting – it does not exist! Of its own accord must it ever overcome itself anew.

With your values and formulae of good and evil, you exercise power, you valuing ones: and that is your secret love, and the sparkling, trembling, and overflowing of your souls.

But a stronger power grows out of your values, and a new overcoming: by it breaks egg and egg-shell.

And he who has to be a creator in good and evil – verily, he has first to be a destroyer, and break values in pieces.

Thus does the greatest evil pertain to the greatest good: that, however, is the creating good.

Let us speak thereof, you wisest ones, even though it be bad. To be silent is worse; all suppressed truths become poisonous.

And let everything break up which – can break up by our truths! Many a house is still to be built!'

Thus spoke Zarathustra.

35. The Sublime Ones

'CALM is the bottom of my sea: who would guess that it hides droll monsters!

Unmoved is my depth: but it sparkles with swimming enigmas and laughters.

A sublime one saw I today, a solemn one, a penitent of the spirit: Oh, how my soul laughed at his ugliness!

With upraised breast, and like those who draw in their breath: thus did he stand, the sublime one, and in silence:

O'erhung with ugly truths, the spoil of his hunting, and rich in torn raiment; many thorns also hung on him – but I saw no rose. Not yet had he learned laughing and beauty. Gloomy did this hunter return from the forest of knowledge.

From the fight with wild beasts returned he home: but even yet a wild beast gazes out of his seriousness – an unconquered wild beast!

As a tiger does he ever stand, on the point of springing; but I do not like those strained souls; ungracious is my taste towards all those self-engrossed ones.

And you tell me, friends, that there is to be no dispute about taste and tasting? But all life is a dispute about taste and tasting!

Taste: that is weight at the same time, and scales and weigher; and alas for every living thing that would live without dispute about weight and scales and weigher!

Should he become weary of his sublimeness, this sublime one, then only will his beauty begin – and then only will I taste him and find him savoury.

And only when he turns away from himself will he o'erleap his own shadow – and verily! into his sun.

Far too long did he sit in the shade; the cheeks of the penitent of the spirit became pale; he almost starved on his expectations.

Contempt is still in his eye, and loathing hides in his mouth. To be sure, he now rests, but he has not yet taken rest in the sunshine.

As the ox ought he to do; and his happiness should smell of the earth, and not of contempt for the earth.

As a white ox would I like to see him, which, snorting and lowing, walks before the plough-share: and his lowing should also laud all that is earthly!

Dark is still his countenance; the shadow of his hand dances upon it. O'ershadowed is still the sense of his eye.

His deed itself is still the shadow upon him: his doing obscures the doer. Not yet has he overcome his deed.

To be sure, I love in him the shoulders of the ox: but now do I want to see also the eye of the angel.

Also his hero-will has he still to unlearn: an exalted one shall he be, and not only a sublime one: the ether itself should raise him, the will-less one!

He has subdued monsters, he has solved enigmas. But he should also redeem his monsters and enigmas; into heavenly children should he transform them.

As yet has his knowledge not learned to smile, and to be without jealousy; as yet has his gushing passion not become calm in beauty.

Not in satiety shall his longing cease and disappear, but in beauty! Gracefulness belongs to the munificence of the magnanimous.

His arm across his head: thus should the hero repose; thus should he also overcome his repose.

But precisely to the hero is beauty the hardest thing of all. Unattainable is beauty by all ardent wills.

A little more, a little less: precisely this is much here, it is the most here.

To stand with relaxed muscles and with unharnessed will: that is the hardest for all of you, you sublime ones!

When power becomes gracious and descends into the visible – I call such condescension, beauty.

And from no one do I want beauty so much as from you, you powerful one: let your goodness be your last self-conquest.

All evil do I accredit to you: therefore do I desire of you the good.

I have often laughed at the weaklings, who think themselves good because they have crippled paws!

The virtue of the pillar shall you strive after: more beautiful does it ever become, and more graceful – but internally harder and more sustaining – the higher it rises.

Yes, you sublime one, one day shall you also be beautiful, and hold up the mirror to your own beauty.

Then will your soul thrill with divine desires; and there will be adoration even in your vanity!

For this is the secret of the soul: when the hero has abandoned it, then only approach it in dreams – the super-hero.'

Thus spoke Zarathustra.

36. The Land of Culture

'TOO far did I fly into the future: a horror seized upon me.

And when I looked around me, behold, there time was my sole contemporary.

Then did I fly backwards, homewards – and always faster. Thus did I come to you: you present-day men, and into the land of culture.

For the first time brought I an eye to see you, and good desire: verily, with longing in my heart did I come.

But how did it turn out with me? Although so alarmed – I had yet to laugh! Never did my eye see anything so motley-coloured!

I laughed and laughed, while my foot still trembled, and my heart as well. "Here, is the home of all the paint-pots", – said I.

With fifty patches painted on faces and limbs – so sat ye there to my astonishment, ye present-day men!

And with fifty mirrors around you, which flattered your play of colours, and repeated it!

Verily, ye could wear no better masks, ye present-day men, than your own faces! Who could – *recognize* you!

Written all over with the characters of the past, and these characters also pencilled over with new characters – thus have ye concealed yourselves well from all decipherers!

And though one be a trier of the reins, who still believeth that ye have reins! Out of colours ye seem to be baked, and out of glued scraps.

All times and peoples gaze divers-coloured out of your veils; all customs and beliefs speak divers-coloured out of your gestures.

He who would strip you of veils and wrappers, and paints and gestures, would just have enough left to scare the crows.

Verily, I myself am the scared crow that once saw you naked, and without paint; and I flew away when the skeleton ogled at me.

Rather would I be a day-labourer in the nether-world, and among the shades of the by – gone! – Fatter and fuller than ye, are the nether-worldlings!

This, yea this, is bitterness to my bowels, that I can neither endure you naked nor clothed, ye present-day men!

All that is unhomelike in the future, and whatever maketh strayed birds shiver, is verily more homelike and familiar than your 'reality.'

For thus speak you: "Real are we wholly, and without faith and superstition": thus do you plume yourselves – alas! even without plumes!

Indeed, how would ye be *able* to believe, you divers-coloured ones! You who are pictures of all that has ever been believed!

Perambulating refutations are you, of belief itself, and a dislocation of all thought. Untrustworthy ones: thus do I call you, you real ones!

All periods prate against one another in your spirits; and the dreams and pratings of all periods were even realer than your awakeness!

Unfruitful are you: therefore do you lack belief. But he who had to create, had always his presaging dreams and astral premonitions – and believed in believing!

Half-open doors are you, at which gravediggers wait. And this is your reality: "Everything deserves to perish."

Alas, how you stand there before me, you unfruitful ones; how lean your ribs! And many of you surely have had knowledge thereof.

Many a one has said: "There has surely a God filched something from me secretly whilst I slept? Enough to make a girl for himself therefrom!"

"Amazing is the poverty of my ribs!" thus has spoken many a present-day man.

Yes, you are laughable to me, you present-day men! And especially when you marvel at yourselves!

And woe to me if I could not laugh at your marvelling, and had to swallow all that is repugnant in your platters!

As it is, however, I will make lighter of you, since I have to carry what is heavy; and what matter if beetles and May bugs also alight on my load!

It shall not on that account become heavier to me! And not from you, you present-day men, shall my great weariness arise.

Ah, where shall I now ascend with my longing! From all mountains do I look out for fatherlands and motherlands.

But a home have I found nowhere: unsettled am I in all cities, and decamping at all gates.

Alien to me, and a mockery, are the present-day men, to whom of late my heart impelled me; and exiled am I from fatherlands and motherlands.

Thus do I love only my children's land, the undiscovered in the remotest sea: for it do I bid my sails search and search.

To my children will I make amends for being the child of my fathers: and to all the future – for this present-day!'

Thus spoke Zarathustra.

37. *Immaculate Perception*

'WHEN yester-eve the moon arose, then did I fancy it about to bear a sun: so broad and teeming did it lie on the horizon.

But it was a liar with its pregnancy; and sooner will I believe in the man in the moon than in the woman.

To be sure, little of a man is he also, that timid night-reveller. With a bad conscience does he stalk over the roofs.

For he is covetous and jealous, the monk in the moon; covetous of the earth, and all the joys of lovers.

No, I like him not, that tom-cat on the roofs! Hateful to me are all that slink around half-closed windows!

Piously and silently does he stalk along on the star-carpets: but I like no light-treading human feet, on which not even a spur jingles.

Every honest one's step speaks; the cat however, steals along over the ground. Behold, cat-like does the moon come along, and dishonestly.

This parable speak I to you sentimental dissemblers, to you, the "pure discerners!" You do I call – covetous ones!

Also you love the earth, and the earthly: I have divined you well! But shame is in your love, and a bad conscience – you are like the moon!

To despise the earthly has your spirit been persuaded, but not your bowels: these, however, are the strongest in you!

And now is your spirit ashamed to be at the service of your bowels, and goes in byways and lying ways to escape its own shame.

"That would be the highest thing for me" – so says your lying spirit to itself – "to gaze upon life without desire, and not like the dog, with hanging-out tongue:

To be happy in gazing: with dead will, free from the grip and greed of selfishness – cold and ashy grey all over, but with intoxicated moon-eyes!

That would be the dearest thing to me" – thus does the seduced one seduce himself, "to love the earth as the moon loves it, and with the eye only to feel its beauty.

And this do I call immaculate perception of all things: to want nothing else from them, but to be allowed to lie before them as a mirror with a hundred facets."

Oh, you sentimental dissemblers, you covetous ones! You lack innocence in your desire: and now do you defame desiring on that account!

Not as creators, as procreators, or as jubilators do you love the earth!

Where is innocence? Where there is will to procreation. And he who seeks to create beyond himself, has for me the purest will.

Where is beauty? Where I must will with my whole Will; where I will love and perish, that an image may not remain merely an image.

Loving and perishing: these have rhymed from eternity. Will to love: that is to be ready also for death. Thus do I speak to you cowards!

But now does your emasculated ogling profess to be "contemplation!" And that which can be examined with cowardly eyes is to be christened "beautiful!" Oh, you violators of noble names!

But it shall be your curse, you immaculate ones, you pure discerners, that you shall never bring forth, even though you lie broad and teeming on the horizon!

You fill your mouth with noble words: and we are to believe that your heart overflows, you cozeners?

But my words are poor, contemptible, stammering words: gladly do I pick up what falls from the table at your repasts.

Yet still can I say therewith the truth – to dissemblers! Yes, my fish-bones, shells, and prickly leaves shall – tickle the noses of dissemblers!

Bad air is always about you and your repasts: your lascivious thoughts, your lies, and secrets are indeed in the air!

Dare only to believe in yourselves – in yourselves and in your inward parts! He who does not believe in himself always lies.

A God's mask have you hung in front of you, you "pure ones": into a God's mask has your execrable coiling snake crawled.

Verily you deceive, you "contemplative ones!" Even Zarathustra was once the dupe of your godlike exterior; he did not divine the serpent's coil with which it was stuffed.

A God's soul, I once thought I saw playing in your games, you pure discerners! No better arts did I once dream of than your arts!

Serpents' filth and evil odour, the distance concealed from me: and that a lizard's craft prowled thereabouts lasciviously.

But I came near to you: then came to me the day, and now comes it to you, at an end is the moon's love affair!

See there! Surprised and pale does it stand – before the rosy dawn!

For already she comes, the glowing one, her love to the earth comes! Innocence, and creative desire, is all solar love!

See there, how she comes impatiently over the sea! Do you not feel the thirst and the hot breath of her love?

At the sea would she suck, and drink its depths to her height: now rises the desire of the sea with its thousand breasts.

Kissed and sucked would it be by the thirst of the sun; vapour would it become, and height, and path of light, and light itself!

Like the sun do I love life, and all deep seas.

And this means to me knowledge: all that is deep shall ascend – to my height!'

Thus spoke Zarathustra.

38. Scholars

'WHEN I lay asleep, then did a sheep eat at the ivy-wreath on my head, it ate, and said thereby: "Zarathustra is no longer a scholar."

It said this, and went away clumsily and proudly. A child told it to me.

I like to lie here where the children play, beside the ruined wall, among thistles and red poppies.

A scholar am I still to the children, and also to the thistles and red poppies. Innocent are they, even in their wickedness.

But to the sheep I am no longer a scholar: so wills my lot-blessings upon it!

For this is the truth: I have departed from the house of the scholars, and the door have I also slammed behind me.

Too long did my soul sit hungry at their table: not like them have I got the knack of investigating, as the knack of nut-cracking.

Freedom do I love, and the air over fresh soil; rather would I sleep on ox-skins than on their honours and dignities.

I am too hot and scorched with my own thought: often is it ready to take away my breath. Then have I to go into the open air, and away from all dusty rooms.

But they sit cool in the cool shade: they want in everything to be merely spectators, and they avoid sitting where the sun burns on the steps.

Like those who stand in the street and gape at the passers-by: thus do they also wait, and gape at the thoughts which others have thought.

Should one lay hold of them, then do they raise a dust like flour-sacks, and involuntarily: but who would divine that their dust came from corn, and from the yellow delight of the summer fields?

When they give themselves out as wise, then do their petty sayings and truths chill me: in their wisdom there is often an odour as if it came from the swamp; and verily, I have even heard the frog croak in it!

Clever are they – they have dexterous fingers: what does my simplicity pretend to beside their multiplicity! All threading and knitting and weaving do their fingers understand: thus do they make the hose of the spirit!

Good clockworks are they: only be careful to wind them up properly! Then do they indicate the hour without mistake, and make a modest noise thereby.

Like millstones do they work, and like pestles: throw only seed-corn to them! They know well how to grind corn small, and make white dust out of it.

They keep a sharp eye on one another, and do not trust each

other the best. Ingenious in little artifices, they wait for those whose knowledge walks on lame feet, like spiders do they wait.

I saw them always prepare their poison with precaution; and always did they put glass gloves on their fingers in doing so.

They also know how to play with false dice; and so eagerly did I find them playing, that they perspired thereby.

We are alien to each other, and their virtues are even more repugnant to my taste than their falsehoods and false dice.

And when I lived with them, then did I live above them. Therefore did they take a dislike to me.

They want to hear nothing of any one walking above their heads; and so they put wood and earth and rubbish between me and their heads.

Thus did they deafen the sound of my tread: and least have I hitherto been heard by the most learned.

All mankind's faults and weaknesses did they put between themselves and me: they call it "false ceiling" in their houses.

But nevertheless I walk with my thoughts above their heads; and even should I walk on my own errors, still would I be above them and their heads.

For men are not equal: so speaks justice. And what I will, they may not will!'

Thus spoke Zarathustra.

39. Poets

'SINCE I have known the body better' – said Zarathustra to one of his disciples – 'the spirit has only been to me symbolically spirit; and all the 'imperishable' – that is also but a parable.'

'So have I heard you say once before,' answered the disciple, 'and then you added: "But the poets lie too much." Why did you say that the poets lie too much?'

'Why?' said Zarathustra. 'You ask why? I do not belong to those who may be asked after their Why.

Is my experience but of yesterday? It is long ago that I experienced the reasons for my opinions.

Should I not have to be a cask of memory, if I also wanted to have my reasons with me?

It is already too much for me even to retain my opinions; and many a bird flies away.

And sometimes, also, do I find a fugitive creature in my dovecote, which is alien to me, and trembles when I lay my hand upon it.

But what did Zarathustra once say to you? That the poets lie too much? – But Zarathustra also is a poet.

Believe you that he there spoke the truth? Why do you believe it?'

The disciple answered: 'I believe in Zarathustra.' But Zarathustra shook his head and smiled.

'Belief does not sanctify me', said he, 'least of all the belief in myself.

But granting that some one did say in all seriousness that the poets lie too much: he was right – we do lie too much.

We also know too little, and are bad learners: so we are obliged to lie.

And which of us poets has not adulterated his wine? Many a poisonous hotchpotch has evolved in our cellars: many an indescribable thing has there been done.

And because we know little, therefore are we pleased from the heart with the poor in spirit, especially when they are young women!

And even of those things are we desirous, which old women tell one another in the evening. This do we call the eternally feminine in us.

And as if there were a special secret access to knowledge, which chokes up for those who learn anything, so do we believe in the people and in their "wisdom."

This, however, do all poets believe: that whoever pricks up his ears when lying in the grass or on lonely slopes, learns something of the things that are between heaven and earth.

And if there come to them tender emotions, then do the poets always think that nature herself is in love with them:

And that she steals to their ear to whisper secrets into it, and amorous flatteries: of this do they plume and pride themselves, before all mortals!

Ah, there are so many things between heaven and earth of which only the poets have dreamed!

And especially above the heavens: for all gods are poet-symbolizations, poet-sophistications!

Ever are we drawn aloft – that is, to the realm of the clouds: on these do we set our gaudy puppets, and then call them gods and supermen:

Are not they light enough for those chairs! All these gods and supermen?

Ah, how I am weary of all the inadequate that is insisted on as actual! Ah, how I am weary of the poets!'

When Zarathustra so spoke, his disciple resented it, but was silent. And Zarathustra also was silent; and his eye directed itself inwardly, as if it gazed into the far distance. At last he sighed and drew breath.

'I am of today and heretofore', said he then; 'but something is in me that is of the morrow, and the day following, and the hereafter.

I became weary of the poets, of the old and of the new: superficial are they all to me, and shallow seas.

They did not think sufficiently into the depth; therefore their feeling did not reach to the bottom.

Some sensation of voluptuousness and some sensation of tedium: these have as yet been their best contemplation.

Ghost-breathing and ghost-whisking, seems to me all the jingle-jangling of their harps; what have they known hitherto of the fervour of tones!

They are also not pure enough for me: they all muddle their water that it may seem deep.

And rather would they thereby prove themselves reconcilers: but mediaries and mixers are they to me, and half-and-half, and impure!

Ah, I cast indeed my net into their sea, and meant to catch good fish; but always did I draw up the head of some ancient God.

Thus did the sea give a stone to the hungry one. And they themselves may well originate from the sea.

Certainly, one finds pearls in them: thereby they are the more like hard molluscs. And instead of a soul, I have often found in them salt slime.

They have learned from the sea also its vanity: is not the sea the peacock of peacocks?

Even before the ugliest of all buffaloes does it spread out its tail; never does it tire of its lace-fan of silver and silk.

Disdainfully does the buffalo glance thereat, nigh to the sand with its soul, closer still to the thicket, nighest, however, to the swamp.

What is beauty and sea and peacock-splendour to it! This parable I speak to the poets.

Their spirit itself is the peacock of peacocks, and a sea of vanity!

Spectators seeks the spirit of the poet – should they even be buffaloes!

But of this spirit became I weary; and I see the time coming when it will become weary of itself.

Yes, changed have I seen the poets, and their glance turned towards themselves.

Penitents of the spirit have I seen appearing; they grew out of the poets.'

Thus spoke Zarathustra.

40. Great Events

THERE is an isle in the sea – not far from the Blessed isles of Zarathustra – on which a volcano ever smokes; of which isle the people, and especially the old women amongst them, say that it is placed as a rock before the gate of the underworld; but that through the volcano itself the narrow way leads downwards which conducts to this gate.

Now about the time that Zarathustra sojourned on the Blessed isles, it happened that a ship anchored at the isle on which stands the smoking mountain, and the crew went ashore to shoot rabbits. About the noontide hour, however, when the captain and his men were together again, they saw suddenly a man coming towards them through the air, and a voice said distinctly: 'It is time! It is the highest time!' But when the figure was nearest to them (it flew past quickly, however, like a shadow, in the direction of the volcano), then did they recognize with the greatest surprise that it was Zarathustra; for they had all seen him before except the captain himself, and they loved him as the people love: in such wise that love and awe were combined in equal degree.

'Behold!' said the old helmsman, 'there goes Zarathustra to hell!'

About the same time that these sailors landed on the fire-isle, there was a rumour that Zarathustra had disappeared; and when his friends were asked about it, they said that he had gone on board a ship by night, without saying where he was going.

Thus there arose some uneasiness. After three days, however, there came the story of the ship's crew in addition to this uneasiness – and then did all the people say that the devil had taken Zarathustra. His disciples laughed, sure enough, at this talk; and one of them said even: 'Sooner would I believe that Zarathustra has taken the devil.' But at the bottom of their hearts they were all full of anxiety and longing: so their joy was great when on the fifth day Zarathustra appeared amongst them.

And this is the account of Zarathustra's interview with the fire-dog:

'The earth', said he, 'has a skin; and this skin has diseases. One of these diseases, for example, is called "man."

And another of these diseases is called "the fire-dog": concerning him men have greatly deceived themselves, and let themselves be deceived.

To fathom this mystery did I go o'er the sea; and I have seen the truth naked, verily! barefooted up to the neck.

Now do I know how it is concerning the fire-dog; and likewise concerning all the spouting and subversive devils, of which not only old women are afraid.

"Up with you, fire-dog, out of your depth!" cried I, "and

confess how deep that depth is! Whence comes that which you snort up?

You drink copiously at the sea: that does your embittered eloquence betray! In sooth, for a dog of the depth, you take your nourishment too much from the surface!

At the most, I regard you as the ventriloquist of the earth: and ever, when I have heard subversive and spouting devils speak, I have found them like you: embittered, mendacious, and shallow.

You understand how to roar and obscure with ashes! You are the best braggarts, and have sufficiently learned the art of making dregs boil.

Where you are, there must always be dregs at hand, and much that is spongy, hollow, and compressed: it wants to have freedom.

'Freedom' you all roar most eagerly: but I have unlearned the belief in 'great events,' when there is much roaring and smoke about them.

And believe me, friend Hullabaloo! The greatest events – are not our noisiest, but our still hours.

Not around the inventors of new noise, but around the inventors of new values, does the world revolve; inaudibly it revolves.

And just own to it! Little had ever taken place when your noise and smoke passed away. What, if a city did become a mummy, and a statue lay in the mud!

And this do I say also to the o'erthrowers of statues: It is certainly the greatest folly to throw salt into the sea, and statues into the mud.

In the mud of your contempt lay the statue: but it is just its law, that out of contempt, its life and living beauty grow again!

With diviner features does it now arise, seducing by its suffering; and verily! it will yet thank you for o'erthrowing it, you subverters!

This counsel, however, do I counsel to kings and churches, and to all that is weak with age or virtue – let yourselves be o'erthrown! That you may again come to life, and that virtue – may come to you!"

Thus spoke I before the fire-dog: then did he interrupt me sullenly, and asked: "Church? What is that?"

"Church?" answered I, 'that is a kind of state, and indeed the most mendacious. But remain quiet, you dissembling dog! you surely know your own species best!

Like yourself the state is a dissembling dog; like you does it like to speak with smoke and roaring – to make believe, like you, that it speaks out of the heart of things.

For it seeks by all means to be the most important creature on earth, the state; and people think it so."

When I had said this, the fire-dog acted as if mad with envy. "What!" cried he, "the most important creature on earth? And people think it so?" And so much vapour and terrible voices came out of his throat, that I thought he would choke with vexation and envy.

At last he became calmer and his panting subsided; as soon, however, as he was quiet, I said laughingly:

"You are angry, fire-dog: so I am in the right about you!

And that I may also maintain the right, hear the story of another fire-dog; he speaks actually out of the heart of the earth.

Gold does his breath exhale, and golden rain: so does his heart desire. What are ashes and smoke and hot dregs to him!

Laughter flits from him like a variegated cloud; adverse is he to your gargling and spewing and grips in the bowels!

The gold, however, and the laughter – these does he take out of the heart of the earth: for, that you mayst know it, the heart of the earth is of gold."

When the fire-dog heard this, he could no longer endure to listen to me. Abashed did he draw in his tail, said "bow-wow!" in a cowed voice, and crept down into his cave.'

Thus told Zarathustra. His disciples, however, hardly listened to him: so great was their eagerness to tell him about the sailors, the rabbits, and the flying man.

'What am I to think of it!' said Zarathustra. 'Am I indeed a ghost?

But it may have been my shadow. You have surely heard something of the Wanderer and his Shadow?

One thing, however, is certain: I must keep a tighter hold of it; otherwise it will spoil my reputation.'

And once more Zarathustra shook his head and wondered. 'What am I to think of it!' said he once more.

'Why did the ghost cry: "It is time! It is the highest time!" *For what* is it then – the highest time?'

Thus spake Zarathustra.

41. The Soothsayer

'AND I saw a great sadness come over mankind. The best turned weary of their works.

A doctrine appeared, a faith ran beside it: "All is empty, all is alike, all hath been!"

And from all hills there re-echoed: "All is empty, all is alike, all hath been!"

To be sure we have harvested: but why have all our fruits become rotten and brown? What was it fell last night from the evil moon?

In vain was all our labour, poison has our wine become, the evil eye hath singed yellow our fields and hearts.

Arid have we all become; and fire falling upon us, then do we turn dust like ashes: yea, the fire itself have we made aweary.

All our fountains have dried up, even the sea has receded. All the ground tries to gape, but the depth will not swallow!

"Alas! where is there still a sea in which one could be drowned?" so soundeth our plaint – across shallow swamps. Even for dying have we become too weary; now do we keep awake and live on – in sepulchres.'

* * *

Thus did Zarathustra hear a soothsayer speak; and the foreboding touched his heart and transformed him. Sorrowfully did he go about and wearily; and he became like to those of whom the soothsayer had spoken.

Said he to his disciples, 'a little while, and there comes the long twilight. Alas, how shall I preserve my light through it!

That it may not smother in this sorrowfulness! To remoter worlds shall it be a light, and also to remotest nights!'

Thus did Zarathustra go about grieved in his heart, and for three days he did not take any meat or drink: he had no rest, and lost his speech. At last it came to pass that he fell into a deep sleep. His disciples, however, sat around him in long night-watches, and waited anxiously to see if he would awake, and speak again, and recover from his affliction.

And this is what Zarathustra said when he awoke; his voice, however, came to his disciples as from afar:

'Hear, I pray you, the dream that I dreamed, my friends, and help me to divine its meaning!

A riddle is it still to me, this dream; the meaning is hidden in it and encaged, and do not yet fly above it on free pinions.

All life had I renounced, so I dreamed. Night-watchman and grave-guardian had I become, aloft, in the lone mountain-fortress of Death.

There did I guard his coffins: full stood the musty vaults of those trophies of victory. Out of glass coffins did vanquished life gaze upon me.

The odour of dust-covered eternities did I breathe: sultry and dust-covered lay my soul. And who could have aired his soul there!

Brightness of midnight was ever around me; lonesomeness cowered beside her; and as a third, death-rattle stillness, the worst of my female friends.

Keys did I carry, the rustiest of all keys; and I knew how to open with them the most creaking of all gates.

Like a bitterly angry croaking ran the sound through the long corridors when the leaves of the gate opened: ungraciously did this bird cry, unwillingly was it awakened.

But more frightful even, and more heart-strangling was it, when it again became silent and still all around, and I alone sat in that malignant silence.

Thus did time pass with me, and slip by, if time there still was: what do I know thereof! But at last there happened that which awoke me.

Thrice did there peal peals at the gate like thunders, thrice did the vaults resound and howl again: then did I go to the sate.

Alpa! cried I, who carries his ashes to the mountain? Alpa! Alpa! who carries his ashes to the mountain?

And I pressed the key, and pulled at the gate, and exerted myself. But not a finger's-breadth was it yet open:

Then did a roaring wind tear the folds apart: whistling, whizzing, and piercing, it threw to me a black coffin.

And in the roaring and whistling and whizzing, the coffin burst open, and spouted out a thousand peals of laughter.

And a thousand caricatures of children, angels, owls, fools, and child-sized butterflies laughed and mocked, and roared at me.

Fearfully was I terrified thereby: it prostrated me. And I cried with horror as I ne'er cried before.

But my own crying awoke me: and I came to myself.'

Thus did Zarathustra relate his dream, and then was silent: for as yet he knew not the interpretation thereof. But the disciple whom he loved most arose quickly, seized Zarathustra's hand, and said:

'Your life itself interprets to us this dream, O Zarathustra!

Are you not yourself the wind with shrill whistling, which bursts open the gates of the fortress of Death?

Are you not yourself the coffin full of many-hued malices and angel – caricatures of life?

Like a thousand peals of children's laughter comes Zarathustra into all sepulchres, laughing at those night-watchmen and grave-guardians, and whoever else rattles with sinister keys.

With your laughter will you frighten and prostrate them: fainting and recovering will you demonstrate your power over them.

And when the long twilight comes and the mortal weariness, even then will you not disappear from our firmament, you advocate of life!

New stars have you made us see, and new nocturnal glories: verily, laughter itself have you spread out over us like a many-hued canopy.

Now will children's laughter ever from coffins flow; now will a strong wind ever come victoriously to all mortal weariness: of this you are yourself the pledge and the prophet!

They themselves did you dream, your enemies: that was your sorest dream.

But as you awoke from them and came to yourself, so shall they awaken from themselves – and come to you!'

Thus spoke the disciple; and all the others then thronged around Zarathustra, grasped him by the hands, and tried to persuade him to leave his bed and his sadness, and return to them. Zarathustra, however, sat upright on his couch, with an absent look. Like one returning from long foreign sojourn did he look on his disciples, and examined their features; but still he knew them not. When, however, they raised him, and set him upon his feet, behold, all on a sudden his eye changed; he understood everything that had happened, stroked his beard, and said with a strong voice:

'Well! This has just its time; but see to it, my disciples, that we have a good repast; and without delay! Thus do I mean to make amends for bad dreams!

The soothsayer, however, shall eat and drink at my side: and verily, I will yet show him a sea in which he can drown himself!'

Thus spoke Zarathustra. Then did he gaze long into the face of the disciple who had been the dream-interpreter, and shook his head.

42. *Redemption*

WHEN Zarathustra went one day over the great bridge, then did the cripples and beggars surround him, and a hunchback spoke thus to him:

'Behold, Zarathustra! Even the people learn from you, and acquire faith in your teaching: but for them to believe fully in you, one thing is still needful – you must first of all convince us cripples! Here have you now a fine selection, and verily, an opportunity with more than one forelock! The blind can you heal, and make the lame run; and from him who has too much behind, could you well, also, take away a little; – that, I think, would be the right method to make the cripples believe in Zarathustra!'

Zarathustra, however, answered thus to him who so spoke: "When one takes his hump from the hunchback, then does one take from him his spirit – so do the people teach. And when one gives the blind man eyes, then does he see too many bad things on the earth: so that he curses him who healed him. He, however, who makes the lame man run, inflicts upon him the greatest injury; for hardly can he run, when his vices run away with him – so do the people teach concerning cripples. And why should not Zarathustra also learn from the people, when the people learn from Zarathustra?

It is, however, the small thing to me since I have been amongst men, to see one person lacking an eye, another an ear, and a third a leg, and that others have lost the tongue, or the nose, or the head.

I see and have seen worse things, and divers things so hideous, that I should neither like to speak of all matters, nor even keep silent about some of them: namely, men who lack everything, except that they have too much of one thing – men who are nothing more than a big eye, or a big mouth, or a big belly, or something else big, reversed cripples, I call such men.

And when I came out of my solitude, and for the first time passed over this bridge, then I could not trust my eyes, but looked again and again, and said at last: "That is an ear! An ear as big as a man!" I looked still more attentively – and actually there did move under the ear something that was pitiably small and poor and slim. And in truth this immense ear was perched on a small thin stalk – the stalk, however, was a man! A person putting a glass to his eyes, could even recognize further a small envious countenance, and also that a bloated little soul dangled at the stalk. The people told me, however, that the big ear was not only a man, but a great man, a genius. But I never believed in the people when they spoke of great men – and I hold to my belief that it was a reversed cripple, who had too little of everything, and too much of one thing.'

When Zarathustra had spoken thus to the hunchback, and to those of whom the hunchback was the mouthpiece and advocate, then did he turn to his disciples in profound dejection, and said:

'My friends, I walk amongst men as amongst the fragments and limbs of human beings!

This is the terrible thing to my eye, that I find man broken up, and scattered about, as on a battle- and butcher-ground.

And when my eye flees from the present to the bygone, it finds ever the same: fragments and limbs and fearful chances – but no men!

The present and the bygone upon earth – ah! my friends – that is my most unbearable trouble; and I should not know how to live, if I were not a seer of what is to come.

A seer, a purposer, a creator, a future itself, and a bridge to the future – and alas! also as it were a cripple on this bridge: all that is Zarathustra.

And you also asked yourselves often: "Who is Zarathustra to us? What shall he be called by us?" And like me, did you give yourselves questions for answers.

Is he a promiser? Or a fulfiller? A conqueror? Or an inheritor? A harvest? Or a ploughshare? A physician? Or a healed one?

Is he a poet? Or a genuine one? An emancipator? Or a subjugator? A good one? Or an evil one?

I walk amongst men as the fragments of the future: that future which I contemplate.

And it is all my poetisation and aspiration to compose and collect into unity what is fragment and riddle and fearful chance.

And how could I endure to be a man, if man were not also the composer, and riddle-reader, and redeemer of chance!

To redeem what is past, and to transform every "It was" into "Thus would I have it!" – that only do I call redemption!

Will – so is the emancipator and joy-bringer called: thus have I taught you, my friends! But now learn this likewise: the Will itself is still a prisoner.

Willing emancipates: but what is that called which still puts the emancipator in chains?

"It was": thus is the Will's teeth-gnashing and most lonesome tribulation called. Impotent towards what has been done – it is a malicious spectator of all that is past.

Not backward can the Will will; that it cannot break time and time's desire – that is the Will's most lonesome tribulation.

Willing emancipates: what does Willing itself create in order to get free from its tribulation and mock at its prison?

Ah, a fool becomes every prisoner! Foolishly delivers itself also the imprisoned Will.

That time does not run backward – that is its animosity: "That which was": so is the stone which it cannot roll called.

And thus does it roll stones out of animosity and ill-humour, and takes revenge on whatever does not, like it, feel rage and ill-humour.

Thus did the Will, the emancipator, become a torturer; and on all that is capable of suffering it takes revenge, because it cannot go backward.

This, yes, this alone is revenge itself: the Will's antipathy to time, and its "It was."

A great folly dwells in our Will; and it became a curse to all humanity, that this folly acquired spirit!

The spirit of revenge: my friends, that has hitherto been man's best contemplation; and where there was suffering, it was claimed there was always penalty.

"Penalty," so calls itself revenge. With a lying word it feigns a good conscience.

And because in the willer himself there is suffering, because he cannot will backwards – thus was Willing itself, and all life, claimed – to be penalty!

And then did cloud after cloud roll over the spirit, until at last madness preached: "Everything perishes, therefore everything deserves to perish!"

"And this itself is justice, the law of time – that he must devour his children:" thus did madness preach.

"Morally are things ordered according to justice and penalty. Oh, where is there deliverance from the flux of things and from the 'existence' of penalty?" Thus did madness preach.

"Can there be deliverance when there is eternal justice? Alas, unrollable is the stone, 'It was': eternal must also be all penalties!" Thus did madness preach.

"No deed can be annihilated: how could it be undone by the penalty! This, this is what is eternal in the 'existence' of penalty, that existence also must be eternally recurring deed and guilt!

Unless the Will should at last deliver itself, and Willing become non-Willing:" but you know, my brothers, this fabulous song of madness!

Away from those fabulous songs did I lead you when I taught you: "The Will is a creator."

All "It was" is a fragment, a riddle, a fearful chance – until the creating Will says thereto: "But thus would I have it."

Until the creating Will says thereto: "But thus do I will it! Thus shall I will it!"

But did it ever speak thus? And when does this take place? Has the Will been unharnessed from its own folly?

Has the Will become its own deliverer and joy-bringer? Has it unlearned the spirit of revenge and all teeth-gnashing?

And who has taught it reconciliation with time, and something higher than all reconciliation?

Something higher than all reconciliation must the Will will which is the Will to Power: but how does that take place? Who has taught it also to will backwards?'

—But at this point it chanced that Zarathustra suddenly paused, and looked like a person in the greatest alarm. With terror in his eyes did he gaze on his disciples; his glances pierced as with arrows their thoughts and arrear-thoughts. But after a brief space he again laughed, and said soothedly:

'It is difficult to live amongst men, because silence is so difficult – especially for a babbler.'

Thus spoke Zarathustra. The hunchback, however, had listened to the conversation and had covered his face during the time; but when he heard Zarathustra laugh, he looked up with curiosity, and said slowly:

'But why does Zarathustra speak otherwise to us than to his disciples?'

Zarathustra answered: 'What is there to be wondered at! With hunchbacks one May well speak in a hunchbacked way!'

'Very good,' said the hunchback; 'and with pupils one may well tell tales out of school.

But why does Zarathustra speak otherwise to his pupils – than to himself?'

43. *Manly Prudence*

'NOT the height, it is the declivity that is terrible!

The declivity, where the gaze shoots downwards, and the hand grasps upwards. There does the heart become giddy through its double will.

Ah, friends, do you divine also my heart's double will?

This, this is my declivity and my danger, that my gaze shoots towards the summit, and my hand would rather clutch and lean – on the depth!

To man clings my will; with chains do I bind myself to man, because I am pulled upwards to the Superman: for there does my other will tend.

And therefore do I live blindly among men, as if I knew them not: that my hand may not entirely lose belief in firmness.

I know not you men: this gloom and consolation is often spread around me.

I sit at the gateway for every rogue, and ask: Who wishes to deceive me?

This is my first manly prudence, that I allow myself to be deceived, so as not to be on my guard against deceivers.

Ah, if I were on my guard against man, how could man be an anchor to my ball! Too easily would I be pulled upwards and away!

This providence is over my fate, that I have to be without foresight.

And he who would not languish amongst men, must learn to drink out of all glasses; and he who would keep clean amongst men, must know how to wash himself even with dirty water.

And thus spoke I often to myself for consolation: "Courage! Cheer up! old heart! An unhappiness has failed to befall you: enjoy that as thy – happiness!"

This, however, is my other manly prudence: I am more forbearing to the vain than to the proud.

Is not wounded vanity the mother of all tragedies? Where, however, pride is wounded, there there grows up something better than pride.

That life may be fair to behold, its game must be well played; for that purpose, however, it needs good actors.

Good actors have I found all the vain ones: they play, and wish people to be fond of beholding them – all their spirit is in this wish.

They represent themselves, they invent themselves; in their neighbourhood I like to look upon life – it cures of melancholy.

Therefore am I forbearing to the vain, because they are the physicians of my melancholy, and keep me attached to man as to a drama.

And further, who conceives the full depth of the modesty of the vain man! I am favourable to him, and sympathetic on account of his modesty.

From you would he learn his belief in himself; he feeds upon your glances, he eates praise out of your hands.

Your lies does he even believe when you lie favourably about him: for in its depths sighs his heart: "What am I?"

And if that be the true virtue which is unconscious of itself – well, the vain man is unconscious of his modesty!

This is, however, my third manly prudence: I am not put out of conceit with the wicked by your timorousness.

I am happy to see the marvels the warm sun hatches: tigers and palms and rattlesnakes.

Also amongst men there is a beautiful brood of the warm sun, and much that is marvellous in the wicked.

In truth, as your wisest did not seem to me so very wise, so found I also human wickedness below the fame of it.

And oft did I ask with a shake of the head: Why still rattle, you rattlesnakes?

There is still a future even for evil! And the warmest south is still undiscovered by man.

How many things are now called the worst wickedness, which are only twelve feet broad and three months long! Some day, however, will greater dragons come into the world.

For that the Superman may not lack his dragon, the super-dragon that is worthy of him, there must still much warm sun glow on moist virgin forests!

Out of your wild cats must tigers have evolved, and out of your poison-toads, crocodiles: for the good hunter shall have a good hunt!

And verily, you good and just! In you there is much to be laughed at, and especially your fear of what has hitherto been called "the devil!"

So alien are you in your souls to what is great, that to you the Superman would be frightful in his goodness!

And you wise and knowing ones, you would flee from the solar-glow of the wisdom in which the Superman joyfully baths his nakedness!

You highest men who have come within my ken! This is my doubt of you, and my secret laughter: I suspect you would call my Superman – a devil!

Ah, I became tired of those highest and best ones: from their "height" did I long to be up, out, and away to the Superman!

A horror came over me when I saw those best ones naked: then there grew for me the pinions to soar away into distant futures.

Into more distant futures, into more southern souths than ever artist dreamed of: there, where gods are ashamed of all clothes!

But disguised do I want to see you, you neighbours and fellowmen, and well-attired and vain and estimable, as "the good and just;" –

And disguised will I myself sit amongst you – that I may mistake you and myself: for that is my last manly prudence.'

Thus spoke Zarathustra.

44. The Stillest Hour

'WHAT has happened to me, my friends? You see me troubled, driven forth, unwillingly obedient, ready to go – alas, to go away from you!

Yes, once more must Zarathustra retire to his solitude: but unjoyously this time does the bear go back to his cave!

What has happened to me? Who orders this? – Ah, my angry mistress wishes it so; she spoke to me. Have I ever named her name to you?

Yesterday towards evening there spoke to me my still hour: that is the name of my terrible mistress.

And thus did it happen – for everything must I tell you, that your heart may not harden against the suddenly departing one!

Do you know the terror of him who falls asleep?

To the very toes he is terrified, because the ground gives way under him, and the dream begins.

This do I speak to you in parable. Yesterday at the still hour did the ground give way under me: the dream began.

The hour-hand moved on, the timepiece of my life drew breath – never did I hear such stillness around me, so that my heart was terrified.

Then was there spoken to me without voice: "You know it, Zarathustra?"

And I cried in terror at this whispering, and the blood left my face: but I was silent.

Then was there once more spoken to me without voice: "You know it, Zarathustra, but you do not speak it!"

And at last I answered, like one defiant: "Yes, I know it, but I will not speak it!"

Then was there again spoken to me without voice: "You will not, Zarathustra? Is this true? Conceal yourself not behind your defiance!"

And I wept and trembled like a child, and said: 'Ah, I would indeed, but how can I do it! Exempt me only from this! It is beyond my power!'

Then was there again spoken to me without voice: "What matter about yourself, Zarathustra! Speak your word, and perish!"

And I answered: "Ah, is it my word? Who am I? I await the worthier one; I am not worthy even to perish by it."

Then was there again spoken to me without voice: "What matter about yourself? You are not yet humble enough for me. Humility has the hardest skin."

And I answered: "What has not the skin of my humility endured! At the foot of my height do I dwell: how high are my summits, no one has yet told me. But well do I know my valleys."

Then was there again spoken to me without voice: "O Zarathustra, he who has to remove mountains removes also valleys and plains."

And I answered: "As yet has my word not removed mountains, and what I have spoken has not reached man. I went, indeed, to men, but not yet have I attained to them."

Then was there again spoken to me without voice: "What know you thereof! The dew falls on the grass when the night is most silent."

And I answered: "They mocked me when I found and walked in my own path; and certainly did my feet then tremble.

And thus did they speak to me: you forgot the path before, now do you also forget how to walk!"

Then was there again spoken to me without voice: "What matter about their mockery! You are one who have unlearned to obey: now shall you command!

Know you not who is most needed by all? He who commands great things.

To execute great things is difficult: but the more difficult task is to command great things.

This is your most unpardonable obstinacy: you have the power, and you will not rule."

And I answered: "I lack the lion's voice for all commanding."

Then was there again spoken to me as a whispering: 'It is the still words which bring the storm. Thoughts that come with doves' footsteps guide the world.

O Zarathustra, you shall go as a shadow of that which is to come: thus will you command, and in commanding go foremost."

And I answered: "I am ashamed."

Then was there again spoken to me without voice: "You must yet become a child, and be without shame.

The pride of youth is still upon you; late have you become young: but he who would become a child must overcome even his youth."

And I considered a long while, and trembled. At last, however, did I say what I had said at first. "I will not."

Then did a laughing take place all around me. Alas, how that laughing lacerated my bowels and cut into my heart!

And there was spoken to me for the last time: "O Zarathustra, your fruits are ripe, but you are not ripe for your fruits!

So must you go again into solitude: for you shall yet become mellow."

And again was there a laughing, and it fled: then did it become still around me, as with a double stillness. I lay, however, on the ground, and the sweat flowed from my limbs.

—Now have you heard all, and why I have to return into my solitude. Nothing have I kept hidden from you, my friends.

But even this have you heard from me, who is still the most reserved of men – and will be so!

Ah, my friends! I should have something more to say to you! I should have something more to give to you! Why do I not give it? Am I then a niggard?'

When, however, Zarathustra had spoken these words, the violence of his pain, and a sense of the nearness of his departure from his friends came over him, so that he wept aloud; and no one knew how to console him. In the night, however, he went away alone and left his friends.

PART THREE

45. The Wanderer

THEN, when it was about midnight, Zarathustra went his way over the ridge of the isle, that he might arrive early in the morning at the other coast; because there he meant to embark. For there was a good roadstead there, in which foreign ships also liked to anchor: those ships took many people with them, who wished to cross over from the Blessed isles. So when Zarathustra thus ascended the mountain, he thought on the way of his many solitary wanderings from youth onwards, and how many mountains and ridges and summits he had already climbed.

'I am a wanderer and mountain-climber', said he to his heart. 'I love not the plains, and it seems I cannot long sit still.

And whatever may still overtake me as fate and experience – a wandering will be therein, and a mountain-climbing: in the end one experiences only oneself.

The time is now past when accidents could befall me; and what *could* now fall to my lot which would not already be my own!

It returns only, it comes home to me at last – my own Self, and such of it as has been long abroad, and scattered among things and accidents.

And one thing more do I know: I stand now before my last summit, and before that which has been longest reserved for me. Ah, my hardest path must I ascend! Ah, I have begun my most lonesome wandering!

Yet he who is of my nature does not avoid such an hour: the hour that says to him: Now only do you go the way to your greatness! Summit and abyss – these are now comprised together!

You go the way to your greatness: now has it become your last refuge, what was hitherto your last danger!

You go the way to your greatness: it must now be your best courage that there is no longer any path behind you!

You go the way to your greatness: here shall no one steal after you! Your foot itself has effaced the path behind you, and over it stands written: Impossibility.

And if all ladders henceforth fail you, then must you learn to mount upon your own head: how could you mount upward otherwise?

Upon your own head, and beyond your own heart! Now must the gentlest in you become the hardest.

He who has always much-indulged himself, sickens at last by his much-indulgence. Praises on what makes hardy! I do not praise the land where butter and honey – flow!

To learn to look away from oneself, is necessary in order to see many things – this hardiness is needed by every mountain-climber.

Yet he who is obtrusive with his eyes as a discerner, how can he ever see more of anything than its foreground!

But you, O Zarathustra, would view the ground of everything, and its background: thus must you mount even above yourself – up, upwards, until you have even your stars under you!

Yes! To look down upon myself, and even upon my stars: that only would I call my summit, that has remained for me as my last summit!'

Thus spoke Zarathustra to himself while ascending, comforting his heart with harsh maxims: for he was sore at heart as he had never been before. And when he had reached the top of the mountain-ridge, behold, there lay the other sea spread out before him; and he stood still and was long silent. The night, however, was cold at this height, and clear and starry.

'I recognize my destiny', said he at last, sadly. 'Well! I am ready. Now has my last lonesomeness begun.

Ah, this sombre, sad sea, below me! Ah, this sombre nocturnal vexation! Ah, fate and sea! To you must I now go down!

Before my highest mountain do I stand, and before my longest wandering: therefore must I first go deeper down than I ever ascended:

—Deeper down into pain than I ever ascended, even into its darkest flood! So wills my fate. Well! I am ready.

Whence come the highest mountains? So did I once ask. Then did I learn that they come out of the sea.

That testimony is inscribed on their stones, and on the walls of their summits. Out of the deepest must the highest come to its height.'

Thus spoke Zarathustra on the ridge of the mountain where it was cold: when, however, he came into the vicinity of the sea, and at last stood alone amongst the cliffs, then had he become weary on his way, and eagerer than ever before.

'Everything as yet sleeps', said he; 'even the sea sleeps. Drowsily and strangely does its eye gaze upon me.

But it breaths warmly – I feel it. And I feel also that it dreams. It tosses about dreamily on hard pillows.

Hark! Hark! How it groans with evil recollections! Or evil expectations?

Ah, I am sad along with you, you dusky monster, and angry with myself even for your sake.

Ah, that my hand has not strength enough! Gladly, indeed, would I free you from evil dreams!'

And while Zarathustra thus spoke, he laughed at himself with melancholy and bitterness. 'What! Zarathustra', said he, 'will you even sing consolation to the sea?

Ah, you amiable fool, Zarathustra, you too-blindly confiding one! But thus have you ever been: ever have you approached confidently all that is terrible.

Every monster would you caress. A whiff of warm breath, a little soft tuft on its paw: and immediately were you ready to love and lure it.

Love is the danger of the most lonesome one, love to anything, if it only live! Laughable, verily, is my folly and my modesty in love!'

Thus spoke Zarathustra, and laughed thereby a second time. Then, however, he thought of his abandoned friends – and as if he had done them a wrong with his thoughts, he upbraided himself because of his thoughts. And forthwith it came to pass that the laugher wept – with anger and longing wept Zarathustra bitterly.

46. *The Vision and the Riddle*

1

WHEN it got abroad among the sailors that Zarathustra was on board the ship – for a man who came from the Blessed isles had gone on board along with him, there was great curiosity and expectation. But Zarathustra kept silent for two days, and was cold and deaf with sadness; so that he neither answered looks nor questions. On the evening of the second day, however, he again opened his ears, though he still kept silent: for there were many curious and dangerous things to be heard on board the ship, which came from afar, and was to go still further. Zarathustra, however, was fond of all those who make distant voyages, and dislike to live without danger. And behold! When listening, his own tongue was at last loosened, and the ice of his heart broke. Then did he begin to speak thus:

'To you, the daring venturers and adventurers, and whoever has embarked with cunning sails upon frightful seas,

To you the enigma-intoxicated, the twilight-enjoyers, whose souls are allured by flutes to every treacherous gulf:

—For you dislike to grope at a thread with cowardly hand; and where you can divine, there do you hate to calculate.

To you only do I tell the enigma that I saw – the vision of the most lonesome one.

Gloomily walked I lately in corpse-coloured twilight – gloomily and sternly, with compressed lips. Not only one sun had set for me.

A path which ascended daringly among boulders, an evil, lonesome path, which neither herb nor shrub any longer cheered, a mountain-path, crunched under the daring of my foot.

Mutely marching over the scornful clinking of pebbles, trampling the stone that let it slip: thus did my foot force its way upwards.

Upwards: in spite of the spirit that drew it downwards, towards the abyss, the spirit of gravity, my devil and archenemy.

Upwards: although it sat upon me, half-dwarf, half-mole; paralysed, paralysing; dripping lead in my ear, and thoughts like drops of lead into my brain.

"O Zarathustra," it whispered scornfully, syllable by syllable, 'you stone of wisdom! you threw yourself high, but every thrown stone must – fall!

O Zarathustra, you stone of wisdom, you sling-stone, you star-destroyer! Yourself threw you so high, but every thrown stone – must fall!

Condemned of yourself, and to your own stoning: O Zarathustra, far indeed threw you your stone – but upon yourself will it recoil!"

Then was the dwarf silent; and it lasted long. The silence, however, oppressed me; and to be thus in pairs, one is verily lonesomer than when alone!

I ascended, I ascended, I dreamt, I thought, but everything oppressed me. A sick one did I resemble, whom bad torture wearies, and a worse dream reawakens out of his first sleep.

But there is something in me which I call courage: it has hitherto slain for me every dejection. This courage at last bade me stand still and say: "Dwarf! Thou! Or I!"—

For courage is the best killer, courage which attacks: for in every attack there is sound of triumph. Man, however, is the most courageous animal: thereby has he overcome every animal. With sound of triumph has he overcome every pain; human pain, however, is the sorest pain.

Courage kills also giddiness at abysses: and where does man not stand at abysses! Is not seeing itself – seeing abysses?

Courage is the best killer: courage kills also fellow-suffering. Fellow-suffering, however, is the deepest abyss: as deeply as man looks into life, so deeply also does he look into suffering.

Courage, however, is the best killer, courage which attacks: it kills even death itself; for it says: "Was that life? Well! Once more!"

In such speech, however, there is much sound of triumph. He who has ears to hear, let him hear.'

2

'"Halt, dwarf!" said I. "Either I – or you! I, however, am the stronger of the two: you knowest not my abysmal thought! It – could you not endure!"

Then happened that which made me lighter: for the dwarf sprang from my shoulder, the prying sprite! And it squatted on a stone in front of me. There was however a gateway just where we halted.

"Look at this gateway! Dwarf!" I continued, "it has two faces. Two roads come together here: these has no one yet gone to the end of.

This long lane backwards: it continues for an eternity. And that long lane forward – that is another eternity.

They are antithetical to one another, these roads; they directly abut on one another: and it is here, at this gateway that they come together. The name of the gateway is inscribed above: 'This Moment.'

But should one follow them further – and ever further and further on, think you, dwarf, that these roads would be eternally antithetical?"

"Everything straight lies," murmured the dwarf, contemptuously. "All truth is crooked; time itself is a circle."

"You spirit of gravity!" said I wrathfully, "do not take it too lightly! Or I shall let you squat where you squat, Haltfoot, and I carried you high!"

"Observe," continued I, "This Moment! From the gateway, This Moment, there runs a long eternal lane backwards: behind us lies an eternity.

Must not whatever can run its course of all things, have already run along that lane? Must not whatever can happen of all things have already happened, resulted, and gone by?

And if everything has already existed, what think you, dwarf, of This Moment? Must not this gateway also – have already existed?

And are not all things closely bound together in such wise that This Moment draws all coming things after it? Consequently – itself also?

For whatever can run its course of all things, also in this long lane outward – must it once more run!

And this slow spider which creeps in the moonlight, and this moonlight itself, and you and I in this gateway whispering together, whispering of eternal things – must we not all have already existed?

—And must we not return and run in that other lane out before us, that long weird lane – must we not eternally return?"

Thus did I speak, and always more softly: for I was afraid of my own thoughts, and arrear-thoughts. Then, suddenly did I hear a dog howl near me.

Had I ever heard a dog howl thus? My thoughts ran back. Yes! When I was a child, in my most distant childhood:

—Then did I hear a dog howl thus. And saw it also, with hair bristling, its head upwards, trembling in the still midnight, when even dogs believe in ghosts:

—So that it excited my commiseration. For just then went the full moon, silent as death, over the house; just then did it stand still, a glowing globe – at rest on the flat roof, as if on someone's property:

Thereby had the dog been terrified: for dogs believe in thieves and ghosts. And when I again heard such howling, then did it excite my commiseration once more.

Where was now the dwarf? And the gateway? And the spider? And all the whispering? Had I dreamt? Had I awakened? 'Twixt rugged rocks did I suddenly stand alone, dreary in the dreariest moonlight.

But there lay a man! And there! The dog leaping, bristling, whining – now did it see me coming – then did it howl again, then did it cry: had I ever heard a dog cry so for help?

And verily, what I saw, the like had I never seen. A young shepherd did I see, writhing, choking, quivering, with distorted countenance, and with a heavy black serpent hanging out of his mouth.

Had I ever seen so much loathing and pale horror on one countenance? He had perhaps gone to sleep? Then had the serpent crawled into his throat – there had it bitten itself fast.

My hand pulled at the serpent, and pulled: in vain! I failed to pull the serpent out of his throat. Then there cried out of me: "Bite! Bite! Its head off! Bite!" – so cried it out of me; my horror, my hatred, my loathing, my pity, all my good and my bad cried with one voice out of me.

You daring ones around me! You venturers and adventurers, and whoever of you have embarked with cunning sails on unexplored seas! You enigma-enjoyers!

Solve to me the enigma that I then beheld, interpret to me the vision of the most lonesome one!

For it was a vision and a foresight: what did I then behold in parable? And who is it that must come some day?

Who is the shepherd into whose throat the serpent thus crawled? Who is the man into whose throat all the heaviest and blackest will thus crawl?

—The shepherd however bit as my cry had admonished him; he bit with a strong bite! Far away did he spit the head of the serpent: and sprang up.

No longer shepherd, no longer man – a transfigured being, a light-surrounded being, that laughed! Never on earth laughed a man as he laughed!

O my brothers, I heard a laughter which was no human laughter, and now gnaws a thirst at me, a longing that is never allayed.

My longing for that laughter gnaws at me: oh, how can I still endure to live! And how could I endure to die at present!'

Thus spoke Zarathustra.

47. Involuntary Bliss

WITH such enigmas and bitterness in his heart did Zarathustra sail o'er the sea. When, however, he was four day-journeys from the Blessed isles and from his friends, then had he overcame all his pain: triumphantly and with firm foot did he again accept his fate. And then talked Zarathustra in this wise to his exulting conscience:

'Alone am I again, and like to be so, alone with the pure heaven, and the open sea; and again is the afternoon around me.

On an afternoon did I find my friends for the first time; on an afternoon, also, did I find them a second time: at the hour when all light becomes stiller.

For whatever happiness is still on its way 'twixt heaven and earth, now seeks for lodging a luminous soul: with happiness has all light now become stiller.

O afternoon of my life! Once did my happiness also descend to the valley that it might seek a lodging: then did it find those open hospitable souls.

O afternoon of my life! What did I not surrender that I might have one thing: this living plantation of my thoughts, and this dawn of my highest hope!

Companions did the creator once seek, and children of his hope: and lo, it turned out that he could not find them, except he himself should first create them.

Thus am I in the midst of my work, to my children going, and from them returning: for the sake of his children must Zarathustra perfect himself.

For in one's heart one loves only one's child and one's work; and where there is great love to oneself, then is it the sign of pregnancy: so have I found it.

Still are my children verdant in their first spring, standing nigh one another, and shaken in common by the winds, the trees of my garden and of my best soil.

And verily, where such trees stand beside one another, there are Blessed isles!

But one day will I take them up, and put each by itself alone: that it may learn solitude and defiance and prudence.

Gnarled and crooked and with flexible hardness shall it then stand by the sea, a living lighthouse of unconquerable life.

Yonder where the storms rush down into the sea, and the snout of the mountain drinks water, shall each on a time have his day and night watches, for his testing and recognition.

Recognized and tested shall each be, to see if he be of my type and lineage: if he be master of a long will, silent even when he speaks, and giving in such wise that he takes in giving:

—So that he may one day become my companion, a fellow-creator and fellow-enjoyer with Zarathustra: such a one as writes my will on my law-tablets, for the fuller perfection of all things.

And for his sake and for those like him, must I perfect myself: therefore do I now avoid my happiness, and present myself to every misfortune – for my final testing and recognition.

And verily, it were time that I went away; and the wanderer's shadow and the longest tedium and the still hour – have all said to me: "It is the highest time!"

The word blew to me through the keyhole and said "Come!" The door sprang subtly open to me, and said "Go!"

But I lay enchained to my love for my children: desire spread this snare for me – the desire for love – that I should become the prey of my children, and lose myself in them.

Desiring – that is now for me to have lost myself. I possess you, my children! In this possessing shall everything be assurance and nothing desire.

But brooding lay the sun of my love upon me, in his own juice stewed Zarathustra, then did shadows and doubts fly past me.

For frost and winter I now longed: "Oh, that frost and winter would again make me crack and crunch!" sighed I: then arose icy mist out of me.

My past burst its tomb, many pains buried alike woke up: fully slept had they merely, concealed in corpse-clothes.

So called everything to me in signs: "It is time!" But I – heard not, until at last my abyss moved, and my thought bit me.

Ah, abysmal thought, which are my thought! When shall I find strength to hear you burrowing, and no longer tremble?

To my very throat throbs my heart when I hear them burrowing! Your muteness even is like to strangle me, you abysmal mute one!

As yet have I never ventured to call you up; it has been enough that I – have carried you about with me! As yet have I not been strong enough for my final lion-wantonness and playfulness.

Sufficiently formidable to me has your weight ever been: but one day shall I yet find the strength and the lion's voice which will call you up!

When I shall have overcome myself therein, then will I overcome myself also in that which is greater; and a victory shall be the seal of my perfection!

Meanwhile do I sail along on uncertain seas; chance flatters me, smooth-tongued chance; forward and backward do I gaze, still see I no end.

As yet has the hour of my final struggle not come to me – or does it come to me perhaps just now? With insidious beauty do sea and life gaze upon me round about:

O afternoon of my life! O happiness before eventide! O haven upon high seas! O peace in uncertainty! How I distrust all of you!

Distrustful am I of your insidious beauty! Like the lover am I, who distrusts too sleek smiling.

As he pushes the best-beloved before him – tender even in severity, the jealous one, so do I push this blissful hour before me.

Away with you, you blissful hour! With you has there come to me an involuntary bliss! Ready for my severest pain do I here stand: at the wrong time have you come!

Away with you, you blissful hour! Rather harbour there – with my children! Hasten! and bless them before eventide with my happiness!

There, already approaches eventide: the sun sinks. Away – my happiness!'

Thus spoke Zarathustra. And he waited for his misfortune the whole night; but he waited in vain. The night remained clear and calm, and happiness itself came closer and closer to him. Towards morning, however, Zarathustra laughed to his heart, and said mockingly: 'Happiness runs after me. That is because I do not run after women. Happiness, however, is a woman.'

48. Before Sunrise

'O HEAVEN above me, you pure, you deep heaven! You abyss of light! Gazing on you, I tremble with divine desires.

Up to your height to toss myself – that is my depth! In your purity to hide myself – that is my innocence!

The God veils his beauty: thus hide you your stars. You speak not: thus proclaim you your wisdom to me.

Mute o'er the raging sea have you risen for me today; your love and your modesty make a revelation to my raging soul.

In that you came to me beautiful, veiled in your beauty, in that you spoke to me mutely, obvious in your wisdom:

Oh, how could I fail to divine all the modesty of your soul! Before the sun did you come to me – the most lonesome one.

We have been friends from the beginning: to us are grief, gruesomeness, and ground common; even the sun is common to us.

We do not speak to each other, because we know too much: we keep silent to each other, we smile our knowledge to each other.

Are you not the light of my fire? Have you not the sister-soul of my insight?

Together did we learn everything; together did we learn to ascend beyond ourselves to ourselves, and to smile uncloudedly:

—Uncloudedly to smile down out of luminous eyes and out of miles of distance, when under us constraint and purpose and guilt stream like rain.

And wandered I alone, for what did my soul hunger by night and in labyrinthine paths? And climbed I mountains, whom did I ever seek, if not you, upon mountains?

And all my wandering and mountain-climbing: a necessity was it merely, and a makeshift of the unhandy one: to fly only, wants my entire will, to fly into you!

And what have I hated more than passing clouds, and whatever taints you? And my own hatred have I even hated, because it tainted you!

The passing clouds I detest – those stealthy cats of prey: they take from you and me what is common to us – the vast unbounded Yes – and Amen – saying.

These mediators and mixers we detest – the passing clouds: those half-and-half ones, that have neither learned to bless nor to curse from the heart.

Rather will I sit in a tub under a closed heaven, rather will I sit in the abyss without heaven, than see you, you luminous heaven, tainted with passing clouds!

And oft have I longed to pin them fast with the jagged gold-wires of lightning, that I might, like the thunder, beat the drum upon their kettle-bellies:

—An angry drummer, because they rob me of your Yes and Amen! you heaven above me, you pure, you luminous heaven! You abyss of light! Because they rob you of my Yes and Amen.

For rather will I have noise and thunders and tempest-blasts, than this discreet, doubting cat-repose; and also amongst men do I hate most of all the soft-treaders, and half-and-half ones, and the doubting, hesitating, passing clouds.

And "he who cannot bless shall learn to curse!" – this clear teaching dropt to me from the clear heaven; this star stands in my heaven even in dark nights.

I, however, am a blesser and a Yes-sayer, if you be but around me, you pure, you luminous heaven! You abyss of light! Into all abysses do I then carry my beneficent Yes-saying.

A blesser have I become and a Yes-sayer: and therefore strove I long and was a striver, that I might one day get my hands free for blessing.

This, however, is my blessing: to stand above everything as its own heaven, its round roof, its azure bell and eternal security: and blessed is he who thus blesses!

For all things are baptized at the font of eternity, and beyond good and evil; good and evil themselves, however, are but fugitive shadows and damp afflictions and passing clouds.

It is a blessing and not a blasphemy when I teach that "above all things there stands the heaven of chance, the heaven of innocence, the heaven of hazard, the heaven of wantonness."

"Of Hazard" – that is the oldest nobility in the world; that gave I back to all things; I emancipated them from bondage under purpose.

This freedom and celestial serenity did I put like an azure bell above all things, when I taught that over them and through them, no "eternal Will" – wills.

This wantonness and folly did I put in place of that Will, when I taught that "In everything there is one thing impossible – rationality!"

A little reason, to be sure, a germ of wisdom scattered from star to star – this leaven is mixed in all things: for the sake of folly, wisdom is mixed in all things!

A little wisdom is indeed possible; but this blessed security have I found in all things, that they prefer – to dance on the feet of chance.

O heaven above me! You pure, you lofty heaven! This is now your purity to me, that there is no eternal reason-spider and reason-cobweb: That you are to me a dancing-floor for divine chances, that you are to me a table of the Gods, for divine dice and dice-players!

But you blush? Have I spoken unspeakable things? Have I abused, when I meant to bless you?

Or is it the shame of being two of us that makes you blush! Do you bid me go and be silent, because now – day comes?

The world is deep: and deeper than e'er the day could read. Not everything may be uttered in presence of day. But day comes: so let us part!

O heaven above me, you modest one! You glowing one! O you, my happiness before sunrise! The day comes: so let us part!'

Thus spoke Zarathustra.

49. Virtue That Diminishes

1

WHEN Zarathustra was again on the continent, he did not go straightway to his mountains and his cave, but made many wanderings and questionings, and ascertained this and that; so that he said of himself jestingly: 'Lo, a river that flows back to its source in many windings!' For he wanted to learn what had taken place among men during the interval: whether they had become greater or smaller. And once, when he saw a row of new houses, he marvelled, and said:

'What do these houses mean? No great soul put them up as its simile!

Did perhaps a silly child take them out of its toy-box? Would that another child put them again into the box!

And these rooms and chambers – can men go out and in there? They seem to be made for silk dolls; or for dainty-eaters, who perhaps let others eat with them.'

And Zarathustra stood still and meditated. At last he said sorrowfully: 'There has everything become smaller!

Everywhere do I see lower doorways: he who is of my type can still go therethrough, but – he must stoop!

Oh, when shall I arrive again at my home, where I shall no longer have to stoop – shall no longer have to stoop before the small ones!' – And Zarathustra sighed, and gazed into the distance.

The same day, however, he spoke on the virtue that makes small.

2

'I pass through this people and keep my eyes open: they do not forgive me for not envying their virtues.

They bite at me, because I say to them that for small people, small virtues are necessary – and because it is hard for me to understand that small people are necessary!

Here am I still like a cock in a strange farm-yard, at which even the hens peck: but on that account I am not unfriendly to the hens.

I am courteous towards them, as towards all small annoyances; to be prickly towards what is small, seems to me wisdom for hedgehogs.

They all speak of me when they sit around their fire in the evening – they speak of me, but no one thinks – of me!

This is the new stillness which I have experienced: their noise around me spreads a mantle over my thoughts.

They shout to one another: "What is this gloomy cloud about to do to us? Let us see that it does not bring a plague upon us!"

And recently did a woman seize upon her child that was coming to me: "Take the children away," cried she, "such eyes scorch children's souls."

They cough when I speak: they think coughing an objection to strong winds – they divine nothing of the boisterousness of my happiness!

"We have not yet time for Zarathustra" – so they object; but what matter about a time that "has no time" for Zarathustra?

And if they should altogether praise me, how could I go to sleep on their praise? A girdle of spines is their praise to me: it scratches me even when I take it off.

And this also did I learn among them: the praiser does as if he gave back; in truth, however, he wants more to be given him!

Ask my foot if their lauding and luring strains please it! To such measure and ticktack, it likes neither to dance nor to stand still.

To small virtues would they rather lure and laud me; to the ticktack of small happiness would they rather persuade my foot.

I pass through this people and keep my eyes open; they have become smaller, and ever become smaller: the reason thereof is their doctrine of happiness and virtue.

For they are moderate also in virtue, because they want comfort. With comfort, however, moderate virtue only is compatible.

To be sure, they also learn in their way to stride on and stride forward: that, I call their hobbling. – Thereby they become a hindrance to all who are in haste.

And many of them go forward, and look backwards thereby, with stiffened necks: those do I like to run up against.

Foot and eye shall not lie, nor give the lie to each other. But there is much lying among small people.

Some of them will, but most of them are willed. Some of them are genuine, but most of them are bad actors.

There are actors without knowing it amongst them, and actors without intending it, the genuine ones are always rare, especially the genuine actors.

Of man there is little here: therefore do their women masculinize themselves. For only he who is man enough, will – save the woman in woman.

And this hypocrisy found I worst amongst them, that even those who command feign the virtues of those who serve.

"I serve, you serve, we serve" – so chants here even the hypocrisy of the rulers – and alas! if the first lord be only the first servant!

Ah, even upon their hypocrisy did my eyes' curiosity alight; and well did I divine all their fly – happiness, and their buzzing around sunny window-panes.

So much kindness, so much weakness do I see. So much justice and pity, so much weakness.

Round, fair, and considerate are they to one another, as grains of sand are round, fair, and considerate to grains of sand.

Modestly to embrace a small happiness – that do they call 'submission'! and at the same time they peer modestly after a new small happiness.

In their hearts they want simply one thing most of all: that no one hurt them. Thus do they anticipate every one's wishes and do well to every one.

That, however, is cowardice, though it be called "virtue."

And when they chance to speak harshly, those small people, then do I hear therein only their hoarseness – every draught of air makes them hoarse.

Shrewd indeed are they, their virtues have shrewd fingers. But they lack fists: their fingers do not know how to creep behind fists.

Virtue for them is what makes modest and tame: therewith have they made the wolf a dog, and man himself man's best domestic animal.

"We set our chair in the midst" – so says their smirking to me – "and as far from dying gladiators as from satisfied swine."

That, however, is – mediocrity, though it be called moderation.'

3

'I pass through this people and let fall many words: but they know neither how to take nor how to retain them.

They wonder why I came not to revile venery and vice; and verily, I came not to warn against pickpockets either!

They wonder why I am not ready to abet and whet their wisdom: as if they had not yet enough of wiseacres, whose voices grate on my ear like slate-pencils!

And when I call out: "Curse all the cowardly devils in you, that would rather whimper and fold the hands and adore" – then do they shout: "Zarathustra is godless."

And especially do their teachers of submission shout this; – but precisely in their ears do I love to cry: "Yes! I am Zarathustra, the godless!"

Those teachers of submission! Wherever there is anything puny, or sickly, or scabby, there do they creep like lice; and only my disgust prevents me from cracking them.

Well! This is my sermon for their ears: I am Zarathustra the godless, who says: "Who is more godless than I, that I may enjoy his teaching?"

I am Zarathustra the godless: where do I find my equal? And all those are my equals who give to themselves their Will, and divest themselves of all submission.

I am Zarathustra the godless! I cook every chance in my pot. And only when it has been quite cooked do I welcome it as my food.

And verily, many a chance came imperiously to me: but still more imperiously did my Will speak to it, then did it lie imploringly upon its knees—

—Imploring that it might find home and heart with me, and saying flatteringly: 'See, O Zarathustra, how friend only comes to friend!"—

But why talk I, when no one has my ears! And so will I shout it out to all the winds:

You ever become smaller, you small people! You crumble away, you comfortable ones! You will yet perish—

—By your many small virtues, by your many small omissions, and by your many small submissions!

Too tender, too yielding: so is your soil! But for a tree to become great, it seeks to twine hard roots around hard rocks!

Also what you omit weaves at the web of all the human future; even your naught is a cobweb, and a spider that lives on the blood of the future.

And when you take, then is it like stealing, you small virtuous ones; but even among knaves honour says that "one shall only steal when one cannot rob."

"It gives itself" – that is also a doctrine of submission. But I say to you, you comfortable ones, that it takes to itself, and will ever take more and more from you!

Ah, that you would renounce all half-willing, and would decide for idleness as you decide for action!

Ah, that you understood my word: 'Do ever what you will – but first be such as can will.

Love ever your neighbour as yourselves – but first be such as love themselves—

—Such as love with great love, such as love with great contempt!" Thus speaks Zarathustra the godless.

But why talk I, when no one has my ears! It is still an hour too early for me here.

My own forerunner am I among this people, my own cockcrow in dark lanes.

But their hour comes! And there comes also mine! Hourly do they become smaller, poorer, unfruitfuller, poor herbs! poor earth!

And soon shall they stand before me like dry grass and prairie, and verily, weary of themselves – and panting for fire, more than for water!

O blessed hour of the lightning! O mystery before noontide! Running fires will I one day make of them, and heralds with flaming tongues:

—Herald shall they one day with flaming tongues: It comes, it is nigh, the great noontide!'

Thus spoke Zarathustra.

50. The Mount of Olives

'WINTER, a bad guest, sits with me at home; blue are my hands with his friendly hand-shaking.

I honour him, that bad guest, but gladly leave him alone. Gladly do I run away from him; and when one runs well, then one escapes him!

With warm feet and warm thoughts do I run where the wind is calm – to the sunny corner of my olive-mount.

There do I laugh at my stern guest, and am still fond of him; because he clears my house of flies, and quiets many little noises.

For he suffers it not if a gnat wants to buzz, or even two of them; also the lanes makes he lonesome, so that the moonlight is afraid there at night.

A hard guest is he, but I honour him, and do not worship, like the tenderlings, the pot-bellied fire-idol.

Better even a little teeth-chattering than idol-adoration! So wills my nature. And especially have I a grudge against all ardent, steaming, steamy fire-idols.

Him whom I love, I love better in winter than in summer; better do I now mock at my enemies, and more heartily, when winter sits in my house.

Heartily, verily, even when I creep into bed: there, still laughs and wantons my hidden happiness; even my deceptive dream laughs.

I, a – creeper? Never in my life did I creep before the powerful; and if ever I lied, then did I lie out of love. Therefore am I glad even in my winter-bed.

A poor bed warms me more than a rich one, for I am jealous of my poverty. And in winter she is most faithful to me.

With a wickedness do I begin every day: I mock at the winter with a cold bath: on that account grumbles my stern house-mate.

Also do I like to tickle him with a wax-taper, that he may finally let the heavens emerge from ashy-grey twilight.

For especially wicked am I in the morning: at the early hour when the pail rattles at the well, and horses neigh warmly in grey lanes:

Impatiently do I then wait, that the clear sky may finally dawn for me, the snow-bearded winter-sky, the hoary one, the white-head,

—The winter-sky, the silent winter-sky, which often stifles even its sun!

Did I perhaps learn from it the long clear silence? Or did it learn it from me? Or has each of us created it himself?

Of all good things the origin is a thousandfold, all good roguish things spring into existence for joy: how could they always do so – for once only!

A good roguish thing is also the long silence, and to look, like the winter-sky, out of a clear, round-eyed countenance:

—Like it to stifle one's sun, and one's inflexible solar will: verily, this art and this winter-roguishness have I learned well!

My best-loved wickedness and art is it, that my silence has learned not to betray itself by silence.

Clattering with diction and dice, I outwit the solemn assistants: all those stern watchers, shall my will and purpose elude.

That no one might see down into my depth and into my ultimate will – for that purpose did I create the long clear silence.

Many a shrewd one did I find: he veiled his countenance and made his water muddy, that no one might see therethrough and thereunder.

But precisely to him came the shrewder distrusters and nut -crackers: precisely from him did they fish his best-concealed fish!

But the clear, the honest, the transparent – these are for me the wisest silent ones: in them, so profound is the depth that even the clearest water does not – betray it.

You snow-bearded, silent, winter-sky, you round-eyed whitehead above me! Oh, you heavenly parable of my soul and its wantonness!

And must I not conceal myself like one who has swallowed gold – lest my soul should be ripped up?

Must I not wear stilts, that they may overlook my long legs – all those enviers and injurers around me?

Those dingy, fire-warmed, used-up, green-tinted, ill-natured souls – how could their envy endure my happiness!

Thus do I show them only the ice and winter of my peaks – and not that my mountain winds all the solar girdles around it!

They hear only the whistling of my winter-storms: and know not that I also travel over warm seas, like longing, heavy, hot south-winds.

They commiserate also my accidents and chances: but my word says: "Suffer the chance to come to me: innocent is it as a little child!"

How could they endure my happiness, if I did not put around it accidents, and winter-privations, and bear-skin caps, and enmantling snowflakes!

—If I did not myself commiserate their pity, the pity of those enviers and injurers!

—If I did not myself sigh before them, and chatter with cold, and patiently let myself be swathed in their pity!

This is the wise waggish-will and good-will of my soul, that it conceals not its winters and glacial storms; it conceals not its chilblains either.

To one man, solitude is the flight of the sick one; to another, it is the flight from the sick ones.

Let them hear me chattering and sighing with winter-cold, all those poor squinting knaves around me! With such sighing and chattering do I flee from their heated rooms.

Let them sympathize with me and sigh with me on account of my chilblains: "At the ice of knowledge will he yet freeze to death!" – so they mourn.

Meanwhile do I run with warm feet here and there on my olive-mount: in the sunny corner of my olive-mount do I sing, and mock at all pity.'

Thus sang Zarathustra.

51. Passing By

THUS slowly wandering through many peoples and divers cities, did Zarathustra return by round-about roads to his mountains and his cave. And behold, thereby came he unawares also to the gate of the great city. Here, however, a foaming fool, with extended hands, sprang forward to him and stood in his way. It was the same fool whom the people called 'the ape of Zarathustra:' for he had learned from him something of the expression and modulation of language, and perhaps liked also to borrow from the store of his wisdom. And the fool talked thus to Zarathustra:

'O Zarathustra, here is the great city: here have you nothing to seek and everything to lose.

Why would you wade through this mire? Have pity upon your foot! Spit rather on the gate of the city, and – turn back!

Here is the hell for hermits' thoughts: here are great thoughts seethed alive and boiled small.

Here do all great sentiments decay: here may only rattle-boned sensations rattle!

Smell you not already the shambles and cookshops of the spirit? Steams not this city with the fumes of slaughtered spirit?

See you not the souls hanging like limp dirty rags? – And they make newspapers also out of these rags!

Hear you not how spirit has here become a verbal game? Loathsome verbal swill does it vomit forth! And they make newspapers also out of this verbal swill.

They hound one another, and know not where! They inflame one another, and know not why! They tinkle with their pinchbeck, they jingle with their gold.

They are cold, and seek warmth from distilled waters: they are inflamed, and seek coolness from frozen spirits; they are all sick and sore through public opinion.

All lusts and vices are here at home; but here there are also the virtuous; there is much appointable appointed virtue:

Much appointable virtue with scribe-fingers, and hardy sitting-flesh and waiting-flesh, blessed with small breast-stars, and padded, haunchless daughters.

There is here also much piety, and much faithful spittle-licking and spittle-backing, before the God of Hosts.

"From on high," drips the star, and the gracious spittle; for the high, longs every starless bosom.

The moon has its court, and the court has its moon-calves: to all, however, that comes from the court do the mendicant people pray, and all appointable mendicant virtues.

"I serve, you serve, we serve" – so prays all appointable virtue to the prince: that the merited star may at last stick on the slender breast!

But the moon still revolves around all that is earthly: so revolves also the prince around what is earthliest of all – that, however, is the gold of the shopman.

The God of the Hosts of war is not the God of the golden bar; the prince proposes, but the shopman – disposes!

By all that is luminous and strong and good in you, O Zarathustra! Spit on this city of shopmen and return back!

Here flows all blood putridly and tepidly and frothily through all veins: spit on the great city, which is the great slum where all the scum froths together!

Spit on the city of compressed souls and slender breasts, of pointed eyes and sticky fingers –

—On the city of the obtrusive, the brazen – faced, the pen – demagogues and tongue – demagogues, the overheated ambitious:

Where everything maimed, ill-famed, lustful, untrustful, over – mellow, sickly-yellow and seditious, festers perniciously:

—Spit on the great city and turn back!'

Here, however, did Zarathustra interrupt the foaming fool, and shut his mouth.

'Stop this at once!' called out Zarathustra, 'long have your speech and your species disgusted me!

Why did you live so long by the swamp, that you yourself had to become a frog and a toad?

Flows there not a tainted, frothy, swamp-blood in your own veins, when you have thus learned to croak and revile?

Why went you not into the forest? Or why did you not till the ground? Is the sea not full of green islands?

I despise your contempt; and when you warned me – why did you not warn yourself?

Out of love alone shall my contempt and my warning bird take wing; but not out of the swamp!

They call you my ape, you foaming fool: but I call you my grunting-pig, by your grunting, you spoil even my praise of folly.

What was it that first made you grunt? Because no one sufficiently flattered you: therefore did you seat yourself beside this filth, that you might have cause for much grunting,

—That you might have cause for much vengeance! For vengeance, you vain fool, is all your foaming; I have divined you well!

But your fools'-word injures me, even when you are right! And even if Zarathustra's word were a hundred times justified, you would ever – do wrong with my word!'

Thus spoke Zarathustra. Then did he look on the great city and sighed, and was long silent. At last he spoke thus:

'I loathe also this great city, and not only this fool. Here and there – there is nothing to better, nothing to worsen.

Woe to this great city! And I would that I already saw the pillar of fire in which it will be consumed!

For such pillars of fire must precede the great noontide. But this has its time and its own fate.

This precept, however, give I to you, in parting, you fool: Where one can no longer love, there should one – pass by!'

Thus spoke Zarathustra, and passed by the fool and the great city.

52. The Apostates

1

'AH, LIES everything already withered and grey which but lately stood green and many-hued on this meadow! And how much honey of hope did I carry hence into my beehives!

Those young hearts have already all become old – and not old even! Only weary, ordinary, comfortable: they declare it: "We have again become pious."

Of late did I see them run forth at early morn with valorous steps: but the feet of their knowledge became weary, and now do they malign even their morning valour!

Many of them once lifted their legs like the dancer; to them winked the laughter of my wisdom: then did they bethink themselves. Just now have I seen them bent down – to crawl before the cross.

Around light and liberty did they once flutter like gnats and young poets. A little older, a little colder: and already are they mystifiers, and mumblers and mollycoddles.

Did perhaps their hearts despond, because solitude had swallowed me like a whale? Did their ear perhaps hearken yearningly-long for me in vain, and for my trumpet-notes and herald-calls?

—Ah! Ever are there but few of those whose hearts have persistent courage and exuberance; and in such remains also the spirit patient. The rest, however, are cowardly.

The rest: these are always the great majority, the common-place, the superfluous, the all-too-many – those all are cowardly!

Him who is of my type, will also the experiences of my type meet on the way: so that his first companions must be corpses and fools.

His second companions, however – they will call themselves his believers, will be a living host, with much love, much folly, much unbearded veneration.

To those believers shall he who is of my type among men not bind his heart; in those spring-times and many-hued meadows shall he not believe, who knows the fickly faint-hearted human species!

Could they do otherwise, then would they also will otherwise. The half-and-half spoil every whole. That leaves become withered, what is there to lament about that!

Let them go and fall away, O Zarathustra, and do not lament! Better even to blow amongst them with rustling winds,

—Blow amongst those leaves, O Zarathustra, that everything withered may run away from you the faster!'

2

'"We have again become pious" – so do those apostates confess; and some of them are still too pusillanimous thus to confess. To them I look into the eye, before them I say it to their face and to the blush on their cheeks: You are those who again pray!

It is shameful to pray! Not for all, but for you, and me, and whoever has his conscience in his head. For you it is shameful to pray!

You know it well: the faint-hearted devil in you, which would rather fold its arms, and place its hands in its bosom, and take it easier: this faint-hearted devil persuades you that "there is a God!"

Thereby, however, do you belong to the light-dreading type, to whom light never permits repose: now must you daily thrust your head deeper into obscurity and vapour!

And verily, you choose the hour well: for just now do the nocturnal birds again fly abroad. The hour has come for all light-dreading people, the vesper hour and leisure hour, when they do not – "take leisure."

I hear it and smell it: it has come – their hour for hunt and procession, not indeed for a wild hunt, but for a tame, lame, snuffling, soft-treaders', soft-prayers' hunt.

—For a hunt after susceptible simpletons: all mouse-traps for the heart have again been set! And whenever I lift a curtain, a night-moth rushes out of it.

Did it perhaps squat there along with another night-moth? For everywhere do I smell small concealed communities; and wherever there are closets there are new devotees therein, and the atmosphere of devotees.

They sit for long evenings beside one another, and say: "Let us again become like little children and say, 'good God!'" – ruined in mouths and stomachs by the pious confectioners.

Or they look for long evenings at a crafty, lurking cross-spider, that preaches prudence to the spiders themselves, and teaches that "under crosses it is good for web-spinning!"

Or they sit all day at swamps with angle-rods, and on that account think themselves profound; but whoever fishes where there are no fish, I do not even call him superficial!

Or they learn in godly-gay style to play the harp with a hymn – poet, who would rather harp himself into the heart of young girls: for he has tired of old girls and their praises.

Or they learn to shudder with a learned semi-madcap, who waits in darkened rooms for spirits to come to him – and the spirit runs away entirely!

Or they listen to an old roving howl- and growl-piper, who has learned from the sad winds the sadness of sounds; now pips he as the wind, and preaches sadness in sad strains.

And some of them have even become night-watchmen: they know now how to blow horns, and go about at night and awaken old things which have long fallen asleep.

Five words about old things did I hear last night at the garden-wall: they came from such old, sorrowful, arid night-watchmen.

"For a father he cares not sufficiently for his children: human fathers do this better!"—

"He is too old! He now cares no more for his children," – answered the other night-watchman.

"Has he then children? No one can prove it unless he himself prove it! I have long wished that he would for once prove it thoroughly."

"Prove? As if he had ever proved anything! Proving is difficult to him; he lays great stress on one's believing him."

"Ay! Ay! Belief saves him; belief in him. That is the way with old people! So it is with us also!"—

—Thus spoke to each other the two old night-watchmen and light-scarers, and tooted then sorrowfully on their horns: so did it happen last night at the garden-wall.

To me, however, did the heart writhe with laughter, and was like to break; it knew not where to go, and sunk into the midriff.

It will be my death yet – to choke with laughter when I see asses drunken, and hear night-watchmen thus doubt about God.

Has the time not long since passed for all such doubts? Who may nowadays awaken such old slumbering, light-shunning things!

With the old Deities has it long since come to an end: and verily, a good joyful Deity-end had they!

They did not "twilight" themselves to death – that do people fabricate! On the contrary, they – laughed themselves to death once on a time!

That took place when the ungodliest utterance came from a God himself – the utterance: 'There is but one God! You shall have no other gods before me!'—

—An old grim-beard of a God, a jealous one, forgot himself in such wise:

And all the gods then laughed, and shook upon their thrones, and exclaimed: "Is it not just divinity that there are gods, but no God?"

He that has an ear let him hear.'

Thus talked Zarathustra in the city he loved, which is surnamed The Pied Cow. For from here he had but two days to travel to reach once more his cave and his animals; his soul, however, rejoiced unceasingly on account of the nighness of his return home.

53. The Return Home

'O SOLITUDE! My home, solitude! Too long have I lived wildly in wild remoteness, to return to you without tears!

Now threaten me with the finger as mothers threaten; now smile upon me as mothers smile; now say just: "Who was it that like a whirlwind once rushed away from me?

—Who when departing called out: 'Too long have I sat with solitude; there have I unlearned silence!' That have you learned now – surely?

O Zarathustra, everything do I know; and that you were more forsaken amongst the many, you unique one, than you ever were with me!

One thing is forsakenness, another matter is solitude: that have you now learned! And that amongst men you will ever be wild and strange:

—Wild and strange even when they love you: for above all they want to be treated indulgently!

Here, however, are you at home and house with yourself; here can you utter everything, and unbosom all motives; nothing is here ashamed of concealed, congealed feelings.

Here do all things come caressingly to your talk and flatter you: for they want to ride upon your back. On every simile do you here ride to every truth.

Honestly and openly may you here talk to all things: and verily, it sounds as praise in their ears, for one to talk to all things – directly!

Another matter, however, is forsakenness. For, do you remember, O Zarathustra? When your bird screamed overhead, when you stood in the forest, irresolute, ignorant where to go, beside a corpse:

—When you spoke: 'Let my animals lead me! More dangerous have I found it among men than among animals:' – That was forsakenness!

And do you remember, O Zarathustra? When you sat in your isle, a well of wine giving and granting amongst empty buckets, giving and distributing amongst the thirsty:

– Until at last you alone sat thirsty amongst the drunken ones, and wailed nightly: 'Is taking not more blessed than giving? And stealing yet more blessed than taking?' – That was forsakenness!

And do you remember, O Zarathustra? When your still hour came and drove you forth from yourself, when with wicked whispering it said: 'Speak and perish!'—

—When it disgusted you with all your waiting and silence, and discouraged your humble courage: That was forsakenness!' –

O solitude! My home, solitude! How blessedly and tenderly speaks your voice to me!

We do not question each other, we do not complain to each other; we go together openly through open doors.

For all is open with you and clear; and even the hours run here on lighter feet. For in the dark, time weighs heavier upon one than in the light.

Here fly open to me all beings' words and word-cabinets: here all being wants to become words, here all becoming wants to learn of me how to talk.

Down there, however – all talking is in vain! There, forgetting and passing-by are the best wisdom: that have I learned now!

He who would understand everything in man must handle everything. But for that I have too clean hands.

I do not like even to inhale their breath; alas! That I have lived so long among their noise and bad breaths!

O blessed stillness around me! O pure odours around me! How from a deep breast this stillness fetches pure breath! How it hearkens, this blessed stillness!

But down there – there speaks everything, there is everything misheard. If one announce one's wisdom with bells, the shopmen in the marketplace will out-jingle it with pennies!

Everything among them talks; no one knows any longer how to understand. Everything falls into the water; nothing falls any longer into deep wells.

Everything among them talks, nothing succeeds any longer and accomplishes itself. Everything cackles, but who will still sit quietly on the nest and hatch eggs?

Everything among them talks, everything is out-talked. And that which yesterday was still too hard for time itself and its tooth, hangs today, outchamped and outchewed, from the mouths of the men of today.

Everything among them talks, everything is betrayed. And what was once called the secret and secrecy of profound souls, belongs today to the street-trumpeters and other butterflies.

O human hubbub, you wonderful thing! You noise in dark streets! Now are you again behind me: my greatest danger lies behind me!

In indulging and pitying lay ever my greatest danger; and all human hubbub wishes to be indulged and tolerated.

With suppressed truths, with fool's hand and befooled heart, and rich in petty lies of pity: thus have I ever lived among men.

Disguised did I sit amongst them, ready to misjudge myself that I might endure them, and willingly saying to myself: 'You fool, you do not know men!"

One unlearns men when one lives amongst them: there is too much foreground in all men – what can far-seeing, far-longing eyes do there!

And, fool that I was, when they misjudged me, I indulged them on that account more than myself, being habitually hard on myself, and often even taking revenge on myself for the indulgence.

Stung all over by poisonous flies, and hollowed like the stone by many drops of wickedness: thus did I sit among them, and still said to myself: "Innocent is everything petty of its pettiness!"

Especially did I find those who call themselves "the good," the most poisonous flies; they sting in all innocence, they lie in all innocence; how could they – be just towards me!

He who lives amongst the good – pity teaches him to lie. Pity makes stifling air for all free souls. For the stupidity of the good is unfathomable.

To conceal myself and my riches – that did I learn down there: for every one did I still find poor in spirit. It was the lie of my pity, that I knew in every one.

—That I saw and scented in every one, what was enough of spirit for him, and what was too much!

Their stiff wise men: I call them wise, not stiff – thus did I learn to slur over words.

The grave-diggers dig for themselves diseases. Under old rubbish rest bad vapours. One should not stir up the marsh. One should live on mountains.

With blessed nostrils do I again breathe mountain-freedom. Freed at last is my nose from the smell of all human hubbub!

With sharp breezes tickled, as with sparkling wine, sneezes my soul – sneezes, and shouts self-congratulatingly: "Health to you!"'

Thus spoke Zarathustra.

54. The Three Evils

1

'IN MY dream, in my last morning-dream, I stood today on a promontory – beyond the world; I held a pair of scales, and weighed the world.

Alas, that the rosy dawn came too early to me: she glowed me awake, the jealous one! Jealous is she always of the glows of my morning-dream.

Measurable by him who has time, weighable by a good weigher, attainable by strong pinions, divinable by divine nutcrackers: thus did my dream find the world:

My dream, a bold sailor, half-ship, half-hurricane, silent as the butterfly, impatient as the falcon: how had it the patience and leisure today for world-weighing!

Did my wisdom perhaps speak secretly to it, my laughing, wide-awake day-wisdom, which mocks at all "infinite worlds"? For it says: "Where force is, there becomes number the master: it has more force."

How confidently did my dream contemplate this finite world, not new-fangledly, not old-fangledly, not timidly, not entreatingly:

—As if a big round apple presented itself to my hand, a ripe golden apple, with a coolly-soft, velvety skin: thus did the world present itself to me:

—As if a tree nodded to me, a broad-branched, strong-willed tree, curved as a recline and a foot-stool for weary travellers: thus did the world stand on my promontory:

—As if delicate hands carried a casket towards me – a casket open for the delectation of modest adoring eyes: thus did the world present itself before me today:

—Not riddle enough to scare human love from it, not solution enough to put to sleep human wisdom: a humanly good thing was the world to me today, of which such bad things are said!

How I thank my morning-dream that I thus at today's dawn, weighed the world! As a humanly good thing did it come to me, this dream and heart-comforter!

And that I may do the like by day, and imitate and copy its best, now will I put the three worst things on the scales, and weigh them humanly well.

He who taught to bless taught also to curse: what are the three best cursed things in the world? These will I put on the scales.

Voluptuousness, passion for power, and selfishness: these three things have hitherto been best cursed, and have been in worst and falsest repute – these three things will I weigh humanly well.

Well! Here is my promontory, and there is the sea – it rolls here to me, shaggily and fawningly, the old, faithful, hundred-headed dog-monster that I love!

Well! Here will I hold the scales over the weltering sea: and also a witness do I choose to look on – you, the hermit-tree, you, the strong-odoured, broad-arched tree that I love!

On what bridge goes the now to the hereafter? By what constraint do the high stoop to the low? And what enjoins even the highest still – to grow upwards?

Now stand the scales poised and at rest: three heavy questions have I thrown in; three heavy answers carries the other scale.'

2

'Voluptuousness: to all hair-shirted despisers of the body, a sting and stake; and, cursed as "the world," by all the afterworldly: for it mocks and befools all erring, misinferring teachers.

Voluptuousness: to the rabble, the slow fire at which it is burnt; to all wormy wood, to all stinking rags, the prepared heat and stew furnace.

Voluptuousness: to free hearts, a thing innocent and free, the garden-happiness of the earth, all the future's thanks – overflow to the present.

Voluptuousness: only to the withered a sweet poison; to the lion-willed, however, the great cordial, and the reverently saved wine of wines.

Voluptuousness: the great symbolic happiness of a higher happiness and highest hope. For to many is marriage promised, and more than marriage,

—To many that are more unknown to each other than man and woman: and who has fully understood how unknown to each other are man and woman!

Voluptuousness: but I will have hedges around my thoughts, and even around my words, lest swine and libertine should break into my gardens!

Passion for power: the glowing scourge of the hardest of the heart-hard; the cruel torture reserved for the cruel themselves; the gloomy flame of living pyres.

Passion for power: the wicked gadfly which is mounted on the vainest peoples; the scorner of all uncertain virtue; which rides on every horse and on every pride.

Passion for power: the earthquake which breaks and upbreaks

all that is rotten and hollow; the rolling, rumbling, punitive demolisher of whited sepulchres; the flashing interrogative-sign beside premature answers.

Passion for power: before whose glance man creeps and crouches and drudges, and becomes lower than the serpent and the swine: until at last great contempt cries out of him,

Passion for power: the terrible teacher of great contempt, which preaches to their face to cities and empires: "Away with you!" – until a voice cries out of themselves: "Away with me!"

Passion for power: which, however, mounts alluringly even to the pure and lonesome, and up to self-satisfied elevations, glowing like a love that paints purple felicities alluringly on earthly heavens.

Passion for power: but who would call it passion, when the height longs to stoop for power! Nothing sick or diseased is there in such longing and descending!

That the lonesome height may not forever remain lonesome and self-sufficing; that the mountains may come to the valleys and the winds of the heights to the plains:

Oh, who could find the right prenomen and honouring name for such longing! "Giving virtue" – thus did Zarathustra. Once name the unnamable.

And then it happened also, and verily, it happened for the first time! That his word blessed selfishness, the wholesome, healthy selfishness, that springs from the powerful soul:

—From the powerful soul, to which the high body appertains, the handsome, triumphing, refreshing body, around which everything becomes a mirror:

—The pliant, persuasive body, the dancer, whose symbol and epitome is the self-enjoying soul. Of such bodies and souls the self-enjoyment calls itself "virtue."

With its words of good and bad does such self-enjoyment shelter itself as with sacred groves; with the names of its happiness does it banish from itself everything contemptible.

Away from itself does it banish everything cowardly; it says: "Bad – that is cowardly!" Contemptible seem to it the ever-solicitous, the sighing, the complaining, and whoever pick up the most trifling advantage.

It despises also all bitter-sweet wisdom: for verily, there is also wisdom that blooms in the dark, a night-shade wisdom, which ever sighs: "All is vain!"

Shy distrust is regarded by it as base, and every one who wants oaths instead of looks and hands: also all over-distrustful wisdom, for such is the mode of cowardly souls.

Baser still it regards the obsequious, doggish one, who immediately lies on his back, the submissive one; and there is also wisdom that is submissive, and doggish, and pious, and obsequious.

Hateful to it altogether, and a loathing, is he who will never defend himself, he who swallows down poisonous spittle and bad looks, the all-too-patient one, the all-endurer, the all-satisfied one: for that is the mode of slaves. Whether they be servile before gods and divine spurnings, or before men and stupid human opinions: at all kinds of slaves does it spit, this blessed selfishness!

Bad: thus does it call all that is spirit-broken, and sordidly-servile – constrained, blinking eyes, depressed hearts, and the false submissive style, which kisses with broad cowardly lips.

And spurious wisdom: so does it call all the wit that slaves, and hoary-headed and weary ones affect; and especially all the cunning, spurious-witted, curious-witted foolishness of priests!

The spurious wise, however, all the priests, the world-weary, and those whose souls are of feminine and servile nature – oh, how has their game all along abused selfishness!

And precisely that was to be virtue and was to be called virtue – to abuse selfishness! And "selfless" – so did they wish themselves with good reason, all those world-weary cowards and cross-spiders!

But to all those comes now the day, the change, the sword of judgment, the great noontide: then shall many things be revealed!

And he who proclaims the ego wholesome and sacred, and selfishness blessed, verily, he, the prognosticator, speaks also what he knows: "Behold, it comes, it is night, the great noontide!"'

Thus spoke Zarathustra.

55. The Spirit of Gravity

1

'MY MOUTHPIECE – is of the people: too coarsely and cordially do I talk for Angora rabbits. And still stranger sounds my word to all ink-fish and pen-foxes.

My hand – is a fool's hand: woe to all tables and walls, and whatever has room for fool's sketching, fool's scrawling!

My foot – is a horse-foot; therewith do I trample and trot over stick and stone, in the fields up and down, and am bedevilled with delight in all fast racing.

My stomach – is surely an eagle's stomach? For it prefers lamb's flesh. Certainly it is a bird's stomach.

Nourished with innocent things, and with few, ready and impatient to fly, to fly away – that is now my nature: why should there not be something of bird-nature therein!

And especially that I am hostile to the spirit of gravity, that is bird-nature: verily, deadly hostile, supremely hostile, originally hostile! Oh, where has my hostility not flown and misflown!

Thereof could I sing a song – and will sing it: though I be alone in an empty house, and must sing it to my own ears.

Other singers are there, to be sure, to whom only the full house makes the voice soft, the hand eloquent, the eye expressive, the heart wakeful: those do I not resemble.

2

He who one day teaches men to fly will have shifted all landmarks; to him will all landmarks themselves fly into the air; the earth will he christen anew – as "the light body."

The ostrich runs faster than the fastest horse, but it also thrusts its head heavily into the heavy earth: thus is it with the man who cannot yet fly.

Heavy to him are earth and life, and so wills the spirit of gravity! But he who would become light, and be a bird, must love himself: thus do I teach.

Not, to be sure, with the love of the side and infected, for with them stinks even self-love!

One must learn to love oneself – thus do I teach – with a wholesome and healthy love: that one may endure to be with oneself, and not go roving about.

Such roving about christens itself "brotherly love"; with these words has there hitherto been the best lying and dissembling, and especially by those who have been burdensome to every one.

And verily, it is no commandment for today and tomorrow to learn to love oneself. Rather is it of all arts the finest, subtlest, last and patientest.

For to its possessor is all possession well concealed, and of all treasure-pits one's own is last excavated – so causes the spirit of gravity.

Almost in the cradle are we apportioned with heavy words and worths: "good" and "evil" – so calls itself this dowry. For the sake of it we are forgiven for living.

And therefore suffers one little children to come to one, to forbid them betimes to love themselves – so causes the spirit of gravity.

And we – we bear loyally what is apportioned to us, on hard shoulders, over rugged mountains! And when we sweat, then do people say to us: "Yes, life is hard to bear!"

But man himself only is hard to bear! The reason thereof is that he carries too many extraneous things on his shoulders. Like the camel kneels he down, and lets himself be well laden.

Especially the strong load-bearing man in whom reverence resides. Too many extraneous heavy words and worths loads he upon himself – then seems life to him a desert!

And verily! Many a thing also that is our own is hard to bear! And many internal things in man are like the oyster – repulsive and slippery and hard to grasp;—

So that an elegant shell, with elegant adornment, must plead for them. But this art also must one learn: to have a shell, and a fine appearance, and sagacious blindness!

Again, it deceives about many things in man, that many a shell is poor and pitiable, and too much of a shell. Much concealed goodness and power is never dreamt of; the choicest dainties find no tasters!

Women know that, the choicest of them: a little fatter a little leaner – oh, how much fate is in so little!

Man is difficult to discover, and to himself most difficult of all; often lies the spirit concerning the soul. So causes the spirit of gravity.

He, however, has discovered himself who says: This is my good and evil: therewith has he silenced the mole and the dwarf, who say: "Good for all, evil for all."

Neither do I like those who call everything good, and this world the best of all. Those do I call the all – satisfied.

All-satisfiedness, which knows how to taste everything, that is not the best taste! I honour the refractory, fastidious tongues and stomachs, which have learned to say "I" and "Yes" and "No."

To chew and digest everything, however – that is the genuine swine-nature! Ever to say YEA – that has only the ass learned, and those like it!

Deep yellow and hot red – so wants my taste – it mixes blood with all colours. Yet he who whitewashes his house, betrays to me a whitewashed soul.

With mummies, some fall in love; others with phantoms: both alike hostile to all flesh and blood – oh, how repugnant are both to my taste! For I love blood.

And there will I not reside and abide where every one spits and spews: that is now my taste, rather would I live amongst thieves and perjurers. Nobody carries gold in his mouth.

Still more repugnant to me, however, are all lick-spittles; and the most repugnant animal of man that I found, did I christen "parasite": it would not love, and would yet live by love.

Unhappy do I call all those who have only one choice: either to become evil beasts, or evil beast-tamers. Amongst such would I not build my tabernacle.

Unhappy do I also call those who have ever to wait, they are repugnant to my taste – all the toll-gatherers and traders, and kings, and other landkeepers and shopkeepers.

I learned waiting also, and thoroughly so, but only waiting for myself. And above all did I learn standing and walking and running and leaping and climbing and dancing.

This however is my teaching: he who wishes one day to fly, must first learn standing and walking and running and climbing and dancing: one does not fly into flying!

With rope-ladders learned I to reach many a window, with nimble legs did I climb high masts: to sit on high masts of perception seemed to me no small bliss;—

—To flicker like small flames on high masts: a small light, certainly, but a great comfort to cast-away sailors and ship-wrecked ones!

By divers ways and wendings did I arrive at my truth; not by one ladder did I mount to the height where my eye roves into my remoteness.

And unwillingly only did I ask my way – that was always counter to my taste! Rather did I question and test the ways themselves.

A testing and a questioning has been all my travelling: and verily, one must also learn to answer such questioning! That, however, is my taste:

—Neither a good nor a bad taste, but my taste, of which I have no longer either shame or secrecy.

"This – is now my way, where is yours?" Thus did I answer those who asked me "the way." For the way – it does not exist!'

Thus spoke Zarathustra.

56. Old and New Tablets

1

'HERE do I sit and wait, old broken law-tablets around me and also new half-written law-tablets. When comes my hour?

—The hour of my descent, of my down-going: for once more will I go to men.

For that hour do I now wait: for first must the signs come to me that it is my hour – namely, the laughing lion with the flock of doves.

Meanwhile do I talk to myself as one who has time. No one tells me anything new, so I tell myself my own story.'

2

'When I came to men, then found I them resting on an old infatuation: all of them thought they had long known what was good and bad for men.

An old wearisome business seemed to them all talk of virtue; and he who wished to sleep well spoke of "good" and "bad" before retiring to rest.

This somnolence did I disturb when I taught that no one yet knows what is good and bad: unless it be the creator!

—It is he, however, who creates man's goal, and gives to the earth its meaning and its future: he only effects it that anything is good or bad.

And I bade them upset their old academic chairs, and wherever that old infatuation had sat; I bade them laugh at their great moralists, their saints, their poets, and their saviours.

At their gloomy sages did I bid them laugh, and whoever had sat admonishing as a black scarecrow on the tree of life.

On their great grave-highway did I seat myself, and even beside the carrion and vultures – and I laughed at all their bygone and its mellow decaying glory.

Like penitential preachers and fools did I cry wrath and shame on all their greatness and smallness. Oh, that their best is so very small! Oh, that their worst is so very small! Thus did I laugh.

Thus did my wise longing, born in the mountains, cry and laugh in me; a wild wisdom, verily! My great pinion-rustling longing.

And oft did it carry me off and up and away and in the midst of laughter; then flew I quivering like an arrow with sun-intoxicated rapture:

—Out into distant futures, which no dream has yet seen, into warmer souths than ever sculptor conceived, where gods in their dancing are ashamed of all clothes:

(That I may speak in parables and halt and stammer like the poets: and verily I am ashamed that I have still to be a poet!)

Where all becoming seemed to me dancing of gods, and wantoning of gods, and the world unloosed and unbridled and fleeing back to itself:

—As an eternal self-fleeing and re-seeking of one another of many gods, as the blessed self-contradicting, recommuning, and re-fraternizing with one another of many gods:

Where all time seemed to me a blessed mockery of moments, where necessity was freedom itself, which played happily with the goad of freedom:

Where I also found again my old devil and arch-enemy, the spirit of gravity, and all that it created: constraint, law, necessity and consequence and purpose and will and good and evil:

For must there not be that which is danced over, danced beyond? Must there not, for the sake of the nimble, the nimblest, be moles and clumsy dwarfs?'

3

'There was it also where I picked up from the path the word "Superman," and that man is something that must be overcome.

—That man is a bridge and not a goal – rejoicing over his noontides and evenings, as advances to new rosy dawns:

—The Zarathustra word of the great noontide, and whatever else I have hung up over men like purple evening-afterglows.

Also new stars did I make them see, along with new nights; and over cloud and day and night, did I spread out laughter like a gay-coloured canopy.

I taught them all my poetization and aspiration: to compose and collect into unity what is fragment in man, and riddle and fearful chance;—

—As composer, riddle-reader, and redeemer of chance, did I teach them to create the future, and all that has been – to redeem by creating.

The past of man to redeem, and every "It was" to transform, until the Will says: "But so did I will it! So shall I will it –"

—This did I call redemption; this alone taught I them to call redemption.—

Now do I await my redemption – that I may go to them for the last time.

For once more will I go to men: amongst them will my sun set; in dying will I give them my choicest gift!

From the sun did I learn this, when it goes down, the exuberant one: gold does it then pour into the sea, out of inexhaustible riches,

—So that the poorest fisherman rows even with golden oars! For this did I once see, and did not tire of weeping in beholding it. –

Like the sun will also Zarathustra go down: now sits he here and waits, old broken law–tablets around him, and also new law-tablets – half-written.'

4

'Behold, here is a new table; but where are my brothers who will carry it with me to the valley and into hearts of flesh?

Thus demands my great love to the remotest ones: be not considerate of your neighbour! Man is something that must be overcome.

There are many divers ways and modes of overcoming: see you thereto! But only a fool thinks: "man can also be overleapt."

Overcome yourself even in your neighbour: and a right which you can seize upon, shall you not allow to be given you!

What you do can no one do to you again. Lo, there is no requital.

He who cannot command himself shall obey. And many a one can command himself, but still sorely lacks self-obedience!'

5

'Thus wishes the type of noble souls: they desire to have nothing gratuitously, least of all, life.

He who is of the rabble wishes to live gratuitously; we others, however, to whom life has given itself – we are ever considering what we can best give in return!

And verily, it is a noble dictum which says: "What life promises us, that promise will we keep – to life!"

One should not wish to enjoy where one does not contribute to the enjoyment. And one should not wish to enjoy!

For enjoyment and innocence are the most bashful things. Neither like to be sought for. One should have them, but one should rather seek for guilt and pain!'

6

'O my brothers, he who is a firstling is ever sacrificed. Now, however, are we firstlings!

We all bleed on secret sacrificial altars, we all burn and broil in honour of ancient idols.

Our best is still young: this excites old palates. Our flesh is tender, our skin is only lambs' skin: how could we not excite old idol-priests!

In ourselves dwells he still, the old idol-priest, who broils our best for his banquet. Ah, my brothers, how could firstlings fail to be sacrifices!

But so wishes our type; and I love those who do not wish to preserve themselves, the down-going ones do I love with my entire love: for they go beyond.'

7

'To be true – that can few be! And he who can, will not! Least of all, however, can the good be true.

Oh, those good ones! Good men never speak the truth. For the spirit, thus to be good, is a malady.

They yield, those good ones, they submit themselves; their heart repeats, their soul obeys: yet he who obeys, does not listen to himself!

All that is called evil by the good, must come together in order that one truth may be born. O my brothers, are you also evil enough for this truth?

The daring venture, the prolonged distrust, the cruel No, the tedium, the cutting-into-the-quick – how seldom do these come together! Out of such seed, however – is truth produced!

Beside the bad conscience has hitherto grown all knowledge! Break up, break up, you discerning ones, the old law-tablets!'

8

'When the water has planks, when gangways and railings o'erspan the stream, verily, he is not believed who then says: 'All is in flux.'

But even the simpletons contradict him. "What?" say the simpletons, "all in flux? Planks and railings are still over the stream!

Over the stream all is stable, all the values of things, the bridges and bearings, all 'good' and 'evil': these are all stable!"—

Comes, however, the hard winter, the stream-tamer, then learn even the wittiest distrust, and verily, not only the simpletons then say: 'Should not everything – stand still?'

"Fundamentally stands everything still" – that is an appropriate winter doctrine, good cheer for an unproductive period, a great comfort for winter-sleepers and fireside-loungers.

"Fundamentally stands everything still": but contrary thereto, preaches the thawing wind!

The thawing wind, a bullock, which is no ploughing bullock – a furious bullock, a destroyer, which with angry horns breaks the ice! The ice however – breaks gangways!

O my brothers, is not everything at present in flux? Have not all railings and gangways fallen into the water? Who would still hold on to "good" and "evil"?

"Woe to us! Hail to us! The thawing wind blows!" – Thus preach, my brothers, through all the streets!'

9

'There is an old illusion – it is called good and evil. Around soothsayers and astrologers has hitherto revolved the orbit of this illusion.

Once did one believe in soothsayers and astrologers; and therefore did one believe, "Everything is fate: you shall, for you must!"

Then again did one distrust all soothsayers and astrologers; and therefore did one believe, 'Everything is freedom: you can, for you will!'

O my brothers, concerning the stars and the future there has hitherto been only illusion, and not knowledge; and therefore concerning good and evil there has hitherto been only illusion and not knowledge!'

10

'"You shall not rob! You shall not kill!" – such precepts were once called sacred; before them did one bow the knee and the head, and take off one's shoes.

But I ask you: Where have there ever been better robbers and killers in the world than such sacred precepts?

Is there not even in all life – robbing and killing? And for such precepts to be called sacred, was not truth itself thereby – slain?

—Or was it a sermon of death that called sacred what contradicted and dissuaded from life? – O my brothers, break up, break up for me the old law-tablets!'

11

'It is my sympathy with all the past that I see it is abandoned,

—Abandoned to the favour, the spirit and the madness of every generation that comes, and reinterprets all that has been as its bridge!

A great potentate might arise, an artful prodigy, who with approval and disapproval could strain and constrain all the past, until it became for him a bridge, a harbinger, a herald, and a cock-crowing.

This however is the other danger, and my other sympathy: he who is of the rabble, his thoughts go back to his grandfather, with his grandfather, however, does time cease.

Thus is all the past abandoned: for it might some day happen for the rabble to become master, and drown all time in shallow waters.

Therefore, O my brothers, a new nobility is needed, which shall be the adversary of all rabble and potentate rule, and shall inscribe anew the word "noble" on new law-tablets.

For many noble ones are needed, and many kinds of noble ones, for a new nobility! Or, as I once said in parable: "That is just divinity, that there are gods, but no God!"'

12

'O my brothers, I consecrate you and point you to a new nobility: you shall become procreators and cultivators and sowers of the future;—

—Verily, not to a nobility which you could purchase like traders with traders' gold; for little worth is all that has its price.

Let it not be your honour henceforth whence you come, but where you go! Your Will and your feet which seek to overcome you – let these be your new honour!

Not that you have served a prince – of what account are princes now! nor that you have become a bulwark to that which stands, that it may stand more firmly.

Not that your family have become courtly at courts, and that you have learned – gay-coloured, like the flamingo – to stand long hours in shallow pools:

(For ability-to-stand is a merit in courtiers; and all courtiers believe that to blessedness after death pertains – permission-to-sit!)

Nor even that a Spirit called Holy, led your forefathers into promised lands, which I do not praise: for where the worst of all trees grew – the cross, in that land there is nothing to praise!

– And verily, wherever this "Holy Spirit" led its knights, always in such campaigns did – goats and geese, and wry-heads and guy-heads run foremost!

O my brothers, not backward shall your nobility gaze, but outward! Exiles shall you be from all fatherlands and forefatherlands!

Your children's land shall you love: let this love be your new nobility, the undiscovered in the remotest seas! For it do I bid your sails search and search!

To your children shall you make amends for being the children of your fathers: all the past shall you thus redeem! This new table do I place over you!'

13

'"Why should one live? All is vain! To live – that is to thresh straw; to live – that is to burn oneself and yet not get warm."

Such ancient babbling still passes for 'wisdom'; because it is old, however, and smells mustily, therefore is it the more honoured. Even mould ennobles.

Children might thus speak: they shun the fire because it has burnt them! There is much childishness in the old books of wisdom.

And he who ever 'threshes straw,' why should he be allowed to rail at threshing! Such a fool one would have to muzzle!

Such persons sit down to the table and bring nothing with them, not even good hunger: and then do they rail: 'All is vain!'

But to eat and drink well, my brothers, is verily no vain art! Break up, break up for me the law-tablets of the never-joyous ones!'

14

'"To the clean are all things clean" – thus say the people. I, however, say to you: To the swine all things become swinish!

Therefore preach the visionaries and bowed-heads (whose hearts are also bowed down): "The world itself is a filthy monster."

For these are all unclean spirits; especially those, however, who have no peace or rest, unless they see the world from the backside – the afterworldly!

To those do I say it to the face, although it sound unpleasantly: the world resembles man, in that it has a backside, so much is true!

There is in the world much filth: so much is true! But the world itself is not therefore a filthy monster!

There is wisdom in the fact that much in the world smells badly: loathing itself creates wings, and fountain-divining powers!

In the best there is still something to loathe; and the best is still something that must be overcome!

O my brothers, there is much wisdom in the fact that much filth is in the world!'

15

'Such sayings did I hear pious afterworldly speak to their consciences, and verily without wickedness or guile, although there is nothing more guileful in the world, or more wicked.

"Let the world be as it is! Raise not a finger against it!"

"Let whoever will choke and stab and skin and scrape the people: raise not a finger against it! Thereby will they learn to renounce the world."

"And your own reason – this shall you yourself stifle and choke; for it is a reason of this world, thereby will you learn yourself to renounce the world."—

—Shatter, shatter, O my brothers, those old law-tablets of the pious! Tatter the maxims of the world-maligners!'

16

'"He who learns much unlearns all violent cravings" – that do people now whisper to one another in all the dark lanes.

"Wisdom wearies, nothing is worth while; you shall not crave!" – this new table found I hanging even in the public markets.

Break up for me, O my brothers, break up also that new table! The weary-o'-the-world put it up, and the preachers of death and the jailer: for lo, it is also a sermon for slavery:

Because they learned badly and not the best, and everything too early and everything too fast; because they ate badly: from thence has resulted their ruined stomach; –

—For a ruined stomach, is their spirit: it persuades to death! For verily, my brothers, the spirit is a stomach!

Life is a well of delight, but to him in whom the ruined stomach speaks, the father of affliction, all fountains are poisoned.

To discern: that is delight to the lion-willed! But he who has become weary, is himself merely "willed"; with him play all the waves.

And such is always the nature of weak men: they lose themselves on their way. And at last asks their weariness: "Why did we ever go on the way? All is indifferent!"

To them sounds it pleasant to have preached in their ears: "Nothing is worth while! You shall not will!" That, however, is a sermon for slavery.

O my brothers, a fresh blustering wind comes Zarathustra to all way-weary ones; many noses will he yet make sneeze!

Even through walls blows my free breath, and into prisons and imprisoned spirits!

Willing emancipates: for willing is creating: so do I teach. And only for creating shall you learn!

And also the learning shall you learn only from me, the learning well! He who has ears let him hear!'

17

There stands the boat – there goes it over, perhaps into vast nothingness – but who wills to enter into this "Perhaps"?

None of you want to enter into the death-boat! How should you then be world-weary ones!

World-weary ones! And have not even withdrawn from the earth! Eager did I ever find you for the earth, amorous still of your own earth-weariness!

Not in vain does your lip hang down: a small worldly wish still sits on it! And in your eye – floats there not a little cloud of unforgotten earthly bliss?

There are on the earth many good inventions, some useful, some pleasant: for their sake is the earth to be loved.

And many such good inventions are there, that they are like

woman's breasts: useful at the same time, and pleasant.

You world-weary ones, however! You earth-idlers! You, shall one beat with stripes! With stripes shall one again make you sprightly limbs.

For if you be not invalids, or decrepit creatures, of whom the earth is weary, then are you sly sloths, or dainty, sneaking pleasure-cats. And if you will not again run gaily, then shall you – pass away!

To the incurable shall one not seek to be a physician: thus teaches Zarathustra: so shall you pass away!

But more courage is needed to make an end than to make a new verse: that do all physicians and poets know well.'

18

'O my brothers, there are law-tablets which weariness framed, and law-tablets which slothfulness framed, corrupt slothfulness: although they speak similarly, they want to be heard differently.

See this languishing one! Only a span-breadth is he from his goal; but from weariness has he lain down obstinately in the dust, this brave one!

From weariness yawns he at the path, at the earth, at the goal, and at himself: not a step further will he go, this brave one!

Now glows the sun upon him, and the dogs lick at his sweat: but he lies there in his obstinacy and preferrs to languish:

—A span-breadth from his goal, to languish! You will have to drag him into his heaven by the hair of his head – this hero!

Better still that you let him lie where he has lain down, that sleep may come to him, the comforter, with cooling patter-rain.

Let him lie, until of his own accord he awakens, until of his own accord he repudiates all weariness, and what weariness has taught through him!

Only, my brothers, see that you scare the dogs away from him, the idle skulkers, and all the swarming vermin:

—All the swarming vermin of the "cultured," that – feast on the sweat of every hero!'

19.

'I form circles around me and sacred boundaries; ever fewer ascend with me ever higher mountains: I build a mountain-range out of ever holier mountains.

But wherever you would ascend with me, O my brothers, take care lest a parasite ascend with you!

A parasite: that is a reptile, a creeping, cringing reptile, that tries to fatten on your infirm and sore places.

And this is its art: it divines where ascending souls are weary, in your trouble and dejection, in your sensitive modesty, does it build its loathsome nest.

Where the strong are weak, where the noble are all-too-gentle – there builds it its loathsome nest; the parasite lives where the great have small sore-places.

What is the highest of all species of being, and what is the lowest? The parasite is the lowest species; yet he who is of the highest species feeds most parasites.

For the soul which has the longest ladder, and can go deepest down: how could there fail to be most parasites upon it?

—The most comprehensive soul, which can run and stray and rove furthest in itself; the most necessary soul, which out of joy flings itself into chance:

—The soul in Being, which plunges into Becoming; the possessing soul, which seeks to attain desire and longing:

—The soul fleeing from itself, which overtakes itself in the widest circuit; the wisest soul, to which folly speaks most sweetly:

—The soul most self – loving, in which all things have their current and counter – current, their ebb and their flow: oh, how could the loftiest soul fail to have the worst parasites?'

20

'O my brothers, am I then cruel? But I say: What falls, that shall one also push!

Everything of today – it falls, it decays; who would preserve it! But I – I wish also to push it!

Know you the delight which rolls stones into precipitous depths? – Those men of today, see just how they roll into my depths!

A prelude am I to better players, O my brothers! An example! Do according to my example!

And him whom you do not teach to fly, teach I pray you – to fall faster!'

21

'I love the brave: but it is not enough to be a swordsman, one must also know whereon to use swordsmanship!

And often is it greater bravery to keep quiet and pass by, that thereby one may reserve oneself for a worthier foe!

You shall only have foes to be hated; but not foes to be despised: you must be proud of your foes. Thus have I already taught.

For the worthier foe, O my brothers, shall you reserve yourselves: therefore must you pass by many a one,

—Especially many of the rabble, who din your ears with noise about people and peoples.

Keep your eye clear of their For and Against! There is there much right, much wrong: he who looks on becomes wroth.

Therein viewing, therein hewing – they are the same thing: therefore depart into the forests and lay your sword to sleep!

Go your ways! and let the people and peoples go theirs! Gloomy ways, verily, on which not a single hope glints any more!

Let there the trader rule, where all that still glitters is – traders' gold. It is the time of kings no longer: that which now calls itself the people is unworthy of kings.

See how these peoples themselves now do just like the traders: they pick up the small advantage out of all kinds of rubbish!

They lay lures for one another, they lure things out of one another, that they call "good neighbourliness." O blessed remote period when a people said to itself: "I will be – master over peoples!"

For, my brothers, the best shall rule, the best also wills to rule! And where the teaching is different, there – the best is lacking.'

22

'If they had – bread for nothing, alas! For what would they cry! Their maintainment – that is their true entertainment; and they shall have it hard!

Beasts of prey, are they: in their "working" – there is even plundering, in their "earning" – there is even over-reaching! Therefore shall they have it hard!

Better beasts of prey shall they thus become, subtler, cleverer, more man-like: for man is the best beast of prey.

All the animals has man already robbed of their virtues: that is why of all animals it has been hardest for man.

Only the birds are still beyond him. And if man should yet learn to fly, alas! To what height – would his rapacity fly!'

23

'Thus would I have man and woman: fit for war, the one; fit for maternity, the other; both, however, fit for dancing with head and legs.

And lost be the day to us in which a measure has not been danced. And false be every truth which has not had laughter along with it!'

24

'Your marriage-arranging: see that it be not a bad arranging! You have arranged too hastily: so there follows therefrom – marriage-breaking!

And better marriage-breaking than marriage-bending, marriage-lying! Thus spoke a woman to me: "Indeed, I broke the marriage, but first did the marriage break – me!"

The badly paired found I ever the most revengeful: they make every one suffer for it that they no longer run singly.

On that account want I the honest ones to say to one another: "We love each other: let us see to it that we maintain our love! Or shall our pledging be blundering?"

—"Give us a set term and a small marriage, that we may see if we are fit for the great marriage! It is a great matter always to be twain."

Thus do I counsel all honest ones; and what would be my love to the Superman, and to all that is to come, if I should counsel and speak otherwise!

Not only to propagate yourselves onwards but upwards – thereto, O my brothers, may the garden of marriage help you!'

25

'He who has grown wise concerning old origins, lo, he will at last seek after the fountains of the future and new origins.

O my brothers, not long will it be until new peoples shall arise and new fountains shall rush down into new depths.

For the earthquake – it chokes up many wells, it causes much languishing: but it brings also to light inner powers and secrets.

The earthquake discloses new fountains. In the earthquake of old peoples new fountains burst forth.

And whoever calls out: "Lo, here is a well for many thirsty ones, one heart for many longing ones, one will for many instruments": around him collects a people, that is to say, many attempting ones.

Who can command, who must obey – that is there attempted! Ah, with what long seeking and solving and failing and learning and re-attempting!

Human society: it is an attempt – so I teach – a long seeking: it seeks however the ruler!

—An attempt, my brothers! And no "contract"! Destroy, I pray you, destroy that word of the soft-hearted and half-and-half!'

26

'O my brothers! With whom lies the greatest danger to the whole human future? Is it not with the good and just?

—As those who say and feel in their hearts: "We already know what is good and just, we possess it also; woe to those who still seek thereafter!"

And whatever harm the wicked may do, the harm of the good is the harmfulest harm!

And whatever harm the world-maligners may do, the harm of the good is the harmfulest harm!

O my brothers, into the hearts of the good and just looked some one once on a time, who said: "They are the Pharisees." But people did not understand him.

The good and just themselves were not free to understand him; their spirit was imprisoned in their good conscience. The stupidity of the good is unfathomably wise.

It is the truth, however, that the good must be Pharisees – they have no choice!

The good must crucify him who creates his own virtue! That is the truth!

The second one, however, who discovered their country – the country, heart and soil of the good and just, it was he who asked: "Whom do they hate most?"

The creator, hate they most, him who breaks the law-tablets and old values, the breaker, him they call the law-breaker.

For the good – they cannot create; they are always the beginning of the end:

—They crucify him who writes new values on new law-tablets, they sacrifice to themselves the future – they crucify the whole human future!

The good – they have always been the beginning of the end.'

27

'O my brothers, have you also understood this word? And what I once said of the "last man"?—

With whom lies the greatest danger to the whole human future? Is it not with the good and just?

Break up, break up, I pray you, the good and just! O my brothers, have you understood also this word?'

28

'You flee from me? You are frightened? You tremble at this word?

O my brothers, when I enjoined you to break up the good, and the law-tablets of the good, then only did I embark man on his high seas.

And now only comes to him the great terror, the great outlook, the great sickness, the great nausea, the great seasickness.

False shores and false securities did the good teach you; in the lies of the good were you born and bred. Everything has been radically contorted and distorted by the good.

But he who discovered the country of "man," discovered also the country of "man's future." Now shall you be sailors for me, brave, patient!

Keep yourselves up betimes, my brothers, learn to keep yourselves up! The sea storms: many seek to raise themselves again by you.

The sea storms: all is in the sea. Well! Cheer up! You old seaman-hearts!

What of fatherland! There strives our helm where our children's land is! Therewards, stormier than the sea, storms our great longing!'

29

'"Why so hard!" – said to the diamond one day the charcoal; "are we then not near relatives?"—

Why so soft? O my brothers; thus do I ask you: are you then not – my brothers?

Why so soft, so submissive and yielding? Why is there so much negation and abnegation in your hearts? Why is there so little fate in your looks?

And if you will not be fates and inexorable ones, how can you one day – conquer with me?

And if your hardness will not glance and cut and chip to pieces, how can you one day – create with me?

For the creators are hard. And blessed must it seem to you to press your hand upon millenniums as upon wax,

—Blessed to write upon the will of millenniums as upon brass, harder than brass, nobler than brass. Entirely hard is only the noblest.

This new table, O my brothers, put I up over you: Become hard!'

30

'O you, my Will! You change of every need, my needfulness! Preserve me from all small victories!

You fatedness of my soul, which I call fate! you In-me! Over-me! Preserve and spare me for one great fate!

And your last greatness, my Will, spare it for your last – that you may be inexorable in your victory! Ah, who has not perished to his victory!

Ah, whose eye has not bedimmed in this intoxicated twilight! Ah, whose foot has not faltered and forgotten in victory – how to stand!

—That I may one day be ready and ripe in the great noon-tide: ready and ripe like the glowing ore, the lightning-bearing cloud, and the swelling milk-udder:

—Ready for myself and for my most hidden Will: a bow eager for its arrow, an arrow eager for its star:

—A star, ready and ripe in its noontide, glowing, pierced, blessed, by annihilating sun-arrows:

—A sun itself, and an inexorable sun-will, ready for annihilation in victory!

O Will, you change of every need, my needfulness! Spare me for one great victory!'

Thus spoke Zarathustra.

57. The Convalescent

1

ONE morning, not long after his return to his cave, Zarathustra sprang up from his couch like a madman, crying with a frightful voice, and acting as if someone still lay on the couch who did not wish to rise. Zarathustra's voice also resounded in such a manner that his animals came to him frightened, and out of all the neighbouring caves and lurking-places all the creatures slipped away

– flying, fluttering, creeping or leaping, according to their variety of foot or wing. Zarathustra, however, spoke these words:

'Up, abysmal thought out of my depth! I am your cock and morning dawn, you overslept reptile: Up! Up! My voice shall soon crow you awake!

Unbind the fetters of your ears: listen! For I wish to hear you! Up! Up! There is thunder enough to make the very graves listen!

And rub the sleep and all the dimness and blindness out of your eyes! Hear me also with your eyes: my voice is a medicine even for those born blind.

And once you are awake, then shall you ever remain awake. It is not my custom to awake great-grandmothers out of their sleep that I may bid them – sleep on!

You stir, stretch yourself, wheeze? Up! Up! Not wheeze, shall you, but speak to me! Zarathustra calls you, Zarathustra the godless!

I, Zarathustra, the advocate of living, the advocate of suffering, the advocate of the circuit – you do I call, my most abysmal thought!

Joy to me! you come, I hear you! My abyss speaks, my lowest depth have I turned over into the light!

Joy to me! Come here! Give me your hand – ha! let be! aha! – Disgust, disgust, disgust – alas to me!'

2

Hardly, however, had Zarathustra spoken these words, when he fell down as one dead, and remained long as one dead. When however he again came to himself, then was he pale and trembling, and remained lying; and for long he would neither eat nor drink. This condition continued for seven days; his animals, however, did not leave him day nor night, except that the eagle flew forth to fetch food. And what it fetched and foraged, it laid on Zarathustra's couch: so that Zarathustra at last lay among yellow and red berries, grapes, rosy apples, sweet-smelling herbage, and pine-cones. At his feet, however, two lambs were stretched, which the eagle had with difficulty carried off from their shepherds.

At last, after seven days, Zarathustra raised himself upon his couch, took a rosy apple in his hand, smelt it and found its smell pleasant. Then did his animals think the time had come to speak to him.

'O Zarathustra,' said they, 'now have you lain thus for seven days with heavy eyes: will you not set yourself again upon your feet?

Step out of your cave: the world waits for you as a garden. The wind plays with heavy fragrance which seeks for you; and all brooks would like to run after you.

All things long for you, since you have remained alone for seven days – step forth out of your cave! All things want to be your physicians!

Did perhaps a new knowledge come to you, a bitter, grievous knowledge? Like leavened dough lay you, your soul arose and swelled beyond all its bounds.'

—O my animals, answered Zarathustra, talk on thus and let me listen! It refreshes me so to hear your talk: where there is talk, there is the world as a garden to me.

How charming it is that there are words and tones; are not words and tones rainbows and seeming bridges 'twixt the eternally separated?

To each soul belongs another world; to each soul is every other soul a back-world.

Among the most alike does semblance deceive most delightfully: for the small gap is most difficult to bridge over.

For me – how could there be an outside-of-me? There is no outside! But this we forget on hearing tones; how delightful it is that we forget!

Have not names and tones been given to things that man may refresh himself with them? It is a beautiful folly, speaking; therewith dances man over everything.

How lovely is all speech and all falsehoods of tones! With tones dances our love on variegated rainbows.'

'O Zarathustra,' said then his animals, 'to those who think like us, things all dance themselves: they come and hold out the hand and laugh and flee – and return.

Everything goes, everything returns; eternally rolls the wheel of existence. Everything dies, everything blossoms forth again; eternally runs on the year of existence.

Everything breaks, everything is integrated anew; eternally builds itself the same house of existence. All things separate, all things again greet one another; eternally true to itself remains the ring of existence.

Every moment begins existence, around every "Here" rolls the ball "There." The middle is everywhere. Crooked is the path of eternity.'—

—'O you wags and barrel-organs!' answered Zarathustra, and smiled once more, how well do you know what had to be fulfilled in seven days:

—And how that monster crept into my throat and choked me! But I bit off its head and spat it away from me.

And you – you have made a lyre-lay out of it? Now, however, do I lie here, still exhausted with that biting and spitting-away, still sick with my own salvation.

And you looked on at it all? O my animals, are you also cruel? Did you like to look at my great pain as men do? For man is the cruel animal.

At tragedies, bull-fights, and crucifixions has he hitherto been happiest on earth; and when he invented his hell, behold, that was his heaven on earth.

When the great man cries: immediately runs the little man there, and his tongue hangs out of his mouth for very lusting. Yet he calls it his "pity."

The little man, especially the poet – how passionately does he accuse life in words! Hearken to him, but do not fail to hear the delight which is in all accusation!

Such accusers of life – them life overcomes with a glance of the eye. "You love me?" says the insolent one; "wait a little, as yet have I no time for you."

Towards himself man is the cruel animal; and in all who call themselves "sinners" and "bearers of the cross" and "penitents," do not overlook the voluptuousness in their plaints and accusations!

And I myself – do, I thereby want to be man's accuser? Ah, my animals, this only have I learned hitherto, that for man his evil is necessary for his best,

—That all that is evil is the best power, and the hardest stone for the highest creator; and that man must become better and more evil:

Not to this torture-stake was I tied, that I know man is bad, but I cried, as no one has yet cried:

"Ah, that his evil is so very small! Ah, that his best is so very small!"

The great disgust at man – it strangled me and had crept into my throat: and what the soothsayer had presaged: "All is alike, nothing is worth while, knowledge strangles."

A long twilight limped on before me, a fatally weary, fatally intoxicated sadness, which spoke with yawning mouth.

"Eternally he returns, the man of whom you are weary, the small man" – so yawned my sadness, and dragged its foot and could not go to sleep.

A cavern, became the human earth to me; its breast caved in; everything living became to me human dust and bones and mouldering past.

My sighing sat on all human graves, and could no longer arise: my sighing and questioning croaked and choked, and gnawed and nagged day and night:

—"Ah, man returns eternally! The small man returns eternally!"

Naked had I once seen both of them, the greatest man and the small man: all too like one another – all too human, even the greatest man!

All too small, even the greatest man! That was my disgust at man! And the eternal return also of the small man! That was my disgust at all existence!

Ah, Disgust! Disgust! Disgust!' – Thus spoke Zarathustra, and sighed and shuddered; for he remembered his sickness. Then did his animals prevent him from speaking further.

'Do not speak further, you convalescent!' – so answered his animals, 'but go out where the world waits for you like a garden.

Go out to the roses, the bees, and the flocks of doves! Especially, however, to the singing-birds, to learn singing from them!

For singing is for the convalescent; the sound ones may talk. And when the sound also want songs, then want they other songs than the convalescent.'

—'O you wags and barrel – organs, do be silent!' answered Zarathustra, and smiled at his animals. 'How well you know what consolation I created for myself in seven days!

That I have to sing once more – that consolation did I create for myself, and this convalescence: would you also make another lyre-lay thereof?'

—'Do not talk further,' answered his animals once more; 'rather, you convalescent, prepare for yourself first a lyre, a new lyre! For behold, O Zarathustra! For your new lays there are needed new lyres.

Sing and bubble over, O Zarathustra, heal your soul with new lays: that you may bear your great fate, which has not yet been any one's fate!

For your animals know it well, O Zarathustra, who you are and must become: behold, you are the teacher of the eternal return, that is now your fate!

That you must be the first to teach this teaching – how could this great fate not be your greatest danger and infirmity!

Behold, we know what you teach: that all things eternally return, and ourselves with them, and that we have already existed times without number, and all things with us.

You teach that there is a great year of Becoming, a prodigy of a great year; it must, like a sand-glass, ever turn up anew, that it may anew run down and run out:

—So that all those years are like one another in the greatest and also in the small, so that we ourselves, in every great year, are like ourselves in the greatest and also in the small.

And if you would now die, O Zarathustra, behold, we know also how you would then speak to yourself: but your animals beseech you not to die yet!

You would speak, and without trembling, buoyant rather with bliss, for a great weight and worry would be taken from you, you patientest one!

"Now do I die and disappear," would you say, "and in a moment I am nothing. Souls are as mortal as bodies.

But the plexus of causes returns in which I am intertwined, it will again create me! I myself pertain to the causes of the eternal return.

I come again with this sun, with this earth, with this eagle, with this serpent – not to a new life, or a better life, or a similar life:

—I come again eternally to this identical and selfsame life, in its greatest and its small, to teach again the eternal return of all things,

—To speak again the word of the great noontide of earth and man, to announce again to man the Superman.

I have spoken my word. I break down by my word: so wills my eternal fate – as announcer do I perish!

The hour has now come for the down-goer to bless himself. Thus – ends Zarathustra's down-going".'—

When the animals had spoken these words they were silent and waited, so that Zarathustra might say something to them; but Zarathustra did not hear that they were silent. On the contrary, he lay quietly with closed eyes like a person sleeping, although he did not sleep; for he communed just then with his soul. The serpent, however, and the eagle, when they found him silent in such wise, respected the great stillness around him, and prudently retired.

58. *The Great Longing*

'O MY soul, I have taught you to say "today" as "once on a time" and "formerly," and to dance your measure over every Here and There and Yonder.

O my soul, I delivered you from all by-places, I brushed down from you dust and spiders and twilight.

O my soul, I washed the petty shame and the by-place virtue from you, and persuaded you to stand naked before the eyes of the sun.

With the storm that is called "spirit" did I blow over your surging sea; all clouds did I blow away from it; I strangled even the strangler called "sin."

O my soul, I gave you the right to say No like the storm, and to say Yes as the open heaven says Yes: calm as the light remain you, and now walk through denying storms.

O my soul, I restored to you liberty over the created and the uncreated; and who knows, as you know, the voluptuousness of the future?

O my soul, I taught you the contempt which does not come like worm-eating, the great, the loving contempt, which loves most where it contemns most.

O my soul, I taught you so to persuade that you persuade even the grounds themselves to you: like the sun, which persuades even the sea to its height.

O my soul, I have taken from you all obeying and knee-bending and homage-paying; I have myself given you the names, "Change of need" and "Fate."

O my soul, I have given you new names and gay-coloured playthings, I have called you "Fate" and "the Circuit of circuits" and "the Navel-string of time" and "the Azure bell."

O my soul, to your domain gave I all wisdom to drink all new wines, and also all immemorially old strong wines of wisdom.

O my soul, every sun shed I upon you, and every night and every silence and every longing: then grew you up for me as a vine.

O my soul, exuberant and heavy do you now stand forth, a vine with swelling udders and full clusters of brown golden grapes:

—Filled and weighted by your happiness, waiting from superabundance, and yet ashamed of your waiting.

O my soul, there is nowhere a soul which could be more loving and more comprehensive and more extensive! Where could future and past be closer together than with you?

O my soul, I have given you everything, and all my hands have become empty by you: and now! Now say you to me, smiling and full of melancholy: "Which of us owes thanks?

—Does the giver not owe thanks because the receiver received? Is giving not a necessity? Is receiving not – pitying?"

O my soul, I understand the smiling of your melancholy: your over-abundance itself now stretches out longing hands!

Your fullness looks forth over raging seas, and seeks and waits: the longing of over-fullness looks forth from the smiling heaven of your eyes!

And verily, O my soul! Who could see your smiling and not melt into tears? The angels themselves melt into tears through the over-graciousness of your smiling.

Your graciousness and over-graciousness, is it which will not complain and weep: and yet, O my soul, longs your smiling for tears, and your trembling mouth for sobs.

"Is not all weeping complaining? And all complaining, accusing?" Thus speak you to yourself; and therefore, O my soul, will you rather smile than pour forth your grief –

—Than in gushing tears pour forth all your grief concerning your fulness, and concerning the craving of the vine for the vintager and vintage-knife!

But will you not weep, will you not weep forth your purple melancholy, then will you have to sing, O my soul! Behold, I smile myself, who foretell you this:

—You will have to sing with passionate song, until all seas turn calm to hearken to your longing,

—Until over calm longing seas the bark glides, the golden marvel, around the gold of which all good, bad, and marvellous things frisk:

—Also many large and small animals, and everything that has light marvellous feet, so that it can run on violet-blue paths,

—Towards the golden marvel, the spontaneous bark, and its master: he, however, is the vintager who waits with the diamond vintage-knife,

—Your great deliverer, O my soul, the nameless one – for whom future songs only will find names! And verily, already has your breath the fragrance of future songs,

—Already glow you and dream, already drink you thirstily at all deep echoing wells of consolation, already reposes your melancholy in the bliss of future songs!—

O my soul, now have I given you all, and even my last possession, and all my hands have become empty by you: that I bade you sing, behold, that was my last thing to give!

That I bade you sing, say now, say: which of us now – owes thanks? – Better still, however: sing to me, sing, O my soul! And let me thank you!'

Thus spoke Zarathustra.

59. The Second Dance Song

1

'INTO thy eyes gazed I lately, O Life: gold saw I gleam in your night-eyes, my heart stood still with delight:

—A golden bark saw I gleam on darkened waters, a sinking, drinking, reblinking, golden swing-bark!

At my dance-frantic foot, do you cast a glance, a laughing, questioning, melting, thrown glance:

Twice only moved you your rattle with your little hands – then did my feet swing with dance-fury.

My heels reared aloft, my toes they hearkened, you they would know: has not the dancer his ear – in his toe!

To you did I spring: then fled you back from my bound; and towards me waved your fleeing, flying tresses round!

Away from you did I spring, and from your snaky tresses: then stood you there half-turned, and in your eye caresses.

With crooked glances – do you teach me crooked courses; on crooked courses learn my feet – crafty fancies!

I fear you near, I love you far; your flight allures me, your seeking secures me: I suffer, but for you, what would I not gladly bear!

For you, whose coldness inflames, whose hatred misleads, whose flight enchains, whose mockery – pleads:

—Who would not hate you, you great bindress, in windress, temptress, seekress, findress! Who would not love you, you innocent, impatient, wind-swift, child-eyed sinner!

Where pull you me now, you paragon and tomboy? And now fool you me fleeing; you sweet romp does annoy!

I dance after you, I follow even faint traces lonely. Where are you? Give me your hand! Or your finger only!

Here are caves and thickets: we shall go astray! Halt! Stand still! See you not owls and bats in fluttering fray?

You bat! You owl! You would play me foul? Where are we? From the dogs have you learned thus to bark and howl.

You gnash on me sweetly with little white teeth; your evil eyes shoot out upon me, your curly little mane from underneath!

This is a dance over stock and stone: I am the hunter, will you be my hound, or my chamois anon?

Now beside me! And quickly, wickedly springing! Now up! And over! Alas! I have fallen myself overswinging!

Oh, see me lying, you arrogant one, and imploring grace! Gladly would I walk with you – in some lovelier place!

—In the paths of love, through bushes variegated, quiet, trim! Or there along the lake, where gold-fishes dance and swim!

You are now a-weary? There above are sheep and sun-set stripes: is it not sweet to sleep – the shepherd pipes?

You are so very weary? I carry you there; let just your arm sink!

And are you thirsty – I should have something; but your mouth would not like it to drink!

—Oh, that cursed, nimble, supple serpent and lurking-witch! Where are you gone? But in my face do I feel through your hand, two spots and red blotches itch!

I am verily weary of it, ever your sheepish shepherd to be. You witch, if I have hitherto sung to you, now shall you – cry to me!

To the rhythm of my whip shall you dance and cry! I forget not my whip? – Not I!'—

2

'Then did Life answer me thus, and kept thereby her fine ears closed:

"O Zarathustra! Crack not so terribly with your whip! You know surely that noise kills thought, and just now there came to me such delicate thoughts.

We are both of us genuine ne'er-do-wells and ne'er-do-ills. Beyond good and evil found we our island and our green meadow – we two alone! Therefore must we be friendly to each other!

And even should we not love each other from the bottom of our hearts, must we then have a grudge against each other if we do not love each other perfectly?

And that I am friendly to you, and often too friendly, that know you: and the reason is that I am envious of your Wisdom. Ah, this mad old fool, Wisdom!

If your Wisdom should one day run away from you, ah! Then would also my love run away from you quickly."—

Then did Life look thoughtfully behind and around, and said softly: "O Zarathustra, you are not faithful enough to me!

You love me not nearly so much as you say; I know you think of soon leaving me.

There is an old heavy, heavy, booming-clock: it booms by night up to your cave:

—When you hear this clock strike the hours at midnight, then think you between one and twelve thereon—

—You think thereon, O Zarathustra, I know it – of soon leaving me!"—

"Yes," answered I, hesitatingly, "but you know it also" – And I said something into her ear, in amongst her confused, yellow, foolish tresses.

"You know that, O Zarathustra? That knows no one—"

And we gazed at each other, and looked at the green meadow o'er which the cool evening was just passing, and we wept together. – Then, however, was Life dearer to me than all my Wisdom had ever been.'

Thus spoke Zarathustra.

3

One!

'O man! Take heed!'

Two!

'What says deep midnight's voice indeed?'

Three!

'I slept my sleep—

Four!

'From deepest dream I've woke and plead: '

Five!

'The world is deep,'

Six!

'And deeper than the day could read.'

Seven!

'Deep is its woe—'

Eight!

'Joy – deeper still than grief can be:'

Nine!

'Woe says: Hence! Go!'

Ten!

'But joys all want eternity—'

Eleven!

'Want deep profound eternity!'

Twelve!

60. The Seven Seals (or, The Yes and Amen Song)

1

'IF I be a diviner and full of the divining spirit which wanders on high mountain-ridges, 'twixt two seas,

Wanders 'twixt the past and the future as a heavy cloud – hostile to sultry plains, and to all that is weary and can neither die nor live:

Ready for lightning in its dark bosom, and for the redeeming flash of light, charged with lightnings which say Yes! which laugh Yes! ready for divining flashes of lightning:

—Blessed, however, is he who is thus charged! And verily, long must he hang like a heavy tempest on the mountain, who shall one day kindle the light of the future!

Oh, how could I not be ardent for Eternity and for the marriage-ring of rings – the ring of the return?

Never yet have I found the woman by whom I should like to have children, unless it be this woman whom I love: for I love you, O Eternity!

For I love you, O Eternity!'

2

'If ever my wrath has burst graves, shifted landmarks, or rolled old shattered law-tablets into precipitous depths:

If ever my scorn has scattered mouldered words to the winds, and if I have come like a besom to cross-spiders, and as a cleansing wind to old charnel-houses:

If ever I have sat rejoicing where old gods lie buried, world-blessing, world-loving, beside the monuments of old world-maligners:

—For even churches and gods' – graves do I love, if only heaven looks through their ruined roofs with pure eyes; gladly do I sit like grass and red poppies on ruined churches –

Oh, how could I not be ardent for Eternity, and for the marriage – ring of rings – the ring of the return?

Never yet have I found the woman by whom I should like to have children, unless it be this woman whom I love: for I love you, O Eternity!

For I love you, O Eternity!'

3

'If ever a breath has come to me of the creative breath, and of the heavenly necessity which compels even chances to dance star-dances:

If ever I have laughed with the laughter of the creative lightning, to which the long thunder of the deed follows, grumbling, but obedient:

If ever I have played dice with the gods at the divine table of the earth, so that the earth quaked and ruptured, and snorted forth fire-streams:

—For a divine table is the earth, and trembling with new active dictums and dice-casts of the gods:

Oh, how could I not be ardent for Eternity, and for the marriage-ring of rings – the ring of the return?

Never yet have I found the woman by whom I should like to have children, unless it be this woman whom I love: for I love you, O Eternity!

For I love you, O Eternity!'

4

'If ever I have drunk a full draught of the foaming spice – and confection-bowl in which all things are well mixed:

If ever my hand has mingled the furthest with the nearest, fire with spirit, joy with sorrow, and the harshest with the kindest:

If I myself am a grain of the saving salt which makes everything in the confection-bowl mix well:

—For there is a salt which unites good with evil; and even the evilest is worthy, as spicing and as final over-foaming:

Oh, how could I not be ardent for Eternity, and for the marriage-ring of rings – the ring of the return?

Never yet have I found the woman by whom I should like to have children, unless it be this woman whom I love: for I love you, O Eternity!

For I love you, O Eternity!'

5

'If I be fond of the sea, and all that is of the sea, and fondest of it when it angrily contradicts me:

If the exploring delight be in me, which impels sails to the undiscovered, if the seafarer's delight be in my delight:

If ever my rejoicing has called out: "The shore has vanished, now has fallen from me the last chain—

The boundless roars around me, far away sparkle for me space and time, well! Cheer up! Old heart!"—

Oh, how could I not be ardent for Eternity, and for the marriage-ring of rings – the ring of the return?

Never yet have I found the woman by whom I should like to have children, unless it be this woman whom I love: for I love you, O Eternity!

For I love you, O Eternity!'

6

'If my virtue be a dancer's virtue, and if I have often sprung with both feet into golden-emerald rapture:

If my wickedness be a laughing wickedness, at home among rose-banks and hedges of lilies:

—or in laughter is all evil present, but it is sanctified and absolved by its own bliss:

And if it be my Alpha and Omega that everything heavy shall become light, everybody a dancer, and every spirit a bird: and verily, that is my Alpha and Omega!

Oh, how could I not be ardent for Eternity, and for the marriage-ring of rings – the ring of the return?

Never yet have I found the woman by whom I should like to have children, unless it be this woman whom I love: for I love you, O Eternity!

For I love you, O Eternity!'

7

'If ever I have spread out a tranquil heaven above me, and have flown into my own heaven with my own pinions:

If I have swum playfully in profound luminous distances, and if my freedom's avian wisdom has come to me:

—Thus however speaks avian wisdom: 'Lo, there is no above and no below! Throw yourself about, outward, backward, you light one! Sing! Speak no more!

—Are not all words made for the heavy? Do not all words lie to the light ones? Sing! speak no more!'—

Oh, how could I not be ardent for Eternity, and for the marriage-ring of rings – the ring of the return?

Never yet have I found the woman by whom I should like to have children, unless it be this woman whom I love: for I love you, O Eternity!

For I love you, O Eternity!'

PART FOUR

61. The Honey Sacrifice

—AND again passed moons and years over Zarathustra's soul, and he heeded it not; his hair, however, became white. One day when he sat on a stone in front of his cave, and gazed calmly into the distance – one there gazes out on the sea, and away beyond sinuous abysses, then went his animals thoughtfully round about him, and at last set themselves in front of him.

'O Zarathustra,' said they, 'gaze you out perhaps for your happiness?' – 'Of what account is my happiness!' answered he, 'I have long ceased to strive any more for happiness, I strive for my work.' – 'O Zarathustra,' said the animals once more, 'that say you as one who has overmuch of good things. Lie you not in a sky-blue lake of happiness?' – 'You wags,' answered Zarathustra, and smiled, 'how well did you choose the simile! But you know also that my happiness is heavy, and not like a fluid wave of water: it presses me and will not leave me, and is like molten pitch.'—

Then went his animals again thoughtfully around him, and placed themselves once more in front of him. 'O Zarathustra,' said they, 'it is consequently *for that reason* that you yourself always becomes yellower and darker, although your hair looks white and flaxen? Lo, you sit in your pitch!' – 'What do you say, my animals?' said Zarathustra, laughing; 'verily I reviled when I spoke of pitch. As it happens with me, so is it with all fruits that turn ripe. It is the *honey* in my veins that makes my blood thicker, and also my soul stiller.' – 'So will it be, O Zarathustra,' answered his animals, and pressed up to him; 'but will you not today ascend a high mountain? The air is pure, and today one sees more of the world than ever.' – 'Yes, my animals,' answered he, 'you counsel admirably and according to my heart: I will today ascend a high mountain! But see that honey is there ready to hand, yellow, white, good, ice-cool, golden-comb-honey. For know that when aloft I will make the honey-sacrifice.'—

When Zarathustra, however, was aloft on the summit, he sent his animals home that had accompanied him, and found that he was now alone: then he laughed from the bottom of his heart, looked around him, and spoke thus:

'That I spoke of sacrifices and honey-sacrifices, it was merely a ruse in talking and verily, a useful folly! Here aloft can I now speak freer than in front of mountain-caves and hermits' domestic animals.

What to sacrifice! I squander what is given me, a squanderer with a thousand hands: how could I call that – sacrificing?

And when I desired honey I only desired bait, and sweet mucus and mucilage, for which even the mouths of growling bears, and strange, sulky, evil birds, water:

—The best bait, as huntsmen and fishermen require it. For if the world be as a gloomy forest of animals, and a pleasure-ground for all wild huntsmen, it seems to me rather – and preferably – a fathomless, rich sea;

—A sea full of many – hued fishes and crabs, for which even the gods might long, and might be tempted to become fishers in it, and casters of nets, so rich is the world in wonderful things, great and small!

Especially the human world, the human sea: towards it do I now throw out my golden angle-rod and say: Open up, you human abyss!

Open up, and throw to me your fish and shining crabs! With my best bait shall I allure to myself today the strangest human fish!

—My happiness itself do I throw out into all places far and wide 'twixt orient, noontide, and occident, to see if many human fish will not learn to hug and tug at my happiness;—

Until, biting at my sharp hidden hooks, they have to come up to my height, the motleyest abyss-groundlings, to the wickedest of all fishers of men.

For this am I from the heart and from the beginning – drawing, here-drawing, upward-drawing, upbringing; a drawer, a trainer, a training-master, who not in vain counselled himself once on a time: "Become what you are!"

Thus may men now come up to me; for as yet do I await the signs that it is time for my down-going; as yet do I not myself go down, as I must do, amongst men.

Therefore do I here wait, crafty and scornful upon high mountains, no impatient one, no patient one; rather one who has even unlearnt patience, because he no longer "suffers."

For my fate gives me time: it has forgotten me perhaps? Or does it sit behind a big stone and catch flies?

And verily, I am well-disposed to my eternal fate, because it does not hound and hurry me, but leaves me time for merriment and mischief; so that I have today ascended this high mountain to catch fish.

Did ever any one catch fish upon high mountains? And though it be a folly what I here seek and do, it is better so than that down below I should become solemn with waiting, and green and yellow—

—A posturing wrath – snorter with waiting, a holy howl – storm from the mountains, an impatient one that shouts down into the valleys: "Hearken, else I will scourge you with the scourge of God!"

Not that I would have a grudge against such wrathful ones on that account: they are well enough for laughter to me! Impatient must they now be, those big alarm-drums, which find a voice now or never!

Myself, however, and my fate – we do not talk to the Present, neither do we talk to the Never: for talking we have patience and time and more than time. For one day must it yet come, and may not pass by.

What must one day come and may not pass by? Our great Hazar, that is to say, our great, remote human-kingdom, the Zarathustra-kingdom of a thousand years—

How remote may such "remoteness" be? What does it concern me? But on that account it is none the less sure to me – , with both feet stand I secure on this ground;

—On an eternal ground, on hard primary rock, on this highest, hardest, primary mountain-ridge, to which all winds come, as to the storm-parting, asking Where? and Whence? and Where?

Here laugh, laugh, my hearty, healthy wickedness! From high mountains cast down your glittering scorn-laughter! Allure for me with your glittering the finest human fish!

And whatever belongs to me in all seas, my in-and-for-me in all things – fish that out for me, bring that up to me: for that do I wait, the wickedest of all fish-catchers. Out! out! my fishing-hook! In and down, you bait of my happiness! Drip your sweetest dew, you honey of my heart! Bite, my fishing-hook, into the belly of all black affliction!

Look out, look out, my eye! Oh, how many seas round about me, what dawning human futures! And above me – what rosy red stillness! What unclouded silence!'

62. *The Cry of Distress*

THE next day sat Zarathustra again on the stone in front of his cave, whilst his animals roved about in the world outside to bring home new food, also new honey: for Zarathustra had spent and wasted the old honey to the very last particle. When he thus sat, however, with a stick in his hand, tracing the shadow of his figure on the earth, and reflecting – verily! Not upon himself and his shadow, all at once he startled and shrank back: for he saw another shadow beside his own. And when he hastily looked around and stood up, behold, there stood the soothsayer beside him, the same whom he had once given to eat and drink at his table, the proclaimer of the great weariness, who taught: 'All is alike, nothing is worth while, the world is without meaning, knowledge strangles.' But his face had changed since then; and when Zarathustra looked into his eyes, his heart was startled once more: so much evil announcement and ashy-grey lightnings passed over that countenance.

The soothsayer, who had perceived what went on in Zarathustra's soul, wiped his face with his hand, as if he would wipe out the impression; the same did also Zarathustra. And when both of them had thus silently composed and strengthened themselves, they gave each other the hand, as a token that they wanted once more to recognize each other.

'Welcome here,' said Zarathustra, 'you soothsayer of the great weariness, not in vain shall you once have been my messmate and guest. Eat and drink also with me today, and forgive it that a cheerful old man sits with you at table!' – 'A cheerful old man?' answered the soothsayer, shaking his head, 'but whoever you are, or would be, O Zarathustra, you have been here aloft the longest time, in a little while your bark shall no longer rest on dry land!' – 'Do I then rest on dry land?' – asked Zarathustra, laughing. – 'The waves around your mountain,' answered the soothsayer, 'rise and rise, the waves of great distress and affliction: they will soon raise your bark also and carry you away.' – Then was Zarathustra silent and wondered. – 'Do you still hear nothing?' continued the soothsayer: 'does it not rush and roar out of the depth?' – Zarathustra was silent once more and listened: then heard he a long, long cry, which the abysses threw to one another and passed on; for none of them wished to retain it: so evil did it sound.

'You ill announcer,' said Zarathustra at last, 'that is a cry of distress, and the cry of a man; it may come perhaps out of a black sea. But what does human distress matter to me! My last sin which has been reserved for me, know you what it is called?'

—'Pity!' answered the soothsayer from an overflowing heart, and raised both his hands aloft – 'O Zarathustra, I have come that I may seduce you to your last sin!'—

And hardly had those words been uttered when there sounded the cry once more, and longer and more alarming than before – also much nearer. 'Hear you? Hear you, O Zarathustra?' called out the soothsayer, 'the cry concerns you, it calls you: Come, come, come; it is time, it is the highest time!'—

Zarathustra was silent then, confused and staggered; at last he asked, like one who hesitates in himself: 'And who is it that there calls me?'

'But you know it, certainly,' answered the soothsayer warmly, 'why do you conceal yourself? It is the higher man that cries for you!'

'The higher man?' cried Zarathustra, horror-stricken: 'What wants he? What wants he? The higher man! What wants he here?' – and his skin covered with perspiration.

The soothsayer, however, did not heed Zarathustra's alarm, but listened and listened in the downward direction. When, however, it had been still there for a long while, he looked behind, and saw Zarathustra standing trembling.

'O Zarathustra,' he began, with sorrowful voice, 'you do not stand there like one whose happiness makes him giddy: you will have to dance lest you tumble down!

But although you should dance before me, and leap all your side-leaps, no one may say to me: "Behold, here dances the last joyous man!"

In vain would any one come to this height who sought him here: caves would he find, indeed, and back-caves, hiding-places for hidden ones; but not lucky mines, nor treasure-chambers, nor new gold-veins of happiness.

Happiness – how indeed could one find happiness among such buried-alive and solitary ones! Must I yet seek the last happiness on the Blessed isles, and far away among forgotten seas?

But all is alike, nothing is worth while, no seeking is of service, there are no longer any Blessed isles!'—

Thus sighed the soothsayer; with his last sigh, however, Zarathustra again became serene and assured, like one who has come out of a deep chasm into the light. 'No! No! Three times No!' exclaimed he with a strong voice, and stroked his beard – 'that do I know better! There are still Blessed isles! Silence then, you sighing sorrow-sack!

Cease to splash, you rain – cloud of the forenoon! Do I not already stand here wet with your misery, and drenched like a dog?

Now do I shake myself and run away from you, that I may again become dry: thereat may you not wonder! Do I seem to you discourteous? Here however is my court.

But as regards the higher man: well! I shall seek him at once in those forests: from thence came his cry. Perhaps he is there hard beset by an evil beast.

He is in my domain: therein shall he receive no scath! And verily, there are many evil beasts about me.'—

With those words Zarathustra turned around to depart. Then said the soothsayer: 'O Zarathustra, you are a rogue!

I know it well: you would rather be rid of me! Rather would you run into the forest and lay snares for evil beasts!

But what good will it do you? In the evening will you have me again: in your own cave will I sit, patient and heavy like a block – and wait for you!'

'So be it!' shouted back Zarathustra, as he went away: 'and what is mine in my cave belongs also to you, my guest!

Should you however find honey therein, well! Just lick it up, you growling bear, and sweeten your soul! For in the evening we want both to be in good spirits; – In good spirits and joyful, because this day has come to an end! And you yourself shall dance to my lays, as my dancing-bear.

Thou dost not believe this? Thou shakest thy head? Well! Cheer up, old bear! But I also – am a soothsayer.'

Thus spoke Zarathustra.

63. Talk with the Kings

1

ERE Zarathustra had been an hour on his way in the mountains and forests, he saw all at once a strange procession. Right on the path which he was about to descend came two kings walking, bedecked with crowns and purple girdles, and variegated like flamingoes: they drove before them a laden ass. 'What do these kings want in my domain?' said Zarathustra in astonishment to his heart, and hid himself hastily behind a thicket. When however the kings approached to him, he said half-aloud, like one speaking only to himself: 'Strange! Strange! How does this harmonize? Two kings do I see – and only one ass!'

Then the two kings made a halt; they smiled and looked towards the spot whence the voice proceeded, and afterwards looked into each other's faces. 'Such things do we also think among ourselves,' said the king on the right, 'but we do not utter them.'

The king on the left, however, shrugged his shoulders and answered: 'That may perhaps be a goat-herd. Or an hermit who has lived too long among rocks and trees. For no society at all spoils also good manners.'

'Good manners?' replied angrily and bitterly the other king: 'what then do we run out of the way of? Is it not "good manners"? Our "good society"?

Better, verily, to live among hermits and goat-herds, than with our gilded, false, over-rouged rabble – though it call itself 'good society.'

—Though it call itself "nobility." But there all is false and foul, above all the blood – thanks to old evil diseases and worse curers.

The best and dearest to me at present is still a sound peasant, coarse, artful, obstinate and enduring: that is at present the noblest type.

The peasant is at present the best; and the peasant type should be master! But it is the kingdom of the rabble – I no longer allow anything to be imposed upon me. The rabble, however – that means, hodgepodge.

Rabble-hodgepodge: therein is everything mixed with everything, saint and swindler, gentleman and Jew, and every beast out of Noah's ark.

Good manners! Everything is false and foul with us. No one knows any longer how to reverence: it is that precisely that we run away from. They are fulsome obtrusive dogs; they gild palm-leaves.

This loathing chokes me, that we kings ourselves have become false, draped and disguised with the old faded pomp of our ancestors, show-pieces for the stupidest, the craftiest, and whosoever at present trafficks for power.

We are not the first men – and have nevertheless to stand for them: of this imposture have we at last become weary and disgusted.

From the rabble have we gone out of the way, from all those bawlers and scribe – blowflies, from the trader-stench, the ambition-fidgeting, the bad breath: fie, to live among the rabble;

—Fie, to stand for the first men among the rabble! Ah, loathing! Loathing! Loathing! What does it now matter about us kings!'—

'Thine old sickness seizes you,' said here the king on the left, 'thy loathing seizes you, my poor brother. You know, however, that some one hears us.'

Immediately then, Zarathustra, who had opened ears and eyes to this talk, rose from his hiding-place, advanced towards the kings, and thus began:

'He who hearkens to you, he who gladly hearkens to you, is called Zarathustra.

I am Zarathustra who once said: "What does it now matter about kings!" Forgive me; I rejoiced when you said to each other: "What does it matter about us kings!"

Here, however, is my domain and jurisdiction: what may you be seeking in my domain? Perhaps, however, you have found on your way what I seek: namely, the higher man.'

When the kings heard this, they beat upon their breasts and said with one voice: 'We are recognized!

With the sword of your utterance severest you the thickest darkness of our hearts. You have discovered our distress; for behold, we are on our way to find the higher man—

—The man that is higher than we, although we are kings. To him do we convey this ass. For the highest man shall also be the highest lord on earth.

There is no sorer misfortune in all human destiny, than when the mighty of the earth are not also the first men. Then everything becomes false and distorted and monstrous.

And when they are even the last men, and more beast than man, then riseth and riseth the populace in honour, and at last says even the populace-virtue: "Lo, I alone am virtue!"'—

'What have I just heard?' answered Zarathustra. 'What wisdom in kings! I am enchanted, and verily, I have already promptings to make a rhyme thereon:

—Even if it should happen to be a rhyme not suited for every one's ears. I unlearned long ago to have consideration for long ears. Well then! Well now!

(Here, however, it happened that the ass also found utterance: it said distinctly and with malevolence, YE-A.)

'Twas once – methinks year one of our blessed Lord, –
Drunk without wine, the Sybil thus deplored:
'How ill things go!
Decline! Decline! Ne'er sank the world so low!
Rome now has turned harlot and harlot-stew,
Rome's Caesar a beast, and God – has turned Jew!'

2

With those rhymes of Zarathustra the kings were delighted; the king on the right, however, said: 'O Zarathustra, how well it was that we set out to see you!

For thine enemies showed us thy likeness in their mirror: there lookedst thou with the grimace of a devil, and sneeringly: so that we were afraid of thee.

But what good did it do! Always didst thou prick us anew in heart and ear with thy sayings. Then did we say at last: What does it matter how he look!

We must hear him; him who teaches: "You shall love peace as a means to new wars, and the short peace more than the long!"

No one ever spoke such warlike words: "What is good? To be brave is good. It is the good war that hallows every cause."

O Zarathustra, our fathers' blood stirred in our veins at such words: it was like the voice of spring to old wine-casks.

When the swords ran among one another like red-spotted serpents, then did our fathers become fond of life; the sun of every peace seemed to them languid and lukewarm, the long peace, however, made them ashamed.

How they sighed, our fathers, when they saw on the wall brightly furbished, dried-up swords! Like those they thirsted for war. For a sword thirsts to drink blood, and sparkles with desire.'—

—When the kings thus discoursed and talked eagerly of the happiness of their fathers, there came upon Zarathustra no little desire to mock at their eagerness: for evidently they were very peaceable kings whom he saw before him, kings with old and refined features. But he restrained himself. 'Well!' said he, 'there leads the way, there lies the cave of Zarathustra; and this day is to have a long evening! At present, however, a cry of distress calls me hastily away from you.

It will honour my cave if kings want to sit and wait in it: but, to be sure, you will have to wait long!

Well! What of that! Where does one at present learn better to wait than at courts? And the whole virtue of kings that has remained to them – is it not called today: Ability to wait?'

Thus spoke Zarathustra.

64. *The Leech*

AND Zarathustra went thoughtfully on, further and lower down, through forests and past moory bottoms; as it happens, however, to every one who meditates upon hard matters, he trod thereby unawares upon a man. And lo, there spurted into his face all at once a cry of pain, and two curses and twenty bad invectives, so that in his fright he raised his stick and also struck the trodden one. Immediately afterwards, however, he regained his composure, and his heart laughed at the folly he had just committed.

'Pardon me,' said he to the trodden one, who had got up enraged, and had seated himself, 'pardon me, and hear first of all a parable.

As a wanderer who dreams of remote things on a lonesome highway, runs unawares against a sleeping dog, a dog which lies in the sun:

—As both of them then start up and snap at each other, like deadly enemies, those two beings mortally frightened – so did it happen to us.

And yet! And yet – how little was lacking for them to caress each other, that dog and that lonesome one! Are they not both – lonesome ones!'

—'Whoever thou art,' said the trodden one, still enraged, 'thou treadest also too nigh me with thy parable, and not only with thy foot!

Lo! am I then a dog?' – And then the sitting one got up, and pulled his naked arm out of the swamp. For at first he had lain outstretched on the ground, hidden and indiscernible, like those who lie in wait for swamp-game.

'But whatever are you about' called out Zarathustra in alarm, for he saw a deal of blood streaming over the naked arm, 'what has hurt you? Has an evil beast bit you, you unfortunate one?'

The bleeding one laughed, still angry, 'What matter is it to you!' said he, and was about to go on. 'Here am I at home and in my province. Let him question me whoever will: to a dolt, however, I shall hardly answer.'

'You are mistaken,' said Zarathustra sympathetically, and held him fast; 'you are mistaken. Here you are not at home, but in my domain, and therein shall no one receive any hurt.

Call me however what you wilt – I am who I must be. I call myself Zarathustra.

Well! Up there is the way to Zarathustra's cave: it is not far, will you not attend to your wounds at my home?

It has gone badly with you, you unfortunate one, in this life: first a beast bit you, and then – a man trod upon you!' –

When however the trodden one had heard the name of Zarathustra he was transformed. 'What happens to me!' he exclaimed, 'who preoccupies me so much in this life as this one man, namely Zarathustra, and that one animal that lives on blood, the leech?

For the sake of the leech did I lie here by this swamp, like a fisher, and already had my outstretched arm been bitten ten times, when there bites a still finer leech at my blood, Zarathustra himself!

O happiness! O miracle! Praised be this day which enticed me into the swamp! Praised be the best, the livest cupping-glass, that at present lives; praised be the great conscience-leech Zarathustra!'—

Thus spoke the trodden one, and Zarathustra rejoiced at his words and their refined reverential style. 'Who are you?' asked he, and gave him his hand, 'there is much to clear up and elucidate between us, but already methinks pure clear day is dawning.'

'I am the spiritually conscientious one,' answered he who was asked, 'and in matters of the spirit it is difficult for any one to take it more rigorously, more restrictedly, and more severely than I, except him from whom I learnt it, Zarathustra himself.

Better know nothing than half-know many things! Better be a fool on one's own account, than a sage on other people's approbation! I – go to the basis:

—What matter if it be great or small? If it be called swamp or sky? A handbreadth of basis is enough for me, if it be actually basis and ground!

—A handbreadth of basis: there can one stand. In the true knowing-knowledge there is nothing great and nothing small.'

'Then you are perhaps an expert on the leech?' asked Zarathustra; 'and you investigate the leech to its ultimate basis, you conscientious one?'

'O Zarathustra,' answered the trodden one, 'that would be something immense; how could I presume to do so!

That, however, of which I am master and knower, is the brain of the leech: that is my world!

And it is also a world! Forgive it, however, that my pride here finds expression, for here I have not my equal. Therefore said I: "here am I at home."

How long have I investigated this one thing, the brain of the leech, so that here the slippery truth might no longer slip from me! Here is my domain!

—For the sake of this did I cast everything else aside, for the sake of this did everything else become indifferent to me; and close beside my knowledge lies my black ignorance.

My spiritual conscience requires from me that it should be so – that I should know one thing, and not know all else: they are a loathing to me, all the semi-spiritual, all the hazy, hovering, and visionary.

Where my honesty ceases, there am I blind, and want also to be blind. Where I want to know, however, there want I also to be honest – namely, severe, rigorous, restricted, cruel and inexorable.

Because you once said, O Zarathustra: "Spirit is life which itself cuts into life"; – that led and allured me to your doctrine. And verily, with my own blood have I increased my own knowledge!'

—'As the evidence indicates,' broke in Zarathustra; for still was the blood flowing down on the naked arm of the conscientious one. For there had ten leeches bitten into it.

'O you strange fellow, how much does this very evidence teach me – namely, you yourself! And not all, perhaps, might I pour into your rigorous ear!

Well then! We part here! But I would rather find you again. Up there is the way to my cave: tonight shall you there by my welcome guest!

Fain would I also make amends to your body for Zarathustra treading upon you with his feet: I think about that. Just now, however, a cry of distress calls me hastily away from you.'

Thus spoke Zarathustra.

65. The Magician

1

WHEN however Zarathustra had gone round a rock, then saw he on the same path, not far below him, a man who threw his limbs about like a maniac, and at last tumbled to the ground on his belly. 'Halt!' said then Zarathustra to his heart, 'he there must surely be the higher man, from him came that dreadful cry of distress, I will see if I can help him.' When, however, he ran to the spot where the man lay on the ground, he found a trembling old man with fixed eyes; and in spite of all Zarathustra's efforts to lift him and set him again on his feet, it was all in vain. The unfortunate one, also, did not seem to notice that some one was beside him; on the contrary, he continually looked around with moving gestures, like one forsaken and isolated from all the world. At last, however, after much trembling, and convulsion, and curling-himself-up, he began to lament thus:

'Who warm'th me, who lov'th me still?
Give ardent fingers!
Give heartening charcoal-warmers!
Prone, outstretched, trembling,
Like him, half dead and cold, whose feet one warm'th—
And shaken, ah! By unfamiliar fevers,
Shivering with sharpened, icy-cold frost-arrows,
By you pursued, my fancy!
Ineffable! Recondite! Sore-frightening!
You huntsman 'hind the cloud-banks! Now lightning-struck by you,
You mocking eye that me in darkness watches:
—Thus do I lie,
Bend myself, twist myself, convulsed
With all eternal torture,
And smitten
By you, cruel huntsman,
You unfamiliar – God...

Smite deeper!
Smite yet once more!
Pierce through and rend my heart!
What mean'th this torture
With dull, indented arrows?
Why look'st you hither,
Of human pain not weary,
With mischief-loving, godly flash-glances?
Not murder will you,
But torture, torture?
For why – me torture,
You mischief-loving, unfamiliar God?

Ha! Ha!
You stealest nigh
In midnight's gloomy hour?...
What will you?
Speak!
You crowd me, pressest –
Ha! Now far too closely!
You hearst me breathing,
You o'erhearst my heart,
You ever jealous one! – Of what, pray, ever jealous?
Off! Off!
For why the ladder?
Would you get in?
To heart in-clamber?
To mine own secretest
Conceptions in-clamber?
Shameless one! You unknown one! Thief!
What seekst you by your stealing?
What seekst you by your hearkening?
What seekst you by your torturing?
You torturer!
You – hangman-God!

Or shall I, as the mastiffs do,
Roll me before you?
And cringing, enraptured, frantical,
My tail friendly – waggle!

In vain!
Goad further!
Cruel goader!
No dog – your game just am I,
Cruel huntsman!
Your proudest of captives,
You robber 'hind the cloud-banks...
Speak finally!
You lightning-veiled one! You unknown one! Speak!
What will you, highway-ambusher, from – me?
What will you, unfamiliar – God?
What?
Ransom-gold?
How much of ransom-gold? Solicit much – that bid'th my pride!
And be concise – that bid'th mine other pride!

Ha! Ha!
Me – wantst you? me?
—Entire?...

Ha! Ha!
And torturest me, fool that you are,
Dead-torturest quite my pride?
Give love to me – who warm'th me still?
Who lov'th me still?
Give ardent fingers
Give heartening charcoal-warmers,
Give me, the most lonesome,
The ice (ah! seven-fold frozen ice
For very enemies,

For foes, do make one thirst).
Give, yield to me,
Cruel foe,
—Yourself!—

Away!
There fled he surely,
My final, only comrade,
My greatest foe,
Mine unfamiliar—
My hangman – God!...

—No!
Come you back!
With all of your great tortures! To me the last of lonesome ones,
Oh, come you back!
All my hot tears in streamlets trickle
Their course to you!
And all my final hearty fervour—
Up-glow'th to you!
Oh, come you back,
Mine unfamiliar God! my pain!
My final bliss!'

2

—Here, however, Zarathustra could no longer restrain himself; he took his staff and struck the wailer with all his might. 'Stop this,' cried he to him with wrathful laughter, 'stop this, you stage-player! You false coiner! you liar from the very heart! I know you well!

I will soon make warm legs to you, you evil magician: I know well how – to make it hot for such as you!'

—'Leave off,' said the old man, and sprang up from the ground, 'strike me no more, O Zarathustra! I did it only for amusement!

That kind of thing belongs to my art. You yourself, I wanted to put to the proof when I gave this performance. And verily, you have well detected me!

But you yourself – have given me no small proof of yourself: you are hard, you wise Zarathustra! Hard strike you with your "truths," your cudgel forces from me – this truth!'

—'Flatter not,' answered Zarathustra, still excited and frowning, 'you stage-player from the heart! you are false: why speak you – of truth!

You peacock of peacocks, you sea of vanity; what did you represent before me, you evil magician; whom was I meant to believe in when you wailed in such wise?'

'The penitent in spirit,' said the old man, 'it was him – I represented; you yourself once created this expression—

—The poet and magician who at last turns his spirit against himself, the transformed one who freezes to death by his bad science and conscience.

And just acknowledge it: it was long, O Zarathustra, before you discovered my trick and lie! You believed in my distress when you held my head with both your hands,

—I heard you lament "we have loved him too little, loved him too little!" Because I so far deceived you, my wickedness rejoiced in me.'

'You may have deceived subtler ones than I,' said Zarathustra sternly. 'I am not on my guard against deceivers; I have to be without precaution: so wills my lot.

You, however, must deceive: so far do I know you! You must ever be equivocal, trivocal, quadrivocal, and quinquivocal! Even what you have now confessed, is not nearly true enough nor false enough for me!

You bad false coiner, how could you do otherwise! Your very malady would you whitewash if you showed yourself naked to your physician.

Thus did you whitewash your lie before me when you said: "I did so only for amusement!" There was also seriousness therein, you are something of a penitent-in-spirit!

I divine you well: you have become the enchanter of all the world; but for yourself you have no lie or artifice left, you are disenchanted to yourself!

You have reaped disgust as your one truth. No word in you is any longer genuine, but your mouth is so: that is to say, the disgust that cleaves to your mouth.'—

—'Who are you at all!' cried here the old magician with defiant voice, 'who dares to speak thus to me, the greatest man now living?' – and a green flash shot from his eye at Zarathustra. But immediately after he changed, and said sadly:

'O Zarathustra, I am weary of it, I am disgusted with my arts, I am not great, why do I dissemble! But you know it well – I sought for greatness!

A great man I wanted to appear, and persuaded many; but the lie has been beyond my power. On it do I collapse.

O Zarathustra, everything is a lie in me; but that I collapse – this my collapsing is genuine!'—

'It honours you,' said Zarathustra gloomily, looking down with sidelong glance, 'it honours you that you sought for greatness, but it betrays you also. You are not great.

You bad old magician, that is the best and the honestest thing I honour in you, that you have become weary of yourself, and have expressed it: "I am not great."

Therein do I honour you as a penitent-in-spirit, and although only for the twinkling of an eye, in that one moment wast you – genuine.

But tell me, what seek you here in my forests and rocks? And if you have put yourself in my way, what proof of me would you have?

—Wherein did you put me to the test?'

Thus spoke Zarathustra, and his eyes sparkled. But the old magician kept silence for a while; then said he: 'Did I put you to the test? I – seek only.

O Zarathustra, I seek a genuine one, a right one, a simple one, an unequivocal one, a man of perfect honesty, a vessel of wisdom, a saint of knowledge, a great man!

Know you it not, O Zarathustra? I seek Zarathustra.'

—And here there arose a long silence between them: Zarathustra, however, became profoundly absorbed in thought, so that he shut his eyes. But afterwards coming back to the situation, he grasped the hand of the magician, and said, full of politeness and policy:

'Well! Up there leads the way, there is the cave of Zarathustra. In it may you seek him whom you would rather find.

And ask counsel of my animals, my eagle and my serpent: they shall help you to seek. My cave however is large.

I myself, to be sure – I have as yet seen no great man. That which is great, the acutest eye is at present insensible to it. It is the kingdom of the rabble.

Many a one have I found who stretched and inflated himself, and the people cried: "Behold; a great man!" But what good do all bellows do! The wind comes out at last.

At last bursts the frog which has inflated itself too long: then comes out the wind. To prick a swollen one in the belly, I call good pastime. Hear that, you boys!

Our today is of the popular: who still knows what is great and what is small! Who could there seek successfully for greatness! A fool only: it succeeds with fools.

You seek for great men, you strange fool? Who taught that to you? Is today the time for it? Oh, you bad seeker, why do you – tempt me?'—

Thus spoke Zarathustra, comforted in his heart, and went laughing on his way.

66. *Out of Service*

NOT long, however, after Zarathustra had freed himself from the magician, he again saw a person sitting beside the path which he followed, namely a tall, black man, with a haggard, pale countenance: this man grieved him exceedingly. 'Alas,' said he to his heart, 'there sits disguised affliction; methinks he is of the type of the priests: what do they want in my domain?

What! Hardly have I escaped from that magician, and must another necromancer again run across my path,

—Some sorcerer with laying-on-of-hands, some sombre wonder-worker by the grace of God, some anointed world-maligner, whom, may the devil take!

But the devil is never at the place which would be his right place: he always comes too late, that cursed dwarf and club-foot!'—

Thus cursed Zarathustra impatiently in his heart, and considered how with averted look he might slip past the black man. But behold, it came about otherwise. For at the same moment had the sitting one already perceived him; and not unlike one whom an unexpected happiness overtakes, he sprang to his feet, and went straight towards Zarathustra.

'Whoever you are, you traveller,' said he, 'help a strayed one, a seeker, an old man, who may here easily come to grief!

The world here is strange to me, and remote; wild beasts also did I hear howling; and he who could have given me protection – he is himself no more.

I was seeking the pious man, a saint and an hermit, who, alone in his forest, had not yet heard of what all the world knows at present.'

'What does all the world know at present?' asked Zarathustra. 'Perhaps that the old God no longer lives, in whom all the world once believed?'

'You say it,' answered the old man sorrowfully. 'And I served that old God until his last hour.

Now, however, am I out of service, without master, and yet not free; likewise am I no longer merry even for an hour, except it be in recollections.

Therefore did I ascend into these mountains, that I might finally have a festival for myself once more, as becomes an old pope and church-father: for know it, that I am the last pope! A festival of pious recollections and divine services.

Now, however, is he himself dead, the most pious of men, the saint in the forest, who praised his God constantly with singing and mumbling.

He himself found I no longer when I found his cot – but two wolves found I therein, which howled on account of his death, for all animals loved him. Then did I haste away.

Had I thus come in vain into these forests and mountains? Then did my heart determine that I should seek another, the most pious of all those who believe not in God, my heart determined that I should seek Zarathustra!'

Thus spoke the hoary man, and gazed with keen eyes at him who stood before him. Zarathustra however seized the hand of the old pope and regarded it a long while with admiration.

'Lo! You venerable one,' said he then, 'what a fine and long hand! That is the hand of one who has ever dispensed blessings. Now, however, does it hold fast him whom you seek, me, Zarathustra.

It is I, the ungodly Zarathustra, who says: "Who is ungodlier than I, that I may enjoy his teaching?"'—

Thus spoke Zarathustra, and penetrated with his glances the thoughts and arrear-thoughts of the old pope. At last the latter began:

'He who most loved and possessed him has now also lost him most:

—Lo, I myself am surely the most godless of us at present? But who could rejoice at that!'—

—'You served him to the last?' asked Zarathustra thoughtfully, after a deep silence, 'you know how he died? Is it true what they say, that sympathy choked him;

—That he saw how man hung on the cross, and could not endure it; – that his love to man became his hell, and at last his death?'—

The old pope however did not answer, but looked aside timidly, with a painful and gloomy expression.

'Let him go,' said Zarathustra, after prolonged meditation, still looking the old man straight in the eye.

'Let him go, he is gone. And though it honours you that you speak only in praise of this dead one, yet you know as well as I who he was, and that he went curious ways.'

'To speak before three eyes,' said the old pope cheerfully (he was blind of one eye), 'in divine matters I am more enlightened than Zarathustra himself – and may well be so.

My love served him long years, my will followed all his will. A good servant, however, knows everything, and many a thing even which a master hides from himself.

He was a hidden God, full of secrecy. He did not come by his son otherwise than by secret ways. At the door of his faith stands adultery.

Whoever extolls him as a God of love, does not think highly enough of love itself. Did not that God want also to be judge? But the loving one loves irrespective of reward and requital.

When he was young, that God out of the Orient, then was he harsh and revengeful, and built himself a hell for the delight of his favourites.

At last, however, he became old and soft and mellow and pitiful, more like a grandfather than a father, but most like a tottering old grandmother.

There did he sit shrivelled in his chimney-corner, fretting on account of his weak legs, world-weary, will-weary, and one day he suffocated of his all-too-great pity.' –

'You old pope,' said here Zarathustra interposing, 'have you seen that with your eyes? It could well have happened in that way: in that way, and also otherwise. When gods die they always die many kinds of death.

Well! At all events, one way or other – he is gone! He was counter to the taste of my ears and eyes; worse than that I should not like to say against him.

I love everything that looks bright and speaks honestly. But he – you know it, you old priest, there was something of your type in him, the priest-type – he was equivocal.

He was also indistinct. How he raged at us, this wrath-snorter, because we understood him badly! But why did he not speak more clearly?

And if the fault lay in our ears, why did he give us ears that heard him badly? If there was dirt in our ears, well! Who put it in them?

Too much miscarried with him, this potter who had not learned thoroughly! That he took revenge on his pots and creations, however, because they turned out badly – that was a sin against good taste.

There is also good taste in piety: this at last said: "Away with such a God! Better to have no God, better to set up destiny on one's own account, better to be a fool, better to be God oneself!"'

—'What do I hear!' said then the old pope, with intent ears; 'O Zarathustra, you are more pious than you believe, with such an unbelief! Some god in you has converted you to your ungodliness.

Is it not your piety itself which no longer lets you believe in a God? And your over-great honesty will yet lead you even beyond good and evil!

Behold, what has been reserved for you? You have eyes and hands and mouth, which have been predestined for blessing from eternity. One does not bless with the hand alone.

Near to you, though you profess to be the ungodliest one, I feel a hale and holy odour of long benedictions: I feel glad and grieved thereby.

Let me be your guest, O Zarathustra, for a single night! Nowhere on earth shall I now feel better than with you!'—

'Amen! So shall it be!' said Zarathustra, with great astonishment; 'up there leads the way, there lies the cave of Zarathustra.

Gladly would I conduct you there myself, you venerable one; for I love all pious men. But now a cry of distress calls me hastily away from you.

In my domain shall no one come to grief; my cave is a good haven. And best of all would I like to put every sorrowful one again on firm land and firm legs.

Who, however, could take your melancholy off your shoulders? For that I am too weak. Long, verily, should we have to wait until some one re-awoke your God for you.

For that old God lives no more: he is indeed dead.'—

Thus spoke Zarathustra.

67. *The Ugliest Man*

—AND again did Zarathustra's feet run through mountains and forests, and his eyes sought and sought, but nowhere was he to be seen whom they wanted to see – the sorely distressed sufferer and crier. On the whole way, however, he rejoiced in his heart and was full of gratitude. 'What good things,' said he, 'has this day given me, as amends for its bad beginning! What strange interlocutors have I found!

At their words will I now chew a long while as at good corn; small shall my teeth grind and crush them, until they flow like milk into my soul!'—

When, however, the path again curved round a rock, all at once the landscape changed, and Zarathustra entered into a realm of death. Here bristled aloft black and red cliffs, without any grass, tree, or bird's voice. For it was a valley which all animals avoided, even the beasts of prey, except that a species of ugly, thick, green serpent came here to die when they became old. Therefore the shepherds called this valley: 'Serpent-death.'

Zarathustra, however, became absorbed in dark recollections, for it seemed to him as if he had once before stood in this valley. And much heaviness settled on his mind, so that he walked slowly and always more slowly, and at last stood still. Then, however, when he opened his eyes, he saw something sitting by the wayside shaped like a man, and hardly like a man, something nondescript. And all at once there came over Zarathustra a great shame, because he had gazed on such a thing. Blushing up to the very roots of his white hair, he turned aside his glance, and raised his foot that he might leave this ill-starred place. Then, however, became the dead wilderness vocal: for from the ground a noise welled up, gurgling and rattling, as water gurgles and rattles at night through stopped-up water-pipes;

and at last it turned into human voice and human speech: it sounded thus:

'Zarathustra! Zarathustra! Read my riddle! Say, say! What is the revenge on the witness?

I entice you back; here is smooth ice! See to it, see to it, that your pride does not here break its legs!

You think yourself wise, you proud Zarathustra! Read then the riddle, you hard nut-cracker, the riddle that I am! Say then: who am I!'

—When however Zarathustra had heard these words, what think you then took place in his soul? Pity overcame him; and he sank down all at once, like an oak that has long withstood many tree-fellers, heavily, suddenly, to the terror even of those who meant to fell it. But immediately he got up again from the ground, and his countenance became stern.

'I know you well,' said he, with a brazen voice, 'you are the murderer of God! Let me go.

You could not endure him who beheld you, who ever beheld you through and through, you ugliest man. You took revenge on this witness!'

Thus spoke Zarathustra and was about to go; but the nondescript grasped at a corner of his garment and began anew to gurgle and seek for words. 'Stay,' said he at last—

—'Stay! Do not pass by! I have divined what axe it was that struck you to the ground: hail to you, O Zarathustra, that you are again upon your feet!

You have divined, I know it well, how the man feels who killed him, the murderer of God. Stay! Sit down here beside me; it is not to no purpose.

To whom would I go but to you? Stay, sit down! Do not however look at me! Honour thus – my ugliness!

They persecute me: now are you my last refuge. Not with their hatred, not with their bailiffs; – Oh, such persecution would I mock at, and be proud and cheerful!

Has not all success hitherto been with the well-persecuted ones?

And he who persecutes well learns readily to be obsequent – when once he is – put behind! But it is their pity—

—Their pity is it from which I flee away and flee to you. O Zarathustra, protect me, you, my last refuge, you sole one who divined me:

—You have divined how the man feels who killed him. Stay! And if you will go, you impatient one, go not the way that I came. That way is bad.

Are you angry with me because I have already racked language too long? Because I have already counselled you? But know that it is I, the ugliest man,

—Who have also the largest, heaviest feet. Where I have gone, the way is bad. I tread all paths to death and destruction.

But that you passed me by in silence, that you blushed – I saw it well: thereby did I know you as Zarathustra.

Every one else would have thrown to me his alms, his pity, in look and speech. But for that – I am not beggar enough: that did you divine.

For that I am too rich, rich in what is great, frightful, ugliest, most unutterable! Your shame, O Zarathustra, honoured me!

With difficulty did I get out of the crowd of the pitiful, that I might find the only one who at present teaches that "pity is obtrusive" – yourself, O Zarathustra!

—Whether it be the pity of a God, or whether it be human pity, it is offensive to modesty. And unwillingness to help may be nobler than the virtue that rushes to do so.

That however – namely, pity – is called virtue itself at present by all petty people: they have no reverence for great misfortune, great ugliness, great failure.

Beyond all these do I look, as a dog looks over the backs of thronging flocks of sheep. They are petty, good-wooled, good-willed, grey people.

As the heron looks contemptuously at shallow pools, with backward-bent head, so do I look at the throng of grey little waves and wills and souls.

Too long have we acknowledged them to be right, those petty people: so we have at last given them power as well; – and now do they teach that "good is only what petty people call good."

And "truth" is at present what the preacher spoke who himself sprang from them, that singular saint and advocate of the petty people, who testified of himself: "I – am the truth."

That shameless one has long made the petty people greatly puffed up, he who taught no small error when he taught: "I – am the truth."

Has a shameless one ever been answered more courteously? – You, however, O Zarathustra, passed him by, and said: "No! No! Three times No!"

You warned against his error; you warned – the first to do so – against pity: not every one, not none, but yourself and your type.

You are ashamed of the shame of the great sufferer; and verily when you say: "From pity there comes a heavy cloud; take heed, you men!"

—When you teach: "All creators are hard, all great love is beyond their pity:" O Zarathustra, how well versed do you seem to me in weather-signs!

You yourself, however, warn yourself also against your pity! For many are on their way to you, many suffering, doubting, despairing, drowning, freezing ones—

I warn you also against myself. You have read my best, my worst riddle, myself, and what I have done. I know the axe that fells you.

But he – had to die: he looked with eyes which beheld everything, he beheld men's depths and dregs, all his hidden ignominy and ugliness.

His pity knew no modesty: he crept into my dirtiest corners. This most prying, over-intrusive, over-pitiful one had to die.

He ever beheld me: on such a witness I would have revenge – or not live myself.

The God who beheld everything, and also man: that God had to die! Man cannot endure it that such a witness should live.'

Thus spoke the ugliest man. Zarathustra however got up, and prepared to go on: for he felt frozen to the very bowels.

'You nondescript,' said he, 'you warned me against your path. As thanks for it I praise mine to you. Behold, up there is the cave of Zarathustra.

My cave is large and deep and has many corners; there finds he that is most hidden his hiding-place. And close beside it, there are a hundred lurking-places and by-places for creeping, fluttering, and hopping creatures.

You outcast, who have cast yourself out, you will not live amongst men and men's pity? Well then, do like me! Thus will you learn also from me; only the doer learns.

And talk first and foremost to my animals! The proudest animal and the wisest animal – they might well be the right counsellors for us both!'—

Thus spoke Zarathustra and went his way, more thoughtfully and slowly even than before: for he asked himself many things, and hardly knew what to answer.

'How poor indeed is man,' thought he in his heart, 'how ugly, how wheezy, how full of hidden shame!

They tell me that man loves himself. Ah, how great must that self-love be! How much contempt is opposed to it!

Even this man has loved himself, as he has despised himself, a great lover methinks he is, and a great despiser.

No one have I yet found who more thoroughly despised himself: even that is elevation. Alas, was this perhaps the higher man whose cry I heard?

I love the great despisers. Man is something that has to be overcome.'—

68. *The Voluntary Beggar*

WHEN Zarathustra had left the ugliest man, he was chilled and felt lonesome: for much coldness and lonesomeness came over his spirit, so that even his limbs became colder thereby. When, however, he wandered on and on, uphill and down, at times past green meadows, though also sometimes over wild stony couches where once perhaps an impatient brook had made its bed, then he turned all at once warmer and heartier again.

'What has happened to me?' he asked himself, 'something warm and living quickens me; it must be in the neighbourhood.

Already am I less alone; unconscious companions and brothers rove around me; their warm breath touches my soul.'

When, however, he spied about and sought for the comforters of his lonesomeness, behold, there were cows there standing together on an eminence, whose proximity and smell had warmed his heart. The cows, however, seemed to listen eagerly to a speaker, and took no heed of him who approached. When, however, Zarathustra was quite near to them, then did he hear plainly that a human voice spoke in the midst of the cows, and apparently all of them had turned their heads towards the speaker.

Then ran Zarathustra up speedily and drove the animals aside; for he feared that someone had here met with harm, which the pity of the kine would hardly be able to relieve. But in this he was deceived; for behold, there sat a man on the ground who seemed to be persuading the animals to have no fear of him, a peaceable man and Preacher-on-the-Mount, out of whose eyes kindness itself preached. 'What do you seek here?' called out Zarathustra in astonishment.

'What do I here seek?' answered he: 'the same that you seek, you mischief-maker; that is to say, happiness upon earth.

To that end, however, I would rather learn of these cows. For I tell you that I have already talked half a morning to them, and just now were they about to give me their answer. Why do you disturb them?

Except we be converted and become as cattle, we shall in no wise enter into the kingdom of heaven. For we ought to learn from them one thing: ruminating.

And verily, although a man should gain the whole world, and

yet not learn one thing, ruminating, what would it profit him! He would not be rid of his affliction,

—His great affliction: that, however, is at present called disgust. Who has not at present his heart, his mouth and his eyes full of disgust? You also! You also! But behold these cows!' –

Thus spoke the Preacher-on-the-Mount, and turned then his own look towards Zarathustra – for hitherto it had rested lovingly on the cows: then, however, he put on a different expression. 'Who is this with whom I talk?' he exclaimed, frightened, and sprang up from the ground.

'This is the man without disgust, this is Zarathustra himself, the overcomer of the great disgust, this is the eye, this is the mouth, this is the heart of Zarathustra himself.'

And whilst he thus spoke he kissed with o'erflowing eyes the hands of him with whom he spoke, and behaved altogether like one to whom a precious gift and jewel has fallen unawares from heaven. The cattle, however, gazed at it all and wondered.

'Speak not of me, you strange one; you amiable one!' said Zarathustra, and restrained his affection, 'speak to me firstly of yourself! Are you not the voluntary beggar who once cast away great riches,

—Who was ashamed of his riches and of the rich, and fled to the poorest to give upon them his abundance and his heart? But they received him not.'

'But they received me not,' said the voluntary beggar, 'you know it, forsooth. So I went at last to the animals and to those cows.'

'Then learned you,' interrupted Zarathustra, 'how much harder it is to give properly than to take properly, and that giving well is an art – the last, subtlest master-art of kindness.

'Especially nowadays,' answered the voluntary beggar: 'at present, that is to say, when everything low has become rebellious and exclusive and haughty in its manner – in the manner of the rabble.

For the hour has come, you know it, for the great, evil, long, slow mob-and-slave-insurrection: it extends and extends!

Now does it provoke the lower classes, all benevolence and petty giving; and the overrich may be on their guard!

Whoever at present drip, like bulgy bottles out of all-too-small necks: of such bottles at present one willingly breaks the necks.

Wanton avidity, bilious envy, careworn revenge, rabble-pride: all these struck my eye. It is no longer true that the poor are blessed. The kingdom of heaven, however, is with the cows.'

'And why is it not with the rich?' asked Zarathustra temptingly, while he kept back the cattle which sniffed familiarly at the peaceful one.

'Why do you tempt me?' answered the other. 'You know it yourself better even than I. What was it drove me to the poorest, O Zarathustra? Was it not my disgust at the richest?

—At the culprits of riches, with cold eyes and rank thoughts, who pick up profit out of all kinds of rubbish – at this rabble that stinks to heaven,

—At this gilded, falsified rabble, whose fathers were pick-pockets, or carrion-crows, or rag-pickers, with wives compliant, lewd and forgetful: for they are all of them not far different from harlots—

Rabble above, rabble below! What are "poor" and "rich" at present! That distinction did I unlearn, then did I flee away further and ever further, until I came to those cows.'

Thus spoke the peaceful one, and puffed himself and perspired with his words: so that the cattle wondered anew. Zarathustra, however, kept looking into his face with a smile, all the time the man talked so severely – and shook silently his head.

'You do violence to yourself, you Preacher-on-the-Mount, when you use such severe words. For such severity neither your mouth nor your eye have been given you.

Nor, methinks, has your stomach either: to it all such rage and hatred and foaming-over is repugnant. Your stomach wants softer things: you are not a butcher.

Rather seem you to me a plant-eater and a root-man. Perhaps you grind corn. Certainly, however, you are averse to fleshly joys, and you love honey.'

'You have divined me well,' answered the voluntary beggar, with lightened heart. 'I love honey, I also grind corn; for I have sought out what tastes sweetly and makes pure breath:

—Also what requires a long time, a day's-work and a mouth's-work for gentle idlers and sluggards.

Furthest, to be sure, have those cows carried it: they have created ruminating and lying in the sun. They also abstain from all heavy thoughts which inflate the heart.'

—'Well!' said Zarathustra, 'you should also see my animals, my eagle and my serpent, their like do not at present exist on earth.

Behold, there leads the way to my cave: be tonight its guest. And talk to my animals of the happiness of animals,

—Until I myself come home. For now a cry of distress calls me hastily away from you. Also, should you find new honey with me, ice-cold, golden-comb-honey, eat it!

Now, however, take leave at once of your cattle, you strange one! You amiable one! Though it be hard for you. For they are your warmest friends and preceptors!'—

—'One excepted, whom I hold still dearer,' answered the voluntary beggar. 'You yourself are good, O Zarathustra, and better even than a cow!'

'Away, away with you! you evil flatterer!' cried Zarathustra mischievously, 'why do you spoil me with such praise and flattery – honey?'

'Away, away from me!' cried he once more, and heaved his stick at the fond beggar, who, however, ran nimbly away.

69. The Shadow

SCARCELY however was the voluntary beggar gone in haste, and Zarathustra again alone, when he heard behind him a new voice which called out: 'Stay! Zarathustra! Do wait! It is myself, O Zarathustra, myself, your shadow!' But Zarathustra did not wait; for a sudden irritation came over him on account of the crowd and the crowding in his mountains. 'Where has my lonesomeness gone?' spoke he.

'It is verily becoming too much for me; these mountains swarm; my kingdom is no longer of this world; I require new mountains.

My shadow calls me? What matter about my shadow! Let it run after me! I – run away from it.'

Thus spoke Zarathustra to his heart and ran away. But the one behind followed after him, so that immediately there were three runners, one after the other – namely, foremost the voluntary beggar, then Zarathustra, and thirdly, and hindmost, his shadow. But not long had they run thus when Zarathustra became conscious of his folly, and shook off with one jerk all his irritation and detestation.

'What!' said he, 'have not the most ludicrous things always happened to us old hermits and saints?

My folly has grown big in the mountains! Now do I hear six old fools' legs rattling behind one another!

But does Zarathustra need to be frightened by his shadow? Also, methinks that after all it has longer legs thin mine.'

Thus spoke Zarathustra, and, laughing with eyes and entrails, he stood still and turned round quickly – and behold, he almost thereby threw his shadow and follower to the ground, so closely had the latter followed at his heels, and so weak was he. For when Zarathustra scrutinized him with his glance he was frightened as by a sudden apparition, so slender, swarthy, hollow and worn out did this follower appear.

'Who are you?' asked Zarathustra vehemently, 'what do you here? And why call you yourself my shadow? You are not pleasing to me.'

'Forgive me,' answered the shadow, 'that it is I; and if I please you not – well, O Zarathustra! Therein do I admire you and your good taste.

A wanderer am I, who have walked long at your heels; always on the way, but without a goal, also without a home: so that verily, I lack little of being the eternally Wandering Jew, except that I am not eternal and not a Jew.

What? Must I ever be on the way? Whirled by every wind, unsettled, driven about? O earth, you have become too round for me!

On every surface have I already sat, like tired dust have I fallen asleep on mirrors and window-panes: everything takes from me, nothing gives; I become thin – I am almost equal to a shadow.

After you, however, O Zarathustra, did I fly and hie longest; and though I hid myself from you, I was nevertheless your best shadow: wherever you have sat, there sat I also.

With you have I wandered about in the remotest, coldest worlds, like a phantom that voluntarily haunts winter roofs and snows.

With you have I pushed into all the forbidden, all the worst and the furthest: and if there be anything of virtue in me, it is that I have had no fear of any prohibition.

With you have I broken up whatever my heart revered; all boundary-stones and statues have I o'erthrown; the most dangerous wishes did I pursue, verily, beyond every crime did I once go.

With you did I unlearn the belief in words and worths and in great names. When the devil casts his skin, does not his name also fall away? It is also skin. The devil himself is perhaps – skin.

"Nothing is true, all is permitted": so said I to myself. Into the coldest water did I plunge with head and heart. Ah, how oft did I stand there naked on that account, like a red crab!

Ah, where have gone all my goodness and all my shame and all my belief in the good! Ah, where is the lying innocence which I once possessed, the innocence of the good and of their noble lies!

Too oft, verily, did I follow close to the heels of truth: then did it kick me on the face. Sometimes I meant to lie, and behold! Then only did I hit – the truth.

Too much has become clear to me: now it does not concern me any more. Nothing lives any longer that I love, how should I still love myself?

"To live as I incline, or not to live at all": so do I wish; so wishes also the holiest. But alas! how have I still – inclination?

Have I – still a goal? A haven towards which my sail is set?

A good wind? Ah, he only who knows where he sails, knows what wind is good, and a fair wind for him.

What still remains to me? A heart weary and flippant; an unstable will; fluttering wings; a broken backbone.

This seeking for my home: O Zarathustra, do you know that this seeking has been my home-sickening; it eats me up.

"Where is – my home?" For it do I ask and seek, and have sought, but have not found it. O eternal everywhere, O eternal nowhere, O eternal – in-vain!'

Thus spoke the shadow, and Zarathustra's countenance lengthened at his words. 'You are my shadow!' said he at last sadly.

'Your danger is not small, you free spirit and wanderer! you have had a bad day: see that a still worse evening does not overtake you!

To such unsettled ones as you, seems at last even a prisoner blessed. Did you ever see how captured criminals sleep? They sleep quietly, they enjoy their new security.

Beware lest in the end a narrow faith capture you, a hard, rigorous delusion! For now everything that is narrow and fixed seduces and tempts you.

You have lost your goal. Alas, how will you forego and forget that loss? Thereby – have you also lost your way!

You poor rover and rambler, you tired butterfly! Will you have a rest and a home this evening? Then go up to my cave!

There leads the way to my cave. And now will I run quickly away from you again. Already lies as it were a shadow upon me.

I will run alone, so that it may again become bright around me. Therefore must I still be a long time merrily upon my legs. In the evening, however, there will be – dancing with me!'—

Thus spoke Zarathustra.

70. At Noontide

—AND Zarathustra ran and ran, but he found no one else, and was alone and ever found himself again; he enjoyed and quaffed his solitude, and thought of good things – for hours. About the hour of noontide, however, when the sun stood exactly over Zarathustra's head, he passed an old, bent and gnarled tree, which was encircled round by the ardent love of a vine, and hidden from itself; from this there hung yellow grapes in abundance, confronting the wanderer. Then he felt inclined to quench a little thirst, and to break off for himself a cluster of grapes. When, however, he had already his arm out-stretched for that purpose, he felt still more inclined for something else – namely, to lie down beside the tree at the hour of perfect noontide and sleep.

This Zarathustra did; and no sooner had he laid himself on the ground in the stillness and secrecy of the variegated grass, than he had forgotten his little thirst, and fell asleep. For as the aphorism of Zarathustra says: 'One thing is more necessary than the other.' Only that his eyes remained open: for they never grew weary of viewing and admiring the tree and the love of the vine. In falling asleep, however, Zarathustra spoke thus to his heart:

'Hush! Hush! Has not the world now become perfect? What has happened to me?

As a delicate wind dances invisibly upon parqueted seas, light, feather-light, so – dances sleep upon me.

No eye does it close to me, it leaves my soul awake. Light is it, verily, feather-light.

It persuades me, I know not how, it touches me inwardly with a caressing hand, it constrains me. Yes, it constrains me, so that my soul stretches itself out:

—How long and weary it becomes, my strange soul! Has a seventh-day evening come to it precisely at noontide? Has it already wandered too long, blissfully, among good and ripe things?

It stretches itself out, long – longer! It lies still, my strange soul. Too many good things has it already tasted; this golden sadness oppresses it, it distorts its mouth.

—As a ship that puts into the calmest cove: it now draws up to the land, weary of long voyages and uncertain seas. Is not the land more faithful?

As such a ship hugs the shore, tugs the shore: then it suffices for a spider to spin its thread from the ship to the land. No stronger ropes are required there.

As such a weary ship in the calmest cove, so do I also now repose, nigh to the earth, faithful, trusting, waiting, bound to it with the lightest threads.

O happiness! O happiness! Will you perhaps sing, O my soul? You lie in the grass. But this is the secret, solemn hour, when no shepherd plays his pipe.

Take care! Hot noontide sleeps on the fields. Do not sing! Hush! The world is perfect.

Do not sing, you prairie-bird, my soul! Do not even whisper! Lo – hush! The old noontide sleeps, it moves its mouth: does it not just now drink a drop of happiness—

—An old brown drop of golden happiness, golden wine? Something whisks over it, its happiness laughs. Thus – laughs a God. Hush!

—"For happiness, how little suffices for happiness!" Thus spoke I once and thought myself wise. But it was a blasphemy: that have I now learned. Wise fools speak better.

The least thing precisely, the gentlest thing, the lightest thing, a lizard's rustling, a breath, a whisk, an eye-glance – little makes up the best happiness. Hush!

—What has befallen me: Hark! has time flown away? Do I not fall? Have I not fallen – hark! into the well of eternity?

—What happens to me? Hush! It stings me – alas – to the heart? To the heart! Oh, break up, break up, my heart, after such happiness, after such a sting!

—What? has not the world just now become perfect? Round and ripe? Oh, for the golden round ring – where does it fly? Let me run after it! Quick!

Hush—' (and here Zarathustra stretched himself, and felt that he was asleep.)

'Up!' said he to himself, 'you sleeper! you noontide sleeper! Well then, up, you old legs! It is time and more than time; many a good stretch of road is still awaiting you—

Now have you slept your fill; for how long a time? A half-eternity! Well then, up now, my old heart! For how long after such a sleep may you – remain awake?'

(But then did he fall asleep anew, and his soul spoke against him and defended itself, and lay down again) – 'Leave me alone! Hush! Has not the world just now become perfect? Oh, for the golden round ball!'

'Get up,' said Zarathustra, 'you little thief, you sluggard! What! Still stretching yourself, yawning, sighing, failing into deep wells?

Who are you then, O my soul!' (and here he became frightened, for a sunbeam shot down from heaven upon his face.)

'O heaven above me,' said he sighing, and sat upright, 'you gaze at me? You hearken to my strange soul?

When will you drink this drop of dew that fell down upon all earthly things, when will you drink this strange soul –

—When, you well of eternity! You joyous, awful, noontide abyss! When will you drink my soul back into you?'

Thus spoke Zarathustra, and rose from his couch beside the tree, as if awakening from a strange drunkenness: and behold! There stood the sun still exactly above his head. One might, however, rightly infer therefrom that Zarathustra had not then slept long.

71. The Greeting

IT WAS late in the afternoon only when Zarathustra, after long useless searching and strolling about, again came home to his cave. When, however, he stood over against it, not more than twenty paces therefrom, the thing happened which he now least of all expected: he heard anew the great cry of distress. And extraordinary! This time the cry came out of his own cave. It was a long, manifold, peculiar cry, and Zarathustra plainly distinguished that it was composed of many voices: although heard at a distance it might sound like the cry out of a single mouth.

Then Zarathustra rushed forward to his cave, and behold! What a spectacle awaited him after that concert! For there did they all sit together whom he had passed during the day: the king on the right and the king on the left, the old magician, the pope, the voluntary beggar, the shadow, the intellectually conscientious one, the sorrowful soothsayer, and the ass; the ugliest man, however, had set a crown on his head, and had put round him two purple girdles, for he liked, like all ugly ones, to disguise himself and play the handsome person. In the midst, however, of that sorrowful company stood Zarathustra's eagle, ruffled and disquieted, for it had been called upon to answer too much for which its pride had not any answer; the wise serpent however hung round its neck.

All this did Zarathustra behold with great astonishment; then however he scrutinized each individual guest with courteous curiosity, read their souls and wondered anew. In the meantime the assembled ones had risen from their seats, and waited with reverence for Zarathustra to speak. Zarathustra however spoke thus:

'You despairing ones! You strange ones! So it was your cry of distress that I heard? And now do I know also where he is to be sought, whom I have sought for in vain today: the higher man:

—In my own cave sits he, the higher man! But why do I wonder! Have not I myself allured him to me by honey-offerings and artful lure-calls of my happiness?

But it seems to me that you are badly adapted for company: you make one another's hearts fretful, you that cry for help, when you sit here together? There is one that must first come,

—One who will make you laugh once more, a good jovial fool, a dancer, a wind, a wild romp, some old fool: what think ye?

Forgive me, however, you despairing ones, for speaking such trivial words before you, unworthy, verily, of such guests! But you do not divine what makes my heart wanton:

—You yourselves do it, and your aspect, forgive it me! For every one becomes courageous who beholds a despairing one. To encourage a despairing one – every one thinks himself strong enough to do so.

To myself have you given this power, a good gift, my honourable guests! An excellent guest's-present! Well, do not then upbraid when I also offer you something of mine.

This is my empire and my dominion: that which is mine, however, shall this evening and tonight be yours. My animals shall serve you: let my cave be your resting-place!

At house and home with me shall no one despair: in my purlieus do I protect every one from his wild beasts. And that is the first thing which I offer you: security!

The second thing, however, is my little finger. And when you have that, then take the whole hand also, yes and the heart with it! Welcome here, welcome to you, my guests!'

Thus spoke Zarathustra, and laughed with love and mischief. After this greeting his guests bowed once more and were reverentially silent; the king on the right, however, answered him in their name.

'O Zarathustra, by the way in which you have given us your hand and your greeting, we recognize you as Zarathustra. You have humbled yourself before us; almost have you hurt our reverence:

—Who however could have humbled himself as you have done, with such pride? That uplifts us ourselves; a refreshment is it, to our eyes and hearts.

To behold this, merely, gladly would we ascend higher mountains than this. For as eager beholders have we come; we wanted to see what brightens dim eyes.

And lo! Now is it all over with our cries of distress. Now are our minds and hearts open and enraptured. Little is lacking for our spirits to become wanton.

There is nothing, O Zarathustra, that grows more pleasingly on earth than a lofty, strong will: it is the finest growth. An entire landscape refreshes itself at one such tree.

To the pine do I compare him, O Zarathustra, which grows up like you – tall, silent, hardy, solitary, of the best, supplest wood, stately,

—In the end, however, grasping out for its dominion with strong, green branches, asking weighty questions of the wind, the storm, and whatever is at home on high places;

—Answering more weightily, a commander, a victor! Oh! Who should not ascend high mountains to behold such growths?

At your tree, O Zarathustra, the gloomy and ill-constituted also refresh themselves; at your look even the wavering become steady and heal their hearts.

And verily, towards your mountain and your tree do many eyes turn today; a great longing has arisen, and many have learned to ask: "Who is Zarathustra?"

And those into whose ears you have at any time dripped your song and your honey: all the hidden ones, the lone-dwellers and the twain-dwellers, have simultaneously said to their hearts:

"Does Zarathustra still live? It is no longer worth while to live, everything is indifferent, everything is useless: or else – we must live with Zarathustra!

Why does he not come who has so long announced himself?" Thus do many people ask; "has solitude swallowed him up? Or should we perhaps go to him?"

Now does it come to pass that solitude itself becomes fragile and breaks open, like a grave that breaks open and can no longer hold its dead. Everywhere one sees resurrected ones.

Now do the waves rise and rise around your mountain, O Zarathustra. And however high be your height, many of them must rise up to you: your boat shall not rest much longer on dry ground.

And that we despairing ones have now come into your cave, and already no longer despair: it is but a prognostic and a presage that better ones are on the way to you,

—For they themselves are on the way to you, the last remnant of God among men – that is to say, all the men of great longing, of great loathing, of great satiety,

—All who do not want to live unless they learn again to hope – unless they learn from you, O Zarathustra, the great hope!'

Thus spoke the king on the right, and seized the hand of

Zarathustra in order to kiss it; but Zarathustra checked his veneration, and stepped back frightened, fleeing as it were, silently and suddenly into the far distance. After a little while, however, he was again at home with his guests, looked at them with clear scrutinizing eyes, and said:

'My guests, you higher men, I will speak plain language and plainly with you. It is not for you that I have waited here in these mountains.'

("'Plain language and plainly?' Good God!" said here the king on the left to himself; "one sees he does not know the good Occidentals, this sage out of the Orient!

But he means 'blunt language and bluntly' – well! That is not the worst taste in these days!")

'You may, verily, all of you be higher men,' continued Zarathustra; 'but for me – you are neither high enough, nor strong enough.

For me, that is to say, for the inexorable which is now silent in me, but will not always be silent. And if you appertain to me, still it is not as my right arm.

For he who himself stands, like you, on sickly and tender legs, wishes above all to be treated indulgently, whether he be conscious of it or hide it from himself.

My arms and my legs, however, I do not treat indulgently, I do not treat my warriors indulgently: how then could you be fit for my warfare?

With you I should spoil all my victories. And many of you would tumble over if you but heard the loud beating of my drums.

Moreover, you are not sufficiently beautiful and well-born for me. I require pure, smooth mirrors for my doctrines; on your surface even my own likeness is distorted.

On your shoulders presses many a burden, many a recollection; many a mischievous dwarf squats in your corners. There is concealed rabble also in you.

And though you be high and of a higher type, much in you is crooked and misshapen. There is no smith in the world that could hammer you right and straight for me.

You are only bridges: may higher ones pass over upon you! You signify steps: so do not upbraid him who ascends beyond you into his height!

Out of your seed there may one day arise for me a genuine son and perfect heir: but that time is distant. You yourselves are not those to whom my heritage and name belong.

Not for you do I wait here in these mountains; not with you may I descend for the last time. You have come to me only as a presage that higher ones are on the way to me,

—Not the men of great longing, of great loathing, of great satiety, and that which you call the remnant of God;

—No! No! Three times No! For others do I wait here in these mountains, and will not lift my foot from thence without them;

—For higher ones, stronger ones, triumphanter ones, merrier ones, for such as are built squarely in body and soul: laughing lions must come!

O my guests, you strange ones – have you yet heard nothing of my children? And that they are on the way to me?

Do speak to me of my gardens, of my Blessed isles, of my new beautiful race – why do you not speak to me thereof?

This guests'-present do I solicit of your love, that you speak to me of my children. For them am I rich, for them I became poor: what have I not surrendered.

What would I not surrender that I might have one thing these children, this living plantation, these life-trees of my will and of my highest hope!'

Thus spoke Zarathustra, and stopped suddenly: for his longing came over him, and he closed his eyes and his mouth, because of the agitation of his heart. And all his guests also were silent, and stood still and confounded: except only that the old soothsayer made signs with his hands and his gestures.

72. The Last Supper

FOR at this point the soothsayer interrupted the greeting of Zarathustra and his guests: he pressed forward as one who had no time to lose, seized Zarathustra's hand and exclaimed: 'But Zarathustra!

One thing is more necessary than the other, so say you yourself: well, one thing is now more necessary to me than all others.

A word at the right time: did you not invite me to table? And here are many who have made long journeys. You do not mean to feed us merely with speeches?

Besides, all of you have thought too much about freezing, drowning, suffocating, and other bodily dangers: none of you, however, have thought of my danger, namely, perishing of hunger—'

(Thus spoke the soothsayer. When Zarathustra's animals, however, heard these words, they ran away in terror. For they saw that all they had brought home during the day would not be enough to fill the one soothsayer.)

'Likewise perishing of thirst,' continued the soothsayer. 'And although I hear water splashing here like words of wisdom – that is to say, plenteously and unweariedly, I – want wine!

Not every one is a born water-drinker like Zarathustra. Neither does water suit weary and withered ones: we deserve wine – it alone gives immediate vigour and improvised health!'

On this occasion, when the soothsayer was longing for wine, it happened that the king on the left, the silent one, also found expression for once. 'We took care,' said he, 'about wine, I, along with my brother the king on the right: we have enough of wine, a whole ass-load of it. So there is nothing lacking but bread.'

'Bread,' replied Zarathustra, laughing when he spoke, 'it is precisely bread that hermits have not. But man does not live by bread alone, but also by the flesh of good lambs, of which I have two:

—These shall we slaughter quickly, and cook spicily with sage: it is so that I like them. And there is also no lack of roots and fruits, good enough even for the fastidious and dainty, nor of nuts and other riddles for cracking.

Thus will we have a good repast in a little while. But whoever wishes to eat with us must also give a hand to the work, even the kings. For with Zarathustra even a king may be a cook.'

This proposal appealed to the hearts of all of them, save that the voluntary beggar objected to the flesh and wine and spices.

'Just hear this glutton Zarathustra!' said he jokingly: 'does one go into caves and high mountains to make such repasts?

Now indeed do I understand what he once taught us: "Blessed be moderate poverty!" And why he wishes to do away with beggars.'

'Be of good cheer,' replied Zarathustra, 'as I am. Abide by your customs, you excellent one: grind your corn, drink your water, praise your cooking, if only it make you glad!

I am a law only for my own; I am not a law for all. Yet he who belongs to me must be strong of bone and light of foot,

—Joyous in fight and feast, no sulker, no John o' Dreams, ready for the hardest task as for the feast, healthy and hale.

The best belongs to mine and me; and if it be not given us, then do we take it: the best food, the purest sky, the strongest thoughts, the fairest women!'—

Thus spoke Zarathustra; the king on the right however answered and said: 'Strange! Did one ever hear such sensible things out of the mouth of a wise man?

And verily, it is the strangest thing in a wise man, if over and above, he be still sensible, and not an ass.'

Thus spoke the king on the right and wondered; the ass however, with ill-will, said YE-A to his remark. This however was the beginning of that long repast which is called 'The Supper' in the history-books. At this there was nothing else spoken of but *the higher man*.

73. *The Higher Man*

1

'WHEN I came to men for the first time, then did I commit the hermit folly, the great folly: I appeared on the marketplace.

And when I spoke to all, I spoke to none. In the evening, however, rope-dancers were my companions, and corpses; and I myself almost a corpse.

With the new morning, however, there came to me a new truth: then did I learn to say: "Of what account to me are marketplace and rabble and rabble-noise and long rabble-cars!"

You higher men, learn this from me: On the marketplace no one believes in higher men. But if you will speak there, very well! The rabble, however, blinks: "We are all equal."

"You higher men," – so blinks the rabble – "there are no higher men, we are all equal; man is man, before God – we are all equal!"

Before God! Now, however, this God has died. Before the rabble, however, we will not be equal. You higher men, away from the marketplace!

2

'Before God! Now however this God has died! You higher men, this God was your greatest danger.

Only since he lay in the grave have you again arisen. Now only comes the great noontide, now only does the higher man become – master!

Have you understood this word, O my brothers? You are frightened: do your hearts turn giddy? does the abyss here yawn for you? does the hellhound here yelp at you?

Well! Take heart! you higher men! Now only travails the mountain of the human future. God has died: now do we desire – the Superman to live.'

3

'The most careful ask today: "How is man to be maintained?" Zarathustra however asks, as the first and only one: "How is man to be overcome?"

The Superman, I have at heart; that is the first and only thing to me – and not man: not the neighbour, not the poorest, not the sorriest, not the best.

O my brothers, what I can love in man is that he is an over-going and a down-going. And also in you there is much that makes me love and hope.

In that you have despised, you higher men, that makes me hope. For the great despisers are the great reverers.

In that you have despaired, there is much to honour. For you have not learned to submit yourselves, you have not learned petty policy.

For today have the petty people become master: they all preach submission and humility and policy and diligence and consideration and the long et cetera of petty virtues.

Whatever is of the effeminate type, whatever originates from the servile type, and especially the rabble-mishmash: that wishes now to be master of all human destiny – O disgust! Disgust! Disgust!

That asks and asks and never tires: "How is man to maintain himself best, longest, most pleasantly?" Thereby – are they the masters of today.

These masters of today – overcome them, O my brothers – these petty people: they are the Superman's greatest danger!

Overcome, you higher men, the petty virtues, the petty policy, the sand-grain considerateness, the ant-hill trumpery, the pitiable comfortableness, the "happiness of the greatest number"—!

And rather despair than submit yourselves. And verily, I love you, because you know not today how to live, you higher men! For thus do you live – best!'

4

'Have you courage, O my brothers? Are you stout-hearted? Not the courage before witnesses, but hermit and eagle courage, which not even a God any longer beholds?

Cold souls, mules, the blind and the drunken, I do not call stout-hearted. He has heart who knows fear, but vanquishes it; who sees the abyss, but with pride.

He who sees the abyss, but with eagle's eyes, he who with eagle's talons grasps the abyss: he has courage.'—

5

'"Man is evil" – so said to me for consolation, all the wisest ones. Ah, if only it be still true today! For the evil is man's best force.

"Man must become better and eviler" – so do I teach. The evilest is necessary for the Superman's best.

It may have been well for the preacher of the petty people to suffer and be burdened by men's sin. I, however, rejoice in great sin as my great consolation.

Such things, however, are not said for long ears. Every word, also, is not suited for every mouth. These are fine far-away things: at them sheep's claws shall not grasp!'

6

'You higher men, think you that I am here to put right what you have put wrong?

Or that I wished henceforth to make snugger couches for you sufferers? Or show you restless, miswandering, misclimbing ones, new and easier footpaths?

No! No! Three times No! Always more, always better ones of your type shall perish, for you shall always have it worse and harder. Thus only—

—Thus only grows man aloft to the height where the lightning strikes and shatters him: high enough for the lightning!

Towards the few, the long, the remote go forth my soul and my seeking: of what account to me are your many little, short miseries!

You do not yet suffer enough for me! For you suffer from yourselves, you have not yet suffered from man. You would lie if you spoke otherwise! None of you suffers from what I have suffered.'—

7

'It is not enough for me that the lightning no longer does harm. I do not wish to conduct it away: it shall learn – to work for me.

My wisdom has accumulated long like a cloud, it becomes stiller and darker. So does all wisdom which shall one day bear lightnings.

To these men of today will I not be light, nor be called light. Them – will I blind: lightning of my wisdom! Put out their eyes!'

8

'Do not will anything beyond your power: there is a bad falseness in those who will beyond their power.

Especially when they will great things! For they awaken distrust in great things, these subtle false-coiners and stage-players:

– Until at last they are false towards themselves, squint-eyed, whited cankers, glossed over with strong words, parade virtues and brilliant false deeds.

Take good care there, you higher men! For nothing is more precious to me, and rarer, than honesty.

Is this today not that of the rabble? The rabble however knows not what is great and what is small, what is straight and what is honest: it is innocently crooked, it ever lies.'

9

'Have a good distrust today you, higher men, you enheartened ones! You open-hearted ones! And keep your reasons secret! For this today is that of the rabble.

What the rabble once learned to believe without reasons, who could – refute it to them by means of reasons?

And on the marketplace one convinces with gestures. But reasons make the rabble distrustful.

And when truth has once triumphed there, then ask yourselves with good distrust: "What strong error has fought for it?"

Be on your guard also against the learned! They hate you, because they are unproductive! They have cold, withered eyes before which every bird is unplumed.

Such persons vaunt about not lying: but inability to lie is still far from being love to truth. Be on your guard!

Freedom from fever is still far from being knowledge! Refrigerated spirits I do not believe in. He who cannot lie, does not know what truth is.'

10

'If you would go up high, then use your own legs! Do not get yourselves carried aloft; do not seat yourselves on other people's backs and heads!

You have mounted, however, on horseback? You now ride briskly up to your goal? Well, my friend! But your lame foot is also with you on horseback!

When you reach your goal, when you alight from your horse: precisely on your height, you higher man, then will you stumble!'

11

'You creators, you higher men! One is only pregnant with one's own child.

Do not let yourselves be imposed upon or put upon! Who then is your neighbour? Even if you act "for your neighbour" – you still do not create for him!

Unlearn, I pray you, this "for," you creators: your very virtue wishes you to have naught to do with "for" and "on account of" and "because." Against these false little words shall you stop your ears.

"For one's neighbour," is the virtue only of the petty people: there it is said "like and like," and "hand washes hand": they have neither the right nor the power for your self-seeking!

In your self-seeking, you creators, there is the foresight and foreseeing of the pregnant! What no one's eye has yet seen, namely, the fruit – this, shelters and saves and nourishes your entire love.

Where your entire love is, namely, with your child, there is also your entire virtue! Your work, your will is your "neighbour": let no false values impose upon you!'

12

'You creators, you higher men! Whoever has to give birth is sick; whoever has given birth, however, is unclean.

Ask women: one gives birth, not because it gives pleasure. The pain makes hens and poets cackle.

You creators, in you there is much uncleanliness. That is because you have had to be mothers.

A new child: oh, how much new filth has also come into the world! Go apart! He who has given birth shall wash his soul!'

13

'Be not virtuous beyond your powers! And seek nothing from yourselves opposed to probability!

Walk in the footsteps in which your fathers' virtue has already walked! How would you rise high, if your fathers' will should not rise with you?

Yet he who would be a firstling, let him take care lest he also become a lastling! And where the vices of your fathers are, there should you not set up as saints!

He whose fathers were inclined for women, and for strong wine and flesh of wildboar swine; what would it be if he demanded chastity of himself?

A folly would it be! Much, verily, does it seem to me for such a one, if he should be the husband of one or of two or of three women.

And if he founded monasteries, and inscribed over their portals: "The way to holiness," – I should still say: What good is it! it is a new folly!

He has founded for himself a penance-house and refuge-house: much good may it do! But I do not believe in it.

In solitude there grows what any one brings into it – also the brute in one's nature. Thus is solitude inadvisable to many.

Has there ever been anything filthier on earth than the saints of the wilderness? Around them was not only the devil loose – but also the swine.'

14

'Shy, ashamed, awkward, like the tiger whose spring has failed – thus, you higher men, have I often seen you slink aside. A cast which you made had failed.

But what does it matter, you dice-players! You had not learned to play and mock, as one must play and mock! Do we not ever sit at a great table of mocking and playing?

And if great things have been a failure with you, have you yourselves therefore – been a failure? And if you yourselves have been a failure, has man therefore – been a failure? If man, however, has been a failure: well then! never mind!'

15

'The higher its type, always the seldomer does a thing succeed. You higher men here, have you not all – been failures?

Be of good cheer; what does it matter? How much is still possible! Learn to laugh at yourselves, as you ought to laugh!

What wonder even that you have failed and only half – succeeded, you half-shattered ones! Do not – man's future strive and struggle in you?

Man's furthest, profoundest, star-highest issues, his prodigious powers – do not all these foam through one another in your vessel?

What wonder that many a vessel shatters! Learn to laugh at yourselves, as you ought to laugh! You higher men, Oh, how much is still possible!

And verily, how much has already succeeded! How rich is this earth in small, good, perfect things, in well-constituted things!

Set around you small, good, perfect things, you higher men. Their golden maturity heals the heart. The perfect teaches one to hope.'

16

'What has hitherto been the greatest sin here on earth? Was it not the word of him who said: "Woe to them that laugh now!"

Did he himself find no cause for laughter on the earth? Then he sought badly. A child even finds cause for it.

He – did not love sufficiently: otherwise would he also have loved us, the laughing ones! But he hated and hooted us; wailing and teeth-gnashing did he promise us.

Must one then curse immediately, when one does not love? That – seems to me bad taste. Thus did he, however, this absolute one. He sprang from the rabble.

And he himself just did not love sufficiently; otherwise would he have raged less because people did not love him. All great love does not seek love: it seeks more.

Go out of the way of all such absolute ones! They are a poor sickly type, a rabble-type: they look at this life with ill-will, they have an evil eye for this earth.

Go out of the way of all such absolute ones! They have heavy feet and sultry hearts: they do not know how to dance. How could the earth be light to such ones!'

17

'Tortuously do all good things come nigh to their goal. Like cats they curve their backs, they purr inwardly with their approaching happiness, all good things laugh.

His step betrays whether a person already walks on his own path: just see me walk! Yet he who comes nigh to his goal, dances.

And verily, a statue have I not become, not yet do I stand there stiff, stupid and stony, like a pillar; I love fast racing.

And though there be on earth fens and dense afflictions, he who has light feet runs even across the mud, and dances, as upon well-swept ice.

Lift up your hearts, my brothers, high, higher! And do not forget your legs! Lift up also your legs, you good dancers, and better still, if you stand upon your heads!'

18

'This crown of the laughter, this rose-garland crown: I myself have put on this crown, I myself have consecrated my laughter. No one else have I found today potent enough for this.

Zarathustra the dancer, Zarathustra the light one, who beckons with his pinions, one ready for flight, beckoning to all birds, ready and prepared, a blissfully light-spirited one:

Zarathustra the soothsayer, Zarathustra the sooth-laugher, no impatient one, no absolute one, one who loves leaps and side-leaps; I myself have put on this crown!'

19

'Lift up your hearts, my brothers, high, higher! And do not forget your legs! Lift up also your legs, you good dancers, and better still if you stand upon your heads!

There are also heavy animals in a state of happiness, there are club-footed ones from the beginning. Curiously do they exert themselves, like an elephant which endeavours to stand upon its head.

Better, however, to be foolish with happiness than foolish with misfortune, better to dance awkwardly than walk lamely. So learn, I pray you, my wisdom, you higher men: even the worst thing has two good reverse sides,

—Even the worst thing has good dancing-legs: so learn, I pray you, you higher men, to put yourselves on your proper legs!

So unlearn, I pray you, the sorrow-sighing, and all the rabble - sadness! Oh, how sad the fools of the rabble seem to me today! This today, however, is that of the rabble.'

20

'Do like to the wind when it rushes forth from its mountain-caves: to its own piping will it dance; the seas tremble and leap under its footsteps.

That which gives wings to asses, that which milks the lionesses: praised be that good, unruly spirit, which comes like a hurricane to all the present and to all the rabble,

—Which is hostile to thistle-heads and puzzle-heads, and to all withered leaves and weeds: praised be this wild, good, free spirit of the storm, which dances upon fens and afflictions, as upon meadows!

Which hates the consumptive rabble-dogs, and all the ill-constituted, sullen brood: praised be this spirit of all free spirits, the laughing storm, which blows dust into the eyes of all the melanopic and melancholic!

You higher men, the worst thing in you is that you have none of you learned to dance as you ought to dance – to dance beyond yourselves! What does it matter that you have failed!

How many things are still possible! So learn to laugh beyond yourselves! Lift up your hearts, you good dancers, high! Higher! And do not forget the good laughter!

This crown of the laughter, this rose-garland crown: to you, my brothers, do I cast this crown! Laughing have I consecrated; you higher men, learn, I pray you – to laugh!'

74. The Song of Melancholy

1

WHEN Zarathustra spoke these sayings, he stood nigh to the entrance of his cave; with the last words, however, he slipped away from his guests, and fled for a little while into the open air.

'O pure odours around me,' cried he, 'O blessed stillness around me! But where are my animals? Here, here, my eagle and my serpent!

Tell me, my animals: these higher men, all of them – do they perhaps not smell well? O pure odours around me! Now only do I know and feel how I love you, my animals.'

—And Zarathustra said once more: 'I love you, my animals!' The eagle, however, and the serpent pressed close to him when he spoke these words, and looked up to him. In this attitude were they all three silent together, and sniffed and sipped the good air with one another. For the air here outside was better than with the higher men.

2

Hardly, however, had Zarathustra left the cave when the old magician got up, looked cunningly about him, and said: 'He is gone!

And already, you higher men – let me tickle you with this complimentary and flattering name, as he himself does – already does my evil spirit of deceit and magic attack me, my melancholy devil,

—Which is an adversary to this Zarathustra from the very heart: forgive it for this! Now does it wish to beseech before you, it has just its hour; in vain do I struggle with this evil spirit.

To all of you, whatever honours you like to assume in your names, whether you call yourselves "the free spirits" or "the conscientious," or "the penitents of the spirit," or "the unfettered," or "the great longers,"

—To all of you, who like me suffer from the great loathing, to whom the old God has died, and as yet no new God lies in cradles and swaddling clothes – to all of you is my evil spirit and magic – devil favourable.

I know you, you higher men, I know him, I know also this fiend whom I love in spite of me, this Zarathustra: he himself often seems to me like the beautiful mask of a saint,

—Like a new strange mummery in which my evil spirit, the melancholy devil, delights: I love Zarathustra, so does it often seem to me, for the sake of my evil spirit.

But already does it attack me and constrain me, this spirit of melancholy, this evening-twilight devil: and verily, you higher men, it has a longing—

—Open your eyes! It has a longing to come naked, whether male or female, I do not yet know: but it comes, it constrains me, alas! Open your wits!

The day dies out, to all things comes now the evening, also to the best things; hear now, and see, you higher men, what devil – man or woman – this spirit of evening-melancholy is!'

Thus spoke the old magician, looked cunningly about him, and then seized his harp.

3

'In evening's limpid air,
What time the dew's soothings
To the earth downpour,
Invisibly and unheard—
For tender shoe-gear wear
The soothing dews, like all that's kind-gentle:
Bethinkst you then, bethinkst you, burning heart,
How once you thirstedest
For heaven's kindly teardrops and dew's down-droppings,
All singed and weary thirstedest,
What time on yellow grass-pathways
Wicked, occidental sunny glances
Through sombre trees about you sported,
Blindingly sunny glow-glances, gladly-hurting?

"Of truth the wooer? You?" – so taunted they—
No! Merely poet!
A brute insidious, plundering, grovelling,
That aye must lie,
That wittingly, wilfully, aye must lie:
For booty lusting,
Motley masked,
Self-hidden, shrouded,
Himself his booty—
He – of truth the wooer?
No! Mere fool! Mere poet!
Just motley speaking,
From mask of fool confusedly shouting,
Circumambling on fabricated word-bridges,
On motley rainbow-arches,
'Twixt the spurious heavenly,

And spurious earthly,
Round us roving, round us soaring,
Mere fool! Mere poet!

He – of truth the wooer?
Not still, stiff, smooth and cold,
Become an image,
A godlike statue,
Set up in front of temples,
As a God's own door-guard:
No! Hostile to all such truthfulness-statues,
In every desert homelier than at temples,
With cattish wantonness,
Through every window leaping
Quickly into chances,
Every wild forest a-sniffing,
Greedily-longingly, sniffing,
That you, in wild forests,
'Mong the motley-speckled fierce creatures,
Shouldest rove, sinful-sound and fine-coloured,
With longing lips smacking,
Blessedly mocking, blessedly hellish, blessedly blood-thirsty,
Robbing, skulking, lying – roving:

Or to eagles like which fixedly,
Long adown the precipice look,
Adown their precipice:
Oh, how they whirl down now,
Thereunder, therein,
To ever deeper profoundness whirling!
Then,
Sudden,
With aim aright,
With quivering flight,
On lambkins pouncing,

Headlong down, sore-hungry,
For lambkins longing,
Fierce 'gainst all lamb – spirits,
Furious-fierce all that look
Sheeplike, or lambeyed, or crisp-woolly,
—Grey, with lambsheep kindliness!

Even thus,
Eaglelike, pantherlike,
Are the poet's desires,
Are your own desires 'neath a thousand guises.
You fool! You poet!
You who all mankind viewed—
So God, as sheep:
The God to rend within mankind,
As the sheep in mankind,
And in rending laughing—

That, that is your own blessedness!
Of a panther and eagle – blessedness!
Of a poet and fool – the blessedness!—

In evening's limpid air,
What time the moon's sickle,
Green, 'twixt the purple-glowings,
And jealous, steal'th forth:
—Of day the foe,
With every step in secret,
The rosy garland-hammocks
Downsickling, till they've sunken
Down nightwards, faded, downsunken:

Thus had I sunken one day
From mine own truth-insanity,
From mine own fervid day-longings,

Of day aweary, sick of sunshine,
—Sunk downwards, evenwards, shadowwards:
By one sole trueness
All scorched and thirsty:
—Bethinkst you still, bethinkst you, burning heart,
How then you thirstedest?
That I should banned be
From all the trueness!
Mere fool! Mere poet!'

75. Science

THUS sang the magician; and all who were present went like birds unawares into the net of his artful and melancholy voluptuousness. Only the spiritually conscientious one had not been caught: he at once snatched the harp from the magician and called out: 'Air! Let in good air! Let in Zarathustra! you make this cave sultry and poisonous, you bad old magician!

You seduce, you false one, you subtle one, to unknown desires and deserts. And alas, that such as you should talk and make ado about the truth!

Alas, to all free spirits who are not on their guard against such magicians! It is all over with their freedom: you teach and tempt back into prisons,

—You old melancholy devil, out of your lament sounds a lurement: you resemble those who with their praise of chastity secretly invite to voluptuousness!'

Thus spoke the conscientious one; the old magician, however, looked about him, enjoying his triumph, and on that account put up with the annoyance which the conscientious one caused him. 'Be still!' said he with modest voice, 'good songs want to re-echo well; after good songs one should be long silent.

Thus do all those present, the higher men. You, however, have perhaps understood but little of my song? In you there is little of the magic spirit.'

'You praise me,' replied the conscientious one, 'in that you separate me from yourself; very well! But, you others, what do I see? You still sit there, all of you, with lusting eyes:

You free spirits, where has your freedom gone! You almost seem to me to resemble those who have long looked at bad girls dancing naked: your souls themselves dance!

In you, you higher men, there must be more of that which the magician calls his evil spirit of magic and deceit: we must indeed be different.

And verily, we spoke and thought long enough together before. Zarathustra came home to his cave, for me not to be unaware that we are different.

We seek different things even here aloft, you and I. For I seek more security; on that account have I come to Zarathustra. For he is still the most steadfast tower and will—

—Today, when everything totters, when all the earth quakes. You, however, when I see what eyes you make, it almost seems to me that you seek more insecurity,

—More horror, more danger, more earthquake. You long (it almost seems so to me – forgive my presumption, you higher men)—

—You long for the worst and dangerousest life, which frightens me most, for the life of wild beasts, for forests, caves, steep mountains and labyrinthine gorges.

And it is not those who lead out of danger that please you best, but those who lead you away from all paths, the misleaders. But if such longing in you be actual, it seems to me nevertheless to be impossible.

For fear – that is man's original and fundamental feeling; through fear everything is explained, original sin and original virtue. Through fear there grew also my virtue, that is to say: Science.

For fear of wild animals – that has been longest fostered in man, inclusive of the animal which he conceals and feares in himself: Zarathustra calls it "the beast inside."

Such prolonged ancient fear, at last become subtle, spiritual and intellectual – at present, me thinks, it is called Science.'—

Thus spoke the conscientious one; but Zarathustra, who had just come back into his cave and had heard and divined the last conversation, threw a handful of roses to the conscientious one, and laughed on account of his 'truths.' 'Why!' he exclaimed, 'what did I hear just now? it seems to me, you are a fool, or else I myself am one: and quietly and quickly will I Put your "truth" upside down.

For fear – is an exception with us. Courage, however, and adventure, and delight in the uncertain, in the unattempted – courage seems to me the entire primitive history of man.

The wildest and most courageous animals has he envied and robbed of all their virtues: thus only did he become – man.

This courage, at last become subtle, spiritual and intellectual, this human courage, with eagle's pinions and serpent's wisdom: this, it seems to me, is called at present – '

'Zarathustra!' cried all of them there assembled, as if with one voice, and burst out at the same time into a great laughter; there arose, however, from them as it were a heavy cloud. Even the magician laughed, and said wisely: 'Well! It is gone, my evil spirit!

And did I not myself warn you against it when I said that it was a deceiver, a lying and deceiving spirit?

Especially when it shows itself naked. But what can I do with regard to its tricks! Have I created it and the world?

Well! Let us be good again, and of good cheer! And although Zarathustra looks with evil eye – just see him! he dislikes me:

—Ere night comes will he again learn to love and laud me; he cannot live long without committing such follies.

He – loves his enemies: this art knows he better than any one I have seen. But he takes revenge for it – on his friends!'

Thus spoke the old magician, and the higher men applauded him; so that Zarathustra went round, and mischievously and lovingly shook hands with his friends, like one who has to make amends and apologize to every one for something. When however he had thereby come to the door of his cave, lo, then had he again a longing for the good air outside, and for his animals, and wished to steal out.

76. Among Daughters of the Desert

1

'GO NOT away!' said then the wanderer who called himself Zarathustra's shadow, 'abide with us – otherwise the old gloomy affliction might again fall upon us.

Now has that old magician given us of his worst for our good, and lo! The good, pious pope there has tears in his eyes, and has quite embarked again upon the sea of melancholy.

Those kings may well put on a good air before us still: for that have they learned best of us all at present! Had they however no one to see them, I wager that with them also the bad game would again commence,

—The bad game of drifting clouds, of damp melancholy, of curtained heavens, of stolen suns, of howling autumn-winds,

—The bad game of our howling and crying for help! Abide with us, O Zarathustra! Here there is much concealed misery that wishes to speak, much evening, much cloud, much damp air!

You have nourished us with strong food for men, and powerful aphorisms: do not let the weakly, womanly spirits attack us anew at dessert!

You alone make the air around you strong and clear. Did I ever find anywhere on earth such good air as with you in your cave?

Many lands have I seen, my nose has learned to test and estimate many kinds of air: but with you do my nostrils taste their greatest delight!

Unless it be, unless it be —, do forgive an old recollection! Forgive me an old after-dinner song, which I once composed amongst daughters of the desert:

For with them was there equally good, clear, Oriental air; there was I furthest from cloudy, damp, melancholy Old-Europe!

Then did I love such Oriental maidens and other blue kingdoms of heaven, over which hang no clouds and no thoughts.

You would not believe how charmingly they sat there, when they did not dance, profound, but without thoughts, like little secrets, like beribboned riddles, like dessert-nuts—

Many-hued and foreign, forsooth! But without clouds: riddles which can be guessed: to please such maidens I then composed an after-dinner psalm.'

Thus spoke the wanderer who called himself Zarathustra's shadow; and before any one answered him, he had seized the harp of the old magician, crossed his legs, and looked calmly and sagely around him: with his nostrils, however, he inhaled the air slowly and questioningly, like one who in new countries tastes new foreign air. Afterward he began to sing with a kind of roaring.

2.

'The deserts grow: woe him who does them hide!

—Ha!
Solemnly!
In effect solemnly!
A worthy beginning!
Afric manner, solemnly!
Of a lion worthy,
Or perhaps of a virtuous howl-monkey—
—But it's naught to you,
You friendly damsels dearly loved,
At whose own feet to me,
The first occasion,
To a European under palm-trees,
At seat is now granted. Selah.

Wonderful, truly!
Here do I sit now,
The desert nigh, and yet I am
So far still from the desert,
Even in naught yet deserted:
That is, I'm swallowed down

By this the small oasis:
—It opened up just yawning,
Its loveliest mouth agape,
Most sweet-odoured of all mouthlets:
Then fell I right in,
Right down, right through – in 'mong you,
You friendly damsels dearly loved! Selah.
Hail! Hail! To that whale, fishlike,
If it thus for its guest's convenience
Made things nice! (you well know,
Surely, my learned allusion?)
Hail to its belly,
If it had e'er
A such loveliest oasis-belly
As this is: though however I doubt about it,
—With this come I out of Old-Europe,
That doubt'th more eagerly than do any
Elderly married woman.
May the Lord improve it!
Amen!

Here do I sit now,
In this the small oasis,
Like a date indeed,
Brown, quite sweet, gold-suppurating,
For rounded mouth of maiden longing,
But yet still more for youthful, maidlike,
Ice-cold and snow-white and incisory
Front teeth: and for such assuredly,
Pine the hearts all of ardent date-fruits. Selah.

To the there-named south-fruits now,
Similar, all-too-similar,
Do I lie here; by little
Flying insects

Round-sniffled and round-played,
And also by yet littler,
Foolisher, and peccabler
Wishes and phantasies,
Environed by you,
You silent, presentientest
Maiden-kittens,
Dudu and Suleika,
—Round sphinxed, that into one word
I may crowd much feeling:
(Forgive me, O God,
All such speech-sinning!)
—Sit I here the best of air sniffling,
Paradisal air, truly,
Bright and buoyant air, golden-mottled,
As goodly air as ever
From lunar orb downfell—
Be it by hazard,
Or supervened it by arrogancy?
As the ancient poets relate it.
But doubter, I'm now calling it
In question: with this do I come indeed
Out of Europe,
That doubt'th more eagerly than do any
Elderly married woman.
May the Lord improve it!
Amen.

This the finest air drinking,
With nostrils out-swelled like goblets,
Lacking future, lacking remembrances,
Thus do I sit here, ye
Friendly damsels dearly loved,
And look at the palm-tree there,
How it, to a dance-girl, like,

Do bow and bend and on its haunches bob,
—One does it too, when one view'th it long!
To a dance-girl like, who as it seem'th to me,
Too long, and dangerously persistent,
Always, always, just on single leg has stood?
—Then forgot she thereby, as it seem'th to me,
The other leg?
For vainly I, at least,
Did search for the amissing
Fellow-jewel
—Namely, the other leg—
In the sanctified precincts,
Nigh her very dearest, very tenderest,
Flapping and fluttering and flickering skirting.
Yes, if you should, you beauteous friendly ones,
Quite take my word:
She hath, alas! Lost it!
Hu! Hu! Hu! Hu! Hu!
It is away!
For ever away!
The other leg!
Oh, pity for that loveliest other leg!
Where may it now tarry, all-forsaken weeping?
The most lonesome leg?
In fear perhaps before a
Furious, yellow, blond and curled
Leonine monster? Or perhaps even
Gnawed away, nibbled badly—
Most wretched, woeful! Woeful! Nibbled badly! Selah.

Oh, weep you not,
Gentle spirits!
Weep you not, ye
Date-fruit spirits! Milk-bosoms!
You sweetwood-heart

Purselets!
Weep you no more,
Pallid Dudu!
Be a man, Suleika! Bold! Bold!
—Or else should there perhaps
Something strengthening, heart-strengthening,
Here most proper be?
Some inspiring text?
Some solemn exhortation?
Ha! Up now! Honour!
Moral honour! European honour!
Blow again, continue,
Bellows-box of virtue!
Ha!
Once more your roaring,
Your moral roaring!
As a virtuous lion
Nigh the daughters of deserts roaring!
—For virtue's out-howl,
You very dearest maidens,
Is more than every
European fervour, European hot-hunger!
And now do I stand here,
As European,
I can't be different, God's help to me!
Amen!

The deserts grow: woe him who do them hide!'

77. *The Awakening*

1

AFTER the song of the wanderer and shadow, the cave became all at once full of noise and laughter: and since the assembled guests all spoke simultaneously, and even the ass, encouraged thereby, no longer remained silent, a little aversion and scorn for his visitors came over Zarathustra, although he rejoiced at their gladness. For it seemed to him a sign of convalescence. So he slipped out into the open air and spoke to his animals.

'Where has their distress now gone?' said he, and already did he himself feel relieved of his petty disgust – 'with me, it seems that they have unlearned their cries of distress!

—Though, alas! Not yet their crying.' And Zarathustra stopped his ears, for just then did the YE-A of the ass mix strangely with the noisy jubilation of those higher men.

'They are merry,' he began again, 'and who knows? perhaps at their host's expense; and if they have learned of me to laugh, still it is not my laughter they have learned.

But what matter about that! They are old people: they recover in their own way, they laugh in their own way; my ears have already endured worse and have not become peevish.

This day is a victory: he already yields, he flees, the spirit of gravity, my old arch-enemy! How well this day is about to end, which began so badly and gloomily!

And it is about to end. Already comes the evening: over the sea rides it here, the good rider! How it bobs, the blessed one, the home-returning one, in its purple saddles!

The sky gazes brightly there, the world lies deep. Oh, all you strange ones who have come to me, it is already worth while to have lived with me!'

Thus spoke Zarathustra. And again came the cries and laughter of the higher men out of the cave: then began he anew:

'They bite at it, my bait takes, there departs also from them their enemy, the spirit of gravity. Now do they learn to laugh at themselves: do I hear rightly?

My virile food takes effect, my strong and savoury sayings: and verily, I did not nourish them with flatulent vegetables! But with warrior-food, with conqueror-food: new desires did I awaken.

New hopes are in their arms and legs, their hearts expand. They find new words, soon will their spirits breathe wantonness.

Such food may sure enough not be proper for children, nor even for longing girls old and young. One persuades their bowels otherwise; I am not their physician and teacher.

The disgust departs from these higher men; well! That is my victory. In my domain they become assured; all stupid shame flees away; they empty themselves.

They empty their hearts, good times return to them, they keep holiday and ruminate, they become thankful.

That do I take as the best sign: they become thankful. Not long will it be before they create festivals, and put up memorials to their old joys.

They are convalescents!' Thus spoke Zarathustra joyfully to his heart and gazed outward; his animals, however, pressed up to him, and honoured his happiness and his silence.

2

All on a sudden however, Zarathustra's ear was frightened: for the cave which had hitherto been full of noise and laughter, became all at once still as death; – his nose, however, smelt a sweet-scented vapor and incense-odour, as if from burning pinecones.

'What happens? What are they about?' he asked himself, and stole up to the entrance, that he might be able unobserved to see his guests. But wonder upon wonder! What was he then obliged to behold with his own eyes!

'They have all of them become pious again, they pray, they are mad!' – said he, and was astonished beyond measure. And forsooth! All these higher men, the two kings, the pope out of service, the evil magician, the voluntary beggar, the wanderer and shadow, the old soothsayer, the spiritually conscientious one, and the ugliest man – they all lay on their knees like children and credulous old women, and worshipped the ass. And just then began the ugliest man to gurgle and snort, as if something unutterable in him tried to find expression; when, however, he had actually found words, behold!

it was a pious, strange litany in praise of the adored and censed ass. And the litany sounded thus:

'Amen! And glory and honour and wisdom and thanks and praise and strength be to our God, from everlasting to everlasting!

—The ass, however, here brayed YE-A.

He carried our burdens, he has taken upon him the form of a servant, he is patient of heart and never says No; and he who loves his God chastises him.

—The ass, however, here brayed YE-A.

He speaks not: except that he ever says Yes to the world which he created: thus does he extol his world. It is his artfulness that speaks not: thus is he rarely found wrong.

—The ass, however, here brayed YE-A.

Uncomely goes he through the world. Grey is the favourite colour in which he wraps his virtue. Has he spirit, then does he conceal it; every one, however, believes in his long ears.

—The ass, however, here brayed YE-A.

What hidden wisdom it is to wear long ears, and only to say Yes and never No! Has he not created the world in his own image, namely, as stupid as possible?

—The ass, however, here brayed YE-A.

You go straight and crooked ways; it concerns you little what seems straight or crooked to us men. Beyond good and evil is your domain. It is your innocence not to know what innocence is.

—The ass, however, here brayed YE-A.

Lo! How you spurn none from you, neither beggars nor kings. You suffer little children to come to you, and when the bad boys decoy you, then say you simply, YE-A.

—The ass, however, here brayed YE-A.

You love she-asses and fresh figs, you are no food-despiser. A thistle tickles your heart when you chance to be hungry. There is the wisdom of a God therein.

—The ass, however, here brayed YE-A.

78. The Ass Festival

1

AT THIS place in the litany, however, Zarathustra could no longer control himself; he himself cried out YE-A, louder even than the ass, and sprang into the midst of his maddened guests. 'Whatever are you about, you grown-up children?' he exclaimed, pulling up the praying ones from the ground. 'Alas, if any one else, except Zarathustra, had seen you:

Every one would think you the worst blasphemers, or the very most foolish old women, with your new belief!

And you yourself, you old pope, how is it in accordance with you, to adore an ass in such a manner as God?'—

'O Zarathustra,' answered the pope, 'forgive me, but in divine matters I am more enlightened even than you. And it is right that it should be so.

Better to adore God so, in this form, than in no form at all! Think over this saying, my exalted friend: you will readily divine that in such a saying there is wisdom.

He who said "God is a Spirit" – made the greatest stride and slide hitherto made on earth towards unbelief: such a dictum is not easily amended again on earth!

My old heart leaps and bounds because there is still something to adore on earth. Forgive it, O Zarathustra, to an old, pious pontiff-heart!'

—'And you,' said Zarathustra to the wanderer and shadow, 'you call and think yourself a free spirit? And you here practise such idolatry and hierolatry?

Worse verily, do you here than with your bad brown girls, you bad, new believer!'

'It is sad enough,' answered the wanderer and shadow, 'you are right: but how can I help it! The old God lives again, O Zarathustra, you mayst say what you wilt.

The ugliest man is to blame for it all: he has reawakened him. And if he say that he once killed him, with Gods death is always just a prejudice.'

—'And you,' said Zarathustra, 'you bad old magician, what did you do! Who ought to believe any longer in you in this free age, when you believe in such divine donkeyism?

It was a stupid thing that you didst; how could you, a shrewd man, do such a stupid thing!'

'O Zarathustra,' answered the shrewd magician, 'you are right, it was a stupid thing, it was also repugnant to me.'

—'And you even,' said Zarathustra to the spiritually conscientious one, 'consider, and put your finger to your nose! Does nothing go against your conscience here? Is your spirit not too cleanly for this praying and the fumes of those devotees?'

'There is something therein,' said the spiritually conscientious one, and put his finger to his nose, 'there is something in this spectacle which even does good to my conscience.

Perhaps I dare not believe in God: certain it is however, that God seems to me most worthy of belief in this form.

God is said to be eternal, according to the testimony of the most pious: he who has so much time takes his time. As slow and as stupid as possible: thereby can such a one nevertheless go very far.

And he who has too much spirit might well become infatuated with stupidity and folly. Think of yourself, O Zarathustra!

You yourself – verily! Even you could well become an ass through superabundance of wisdom.

Does not the true sage willingly walk on the crookedest paths? The evidence teaches it, O Zarathustra, your own evidence!'

—'And you yourself, finally,' said Zarathustra, and turned towards the ugliest man, who still lay on the ground stretching up his arm to the ass (for he gave it wine to drink). 'Say, you nondescript, what have you been about!

You seem to me transformed, your eyes glow, the mantle of the sublime covers your ugliness: what did you do?

Is it then true what they say, that you have again awakened him? And why? Was he not for good reasons killed and made away with?

You yourself seem to me awakened: what did you do? Why did you turn round? Why did you get converted? Speak, you nondescript!'

'O Zarathustra,' answered the ugliest man, 'you are a rogue!

Whether he yet lives, or again lives, or is thoroughly dead – which of us both knows that best? I ask you.

One thing however do I know, from yourself did I learn it once, O Zarathustra: he who wants to kill most thoroughly, laughs.

"Not by wrath but by laughter does one kill" – thus spoke you once, O Zarathustra, you hidden one, you destroyer without wrath, you dangerous saint, you are a rogue!'

2

Then, however, did it come to pass that Zarathustra, astonished at such merely roguish answers, jumped back to the door of his cave, and turning towards all his guests, cried out with a strong voice:

'O you wags, all of you, you fools! Why do you dissemble and disguise yourselves before me!

How the hearts of all of you convulsed with delight and wickedness, because you had at last become again like little children – namely, pious,

—Because you at last did again as children do – namely, prayed, folded your hands and said "good God"!

But now leave, I pray you, this nursery, my own cave, where today all childishness is carried on. Cool down, here outside, your hot child-wantonness and heart-tumult!

To be sure: except you become as little children you shall not enter into that kingdom of heaven.' (And Zarathustra pointed aloft with his hands.)

'But we do not at all want to enter into the kingdom of heaven: we have become men, so we want the kingdom of earth.'

3

And once more began Zarathustra to speak. 'O my new friends,' said he, 'you strange ones, you higher men, how well do you now please me,

—Since you have again become joyful! You have, verily, all blossomed forth: it seems to me that for such flowers as you, new festivals are required.

—A little valiant nonsense, some divine service and ass-festival, some old joyful Zarathustra fool, some blusterer to blow your souls bright. Forget not this night and this ass-festival, you higher men! That did you create when with me, that do I take as a good omen, such things only the convalescents create!

And should you celebrate it again, this ass-festival, do it from love to yourselves, do it also from love to me! And in remembrance of me!'

Thus spoke Zarathustra.

79. The Drunken Song

1

MEANWHILE one after another had gone out into the open air, and into the cool, thoughtful night; Zarathustra himself, however, led the ugliest man by the hand, that he might show him his night-world, and the great round moon, and the silvery waterfalls near his cave. There they at last stood still beside one another; all of them old people, but with comforted, brave hearts, and astonished in themselves that it was so well with them on earth; the mystery of the night, however, came closer and closer to their hearts. And anew Zarathustra thought to himself: 'Oh, how well do they now please me, these higher men!' – but he did not say it aloud, for he respected their happiness and their silence.

Then, however, there happened that which in this astonishing long day was most astonishing: the ugliest man began once more and for the last time to gurgle and snort, and when he had at length found expression, behold! there sprang a question plump and plain out of his mouth, a good, deep, clear question, which moved the hearts of all who listened to him.

'My friends, all of you,' said the ugliest man, 'what think ye? For the sake of this day – I am for the first time content to have lived my entire life.

And that I testify so much is still not enough for me. It is worth while living on the earth: one day, one festival with Zarathustra, has taught me to love the earth.

"Was that – life?" will I say to death. "Well! Once more!"

My friends, what think ye? Will you not, like me, say to death: "Was that – life? For the sake of Zarathustra, well! Once more!"'—

Thus spoke the ugliest man; it was not, however, far from midnight. And what took place then, think ye? As soon as the higher men heard his question, they became all at once conscious of their transformation and convalescence, and of him who was the cause thereof: then did they rush up to Zarathustra, thanking, honouring, caressing him, and kissing his hands, each in his own peculiar way; so that some laughed and some wept. The old soothsayer, however, danced with delight; and though he was then, as some narrators suppose, full of sweet wine, he was certainly still fuller of sweet life, and had renounced all weariness. There are even those who narrate that the ass then danced: for not in vain had the ugliest man previously given it wine to drink. That may be the case, or it may be otherwise; and if in truth the ass did not dance that evening, there nevertheless happened then greater and rarer wonders than the dancing of an ass would have been. In short, as the aphorism of Zarathustra says: 'What does it matter!'

2

When, however, this took place with the ugliest man, Zarathustra stood there like one drunken: his glance dulled, his tongue faltered and his feet staggered. And who could divine what thoughts then passed through Zarathustra's soul? Apparently, however, his spirit retreated and fled in advance and was in remote distances, and as it were 'wandering on high mountain-ridges,' as it stands written, ''twixt two seas,

—Wandering 'twixt the past and the future as a heavy cloud.' Gradually, however, while the higher men held him in their arms, he came back to himself a little, and resisted with his hands the crowd of the honouring and caring ones; but he did not speak. All at once, however, he turned his head quickly, for he seemed to hear something: then laid he his finger on his mouth and said: 'Come!'

And immediately it became still and mysterious round about; from the depth however there came up slowly the sound of a clock-bell. Zarathustra listened thereto, like the higher men; then, however, laid he his finger on his mouth the second time, and said again: 'Come! Come! It is getting on to midnight!' – and his voice had changed. But still he had not moved from the spot. Then it became yet stiller and more mysterious, and everything hearkened, even the ass, and Zarathustra's noble animals, the eagle and the serpent, likewise the cave of Zarathustra and the big cool moon, and the night itself. Zarathustra, however, laid his hand upon his mouth for the third time, and said:

'Come! Come! Come! Let us now wander! It is the hour: let us wander into the night!'

3

'You higher men, it is getting on to midnight: then will I say something into your ears, as that old clock-bell says it into my ear,

—As mysteriously, as frightfully, and as cordially as that midnight clock-bell speaks it to me, which has experienced more than one man:

—Which has already counted the smarting throbbings of your fathers' hearts – ah! ah! How it sighs! how it laughs in its dream! The old, deep, deep midnight!

Hush! Hush! Then is there many a thing heard which may not be heard by day; now however, in the cool air, when even all the tumult of your hearts has become still,

—Now does it speak, now is it heard, now does it steal into overwakeful, nocturnal souls: ah! ah! How the midnight sighs! How it laughs in its dream!

—Hear you not how it mysteriously, frightfully, and cordially speaks to you, the old deep, deep midnight?

O man, take heed!'

4

'Woe to me! Where has time gone? Have I not sunk into deep wells? The world sleeps—

Ah! Ah! The dog howls, the moon shins. Rather will I die, rather will I die, than say to you what my midnight-heart now thinks.

Already have I died. It is all over. Spider, why spin you around me? Will you have blood? Ah! Ah! The dew falls, the hour comes – The hour in which I frost and freeze, which asks and asks and asks: "Who has sufficient courage for it?

—Who is to be master of the world? Who is going to say: Thus shall you flow, you great and small streams!"

—The hour approaches: O man, you higher man, take heed! This talk is for fine ears, for your ears – what says deep midnight's voice indeed?'

5

'It carries me away, my soul dances. Day's-work! Day's-work! Who is to be master of the world?

The moon is cool, the wind is still. Ah! Ah! Have you already flown high enough? You have danced: a leg, nevertheless, is not a wing.

You good dancers, now is all delight over: wine has become lees, every cup has become brittle, the sepulchres mutter.

You have not flown high enough: now do the sepulchres mutter: "Free the dead! Why is it so long night? Does not the moon make us drunken?"

You higher men, free the sepulchres, awaken the corpses! Ah, why does the worm still burrow? There approaches, there approaches, the hour,

—There booms the clock-bell, there thrills still the heart, there burrows still the wood-worm, the heart-worm. Ah! Ah! The world is deep!'

6

'Sweet lyre! Sweet lyre! I love your tone, your drunken, ranunculine tone! How long, how far has come to me your tone, from the distance, from the ponds of love!

You old clock-bell, you sweet lyre! Every pain has torn your heart, father-pain, fathers'-pain, forefathers'-pain; your speech has become ripe,

—Ripe like the golden autumn and the afternoon, like my hermit heart – now say you: The world itself has become ripe, the grape turns brown,

—Now does it wish to die, to die of happiness. You higher men, do you not feel it? There wells up mysteriously an odour,

—A perfume and odour of eternity, a rosy-blessed, brown, gold-wine-odour of old happiness.

—Of drunken midnight-death happiness, which sings: the world is deep, and deeper than the day could read!'

7

'Leave me alone! Leave me alone! I am too pure for you. Touch me not! has not my world just now become perfect?

My skin is too pure for your hands. Leave me alone, you dull, doltish, stupid day! Is not the midnight brighter?

The purest are to be masters of the world, the least known, the strongest, the midnight-souls, who are brighter and deeper than any day.

O day, you grope for me? you feel for my happiness? For you am I rich, lonesome, a treasure-pit, a gold chamber?

O world, you want me? Am I worldly for you? Am I spiritual for you? Am I divine for you? But day and world, you are too coarse,

—Have cleverer hands, grasp after deeper happiness, after deeper unhappiness, grasp after some God; grasp not after me:

—My unhappiness, my happiness is deep, you strange day, but yet am I no God, no God's-hell: deep is its woe.'

8

'God's woe is deeper, you strange world! Grasp at God's woe, not at me! What am I! A drunken sweet lyre,

—A midnight-lyre, a bell-frog, which no one understands, but which must speak before deaf ones, you higher men! For you do not understand me!

Gone! Gone! O youth! O noontide! O afternoon! Now have come evening and night and midnight, the dog howls, the wind:

—Is the wind not a dog? It whines, it barks, it howls. Ah! Ah! How she sighs! How she laughs, how she wheezes and pants, the midnight!

How she just now speaks soberly, this drunken poetess! Has she perhaps overdrunk her drunkenness? Has she become overawake? does she ruminate?

—Her woe does she ruminate over, in a dream, the old, deep midnight – and still more her joy. For joy, although woe be deep, joy is deeper still than grief can be.'

9

'You grape-vine! Why do you praise me? Have I not cut you! I am cruel, you bleedest: what means your praise of my drunken cruelty?

"Whatever has become perfect, everything mature – wants to die!" So say you. Blessed, blessed be the vintner's knife! But everything immature wants to live: alas!

Woe says: "Hence! Go! Away, you woe!" But everything that suffers wants to live, that it may become mature and lively and longing,

—Longing for the further, the higher, the brighter. "I want heirs," so says everything that suffers, "I want children, I do not want myself,"

Joy, however, does not want heirs, it does not want children, joy wants itself, it wants eternity, it wants recurrence, it wants everything eternally-like-itself.

Woe says: "Break, bleed, you heart! Wander, you leg! You wing, fly! Onward! Upward! you pain!" Well! Cheer up! O my old heart: Woe says: "Hence! Go!"'

10

'You higher men, what think ye? Am I a soothsayer? Or a dreamer? Or a drunkard? Or a dream-reader? Or a midnight-bell?

Or a drop of dew? Or a fume and fragrance of eternity? Hear you it not? Smell you it not? Just now has my world become perfect, midnight is also midday,

Pain is also a joy, curse is also a blessing, night is also a sun, go away! Or you will learn that a sage is also a fool.

Said you ever Yes to one joy? O my friends, then said you Yes also to all woe. All things are enlinked, enlaced and enamoured,

—Wanted you ever once to come twice; said you ever: "You please me, happiness! Instant! Moment!" then wanted you all to come back again!

—All anew, all eternal, all enlinked, enlaced and enamoured, Oh, then did you love the world,

—You eternal ones, you love it eternally and for all time: and also to woe do you say: Hence! Go! but come back! For joys all want – eternity!'

11

'All joy wants the eternity of all things, it wants honey, it wants lees, it wants drunken midnight, it wants graves, it wants grave-tears' consolation, it wants gilded evening-red—

—What does not joy want! It is thirstier, heartier, hungrier, more frightful, more mysterious, than all woe: it wants itself, it bites into itself, the ring's will wriths in it,

—It wants love, it wants hate, it is over-rich, it gives, it throws away, it begs for some one to take from it, it thanks the taker, it would rather be hated,

—So rich is joy that it thirsts for woe, for hell, for hate, for shame, for the lame, for the world, for this world, Oh, you know it indeed!

You higher men, for you does it long, this joy, this irrepressible, blessed joy – for your woe, you failures! For failures, longs all eternal joy.

For joys all want themselves, therefore do they also want grief! O happiness, O pain! Oh break, you heart! You higher men, do learn it, that joys want eternity.

—Joys want the eternity of all things, they want deep, profound eternity!'

12

'Have you now learned my song? Have you divined what it would say? Well! Cheer up! You higher men, sing now my roundelay!

Sing now yourselves the song, the name of which is "Once more," the signification of which is "To all eternity!" – sing, you higher men, Zarathustra's roundelay!

O man! Take heed!
What says deep midnight's voice indeed?
"I slept my sleep,
From deepest dream I've woke, and plead:
The world is deep,
And deeper than the day could read.
Deep is its woe,
Joy – deeper still than grief can be:
Woe says: Hence! Go!
But joys all want eternity,
Want deep, profound eternity!"'

80. The Sign

IN THE morning, however, after this night, Zarathustra jumped up from his couch, and, having girded his loins, he came out of his cave glowing and strong, like a morning sun coming out of gloomy mountains.

'You great star,' spoke he, as he had spoken once before, 'you deep eye of happiness, what would be all your happiness if you had not those for whom you shine!

And if they remained in their chambers whilst you are already awake, and come and give and distribute, how would your proud modesty upbraid for it!

Well! They still sleep, these higher men, whilst I am awake: they are not my proper companions! Not for them do I wait here in my mountains.

At my work I want to be, at my day: but they understand not what are the signs of my morning, my step – is not for them the awakening-call.

They still sleep in my cave; their dream still drinks at my drunken songs. The audient ear for me – the obedient ear, is yet lacking in their limbs.'

– This had Zarathustra spoken to his heart when the sun arose: then looked he inquiringly aloft, for he heard above him the sharp call of his eagle. 'Well!' called he upwards, 'thus is it pleasing and proper to me. My animals are awake, for I am awake.

My eagle is awake, and like me honours the sun. With eagle-talons does it grasp at the new light. You are my proper animals; I love you.

But still do I lack my proper men!'—

Thus spoke Zarathustra; then, however, it happened that all on a sudden he became aware that he was flocked around and fluttered around, as if by innumerable birds, the whizzing of so many wings, however, and the crowding around his head was so great that he shut his eyes. And verily, there came down upon him as it were a cloud, like a cloud of arrows which pours upon a new enemy. But behold, here it was a cloud of love, and showered upon a new friend.

'What happens to me?' thought Zarathustra in his astonished heart, and slowly seated himself on the big stone which lay close to the exit from his cave. But while he grasped about with his hands, around him, above him and below him, and repelled the tender birds, behold, there then happened to him something still stranger: for he grasped thereby unawares into a mass of thick, warm, shaggy hair; at the same time, however, there sounded before him a roar, a long, soft lion-roar.

'The sign comes,' said Zarathustra, and a change came over his heart. And in truth, when it turned clear before him, there lay a yellow, powerful animal at his feet, resting its head on his knee, unwilling to leave him out of love, and doing like a dog which again finds its old master. The doves, however, were no less eager with their love than the lion; and whenever a dove whisked over its nose, the lion shook its head and wondered and laughed.

When all this went on Zarathustra spoke only a word: 'My children are nigh, my children', then he became quite mute. His heart, however, was loosed, and from his eyes there dropped down tears and fell upon his hands. And he took no further notice of anything, but sat there motionless, without repelling the animals further. Then flew the doves to and fro, and perched on his shoulder, and caressed his white hair, and did not tire of their tenderness and joyousness. The strong lion, however, licked always the tears that fell on Zarathustra's hands, and roared and growled shyly. Thus did these animals do.

All this went on for a long time, or a short time: for properly speaking, there is no time on earth for such things. Meanwhile, however, the higher men had awakened in Zarathustra's cave, and marshalled themselves for a procession to go to meet Zarathustra, and give him their morning greeting: for they had found when they awakened that he no longer tarried with them. When, however, they reached the door of the cave and the noise of their steps had preceded them, the lion started violently; it turned away all at once from Zarathustra, and roaring wildly, sprang towards the cave. The higher men, however, when they heard the lion roaring, cried all aloud as with one voice, fled back and vanished in an instant.

Zarathustra himself, however, stunned and strange, rose from his seat, looked around him, stood there astonished, inquired of his heart, bethought himself, and remained alone. 'What did I hear?' said he at last, slowly, 'What happened to me just now?'

But soon there came to him his recollection, and he took in at a glance all that had taken place between yesterday and today. 'Here is indeed the stone,' said he, and stroked his beard, 'on it sat I yester-morn; and here came the soothsayer to me, and here heard I first the cry which I heard just now, the great cry of distress.

O you higher men, your distress was it that the old soothsayer foretold to me yester-morn,

—To your distress did he want to seduce and tempt me: "O Zarathustra," said he to me, "I come to seduce you to your last sin."

To my last sin?' cried Zarathustra, and laughed angrily at his own words: 'What has been reserved for me as my last sin?'

—And once more Zarathustra became absorbed in himself, and sat down again on the big stone and meditated. Suddenly he sprang up,

'Fellow-suffering! Fellow-suffering with the higher men!' he cried out, and his countenance changed into brass. 'Well! That – has had its time!

My suffering and my fellow-suffering – what matter about them! Do I then strive after happiness? I strive after my work!

Well! The lion has come, my children are nigh, Zarathustra has grown ripe, my hour has come:

This is my morning, my day begins: arise now, arise, you great noontide!'

Thus spoke Zarathustra and left his cave, glowing and strong, like a morning sun coming out of gloomy mountains.